"Designed to serve as a textbook on I[...]
than that genre would suggest. Its 'th[...]
accessible commentary to most of the Epistle, together with well-informed
treatments of topics of relevance—and, in some cases, of controversy—
within the contemporary church. Combining depth with accessibility, the
book will interest both scholars and non-scholars, those in ministry and lay
readers alike."

—Stephen Westerholm, Professor Emeritus of
Early Christianity, McMaster University

"The essays in this volume by an outstanding array of scholars provide in-
sightful expositions of key texts in Romans, elucidations of its major theological themes, and analyses that apply to issues facing the church today.
It not only is an excellent resource that will help scholars stay current on
the enormous quantity of research on Romans, it also will give students
an excellent introduction to the letter with valuable models for how to do
careful exegesis."

—David E. Garland, Professor of Christian Scriptures,
George W. Truett Theological Seminary, Baylor University

"It is not often we see twenty-four New Testament scholars offering fresh
appraisals of significant issues related to the interpretation of Romans. I am
impressed by the quality of all the contributions to this volume, which in
many cases offer new, well-considered approaches to the major sections of
the letter, including matters of interpretation that have long occupied the
minds of scholars. The book will, in my opinion, greatly benefit students and
interpreters of Romans."

—Colin G. Kruse, Emeritus Scholar, Melbourne School of Theology

"This collection of essays on the greatest letter ever written is thought provoking and academically responsible. That is what we would expect since
the editors are expert exegetes who have authored outstanding commentaries on Romans."

—Andy Naselli, Associate Professor of Systematic Theology
and New Testament, Bethlehem College and Seminary

Paul's Letter *to the* Romans

Paul's Letter *to the* Romans

Theological Essays

Edited by Douglas J. Moo, Eckhard J. Schnabel,
Thomas R. Schreiner, and Frank Thielman

HENDRICKSON ACADEMIC

an imprint of Hendrickson Publishing Group

Paul's Letter to the Romans: Theological Essays

© 2023 by Douglas J. Moo, Eckhard J. Schnabel, Thomas R. Schreiner, and Frank Thielman

Published by Hendrickson Academic
an imprint of Hendrickson Publishing Group
Hendrickson Publishers, LLC
P. O. Box 3473
Peabody, Massachusetts 01961-3473
www.hendricksonpublishinggroup.com

ISBN 978-1-4964-8087-3

Printed in the United States of America

First Printing — December 2023

Cover image: P.Mich.inv. 6238 Recto, displaying Romans 11:26–12:8 ($\mathfrak{P}^{46}$). Courtesy of University of Michigan Library.

Library of Congress Control Number: 2023011639

Contents

Abbreviations

General

//	parallel
§(§)	section(s)
AB	Anchor Bible
AD	Anno Domini
ANE	ancient Near East(ern)
AYB	Anchor Yale Bible
BCE	before the Common Era
ca.	*circa*
CE	Common Era
CEB	Common English Bible
cf.	*confer*, compare
ch(s).	chapter(s)
col(s).	column(s)
CSB	Christian Standard Bible
ed.	edition; edited by
e.g.	*exempli gratia*, for example
Eng.	English
esp.	especially
ESV	English Standard Version
et al.	*et alii*, and others
f(f).	and the following (ones)
frag.	fragment
GNT	Good News Translation
Gk.	Greek
Heb.	Hebrew
i.e.	*id est*, that is
KJV	King James Version
Lat.	Latin
LEB	Lexham English Bible
LXX	Septuagint
MS(S)	manuscript(s)
MT	Masoretic Text
n(n).	note(s)
NA28	*Novum Testamentum Graece*, Nestle-Aland, 28th ed.
NAB	New American Bible

NEB	New English Bible
NETS	*A New English Translation of the Septuagint.* Edited by Albert Pietersma and Benjamin G. Wright. New York: Oxford University Press, 2007.
NIV	New International Version
NJB	New Jerusalem Bible
NLT	New Living Translation
NPP	New Perspective on Paul
NRSV	New Revised Standard Version
NRSVue	New Revised Standard Version Updated Edition
NT	New Testament
OPP	Old Perspective on Paul
orig.	originally published
OT	Old Testament
𝔓	Papyrus
pace	"no offense intended"
pref.	prefaced by
passim	found throughout
REB	Revised English Bible
repr.	reprinted
[*sic*]	"thus it was written"
s.v.	*sub verbo*, under the word
trans.	translated by
UBS4	*The Greek New Testament*, United Bible Societies, 4th ed.
v.l.	*varia lectio*, variant reading
v(v).	verse(s)
vol(s).	volume(s)
x	times

Journals, Series, and Reference Works

AB	Anchor Bible
ABD	*Anchor Bible Dictionary.* Edited by David Noel Freedman. 6 vols. New York: Doubleday, 1992.
ABR	*Australian Biblical Review*
AJSR	*Association for Jewish Studies Review*
ANTC	Abingdon New Testament Commentaries
BBR	*Bulletin for Biblical Research*
BBRSup	Bulletin for Biblical Research Supplements
BDAG	Danker, Frederick W., Walter Bauer, William F. Arndt, and F. Wilbur Gingrich. *Greek-English Lexicon of the New*

	Testament and Other Early Christian Literature. 3rd ed. Chicago: University of Chicago Press, 2000.
BDF	Blass, Friedrich, Albert Debrunner, and Robert W. Funk. *A Greek Grammar of the New Testament and Other Early Christian Literature.* Chicago: University of Chicago Press, 1961.
BECNT	Baker Exegetical Commentary on the New Testament
BETL	Bibliotheca Ephemeridum Theologicarum Lovaniensium
BHR	Biblical Hermeneutics Rediscovered
BN	*Biblische Notizen*
BNTC	Black's New Testament Commentary
BTB	*Biblical Theology Bulletin: Journal of Bible and Culture*
BTCP	Biblical Theology for Christian Proclamation
BZAW	Beihefte zur Zeitschrift für die alttestamentliche Wissenschaft
BZNW	Beihefte zur Zeitschrift für die neutestamentliche Wissenschaft
CBQ	*Catholic Biblical Quarterly*
CCSS	Catholic Commentary on Sacred Scripture
CEJL	Commentaries on Early Jewish Literature
COQG	Christian Origins and the Question of God
CRINT	Compendia Rerum Iudaicarum ad Novum Testamentum
CurBR	*Currents in Biblical Research*
Ébib	*Études bibliques*
EGGNT	Exegetical Guide to the Greek New Testament
EKKNT	Evangelisch-katholischer Kommentar zum Neuen Testament
ETL	*Ephemerides Theologicae Lovanienses*
EvQ	*Evangelical Quarterly*
ExAud	*Ex Auditu*
FAT	Forschungen zum Alten Testament
FB	Forschung zur Bibel
FRLANT	Forschungen zur Religion und Literatur des Alten und Neuen Testaments
GFS	GlossaHouse Festschrift Series
GzNT	Grundrisse zum Neuen Testament
HBT	*Horizons in Biblical Theology*
HNT	Handbuch zum Neuen Testament
HTA	Historisch-Theologische Auslegung
HThKNT	Herders Theologischer Kommentar zum Neuen Testament
HTR	*Harvard Theological Review*

HUCA	*Hebrew Union College Annual*
IBC	Interpretation: A Bible Commentary for Teaching and Preaching
IBMR	*International Bulletin for Missions Research*
ICC	International Critical Commentary
IDBSup	*Interpreter's Dictionary of the Bible: Supplementary Volume.* Edited by Keith Crim. Nashville: Abingdon, 1976.
IVPNTC	IVP New Testament Commentary
JBL	*Journal of Biblical Literature*
JCPS	Jewish and Christian Perspectives Series
JETS	*Journal of the Evangelical Theological Society*
JGRChJ	*Journal of Greco-Roman Christianity and Judaism*
JJS	*Journal of Jewish Studies*
JSHJ	*Journal for the Study of the Historical Jesus*
JSJ	*Journal for the Study of Judaism*
JSNT	*Journal for the Study of the New Testament*
JSNTSup	Journal for the Study of the New Testament Supplement Series
JSP	*Journal for the Study of the Pseudepigrapha*
JSPL	*Journal for the Study of Paul and His Letters*
JTI	*Journal of Theological Interpretation*
JTS	*Journal of Theological Studies*
KEK	Kritisch-exegetischer Kommentar über das Neue Testament (Meyer-Kommentar)
KNT	Kommentar zum Neuen Testament
LCL	Loeb Classical Library
LD	Lectio Divina
LEC	Library of Early Christology
LNTS	Library of New Testament Studies
Louw & Nida	Louw, J. P., and E. A. Nida, eds. *Greek-English Lexicon of the New Testament Based on Semantic Domains.* New York: United Bible Societies, 1988.
LPS	Library of Pauline Studies
LSJ	Liddell, Henry George, Robert Scott, Henry Stuart Jones. *A Greek-English Lexicon.* 9th ed. with revised supplement. Oxford: Clarendon, 1996.
LW	*Luther's Works: American Edition.* Vols. 1–30, edited by Jaroslav Pelikan. St. Louis: Concordia, 1955–76. Vols. 31–55, edited by Helmut Lehmann. Philadelphia/Minneapolis: Fortress, 1957–86. Vols. 56–82, edited by Christopher B. Brown. St. Louis: Concordia, 2009ff.

MM	Moulton, James H., and George Milligan. *The Vocabulary of the Greek Testament*. London, 1930. Repr., Peabody, MA: Hendrickson, 1997.
MSHACA	Mnemosyne Supplements, History and Archaeology of Classical Antiquity
MSJ	*The Master's Seminary Journal*
NACSBT	New American Commentary Studies in Bible and Theology
NCB	New Century Bible
Neot	*Neotestamentica*
NICNT	New International Commentary on the New Testament
NIDNTT	*New International Dictionary of New Testament Theology*. Edited by Colin Brown. 4 vols. Grand Rapids: Zondervan, 1975–78.
NIGTC	New International Greek Testament Commentary
NKT	Neukirchener Theologie
NovT	*Novum Testamentum*
NovTSup	Supplements to Novum Testamentum
NPNF[1]	*Nicene and Post-Nicene Fathers*, Series 1
NPNF[2]	*Nicene and Post-Nicene Fathers*, Series 2
NTAb	Neutestamentliche Abhandlungen
NTD	Das Neue Testament Deutsch
NTL	New Testament Library
NTM	New Testament Monographs
NTR	*New Testament Readings*
NTS	*New Testament Studies*
NZSTh	*Neue Zeitschrift für systematische Theologie*
OTL	Old Testament Library
OTP	*The Old Testament Pseudepigrapha*. Edited by James H. Charlesworth. 2 vols. New York: Doubleday, 1983–85.
PAST	*Pauline Studies*
PBM	Paternoster Biblical Monographs
PG	Patrologia Graeca [= *Patrologiae Cursus Completus*: Series Graeca]. Edited by Jacques-Paul Migne. 162 vols. Paris, 1857–86.
PKNT	Papyrologische Kommentare zum Neuen Testament
PL	Patrologia Latina [= *Patrologiae Cursus Completus*: Series Latina]. Edited by Jacques-Paul Migne. 217 vols. Paris, 1844–64.
PNTC	Pillar New Testament Commentary
PWSup	Supplements to *Paulys Real-Encyclopädie der classischen Alterumswissenschaft*. New edition by Georg Wissowa and

	Wilhelm Kroll. 50 vols. in 84 parts. Stuttgart: Metzler and Druckenmüller, 1894–1980.
PSB	*Princeton Seminary Bulletin*
RB	*Revue Biblique*
RBS	Resources for Biblical Study
REC	Reformed Expository Commentary
RevExp	*Review and Expositor*
RNT	Regensburger Neues Testament
RTR	*Reformed Theological Review*
SBJT	*Southern Baptist Journal of Theology*
SBLDS	Society of Biblical Literature Dissertation Series
SBS	Stuttgarter Bibelstudien
SD	Studies and Documents
SDOC	Scritti delle origini Cristiane
SFEG	Schriften der Finnischen Exegetischen Gesellschaft
SGBC	The Story of God Bible Commentary
SHR	Studies in the History of Religions (supplements to *Numen*)
SJT	*Scottish Journal of Theology*
SMBen	Série monographique de Benedictina: Section paulinienne
SNTSMS	Society for New Testament Studies Monograph Series
SNTW	Studies of the New Testament and Its World
SSBT	Shorter Studies in Biblical Theology
TBTöp	Theologische Bibliothek Töpelmann
TDNT	*Theological Dictionary of the New Testament*. Edited by G. Johannes Botterweck and Helmer Ringgren. Translated by Geoffrey W. Bromiley. 10 vols. Grand Rapids: Eerdmans, 1964–76.
TDOT	*Theological Dictionary of the Old Testament*. Edited by G. Johannes Botterweck and Helmer Ringgren. Translated by John T. Willis et al. 8 vols. Grand Rapids: Eerdmans, 1974–2006.
TFSS	The Five Solas Series
THKNT	Theologischer Handkommentar zum Neuen Testament
TLNT	*Theological Lexicon of the New Testament*. C. Spicq. Translated and edited by J. D. Ernest. 3 vols. Peabody, MA: Hendrickson, 1994.
TLZ	*Theologische Literaturzeitung*
TNTC	Tyndale New Testament Commentaries
TOTC	Tyndale Old Testament Commentaries
TS	Texts and Studies
TynBul	*Tyndale Bulletin*
TzF	Texte zur Forschung

WA	*D. Martin Luthers Werke: Kritische Gesamtausgabe (Weimarer Ausgabe).* 73 vols. Weimar: H. Böhlau, 1883–1993.
WBC	Word Biblical Commentary
WMANT	Wissenschaftliche Monographien zum Alten und Neuen Testament
WUNT	Wissenschaftliche Untersuchungen zum Neuen Testament
ZECNT	Zondervan Exegetical Commentary on the New Testament
ZNW	*Zeitschrift für die neutestamentliche Wissenschaft und die Kunde der älteren Kirche*
ZTK	*Zeitschrift für Theologie und Kirche*

Ancient Sources

Deuterocanon/Apocrypha

1–4 Macc	1–4 Maccabees
2 Esd	2 Esdras (4 Ezra)
Add Esth	Additions to Esther
Bar	Baruch
Jdt	Judith
Sir	Sirach
Tob	Tobit
Wis	Wisdom of Solomon

Pseudepigrapha

1 En.	1 Enoch
Jos. Asen.	Joseph and Aseneth
Jub.	Jubilees
LAE	Life of Adam and Eve
Let. Aris.	Letter of Aristeas
Pss. Sol.	Psalms of Solomon
Sib. Or.	Sibylline Oracles
T. Ab.	Testament of Abraham
T. Ab. A	Testament of Abraham (A recension)
T. Ab. B	Testament of Abraham (B recension)
T. Gad	Testament of Gad
T. Jud.	Testament of Judah
T. Naph.	Testament of Naphtali
T. Reub.	Testament of Reuben

Dead Sea Scrolls

11QT	Temple Scroll
4Q274	4Q Tohorot

PHILO
Abr.	*On Abraham*
Cont. Life	*On the Contemplative Life*
Deus	*Quod Deus sit immutabulis (That God is Unchangeable)*
Leg.	*Legum allegoriae (Allegorical Interpretation)*
Mos.	*De vita Mosis (On the Life of Moses)*
QG	*Questions and Answers on Genesis*
Sacr.	*De sacrificiis Abelis et Caini (On the Sacrifices of Abel and Cain)*
Spec.	*De specialibus legibus (On the Special Laws)*

JOSEPHUS
Ag. Ap.	*Against Apion*
Ant.	*Jewish Antiquities*
J. W.	*Jewish War*
Life	*The Life of Josephus*

RABBINIC LITERATURE
b.	Babylonian Talmud
m.	Mishnah
t.	Tosefta
'Abod. Zar.	'Abodah Zarah
Gen. Rab.	Genesis Rabbah
Ḥag.	Ḥagigah
Ḥul	Ḥullin
Lev. Rab.	Leviticus Rabbah
Mak.	Makkot
Makš.	Makširin
Miqw.	Miqwa'ot
Neg.	Nega'im
Nid.	Niddah
Qidd.	Qiddušin
Sanh.	Sanhedrin
Ṭehar.	Ṭeharot

EARLY CHURCH
1 Clem.	1 Clement
Civ.	Augustine, *De civitate Dei (The City of God)*
Dial.	Justin Martyr, *Dialogue with Trypho*
Herm. Mand.	Shepherd of Hermas, Mandates
Nat.	Tertullian, *Ad nationes (To the Heathen)*
Quis div.	Clement of Alexandria, *Quis dives salvetur (Salvation of the Rich)*

GRECO-ROMAN

Am.	Ovid, *Amores*
Ars	Ovid, *Ars amatoria (The Art of Love)*
Diatr.	Epictetus, *Diatribai (Dissertations)*
Ep.	Seneca, *Epistulae morales*
Hist. Rom.	Dio Cassius, *Roman Histories*
Eth. nic.	Aristotle, *Nichomachean Ethics*
[Subl.]	Longinus, *De sublimitate (On the Sublime)*
Symp.	Plato, *Symposium*

Editors' Preface

The essays in this volume have been presented during four sessions of the Consultation on Paul's Letter to the Romans of the Annual Meetings of the Evangelical Theological Society between 2018–2022, interrupted in 2020 by the COVID-19 pandemic. As the Steering Committee, we are grateful to the Evangelical Theological Society for arranging the Consultation that pursued the goal of producing a volume of scholarly essays written by evangelical Pauline scholars that presents analyses of major passages and themes, the *status quaestionis* on contested matters, and which can serve as a textbook.

The editors are grateful to Paul Hendrickson for his readiness to publish the proceedings of the Consultation, to Marco Resendes for his editorial oversight, to Nicole Viera, Tyler Comer, and Kate Walker for proofreading, to Phil Frank for typesetting the book, to Meg Rusick for the cover design, and to Dave Pietrantonio for print production. It is our sincere hope that the volume will be helpful as a textbook for classes on the Letter to the Romans.

Douglas J. Moo
Eckhard J. Schnabel
Thomas R. Schreiner
Frank Thielman

PART ONE

The Gospel, Sin, and Salvation (ETS 2018)

CHAPTER 1

The Centrality of the Gospel in Romans: The Importance of Getting It . . . and Getting It Right

Robert W. Yarbrough

In his 383rd edition of "Select Items," an informal and unpublished summary of important recent publications by Covenant Seminary's longtime librarian Dr. Jim Pakala, Pakala stated:

> I wish we Protestants had much more awareness of and appreciation for all those in the first three-fourths of Christianity following the Apostles. For some centuries now, too many of us have helped secularists get the world to ignore or, if not completely ignore, then demean not only the thinkers and writers but 1,500 hundred years of pre-Renaissance/Reformation Christianity generally.

This brief essay will not delve directly into how Romans was interpreted during that important but neglected 1500 years. But it will seek to sharpen appreciation for an aspect of reading Romans that would have been common during the majority of Christian history, but has been eclipsed by recent generations in so-called critical study.

I will not, however, attempt to rehabilitate appreciation for reading Romans with a fixation on the question of its purpose, a topic that has dominated Romans scholarship for several generations and has not found resolution.[1] I will argue that an overlooked but directly stated purpose—so directly stated that it can hardly be disputed—relates to pastoral reception of the epistle's teaching, and then the instilling of that teaching in church members under that pastoral oversight.

We will begin by touching on the immensity of Romans commentary literature, a reminder of how humble we are advised to be in thinking that our times are apt to generate much in the way of truly fresh and distinct insight into this epistle. We will then observe three ways in which the understanding of the gospel articulated in Romans may be said to be its central component. We will conclude with brief remarks on continuing implications for Romans' gospel center.

---

1. "The reasons-for-Romans debate is one of the longest and most complex within modern biblical scholarship." Michael J. Gorman, *Romans: A Theological and Practical Commentary* (Grand Rapids: Eerdmans, 2022), 24.

Romans Commentating: A Thick Tradition

Robert Matthew Calhoun plausibly defines "the gospel" in Romans. Linking Rom 1:1–4 and 1:16–17 with 1 Cor 15, he states that for the apostle Paul, "The gospel *is* the confirmed death, burial, and resurrection of Christ on behalf of our sins according to the scriptures; we preached it, and you believed it."[2] For purposes of this paper, that will serve as a working definition of the gospel of which Paul speaks in Romans.

This topic calls first for exegetical treatment, and that means consideration of both the Greek text of Romans and the best commentaries. But here we face an immediate challenge. Eckhard Schnabel, in his 2015 two-volume commentary on Romans, noted that there are some 740 commentaries on Romans in existence in over a dozen languages. Forty hail from the time between Origen (the author of the earliest extant Romans commentary) and Luther, sixty-one from Luther ca. 1515 to the year 1600, fifty-three from the 1600s, forty-one from the 1700s, 185 from the 1800s, and 270 from the 1900s.[3] This commentary cornucopia is as likely to be as paralyzing in its magnitude as it is clarifying in its content. Who can do justice to even one or two hundred of them?

Moreover, Schnabel counted 56 additional Romans commentaries in what he called the "still young 21st century," and that was before the appearance of commentaries by, e.g., Stanley Porter, Anthony Thiselton, Richard Longenecker, John Harvey, David Peterson, Frank Thielman, Scott Hahn, Daniel Doriani, Frederick Dale Bruner, and Michael J. Gorman, to say nothing of recent new editions of standard commentaries by Thomas Schreiner and Douglas Moo. This is not to mention works critical to reclaiming an accurate reading of Romans. These followed in the wake of the substantially misguided revolt against historic understanding that was underwritten by the once-mighty New Perspective. I have in mind here Stephen Chester's *Reading Paul with the Reformers*,[4] which does not so much reconcile old and new perspectives as it shows how loosely New Perspective readings of the Reformation regard key facts. There are equally weighty essays in Matthew Barrett's magisterial volume *The Doctrine on Which the Church Stands or Falls: Justification in Biblical, Theological, Historical, and Pastoral Perspective.*[5] Starting from this concession, then,

---

2. Robert Matthew Calhoun, *Paul's Definition of the Gospel in Romans 1*, WUNT 2.316 (Tübingen: Mohr Siebeck, 2011), 221.

3. See Eckhard J. Schnabel, *Der Brief des Paulus an die Römer*, vol. 1: *Kapitel 1–5*; vol. 2: *Kapitel 6–16*, HTA (Witten/Gießen: Brockhaus/Brunnen, 2015–16), 1:71–72.

4. Stephen Chester, *Reading Paul with the Reformers* (Grand Rapids: Eerdmans, 2017).

5. Matthew Barrett, ed., *The Doctrine on Which the Church Stands or Falls: Justification in Biblical, Theological, Historical, and Pastoral Perspective* (Wheaton, IL: Crossway, 2019). Those especially pertaining to a fresh understanding of the gospel in Romans are: Timo Laato, "The New Quest for Paul: A Critique of the New Perspective

that doing justice to the mountain of relevant commentary and other literature impinging on Romans is infeasible, I propose a cautious probe rather than a definitive statement. I will argue that the gospel may be said to be central in Romans by virtue of its ubiquitous, pastoral, and political presence.

The Gospel's Centrality in Romans: Ubiquity

There is widespread agreement that Rom 1:16–17 contains the theme of the entire epistle. It is a statement defining the gospel.

> For I am not ashamed of the gospel, because it is the power of God that brings salvation to everyone who believes: first to the Jew, then to the Gentile. For in the gospel the righteousness of God is revealed—a righteousness that is by faith from first to last, just as it is written: "The righteous will live by faith." (NIV 2011)

As Stanley Porter notes, "These two verses serve to initiate and motivate the major concepts found in the book. Commentators typically see these verses as comprising a theme statement for the entire book."[6] Or again: "Without being overly programmatic, within these two verses Paul has laid out the field of discourse for the body of his letter,"[7] which Porter views as 1:16–11:36, followed by paraenesis in chapters 12–15 and then the closing in chapter 16.[8]

One way to verify the gospel's ubiquity is to note Paul's statement in 1:1 that it is "the gospel of God." It is from God and about God. In particular, God promised it "beforehand through his prophets in the Holy Scriptures," one of only two places where Paul calls the OT Scriptures holy (ἅγιος; ἱερός in 2 Tim 3:15). God verified the gospel by sending his Son as a descendent of David and vindicating him by his resurrection from the dead through the Spirit of holiness (vv. 3–4)—all much debated utterances, but clear in their general thrust. Only God can do such things.

How does this relate to the gospel's centrality in Romans? God—the gospel's source and object—is central in Romans. The word θεός is by far the most prominent word in Romans (153x). The next most prominent word, νόμος, occurs fewer than half as many times. If you add in sixty-five references to Christ, forty-three to Lord, thirty-six to Jesus, and roughly thirty to capital-S Spirit, you have 327 explicit references to triune deity in Romans, which contains only

on Paul," 295–326; David Shaw, "What Next? Justification after the New Perspective," 327–50; and Bruce Baugus, "The Eclipse of Justification: Justification during the Enlightenment and Post-Enlightenment Eras," 769–810.

6. Stanley E. Porter, *The Letter to the Romans: A Linguistic and Literary Commentary*, NTM 37 (Sheffield: Sheffield Phoenix Press, 2015), 57.

7. Porter, *Romans*, 60.

8. See outline in Porter, *Romans*, 36–37.

432 verses. That means about 75 percent of the verses in Romans refer to God directly, with many others doing so indirectly through pronouns or implicit reference.

The gospel is central, then, in Romans because its subject and chief object—God in three persons[9]—are the primary linguistic focus, present virtually everywhere the reader turns.[10] Scott Hahn summarizes the theology of Romans first under the heading "the righteousness of God"[11] in tune with Arland Hultgren's claim that "the primary question in Romans is theocentric."[12] David Peterson's commentary identifies the gospel as the most significant theme in Romans, followed by the Scriptures and God as Trinity.[13] God is also highlighted in connection with Paul's mission and gospel message in the recent Romans commentary by Subhro Sekhar Sircar.[14]

Both God and gospel, then, are everywhere to be found in Romans. Kruse combines these. He finds Romans' *centrum Paulinum*, "the center, heart, or organizing principle of Paul's theology" to be "the gospel of God comprehensively conceived."[15] Elsewhere, Kruse writes that Moo is correct to say that in Romans the gospel "becomes functionally equivalent to 'Christ' or God's intervention in Christ."[16] Yet whether one wishes to highlight (1) God's person and work or (2) Christ's person and work as definitive for the meaning of "gospel" in Romans, both are in evidence at every turn; and in Trinitarian understanding, both are redemptively present even when it is the other who is being highlighted.[17]

The word εὐαγγέλιον occurs nine times in Romans. It is not only at the thematic core in 1:1–4 and 1:16–17 but is also central in Paul's closing flourish in 16:25: "Now to him who is able to establish you in accordance with my gospel, the message I proclaim about Jesus Christ." Moo states that the theme of Romans

---

9. Emphasized as thematic in Romans by Gorman, *Romans*, 15.

10. Recent commentaries that list "God" as at or near the thematic top of Romans include those by Schnabel (God is second; first is the gospel revealed by God) and Colin Kruse (God the Father is first). Schnabel, *Der Brief des Paulus an die Römer: Kapitel 1–5*, 53, 58; Colin G. Kruse, *Paul's Letter to the Romans*, PNTC (Grand Rapids: Eerdmans, 2012), 22.

11. Scott Hahn, *Romans*, CCSS (Grand Rapids: Baker Academic, 2017), xxiv.

12. Arland Hultgren, *Paul's Letter to the Romans: A Commentary* (Grand Rapids: Eerdmans, 2011), 26.

13. David G. Peterson, *Commentary on Romans*, BTCP (Nashville: Holman Reference, 2017), 31–60.

14. Subhro Sekhar Sircar, *Paul's Theology of Mission to the Nations in Romans*, BHR 9 (New Delhi, India: Christian World Imprints, 2017), 4.

15. Kruse, *Romans*, 31, 33.

16. Kruse, *Romans*, 41.

17. Here see Adonis Vidu, *The Same God Who Works All Things: Inseparable Operations in Trinitarian Theology* (Grand Rapids: Eerdmans, 2021). When the Father acts, the Son is implicated (as is the Spirit). And the same holds true, mutatis mutandis, when it is the Son (or Spirit) who is highlighted.

is in fact the gospel, repeating as just asserted that εὐαγγέλιον, εὐαγγελίζω "are particularly prominent in the introduction . . . and conclusion," providing the epistle's "literary frame."[18] Grant Osborne is more cautious but concurs with Moo that in Romans "Paul is summarizing the contents and meaning of the gospel" and that "this comes the closest"[19] to serving as Romans' integrating theme.

Other verses in Romans autobiographically highlight how Paul had long centered his life and ministry on the gospel and its promulgation:

| 1:9 | God, whom I serve in my spirit in preaching *the gospel* of his Son . . . |

| 1:15 | That is why I am so eager to preach *the gospel* also to you who are in Rome. |

| 15:16 | [God] gave me the priestly duty of proclaiming *the gospel* of God, so that the Gentiles might become an offering acceptable to God, sanctified by the Holy Spirit. |

| 15:19–20 | So from Jerusalem all the way around to Illyricum, I have fully proclaimed *the gospel* of Christ. It has always been my ambition to preach *the gospel* where Christ was not known, so that I would not be building on someone else's foundation. |

By design, no part of Romans is free of assertions related to God, Christ, and the Spirit who spark saving faith in those who hear and believe the gospel. It is fair, therefore, to conclude that the revelation of the gospel, the application of the gospel, or both, are foundational for understanding any part of Romans.

The Gospel's Centrality in Romans: Pastoral Edge

Grant Osborne's commentary opens by marveling at the wealth of Romans commentaries already available.[20] But Osborne perceptively notes two things. One is the surfeit of Romans commentaries available to the church in the West "while churches in the rest of the world have been unable to publish what they need."[21] The second Osborne expresses in these words: "Many Western commentaries, for the most part, are too technical for many pastors and nearly all laypersons. Others are too shallow and miss the meaning of the text."[22]

---

18. Douglas J. Moo, *The Epistle to the Romans*, NICNT (Grand Rapids: Eerdmans, 1996), 29.

19. Grant Osborne, *Romans*, IVPNTC (Downers Grove, IL: IVP Academic, 2004), 21; cf. Daniel M. Doriani, *Romans*, REC (Phillipsburg, NJ: P&R, 2021), 7–8.

20. Osborne, *Romans*, 11. He cites over a dozen, from Chrysostom and Calvin to Barth, Cranfield, Wilckens, Moo, Dunn, and Schreiner.

21. Osborne, *Romans*, 11.

22. Osborne, *Romans*, 11–12.

I had a similar impression in 2017 while pondering how to present Romans credibly to some 60 pastors in the Cape Flats, a depressed area called the "dumping ground of apartheid"[23] where people of color were forcibly relocated by the infamous Group Areas Act of 1950. This dense cluster of settlements boasts the highest murder rate in South Africa. Yet it is also a venue rich in ministry opportunity and results at the present time. It is certainly no place for shallow readings of Romans, as pastors want and need meat not milk. Our conference permitted me five one-hour sessions to go deep and give a Reformation-commemorating exposition of the celebrated solas. But in light of Romans' complexities and the lack of consensus among scholars on even what Romans' purpose is, I opted to give five talks on Galatians instead.

At a subsequent pastoral training conference in those same Cape Flats, I took up Romans, having settled on what is an overlooked key to Paul's pastoral intent in writing the letter is Rom 16:17–20:

> I appeal to you, brothers, to watch out for those who cause divisions and create obstacles contrary to the doctrine that you have been taught; avoid them. For such persons do not serve our Lord Christ, but their own appetites, and by smooth talk and flattery they deceive the hearts of the naive. For your obedience is known to all, so that I rejoice over you, but I want you to be wise as to what is good and innocent as to what is evil. The God of peace will soon crush Satan under your feet. The grace of our Lord Jesus Christ be with you.

It is proper to note the possible purposes for Romans as well as its many emphases. Schreiner's commentary lists some of the most common proposals. Romans is: a summary of Paul's theology; a summary of previous letters or last testament; a letter to Jerusalem; a letter to put the Roman church on an apostolic foundation; a counter-imperial letter; a letter to garner support for the Spanish mission; a letter to ease tensions between Jews and Gentiles in Rome and/or Roman congregations.[24] But here I want to argue for consideration of 16:17–20 as a closing flourish that would alert the pastoral leaders of household congregations to what they should make of Paul's letter in its entirety. If that is the case, then Romans is not least—and perhaps more than scholars tend to affirm—a *pastoral* letter with overt *pastoral* application. I will get to specifics shortly. First a historical point and then a logistical conjecture.

The historical point is that the earliest Pauline churches had pastoral leaders who would have administered the content of his letters to the congregations who received them. Acts 14:22 depicts Paul and Barnabas appointing elders in

---

23. Cf. Christopher Clark, "Cape Flats: New hope in 'apartheid's dumping ground.'" CNN Travel. January 26, 2016. https://www.cnn.com/travel/article/cape-town-townships/index.html.

24. Thomas R. Schreiner, *Romans*, 2nd ed., BECNT (Grand Rapids: Baker Academic, 2018), 16–22.

every church. In my reading, these can be likened to the overseers spoken of in 1 Tim 3 and Titus 1. First Thessalonians 5 confirms the leaders' presence in a congregation or group of congregations only recently founded. In 1 Thess 5:27 we read that Paul places the recipients of the letter, surely the leaders, under oath: "I charge you before the Lord to have this letter read to all the brothers and sisters." Some verses earlier (5:12–13) we read directions to the congregation regarding these leaders: "We ask you, brothers, to respect those who labor among you and are over you in the Lord and admonish you, and to esteem them very highly in love because of their work. Be at peace among yourselves" (ESV).[25] While early churches were household gatherings rather than churches as we more typically know them, these household congregations nevertheless had leaders. First Peter 5 addresses the elders of churches receiving that epistle and instructs them on shepherding the flock under Christ the chief Shepherd. Hebrews 13:17 surely rallies church members to cooperation with pastoral overseers when it says, "Obey your leaders and submit to them, for they are keeping watch over your souls, as those who will have to give an account." A major effect of Paul's three pastoral letters is the same.

Given this historical evidence, a logistical conjecture regarding Romans is justified. I suggest there was a similar dynamic at work with the congregational reception of Paul's letter to Roman believers. All believers who heard the letter, or who had it taught to them in the course of time after the letter arrived, would have heard and applied its message. In that sense, Romans was addressed to all the church members who heard it read in their congregations. But if modern literacy studies are correct that not many people could read, and if our understanding of scribal practices is on target,[26] the Roman letter was not mass-copied so that most or even many in the congregations would have daily personal access to it to read and ponder. Its contents would rather have been in the hands of the congregational overseers and other recognized teachers, who would in the course of time read the letter to everyone as 1 Thess 5:27 commands. A similar dynamic is visible as Paul writes regarding his epistle and its apparent twin: "And when this letter [Colossians] has been read among you, have it also read in the church of the Laodiceans; and see that you also read the letter from Laodicea" (Col 4:16).

Pastoral leaders who could read and were charged with shepherding and instructing church members would then labor among house church participants

---

25. The leadership function of these figures is confirmed in an essay on Paul's pastoral strategy at Thessalonica: see Trevor Burke, "Mother, Father, Infant, Orphan, Brother: Paul's Variegated Pastoral Strategy towards His Thessalonian Church Family," in *Paul as Pastor*, ed. Brian Rosner, Andrew Malone, and Trevor Burke (London: T&T Clark, 2018), 139–40.

26. On these two points, see Justo L. González, *The Bible in the Early Church* (Grand Rapids: Eerdmans, 2022), 60–61. He suggests that less than a fourth and perhaps as few as a tenth of the population in the Roman Empire could read.

to help impress Romans' message on them, perhaps in part as Titus 2 describes, with discipleship delegated among various subgroups. Along with this instructional guidance, subgroup overseers would render spiritual oversight, the necessary complement to teaching.

To return to Rom 16:17–20, this passage is not an interpolation, as Paul Jewett has proposed; nor is it a misplaced pericope from some other Pauline letter, as others have thought.[27] I propose that Paul crafted it to alert all readers or listeners, but especially those overseeing the public reading and subsequent instruction in the letter, to ponder the Roman epistle precisely for the sake of fulfilling the surprisingly wide-ranging instructions the brief passage contains. If this conjecture is correct, these verses confirm the centrality of a *pastoral* purpose for the gospel-saturated Romans.

Upon reflection, it is easy to imagine Paul thinking along these lines: he intends to come to Rome, minister the gospel there, and benefit from mutual exchange of spiritual giftedness (1:10–11). But an epistle is justified to announce Paul's eventual arrival and to confirm and expand on what "gospel" means precisely for the Roman congregations receiving the letter in view of Paul's hope for their aid in the upcoming mission to Spain. As 16:17–20 indicates, Paul knows they face possible divisions and obstacles posed by "people . . . not serving our Lord Christ, but their own appetites," and people who "by smooth talk and flattery . . . deceive the minds of naive people" (16:18). They defy the apostolic διδαχή (teaching) Paul and other apostles stand for and are therefore to be shunned, not welcomed or tolerated (16:17).

Paul praises his Roman readers for their obedience (ὑπακοή; 16:19), a word that occurs in 1:5, 15:18, and 16:26, referring (as in 16:19) to the Gentiles' response to the gospel. The Roman readers get what Paul's gospel aims to establish: "the obedience that comes from faith" in Christ, whom the gospel announces among Gentiles like them. But in part to confirm and steady them in their obedience, Paul has written a letter containing διδαχή that will be of great value in their steadfastness and growth in obedience. Paul had written earlier in 6:17, "But thanks be to God that, though you used to be slaves to sin, you have come to obey [from ὑπακούω] from your heart the pattern of teaching [διδαχή] that has now claimed your allegiance."

Calvin in his Romans commentary points to Paul's pastoral aim here: "Men are distracted from the unity of the truth when the truth of God is destroyed by doctrines of human invention. They are alienated from the love of the Gospel when it is made the object of hatred or contempt by various means."[28] Romans provides exhortation and didactic resources for offsetting these calamities.

---

27. Porter, *Romans*, 301.

28. John Calvin, *The Epistles of Paul the Apostle to the Romans and to the Thessalonians*, trans. Ross MacKenzie (Grand Rapids: Eerdmans, 1960), 324.

Whatever else it may be, Paul's Roman letter is a pastoral letter[29] whose every section assists both pastoral and lay recipients in complying with the pastoral admonition found in 16:17–20. It does so by means of its creative, comprehensive, and authoritative exposition and application of the gospel, as already noted. As Schreiner writes, Paul's intention in the letter is not merely evangelistic, but also "to strengthen and edify those who are already believers in Rome."[30] The entire letter seen in the light of its concluding directive edge in 16:17–20 serves that fortifying pastoral aim.

The Gospel's Centrality in Romans: Political Effect

By political here, I mean pertaining to the πόλις, the human community. According to Gen 3 and especially 3:15, that community is marred and menaced by sin and its aftereffects. A chief aftereffect was enmity between Satan and the woman and between Satan's and the woman's descendants. Cain killing Abel in Gen 4 gives an immediate confirmation of the problem. The word in LXX Gen 3:15 that epitomizes the lethal human flaw is ἔχθρα, "enmity." God tells the serpent in 3:15, "I will put enmity between you and the woman, and between your offspring and hers; he will crush your head, and you will strike his heel." God promises to quash the enmity introduced by sin by crushing Satan through the offspring of the woman.

Commentators like Moo, Porter, Peterson, Schnabel, and Hultgren agree that the words in Rom 16:20, "the God of peace will soon crush Satan under your feet," could very well be connected to Gen 3:15.[31] Schreiner argues for this more vigorously, citing Schlatter in support. In Schreiner's words, "Paul is reflecting on Gen. 3:15 MT, which promises victory over the serpent and his offspring."[32] This would not be surprising, given the prominence of the Genesis narrative in Rom 1 (creation), Rom 4 (Abraham), Rom 5 (Christ undoing Adam's trespass), Rom 8 (creation subjected to futility), and Rom 9 (God's electing a people through Rebekah and Isaac and from them Jacob). As Moises Silva has noted, Paul had "a christological view of redemptive history."[33] This observation in connection with Paul's repeated mention of Adam, Eve, or both elsewhere in

---

29. See Gorman, *Romans*, 26.

30. Schreiner, *Romans*, 59.

31. Moo, *Romans*, 932 (with caveats); Porter, *Romans*, 304; Peterson, *Romans*, 547; Schnabel, *Der Brief des Paulus an die Römer: Kapitel 6–16*, 912; Hultgren, *Romans*, 594 (cautiously). See also Andrew David Naselli, *The Serpent and the Serpent Slayer* (Wheaton, IL: Crossway, 2020), 41, 100.

32. Schreiner, *Romans*, 779.

33. Moisés Silva, "Old Testament in Paul," in *Dictionary of Paul and His Letters*, ed. Gerald F. Hawthorne and Ralph P. Martin (Downers Grove, IL: IVP Academic, 1993), 642.

his letters justifies the inference that when Paul advances the good news of the gospel, he does so against the bad news of the fall transformed by God's promise to redeem that debacle through the seed of the woman, one "born of woman" as Gal 4:4 (ESV) puts it, which echoes "her offspring" in Gen 3:15.

For Paul, it is Christ who vanquishes the Gen 3:15 ἔχθρα. He knows it is a problem as he writes Romans and says as much in Rom 8:7, stating that the mindset of the flesh is hostility toward God (ἔχθρα εἰς θεόν). Internally we all harbor enmity; Rom 7 may describe our ongoing wrestling match with it. World history tells the story of our hostility in the warfare of nations, which still rages today, and in the United States, for example, in ongoing mass shootings and bitter partisanship on every side.

But as Paul would write to the Ephesians, Christ "himself is our peace, who has made the two groups one and has destroyed the barrier, the dividing wall of hostility [ἔχθρα]"; he did this "to reconcile both of them to God through the cross, by which he put to death their hostility [ἔχθρα]" (Eph 2:14, 16). This means that all humankind has access to an Edenic restoration, even in the present, through the amazing redemption of a people through a message that justifies the ungodly and begins to transform the core makeup of each individual member of the body of Christ. Paul thus exhorts in Rom 12:1: "Be transformed." That's what the gospel does. Paul lays it out explicitly in Eph 3:6: "This mystery is that through the gospel the Gentiles are heirs together with Israel, members together of one body, and sharers together in the promise in Christ Jesus." The gospel establishes human harmony. This is something that transcends the common grace of natural affection or mere legal respect. It is rather an eschatologically tinged selfless regard for others that biblical writers call ἀγάπη. That "promise in Christ Jesus" is infinitely wide-ranging in application, but for Paul it surely has its center in the fulfillment of God's Gen 3:15 promise of Christ's Satan-destroying work as summarized in Rom 4:25: "He was delivered over to death for our sins and was raised to life for our justification."

The political meaning is that we disciples of the Satan-stomper are Christ's agents of reconciling outreach to others, even as we already now enjoy proleptic heavenly fellowship in ministry as worshippers and co-laborers in what Paul calls "God's household . . . the church of the living God, the pillar and foundation of the truth" (1 Tim 3:15). People like the original readers of Romans contracted (by hearing and believing) and then extended this gospel contagion in Paul's generation. Hence was established the ἐκκλησία. It is still taking shape and expanding, as human ἔχθρα is displaced by εὐαγγέλιον in places like Cape Flats where human animosity is thick, and where Satan and his seed do their stunning worst to ply murder and deception. Yet as scholars point out,[34] despite opposition, the

---

34. See Scott W. Sunquist, *The Unexpected Christian Century: The Reversal and Transformation of Global Christianity, 1900–2000* (Grand Rapids: Baker Academic,

gospel in amazing ways is bringing disparate groups together through forgiveness of sins, impartation of new life, and promotion of human community inter-
mingled with the beauteous grace with which Paul closes Rom 16:20: "the grace
of our Lord Jesus be with you." Looking back, we can see it was and continues.

Romans is about the God of peace making short work of Satan and displac-
ing his mayhem with human affection, flourishing, and the ongoing creation
of a multinational embedded πόλις conveying the gospel that is transforming
us to current and remaining generations. That is an all-too-brief depiction of
the gospel's political centrality in Romans, the capstone of its ubiquitous and
pastoral presence. This is all to God's glory, as Paul highlights in five separate
doxological outbursts from the first chapter of Romans to the last verse, where
we read: "to the only wise God be glory forevermore through Jesus Christ!
Amen" (16:27; see also 1:25; 9:5; 11:36; 15:33).

The Gospel's Centrality in Romans: Some Matters at Stake

Paul's gospel-centric epistle to the Romans has been famously influential in
its revolutionary effect on individuals like Augustine and John Wesley and on
movements like the Protestant Reformation. The church and the whole world
need its power no less today, for many reasons. For brevity's sake I will mention just four.

1. As Paul warns in 16:17–20, divisions and obstacles caused by aberrant
doctrine are continual threats. A not too distant prominent case in point: the
megachurch pastoral leader Andy Stanley in the largest Protestant denomination
in the United States, the Southern Baptist Convention, and his flirtation with
Marcionite-sounding views on the relation of the Old Testament to the New.[35]
Or consider the debates waged by Robert Gagnon against misreadings of Rom 1

2015), 180–81, commenting on what unites Christians worldwide despite significant
differences. And this is not just an academic assertion: since 1989 to the present I have
engaged in theological education and especially pastoral training in Egypt, Romania,
Sudan, South Sudan, and South Africa (including the Cape Flats). In all these locations,
like any corner of the world, there are human animosities presenting a challenge for
(and often in) the church. Hungarians and Romanians have deep historical tensions.
Sudan is rife with tribal strife, in addition to the ongoing clash between Islam and the
non-Islamic population. The legacy of apartheid in South Africa is well known. Yet in
all these locations, I have observed the gospel message transforming people and communities in observable, practical, and effective ways, so that love, respect, and service
emerge by virtue of the gospel's reception and spread. This seems to compare favorably
with the effect of the gospel message that Romans unpacks and that Paul's ministry
often engendered.

35. Major points at issue are reasonably aired by Albert Mohler, "Getting 'Unhitched' from the Old Testament? Andy Stanley Aims at Heresy." https://albertmohler
.com/2018/08/10/getting-unhitched-old-testament-andy-stanley-aims-heresy/.

and its depiction of homosexual sin.[36] In both cases, Romans (with its strong Old Testament stress) gets it right against Stanley and (in Rom 1) against defenders of sexual expression that deviates from God's norms. We need Romans on many fronts to preserve the numerous truths it advances and explores for the sake of the authenticity of the gospel message and way of living we derive from it.

2. The Romans gospel is a missionary gospel, as its proponent Paul the apostle was a missionary apostle, a point stressed by Eckhard Schnabel.[37] We live in a world of missionary gospel expansion. This requires missionaries. Currently there are some 435,000 missionaries worldwide.[38] That number is projected to expand to 450,000 by 2025 and 600,000 by 2050. To sustain that growth will require steady infusion of the gospel vision for which Romans is arguably the sheet anchor. Will enough churches in enough nations grasp Romans, live it out, and pass it along to next generations so that this missionary growth will continue? Or will doctrinal deviance or indifference render null current projections? Attention or inattention to Romans could prove the deciding factor humanly speaking.

3. The Romans gospel is, in keeping with Paul's chapter 16 warning, pervertible. Currently US-based foreign missions, never lavishly funded, gets by on annual donations of some 52 billion USD.[39] We may well thank God for how much he accomplishes with such a relatively negligible sum relative to the enormity of the task and the 435,000 missionaries directly involved. But while foreign mission giving in the US stands at over 50 billion USD annually, it is estimated that ecclesiastical crime ("amounts embezzled by top custodians of Christian monies") skims off 59 billion USD. The worldwide church is robbed of more than it invests in the Great Commission beyond churches' national borders. We need the gospel message of Romans to purify the church, reject and eject pastoral pretenders, and strengthen the church's discernment against such criminal sacrilege, for the sake of conserving always scarce resources for the promulgation of the Romans gospel.

4. Romans only hints (in chapters 5 and 8) at what elsewhere is a prominent Pauline and early church challenge and theme: persecution of Christians.[40] The

---

36. See Robert A. J. Gagnon, *The Bible and Homosexual Practice: Texts and Hermeneutics* (Nashville: Abingdon, 2001). See also his discussion of Rom 1 in chapter 4 of the present volume.

37. Eckhard J. Schnabel, *Paul the Missionary: Realities, Strategies and Methods* (Downers Grove, IL: IVP Academic, 2010).

38. Numbers in this paragraph are from Gina A. Zurlo, Todd M. Johnson, and Peter F. Crossing, "World Christianity and Religions 2022: A Complicated Relationship," *IBMR* 46 (2022): 71–80, esp. 78.

39. Numbers in this paragraph are from Zurlo, Johnson, and Crossing, "World Christianity and Religions 2022", 79.

40. See Eckhard J. Schnabel, "The Persecution of Christians in the First Century," *JETS* 61 (2018): 525–47.

Center for the Study of Global Christianity estimates that currently 90,000 Christians are martyred annually, or 247 daily.[41] That number is projected to hold steady through 2025, but then climb again to 100,000 annually (274 daily) by 2050. How does this relate to Romans? It takes people of strong faith to lay down their lives for gospel conviction. Where does such conviction come from? From God of course: but he uses means, namely, the active hearing and heeding of his word. I would suggest that the church's readiness not only to live abundantly in Christ but also to die readily for Christ will be enhanced, or will fizzle and fade, to the extent that God in his transforming righteousness as manifest by the Romans gospel is heard, heeded, courageously embraced, and spread (Rom 10:14–15).

Bibliography

Barrett, Matthew, ed. *The Doctrine on Which the Church Stands or Falls: Justification in Biblical, Theological, Historical, and Pastoral Perspective.* Wheaton, IL: Crossway, 2019.

Baugus, Bruce. "The Eclipse of Justification: Justification during the Enlightenment and Post-Enlightenment Eras." Pages 769–810 in *The Doctrine on Which the Church Stands or Falls: Justification in Biblical, Theological, Historical, and Pastoral Perspective.* Edited by Matthew Barrett. Wheaton, IL: Crossway, 2019.

Burke, Trevor. "Mother, Father, Infant, Orphan, Brother: Paul's Variegated Pastoral Strategy towards His Thessalonian Church Family." Pages 123–42 in *Paul as Pastor.* Edited by Brian Rosner, Andrew Malone, and Trevor Burke. London: T&T Clark, 2018.

Calhoun, Robert Matthew. *Paul's Definition of the Gospel in Romans 1.* WUNT 2.316. Tübingen: Mohr Siebeck, 2011.

Calvin, John. *The Epistles of Paul the Apostle to the Romans and to the Thessalonians.* Translated by Ross MacKenzie. Grand Rapids: Eerdmans, 1960.

Chester, Stephen. *Reading Paul with the Reformers.* Grand Rapids: Eerdmans, 2017.

Clark, Christopher. "Cape Flats: New hope in 'apartheid's dumping ground.'" CNN Travel. January 26, 2016. https://www.cnn.com/travel/article/cape-town-townships/index.html.

Doriani, Daniel M. *Romans.* REC. Phillipsburg, NJ: P&R, 2021.

Gagnon, Robert A. J. *The Bible and Homosexual Practice: Texts and Hermeneutics.* Nashville: Abingdon, 2001.

González, Justo L. *The Bible in the Early Church.* Grand Rapids: Eerdmans, 2022.

---

41. Numbers in this paragraph are from Zurlo, Johnson, and Crossing, "World Christianity and Religions 2022," 97.

Gorman, Michael J. *Romans: A Theological and Practical Commentary*. Grand Rapids: Eerdmans, 2022.

Hahn, Scott. *Romans*. CCSS. Grand Rapids: Baker Academic, 2017.

Hultgren, Arland. *Paul's Letter to the Romans: A Commentary*. Grand Rapids: Eerdmans, 2011.

Kruse, Colin G. *Paul's Letter to the Romans*. PNTC. Grand Rapids: Eerdmans, 2012.

Laato, Timo. "The New Quest for Paul: A Critique of the New Perspective on Paul." Pages 295–326 in *The Doctrine on Which the Church Stands or Falls: Justification in Biblical, Theological, Historical, and Pastoral Perspective*. Edited by Matthew Barrett. Wheaton, IL: Crossway, 2019.

Mohler, Albert. "Getting 'Unhitched' from the Old Testament? Andy Stanley Aims at Heresy." https://albertmohler.com/2018/08/10/getting-unhitched -old-testament-andy-stanley-aims-heresy/.

Moo, Douglas J. *The Epistle to the Romans*. Grand Rapids: Eerdmans, 1996.

Naselli, Andrew David. *The Serpent and the Serpent Slayer*. SSBT. Wheaton, IL: Crossway, 2020.

Osborne, Grant. *Romans*. IVPNTC. Downers Grove, IL: IVP Academic, 2004.

Peterson, David G. *Commentary on Romans*. BTCP. Nashville: Holman Reference, 2017.

Porter, Stanley E. *The Letter to the Romans: A Linguistic and Literary Commentary*. NTM 37. Sheffield: Sheffield Phoenix Press, 2015.

Rosner, Brian, Andrew Malone, and Trevor Burke, eds. *Paul as Pastor*. London: T&T Clark, 2018.

Silva, Moisés. "Old Testament in Paul." Pages 630–42 in *Dictionary of Paul and His Letters*. Edited by Gerald F. Hawthorne and Ralph F. Martin. Downers Grove, IL: IVP Academic, 1993.

Sircar, Subhro Sekhar. *Paul's Theology of Mission to the Nations in Romans*. BHR 9. New Delhi, India: Christian World Imprints, 2017.

Schnabel, Eckhard J. *Der Brief des Paulus an die Römer: Kapitel 1–5*. 2nd ed. HTA. Witten/Gießen: Brockhaus/Brunnen, 2018.

———. *Der Brief des Paulus an die Römer: Kapitel 6–16*. HTA. Witten/Gießen: Brockhaus/Brunnen, 2016.

———. *Paul the Missionary: Realities, Strategies and Methods*. Downers Grove, IL: IVP Academic, 2010.

———. "The Persecution of Christians in the First Century." *JETS* 61 (2018): 525–47.

Schreiner, Thomas R. *Romans*. 2nd ed. BECNT. Grand Rapids: Baker Academic, 2018.

Shaw, David. "What Next? Justification after the New Perspective." Pages 327–50 in *The Doctrine on Which the Church Stands or Falls: Justification in*

    Biblical, Theological, Historical, and Pastoral Perspective. Edited by Matthew Barrett. Wheaton, IL: Crossway, 2019.

Sunquist, Scott W. *The Unexpected Christian Century: The Reversal and Transformation of Global Christianity, 1900–2000.* Grand Rapids: Baker Academic, 2015.

Vidu, Adonis. *The Same God Who Works All Things: Inseparable Operations in Trinitarian Theology.* Grand Rapids: Eerdmans, 2021.

Zurlo, Gina A., Todd M. Johnson, and Peter F. Crossing. "World Christianity and Religions 2022: A Complicated Relationship." *IBMR* 46 (2022): 71–80.

CHAPTER 2

The Revelation of the Righteousness
of God in Romans

Douglas J. Moo

The phrase "righteousness of God" is especially important to the argument of Romans, since, of Paul's nine uses of the phrase, eight occur in this letter (1:17; 3:5, 21, 22, 25, 26; 10:3 [twice]; the other occurrence is in 2 Cor 5:21).[1] Moreover, the phrase is prominent in precisely those texts that are often considered to state the central theme of the letter: 1:16–17 and 3:21–26. The interpretation of "the righteousness of God" has played a significant role in the interpretation of Paul and of the gospel generally—from Augustine to Luther to E. Käsemann to N. T. Wright. We can group these interpretations into three basic categories.

(1) The expression might refer to *an attribute of God*.[2] Some have identified this attribute as God's justice, or rectitude (*iustitia distributiva*, "distributive justice"). This interpretation was widespread in the early church, where it owed its popularity somewhat to the meaning of the Greek term *dikaiosynē* and its Latin equivalent.[3] Contemporary scholars, while often giving this meaning (or one similar to it) to the phrase in 3:5 and 3:25–26, rarely do so in 1:17;[4] and justly so: the context requires a positive meaning for the phrase. Another option within this "attribute" category takes its point of departure from the alleged OT meaning of "God's righteousness": God's faithfulness, especially to his covenant with Israel. This interpretation also has an ancient pedigree,[5] and has been especially popular in recent literature.[6]

---

1. The substance—and often wording—of this paper duplicates material in *The Letter to the Romans*, 2nd ed., NICNT (Grand Rapids: Eerdmans, 2018).

2. With this meaning, θεοῦ is likely a possessive genitive: "God's own righteousness."

3. See A. E. McGrath, *Iustitia Dei: A History of the Christian Doctrine of Justification*, 2 vols. (Cambridge: Cambridge University Press, 1986–87), 1:52. Some recent interpreters think the phrase refers to the "justice" of God, but define justice in a broad sense, incorporating God's exercise of judgment and salvation, reliability, etc. See Robert Matthew Calhoun, *Paul's Definitions of the Gospel in Romans 1*, WUNT 2.316 (Tübingen: Mohr Siebeck, 2011), 157–68.

4. Though E. Ochsenmeier argues the phrase refers to God's impartial justice, noting especially the prominence of other δικ- words in Rom 1–3 that move in this direction (*Mal, Souffrance et Justice de Dieu selon Romains 1-3: Étude Exégétique et Théologique*, BZNW 155 [Berlin: de Gruyter, 2007], 226–41).

5. See McGrath, *Iustitia Dei*, 1:52, who cites Ambrosiaster.

6. See esp. N. T. Wright, *Paul and the Faithfulness of God*, COQG 4 (Minneapolis: Fortress, 2013), 795–804; Sam K. Williams, "The Righteousness of God in Romans," *JBL*

(2) "Righteousness of God" in 1:17 might refer to a *status given by God*.[7] Luther's personal spiritual struggle ended with his realization that God's righteousness meant not "the righteousness by which he is righteous in himself but the righteousness by which we are made righteous by God."[8] It meant not the strict "distributive justice" (*iustitia distributiva*) by which God impartially rules and governs the world, but a righteousness that is not one's own (*iustitia aliena*), a new standing imparted to the sinner who believes—this was what made Paul's message "good news" to Luther. In contrast to both Augustine and most medieval theologians, Luther viewed this righteousness as purely forensic—a matter of judicial standing, or status, and not of internal renewal or moral transformation.[9] This understanding of the "righteousness of God" stands at the heart of Luther's theology and has been a hallmark of Protestant interpretation.[10] On this view, Paul is asserting that the gospel reveals "the righteous status that is from God."

(3) "Righteousness of God" might denote *an activity of God*.[11] The English word "righteousness" naturally designates an abstract quality, but it is argued that the equivalent Greek term (*dikaiosynē*) in the LXX has a much broader range of meaning—including the dynamic sense of "establishing right." Especially significant are the many places in the Psalms and Isaiah where God's

---

99 (1980): 241–90; Peter T. O'Brien, "Justification in Paul and Some Crucial Issues of the Last Two Decades," in *Right With God: Justification in the Bible and the World*, ed. D. A. Carson (Eugene, OR: Wipf & Stock, 2002), 70–78.

7. This interpretation usually takes θεοῦ as a genitive of source—"righteousness from God"—but a few have followed Luther and taken it as an objective genitive—"righteousness that is valid before God" (cf. A. Oepke, "ΔΙΚΑΙΟΣΥΝΗ ΘΕΟΥ Bei Paulus in Neuer Beleuchtung," *TLZ* 78 (1953): 263 [*TDNT* 3:583]; Francis Watson, *Paul and the Hermeneutics of Faith*, 2nd ed., Cornerstones [London: T&T Clark, 2015], 43–44).

8. *LW* 25.151.

9. McGrath argues that it was this "deliberate and systematic distinction . . . between justification and regeneration" that distinguished Protestant from medieval Roman Catholic theology (*Iustitia Dei*, 1:183–86).

10. As we have seen, however, the occurrences in 3:5 and 3:25–26 are usually exempted and understood to refer to God's justice. A sample of expositors who argue that "righteousness of God" in 1:17 is a status given to human beings by God includes Cranfield; Mark A. Seifrid, *Justification by Faith: The Origin and Development of a Central Pauline Theme*, NovTSup 68 (Leiden: Brill, 1992), 214–15; C. L. Irons, *The Righteousness of God: A Lexical Examination of the Covenant-Faithfulness Interpretation*, WUNT 2.386 (Tübingen: Mohr Siebeck, 2015), 311–18; Rudolf Karl Bultmann ("Δικαιοσύνη Θεοῦ," *JBL* 83 [1964]: 12–16) and many of his followers, such as Hans Conzelmann (*An Outline of the Theology of the New Testament*, NTL [London: SCM Press, 1969], 214–20), G. Klein ("Righteousness in the NT," in *IDBSup*, ed. Keith Crim [New York: Abingdon, 1976], 750–52), and D. Zeller (*Juden Und Heiden in Der Mission Des Paulus: Studien Zum Römerbrief*, FB 1 [Stuttgart: Katholisches Bibelwerk, 1976], 161–80).

11. On this view, θεοῦ is a subjective genitive: "the righteousness that is being shown by God."

"righteousness" refers to his salvific intervention on behalf of his people. In this case, "God's righteousness" would be generally equivalent to his saving action."[12]

Some interpretations of the phrase do not, of course, neatly fit into this simple outline; and it is especially important to note that many interpreters would incorporate two or more of these basic ideas in their definition of the phrase in 1:17. In fact, every possible combination of the three basic interpretations is found in the literature: God's action in making people right and the status of people so made right;[13] God's attribute of "being in the right" and his making sinners right before him;[14] both his being in the right and his gift of righteousness;[15] and, combining all three, God's being in the right, his action of making people right before him, *and* the resultant status of those made right.[16] A particularly significant option along these lines has been advanced by E. Käsemann. He argues that "God's righteousness" is "God's salvation-creating power,"[17] a concept that incorporates the ideas of status given by God and ac-

---

12. J. Cambier, *L'Evangile de La Justice et de La Gràce* (Bruges: Desclée de Brouwer, 1967), 39–40; J. H. Roberts, "Righteousness in Romans with Special Reference to Romans 3:19–31," *Neot* 15 (1981), 18. Perhaps to be included here is the view of Douglas A. Campbell, who thinks that "God's righteousness" is a wholly liberative activity; his sovereign intervention to right wrongs (along the lines, he argues, of the Israelite king's coming to the rescue of the poor and downtrodden [he cites especially Ps 98]) (*The Deliverance of God: An Apocalyptic Rereading of Justification in Paul* [Grand Rapids: Eerdmans, 2009], 675–702). For response, see Douglas J. Moo, "Review Article: The Deliverance of God: An Apocalyptic Rereading of Justification in Paul by Douglas A. Campbell," *JETS* 53 (2010): 143–50; Chris Tilling, ed., *Beyond Old and New Perspectives on Paul* (Eugene, OR: Wipf & Stock, 2014).

13. Harold S. Songer, "New Standing Before God: Romans 3:21–5:21," *RevExp* 73 (1976): 416.

14. David Hill, *Greek Words and Hebrew Meanings: Studies in the Semantics of Soteriological Terms*, SNTS 5 (Eugene, OR: Wipf & Stock, 1967), 160; William Sanday and Arthur Cayley Headlam, *A Critical and Exegetical Commentary on the Epistle to the Romans*, ICC (Edinburgh: T&T Clark, 1895); F. F. Bruce, *The Letter of Paul to the Romans*, TNTC (Downers Grove, IL: IVP Academic, 1985), 74.

15. Leon Morris, *The Apostolic Preaching of the Cross*, 3rd ed. (Grand Rapids: Eerdmans, 1965), 252; C. A. Anderson Scott, *Christianity According to St. Paul* (Cambridge: Cambridge University Press, 1939), 63.

16. James Hardy Ropes, "'Righteousness' and 'the Righteousness of God' in the Old Testament and in St. Paul," *JBL* 22 (1903): 225–26; A. J. M. Wedderburn, *The Reasons for Romans* (Minneapolis: Fortress, 1991), 108–23; Frank Thielman, "God's Righteousness as God's Fairness in Romans 1:17: An Ancient Perspective on a Significant Phrase," *JETS* 54 (2011): 35–48.

17. Germ. "Heilsetzende Macht." For Käsemann's view, see esp. "The Righteousness of God," in *New Testament Questions of Today*, trans. W. J. Montague (Philadelphia: Fortress, 1969), 168–82; *Commentary on Romans*, trans. and ed. Geoffrey W. Bromiley (Grand Rapids: Eerdmans, 1980), 23–30; the appendix to "Justification and Salvation History," in *Perspectives on Paul* (Philadelphia: Fortress, 1971), 76–78. A few of the more important works that defend this general approach—though with differences in specifics—are: Peter Stuhlmacher, *Gerechtigkeit Gottes bei Paulus*, FRLANT 87 (Got-

tivity exercised by God—with the emphasis on the latter—and the addition of nuances such as God's reclaiming of creation for his lordship.

In what follows, we will try to determine what Paul means by the language of "righteousness" or "righteousness of God" in Romans. Four factors influence the decision we reach on this issue: (1) the semantic range of the word *dikaiosynē*; (2) the OT use of the word, particularly when it is qualified by a reference to God; (3) the use of "righteousness" words generally in Paul, and especially in Romans;[18] and (4) the immediate context of Rom 1:17. The difficulty is that they do not all point in the same direction.

The Semantic Range of the Word *Dikaiosynē*

The Greek word *dikaiosynē* belongs to a class of words (ending in *-synē*) that usually denote an abstract quality: in this case the quality of being *dikaios*, "right," or "just." God may be said to possess such an attribute; and so can humans. But it is a bit more difficult to think that a noun of this class could come to denote an action.[19]

In terms of the OT Background, we begin with "righteousness" language generally. Righteousness language occurs in all forms of ancient Greek,[20] but the widespread and theologically significant use of the terminology in the LXX, along with Paul's frequent appeal to the OT in discussing the words, shows that the OT/Jewish background is decisive. Words from the *dik-* root consistently (though not universally) translate words from the *ṣdq* root: the noun *dikaiosynē* ("righteousness") normally translate *ṣedeq* and *ṣədāqâ* (which probably have the same

---

tingen: Vandenhoeck & Ruprecht, 1965) (see, however, the important qualifications he introduces in his essay "The Apostle Paul's View of Righteousness," in *Reconciliation, Law & Righteousness: Essays in Biblical Theology* [Philadelphia: Fortress, 1986], 91–92); Christian Müller, *Gottes Gerechtigkeit und Gottes Volk: Eine Untersuchung zu Römer 9–11*, FRLANT 86 (Göttingen: Vandenhoeck & Ruprecht, 1964), esp. 65–72, 109–14; Karl Kertelge, *Rechtfertigung bei Paulus: Studien zur Struktur und zum Bedeutungsgehalt des Paulinischen Rechtfertigungsbegriffs*, NTA 3 (Münster: Aschendorff, 1967); John A. Ziesler, *The Meaning of Righteousness in Paul: A Linguistic and Theological Inquiry*, SNTSMS 20 (London: Cambridge University Press, 1972), 170–71, 187–88; Arland J. Hultgren, *Paul's Gospel and Mission* (Philadelphia: Fortress, 1985), 31; J. Christiaan Beker, *Paul the Apostle: The Triumph of God in Life and Thought* (Philadelphia: Fortress, 2000), 263–64.

18. These include, in addition to the noun δικαιοσύνη, the adjective δίκαιος ("righteous") and the verb δικαιόω ("justify").

19. See esp. Denny Burk, "The Righteousness of God (Dikaiosunē Theou) and Verbal Genitives: A Grammatical Clarification," *JSNT* 34 (2012): 346–60; also, e.g., Ochsenmeier, *Mal, Souffrance et Justice de Dieu*, 239–41.

20. See the survey in Schrenk, *TDNT* 2:178–225; and also Mark A. Seifrid, "Paul's Use of Righteousness Language Against Its Hellenistic Background," in *Justification and Variegated Nomism: The Paradoxes of Paul*, WUNT 2.181, ed. D. A. Carson, Peter T. O'Brien, and Mark A. Seifrid (Tübingen: Mohr Siebeck, 2004), 39–74.

meaning[21]); *dikaioō* ("justify") usually translates *ṣādaq*; and *dikaios* ("righteous," "just") *ṣāddîq*.[22] By the same token, words from the *ṣdq* root are translated by Greek words from the *dik-* root in the large majority of cases. This considerable linguistic overlap suggests that the meaning of *dik-* words for Greek-speaking Jews like Paul would have been decisively influenced by the meaning of *ṣdq* words.

The denotation of these words has been a matter of long-standing controversy. While heeding Seifrid's warning about not imposing on the rich vocabulary of righteousness in the OT a single "basic concept,"[23] we suggest that these words often, and perhaps even basically, allude to the notion of doing or being "right," the "rightness" being determined by the particular situation in which one is placed.[24] Weights are "right" (*ṣedeq*; LXX *dikaia*) when they conform to agreed-upon standards of measurement (Lev 19:36); Noah is "right" (*ṣāddîq*, LXX *dikaios*) when he conforms to God's will for him (Gen 6:9); a person, whether in covenant relationship or not, is "right" when he or she conforms to the standards built into this world by God (*ṣāddîq*, LXX *dikaios* very often in Proverbs); an Israelite is "right" (*ṣāddîq*, LXX *dikaios*) when he or she conforms to the expectations of the covenant relationship (e.g., Ezek 18:9); God's decrees are "right" (*ṣāddîqim*, LXX *dikaia*) when (and because) they conform to his own person and will (e.g., Deut 4:8; Ps 119 passim); God is "right" (*ṣāddîq*, LXX *dikaios*) when he punishes his people (Neh 9:33), because this judgment is in conformity with God's warning about punishment for covenant unfaithfulness; and, at the same time, God's "righteousness" (*ṣidqî*, LXX *dikaiosynē*) acts to vindicate his people (e.g., Isa 51:4–8) because this, too, is in conformity to his gracious promise to redeem his people after judgment. Righteousness, therefore, often implies a conformity to a norm. But since this "norm" is God's own character and his commitment to "do right," the long-standing debate about whether the language indicates conformity to a norm[25] or "mutual fulfillment of claims arising from a particular relationship"[26] can be put to rest: it is both.

21. E.g., Scullion, *ABD* 5:725–26. Contra, e.g., Mark A. Seifrid, "Righteousness Language in the Hebrew Scriptures and Early Judaism," in *Justification and Variegated Nomism: Complexities of Second Temple Judaism*, WUNT 2.140, ed. D. A. Carson, Peter T. O'Brien, and Mark A. Seifrid (Tübingen: Mohr Siebeck, 2001), 428.

22. Ziesler, *The Meaning of Righteousness*, 22–67, gives a full survey of the OT data.

23. Seifrid, "Righteousness Language," 418.

24. For similar views, see, e.g., Seifrid, "Righteousness Language"; Stephen Westerholm, *Perspectives Old and New on Paul: The "Lutheran" Paul and His Critics* (Grand Rapids: Eerdmans, 2004), 267–78; Thomas R. Schreiner, *Faith Alone: The Doctrine of Justification: What the Reformers Taught ... and Why It Still Matters*, TFSS (Grand Rapids: Zondervan Academic, 2015), 216–29; Irons, *The Righteousness of God*, 131–77.

25. For a concise survey, see John Piper, *The Justification of God: An Exegetical and Theological Study of Romans 9:1–23*, 2nd ed. (Grand Rapids: Baker Academic, 1993), 82–83; Seifrid, "Righteousness Language," 419–22.

26. See esp. Hermann Cremer, *Die Paulinische Rechtfertigungslehre: im Zusammenhange ihrer geschichtlichen Voraussetzungen* (Hansebooks, 1899). This basic ap-

But we are not faced here with either/or propositions. Many instances of "righteousness" language reveal that the norm or relationship that lies behind the word is God's own character or his commitment to do "right" to his creation. At the same time, then, God's decision to bind himself and Israel in a covenant relationship means that many instances of the *ṣdq* root assume that this "rightness" is defined (though certainly not exhausted) in terms of this covenant structure (see below). On the other hand, "righteousness" language will, by a simple extension, often connote the status of a person who has conformed to the expected norm.

The OT Use of *Dikaiosynē Theou*

The actual phrase *dikaiosynē theou* never occurs in the LXX; *dikaiosynē kyriou* ("righteousness of the Lord") occurs twice (1 Sam 12:7; Mic 6:5). But 48 times, mainly in the Psalms and Isaiah, we find *dikaiosynē* modified by a personal pronoun whose antecedent is "God" or "the Lord."[27] In all but six of these occurrences, *dikaiosynē* translates *ṣedeq* (12 times) or *ṣədāqâ* (32 times).[28] In addition to these specific references to "God's righteousness" are more than 50 places where *dikaiosynē* is ascribed to God or where God is said to do or speak *dikaiosynē*, or the like.

In secular Greek, God's *dikaiosynē* is usually a divine attribute, and biblical texts also ascribe "righteousness" to God. Taking as our starting point key passages in Isa 40–66, we read that "in the LORD alone are righteousness and strength" (45:24; NIV adapted); the LORD is "a righteous God and Savior" (45:21); and God's servant is also "righteous" (53:11). But the OT tends to portray God's righteousness as a relational characteristic in regard to humans. Thus, God acts "in righteousness" (41:2; 42:6; 45:13; see 45:23) or "with the hand of my righteousness" (41:10); or "in accordance with the magnitude of his righteousness" (63:7, LXX only; my translation); or "for his righteousness" (42:21). Such language is especially common in the Psalms. In such passages, "righteousness" becomes the norm by which God himself acts.[29]

---

proach to the language has been followed by a large number of modern OT (and NT) scholars.

27. Of these, two are textually uncertain. In 1 Sam 12:7, some MSS read the plural δικαιοσύνας, and the phrase is omitted entirely in some MSS in Ps 71:21.

28. The exceptions are Exod 15:13 and Isa 63:7 (where the Hebrew is חֶסֶד), Isa 38:19 and LXX Dan 9:13 (where the Hebrew is אֱמֶת), and Bar 4:13 and Ps 71:21 (where there is no corresponding Hebrew word).

29. E.g., Ps 51:14 (LXX 50:16), where David prays, "Deliver me from the guilt of bloodshed, O God, you who are God my Savior, and my tongue will sing of your righteousness [τὴν δικαιοσύνη σου]" (LXX 50:16). See also Pss 35:24; 36:6, 10; 71:2; 89:16; 103:17; 111:3; 119:40; 143:1, 11; 145:7; and also Exod 15:13; Isa 38:19. In these texts,

There is considerable debate, as we note above, over whether this norm is an absolute, residing in or an aspect of God's person, or whether the norm is relational, existing because of the covenant to which God has bound himself. In the second sense, God's "righteousness" can sometimes come to refer to the norms of the covenant. Many contemporary scholars therefore think "God's righteousness" in Paul is basically God's "covenant faithfulness."[30] But there are problems with this view.[31] Righteousness language and covenant language are rarely found together (although, in fairness, if covenant is a basic enough category, this is not altogether surprising).[32] Second, as we noted above, there are many contexts in which the "standard" by which God is judged to do "right" goes beyond (and behind) the terms of the covenant. God's righteousness, then, while finding particular historical expression in his faithfulness in maintaining the "right" of his covenant people, is finally rooted more deeply in his own character as God. As Linebaugh says, "a covenantal context does not dilute the notion of normativity which *dikaiosyne* conveys . . . it locates and particularizes the norm."[33]

δικαιοσύνη translates Heb. חֶסֶד ("loving-kindness") twice (Exod 15:13; Isa 63:7), אֱמֶת ("truth") once (Isa 38:19), and is paralleled by words such as ἀλήθεια ("truth"; Pss 36:6; 88:12; 98:2; 143:1; Isa 38:19), ἔλεος ("mercy"; Pss 31:1; 36:6, 10; 88:12; 98:2; 103:17; 143:11), and χρηστότης ("goodness"; Ps 145:7). Note, e.g., Ps 36:5–6a: "Your love [ἔλεος], Lord, reaches to the heavens, your faithfulness [ἀλήθεια] to the skies. Your righteousness [δικιαοσύνη] is like the highest mountains . . ."

30. See esp. N. T. Wright, *Justification: God's Plan & Paul's Vision* (Downers Grove, IL: IVP Academic, 2009), 55–78; Wright, *Paul and the Faithfulness of God*, 1055–71. Reference to "covenant faithfulness" begs a crucial question: what "covenant" are we talking about? Wright refers repeatedly to God's fulfillment of his promises made to Abraham in this regard (e.g., *Justification*, 57). The "covenant" involved, then, is not the Sinai covenant narrowly construed, but the promises that God first made to Abraham and the patriarchs and which he renewed in the Sinai covenant (see esp. Deut 27–30). What, then, is the status of this language in Paul, who importantly distinguishes the Abrahamic covenant from the Mosaic (e.g., Gal 3:15–18)? Michael S. Horton (*Covenant and Salvation: Union with Christ* [Louisville: Westminster John Knox, 2007], 11–36) has drawn attention to the tendency of contemporary NT scholars (and especially those who defend some form of the new perspective) to assume a mono-covenantalism that distorts the biblical categories.

31. The most important critique of the "covenant faithfulness" view is Irons, *Righteousness of God*.

32. Seifrid, "Righteousness Language," 423–24.

33. Jonathan A. Linebaugh, *God, Grace, and Righteousness in Wisdom of Solomon and Paul's Letter to the Romans: Texts in Conversation*, NovTSup 152 (Leiden: Brill, 2013), 131; similarly, Seifrid: "All 'covenant-keeping' is righteous behavior, but not all righteous behavior is 'covenant-keeping'" ("Righteousness Language," 424); see also, e.g., William J. Dumbrell, "Justification in Paul: A Covenantal Perspective," *RTR* 51 (1992): 91–92; Michael F. Bird, "Justification as Forensic Declaration and Covenant Membership: A Via Media Between Reformed and Revisionist Readings of Paul," *TynBul* 57 (2006): 116–18.

In other OT passages, God's "righteousness" is closely bound up with his acting to save his people and/or to judge their enemies. Two passages are particularly important: Isa 51:4–8 and Ps 98:2. Note first Isa 51, esp. vv. 5, 6, and 8:

> **My righteousness** [*ṣidqî; hē dikaiosynē mou*] draws near speedily,
>   **my salvation** [*yiš'î; to sōtērion mou*] is on the way,
>   and my arm will bring justice to the nations.
> But **my salvation** will last forever,
>   **my righteousness** will never fail.
> But **my righteousness** will last forever,
>   **my salvation** through all generations.

Three times God's "salvation" occurs in a parallel line with God's "righteousness." Several other Isaiah texts exhibit a similar pairing (45:8 twice; 46:13; 56:1; 59:16, 17; 61:10; 63:1).

The second key text is Ps 98:2, which features a cluster of words duplicated in Paul. In context (vv. 1–3):[34]

> Sing to the LORD a new song,
>   for he has done marvelous things;
>   his right hand and his holy arm
>   have worked **salvation** for him.
> The LORD has made **his salvation** [*yəšû'ātô; to sōtērion autou*] known
>   and **revealed** [*gillâ; apekalypsen*] his **righteousness** [*ṣidqātô; tēn dikaiosynēn autou*] to **the nations**.
> He has remembered his love
>   and his faithfulness to Israel;
> all **the ends of the earth** have seen
>   the **salvation** of our God.

The close relationship between "righteousness" and "salvation" in these passages[35] might suggest that the two have the same meaning: that "righteousness" *means* "salvation," or "saving acts." But the parallelism need not indicate this, and it is better to see salvation as a manifestation of God's righteousness.[36]

---

34. See, e.g., Richard B. Hays, *Echoes of Scripture in the Letters of Paul* (New Haven: Yale University Press, 1989), 36–37; Ochsenmeier, *Mal, Souffrance et Justice de Dieu*, 69–71; Campbell, *The Deliverance of God*, 688–700. On the importance of the Psalms for righteousness of God in Romans, see Geoffrey Turner, "The Righteousness of God in Psalms and Romans," *SJT* 63 (2010): 285–301.

35. Probably thirteen other texts use "righteousness" with this basic meaning: Pss 22:31; 35:28; 40:10; 69:27; 71:15, 16, 19, 24; 88:12; 98:2; 119:123; Mic 6:5; 7:9.

36. J. A. Motyer comments: "what is essentially a description of the character of God is turned into a description of his acts"; God's saving work "satisfies every standard of God's righteous nature" (*The Prophecy of Isaiah: An Introduction and Commentary*

When God saves his people, he manifests his "being in the right" in that his deliverance fulfills his promises and displays his own glory and faithfulness. Probably most occurrences of the language in this general sense take on a positive sense, simply because the language is being used by or applied to God's own people. But God's righteousness is displayed also when he judges his (and Israel's) enemies. Note, for example, that the end of Ps 98 (see above) returns to the theme of God's righteousness, but now attributes to it God's judgment of the nations: "He will judge the world in righteousness and the peoples with equity" (v. 9b).[37] It is not clear whether this "judging" is neutral—God's "judicial assessment"—or negative—condemnation. However, the important point here is that a negative verdict is at least a possible aspect of God's "judging in righteousness." And this potential negative verdict also applies to God's own people—their stubborn refusal to be faithful to God also earns what God has promised: judgment. In these passages, then, God's saving (quite often) and judging (more rarely) activities are described as manifestations of God's settled determination to "do right."[38] By applying language with a forensic connotation to this activity, these interventions are portrayed as acts of justice.

A frequent objection to any such view of God's righteousness as an "attribute" is that it "intrudes conceptions quite foreign to the Hebrew mind, and for which there is no basis in the naïvely realistic thinking of the Israelite."[39] But such objections, while understandable as a reaction against the tendency of some scholars (particularly in the past) to read European medieval legal norms into the OT, surely have gone too far. What the "Hebrew mind" could or could not conceive can be known only from the pages of the OT. Nor are we seeking to revive the notion that God's righteousness in the OT is a conformity to an ideal ethical norm, as if God were being forced to conform to something outside himself. Nor are we arguing that righteousness is attributed to God as a result of ontological speculation. It is, as we may put it, an experienced attribute, stating the conviction of the Israelites that God can always be

---

[Downers Grove, IL: InterVarsity, 1993], 405). Campbell's distinctive approach focuses on God's righteousness in texts such as Ps. 98 in terms of a monarch bringing liberation to oppressed people (*The Deliverance of God*, 668–703).

37. This "judgment" (צֶדֶק; δικαιοσύνη) probably connotes God's ruling and judging, which can result either in salvation or condemnation. See also, e.g., Pss 7:17; 9:4, 8; 97:2; Isa 59:17. It is God's righteousness in this sense that is given to the king, so that he will be able to "judge your people in righteousness . . . your afflicted ones with justice, . . . defend the afflicted among the people . . . save the children of the needy . . . crush the oppressor" (Ps 72:1–4).

38. God's righteousness is not, then, only a saving righteousness (contra, e.g., Gerhard von Rad, *Old Testament Theology*, 2 vols., OTL [Louisville: Westminster John Knox, 2001], 1:370–77).

39. Walther Eichrodt, *Theology of the Old Testament*, 2 vols., OTL (Philadelphia: Westminster, 1967), 1:240.

depended upon to act in accordance with what is right, as defined by God's person and promises.[40]

To summarize, then, we find that God's *dikaiosynē* in the OT generally refers to God's character as that of a God who will always do what is right (cf. Gen 18:25). God's punishment of his unfaithful covenant partner is a manifestation of that "doing right."[41] But especially significant for God's OT people, suffering in exile, is the glad proclamation that God will manifest his character of "doing right" by intervening to save and vindicate his people. And when he does, the people can be said to enjoy the status of being saved or vindicated.[42]

Two final aspects of the OT teaching are worth mentioning in light of Paul's appropriation of the theme. First, predictions about the revelation of God's righteousness, as some of the texts cited above reveal—especially in Isa 40–66—include the "nations" or Gentiles in his purposes. The theme is especially suited to a letter such as Romans, then, which focuses attention on the inclusion of Gentiles in the people of God. Second, Isaiah and other prophets predict that God will act in his righteousness on behalf of his people Israel. While there are places where God's deliverance is related to people's obedience or righteousness, references to faith in terms of God's righteousness are virtually non-existent. It would fall to Paul to appropriate other OT texts (Hab 2:4; Gen 15:6) that connect "righteousness" and faith to make this connection.

---

40. Evidence of the "cosmic" significance of the phrase, posited, e.g., by Käsemann and his followers, does not have clear textual support and, moreover, severs the connection between righteousness and faith that is fundamental in Paul (see Joseph A. Fitzmyer, *Romans: A New Translation with Introduction and Commentary*, AYBC 33 [New Haven: Yale University Press, 2007], 106–7; Francis Watson, *Paul, Judaism, and the Gentiles: Beyond the New Perspective* [Grand Rapids: Eerdmans, 2007], 238).

41. Although he focuses on "act" as a meaning of the phrase, Irons makes a similar point: God's righteousness is "both his attribute of being a righteous judge who rightly executes his *iustitia distributiva* and the act of deliverance itself so that God's righteousness is conceived of as coming from God and being bestowed on the righteous oppressed" (*The Righteousness of God*, 205).

42. Several scholars have captured this breadth of meaning. Ropes' summary is particularly good: "God's vindication of man can be described either as the righteousness of man or the righteousness of God. It belongs to man as a state into which he is, or hopes to be put; it belongs to God as an attribute, and as the act in which that attribute is exercised" ("Righteousness," 218–19). See also Wright, who distinguishes four related senses: righteous behavior, esp. right relation; law court status; an "attribute of God revealed in action" (esp. in context of covenant); cosmic—covenant faithfulness key (*Paul and the Faithfulness of God*, 796–804). God, Wright claims elsewhere, displays his righteousness in two senses: "covenantal faithfulness and forensic justice, tightly interwoven" (*Paul and the Faithfulness of God*, 942). And Irons, denying any need to separate "distributive" and "saving" righteousness, argues that God's righteousness is "both his attribute of being a righteous judge who rightly executes his *iustitia distributiva* and the act of deliverance itself so that God's righteousness is conceived of as coming from God and being bestowed on the righteous oppressed" (*The Righteousness of God*, 205).

"Righteousness of God" and Other "Righteousness" Language in Paul

Paul uses "righteousness" words in several different ways. One factor, however, is especially clear and important: the tight integration of righteousness language in general and the language of faith. Of course, this has classically been identified as a (or even *the*) key theme of Romans. The references to "righteousness of God" evidence a definite pattern at this point: those in 3:5 and 3:25–26 are not tied directly to faith, and they refer to God's attribute of "faithfulness to his person and promises." On the other hand, Paul links "righteousness of God" closely with the response of faith in 1:17, in 3:21–22, and in 10:3 (note v. 6). This ties the idea of "righteousness" in the phrase "righteousness of God" to Paul's use of the word generally in Romans, where it is typically linked to faith.[43] And "righteousness" is used most often in Romans to denote the "gift of righteousness" (5:17)—a righteous status that God bestows on the one who believes (ch. 4, passim; note also the parallel between "righteousness of God" and "righteousness based on faith" in 10:3–6, and the reference to "righteousness *from* [*ek*] God" in Phil 3:9). Paul's use of "righteousness" language in Romans, then, strongly suggests that "righteousness of God" in 1:17; 3:21, 22; and 10:3 includes reference to the status of righteousness "given" to the believer by God.

The Righteousness of God in the context of Rom 1:17

The fourth consideration is the one that points in the most directions at once. As we have mentioned, Paul connects "the righteousness of God" with faith in 1:17: he claims that it is revealed "on the basis of [Jewish] faith leading to [Gentile] faith" and anchors his claim with a quotation of Hab 2:4, where the cognate word "righteous" designates human status. On the one hand, Paul's use of "reveal"—particularly if it has a dynamic meaning rather than a mere cognitive meaning—makes better sense if "righteousness of God" denotes a divine activity than if it refers to a divine gift. Furthermore, the "revelation of God's wrath" in v. 18 appears to parallel v. 17, and "wrath" in v. 18 also seems to be a divine activity. The contexts in which the related occurrences of "righteousness of God" are found evidence the same ambiguity. First, God's righteousness is "manifested" (3:21) and shown (3:25–26) by his redemptive work in Christ Jesus through faith, also denoting divine activity. Second, the Israelites did not "submit" to God's righteousness because "they sought to establish their own" (10:3). The implied contrast between their righteousness and the righteousness of God suggests a divine activity (making Christ the culmination of the law "for

---

43. This is an important methodological point, for Käsemann and many of his followers insist that δικαιοσύνη θεοῦ be treated as a technical phrase with a meaning all its own.

righteousness"); and yet this righteousness is also "based on" faith, "for all who believe" (10:4)—suggesting gift or status.[44]

Most interpreters make a decision at this point, choosing either activity or status and offering more or less convincing explanations of the data that appear to conflict with the view they have chosen. But we should not too quickly dismiss the first option: that "righteousness of God" refers basically to an attribute of God. "Attribute," however, is a bit too abstract; what is intended is a relational characteristic or aspect of God. This sense of the phrase is suggested by the form and general usage of the word *dikaiosynē* and is arguably the meaning the phrase has in key OT occurrences that are most likely to have influenced Paul—texts that refer to the eschatological revelation of God's righteousness (see esp. Ps 98:2 and Isa 51:5–8 in context). However, in what might seem to be a dubious attempt to have our cake and eat it twice, we would argue that this base concept includes, or at least implies, both God's activity and, more remotely, the status of those who experience God's righteousness.[45] This is also confirmed in Rom 3:26 where God shows his righteousness "in order to be just [*dikaion*] and the one who justifies [*dikaiounta*]." "God's righteousness," then, is an experienced aspect of God in action. When a believer exclaims that "God is good," this "goodness of God" is not so much an "attribute" of God as an experienced aspect of God's character.[46] So "the righteousness of God" is experienced by Jew and Gentile alike in response to belief. And, as a result of that experience, the believer receives the status of righteousness. In the OT, and certainly in the prevalent Jewish view, God's righteousness would be unveiled in saving acts on behalf of his people. But Paul now sees that God's people have been redefined in relationship to Christ. Thus, it is only those—but also, of course *all* those—who believe who benefit from the eschatological revelation of God's righteousness. As Stuhlmacher puts it, "For Paul the righteousness of God is essentially a righteousness that comes by faith."[47]

---

44. Also note the connection between salvation and God's righteousness; Paul prays for them "that they may be saved" (10:1), since "they did not submit to God's righteousness" (10:3).

45. See especially Stuhlmacher, who argues that "righteousness of God" in Paul includes "both poles of the event of justification . . . The gracious activity of God himself and the end result of the divine work in the form of the righteousness granted to the sinner" ("The Theme of Romans," *ABR* 36 [1988]: 339). See also Colin G. Kruse, *Paul's Letter to the Romans*, PNTC (Grand Rapids: Eerdmans, 2012), 69–71.

46. Bird: "God's righteousness is chiefly a way of designating his saving action as it is expressed in his feats of deliverance for his people. The righteousness of God then is the character of God embodied and enacted in his saving works" (*Romans*, SGBC [Grand Rapids: Zondervan, 2016], 111). Thielman, who defends a view very close to our own (though he stresses the idea of "fairness"), refers to a "property" of God ("God's Righteousness," 38). See also Michael Wolter, *Paul: An Outline of His Theology*, trans. Robert L. Brawley (Waco, TX: Baylor University Press, 2015), 121–23.

47. Stuhlmacher, "Paul's View of Righteousness," 80.

With Luther, we stress that what is meant is a status *before* God and not internal moral transformation—God's activity of "making right" is a purely forensic activity, an acquitting, and not an "infusing" of righteousness or a "making right" in a moral sense. To be sure, the person who experiences God's righteousness inevitably and necessarily gives evidence of that in the moral realm, as Paul makes clear in Rom 6. But, while "sanctification" and "justification" are inseparable, they are distinct; and Paul is badly misread if they are confused or combined. To use the imagery of the law court, from which righteousness language is derived, we can picture God's righteousness as the character of the judge who reveals that character by rendering "just" decisions. But the revelation of God's purposes and plans means that his own people can celebrate those "just" decisions as acts of mercy and salvation on their behalf.[48]

Bibliography

Beker, J. Christiaan. *Paul the Apostle: The Triumph of God in Life and Thought.* Philadelphia: Fortress, 2000.

Bird, Michael F. "Justification as Forensic Declaration and Covenant Membership: A Via Media Between Reformed and Revisionist Readings of Paul." *TynBul* 57 (2006): 109–30.

———. *Romans.* SGBC. Grand Rapids: Zondervan Academic, 2016.

Bultmann, Rudolf Karl. "Δικαιοσύνη Θεοῦ." *JBL* 83 (1964): 12–16.

Burk, Denny. "The Righteousness of God (Dikaiosunē Theou) and Verbal Genitives: A Grammatical Clarification." *JSNT* 34 (2012): 346–60.

Bruce, F. F. *The Letter of Paul to the Romans.* TNTC. Downers Grove, IL: IVP Academic, 1985.

Calhoun, Robert Matthew. *Paul's Definitions of the Gospel in Romans 1.* WUNT 2.316. Tübingen: Mohr Siebeck, 2011.

Cambier, J. *L'Evangile de La Justice et de La Grâce.* Bruges: Desclée de Brouwer, 1967.

Campbell, Douglas A. *The Deliverance of God: An Apocalyptic Rereading of Justification in Paul.* Grand Rapids: Eerdmans, 2009.

Conzelmann, Hans. *An Outline of the Theology of the New Testament.* NTL. London: SCM Press, 1969.

Cremer, Hermann. *Die Paulinische Rechtfertigungslehre: im Zusammenhange ihrer geschichtlichen Voraussetzungen.* Hansebooks, 1899.

Dumbrell, William J. "Justification in Paul: A Covenantal Perspective." *RTR* 51 (1992): 91–101.

---

48. I have been immensely helped in my thinking about "righteousness of God" by M. Monkemeier.

Eichrodt, Walther. *Theology of the Old Testament.* 2 vols. OTL. Philadelphia: Westminster, 1967.

Fitzmyer, Joseph A. *Romans: A New Translation with Introduction and Commentary.* AYB 33. New Haven: Yale University Press, 2007.

Hays, Richard B. *Echoes of Scripture in the Letters of Paul.* New Haven: Yale University Press, 1989.

Hill, David. *Greek Words and Hebrew Meanings: Studies in the Semantics of Soteriological Terms.* SNTS 5. Eugene, OR: Wipf & Stock, 1967.

Horton, Michael S. *Covenant and Salvation: Union with Christ.* Louisville: Westminster John Knox, 2007.

Hultgren, Arland J. *Paul's Gospel and Mission.* Philadelphia: Fortress, 1985.

Irons, Charles Lee. *The Righteousness of God: A Lexical Examination of the Covenant-Faithfulness Interpretation.* WUNT 2.386. Tübingen: Mohr Siebeck, 2015.

Käsemann, Ernst. *Commentary on Romans.* Translated and edited by Geoffrey W. Bromiley. Grand Rapids: Eerdmans, 1980.

———. *New Testament Questions of Today.* Translated by W. J. Montague. Philadelphia: Fortress, 1969.

———. *Perspectives on Paul.* Philadelphia: Fortress, 1971.

———. "The Righteousness of God." Pages 168–82 in *New Testament Questions of Today.* Translated by W. J. Montague. Philadelphia: Fortress, 1969.

Kertelge, Karl. *Rechtfertigung Bei Paulus: Studien Zur Struktur Und Zum Bedeutungsgehalt Des Paulinischen Rechtfertigungsbegriffs.* NTA 3. Münster, Germany: Aschendorff, 1967.

Klein, G. "Righteousness in the NT." *IDBSup.* Edited by Keith Crim. New York: Abingdon, 1976.

Kruse, Colin G. *Paul's Letter to the Romans.* PNTC. Grand Rapids: Eerdmans, 2012.

Linebaugh, Jonathan A. *God, Grace, and Righteousness in Wisdom of Solomon and Paul's Letter to the Romans: Texts in Conversation.* NovTSup 152. Leiden: Brill, 2013.

McGrath, Alister E. *Iustitia Dei.* 4th ed. New York: Cambridge University Press, 2020.

Moo, Douglas J. "Review Article: The Deliverance of God: An Apocalyptic Rereading of Justification in Paul by Douglas A. Campbell." *JETS* 53 (2010): 143–50.

———. *The Letter to the Romans.* NICNT. 2nd ed. Grand Rapids: Eerdmans, 2018.

Morris, Leon. *The Apostolic Preaching of the Cross.* 3rd ed. Grand Rapids: Eerdmans, 1965.

Motyer, J. A. *The Prophecy of Isaiah: An Introduction and Commentary.* Downers Grove, IL: IVP Academic, 1993.

Müller, Christian. *Gottes Gerechtigkeit Und Gottes Volk: Eine Untersuchung Zu Römer 9–11*. FRLANT 86. Göttingen: Vandenhoeck & Ruprecht, 1964.

O'Brien, Peter T. "Justification in Paul and Some Crucial Issues of the Last Two Decades." Pages 69–95 in *Right With God: Justification in the Bible and the World*. Edited by D. A. Carson. Eugene, OR: Wipf & Stock, 2002.

Ochsenmeier, Erwin. *Mal, Souffrance et Justice de Dieu Selon Romains 1–3: Étude Exégétique et Théologique*. BZNW 155. Berlin: de Gruyter, 2007.

Oepke, A. "ΔΙΚΑΙΟΣΥΝΗ ΘΕΟΥ Bei Paulus in Neuer Beleuchtung." *TLZ* 78 (1953): 257–64.

Rad, Gerhard von. *Old Testament Theology*. 2 vols. OTL. Louisville: Westminster John Knox, 2001.

Roberts, J. H. "Righteousness in Romans with Special Reference to Romans 3:19–31." *Neot* 15 (1981): 12–33.

Ropes, James Hardy. "'Righteousness' and 'the Righteousness of God' in the Old Testament and in St. Paul." *JBL* 22 (1903): 211–27.

Sanday, William, and Arthur Cayley Headlam. *A Critical and Exegetical Commentary on the Epistle to the Romans*. ICC. Edinburgh: T&T Clark, 1895.

Schreiner, Thomas R. *Faith Alone: The Doctrine of Justification: What the Reformers Taught ... and Why It Still Matters*. TFSS. Grand Rapids: Zondervan Academic, 2015.

Scott, C. A. Anderson. *Christianity According to St. Paul*. Cambridge: Cambridge University Press, 1939.

Seifrid, Mark A. *Justification by Faith: The Origin and Development of a Central Pauline Theme*. NovTSup 68. Leiden: Brill, 1992.

———. "Paul's Use of Righteousness Language Against Its Hellenistic Background." Pages 39–74 in *Justification and Variegated Nomism: The Paradoxes of Paul*. Edited by D. A. Carson, Peter T. O'Brien, and Mark A. Seifrid. WUNT 2.181. Tübingen: Mohr Siebeck, 2004.

———. "Righteousness Language in the Hebrew Scriptures and Early Judaism." Pages 415–42 in *Justification and Variegated Nomism: Complexities of Second Temple Judaism*. Edited by D. A. Carson, Peter T. O'Brien, and Mark A. Seifrid. WUNT 2.140. Tübingen: Mohr Siebeck, 2001.

Songer, Harold S. "New Standing Before God: Romans 3:21–5:21." *RevExp* 73 (1976): 415–24.

Stuhlmacher, Peter. *Gerechtigkeit Gottes Bei Paulus*. FRLANT 87. Gottingen: Vandenhoeck & Ruprecht, 1965.

———. "The Apostle Paul's View of Righteousness." Pages 68–93 in *Reconciliation, Law, & Righteousness: Essays in Biblical Theology*. Philadelphia: Fortress, 1986.

———. "The Theme of Romans." *ABR* 36 (1988): 31–44.

Thielman, Frank. "God's Righteousness as God's Fairness in Romans 1:17: An Ancient Perspective on a Significant Phrase." *JETS* 54 (2011): 35–48.

Tilling, Chris, ed. *Beyond Old and New Perspectives on Paul*. Eugene, OR: Wipf & Stock, 2014.

Turner, Geoffrey. "The Righteousness of God in Psalms and Romans." *SJT* 63 (2010): 285–301.

Watson, Francis. *Paul and the Hermeneutics of Faith*. 2nd ed. Cornerstones. London: T&T Clark, 2015.

———. *Paul, Judaism, and the Gentiles: Beyond the New Perspective*. Grand Rapids: Eerdmans, 2007.

Wedderburn, A. J. M. *The Reasons for Romans*. Minneapolis: Fortress, 1991.

Westerholm, Stephen. *Perspectives Old and New on Paul: The "Lutheran" Paul and His Critics*. Grand Rapids: Eerdmans, 2004.

Williams, Sam K. "The 'Righteousness of God' in Romans." *JBL* 99 (1980): 241–90.

Wolter, Michael. *Paul: An Outline of His Theology*. Translated by Robert L. Brawley. Waco, TX: Baylor University Press, 2015.

Wright, N. T. *Justification: God's Plan & Paul's Vision*. Downers Grove, IL: IVP Academic, 2009.

———. *Paul and the Faithfulness of God*. 2 vols. COQG 4. Minneapolis: Fortress, 2013.

Zeller, D. *Juden Und Heiden in Der Mission Des Paulus: Studien Zum Römerbrief*. FB 1. Stuttgart: Katholisches Bibelwerk, 1976.

Ziesler, John A. *The Meaning of Righteousness in Paul: A Linguistic and Theological Inquiry*. SNTSMS 20. London: Cambridge University Press, 1972.

CHAPTER 3

The Untamed Wrath of God in Romans

Mark A. Seifrid

The Taming of God's Wrath

The ὀργὴ θεοῦ is potently and vividly present in the grand passage of Rom
i.18ff., where we recognize directly the jealous, passionate Yahweh of the Old
Testament, here grown to a God of the universe of fearful power, who pours
out the blazing vials of his wrath over the whole world. In this passage there is
an intuition, genuinely non-rational in character, the sublimity of which has
an almost horrible quality: the commission of sin is the angry God's punishment for sin.[1]

So writes Rudolf Otto in his provocative work, *The Idea of the Holy* (*Das Hei-
lige*), first published in 1917. His thesis concerning the experience of what he
called the "numinous" and the role of religious intuition, appeared as a response
to the liberal theology of the late-nineteenth century, especially as it had been
represented by Friedrich Schleiermacher and Albrecht Ritschl.[2] Schleiermacher
and Ritschl stood within a lengthy tradition of the rationalization of the wrath
of God, in which at least two questions were at work.[3] First, within the Stoic
tradition of divine *apatheia* that had been taken up within Christian theology
it was unthinkable that God could experience passions. What, then, was to be
done with the language of Scripture that ascribes hot anger to God? A second
question was bound to the first. If we allow that God experiences and displays
wrath, should we not understand this wrath as a rational response to evil? The
wrath of God then may be construed safely within the confines of the rational
and moral.[4]

---

1. Rudolf Otto, *The Idea of the Holy: An Inquiry into the Non-Rational Factor in
the Idea of the Divine and Its Relation to the Rational*, trans. and pref. John W. Harvey
(London: Oxford University Press, 1924), 89.

2. Cf. Hans Walter Schütte, "Die Ausscheidung der Lehre vom Zorn Gottes in der
Theologie Schleiermachers und Ritschls," *NZSTh* 10 (1968): 387–97.

3. See footnote 37 below. Cf. Lennart Pinomaa, *Der Zorn Gottes in der Theologie
Luthers* (Helsinki: Finnische Akademie der Wissenschaften, 1938), 587–614; Thomas
Reinhuber, *Kämpfender Glaube: Studien zu Luthers Bekenntnis am Ende von De servo
arbitrio*, TBTöp 104 (Berlin: de Gruyter, 2000), 91–93.

4. Lactantius' *De ira dei* (ca. 311/312) stands at the beginning of the Christian tradition: "(God) is free from the affections that lead to vices; those, however, that belong to

Schleiermacher radicalizes this tradition in a salvation-historical manner. Because we now have been reconciled to God through Christ, we no longer have any need for a doctrine of God's wrath. It belongs to the religion of the Old Testament. All that remains for us in Christian theology to teach is God's displeasure with sin. Ritschl, too, transposes the biblical language of God's wrath, but in the opposite direction. The Old Testament language about a wrathful God has been concentrated in the New Testament in the announcement of a coming, final judgment of divine wrath. In this context, along with Lactantius, it may be understood as a rational response to evil. Consequently, the Christian need only live in the proper fear and respect of this final judgement. We escape the wrath of God by the moral outworking of this fear. Rejecting these conceptions, Otto sought to make a place for the experiential and irrational within religion. He does so, in the passage above, with an appeal to Paul's opening announcement of the revelation of the wrath of God in the letter to Rome. My argument here is that Otto's claim deserves a fresh hearing. Attempts to tame the biblical statements concerning divine wrath, to rationalize and explain them away, have not ceased and undoubtedly will not do so.

Is it true that Paul does not speak of God's wrath as a divine emotion, but merely as the coming, final judgment?[5] The appeal to the inherent connection between a deed and its recompense as it appears within the Scriptures is not merely an appeal to a connection by a natural process—the connection is the work of God. Is it possible, then to separate God's being from God's acts? For his part, in speaking of God's wrath, the apostle employs the scandalous language of the Scriptures: he expects "wrath and indignation" to come upon the disobedient (Rom 2:8).[6]

One may further ask if it is sufficient to say that God's wrath is merely the inverse side of his love.[7] Admittedly, the Scriptures speak of divine judgment reestablishing justice within this fallen world, bringing vengeance on the enemies

---

virtue, i.e., wrath against evil, love for the good, mercy for affliction, which are worthy of divine power, these he has as his own, rightly and truly. If, truly, he did not have them, the whole of human life would be thrown into confusion and the state of things would come into such confusion, that laws would be held in contempt and transgressed, audaciousness alone would reign, so that no one but the strong would be able to prevail: thus as by a band of robbers the entire world would be pillaged. Now, however, can the wicked expect punishment, the good favor, and the afflicted mercy. And therefore there is place for the virtues and the criminals are rare." Lactantius, *Vom Zorne Gottes*, trans. and ed. H. Kraft and A. Wlosok, TzF 4 (Darmstadt: Wissenschaftliche Buchgesellschaft, 1971), 55.

5. Cf. Otfried Hofius, *Paulusstudien*, WUNT 51 (Tübingen: Mohr Siebeck, 1989), 36.

6. In various forms these and related terms appear in connection in the LXX. Cf. Exod 32:11–12; Deut 29:23; Ps 68:25; 77:49; Isa 7:4; 9:18.

7. Cf. Bernd Janowski, *Ein Gott, der straft und tötet?: Zwölf Fragen zum Gottesbild des Alten Testaments*, 3rd ed., NKT (Göttingen: Vandenhoeck & Ruprecht, 2013), 147–74.

of God, and justice for the oppressed, the poor and the weak. But can the wrath of God be said to serve the purpose of the moral education of humanity *solely*?[8] Can this harmless conclusion be squared with the lament of the psalmist, "We are consumed by your anger, by your wrath we are overwhelmed" (Ps 90:7)?[9] Such attempts to reduce and tame the wrath of God may be judged as failures. At this point we may confess with Lactantius that a God who has no wrath can have no grace either.[10]

In considering Paul's letter to Rome, we may further ask, "If justice has been done to the righteous demands of the Law, does the wrath of God lie entirely in the past for the Christian?"[11] Would not an affirmation of this question simply invert the caricature of the traditional view that God had no love toward us before the cross?[12] Doesn't it come perilously close to Schleierm-acher's proposal?

Again, my thesis: the revelation of the wrath of God that Paul announces in Romans resists all such rationalization. To make this claim is not to embrace Rudolf Otto's appeal to religious intuition or his allowance for the finality of the "non-rational." Nevertheless, the picture of God's wrath that emerges from the apostle is more dynamic and dangerous than is generally assumed. While this wrath of God is certainly not *finally* irrational—there is more to say about its outworking on the children of God (Rom 8:31–39)—it remains hidden and unfathomable within the present fallen world in which it is at work. In its brutal force, the wrath of God overthrows all attempts to explain it and tame it.

---

8. Can it be reduced to the propaedeutic function of exposing human violence, emptying itself finally in the suffering and death of Jesus? In this attempt to tame the wrath of God, a bare "cruciform hermeneutic" threatens—with remarkable naiveté—to deify weakness. Cf. Gregory A. Boyd, *The Crucifixion of the Warrior God: Interpreting the Old Testament's Violent Portraits of God in Light of the Cross* (Minneapolis: Fortress, 2017), 1041–98.

9. Admittedly, the psalmist petitions God to teach him to take this truth to heart. But death remains—despite the hope that lies beyond it (Ps 90:13–17). The psalmist thus asks, "Who knows the power of your wrath?" (Ps 90:11a).

10. Lactantius, *Vom Zorne Gottes*, 7.

11. Here it should be noted that in the Scriptures "the righteousness of God" appears as a saving action of God, albeit one which presupposes the retribution of evil. This understanding of God's righteousness has been explored especially by Peter Stuhl-macher, *Gerechtigkeit Gottes bei Paulus*, 2nd ed., FRLANT 87 (Göttingen: Vandenhoeck & Ruprecht, 1966). In his own way, Bernd Janowski shows how deliverance and retribution are joined (*Ein Gott, der straft und tötet?* 33–59).

12. We may readily dispense with a common oversimplification of the traditional view, that God's love toward us was contingent upon Jesus' aversion of the divine wrath. It was God himself, according to Paul, who put forward Jesus as ἱλαστήριον (Rom 3:25). It was *God* who established his love for us in that Christ died for us (Rom 5:5, 8, 15). It furthermore becomes clear in Paul's statement that the divine act cannot rightly be construed as an act of divine child-abuse. God's action notwithstanding, it was Christ, according to Paul, who in his own act and gift, died for the ungodly.

The Wrath of God in Romans

The Wrath of God Revealed and Announced

"For the wrath of God is revealed from heaven" (Rom 1:18). The meaning and import of this announcement are not exhausted at the end of Rom 3. It continues throughout the letter.[13] Admittedly, Paul's argument in Rom 1:18–32 seems at first appearance to run counter to the thesis of this essay. The text is centered on the supreme justice of the divine wrath. Despite being unseen, all that may be known of God—God's eternal power and essential deity—is perceptible through that which God has made (Rom 1:19–20). Any and all human beings who suppress this truth do so "in unrighteousness," exchanging the glory of the incorruptible God for an image of the corruptible human being and other creatures: they are without excuse (Rom 1:18, 20–23). God, according to Paul, responds according to an *ius talionis*: just as idolaters have given up God, God has delivered them "in" (or, perhaps, "to") the desires of their hearts (Rom 1:24). Human bodies—worshiped as idols—are now subject to dishonor, precisely because humanity worships the creature rather than the Creator (Rom 1:24–25).[14] The apostle finally underscores the justice of the divine wrath in a threefold declaration that "God gave them up" (Rom 1:24, 26, 28). Despite the

---

13. This pointed, apostolic announcement serves as an elaboration of Paul's preceding announcement of the saving righteousness of God revealed in the Gospel (Rom 1:16–17). This theme and counter theme continue interwoven throughout the letter. Paul's initial declaration concerning the wrath of God serves, at least in the first instance, to introduce a theological description and condemnation of the pagan world. It is followed by an equally sharp condemnation of a Jewish claim to advantage in the possession of the law, in which Paul reminds his readers—especially his Jewish Christian readers—that they themselves must reckon with the wrath of God that will be revealed at the final judgment (Rom 2:3–8). He again refers again to God's wrath in the close of this section of the letter, taking up the human protest against the justice of this wrath (Rom 3:5–8). Paul's reference to God's wrath in Rom 4:15 echoes his earlier argument and at the same time makes it concrete. He again refers to the wrath of God at the opening of the following, christological section of the letter in Rom 5–8 (Rom 5:9). This reference is likewise significant: it provides an indication that the theme of the wrath of God at the opening section of the letter has not been set aside, but instead taken up and elaborated within the continuing argument. Paul introduces the theme of the wrath of God explicitly again in his discussion of the destiny of Israel (Rom 9:22). Here he again is responding to the protest of the human being to the justice of divine wrath. His response is theologically related to his earlier rhetoric in Rom 3:5. The question of Israel's destiny adds a significant dimension to the issue, as long has been recognized. It is not without significance that in the concluding "paraclesis" Paul twice refers to the significance of God's wrath for the life of the believing community within the world (Rom 12:19; 13:4–5). As the counterpoint to God's saving righteousness, the revelation of God's wrath is integral to the thematic structure of the letter.

14. Paul has in view pagan society as a whole, not merely individuals within it, as if all idolaters were homosexuals or only homosexuals were idolaters. He will go on to

clear and evident justice of the divine response, Rudolf Otto is correct: "the commission of sins is the angry God's punishment for the fundamental sin, the sin of idolatry."[15] According to the apostle, all the evil that human beings work within the world is the result of God's judgment upon the injustice of the human rejection of the Creator. The final judgment threatens a tragic yet just end to this dangerous drama.

Even if the apostolic declaration cannot rightly be described as "intuitive" and the divine wrath is supremely just, it is clear that Paul speaks of the divine wrath as a reality that is hidden from human beings. He *announces* that the wrath of God has been revealed from heaven. He does not presuppose it. Those upon whom it falls remain oblivious to it. In being delivered to "a useless, base mind" human beings practice and approve of deeds that they know are worthy of death, as if there were no God, no wrath, and no death—just as they would like to imagine (Rom 1:28–31; 3:9–18; cf. Pss 14:1–3; 53:1–5). The wrath of God revealed from heaven is the numinous and dreadful counterpart to the revelation of the saving righteousness of in the word of the gospel that Paul announces (Rom 1:16–17).[16]

The Moralistic Judge and the Day of God's Wrath

The deplorable condition of pagan idolaters nevertheless seems to be clear to the Jewish interlocutor who appears in the second movement of Paul's argument (Rom 2:1–29). According to Paul, however, this human being, who arrogates to themselves the role of the judge, does so in blindness to their own guilt. Such persons imagine that they are set apart from the pagans by virtue of their possession and knowledge of the law (Rom 2:12–16, 17–24). The problem with the pagans, Paul's figure supposes, is their lack of moral education: the one who possesses the law imagines that they are a guide to the blind, a light to those in darkness, a moral instructor of the foolish, and a teacher of the morally

---

insist that every human being, including the moral judge, is subject to the justice of the divine wrath.

15. Pace Gerhart Herold (*Zorn und Gerechtigkeit Gottes bei Paulus: Eine Untersuchung zu Röm. 1,16–18*, European University Papers, Series XXIII: Theology 14 [Bern: Peter Lang, 1973], 302–36), Paul's announcement of the revelation of the wrath of God in Rom 1:18 is not to be understood as a reference to the cross, even though the hope of deliverance from enemies is bound to the expectation of the wrath that will come upon them. It is not inappropriate to see the overcoming of divine wrath at work in Paul's reference to Jesus as ἱλαστήριον, but the thought is retrospective and allusive, dependent on the insight of the reader.

16. Cf. Marcus A. Mininger, *Uncovering the Theme of Revelation in Romans 1:16–3:26: Discovering a New Approach to Paul's Argument*, WUNT 2.445 (Tübingen: Mohr Siebeck), 208–12, 267–71, who is correct in his observation that Paul's argument presupposes the present hiddenness of God's work in judgment and salvation.

infantile (Rom 2:19–20).[17] The knowledge of what is right and just, mediated by the gift of the law to Israel, serves as protection against the reprehensible conduct of the pagans.[18] It serves as a shield against the wrath of God.

Here again, however, Paul announces the wrath of God, shifting attention from the present wrath of God to the "day of wrath" that is yet to come (Rom 2:5–11).[19] The two manifestations of divine wrath are inseparable: the numinous divine wrath that is presently at work in the world prepares for the terrible, final day of wrath: "according to your hard and unrepentant heart, you are treasuring up for yourself wrath in the day of wrath" (Rom 2:5). In an ironic play upon the hope of recompense for good deeds, Paul speaks of "wrath" as being stored up as a "treasure" in the day of judgment.[20] He describes unrighteous deeds as manifestations of divine wrath, in a pointed metonym that takes up his preceding declarations in Rom 1. His argument in Rom 2 thus remains anchored in

---

17. Despite its remarkable proximity to Paul's indictment of the pagan world, the parallel description of pagan idolatry found in Wis 13:1–16:29 takes a remarkably exculpatory tone, based on the same stance as Paul's interlocutor: "All people were empty by nature, for whom an ignorance of God was present. From the good things that are seen, they were unable to know the One who is. . . . for such ones there is little blame" (Wis 13:1, 6). Cf. Jonathan A. Linebaugh, "Wisdom of Solomon and Romans 1:18–2:5: God's Wrath Against All," in *Reading Romans in Context: Paul and Second Temple Judaism*, ed. Ben C. Blackwell, John K. Goodrich, and Jason Maston (Grand Rapids: Zondervan, 2015), 38–45.

18. The form of Paul's argument is of significance in this regard. In his opening announcement of the revelation of the wrath of God, he does not quite say that it has fallen upon all humanity. The wording is slightly ambiguous: the wrath of God rests upon "all impiety and unrighteousness of human beings who suppress the truth in unrighteousness" (Rom 1:18). He speaks in the first instance of God's wrath as directed against idolatry, even if he goes on to charge idolaters with an inexcusable rejection of God the Creator. The identity of the idolaters itself remain ambiguous: the participial clause ("[those] who suppress the truth in unrighteousness") might be understood either as descriptive or restrictive. Is the pious Jew among the idolaters or not? The question remains open, even in the indictment of the moralistic judge that follows in Rom 2:1–11. Here, as well as in his engagement with a Jewish interlocutor in Rom 2:17–29, Paul seeks to bring his readers to a self-judgment. He presupposes the blindness of human beings and thus *announces* the wrath of God revealed from heaven.

19. The "day of wrath" is the eschatologically heightened expression of the warning of a coming time of judgment and disaster. The day of God's wrath upon his enemies through his "son" (Ps 110:5) is turned against Israel itself (cf. Zeph 1:14–18; and in the exilic period Ezek 7:1–27 [esp. 7:19]), so that the "day of the Lord" is not one of salvation, but of disaster (Isa 13:6–9; Jer 46:10; Ezek 30:3; Joel 1:15; 2:1,11; 3:14; Amos 5:18–20; Mal 4:5). Already within the biblical tradition "the day of wrath" takes on universal dimensions. The conception of a day of wrath and reckoning for individuals at death or disaster is likewise transposed to a final judgment (Prov 11:4; see Job's embittered response to the idea: Job 21:27–34 [cf. 20:20–29]).

20. On the early Jewish conception of a treasure of reward, see Tob 4:9; 12:8–10; Wis 7:12–14; 2 Esd 6:5; 7:72; Sir 3:4; 29:11; Matt 6:19–21; Mark 10:21.

his preceding announcement of the wrath of God that has surrendered human beings to their own desires.[21]

Those who judge others live in the same ignorance of the divine wrath lying upon them as do the pagan idolaters whom they condemn. Their supposed moral and intellectual superiority blinds them to the truth. They thus misconstrue and despise the delay in judgment that God has allowed in God's "kindness, forbearance, and long-suffering." In his delay, God intends to lead them to repentance. With their "hard and unrepentant heart" they treasure up wrath for themselves "in the day of wrath *and the revelation of the righteous judgment of God*, who will recompense each one according to their works" (Rom 2:5–6). Paul paints a tragic picture. The wrath of God remains just as much unseen and unimagined for the moralistic judge as it does for the pagan. God waits and wants to be merciful. But both God's wrath and God's mercy, as evident as they are, remain hidden to a blind and rebellious humanity. [22]

"The day of wrath," according to Paul, will be "the day of the revelation of the righteous judgment of God" (Rom 2:5). The wrath revealed from heaven— presently ignored and unseen—suddenly comes to light. Hidden from the eyes of the pagans and the pious alike, the wrath of God suddenly becomes manifest. The divine surrender of the human being to unrighteousness becomes absolute and final.[23]

The readers of Romans are granted, of course, insight into what is taking place in the world. This capacity to see the world as it is—if they will accept it—comes through the apostle and depends on their willingness to hear and receive his gospel. That gospel is the source of his own insight into the wrath of God: as God's saving power it opens eyes, ears, and hearts. It is out of the gospel entrusted to him that Paul discerns the lawsuit between God and idolatrous humanity, the divine promise to Abraham, the mysterious singularity of Adam and Christ, the power of sin, death, and the law.

---

21. This connection between the present wrath of God and its end appears in the conclusion of his argument in Rom 1:32: "the righteous judgment of God is that those who do such things are worthy of death."

22. Paul goes on to remind his readers, on the basis of Deuteronomic theology, that this hard heart can be changed only by a work of God the Spirit. Cf. Deut 10:16; 30:6: the same dynamic of a call to change, "to circumcise one's heart" is joined to the announcement that this change finally must be brought about by God.

23. Paul's reference to "the day of wrath" recalls the prophetic announcement of the judgment of God on the transgressions of his people, which are transgressions against him. The language recalls the covenant-lawsuit and sets it now in the context of a contention between God and all humanity. Paul will appeal again to this setting in Rom 3:1–8. Cf. Nicola Wendebourg, *Der Tag des Herrn: Zur Gerichtserwartung im Neuen Testament auf ihrem alttestamentlichen und frühjüdischen Hintergrund*, WMANT 96 (Neukirchen-Vluyn: Neukirchener, 2003), 198–203.

As the bearer of the gospel, Paul does not announce the wrath of God as one who stands above the earthly drama, as if he could see the whole storyline—but as one who has found his place within it. His encounter with the wrath of God as it is at work in the law reveals the true state of all human beings (Rom 7:7–25). The apostle remains within the earthly battle, as one of the sheep given over to slaughter, living in hope in the unseen love of God in Christ (Rom 8:31–39).[24]

The Wrath of God Overcome in the Risen Christ

Paul's single, direct announcement of deliverance from the wrath of God appears near the opening of the argument of Rom 5–8:

> By much more, then, having been justified by his blood, we shall be saved through him from wrath. For if, although we were enemies, we were reconciled to God through the death of his Son, much more, having been reconciled, we shall be saved by his life, And not only this, but we boast in God through our Lord, Jesus Christ, through whom we now have received reconciliation. (Rom 5:9–11)

Paul's focus here rests on the final judgment and the wrath of God that is yet to come. As in Rom 2:5–11, however, his declaration does not exclude, but includes the wrath of God that is at work in the world. Paul associates the final deliverance from wrath with the risen Christ and the power of Christ's life that brings "boasting in God" here and now in the world, where the power of evil remains terrifyingly present (Rom 5:11).[25] The present rule of the risen Christ and the hope of deliverance from divine wrath that Paul here announces is the theme of the whole of Rom 5–8. The deliverance of the human being to the wrath of God that Paul announces in Rom 1:24, 26, 28 appears in the personification of sin and death as evil as powers in Rom 5–8. Sin and death are the horrifying *larvae dei*, the masks of God in God's wrath.[26] They find their end in the personified "grace

---

24. So the early Luther, even before his reformational discovery: "Therefore God accepts only the forsaken, cures only the sick, gives sight only to the blind, restores life only to the dead, sanctifies only the sinners, gives wisdom only to the unwise. In short, He has mercy only on those who are wretched, and gives grace only to those who are not in grace" (*LW* 14:162 = *WA* 1, 183, 36–184, 10; *Seven Penitential Psalms* 1517, on Ps 38:20).

25. It is a boasting that God "is for us" (8:31).

26. One thinks of the words of the psalmist: "All our days come to an end in your wrath. We complete our years as a sigh" (Ps 90:9). The figure of Adam, through whom sin and death entered the world and assumed their reign over humanity, provides the mysterious answer to the question as to the origin of the rejection of the Creator that Paul names in Rom 1:18–23. Rudolf Bultmann, *Theologie des Neuen Testaments* (Tübingen: Mohr Siebeck, 1961), 251: "Sin came into the world through sinning." Otfried Hofius, *Paulusstudien II*, WUNT 143 (Tübingen: Mohr Siebeck, 2002), 82–83.

of God," the power of the life to come that rules through Christ.[27] Christ's saving lordship brings freedom from sin and death. It brings deliverance from the wrath of God that presently is at work in the world—in all too terrifying ways (Rom 6:22–23). Bodily obedience is the necessary anticipation of bodily resurrection.[28]

Paul nevertheless finds it necessary in Rom 6:11–13, 19 to *exhort* the Roman Christians to grasp what has been done for them. Those who belong to Christ remain on the field of battle. Or better stated, they are the field of battle. Eternal life remains located "in Christ Jesus, our Lord" (Rom 6:23). Life under the power of sin remains for the Christian the "impossible possibility."[29] Although in Christ we have been liberated from sin and death, we remain paradoxically subject to sin and death in ourselves. The figure of the human being in the shadow of Adam, "fleshly, sold (as a slave) under sin" in Rom 7:14 is Paul's theological description of both the pagan idolaters of Rom 1:18–32 and the moralistic hypocrite of Rom 2:1–16.[30] The wrath of God in its hidden yet inescapable power remains within the world.

Already in his discussion of Abraham in Rom 4:1–25, Paul explicitly connects the wrath of God to the work of the law: "The law effects wrath. But where there is no law, neither is there transgression" (Rom 4:15). Consequently, the desperate lament of the "wretched person" of Rom 7:24, "Who shall set me free from the body of this death?" is to be understood as the expression of the unbounded desperation of the encounter with the God of wrath as it has been mediated by the law.[31] That this unanswerable lament nevertheless finds an immediate answer in "Jesus Christ, *our Lord*" does not diminish its desperation (Rom 7:25a). The apostle's concluding word concerning the divided human being, which has proved to be a stumbling block to interpreters, forbids such a conclusion (Rom 7:25b). In this wretched figure, the hidden divine wrath, present in the power of sin, and operative in the law of God finally meets with Christ and the gospel. In the voice of the wretched person, Paul speaks as one who understands the triumph of Christ over the power of sin. Nevertheless, as he confesses, in his encounter with the law, he does not understand the strange power that remains operative in him (Rom 7:14–17). He has not yet been removed from the field of battle.

---

27. Rom 5:21; 6:14–15.

28. Cf. Ernst Käsemann, *Commentary on Romans*, trans. and ed. Geoffrey W. Bromiley (Grand Rapids: Eerdmans, 1980), 177.

29. I am obviously playing upon Reinhold Niebuhr, *Moral Man and Immoral Society* (New York: Scribner's Sons, 1932), 53.

30. I borrow the apt expression "in the shadow of Adam" from Hofius, *Paulusstudien II*, 104–54.

31. The "wretched person" of Rom 7:24 may be regarded as the human being in encounter with the law. Mark A. Seifrid, "Romans 7: The Voice of the Law, the Cry of Lament, and the Shout of Thanksgiving," in *Perspectives on Our Struggle with Sin*, ed. Terry L. Wilder (Nashville: Broadman & Holman, 2011), 111–65.

The same paradox is present in the triumph of Christ over death. Death no longer rules over him (Rom 6:9). Those who belong to him have been set free from the law of sin and death (Rom 8:2). Nevertheless, those who belong to Christ have been thrust into the sufferings of Christ (Rom 8:17). Like the people of God in the past, they are surrendered to death by God himself without any apparent cause.[32] Their sufferings, which are without apparent ground or basis, are experienced as accusations (Rom 8:34). They arise not only from natural disasters, but also from those who persecute them (Rom 8:35). They are subject to the shedding of blood, destruction, and misery of those who do not know the way of peace (Rom 3:10–18). The divine wrath that has been loosed in the world strikes even those who belong to Christ and have been delivered from it.[33]

The Wrath of God in Judgment and Mercy

In two loci in Romans, Paul addresses critical questions of the rebellious human being in the face of the divine wrath. The first of these appears in the summary section of his opening argument. Over against the perspective of his rhetorical dialog partner, he reformulates Jewish advantage, locating it in the oracles of God. Although "some" among Israel have not believed the oracles entrusted to them, God's faithfulness to his word remains. Paul contextualizes this affirmation, locating it in a contention between God and the human being, a contention with universal scope.[34] God will be shown to be true, and every human being a liar, "in order that you (God) might be justified in your words and might conquer when you judge" (Rom 3:4; LXX Ps 50:6).[35] The psalmist's confession at once echoes Paul's opening announcement of the present revelation of divine wrath and at the same time shifts the scene to the final judgment. The sin of the psalmist—and that of every human being—took place *in order*

---

32. They are regarded—by God and by the world—as sheep for the slaughter (Rom 8:36). The psalmist's words of lament follow the text that Paul cites: "Awake, Lord! Why do you sleep? Awaken and do not reject us forever! Why do you hide your face? Why do you forget our misery and affliction?" (Ps 44:24–25).

33. Here we may leave aside the references to divine wrath in Rom 12:19–21 and 13:1–7, which obviously deal implications of the divine wrath for the life of the Christian within the world.

34. On the background of Paul's rhetoric in the setting of a divine contention, see James B. Prothro, *Both Judge and Justifier: Biblical Legal Language and the Act of Justifying in Paul*, WUNT 2.461 (Tübingen: Mohr Siebeck, 2018), 166–70. It is not merely that God is defending the law or adjudicating a contention between two others. God is party to the dispute.

35. Paul's introductory assertion, that every human being will be found a liar, metaleptically recalls the language of the psalm, "I sinned and did evil before you, (in order that) . . ." (LXX Ps 50:6a).

that (ὅπως) God might be justified.[36] Paul continues his argument by anticipating the objection of his dialogue partner: "If our unrighteousness demonstrates the righteousness of God, what shall we say?" (Rom 3:5). The apostle forestalls the sacrilegious objection that lies at hand in the following, provocative question: "The God who brings wrath is not unjust, is he?" The response is blunt and assertive: "By no means! Otherwise, how could God judge the world?" (Rom 3:6). God must judge the entire world, Jew and Gentile alike. The dialogue partner is not satisfied and restates the objection: "If the truth of God has abounded by my lie to God's glory, why should I be condemned as a sinner?"[37] In response, Paul again insists on the necessity of the divine judgment. It is not possible for good things to arise from that which is evil. Evil cannot be rewarded with good.[38] The debate ends. The triumph of goodness over evil is not yet in view (cf. Rom 12:21). Despite the necessity of evil, God's right as judge of the world remains.

The question of the justice of divine wrath that Paul has addressed in Rom 3:5–8 takes on a new and deeper dimension in Paul's later reference to "vessels of wrath, fashioned for destruction" (Rom 9:22–23). No longer is it merely the right of God as judge that comes into question. It is now also the right of the Creator to dispose of his creation as the Creator wills, in wrath or in mercy. Here again Paul cuts off the human objection that this divine freedom might be unjust with an abrupt μή γένοιτο. He follows it with an appeal to the Exodus narrative, citing the Lord's response to Moses' overreaching request to see the Lord's glory and thus gain a final, controlling knowledge of God: "I will have mercy on whom I have mercy, and show compassion to whom I show compassion" (Exod 33:19).[39] Correspondingly and consequently, Paul appeals to the divine word to Pharaoh, in whose hardening and destruction the divine freedom is exemplified: God has raised up Pharaoh only in order to display God's power in him and to make God's name known in all the earth. Paul draws the conclusion: "so then, (God) has mercy on whom he wills, and hardens whom he wills" (Rom 9:18).[40] This word concerning the divine freedom provokes the

---

36. The divine surrender of the human being to evil that Paul has announced in Rom 1:18–32 implicitly lies behind his reading of the psalm.

37. The dialogue partner implicitly assumes a rational conception of divine wrath, that corresponds to a philosophical stance extending back at least to Plato, that was operative in the Hellenistic and Roman world. Cf. Reinhard G. Kratz and Hermann Spieckermann, eds., *Divine Wrath and Divine Mercy in the World of Antiquity*, FAT 2.33 (Tübingen: Mohr Siebeck, 2008), 143–52, 153–75, 176–202.

38. That God in Christ and the good has the power to triumph over evil is not yet in view (cf. Rom 12:21).

39. The same dynamic is present in the narrative of the interchange between Moses and God concerning the divine name (Exod 3:13–15).

40. Rom 9:14–18; cf. Exod 33:19; Exod 4:21. It is not without significance that Paul in dealing with the question of Israel's present unbelief and destiny draws on the Exodus narrative of Israel's birth as a nation.

human objection to the justice of it all: "Why then does God find fault, for who can resist God's will?" Paul responds with an appeal to an Isaianic oracle: Like a potter, the Creator has the right to make from the same lump of clay both a vessel for honor as well as a vessel for dishonor.[41] The right of the Creator transcends the question of the creature.

The argument appears complete and might have ended here. Yet Paul continues, adding a remarkable new dimension to the drama: God delays the manifestation of his wrath on "vessels of wrath, prepared for destruction" in order to make known "the riches of his glory on vessels of mercy, prepared beforehand for glory."[42] The counsels of the Creator remain hidden in his freedom, but the glory of the Creator in his freedom is manifest in his mercy. Translated into the terms of Paul's announcement at the beginning of the letter: the wrath of God that delivers all human beings over to sin serves the gospel in which God's righteousness has been revealed.

Summary: God's Untamed Wrath . . . and Mercy

Paul's announcement of the revelation of God's wrath presupposes that God's wrath remains hidden to the rebellious humanity upon whom it falls. The eyes of the blind can be opened only by the revelation of God's righteousness in the gospel. Consequently, although the divine wrath that has been revealed from heaven is manifestly right and rational, it encounters the fallen human being as a hidden power, "numinously," to use Rudolf Otto's language. Only at the day on which God judges human secrets through Jesus Christ will the wrath and righteous judgment of God be revealed in the world (Rom 2:5–6, 11). The relationship between the human creature and the Creator thus takes the form of a drama that ends in mercy or judgment, faith or unbelief. In his larger argument, Paul cuts off both the objection to this final display of God's wrath as well as any questioning of the freedom of the Creator in granting mercy. The God of wrath and judgment is the God of free mercy, whose works and ways remain impenetrable to human reasoning. This divine freedom in mercy is the very point of Paul's entire exposition of God's saving work in Romans. In Christ, God wills to open eyes that have been blinded, so that they may see the difference between the human creature and the Creator, the deep abyss of God's riches, wisdom, and knowledge, the God whose judgments are unsearchable and whose ways are untraceable, the God who wills to have mercy on all

---

41. Rom 9:20–21; cf. Isa 29:16: "That which is formed shall not say to the one who formed it, 'Why did you make me thus?' will it?"

42. The question may remain open as to whether Paul understands the "wrath" that God waits to make manifest as solely that of the final judgment or whether it includes the wrath already that has been revealed from heaven upon blinded humanity.

(Rom 11:32–33). The life of the Christian is thus one of flight from the wrath of God to the grace of God in Jesus Christ (cf. 1 Thess 1:9–10). It is there that we find deliverance from God's wrath, from sin, and from death. This flight is a constant "reckoning" or grasping what Christ has done for us. It is a constant groaning in the anticipation of a hope not yet seen. Rudolf Otto's appeal to human intuition was misplaced, but his intuition that the wrath of God that Paul announces in Romans remains hidden and untamed was entirely correct. According to the apostle, only the God who works the terror of his untamed wrath can display the glory of his untamed mercy.[43] It is this vision that we await, even as our eyes and ears have been opened to the hope that is ours in Jesus Christ. No storyline can contain it—nor should it.

Bibliography

Boyd, Gregory A. *The Crucifixion of the Warrior God: Interpreting the Old Testament's Violent Portraits of God in Light of the Cross*. Minneapolis: Fortress, 2017.

Bultmann, Rudolf. *Theologie des Neuen Testaments*. Tübingen: Mohr Siebeck, 1961.

Herold, Gerhart. *Zorn und Gerechtigkeit Gottes bei Paulus: Eine Untersuchung zu Röm. 1,16–18*. European University Papers, Series XXIII: Theology 14. Bern: Peter Lang, 1973.

Hofius, Otfried. *Paulusstudien*. WUNT 51. Tübingen: Mohr Siebeck, 1989.

———. *Paulusstudien II*. WUNT 143. Tübingen: Mohr Siebeck, 2002.

Janowski, Bernd. *Ein Gott, der straft und tötet? Zwölf Fragen zum Gottesbild des Alten Testaments*. 3rd ed. Neukirchener Theologie. Göttingen: Vandenhoeck & Ruprecht, 2013.

Käsemann, Ernst. *Commentary on Romans*. Translated and edited by Geoffrey W. Bromiley. Grand Rapids: Eerdmans, 1980.

Kratz, Reinhard G., and Hermann Spieckermann, eds. *Divine Wrath and Divine Mercy in the World of Antiquity*. FAT 2.33 Tübingen: Mohr Siebeck, 2008.

Lactantius. *Vom Zorne Gottes*. Translated and edited by H. Kraft and A. Wlosok. TzF 4. Darmstadt: Wissenschaftliche Buchgesellschaft, 1971.

Linebaugh, Jonathan A. "Wisdom of Solomon and Romans 1:18–2:5: God's Wrath Against All." Pages 38–45 in *Reading Romans in Context: Paul and Second Temple Judaism*. Edited by Ben C. Blackwell, John K. Goodrich, and Jason Maston. Grand Rapids: Zondervan, 2015.

Mininger, Marcus A. *Uncovering the Theme of Revelation in Romans 1:16–3:26: Discovering a New Approach to Paul's Argument*. WUNT 2.445. Tübingen: Mohr Siebeck, 2017.

Niebuhr, Reinhold. *Moral Man and Immoral Society*. New York: Scribner's, 1932.

---

43. Cf. Lactantius, *Vom Zorne Gottes*, 7.

Otto, Rudolf. *The Idea of the Holy: An Inquiry into the Non-Rational Factor in the Idea of the Divine and Its Relation to the Rational.* Translated and prefaced by John W. Harvey. London: Oxford University Press, 1924.

Pinomaa, Lennart. *Der Zorn Gottes in der Theologie Luthers.* Helsinki: Finnische Akademie der Wissenschaften, 1938.

Prothro, James B. *Both Judge and Justifier: Biblical Legal Language and the Act of Justifying in Paul.* WUNT 2.461. Tübingen: Mohr Siebeck, 2018.

Reinhuber, Thomas. *Kämpfender Glaube: Studien zu Luthers Bekenntnis am Ende von De servo arbitrio.* TBTöp 104. Berlin: de Gruyter, 2000.

Schütte, Hans Walter. "Die Ausscheidung der Lehre vom Zorn Gottes in der Theologie Schleiermachers und Ritschls." *NZSTh* 10 (1968): 387–97.

Seifrid, Mark A. "Romans 7: The Voice of the Law, the Cry of Lament, and the Shout of Thanksgiving." Pages 111–65 in *Perspectives on Our Struggle with Sin.* Edited by Terry L. Wilder. Nashville: Broadman & Holman, 2011.

Stuhlmacher, Peter. *Gerechtigkeit Gottes bei Paulus.* 2nd ed. FRLANT 87. Göttingen: Vandenhoeck & Ruprecht, 1966.

Wendebourg, Nicola. *Der Tag des Herrn: Zur Gerichtserwartung im Neuen Testament auf ihrem alttestamentlichen und frühjüdischen Hintergrund.* WMANT 96. Neukirchen-Vluyn: Neukirchener, 2003.

CHAPTER 4

Paul's Understanding of Same-Sex Relations in Romans 1: Recent Discussions

Robert A. J. Gagnon

Introduction

The most detailed and explicit discussion of homosexual practice in the NT appears in Paul's remarks in Rom 1:24–27. Otherwise, it comes up for brief mention in vice or offender lists found in Pauline literature; namely, 1 Cor 6:9 and 1 Tim 1:10. The focus of this essay will be on Rom 1:24–27, which I translate as follows:

> [24] Therefore, God gave them over, because of the desires of their hearts (in exchanging the true God for idols), to an uncleanness [or: impurity] consisting of their bodies being dishonored among themselves [25]—the very ones who exchanged the truth about God for the lie and worshiped and served the creature rather than the Creator, who is blessed forever, amen. [26] Because of this God gave them over to passions of dishonor (i.e., dishonorable passions), for even their females exchanged the natural use (i.e., of the male as regards sexual intercourse) for that which is contrary to nature; [27] and likewise also the males, having left behind the natural use of the female (i.e., as regards sexual intercourse), were inflamed with their yearning for one another, males with males committing indecency and in return receiving in themselves the payback which was necessitated by their straying (i.e., from the truth about God to idolatry).[1]

---

1. For translation notes, see my *The Bible and Homosexual Practice: Texts and Hermeneutics* (Nashville: Abingdon, 2001), 231–40. In v. 24 I translate Gk. *en* ("in") causally: "*because of* the desires of their hearts." William Loader, *The New Testament on Sexuality* (Grand Rapids: Eerdmans, 2012), 304, misreads the *en* as equivalent to the *eis* ("into," "to") in 1:26: God giving them over "*to* the passions of dishonor." It is better to understand the *eis akatharsia* ("to uncleanness") in 1:24 as parallel to the *eis pathē atimias* ("to passions of dishonor") in 1:26. Paul is not saying in 1:24, "God handed them over *to* (Gk. *en*) the desires of their hearts *to* (Gk. *eis*) uncleanness." Ancient Greek consistently denotes the thing or person "to" which one is handed over either by an εἰς + accusative (normally a thing) or by a simple dative (normally a person), not by an ἐν + dative. See my "Heart of Wax and a Teaching That Stamps: τύπος διδαχῆς (Rom 6:17b) Once More," *JBL* 112.4 (1993): 669–70.

These verses are part of a larger section in 1:18–3:20 in which Paul explains to an imaginary Jewish interlocutor why God must save by some means other than through "works of the law" (deeds stipulated by the law of Moses to be done; 3:20, 28). Paul provides a summary back-reference to this section in 3:22d–23 (cf. 10:12): "For there is no distinction (i.e., between Jew and Greek), for all (have) sinned and are lacking in [or: fall short of] the glory of God." Salvation cannot be based on human doing, not even for Jews, because no human being can maintain God's standard of righteousness to a degree sufficient to escape God's judgment for sin (3:9–20).

Paul's remarks in 1:18–32 lay out the case for Gentile sin, and in 2:1–3:20 the case for Jewish sin. The opening heading in 1:18 asserts not only that God's wrath is in the process of being "revealed" (manifested) "on every irreverence and unrighteousness of humans," but also that humans sin by knowingly "holding down the truth." Humans cannot claim, "we sinned in ignorance." They sinned rather in deliberate suppression of the truth accessible to them in both indirect and direct revelation.

In terms of overall plot structure, four stages follow the opening thesis statement in 1:18:

- Stage 1: God's power and divinity is visibly manifested in creation (1:19–20)

- Stage 2: Humans suppress this truth and foolishly "*exchange*" the true God for idols (1:21–23, 25, 28).

  - 1:23: "They *exchanged* the glory of the imperishable God for the likeness of an image of a perishable human and birds and four-footed animals and reptiles."

  - 1:25: ". . . who *exchanged* the truth of God for a lie and worshiped and served the creation rather than the Creator."

  - 1:28a: "and just as they did not think it fit to have God in their knowledge . . ."

- Stage 3: God's wrath is manifested in "giving over" humans to self-degrading desires (1:24, 26, 28).

  - 1:24: "Therefore God *gave* them *over* in the desires of their hearts to an uncleanness consisting of their bodies being dishonored among them."

  - 1:26: "Because of this God *gave* them *over* to dishonorable passions . . ."

  - 1:28a: "God *gave* them *over* to an unfit mind, to do what was not proper."

- Some humans even "exchanged" natural intercourse for unnatural intercourse (1:24–25, 27); all committed some form of improper acts (1:28–31).

- Stage 4: These sinful deeds merit death—i.e., God's cataclysmic judgment on the Day of the Lord (1:32–2:11).

In 1:19–31, Paul offers up an extended vice list in which he pauses to give special attention to the two vices that typically begin such lists in either order, idolatry (vv. 19–23) and sexual immorality (vv. 24–27),[2] before resuming an array of other mostly non-sexual social vices (vv. 28–31).[3] After a general reference to sexual "impurity" or "uncleanness" (Gk. *akatharsia*) in 1:24,[4] which elsewhere in the Pauline corpus often parallels the terms "sexual immorality" (Gk. *porneia*) and "licentiousness" (Gk. *aselgeia*),[5] and a back-reference in 1:25 to the idolatry argument in 1:19–23, Paul targets in 1:26–27 a specific form of sexual immorality that underscores his point about people suppressing the transparent truth accessible to them: same-sex intercourse.

---

2. Gal 5:19–21; 1 Cor 6:9–10; cf. 1 Thess 1:9 with 4:2–8; 2 Cor 12:21; Col 3:5, 8–9; Eph 4:17; 5:3–5; 1 Tim 1:9–10.

3. William Loader, *Sexuality in the New Testament: Understanding the Key Texts* (Louisville: Westminster John Knox, 2010), 17, is in error when he denies that Rom 1:18–32 constitutes an extended vice list. According to Loader, Paul "is not making a list of sins, the first of which is idolatry and the second, same-sex relations, for the second flows as a consequence of the first." As an *extended* vice list, it is certainly *more* than just a bare mention of idolatry and sexual immorality (impurity) but not *less than* or *other than* an annotated vice list (as confirmed by the rapid enumeration of vices in 1:29–31). The fact that there is a relationship between the first vice of idolatry and the second vice of sexual impurity is not a sufficient argument to the contrary.

4. It is possible that Paul is already referencing same-sex intercourse when he refers to "an uncleanness consisting of their bodies being dishonored among themselves" (note "passions of dishonor" in 1:26), though at this point the description is general enough to be subject to multiple forms of sexual immorality.

5. Paul warned the Thessalonians that "this is the will of God, your holiness; that you abstain from sexual immorality (*porneia*) . . . For God called us not to uncleanness (*akatharsia*) but in holiness" (1 Thess 4:3, 7). He likewise warned the Galatians that "the works of the flesh are obvious, which are: sexual immorality (*porneia*), uncleanness (*akatharsia*), licentiousness (*aselgeia*) (Gal 5:19). To the Corinthians he expressed the fear that "I may have to mourn over many who have continued in their former sinning and did not repent of the uncleanness (*akatharsia*), sexual immorality (*porneia*), and licentiousness (*aselgeia*) that they practiced" (2 Cor 12:21). The message of Colossians and Ephesians is similar: "So put to death the members that belong to the earth: sexual immorality (*porneia*), uncleanness (*akatharsia*), passion, evil desire" (Col 3:5); "no longer walk as the Gentiles walk, . . . who . . . have given themselves up to licentiousness (*aselgeia*) for the doing of every uncleanness (*akatharsia*) . . . Sexual immorality (*porneia*) and uncleanness (*akatharsia*) of any kind . . . must not even be named among you, as is proper among saints. . . . Know this indeed, that every sexually immoral person (*pornos*) or unclean person (*akathartos*) . . . has no inheritance in the kingdom of Christ and of God" (Eph 4:17, 19; 5:3, 5).

The Claims of Brownson and Vines, and Initial Problems

James Brownson[6] and Matthew Vines[7] make a series of arguments that purport to show that the "moral logic" of Rom 1:24–27 is "grounded" not "in biology-based gender complementarity"[8] but in modes of thinking about homosexual practice that today must be viewed as entirely outdated and of no direct relevance to committed homosexual relationships:

1. *An exploitation* or *promiscuity argument*: They allege that Rom 1:24–27 addresses only exploitative or promiscuous activity, such as pederasty, prostitution, or sex with slaves.

---

6. James V. Brownson, *Bible, Gender, Sexuality: Reframing the Church's Debate on Same-Sex Relationships* (Grand Rapids: Eerdmans, 2013), 149–280. For example: "I contend . . . that the same-sex eroticism Paul envisions is either an expression of the monstrous ego of the Roman imperial house, or an expression of prostitution, child abuse, or promiscuity, in absence of mutuality, a neglect of the obligation to procreate, or a failure of persons to express with their bodies what they say with the rest of their lives. . . . Gender complementarity is never directly taught in Scripture. . . . To the extent that language that might suggest gender complementarity appears at all in Scripture, it is a way of speaking about one or several more specific things: the hierarchy of the genders . . . or else as an expression of the procreative purpose of sexuality" (261–62). "We see four forms of moral logic that form the central framework for objections against same-sex erotic relationships in the ancient world: First, Paul viewed these relationships as an expression of excessive lust . . . driven to increasingly exotic forms of stimulation. . . . The notion that someone might not be significantly attracted to persons of the opposite sex—but to persons of the same sex—is never even considered by early Jewish or Christian writers. Second, he viewed these relationships as shameful . . . because they treated a man as a woman, inherently degrading the passive partner, and more generally because they violated understood gender roles. . . . Third, because same-sex relationships are nonprocreative, Paul regarded these relationships as selfish and socially irresponsible, neglecting the obligation of procreation. Finally, . . . they violated ancient society's understanding of the natural order, the commonly accepted synthesis of . . . individual disposition, larger social values, and the surrounding physical world" (266–67).

7. Matthew Vines, *God and the Gay Christian: The Biblical Case in Support of Same-Sex Relationships* (New York: Convergent Books, 2014), 31–41, 95–115. For example: "Same-sex relations challenged . . . beliefs about nature and sex by putting a male in the passive role or a female in the active role. This inversion of accepted gender roles, combined with the non-procreative character of same-sex unions, is why ancient writers called same-sex behavior "unnatural." . . . Anatomical complementarity . . . is not supported by [Romans 1]. . . . Male passivity, female dominance, and a total lack of self-control made same-sex behavior both the height of sexual excess and the pinnacle of dishonor for many conservative moralists in Paul's day. . . . For Paul, same-sex desire did not characterize a small minority of people. . . . It represented an innate potential for excess within *all* of fallen humanity. . . . It became "unnatural" in the sense that it subverted conventional, patriarchal gender norms" (108–14).

8. Brownson, *Bible, Gender, Sexuality*, 280.

2. *An orientation* or *excess argument*: They claim that Paul presumes that the participants are bored heterosexuals or bisexuals seeking novel ways to express excessive, insatiable lust. "The ancient world had no notion of sexual orientation."[9] Paul would not have forced exclusively oriented "gay" and lesbian Christians into compulsory celibacy.

3. *A misogyny argument*: They contend that Paul viewed "nature" not as male-female anatomical complementarity (allegedly unknown in the ancient world) but rather as patriarchy predicated on female inferiority. They treated as "unnatural" the violation of *conventional* gender roles. Instead of men taking the active-penetrative role in sex and women the passive-receptive role, one man in man-male relations[10] plays the inferior passive role of women and one woman in female-female relations adopts the superior active role of men. Egalitarian relationships were unknown.

4. *A compulsory procreation argument*: They assume that Paul would have allowed sexual relations only in the context of a marriage entered for the procreation of children.

Right out of the starting gate a fair-minded observer could see four fundamental problems with their argumentation.

First, there is the obvious air of historical unreality to their proposition, especially as regards their first two arguments. Knowing that the view against

---

9. Brownson, *Bible, Gender, Sexuality*, 255. This remark is found in the summary of his chapter on nature. It contradicts his earlier concession in that same chapter that my work does show that "an awareness of a "natural" orientation toward same-sex relations is attested in some Greek and Roman sources" (229). Brownson contends wrongly on the basis of this argument from silence that the fact that such theories are not mentioned in Jewish and Christian sources means that "Jews and Christians did not recognize even the possibility that persons might be naturally inclined . . . toward desiring others of the same sex" (229). He claims that "to concede such a possibility would allow a construal of nature that violated their understanding of divine law and thus it would be understood as unacceptable a priori" (230–31). This claim flies in the face of Paul's view of sin as an innate impulse. Does Brownson really want to argue that the existence of innate sinful desires is a contradiction of natural law? For obvious reasons Paul (like the Stoics) did not view innate desires, sexual or otherwise, as reliable indicators of natural law in the same way that he viewed material structures of nature still intact despite the entrance of sin into the world. Were it otherwise, Jesus should not have extrapolated the limitation of two persons to a sexual union on the basis of God's creation of two primary sexes, male and female, but rather should have endorsed polyamorous unions based on innate sexual desires for multiple partners.

10. My use of the expression "man-male" is intentional, calling to mind Lev 20:13, which forbids a "man" (Heb. *'îš*) from having sexual relations with a "male" (Heb. *zākār*). As b. Sanh. 54a notes, "man" (the active partner) "excludes a minor" while "male" (the passive partner) can be "an adult or minor."

homosexual practice is more strenuous in ancient Israel, early Judaism, and early Christianity than anywhere else in the ancient Near East or Greco-Roman world, do Brownson and Vines really believe that if a Christian "gay" couple expressing lifelong commitment to each other and insisting that they experienced no sexual attraction for the other sex came up to Paul and asked his blessing on their "marriage," that Paul would grant it instead of recoiling in horror? Let's add also, for good measure, that the couple is too old to procreate with a heterosexual partner even if they wanted to do so, but is willing to adopt. I submit to readers that anyone who thinks that these considerations would have made any more difference to Paul's acceptance of a homosexual union than, say, to an incestuous one is simply not thinking historically but ideologically.

Second, a moment's consideration would show that some of these arguments create internal contradictions. The exploitation and orientation arguments (arguments 3 and 4) suggest that if Paul had only known about committed homosexual relationships conducted by exclusively homosexual persons (arguments 1 and 2), he would have condoned such unions. Yet their misogyny and compulsory-procreation arguments render considerations of commitment and sexual orientation irrelevant. A committed homosexual relationship between homosexually oriented persons would still upset the patriarchy and still shirk a responsibility to procreate, and thus still be rejected. Given the internal contradictions of their arguments, the impression received by the reader is that they are attempting to throw as many things at the wall as they can, hoping something, anything, will stick. That does not inspire confidence in their argumentation.

Third, although Brownson and Vines reject "gender complementarity" as a grounding for Paul's opposition to homosexual practice, two of their arguments presuppose it. How exactly does one speak of the male's active sexual role in penetration and the female's passive sexual role in being penetrated, much less the prospect of procreation only through such an act, without having any awareness that both anatomically and physiologically males and females are true gender complements or sexual counterparts? Logically, this makes no sense.

Fourth, even though Brownson and Vines insist that Paul did much to undermine both the patriarchy and compulsory procreation, they can point to no corresponding reduction in the intensity of Paul's argument against homosexual practice. Brownson has two whole chapters on how the Bible, especially Paul, undermines the patriarchy (ch. 4) and compulsory procreation (ch. 6).[11]

---

11. In ch. 4, Brownson contends for "two countervailing streams with respect to patriarchy in Scripture," one assuming "a patriarchal framework" that is "shaped by the structures of creation," and another toward "a more egalitarian vision" that looks toward "the new creation" as in Gal 3:28 ("no longer male and female"). "Paul's assertion that both spouses exercise authority over the bodies of the other (1 Cor. 7:3-4)

Vines feels the same way: "Paul . . . may not have endorsed fully equal roles for men and women, but his views were remarkably egalitarian within his cultural context. . . . Tarring Paul as sexist is inaccurate."[12] He too notes Paul's female co-workers, and insists that "Paul undermined the belief that patriarchy has a place in the kingdom of God" when in Gal 3:28 he detached "our ultimate status in Christ" from "worldly hierarchies of ethnicity, class, and gender."[13] Yet, in spite of the fact that Brownson and Vines take pains to show that Paul is not deeply mired in either patriarchy or compulsory procreation as essential components of marriage and human sexuality, we see no loosening of Paul's resolve around a male-female prerequisite of marriage. Would that not rather suggest that Paul's opposition to homosexual practice is not deeply mired in patriarchy and procreation? Logically, one would think so.

Design Complementarity in the Ancient World

According to Brownson, "the notion of 'anatomical gender complementarity' is really a modern concept."[14] As noted above, this is a bizarre claim given that they attribute to Paul a procreation argument, which of necessity premises physiological complementarity on the anatomical compatibility of male-female sex organs. Cicero makes this very point: "The conformation of the body and its members . . . are enough to show that nature's scheme included the procreation of children" (*De finibus* 3.62).[15] Here "nature's scheme" clearly refers to nature's hand in developing complementary male-female sex organs that make procreation possible.

Brownson and Vines misconstrue the procreation argument that was commonly used in the ancient world to explain, in part, why homosexual relation-

---

presents a striking contrast to prevailing patriarchal assumptions," to a point where it "removes hierarchical relationships from the sex act itself" (*Bible, Gender, Sexuality*, 80–81). He cites "many cases throughout the New Testament in which women appear in significant positions of leadership and wield notable authority," especially among Paul's coworkers (61–62).

Likewise, in ch. 6 Brownson argues that Paul "moved" procreation "to the periphery" in "the 'interim' period" between Jesus' resurrection and the kingdom of God. Marriage "has as its purpose not the bearing of children but the exercise of mutual care and the avoidance of uncontrolled lust (1 Cor. 7:2-9)." In Brownson's view, "the moral logic of the Bible is thus fairly clear. . . . Marriage has something more than procreation as its essential reason for being. When we consider some of the most extensive discussions of marriage in Scripture, including Genesis 2, Song of Songs, Ephesians 5:21-33, and 1 Corinthians 7, procreation is entirely absent from the discussion, and the focus falls on kinship, sharing, mutual support, self-control, and intimacy" (117–18).

12. Vines, *God and the Gay Christian*, 110.
13. Vines, *God and the Gay Christian*, 92–93.
14. Brownson, *Bible, Gender, Sexuality*, 243.
15. Ironically, a text noted by Brownson himself (*Bible, Gender, Sexuality*, 243n41).

ships are contrary to nature, from Plato on.[16] Even though Paul did not stress procreation as a requirement for marriage (cf. 1 Cor 7:2, 5, 9, 36; Eph 5:21–33) or view sterility in marriage as grounds for divorce (1 Cor 7:8–11), he did not reduce his opprobrium for homosexual unions. Jews and Christians did not view infertile heterosexual unions as an offense comparable to the immorality of a homosexual unions. Paul viewed procreation primarily in heuristic, rather than prescriptive, terms. The structural incapacity for fertility in homosexual relationships was for Paul, as for the ancients generally, a clue to (and a symptom of) the fundamental asymmetry of such relationships. This means, in turn, that for Paul the procreation argument was not (as Brownson and Vines contend) a "*compulsory* procreation" argument, a point that makes it harder for Brownson and Vines to dismiss the argument in today's context. Even when the "equipment" malfunctions, it still tells us something about the natural fit of male and female.

The ancients were manifestly aware that "the parts fit" male-to-female; indeed, it is absurd to argue that the Greeks and Romans did not realize this. For example, the second-century physician Soranus referred to *molles*, "soft men" eager for penetration (i.e., the Latin equivalent for the Greek term *malakoi* in 1 Cor 6:9), as those who "subjugated to obscene uses parts not so intended" and disregarded "the places of our body which divine providence destined for definite functions" (*On Chronic Diseases* 4.9.131).

In Plutarch's *Dialogue on Love* (early second century CE), a proponent of the superiority of male-female love contends that sex between males is always "contrary to nature," even when conducted with consent and kindness, because a male is not designed for penetration by, and procreation with, another male (751D–E).[17] An advocate for the superiority of male-male love counters this notion of anatomical and physiological complementarity by ridiculing those who correlate love with men who "are locked like dogs by their sexual parts

---

16. "When male unites with female for procreation, the pleasure experienced is held to be in accordance with nature (*kata physin*), but contrary to nature (*para physin*) when male mates with male or female with female." E.g., Plato, *Laws*, 636C.

17. "If sexual intercourse that is contrary to nature (*para physin*) with males does not do away with or damage amorous goodwill [or: a lover's kindness], how much more reasonable is it that the love of women and men, making use of [or: living under] nature, develops into friendship through (sexual) favor.   But the intercourse that comes about from (the joining of) males, either unwillingly with force and plunder, or willingly with softness (Gk. *malakia*) and effeminacy (Gk. *thēlytēs*), surrendering themselves, according to Plato, 'to be mounted in the custom of four-footed animals and to be sowed as to produce children contrary to nature (*para physin*)' (*Phaedrus* 250E)— this is an entirely ill-favored favor, shameful and contrary to Aphrodite." Daphnaeus' argument regarding the superiority of male-female love over male-male love cannot be reduced to misogyny since in context he is lifting up women as suitable partners and friends for men. He is obviously referring at least in part to the unnatural treatment of the male anus as a receptacle for penetration and semen.

to the female" (752B–C). In a later debate over the superiority of male-male or male-female love in the pseudo-Lucianic text *Affairs of the Heart* (ca. 300 CE), an advocate for male-female love asserts that male-male love is an erotic attraction for what one already is as a sexual being, including but not limited to anatomy. Men who have sex with males "transgressed the laws of nature" by bringing together "one nature . . . in one bed," not unaware of what they are doing but rather "seeing themselves in one another" (19–20).

What I am proposing is not a novel view. According to Thomas Hubbard, a classicist who has written the premier sourcebook of texts on homosexuality in ancient Greece and Rome: "Basic to the heterosexual position [against homosexual practice in the first few centuries CE] is the characteristic Stoic appeal to the providence of Nature, which has matched and fitted the sexes to each other."[18] Similarly, classicist William Schoedel acknowledged that ancient writers "who appeal to nature against same-sex *eros* find it convenient to concentrate on the more or less obvious uses of the orifices of the body to suggest the proper channel for the more diffused sexual impulses of the body."[19]

Thus, when Paul speaks of "the males, having left behind the natural use of the female," being "inflamed with their yearning for one another, males with males," it is obvious that by "natural use" he is referring to both the anatomical and physiological design complementarity of the female in sexual intercourse with the male. By the same token, Paul's prior mention of "their females exchang[ing] the natural use for that which is contrary to nature" likely refers to the female's natural use *of the male* in sexual intercourse.

Philo of Alexandria and the Mixing of Gender Complementarity with Misogyny

According to Brownson, "what [the] early Jewish texts [cited by Gagnon] have in mind is not anatomical complementarity but the violation of socially normed gender roles. . . . These texts hardly support an interpretation of nature as referring to 'the anatomical fittedness of the male penis and the female vagina.'"[20] This is an example of Brownson making a "not this but that" out of a "both . . . and" in order to buttress his shaky arguments.

Philo of Alexandria's critique of the discomplementarity of male homosexual relations merged issues of anatomy and physiology with misogynistic

18. Thomas K. Hubbard, *Homosexuality in Greece and Rome: A Sourcebook of Basic Documents* (Berkeley: University of California Press, 2003), 444.

19. William R. Schoedel, "Same-Sex Eros: Paul and the Greco-Roman Tradition," in *Homosexuality, Science, and the "Plain Sense" of Scripture*, ed. David L. Balch (Grand Rapids: Eerdmans, 2000), 46.

20. Brownson, *Bible, Gender, Sexuality*, 242–43 (citing me, *The Bible and Homosexual Practice*, 169–76).

attitudes about women. In other words, Philo mixed entirely appropriate nature arguments with inappropriate sexist biases about female inferiority. Brownson and Vines are unwilling to dissect one from the other because it does not suit their ideological agenda to do so.[21] Instead, they take the reductionistic approach of focusing on Philo's regrettable misogyny to the detriment of his legitimate concerns arising out of anatomical complementarity.

For example, Philo described in his work *On Abraham* how "the Sodomites . . . threw off from their necks the law of nature" (135). Is this all about the conventional misogyny of the day or are there elements that still make sense in our current cultural context? When Philo talks about pederastic "men *mounting* males, the doers (*hoi drōntes*; the active, penetrative partners) not standing in awe of the nature held in common with those who had it done to them (*hoi paschontes*; the passive, penetrated partners)," he obviously is thinking in part about how males are not anatomically suited for sexual penetration because the two males are of the same "nature" as males and thus not sexual complements (135–37; emphasis mine). In another work, Philo compares man-male sexual relationships negatively even to male-female fornication and adultery, noting that promiscuous male-female practices at least "pay tribute to the laws of nature," whereas "men (mad) after males" are "differing from them only in age" (*Cont. Life* 59). At every level, the participants in homosexual union are too much alike, not enough "other."

Returning to his remarks in *Abr.*, when Philo further expresses outrage that the older active partners supplement the act of intercourse with efforts "little by little" at "accustoming *those who had been born men* to put up with feminine things, . . . not only feminizing their bodies . . . but also . . . their very souls," he rightly recognizes inappropriate efforts at socializing birth-males to enjoy undermining their own biological masculinity (*Abr.* 136; emphasis mine). In *Spec.* 3.37–38 and 40, Philo expands on the actions of these highly feminized males ("men-women"): braiding their hair to resemble female hairstyles, painting their faces with makeup, parading themselves with a feminine gait, some of whom even go so far as to "cut off their procreative organs" in a vain effort to effect "a more complete change into women." Brownson and Vines have argued that Philo's complaint has little or nothing to do with anatomical complementarity. Yet Philo's graphic reference to males trying to erase their masculinity by cutting off their penis seems a good indication that sex-specific genitalia are very much at issue.[22] The other male attempts at self-feminization speak to

21. Brownson, *Bible, Gender, Sexuality*, cites Philo intermittently (155, 227–28, 235–36, 239, 242–43); similarly, Vines, *God and the Gay Christian*, 69–71, 87, 89, 108–9).
22. Even Brownson at this point is forced to acknowledge that castration concerns anatomy. Nevertheless, he tries to wriggle out of the significance of this admission by saying that "this concern with anatomy is only one element in a much larger concern of Philo in this passage: the blurring of gender roles defined in terms of dress,

cultural gender markers. Still, two millennia later in a very different culture, such behavior comes across as an attempt (in Philo's words) "to transform the male nature into female" or of "counterfeiting the coin of nature."

Earlier in *Spec.*, Philo castigated pederasts for using their "procreative organs" to "force the male type of nature to debase and convert itself into the feminine form, just to indulge a polluted and accursed passion" (2.50). Why does Philo think that for a man to penetrate another male in the anus with his "procreative organ" is already beginning the process of coding the male as a female? Brownson and Vines will say: Because females in Philo's day are coded as passive and submissive while males are coded as active and dominant. I submit that of equal significance to Philo is the obvious anatomical and physiological fact that males are not designed by God with an orifice for sexual penetration, as illustrated both by fit and purpose.

Philo goes on in his treatise *Abr.* to treat the non-procreative dimension of man-male unions, excoriating those who fail in their social responsibility to populate regions (which Philo calls "a pleasure that is contrary to nature" in *Spec.* 3.39) and praising "unions in accordance with nature, having come into being for the sake of the procreation of children" (*Abr.* 137). Whether or not one accepts an intrinsic connection between marriage and procreation, one cannot contest that Philo's argument at this point is deduced substantially from male-female anatomical and physiological complementarity.

There is nothing inherently misogynistic about some of the key facets of Philo's view. Certainly, a person who believes in the equal worth and dignity of women can endorse many elements of his presentation, stripped of its misogyny. Nor is Philo's case merely "conventional," as though disconnected from biological realities. To claim, as Brownson and Vines do, that there is no significant anatomical or biological components to Philo's presentation is playing fast and loose with historical reality. It is only when Philo tacks on to these ideas a

---

behavior, and authority/control. It is this latter problem, rather than the violation of an 'anatomical norm,' that shapes Philo's discourse as a whole" (*Bible, Gender, Sexuality*, 243). I certainly agree that anatomical complementarity is one element; procreative complementarity is a second element; and a concern for self-presentation (hairstyle, dress, mannerisms) consistent with biological realities from birth as reflected in cultural codes is a third element. To be sure, the "cultural codes" clearly contain misogynistic features. However, it does not relegate the entire discourse to the dustbin of history. Brownson immediately follows the claim cited above, which is at least somewhat nuanced (though inadequately so) with an unnuanced summary: "Even though Gagnon wishes to interpret nature in Romans 1 as referring to "anatomical complementarity," the texts that he cites to support this claim fail to do so. . . . The notion of "anatomical gender complementarity" is really a modern concept rather than a category that actually shaped ethical thought about sex in the ancient world" (*Bible, Gender, Sexuality*, 243). The claim borders on the comical: It never dawned on Jewish critics of homosexual practice in the ancient world that God had shaped the male and female sex organs in compatible ways that suggest divine intentionality for male-female pairings?

rigid view of men always in all spheres of life being dominant and women passive, or when he talks about emasculated males being infected with a "female disease" (*Abr.* 136; also *Cont. Life* 60; *Spec.* 1.325; 3.37), as though expressing revulsion not just for men giving up masculinity but for femininity in women as well, that we reach a point where we must separate out the biological from the cultural.

Since Paul does not breathe the same misogynistic air as Philo, nor apparently treat procreation as a *sine qua non* for entering and maintaining marriages, we can safely assume that Paul himself has engaged at least to some extent in this teasing-out process.

Why Paul Singled Out Homosexual Practice in Romans 1:24–27

It is telling that Brownson and Vines offer no explanation for why Paul singled out same-sex intercourse from among sexual sins in the context of the extended vice list in Rom 1:18–32. My own position is that Paul selects homosexual practice because it provides the perfect corollary to his argument about idolatry in 1:18–23: In both instances humans suppress the truth that God has made transparent in the material structures of creation. In the case of homosexual practice Paul is referring by his nature argument to observable male-female complementarity, including anatomy.

In the midst of his discussion of the vice of idolatry (1:19–23) Paul contends that idolaters "suppress the truth"

> because the knowable aspect of God is transparent[23] to them, for God made (it) transparent to them. For his invisible attributes, since the creation of the world, are being clearly seen, being mentally apprehended by (means of) the things made, both his eternal power and divinity, so that they are without excuse. (Rom 1:19–20)

When Paul then turns to the vice of sexual "impurity" in 1:24 he could have chosen from various options, including adultery, fornication, sex with prostitutes, and incest. Instead, he fixated on same-sex intercourse in 1:26–27. Why? The answer is self-evident: Same-sex intercourse provided the clearest example of a case of sexual immorality that, like idolatry, consisted of a suppression of truth that could be "clearly seen" and "mentally apprehended by means of the things made" by God at "creation" and still observable in "nature." Simply put, even Gentiles without the direct revelation of Scripture have the indirect revelation of nature that human sexual anatomy and function fit female to male and not female to female or male to male. Same-sex intercourse constitutes a deliberate suppression of such transparent knowledge deducible from material structures made by God.

---

23. Or: visible, apparent, conspicuous, plain, evident, obvious (Gk. *phaneros*).

In short, just as the truth about God is visible and apparent in material creation (1:19–20), so too the truth about God's will for sex is visible in our gendered bodies (1:26–27). Pagans do not have to have Genesis or Leviticus to be held accountable for this knowledge. They are "without excuse" (Gk. *anapologētoi*) here, as much as they are when they worship idols (1:20).

Brownson (followed by Vines) claims that I have confused matters:

> This reading [of Rom 1:19–20 as informing 1:24–27] confuses Paul's meaning. What Paul actually says . . . is that what can be known about God is plain or visible in the creation, specifically God's eternal power and divine nature. The focus here is not on knowledge of human things but on the knowledge of God. . . . Gagnon confuses the initial revelation about God suppressed by idolatrous humans (which focuses on visible things) with the later "handing over" of humans into depravity (which focuses on lust, shame, and the violation of what is "natural"). Romans 1 says nothing particular at all about the "visible" quality of nature.[24]

I am not "confusing" the vertical and horizontal dimensions but rather noting an analogous or parallel use. It is Brownson and Vines who are confusing matters by their own arbitrary and tendentious insistence that this same theme, previously applied vertically to God's attributes, cannot then be reapplied by Paul horizontally to the way God made male and female as complementary sexual beings. Brownson and Vines want us to believe that Paul saw no correlation between humans foolishly ignoring the evidence about God and humans foolishly ignoring the evidence about how God designed humans sexually. They want us to believe, further, that Paul saw no correlation between "the things made" by God and our gendered bodies made by God. If God is known by means of the things that God made, why isn't God's will for human sexuality also known by means of the way he shapes our bodies sexually?

Paul is clearly connecting the two sections of 1:18–23 (idolatry) and 1:24–27 (the impurity of same-sex intercourse). First, the thematic heading in v. 18 that refers to humans "suppressing the truth" likely applies not only vertically to suppressing God's visible attributes, but also horizontally to suppressing God's visible design of male and female as complementary sexual beings. Second, Paul in v. 25 summarizes the argument of vv. 18–23 in the midst of discussing sexual impurity in vv. 24, 26–27: "the very ones who exchanged the truth about God for the lie and worshiped and served the creation [or: creature] rather than the Creator." Third, Paul's reference to females horizontally "exchanging" the natural use (of the male) in 1:26 interlocks with the vertical "exchanging" both of the glory of God for idols in 1:23 and of "the truth about God for a lie" in 1:25 (summarizing 1:18–23). Fourth, Paul's references to "the creation" and "by

---

24. Brownson, *Bible, Gender, Sexuality*, 241; similarly, Vines, *God and the Gay Christian*, 204–5n27.

means of the things made" in 1:20, and to "the Creator" in 1:25, tie into Paul's remarks about same-sex intercourse as "contrary to nature" in 1:26–27. "Nature" is what is in place after the act of creation. Fifth, v. 27 again alludes back to vv. 18–23 when referring to the "payback" men lying with males received for their "wandering" or "straying" (*planē*), that is, from the truth about God. Thus, Paul gives multiple indicators to readers that they should link the discussions of idolatry and sexual impurity as prime instances of human suppression of truth accessible through material structures.

In early Judaism we find the following principle: Humans are being "punished by the very things by which one sins" (Wis 11:16 NRSVue; cf. T. Gad 5:9–11). That precisely fits what we see in Rom 1:24–27. Humans foolishly rejected obvious indicators of God's glorious transcendence in the visible structures made by God at creation, preferring instead statues in the image not only of humans but even of animals (1:23). So God "handed them over to desires" that foolishly ignored the evidence of nature's handiwork in male and female bodies (1:24, 26–27). Those who foolishly refused to "glorify God as God" (1:21) now foolishly "dishonor their bodies among themselves" (1:24) through "passions of dishonor" (1:26). Just as idolatry mocks it practitioners, so too does homosexual practice. This is the "payback" that they "receive in themselves" for "straying" from the truth about God to idolatry (1:27).

Brownson makes much of the fact that Rom 1:24–27 focuses on desires while saying nothing explicit about nature's visibility: "the desires of their hearts" (v. 24); "passions of dishonor" (v. 26); males "inflamed with their yearning for one another" (1:27). However, there is no either-or here. In 1:21–22 Paul contrasts the visible structures of God's creation with humans who operate out of skewed thoughts and desires. He refers to people who "were rendered worthless in their reasonings," whose *"senseless heart was darkened,"* and who, "though claiming to be wise, were made foolish." In 1:24 Paul picks up on these remarks in 1:21–22 when noting that "God handed them over in (= because of) *the desires of their hearts* to sexual impurity." Again, in 1:26 Paul starts with *"because of this"* God handed them over to dishonorable passions." The "this" refers back to the foolish "desires" in 1:24, which in turn alludes back to the worthless thinking and senseless heart of 1:21–22.

As with 1:19–23, there is an implicit contrast in 1:24–27 between innate desires, which are poor indicators of the Creator's will, and material structures in our gendered bodies, which, given universal sin, provide far more convincing evidence of the Creator's will expressed in nature. In short, the desires that lead people to discount the natural revelation given in our gendered bodies are an extension of the same desires that led them to discount natural revelation given in the grandeur and majesty of the cosmos.[25]

---

25. Brownson grossly misunderstands a point that I made: "Gagnon is certainly wrong when he declares, 'Passions, which are not material and hence not visible to

In Paul's thinking, "nature" (*physis*) and "natural" (*physikos*) in 1:26–27 clearly parallel both "creation" (*ktisis*) and "the things made" by God in 1:20, not mere social convention. Creation refers to an event at the beginning of time while nature here designates the ongoing state or result issuing from that event. Even that distinction between creation and nature collapses in vv. 19–27 because Paul means by "since the creation of the world" (v. 20) the way things turned out after the initial act of creating. Similarly, an improper use of the "creation" or "creature" (*ktisis*, same word as in v. 20) leads to an improper "use" of "nature" (vv. 25–26). For those who "exchanged" worship of "the Creator" for worship of "the creation" (v. 25) were then "handed over" by God to "dishonorable passions" that impelled them to "exchange the natural use" for a use of sexual bodies "contrary to nature" (v. 26).

Creation and nature are also correlated in T. Naph. 3:2–5, which in a manner similar to Rom 1:18–27 connects two things: (1) Gentile failure to distinguish the Lord from his "workmanship," leading to worship of what "the Lord . . . made" and (2) "Sodom, which changed the order of its nature." The latter in context probably refers to self-evident incongruity of sexual relations between males, as discerned in the "workmanship the Lord . . . made" in their bodies.[26]

Creation and Creator are also correlated with nature's material and often visible structures in Philo of Alexandria. Nature "is personified as the creator and sustainer of the world" so that at times "what is said about nature glides almost imperceptibly into what is said about God," including the power to

---

sight, are excluded from consideration as indications of God's intentions manifest in nature' (Gagnon, *The Bible and Homosexual Practice*, 257–58). Paul refers explicitly to lust and passion throughout this passage in the closest possible connection with what is 'unnatural' (Rom. 1:24, 26, 27)" (*Bible, Gender, Sexuality*, 242n37). I am obviously *not* arguing that Paul fails to refer to lust and passion in 1:24–27 since I provided over ten pages of translation notes to my translation of Rom 1:24–27 which clearly address such (*The Bible and Homosexual Practice*, 230–40). My point was rather that Paul clearly did not regard passions (innate or otherwise) as necessary indicators of a behavior's *conformity to nature* since Paul views these passions for homosexual relations as unnatural passions that ignore an obvious design for sexuality given in the material structures of nature. I make the point because proponents of homosexual unions often argue erroneously that an innate homosexual orientation is "natural" simply by virtue of it being innate desire.

26. *The Bible and Homosexual Practice*, 88–89n121. "Naphtali" exhorts his children not to "change the law of God in disordered deeds," just as "sun and moon and stars do not change their order," and to avoid the example of Gentiles who, "having gone astray and left the Lord, changed their order and followed after stones and trees." They should recognize "in all the pieces of workmanship the Lord who made all these things (sun, moon, stars, firmament, earth, sea, etc.), in order that you may not become like Sodom, which changed the order of its nature. And likewise also the Watchers changed the order of their nature, whom the Lord cursed at the flood."

bestow on men and women distinct functions in procreation.[27] It often "denotes the world of visible things," including all things visible in the heavens and on earth.[28]

Contrary to what Brownson claims,[29] my point is not that nature always refers to visible or material structures but that it often does, with this sense fitting the context of Rom 1:18–27 quite well. Male and female are designed by God as sexual complements and counterparts, and this ought to be obvious to anyone not actively engaged in suppressing the truth about God and the way God made us.

Paul's Clear Intertextual Echo of Genesis 1:26–27

It would be bizarre to argue that "the things made" at "creation" by God (1:20) "the Creator" (1:25) could not extend in Paul to include the gendered bodies of male and female, particularly since the creation texts in Gen 1–2 include such an extension (Gen 1:26–28; 2:7, 21–24). Indeed, there is a very clear echo of one of the two most pivotal creation texts, Gen 1:26–27, in Rom 1:23, 26–27, establishing definitively that Paul means by "nature" what God created. There are eight points of correspondence, in a similar relative order: *human, image, likeness; birds, cattle, reptiles; male, female.* Paul could easily have spoken in Rom 1:26–27 of *women* (not females) having unnatural sex and of *men* (not males) having unnatural sex with *men* (not males). The reason why he stuck

---

27. *TDNT* 9:267, 267n166; citing *Sacr.* 98–100 (nature, like God, is uncreated and unchangeable; it assigns to humankind various gifts, virtues, and functions, including "functions which fitly belong to [one or] the other sex," so that the ability "to sow and beget belongs to the man" and "welfare in child-bearing is a good thing belonging to women" [LCL]) and *Who Is the Heir* 114–16 ("the beginning of things both material and immaterial are found to be by God only. . . . [The beginnings of plants and the generation of people and of the other living creatures are] the invisible works of invisible nature," "the original, the earliest and the real cause. . . . Is not nature the underlying fact" of the arts and sciences?").

28. *TDNT* 9:268, citing *Abr.* 58 (the sight of the eyes allows us to apprehend what nature shows, including the sun, moon, and "the whole heaven and earth" [cp. Rom 1:19-21] while the sight of the mind allows us to see "the Father and Maker of all"); *Every Good Man Is Free* 108 (Zeno showed his moral purpose to be "mightier than the strongest things in nature, fire and iron"); *Mos.* 1.130 (the dog-fly is the fiercest of all the creatures "in nature"). Brownson cites a text in Philo (*Decalogue* 142) that refers to "all the passions of the soul . . . agitating it *contrary to nature,* and not permitting it to remain in a healthy state" (*Bible, Gender, Sexuality,* 242). Ironically for Brownson, negative health often does manifest itself in visible and/or tangible ways, affecting material structures adversely. A passion for eating too many sweets, for example, can lead to rotten teeth, a swollen belly, and hosts of other side effects to the body (visible or not).

29. Brownson, *Bible, Gender, Sexuality,* 242.

to the nomenclature of "male" and "female" was to continue the link to Gen 1 that had begun with Rom 1:23.

LXX Gen 1:26–27	Rom 1:23, 26–27
A. God's likeness and image in humans	
(1) human (*anthrōpos*)	(3) likeness (*homoiōma*)
(2) image (*eikon*)	(2) image (*eikon*)
(3) likeness (*homoiōsis*)	(1) human (*anthrōpos*)
B. Dominion over the animal kingdom	
(4) birds (*peteinōn*)	(4) birds (*peteinōn*)
(5) cattle (*ktēnōn*)	(5) quadrupeds (*tetrapodōn*)
(6) reptiles (*herpetōn*)	(6) reptiles (*herpetōn*)
C. Male-female differentiation	
(7) male (*arsen*)	(8) females (*thēleiai*)
(8) female (*thēlys*)	(7) males (*arsenes*)[30]

What is the point of these echoes of Gen 1:26–27? Gentiles can ascertain through observable, material creation some basic information about God and the way God made us as sexual beings, information that is known with even greater clarity to the people of God who have access to the direct revelation of Scripture. What is that information? Idolatry and same-sex intercourse together constitute a frontal assault on the work of the Creator in nature. However, instead of recognizing their creation in God's image and dominion over animals, humans worshipped statues in the likeness of humans and even animals. Similarly, instead of acknowledging that God made them "male and female," some humans went so far as to deny the transparent complementarity of their sexuality by engaging in sex with the same sex. Those who had suppressed the truth about God visible in creation went on to suppress the truth about the way God made them, visible in nature, choosing instead to gratify contrary innate impulses.

---

30. The two places where the order is inverted in Rom 1 can be easily explained. The inversion of "image" and "likeness" is due to a second intertextual echo in Rom 1:23 to Ps 106:20: "*they* (i.e., the Israelites in the golden calf episode) *exchanged* their [or: his] *glory for the likeness of* a calf eating grass." Romans 1:23 starts with an echo of this verse and then merges with an echo of Gen 1:26: "*they exchanged* the *glory* of the imperishable *God for the likeness of* an *image* of a perishable *human.*" The inversion of "male" and "female" is due to the rhetorical exigencies of Paul's argument. Paul begins with the easiest indictment of homoerotic relations first, an indictment that nearly all would concede (female-female intercourse), and then proceeds to the more disputed case in the ancient world (male-male intercourse).

Brownson did not take note of this intertextual echo that I cited in work subsequent to my first book.[31] Vines does acknowledge it but is confused about its application, asserting that Paul echoes Gen 1:27 to reject only especially "lustful [forms of] same-sex behavior."[32] Yet Paul's echoing of Gen 1:27 clearly sets up a male-female standard ("male and female [God] made them") that necessarily disqualifies all forms of homosexual practice on the grounds of what they can never be: a male-female bond, a union of true sexual complements in terms of anatomy, physiology, and psychology—everything that goes into making a male a male and a female a female.

Romans 1:24–27 is not the only time that Paul echoes a key creation text when he rejects all homosexual practice. Paul's reference to homosexual practice in 1 Cor 6:9 occurs in close proximity to his citation of Gen 2:24b ("the two will become one flesh"), the other pivotal creation text, in 1 Cor 6:16.[33] This makes it very unlikely that Paul is restricting his indictment of homosexual practice in 1 Cor 6:9 only to certain exploitative and promiscuous forms. Nor is this connection between 1 Cor 6:9 and Gen 2:24 conducive to a dismissive misogyny argument since Jesus established Gen 1:27 and 2:24 as foundational standards for sexual ethics. Paul shows himself to be a good disciple of Jesus in applying these two key texts to the issue of homosexual practice. Whereas Brownson and Vines see no contradiction between affirming homosexual practice and the two key creation texts in Gen 1–2, Paul sees an inherent contradiction.

These echoes establish what Paul's main problem with homosexual practice was: It was a violation of God's will for male-female pairing established in creation and visible in nature, not that it was typically exploitative or promiscuous or even that it upset some misogynistic insistence on female inferiority and male dominance. It also shows to be in error Brownson's claim that the phrase "male and female" in Gen 1:27 neither denotes a sexual pair nor establishes a link between a two-sexes prerequisite and divine image-bearing.

---

31. It was available a decade before his own book in Robert A. J. Gagnon, "A Comprehensive and Critical Review Essay of *Homosexuality, Science, and the 'Plain Sense' of Scripture*, Part 2," *HBT* 25 (2003): 179–275, specifically 208–11, 242–46.

32. Vines, *God and the Gay Christian*, 110–11. Vines dismisses the connection to anatomical complementarity because Genesis 1 does not use the word "nature." This misses the point that when Paul chooses to supplement his nature argument with an appeal to Gen 1:27, he is showing that for him, in this context, "nature" is what is left when the creation process is finished.

33. Although the immediate point of the citation is to establish that "the man who joins himself to a prostitute is one body" with her (1 Cor 6:16), there can be little doubt that Paul would have understood its relevance for indicting homosexual practice (as also the vice of adultery mentioned in 6:9). Since Jesus established the significance of these texts for sexual ethics, Paul would be bound to apply them to the issue of homosexual practice. Indeed, Paul's use of Gen 1:27 and 2:21–22 later in the same letter (1 Cor 11:7–12), though it has problems, clearly shows that Paul regarded Gen 1:27 and 2:21–24 as vital for establishing the significance of male-female differentiation in the context of marriage.

Paul's Use of the Word "Nature" Elsewhere

For Paul nature (*physis*) elsewhere corresponds to the essential material, biological, or organic constitution of things as created and set in motion by God. It nowhere corresponds to mere social convention, not even in our thinking, let alone Paul's. In Rom 11:21, 24, branches that are "in accordance with nature" (*kata physin*) are "natural" branches in organic unity with the tree from which they originally sprouted, not "conventional" branches; while branches from a wild olive tree that are grafted in "beyond [or: contrary to] nature" (*para physin*, as in 1:26) into a cultivated olive tree lack an original organic connection. Possibly Paul also had in mind observable differences between cultivated olive trees and wild olive trees in terms of quality of fruit (better from cultivated trees) and root systems (stronger in wild trees), with the production of fine fruit dependent on grafting a shoot from a cultivated tree into a wild tree rather than the reverse (so the successor to Aristotle, Theophrastus, in *Causes of Plants*).[34]

To be enslaved in one's pre-Christian Gentile life to "things that by nature (*physei*) are not gods" (Gal 4:8) is to be enslaved to things that in their created essence are non-gods, not to things that are so by social convention. Those who are "by nature (*physei*) Jews" (Gal 2:15) and "the uncircumcised by nature (*physei*)" (Rom 2:27) are persons who are, respectively, Jews and Gentiles "by biological or physical descent" or "by birth," not by social convention.[35] None of these uses of "nature" involve a subjective human disposition.

One or two uses of *physis* by Paul do refer to a subjective human disposition or inclination, though one biologically determined at birth. Gentiles who do not have the law but nevertheless do by nature (*physei*) what the law requires (Rom 2:14), thereby showing the law to be "written in their hearts" (2:15), are not operating out of social convention but rather out of a capacity for moral discernment implanted by the Creator. BDAG gives a few options for meaning: under meaning 2 (*natural characteristic/disposition*), dative *spontaneously* (cf. *instinctively* [NASB, NRSV, NLT, CSB, CEB]; *through their own innate sense* [NJB]); under meaning 3 (see below), dative *by following the natural order* (of things; cf. REB: *by the light of nature*).[36] The latter sense is

---

34. See Philip F. Esler, *Conflict and Identity in Romans: The Social Setting of Paul's Letter* (Minneapolis: Fortress, 2003), 300–305.

35. BDAG defines all these occurrences under the heading "condition or circumstance as determined by birth, *natural endowment/ condition, nature,* esp. as inherited fr. one's ancestors" (s.v. φύσις 1 [1069]).

36. In Ephesians (written either by Paul or a disciple of Paul's after his death) reference is made to even Jews being "by nature (*physei*) children of wrath like also the rest (of humankind)" because they too do "the wishes of the flesh" (2:3). Nature here means "*our natural condition* (as descendants of Adam)" (BDAG s.v. φύσις 1 [1069]). This is the only time in the Pauline corpus that *physis* designates an innate condition owing to sin. Even this use does not refer to mere social convention but to a birth condition

possible but more likely would have required the phrase *kata physin* (in accordance with nature).

Even in 1 Cor 11:14, Paul appears to have nature proper and not convention in view when he asks rhetorically, "Does not even nature itself teach you that if a man lets the hair on his head grow long it is a disgrace for him, but if a woman lets the hair on her head grow long it is a glorious thing for her?" Paul is making an argument based on the observable reality that women retain head hair throughout life far more than do men; therefore, nature instructs us that a covering for the head is more essential for women than for men, which in turn lends credence to the social convention of reserving long hair and veils for women as a distinguishing feminine feature.[37] While the conclusion from an observable reality in nature may not be compelling, the argument from nature really does hinge on nature proper and not convention.

Brownson (followed by Vines) rejects this reading and argues (with many others) for "nature" as "social convention" or "societal custom," largely on the grounds that the Bible allows long hair for men who take a Nazirite vow (Num 6) and in the case of the tragic hero Samson (Judg 13–16). Yet all that these exceptions show is that, unlike homosexual practice, long hair on men is not a serious offense (unless it is being so worn to communicate one's denial of maleness), so that exceptions can be made to a general rule. Paul himself seems to recognize that his argument from nature is not compelling. While the appeal to nature is the primary argument for Paul's vigorous rejection of homosexual practice in Rom 1:24–27, it is only one of at least five reasons put forward in 1 Cor 11:2–16 for women to have a head covering while praying or prophesying in the church. Moreover, it is obvious that Paul himself distinguishes his nature argument in vv. 14–15 from his argument based on church "custom" in v. 16. Clearly, Paul does not regard the exceptions such as the Nazirite vow and Samson as vitiating his non-custom argument from nature.

What this means is bocth that (1) Paul viewed his nature argument as really a nature argument, not an argument from convention, and that (2) he did not regard the Old Testament exceptions for long hair on men, which doubtless Paul knew, as the kind of devastating obstacle to a nature argument that Brownson and Vines insist on. Furthermore, not only is there a parallel argument in a light-hearted work by the Neoplatonist philosopher Synesius of Cyrene (ca.

---

infecting the whole of humanity. At any rate it has nothing to do with the usage in Rom 1:26 that clearly uses nature in a sense that accords with the will of God.

37. Compare the principle enunciated by the Stoic philosopher Musonius Rufus: "Nature plainly keeps a more careful guard against deficiency than against excess" (XXI). Applied to hair length, what Nature teaches is discerned not from the fact that most men and virtually all women are capable of having an excess of hair but rather from the fact that many men and almost no women experience hair deficiency (baldness).

400 CE),[38] but the argument here resembles arguments that Stoics made for why men should wear beards and not pluck the hairs from their legs.[39] These arguments are based in the first instance on what even we would consider nature arguments and, what's more, on obvious and observable realities in nature that define male-female differences: the fact that men have more body hair than women (except for the head) and the adult male's capacity to grow a beard. Brownson and Vines completely ignore this part of my discussion of 1 Cor 11:14–15.

Now the Stoics did not regard men plucking body hair or shaving facial growth as the end of the world. Yet they were very much concerned that such compromises could lead to more extreme efforts at devaluing or even erasing altogether the masculine stamp from men. Concerns for not eradicating male-female differentiation and so not dishonoring creation distinctives lie behind Paul's remarks in 1 Cor 11:2–16. "Neither male and female" in Gal 3:28 was a statement affirming the equal worth of women before God in the body of Christ, not a program for erasing what makes males male and females female in the time before we receive resurrection bodies (contra Brownson).

In both 1 Cor 11:14 and Rom 1:26, nature refers neither to a subjective individual disposition nor to a social convention but rather to a universal objective

---

38. "Hair of the head" is more "fitting" for women than men, a fact "doubtlessly determined by both custom and nature; by custom, since the hair of the head is good neither for all males, nor everywhere, nor at all times for the same men. . . . but for women it is always and for all women and everywhere a good thing to give serious attention to the treatment of her hair. Yet nature also agrees with custom. . . . If any shedding of hair occurs, (you will say) that this woman suffers from some kind of disease or illness. . . . But of men who are also worthy to be called men it is not easy to say who has not first arrived at this condition (of hair loss as a result) of nature."

39. For example, the first-century (CE) Stoic philosopher Epictetus criticized a young student of rhetoric for plucking the hairs out of his legs:

> Woman is born smooth and dainty by nature, and if she is hairy she is a prodigy, and is exhibited in Rome. . . . But for a man not to be hairy is the same thing, and if by nature he has no hair he is a prodigy, but if he . . . plucks it out himself, what shall we make of him? . . . "I will show you," we say to the audience, "a man who wishes to be a woman rather than a man." What a dreadful spectacle! . . . Man, what reason have you to complain against your nature? Because it brought you into the world as a man? . . . Make a clean sweep of the whole matter; eradicate . . . the cause of your hairiness; make yourself a woman all over, so as not to deceive us, not half-man and half-woman. Whom do you wish to please? Frail womankind? Please them as a man. "Yes, but they like smooth men." Oh, go hang! And if they like sexual perverts, would you become such a pervert? . . . Leave the man a man. . . . How treat your paltry bod, then? As its nature is . . . No, but let's pluck out also the lion's mane . . . and the rooster's comb, for he too ought to be "cleaned up"! Clean? Yes, but clean as a cock, and the other clean as a lion! (*Diatr.* 3.1.27–45)

Epictetus and other Stoics extended this argument to beards (Musonius Rufus XXI; Epictetus, *Diatr.* 1.16.9–14); see Gagnon, *The Bible and Homosexual Practice*, 366.

order in the way God made things that can be discerned by human observation. Brownson's contention that all three meanings are found in each use of "nature" and "natural" in Rom 1:26–27 is not substantiated by any other uses in Pauline literature.

The Exploitation and Promiscuity Argument

There is little to commend the idea that, had Paul and other writers of Scripture been able to fathom the concept of committed homosexual relationships, they might have embraced them. Consider the following:

First, the Levitical prohibitions of man-male intercourse in LXX Lev 18:22 and 20:13, absolutely formulated (no exceptions, alongside absolute prohibitions of incest, adultery, and bestiality), precluded any acceptance of homosexual relations on Paul's part (male same-sex sexual relations explicitly, female same-sex sexual relations implicitly). Indeed, the term *arsenokoitai*, literally "men who lie with a male," found in two Pauline vice or offender lists (1 Cor 6:9; 1 Tim 1:10) was a distinctive Jewish term coined directly from these prohibitions, using the terms for "male" (*arsēn*) and "lying" (the noun *koitē*, "lying, bed," and the passive of the related verb *koimaō*, "to lie"). That Jews of the period construed the Levitical prohibitions of man-male intercourse absolutely and against a backdrop of a male-female requirement is beyond dispute. For example, the first-century Jewish historian Josephus says that "the law [of Moses] recognizes only sexual intercourse that is according to nature, that which is with a woman. . . . But it abhors the intercourse of males with males" (*Ag. Ap.* 2.199). According to b. Sanh. 54a, the "male" (Heb. *zāḵār*) with whom "a man" (Heb. *'îš*) lays in the abstract Hebrew expression *miškāv zāḵār*, "lying with a male," alluding to the Hebrew text of Lev 20:13, may be "an adult or minor," meaning that the prohibition of man-male unions is not limited to pederasty.

Second, as noted above, the obvious intertextual echo of LXX Gen 1:26–27 in Rom 1:23, 26–27 shows that when Paul rejected homosexual practice he had in view not only how well or badly it was done in the ancient world but also what it was not and could never be: a union of true sexual counterparts, "male and female." Similarly, also noted above, Paul's nature argument in Rom 1:24–27, paralleling his creation argument in 1:18–23, underscores that humans who engage in homosexual relations, whether well or badly, suppress the truth about the way God has made them (namely, as sexual complements or counterparts to the other sex). The claim made by Brownson and Vines that Paul meant by "nature" only "convention" or "custom" does not hold up. Nor is there any credibility to Brownson's and Vines' denial that male-female anatomical complementarity was known in the ancient world.

Third, Brownson and Vines fail when they contend that the very terms that Paul uses to describe homosexual practice in Rom 1:24–27 indicate that he had in view only out-of-control, excessive lust that leads to promiscuity and exploitation (pederasty, sex with call boys, and sex with slaves)[40] on the part of men bored with stable relationships with women, over-stimulated by material abundance, and seeking ever more exciting, boundary-crossing novelties.[41] There were indeed such views in the Greco-Roman world, including Philo's account of the Sodomites (*Abr.* 135) and John Chrysostom's reading of Rom 1:26–27.[42]

However, Brownson and Vines overlook the fact that a charge of "excess passion" is not an independent argument. The charge of excess passion is simply a way of further demeaning a desire for something that *on other grounds* has been deemed grossly unacceptable. Otherwise, how would one know to call the desire in question excessive and out-of-control? The worse the violation, the greater the deduction of excess. Promiscuous and exploitative sex would be one kind of manifestation of excessive passion but so too would be "committed" forms of incest, heterosexual sex outside of marriage, homosexual practice, and bestiality.

Philo, for example, thought that gluttonous eating by people could stimulate passions "even for brute beasts" (*Spec.* 3.43). Yet who would seriously argue that Philo mainly opposed bestiality because it was excess passion? Rather, Philo demeaned bestiality as a product of excess passion because the gross discordance of mismatched species was an obvious offense against "the decree of nature" (*Spec.* 3.46). This is how Philo speaks of *any* violation of God's laws:

> Those who resolve to be obedient to the divine utterances will live forever as in unclouded light with the laws themselves as stars illuminating their souls, while all who are rebellious will continue *being burnt and utterly burnt* (*kaiomenoi kai katakaiomenoi*) by their inward *desires/lusts* (*epithymiōn*), which like a flame will ravage the whole life of those who have them. (*Decalogue* 49; LCL, slightly modified)

Philo here depicts *every* rebellion to God's commands, not just particularly promiscuous or exploitative sexual practices, as an instance of excess "desires" or "lusts" (*epithymiai*) that "like a flame will ravage the whole life" and leaves

---

40. Cf. mention of *desires* or *lusts* (*epithymiai*) for sexual behaviors that "dishonor their bodies" (v. 24); and *passions* (*pathē*) of dishonor (= dishonorable passions; v. 25), in which the participants "were *inflamed* (*exekauthēsan*) with their *yearning* [or: appetite] (*orexei*) for one another" (v. 27).

41. Brownson, *Bible, Gender, Sexuality*, 153–56, 228–32; Vines, *God and the Gay Christian*, 31–41, 101–6.

42. For quotations see Gagnon, *The Bible and Homosexual Practice*, 380–82, including 382n48. Brownson (*Bible, Gender, Sexuality*, 154–55) and particularly Vines (*God and the Gay Christian*, 38–39, 104–6) pick up on some of the same.

the rebellious "utterly burnt." Similarly, in an unusual exegesis of the summary prohibition of incest in Lev 18:6, which Philo interprets generally as a global "command to spurn . . . what is akin to the flesh," Philo allows that things necessary for good health must be admitted into one's life. However,

> the superfluous things one must reject with contempt, by which the desires/ lusts (*epithymiai*), on being kindled, consume [or: burn up] (*kataphlegousi*) all the good things with one rush (of fire). So let not our yearnings [or: appetites] (*orexeis*) be stirred up toward all the things dear to the flesh. (*Giants* 34–35; my translation)

Both passages from Philo resonate with Paul's language in Rom 1:24–27 regarding *desires* or *lusts* (*epithymiai*) for sexual behaviors that "dishonor their bodies" (v. 24), *passions* (*pathē*) of dishonor (= dishonorable passions) for unnatural sexual use of the same sex (v. 26) in which the participants "were burned up [or: lit up, inflamed] (*exekauthēsan*) with their yearning [or: appetite] (*orexei*) for one another" (v. 27). *Any* same-sex sexual behavior, whether promiscuous or committed, would have qualified for such a description, as a violation of the absolute and severe prohibition of man-male intercourse in LXX Lev 18:22 and 20:13. The same would apply to any incestuous relationship, whether committed or promiscuous.

Philo contrasts heterosexual immorality, the desires (*epithymiai*) of which at least "pay tribute to the laws of nature," with man-male intercourse that lacks any difference based on sex (*Cont. Life* 59). Philo regarded male penetration of another male (or any other same-sex sexual involvement with a male) as driven by a "madness," a "polluted and accursed passion (*pathos*)" irrespective of whether a committed relationship was involved because it necessarily denied the same male nature of the partner (*Spec.* 2.50; *Abr.* 135). The inevitable gender discomplementarity of the union was the issue. Regularizing it in the context of a committed relationship changed nothing.

Fourth, committed homosexual relationships were well enough known in the Greco-Roman world that, had Paul been referring only to promiscuous and exploitative practices, he could have made exceptions. Already in Plato's *Symposium* (ca. 380 BCE) one finds expressions of committed same-sex love, including this comment from Pausanias: Lovers who love rightly "are prepared to love in the expectation that they will be with them all their life and will share their lives in common," "as if having been fused into a single entity with" the soul of the beloved (181D, 183E). In Plutarch's *Dialogue on Love* (late first to early second century CE), even Daphnaeus, who defends the superiority of male-female love, concedes that homosexual relationships are not necessarily exploitative, for even "sexual intercourse that is contrary to nature with males does not do away with, nor damage, a lover's kindness" (751C). Two second-century CE romances—Xenophon of Ephesus' *An Ephesian Tale* (3.2) and Achilles Tatius' *Leucippe and Clitophon* (1.7–8, 12–14, 33–34)—both include tragic love stories about similar-aged, male lovers. Relationships of a different sort but still attesting to commitment are reported in Rome by the epigrammatist Martial (ca. 40–104 CE; 1.24; 12.42) and by the satirist Juvenal (early second century CE; *Satires* 2): effeminate men who willingly commit themselves as "brides" to another man. Lucian of Samosata (mid-second century CE) tells of two rich women who regard themselves as married, the masculine Megilla of Lesbos and her "wife" Demonassa the Corinthian (*Dialogues of the Courtesans* 5). The astrologer Ptolemy of Alexandria (second century CE) refers to manly women born under a certain constellation who are "lustful for sexual relations contrary to nature" and take the active sexual role with women whom they sometimes call their "lawful wives" (*Tetrabiblos* 3.14; §171–72). Several rabbinic texts forbid marriage of a man to a man; one referring to Egyptian practices even forbids marriage of a woman to a woman (Sifra Lev. 18:3).[43] Clement of Alexandria likewise referred to "women . . . contrary to nature . . . marrying women" (*Paedagogus* 3.3.21.3). Knowledge of such committed homosexual relationships by church fathers and rabbis did not cause them to change their estimate of such relationships as "contrary to nature." There is no reason to believe that they would have changed Paul's assessment.

Fifth, further complicating a claim that Paul had in mind only sex with slaves, prostitutes, or adolescents is that Paul was almost certainly referring to lesbian relationships in Rom 1:26 (which Brownson denies but Vines tends to affirm). (1) The parallel phrasing of vv. 26 and 27, separated by a "likewise also," makes the lesbian interpretation probable.[44] (2) Lesbian intercourse is the form of female intercourse *both* most commonly labeled "contrary to nature" *and* most commonly paired with male homosexual practice in Greco-Roman sources. (3) In the Greco-Roman milieu male attitudes toward female homoeroticism were uniformly negative, even among moralists who favored male homosexual practice. There is no reason that Paul would have shied away from such an indictment, particularly since (as in Pseudo-Lucian's *Affairs of the Heart*) a reference to the wrongness of lesbianism could be used as a clinching argument against supporters of male homosexual unions. (4) The dominant

---

43. Cf. Gen. Rab. 26:6; Lev. Rab. 23:9; b. Ḥul. 92b. Cf. Bernadette J. Brooten, *Love Between Women: Early Christian Responses to Female Homoeroticism* (Chicago: University of Chicago Press, 1996), 65.

44. Hence the wording of the verses: "their females exchanged the natural use for one contrary to nature . . . , and *likewise also* the males, having left the natural use *of the female* were inflamed with their yearning for one another, males with males." For the "likewise also" to have maximum effectiveness, both the thing exchanged (i.e., a person of the other sex) and the thing exchanged *for* (i.e., a person of the same sex) must be comparable.

history of interpretation of Rom 1:26 supports the assumption that lesbianism is in view.[45] A lesbian reference in Rom 1:26 is a big problem for the exploitation argument because lesbianism in antiquity was not typically characterized by pederasty, prostitution, or abuse of slaves.

Sixth, the fact that Paul speaks of males being "inflamed with their yearning for one another" (Rom 1:27; cf. 1:24: "their bodies being dishonored among themselves"), indicating reciprocity of desire, shows that he was not restricting his remarks to coercive or merely commercial acts.

Seventh, the analogy of incest confirms that Paul's rejection of homosexual practice is not limited only to promiscuous or exploitative forms. Brownson unconvincingly argues otherwise. He asserts that the reason that Paul calls incest in 1 Cor 5:3–5 *porneia* (sexual immorality) and not *akatharsia* (impurity, uncleanness) is that the latter term "focuses on the excesses of passion and the absence of self-restraint"; and since incest is always wrong, irrespective of whether it is committed or promiscuous, he avoids calling incest an "impurity." This is a desperate argument. Paul viewed all sexual disobedience to God's commands as by definition excessive and lacking in self-restraint. The terms *porneia* (sexual immorality), *akatharsia* (impurity), and *aselgeia* (licentiousness) and their cognates are used interchangeably in Paul.[46] The word *akatharsia* and its cognates simply stress the "dirty" character of sexual immorality;[47] *porneia* and its cognates the selling of oneself to illicit desire; and *aselgeia* the absence of restraint in not taming unruly desire to conform to the precepts of God. If Paul had wanted to emphasize the aspect of "absence of self-restraint," as Brownson claims, the more precise choice would have been *aselgeia*. The word *akatharsia* is used in early Jewish literature of incest: LXX Lev 20:21 (sex with a brother's wife); LXX Ezek 22:15 (a range of offenses in 22:6–13, including three cases of incest, sex with a menstruant, and adultery); Ps. Sol. 8:22 (a range of sexual

---

45. All the church fathers from Augustine's time (except Augustine) or earlier who commented on what Paul meant by unnatural female intercourse in Rom 1:26 understood it as lesbian intercourse: probably Clement of Alexandria (ca. 200) and the Apocalypse of Peter (second century), certainly "Ambrosiaster" (ca. 370) and John Chrysostom (ca. 390). Augustine (ca. 410) interprets Rom 1:26 as heterosexual anal intercourse, but his interpretation was influenced by his debates with the Pelagians, who in Augustine's view had an overly positive view of sex in marriage apart from its procreative function. See Brooten, *Love Between Women*, 11, 253n106, 257, 361.

46. Homosexual practice is viewed as a subset of the "sexually immoral" (*pornoi*) in 1 Cor 6:9 and 1 Tim 1:10 in addition to an instance of "impurity" in Rom 1:24–27. Adultery in 1 Thess 4:3–7 is called both *porneia* and *akatharsia*. Two or all three of the terms are placed side by side in Gal 5:19; 2 Cor 12:21; Eph 4:19; 5:3, 5.

47. E.g., Philo of Alexandria states that "the tabernacle 'was set up in the midst of our uncleanness' [Lev 16:16] that we may have wherewith to scour and wash away all that defiles our life" (*Who Is the Heir* 113). Note the emphasis on the defiling dirtiness that needs to be scoured and washed.

sins including sex between son and mother, father and daughter; adultery); and T. Jud. 14.5 (Judah's intercourse with his son's wife).

No wonder that even homosexual historian Louis Crompton stated in his massive *Homosexuality and Civilization*:

> According to [one] interpretation, Paul's words were not directed at "bona fide" homosexuals in committed relationships. But such a reading, however well-intentioned, seems strained and unhistorical. Nowhere does Paul or any other Jewish writer of this period imply the least acceptance of same-sex relations under any circumstance. The idea that homosexuals might be redeemed by mutual devotion would have been wholly foreign to Paul or any other Jew or early Christian.[48]

William Loader, an Australian NT scholar who has written more on sexual ethics in early Judaism and Christianity than anyone else, and who is thoroughly supportive of "gay marriage," has acknowledged that Paul's indictment of homosexual practice is inclusive of committed homosexual relationships. In his book *The New Testament on Sexuality* (2012),[49] Loader contends that in Rom 1:26–27 "natural" means "sex with the opposite sex" while "contrary to nature" means same-sex intercourse. Paul cannot mean by *para physin* "simply 'unconventional'" since he is concerned with "what he sees as divine ordering." Nor can it mean merely "beyond nature" since "Paul is concerned about much more than excess. He is concerned about direction." Paul is not "condemning passion or sexual desire, itself, as dishonorable, but only when it is wrongly directed into same-sex engagement." Those who see Rom 1:26 "addressing [female] same-sex sexual relations are almost certainly hearing Paul aright." Romans 1:26–27 "included, but [was] by no means limited to exploitative pederasty," "sexual abuse of male slaves," or "same-sex acts . . . performed within idolatrous ritual contexts." Same-sex relationships in the Greco-Roman world "could include lifelong consensual adult partnerships." "It is inconceivable that [Paul] would approve of any same-sex acts if, as we must assume, he affirmed the prohibitions of Lev 18:22; 20:13 as fellow Jews of his time understood them" and "which had come to be applied to both men and women."[50]

---

48. Louis Crompton, *Homosexuality and Civilization* (Cambridge: Harvard University Press, 2003), 114. Thomas K. Hubbard notes that "Literature of the first century C.E. bears witness to an increasing polarization of attitudes toward homosexual activity, ranging from frank acknowledgment and public display of sexual indulgence on the part of leading Roman citizens to severe moral condemnation of *all* homosexual acts" (*Homosexuality in Greece and Rome*, 383; emphasis mine).

49. Quotations that follow are from pages 307, 309, 311–12, 314, 322, 325.

50. While Loader rejects an exploitation or promiscuity argument, he does employ an orientation argument, rejecting Paul's position on the assumed grounds that Paul was unaware that some persons naturally possess an exclusive homosexual ori-

The Orientation Argument

The idea that Paul and other biblical writers would have changed their mind if they only knew about homosexual orientation is, ironically, undermined by Brownson's and Vines' own misogyny and compulsory-procreation arguments. For, according to their own formulations, even if Paul had known about innate and exclusion same-sex attraction, he still would have rejected homosexual unions on the twin grounds that the sexual act was both damaging to the hierarchical order of male activity and female passivity and incapable of procreation.

As it happens, some in the Greco-Roman world did posit some degree of biological influence on same-sex attraction for at least some participants.[51] In Plato's *Symposium*, the comic Aristophanes spins a tale about the creation splitting of male-male and female-female binary humans as a way of explaining the fact that some people desire sexually only persons of the same sex. He describes men who "are not inclined *by nature* (*physei*) toward marriage and the procreation of children but are compelled to do so by the law or custom," with the sad result that two joined males have to "live their lives out with one another unmarried" (192A–B).[52] The image here is that of an exclusive homosexual orientation in which another of the same sex is viewed as one's sexual "other half."

---

entation. My rebuttal of Brownson's and Vines' use of an orientation argument applies equally to Loader.

51. Contra Vines: "The concept of same-sex orientation didn't exist. . . . In general, people were thought to be capable of both opposite-sex *and* same-sex attraction. . . . Paul's words indicate not only that the people he described exchanged opposite-sex for same-sex relations, but also that they were capable of heterosexual attraction. . . . Same-sex relations in the first century were not thought to be the expression of an exclusive sexual orientation. They were widely understood to be the product of excessive sexual desire. . . . That isn't to say that *no one* pursued only same-sex relationships, or that no same-sex unions were marked by long-term commitment and love. But such examples were rare enough that the overwhelming majority of visible same-sex behavior fit easily into a paradigm of excess" (*God and the Gay Christian*, 102–4).

52. Kenneth J. Dover, *Greek Homosexuality* (Cambridge: Harvard University Press, 1978), 62, cites "the story put into the mouth of Aristophanes by Plato in *Symp.* 189c–193d" as the "clearest" indication of "Greek recognition that some people are more homosexual than others," here "genetically determined." Even if the speech were taken as satire, it would still reflect or play off of the positive view of same-sex eroticism expressed by Phaedrus and Pausanias (present at the symposium at which Aristophanes spoke) and current among some in antiquity.

Plato often presents Socrates as feeling strong desires for beautiful males, not women, but at the same time a model of self-control in resisting these desires. This is the import of Alcibiades' recounting of his attempts at bedding Socrates (*Symp.* 216–18; cf. Gagnon, *The Bible and Homosexual Practice*, 354–55n11). In Plato's *Charmides*, Socrates encounters at a private wrestling school an extraordinarily handsome young man named Charmides, whom Socrates sought to interrogate as regards the condition of his soul. When Charmides sat down beside Socrates and Socrates caught a glimpse inside Charmides' cloak, Socrates found his "previous brash confidence quite gone" and

Aristotelian thought speculated that some males who desired to be penetrated were so disposed "by nature" (i.e., because of sperm ducts leading to the anus, thereby building pressure that requires release through the friction of penetration), and others "from habit" (i.e., owing to pleasurable childhood memories of receptive sex with an adult male and to the reinforcement of repetition), a habit that "becomes like (i.e., takes on the characteristics of) nature." Habit itself was more likely to take hold "in the case of one who is both lustful and soft (*malakos*)"—in modern-day parlance, where a person has a biological predisposition toward gender nonconformity. In instances where sperm ducts led to both the anus and the penis males would desire both to penetrate and to be penetrated. "So for all those for whom nature is the cause, no one would describe these persons as lacking in self-control, any more than they would women because they do not take the active sexual role but the passive." Yet even "the effeminate by nature (*hoi physei thēlydriai*) . . . are constituted contrary to nature (*para physin*)," a mistake or "defect" in nature (Aristotle, *Nicomachean Ethics* 1148b; Pseudo-Aristotle, *Problems* 4.26 [879b–880a]).[53]

The Hippocratic treatise *On Regimen* (1.28–29; fourth century BCE) attributed the degree of manliness or femininity in both men and women to the mixture of male and female sperm at conception, with the sperm of each containing both male and female elements. The extent to which male-based sperm or female-based sperm dominated influenced the extent to which a child would become very manly or very feminine, less manly or less feminine, a male "man-woman" (an *androgynos* in passion, not necessarily in intersexed body) or "a manly woman" (*andreia*). The degree of manliness or femininity would, in turn, influence choice for an active or passive role in sexual intercourse. Biology was not everything, though; diet, education, and habits also played a part.[54] Parmenides, a pre-Socratic philosopher, held a similar conception (as recounted by Soranus in Caelius Aurelianus, *On Chronic Diseases* 4.9.134–35).

"caught on fire and was quite beside" himself (155D; trans. R. K. Sprague in Hubbard, *Homosexuality in Greece and Rome*). A similar story is told of Zeno of Citium, founder of Stoicism: "Being romantically inclined toward Chremonides and sitting next to him . . . , Zeno suddenly stood up. . . . Zeno said, "I understand from good doctors that the best cure for swellings and inflammations [i.e., erections] is rest'" (cited in Diogenes Laertius, *Lives of Eminent Philosophers* 7.17; trans. Thomas K. Hubbard in Hubbard, *Homosexuality in Greece and Rome*).

53. Brooten, *Love Between Women*, 384–85n52; Dover, *Greek Homosexuality*, 168–70; John Boswell, *Christianity, Social Tolerance, and Homosexuality: Gay People in Western Europe from the Beginning of the Christian Era to the Fourteenth Century* (Chicago: University of Chicago Press, 2015), 49–50; Brooten, *Love Between Women*, 149n17; Schoedel, "Same-Sex Eros," 53–54; text and translation in LCL. Schoedel notes that "Philo believes that feminized behavior prevents the natural development of the male heat that leads to the consequent loss of courage in the individual as he matures" (54).

54. Cf. Brooten, *Love Between Women*, 157–58n43; Schoedel, "Same-Sex Eros," 58–59.

Not referring to congenital causation but nevertheless relevant to our discussion here is an old Cretan legend retold by the Roman poet Ovid (43 BC–AD 18). According to the tale, a mother, cognizant of her husband's intense desire for a son, hid from her husband the fact that their new child was a girl. Raised as a boy (we would say: *socialized*), Iphis developed an erotic attraction for females. When she fell in love with Ianthe, another female, she bemoaned her "monstrous" passion because she recognized it to be contrary not only to custom but also to nature and divine law. And yet she was powerless to override this desire. Her tragic circumstances were resolved only when the goddess Isis intervened to change Iphis into a male, thereby enabling her to marry Ianthe.[55] The story illustrates two points: (a) socialization can create a powerful, even irresistible, drive for a homoerotic relationship (in modern terms, nurture becoming nature); and (b) even irresistible drives can be described as contrary to nature and monstrous.

Soranus, an early second-century CE physician in Rome, wrote about why "soft men" desire penetration (*On Chronic Diseases* 4.9).[56] He rejects the idea that there is a physiological cause such as the Aristotelian view that semen flows to the anus instead of the penis (see Ps.-Aristotle, *Problems* 4.26). Rather, the condition is due to "an affliction of the mind." He appears open to the theory of the early fifth-century philosopher Parmenides (also found in the late fifth-century Hippocratic text *On Regimen* 1.28–29) that pathic-effeminate males are determined partly at conception when the "power" contained in the female "seed" (in our day, genes) dominates in a male child. Likewise, active-masculinized females (i.e., women who play the man's role in sex with women) are generated when the male "power" dominates in a female child. Soranus then adds, without criticism, that "many leaders of various (medical) schools" understand this "mental defect" in males to be "an inherited disease" that "enters succeeding generations with the seed."[57] The depiction does not seem to be functionally far afield from modern theories that posit differences in brain structures and genes.

---

55. Cf. Judith P. Hallett, "Female Homoeroticism and the Denial of Roman Reality in Latin Literature," *Yale Journal of Criticism* 3 (1989): 213–14; Brooten, *Love Between Women*, 44. Neither draws the two inferences that I do here.

56. The Greek text of his work no longer survives but a Latin "translation" by the fifth-century writer Caelius Aurelianus does. See the English translation by Lesley Dean Jones in Hubbard, *Homosexuality in Greece and Rome*, 463–65.

57. According to Brooten, "These medical thinkers must have seen male passivity and female desire for other women as arising from something analogous to a mutated gene" (*Love Between Women*, 158). Other theories existed. Various Greco-Roman astrologers from the first to fourth centuries linked up homoerotic desire with the constellation of the stars at the time of one's birth (Dositheos of Sidon, *Carmen Astrologicum* 2.7.6–17; Ptolemy, *Tetrabiblos* 3.14 §171–72; Firmacus Maternus, *Matheseos libri viii* 3.6.6, 9, 15).

One of the interesting features here is that both in Pseudo-Aristotle's *Problems* 4.26 and in Soranus' *Chronic Diseases* 4.9 homosexual conditions that are so "by nature" can still be called "contrary to nature," regarded as defects in nature that do not accord with the natural design and function of body parts. Brownson and Vines miss this point when they argue that, had Paul known about homosexual orientation, he could not have called same-sex attractions "unnatural" or "contrary to nature." On the contrary, if pagan writers could do both, Paul, coming from a Jewish milieu with a much stronger opposition to homosexual practice, certainly could have done the same.

Brownson (followed by Vines) argues that Paul's language in Rom 1:26–27 of females who "exchanged the natural use for that which is contrary to nature" and of males who "left behind the natural use of the female" proves that Paul thought that *all* persons engaging in homosexual relationships were attracted to women. They allegedly pursued promiscuous and exploitative same-sex relationships only out of excessive, insatiable, out-of-control, and lustful desire and passion, bored with stable relationships with women, over-stimulated by material abundance, and seeking ever more exciting, boundary-crossing novelties.[58] There were indeed such views in the Greco-Roman world, including Philo's account of the Sodomites (*Abr.* 135), Dio Chrysostom's comment about men with insatiate sexual appetites (7.149–52), and John Chrysostom's reading of Rom 1:26–27.[59]

However, nothing in Rom 1:26–27 indicates that Paul believed this. First, Paul was not speaking about every person who ever engaged in homosexual practice. He was speaking collectively in the context of a decline-of-civilization narrative. If we apply Brownson's reasoning to 1:19–23, Paul would have believed (absurdly) that all idolaters in the ancient world were constitutional monotheists who once practiced monotheism. For Paul similarly speaks of people who "*exchanged* the glory of the imperishable God for the likeness of an image of a perishable human" and even animals (1:23), restated as those who "*exchanged* the truth about God for the lie and worshipped and served the creation rather than the Creator" (1:25).[60]

Secondly, Paul does not say that people switched from having sex with members of the opposite sex. What was exchanged was an accurate perception of reality that was at least accessible to rational beings through the things God made but was suppressed for an inaccurate perception of reality. Lesbian NT scholar Bernadette Brooten correctly noted that Paul was not limiting his

---

58. Brownson, *Bible, Gender, Sexuality*, 153–56, 228–32; Vines, *God and the Gay Christian*, 31–41, 101–6.

59. For quotations see Gagnon, *Bible and Homosexual Practice*, 380–82, including 382n48. Brownson (*Bible, Gender, Sexuality*, 154–55) and particularly Vines (*God and the Gay Christian*, 38–39, 104–6) pick up on some of the same.

60. Brownson finds this point of mine "inscrutable" but (as with my idolatry analogy) I find his incomprehension puzzling.

remarks to oversexed heterosexuals or bisexuals. Instead, "Paul used the word 'exchanged' to indicate that people knew the natural sexual order of the universe and left it behind."[61]

Third, the fact that Paul says that God "handed them over to dishonorable passions" (1:26) is no more an indication that this was the first experience of homoerotic desire than is the fact that God "handed them over to an unfit mind" (1:28) an indication that this was the first experience of greed, envy, murder, strife, deceit, gossiping, slander, arrogance, bragging, and disobedience to parents (1:29–30). The language of "handing over" implies not the origination of dishonoring desires but instead enslavement to these desires to such a degree that it leads to serial-unrepentant, dishonoring behavior.[62]

As regards whether the ancients knew of *exclusive* homosexual orientation, Thomas K. Hubbard contends: "Homosexuality in this era [i.e., of the early imperial age of Rome] may have ceased to be merely another practice of personal pleasure and began to be viewed as an essential and central category of personal identity, exclusive of and antithetical to heterosexual orientation."[63] Hubbard cites several texts as making the point of exclusivity, including an epigram (short poem) from the late first-century CE writer Martial in which Martial refers to a man named Charidemus who was a "bugger" (*pedico*: anal penetrator) who never had sex with a woman till "poverty" made him do so (11.87; cf. also 6.33; 7.58).[64] An example not cited by Hubbard is that of Pliny the Elder (23–79 CE) who told of a folk remedy that was alleged to create sexual desire for women among "men who hate intercourse with women" (*Natural History* 28.99).[65]

It is hard to believe that the Athenian Callicratidas, advocate for the superiority of man-male love over man-female love in Pseudo-Lucian's *Affairs of the Heart*, experienced any sexual attraction for women. He is described as one who "thought love of women a pit of doom" and whose "hatred for women made him often curse Prometheus" (5, 9). He viewed marriage as nothing more than "a remedy invented to ensure man's necessary perpetuity" (33). He expressed

---

61. Brooten, *Love Between Women*, 244.

62. Loader misunderstands my views when he claims that I view only the homosexual act as sin but not homosexual passion, while Paul treats homosexual desire and orientation as sinful (*The New Testament on Sexuality*, 307, 323). Paul regarded homosexual desires as sinful desires by definition, because they are desires to do what God expressly forbids. So do I. Paul did not attribute moral culpability to persons who merely experience sinful sexual urges such as homoerotic attractions but do not take an active role in gratifying them in thought or deed. Neither do I.

63. Hubbard, *Homosexuality in Greece and Rome*, 386. He also points to a series of later texts from the second to fourth centuries that "reflect the perception that sexual orientation is something fixed and incurable" (446).

64. Hubbard, *Homosexuality in Greece and Rome*, 425–26.

65. Craig Williams, *Roman Homosexuality*, 2nd ed. (Oxford: Oxford University Press, 2010), 188, 382n52.

the wish that "we had no intercourse with women," lamenting that "we are constrained by necessity" to "provide ourselves with heirs." He recommends that "women ... be retained merely for child-bearing but in all else ... may I be rid of them." Women, he says, must spend all day "beautify[ing] themselves with artificial devices" because their "true form is unshapely," requiring them to "have extraneous adornments to beguile the unsightliness of nature" (38). Clearly this man is attracted only to males.[66]

In discussing the actions of the men of Sodom, Philo attributed their erotic desire for penetrating males to a satiety arising out of economic prosperity (*Abr.* 135). However, contrary to Brownson and Vines, we cannot deduce from this interpretation of the particular events at Sodom, constrained as Philo was by both the biblical story and the history of interpretation, that Philo would have attributed *all* active homoerotic desire to such a cause. Philo also recognized an uncontrollable quality to homoerotic impulses. He says regarding the men of Sodom that "they were conquered by a more forcible desire" (*Abr.* 135–36) and speaks generally of the active male partner as consumed by passion for a beloved male (*Cont. Life* 61). It is inconceivable that Paul would have been totally unaware of boys in the Greco-Roman world who, from their earliest period of sexual awareness, were socialized as the receptive partners of insertive males and who, as adults, continued to desire—in many instances exclusively so—sex with other adult males. Philo was aware of adult males who as boys were "accustomed" and "accustomed themselves" to an active process of feminization, including serving as the receptive partner in man-male intercourse, which worked in their very souls a disease "hard to fight against" (*Abr.* 136; *Cont. Life* 60; *Spec.* 3.37). It must surely be obvious that Philo, given his vehement rejection of homosexual practice, would not have excused such behavior arising from an innate, even exclusive, orientation.

We cannot say for certain whether Paul entertained the thought that one or more forms of homosexual behavior could be traced at least partly to innate influences, though I think it is likely that he did. Yet we can say that it would have made little difference to his rejection of homosexual practice, based as it was on his affirmation of a male-female requirement in marriage given in Gen 1–2, buttressed by the Levitical prohibitions (18:22; 20:13), and affirmed by Jesus, further confirmed by the observable complementarity of male and female in anatomy and physiology if not also psychology. In fact, the idea of innate influences on homosexual development coheres nicely with Paul's understanding of sin as an innate impulse, running through the members of the human body, passed on by an ancestor (Adam), and never entirely within human control (Rom 5:12–20; 7:7–23).

---

66. Trans. M. D. Macleod in LCL; reproduced in Hubbard, *Homosexuality in Greece and Rome*, 505–31.

Orientation Is No Excuse for Disobedience

Why would anyone suppose that Paul, or any writer of Scripture, or Jesus, would change God's commands simply because humans might be predisposed to violate them? Put differently, what commands of God are predicated on humans first losing all desires to violate the commands in question? Are not commands and laws instituted precisely because people are disposed to do otherwise? If deep-seated human impulses can trump God's ethical demands, then there are no binding commands of God to constrain human behavior. A monogamy standard would have to succumb to the "polysexual" orientation of most men.

Paul believed that being a faithful follower of Jesus meant being "crucified with Christ," such that believers "no longer live but Christ lives in" them (Gal 2:19–20). Jesus proclaimed the terms of discipleship as "denying oneself, taking up one's cross," and "losing one's life" (Mark 8:34–35). We are not the sum total of our biological urges. We are persons made in God's image to do his will, whatever the cost. God is the kind of God who can say "no" to requests to remove various deprivations and difficulties in our lives precisely because his grace, just knowing him, is "sufficient"; his power is perfected in the midst of our weaknesses, not necessarily by delivering us from hardships (2 Cor 12:9).

Brownson and Vines argue that homosexual relationships have to be accepted because to do otherwise would impose a celibacy requirement on those who are exclusively same-sex-attracted when both Jesus and Paul viewed celibacy as requiring a special gift (Matt 19:11–12; 1 Cor 7:2, 7).[67] This way of thinking puts the cart before the horse in at least three ways.

First, there is no obligatory celibacy imposed on persons with same-sex attractions. Rather, the entirety of Scripture from Gen 1 on establishes a male-female foundation for sexual unions, ratified and made more rigorously consistent by the teaching of Jesus on marriage. There is a major difference between a celibacy requirement and requirements for marriage, even if every requirement for marriage provides significant challenges for some.

Second, the purpose in not requiring the celibacy of those who lack the gift for it is to avoid the commission of sexual immorality (1 Cor 7:2). Eliminating a male-female foundation for marriage to accommodate persons who are not inclined to pair with a true sexual counterpart does not prevent the commission of sexual immorality. Instead, it promotes one of the most severe forms of sexual immorality, that of homosexual practice, which (as Scripture indicates) is abhorrent to God and dishonors the participants.

Third, when we encounter hardships in life, we can presume that God has empowered us and so gifted us to endure such until and unless a "way of escape" is made available that does not lead to the violation of God's commands

---

67. Brownson, *Bible, Gender, Sexuality*, 127–48; Vines, *God and the Gay Christian*, 43–57.

(1 Cor 10:13). Paul encountered incredible hardships on a daily basis in the course of attempting to carry out his apostolic office, far greater than what we are talking about here in connection with same-sex attractions and the institution of marriage (1 Cor 4:9–13; 2 Cor 6:4–10; 11:23–33). The distress that he regularly experienced became a means by which God deepened his relationship with Paul as Paul repeatedly learned not to depend on himself but on "the God who raises from the dead" (2 Cor 1:9). Paul learned to boast in, and think well of, his weaknesses as moments in which "the power of Christ pitches its tent on me" (2 Cor 12:9–10). Instead of concluding from a stressful situation that God must change the rules to make life easier for us, we should see the difficult circumstance as a glorious opportunity for us to be shaped ever more into the image of Jesus Christ, to resemble him more than we otherwise would.

The Misogyny Argument

There are a number of problems with the claim of Brownson and Vines that Paul and other biblical authors were interested in keeping men on top and women on the bottom, literally and figuratively, and not with male-female anatomical complementarity.

(1) *It ignores concerns for structural compatibility.* The argument is reductionistic because even Greco-Roman and Jewish critiques of homosexual practice include consideration of both anatomical and procreative design (see above). Asserting that biblical writers are unconcerned about structural compatibility of the sexes is like arguing that Scripture's only complaint with incest has to do with status issues.

(2) *The link between absolute prohibitions and the priority of gender over status.* In the Greco-Roman world, where status concerns dominate over gender, male homosexual practice is accommodated within a broader misogynistic bent, specifically the right of males to penetrate socially inferior or underdeveloped males such as youths, foreigners, and slaves. Yet for early Judaism and Christianity, where homosexual practice is opposed absolutely, gender differentiation took precedence over gender stratification.

(3) *Women's liberation as a stimulus for opposing all male homosexual unions.* According to the logic of the misogyny argument, the greater the opposition to female equality, the more intense the opposition to homosexual practice. Historically, however, the reverse appears to be the case. As Hubbard puts it, in the age of imperial Rome "the increasingly liberated status of women was crucial to the polarization of sexual preferences." When one looks at ancient debates over whether male-female love or male-male love is superior,[68] one finds that the

---

68. Plutarch, *Dialogue on Love* 1–12; Achilles Tatius, *Luecippe and Clitophon* 35–38; Pseudo-Lucian, *Affairs of the Heart.*

heterosexual position espouses a *higher* view of women as suitable companions and friends deserving of equal pleasure in the sexual bond, "whereas the pederast's position seems in every case to have its origins in a fundamental hatred of women."[69] The Stoic philosopher Musonius Rufus, for example, combined an affirmation of women's capacity for learning philosophy with a strong rejection of homosexual practice (XII). Hence, it is no surprise that as trends developed toward greater roles for women in early Christianity (compared with early Judaism generally) opposition to homosexual practice in no way diminished.

(4) *An absurd corollary of the misogyny argument.* If opposition to homosexual practice were based primarily on a belief in female inferiority and on a strategy to hold women down, then Jews and Christians must have been the biggest misogynists of the ancient world or at least unwittingly complicit with the greatest misogyny. For nowhere in the ancient world was homosexual practice more consistently and strongly opposed than in ancient Israel, early Judaism, and early Christianity. Yet that flies in the face of the evidence that the view of women in the Bible fares well relative to its cultural environments (a point that even Brownson and Vines acknowledge).[70]

(5) *The Jesus factor.* The misogyny argument simply does not fit for Jesus' rigorous application of the sexual binary Gen 1:27 and 2:24 to the issue of additional sexual partners. For Jesus a marital duality follows from a gender binary.[71]

---

69. Hubbard, *Homosexuality in Greece and Rome*, 444–45.

70. In Gen 3:16, a husband's rule over his wife is attributed to the fall. Heroic women in the OT include Miriam, Tamar, Rahab, Deborah, Ruth, prophetess Huldah, and Esther. Jesus allowed female followers, praised women for exemplary acts, and took away from his disciples the right to multiple wives and unilateral divorce. Paul had numerous female coworkers (note the commendations in Rom 16; cf. Phil 4:2–3), emphasized the mutuality of conjugal rights (1 Cor 7:3–4), affirmed women's prophetic roles (1 Cor 11:2–16), and required men to love their wives as Christ loved the church and as they love their own bodies (Eph 5:25–33). Yes, biblical writers, including Paul, maintained a "soft patriarchy." Yet, this should have led to a softening of their stance on homosexual practice, by the logic of the misogyny argument. It did not, which in turn suggests a peripheral role for misogyny in the biblical indictment of homosexual practice.

71. For my critique of Brownson's failure to understand the moral logic of Jesus' appeal to the sexual binary in Mark 10:2–12, see my "Exegetical Case of Traditional Marriage," in *Cultural Engagement: A Crash Course in Contemporary Issues*, ed. Joshua D. Chatraw and Karen Swallow Prior (Grand Rapids: Zondervan, 2019), 72–78. Brownson acknowledges that "Jesus' words . . . presuppose that a man may not be married to more than one woman at the same time (polygyny) . . . If Jesus' words are true, that 'whoever divorces his wife and marries another commits adultery against her [the first wife],' how much more would it be the case that marrying another *without* divorcing the first wife would be considered adultery!" (*Bible, Gender, Sexuality*, 97). He further argues that Jesus arrived at a limitation of two persons to a sexual union solely from the notion of a kinship bond (the citation of "one flesh" in Gen 2:24). This, Brownson insists, is Jesus' moral logic, and not also the creation of two (and only two) sexual counterparts. "*The 'one-flesh' union spoken of in Genesis 2:24 connotes not physical complementarity, but a kinship bond. . . . 'One flesh' means 'one kinship group.' . . . The reference . . . is not*

Conclusion

Brownson and Vines have argued that Paul's moral logic behind Rom 1:24–27 has nothing to do with a normative notion of anatomical or biological gender complementarity between male and female, man and woman. They contend that they are not denying "the authority and truthfulness of Scripture"[72] in viewing Rom 1:24–27 as permitting committed homosexual unions. The evidence put forward above indicates that their claims are both ahistorical (indeed, anti-historical) and unfaithful. Their position rejects the witness of Scripture, in addition to creating an untenable historical reconstruction.

Bibliography

Boswell, John. *Christianity, Social Tolerance, and Homosexuality: Gay People in Western Europe from the Beginning of the Christian Era to the Fourteenth Century*. Chicago: University of Chicago Press, 2015.

Brooten, Bernadette J. *Love Between Women Early Christian Responses to Female Homoeroticism*. Chicago: University of Chicago Press, 2009.

---

to the recovery of a . . . primordial unity, but rather to the establishment of a kinship bond" (32–33). " 'One flesh' . . . focuses attention on the establishment of a new primary kinship bond rather than on the overcoming of the incompleteness of male and female by recovering an alleged original unity of the genders. . . . The link between sex and kinship bonds provides the basic moral logic underlying the Bible's consistent rejection of sexual promiscuity" (86, 88).

Brownson tendentiously makes an *either-or* out of a transparent *both-and*: It is not kinship *or* complementarity for Jesus but kinship *and* complementarity. Brownson's argument about Jesus' moral logic makes little sense for the obvious reason that kinship bonds can be of any number. It also fails to explain why Jesus bothered to cite one third of Gen 1:27, "male and female he made them." The only reason for Jesus to do so is to pinpoint God's intentional creation of a sexual binary as the basis for rejecting more than two persons in a sexual union, whether at any one time (concurrent polygamy) or over time (serial polygamy through remarriage-after-divorce). The twoness of the sexes, ordained by God in creation, is the basis for restricting the number of living sex partners (whether still married or divorced) to two. This means that Jesus regarded the God-designed sexual binary as the foundation of all sexual ethics. The moral logic behind Jesus' citation of this third of Gen 1:27 is paralleled in the document *Damascus Covenant*, where town Essenes rejected "taking two wives in their lives" (i.e., polygyny) because "the foundation of creation is 'male and female he created them' (Gen 1:27)" and because "those who entered (Noah's) ark went in two by two (Gen 7:9)" (4.20–5.1). It is not just that Jesus happened to cite two verses from Gen 1–2 that mention the two sexes, but rather that Jesus intentionally constructed a rigorous monogamy standard on a rigorous application of the foundational scriptural principle of a sexual binary. In all of antiquity there is no greater applier of the logic of the sexual binary for sexual standards than Jesus of Nazareth.

72. Brownson, *Bible, Gender, Sexuality*, 262.

Brownson, James V. *Bible, Gender, Sexuality: Reframing the Church's Debate on Same-Sex Relationships.* Grand Rapids: Eerdmans, 2013.

Crompton, Louis. *Homosexuality and Civilization.* Cambridge: Harvard University Press, 2003.

Dover, Kenneth J. *Greek Homosexuality.* Cambridge: Harvard University Press, 1978.

Esler, Philip F. *Conflict and Identity in Romans: The Social Setting of Paul's Letter.* Minneapolis: Fortress, 2003.

Gagnon, Robert A. J. "A Comprehensive and Critical Review Essay *of Homosexuality, Science, and the 'Plain Sense' of Scripture,* Part 2." *HBT* 25 (2003): 179–275.

———. *The Bible and Homosexual Practice: Texts and Hermeneutics.* Nashville: Abingdon, 2001.

———. "Exegetical Case of Traditional Marriage." Pages 72–78 in *Cultural Engagement: A Crash Course in Contemporary Issues.* Edited by Joshua D. Chatraw and Karen Swallow Prior. Grand Rapids: Zondervan, 2019.

———. "Heart of Wax and a Teaching That Stamps: τύπος διδαχῆς (Rom 6:17b) Once More." *JBL* 112.4 (1993): 667–87.

Hallett, Judith P. "Female Homoeroticism and the Denial of Roman Reality in Latin Literature." *Yale Journal of Criticism* 3 (1989): 209–27.

Hubbard, Thomas K. *Homosexuality in Greece and Rome: A Sourcebook of Basic Documents.* Berkeley: University of California Press, 2003.

Schoedel, William R. "Same-Sex Eros: Paul and the Greco-Roman Tradition." Pages 43–72 in *Homosexuality, Science, and the "Plain Sense" of Scripture.* Edited by David L. Balch. Grand Rapids: Eerdmans, 2000.

Vines, Matthew. *God and the Gay Christian: The Biblical Case in Support of Same-Sex Relationships.* New York: Convergent Books, 2014.

Williams, Craig A. *Roman Homosexuality.* 2nd ed. Oxford: Oxford University Press, 2010.

CHAPTER 5

The Meaning of Εὐαγγέλιον: Lexical and Tradition-Historical Explorations

Patrick Schreiner

Introduction

It would be an understatement to say that the term εὐαγγέλιον, usually translated as "good news" or "gospel," is an important term in the Scriptures.[1] But
what does this term mean? Where did it come from? What sort of context was it
employed in? And did the New Testament authors use it in its typical historical
sense, or did they reconfigure it?

While interpreters need to be careful of different fallacies such as the etymological fallacy, illegitimate totality transfer, and prioritizing the diachronic
rather than synchronic meaning, it is also true that words do not exist in the
pure present.[2] Words cannot be fully separated from their past, and the background to words affects their behavior even if the background does not come to
the foreground.[3] Therefore, it is worthwhile to examine the lexical and historical
background to this important word.

The Greek word itself is the compound form of the adverb εὖ ("well") and
most likely the noun ἄγγελος ("messenger") and has its Hebrew corollary in
the term בָּשַׂר (bāśar). In the Scriptures, and more specifically in Greek, one can
find the noun form εὐαγγέλιον 82 times (76x in the NT, and 6x in the LXX),[4]

---

1. The gloss "gospel" comes from the old English word "godspel" which means
something akin to "good tale." The English is a translation of the Latin term *evangelium*,
which comes from the Greek εὐαγγέλιον.

2. The etymological fallacy claims the present meaning of the word is based on
its origin. Illegitimate totality transfer takes all the possible meanings and applies
this to every use of the word. Prioritizing diachronic meaning means privileging
what the word has meant in the past rather than what it means "in" or "with" time
(synchronic). See D. A. Carson, *Exegetical Fallacies*, 2nd ed. (Grand Rapids: Baker
Academic, 1996).

3. These points are made by Peter J. Leithart, *Deep Exegesis: The Mystery of Reading
Scripture* (Waco, TX: Baylor University Press, 2009).

4. 2 Sam 4:10; 18:20, 22, 25, 27; 2 Kgs 7:9; Matt 11:5; Luke 1:19; 2:10; 3:18; 4:18, 43;
7:22; 8:1; 9:6; 16:16; 20:1; Acts 5:42; 8:4, 12, 25, 35, 40; 10:36; 11:20; 13:32; 14:7, 15, 21; 15:35;
16:10; 17:18; Rom 1:15; 10:15; 15:20; 1 Cor 1:17; 9:16, 18; 15:1–2; 2 Cor 10:16; 11:7; Gal 1:8–9,
11, 16, 23; 4:13; Eph 2:17; 3:8; 1 Thess 3:6; Heb 4:2, 6; 1 Pet 1:12, 25; 4:6; Rev 10:7; 14:6.

the verbal form εὐαγγελίζω 88 times (55x in the NT, 23x in the LXX),[5] while the title εὐαγγελιστής (evangelist) is only found three times.[6]

Overall, my argument is that, historically, εὐαγγέλιον is a media term—a message of good news, a dispatch of victory,[7] and the term is traditionally employed in political contexts, though the more mundane senses are not entirely absent.[8] The NT authors adopt this political sense, but they also clarify and reshape it, largely following the prophet Isaiah. Like Isaiah, the NT authors reshape εὐαγγέλιον in three ways: its scope, primary opposition, and means. This is all based on the arrival and accomplishment of Jesus.

Regarding scope, the NT authors reconfigure εὐαγγέλιον to not only have national implications but cosmic, apocalyptic, and eschatological insinuations. In so doing, the national sense is not erased, but the effect and spread of the message are expanded to the entire world. Secondly, the NT reinterprets εὐαγγέλιον in regard the primary opposition. The main problem is not foreign nations (Rome, Babylon, or Assyria) as in many historical uses of the term, but sin and the spiritual forces that work through flesh and blood. Thirdly, they reshape εὐαγγέλιον in terms of the means by which the victory is accomplished. Εὐαγγέλιον comes not by sword or army, but by suffering.

However, this reshaping does not mean the political sense is washed out. We can affirm a reconfiguring while retaining the political implications. Therefore, the distinction that many dictionaries propose between the secular and religious sense is a false one.[9] By secular, the dictionaries seem to imply this term was used in political and social contexts; then it began to be adapted in a different sense for the religious Jewish community. It is true that Jewish communities began to adopt the term and they certainly put a new spin on some of the associations. However, the implication that the political and social sense disappeared or even got pushed to the periphery is incorrect. The secular, social, cosmic, and religious were not separate spheres in the ancient world. It is thus better to say the term at its most basic level means "good news" and arose especially in contexts related to "political" spheres. It was then remapped under the political reign of Yahweh through his anointed Son Jesus.

---

5. 1 Sam 31:9; 2 Sam 1:20; 4:10; 18:19, 20 (2x), 26, 31; 1 Kgs 1:42; 1 Chr 10:9; Ps 39:10; Ps 67:12; 95:2; Sol 11:1; Joel 3:5; Nah 2:1; Isa 40:9 (2x); 52:7 (2x); 60:6; 61:1; Jer 20:15; Matt 11:5; Luke 1:19; 2:10; 3:18; 4:18, 43; 7:22; 8:1; 9:6; 16:16; 20:1; Acts 5:42; 8:4, 12, 25, 35, 40; 10:36; 11:20; 13:32; 14:7, 15, 21; 15:35; 16:10; 17:18; Rom 1:15; 10:15; 15:20; 1 Cor 1:17; 9:16, 18; 15:1–2; 2 Cor 10:16; 11:7; Gal 1:8–9, 11, 16, 23; 4:13; Eph 2:17; 3:8; 1 Thess 3:6; Heb 4:2, 6; 1 Pet 1:12, 25; 4:6; Rev 10:7; 14:6.

6. Acts 21:8; Eph 4:11; 2 Tim 4:5.

7. Louw & Nida put it under the banner of "Inform, Announce."

8. In 1 Sam 4:17 בָּשַׂר is used for the bad news of Israel being routed by the Philistines. Usually, it is employed in the context of good news.

9. *TDOT* 2:314–15; *TDNT* 2:708; *NIDNTT* 2:107.

I will divide this essay into three parts, arguing in each context that εὐαγγέλιον means good news, but the political pitch was the foundation upon which Isaiah and the rest of NT authors built their cosmic and apocalyptic message. First, I will look to the ANE and OT background, then the Greco-Roman background, and finally to the NT. In the conclusion, I will attempt to define what I do and do not mean by the political sense of εὐαγγέλιον.

Ancient Near Eastern and Old Testament Backgrounds

Paul begins Romans by speaking of the gospel. He asserts he was set apart for the gospel, which God promised beforehand through his prophets in the Holy Scriptures (Rom 1:2). Paul anchors the gospel in salvation history. Therefore, it is to the ANE and OT background that we must turn to understand what Paul means when he refers to εὐαγγέλιον.

In the OT the root בָּשַׂר occurs 30 times in all, and the root is well attested in the ANE.[10] Akkadian has forms that indicate the word itself was neutral—to bring a message (news)—and can be delineated by adding other terms making it "bad news," "good news," or "joyful news." In Ugaritic, the verb means to "bring glad tidings" and appears three times. First, when Anat brings Baal the joyful news of the birth of a bull calf, he calls it good news. Second, the term is employed in the context of conquest. Finally, the term is used when Anat brings Baal the news that a house is going to be built for him.[11] Though the first reference is in the more general context of good news, the second two pertain to political, military, and cosmic victory.

In the OT, readers find the term בָּשַׂר and εὐαγγέλιον only occasionally, but usually connected with some sort of political and/or military context.[12] In LXX 1 Sam 31:9 (and LXX 1 Chr 10:9) the Philistines cut off Saul's head and send the "good news" to all the Philistines.[13] The term is employed in the same context,

---

10. There is a widespread agreement that בָּשַׂר is highly significant for the rise of the verb εὐαγγελίζω. John Dickson, *Mission-Commitment in Ancient Judaism and in the Pauline Communities: The Shape, Extent and Background of Early Christian Mission*, WUNT 2.159 (Tubingen: Mohr Siebeck, 2003), 153–77.

11. For these references see *TDOT* 2:313.

12. Several uses of בָּשַׂר are not translated with ευαγγελ- in the LXX, and in Joel 3:5 εὐαγγελιζόμενοι translates שְׂרִידִים (survivors). At times Jer 20:15 is an exception where it is used in reference to Jeremiah's birth. It can also be employed for bad news (*hamvassēr*), like when Eli is told the sad news of Israel's defeat and the death of his sons (1 Sam 4:17). *TDNT* 2:707 therefore begins the entry on בָּשַׂר stating, "bsr in the OT has the general sense of "proclaiming good news" (1 Kgs 1:42), e.g., the birth of a son (Jer 20:15)." However, with the overwhelming evidence for a political sense, it is probably better to say that the terms semantic range included the broad sense of proclaiming good news, but it was quickly applied to political contexts.

13. Interestingly, in 1 Sam 31:9 the indirect object in the LXX of the good news is "in the temples of their idols." The term therefore has both a military and what we would call a "religious" sense, indicating these are not separate spheres.

but from the Israelite perspective in LXX 2 Sam 1:20, where David tells the people not to not to "tell" (ἀναγγέλλω) of Saul's death in Gath or "announce it" (εὐαγγελίζω) in Ashkelon, because then the Philistines will rejoice.[14] In a few instances, it is related to the reward one receives. In 1 Kgs 1:46, Adonijah expects to hear "good news" from Jonathan in relation to his kingship but ends up hearing that Solomon has been anointed as king. In 2 Kgs 7:9, the good news refers to the flight of the Arameans.

The Psalms continue this designation when David speaks of the good news of righteousness (δικαιοσύνη; ṣedeq; Ps 40:9 [Eng.]; LXX Ps 39:10). Though this could be interpreted in a more individual or personal way, it comes from the mouth of Yahweh who saves and delivers David the king and therefore the nation. Women tell the good news of kings fleeing before Israel in Ps 68:11 (LXX 67:12), and the whole earth is to proclaim the good news of his salvation in the context of Yahweh reigning in Ps 96:2 (LXX 95:2). Already in the Psalms, the בְּשֵׂר is beginning to be expanded to cover the whole earth.

The prophets also use בְּשֵׂר and εὐαγγέλιον in the contexts of political and military victory or at least the promise of this, but they also begin to expand to something bigger than Jerusalem. It concerns all flesh, all creation, and all nations worshipping before Yahweh. In Joel 2:32 (LXX 3:5), the prophet tells of the day when everyone who calls on the name of Yahweh will be saved. He describes this as good news. In Nahum "good news" is employed in the context of the defeat of Assyria's king, allowing those in Judah to celebrate their festivals (Nah 1:15; LXX 2:1). Lingering in the background of all these uses is the covenant Yahweh has made with his people. Good news comes to them because they are his people.

Probably the most important context for the NT use of εὐαγγέλιον comes in the prophet Isaiah. Isaiah employs the term in relationship to the coming reign of Yahweh and the return from exile. Zion and Jerusalem are to proclaim the "good news" of God's return to establish his rule which is further described as Yahweh shepherding his people (Isa 40:9–11). The prophet also declares the bloodied and dusty feet of those who carry good news are beautiful because they proclaim peace, salvation, and tell that God reigns (Isa 52:7). Isaiah 52:7 parallels the good news with God's reign which brings peace and salvation. In Isa 61:1, the anointed one announces the Spirit of Yahweh is upon him to bring good news which is further defined as "binding up the brokenhearted, proclaiming liberty to the captives, the opening of the prison to those who are bound."

The Isaianic gospel therefore pertains to Israel's national salvation through their Messiah who will return them to their land and restore the fortunes of their kingdom. However, Isaiah also expands this term to mean salvation for

---

14. The same sense is found in 2 Sam 4:10; 18:19–31.

the nations. All humanity will see the glory of the Lord when he establishes a new exodus (Isa 40:4–5). It is Yahweh's servant who will accomplish this, and he will do so by suffering. "He will sprinkle the nations. Kings will shut their mouths because of him" (Isa 52:15). Israel will enlarge the site of their tent; their curtains will be stretched out (Isa 54:2).

Though there are a few references that fall outside of the normal political and militaristic contexts, the majority of settings pertain to kings, battles, and victories. What readers will find is that a similar phenomenon occurs in the Greco-Roman background to the term. The Psalms and the Prophets begin to expand this political term to include all nations and all flesh, even giving indications that this victory will be accomplished by suffering rather than the sword.

Greco-Roman Background

Millar Burrows begins his article on the origin of the term "gospel" by stating "the Greek noun εὐαγγέλιον is rarely found in the sense of "good tidings" outside of early Christian literature."[15] In classical Greek, the term means a messenger's rewards.[16] And it is true, we do find this meaning in Homer, Isocrates, Diodorus, Xenophon, Plutarch, and Aristophanes.[17] However, it is not quite right to say it is rarely found in the sense of good tidings. John Dickson clarifies the relationship between the different forms of these words:

> Εὐαγγελίζομαι denotes the activity of the εὐαγγελος, the messenger of ancient Greece who was sent from the field of battle by ship, by horse, or a swift runner, to proclaim to the awaiting city the victory – εὐτυχής [favor] is commonly associated with the announcement – of the army or the death or capture of an enemy or some other significant announcement. The noun εὐαγγέλιον, an adjective used as a substantive, derives from εὐαγγέλος and means simply 'that which is proper to the εὐαγγελος,' thus allowing the two-fold usage of antiquity, 'reward/offering for tidings' and the 'tidings' themselves.[18]

Therefore, the reward is tightly tied to the bringing of the news, and this news was consistently though not exclusively found in political contexts. Michael Bird even states, "In the Greco-Roman world, the noun εὐαγγέλιον was pri-

---

15. Millar Burrows, "The Origin of the Term 'Gospel,'" *JBL* 44.1–2 (1925): 21.

16. BDAG s.v. εὐαγγέλιον (402).

17. Homer, *Odyssey* 14.152, 166; Isocrates, *Aeropagiticus* 7.10; Diodorus, *Historical Library* 15.74.2; Xenophon, *Hellenica*, I.6.37; Plutarch, *Agesilaus* 17.3, 33.4; *Sertorius* 11.4, 26.3; Aristophanes, *Equites* 656.

18. John Dickson, "Gospel as News: εὐαγελλ- from Aristophanes to the Apostle Paul," *NTS* 51 (2005): 212–13.

marily associated with positive news in general and news of military victory in particular."[19]

News of a ruler's birth, the coming of age, enthronement, speeches, decrees, and acts are all put under the banner of "good news."[20] A Priene calendar inscription from 9 BCE speaks of the birth of the emperor Augustus as "the beginning of good news" for the world:

> [Augustus] . . . has made war to cease and . . . put everything in peaceful order; and whereas . . . the birthday of our God signaled the beginning of Good News for the world because of him (τῶν δι' αὐτὸν εὐαγγελἰων).[21]

In one inscription, it states that the day when a son of Augustus takes on the toga is "good news for the city" (εὐαγγελίσθη ἡ πόλις).[22] A papyrus letter from an Egyptian official in the third century AD uses the term "in connection with the accession of emperor Julius Verus Maximus."[23] And an inscription at the Amphiareion of Oropos from around 1 CE mentions the "good news of Rome's victory" (εὐαγγέλια τῆς Ρωμαιων νίκης).[24]

Plutarch speaks of how the Spartans would give a reward to the man who brought good news of victory.[25] He notes that General Quintus Sertorius spoke of military victory in terms of good news.[26] The Roman general Pompey was given the news of the death of his adversary under the umbrella of good news.[27] The Jewish writers Josephus and Philo, who were conversant with the Greco-Roman tradition, wrote of the good news in terms of imperial power. Philo speaks of Gaius Caligula's accession to the throne as "good news."[28] Josephus, likewise, reports Vespasian's accession to the throne saying, "every city celebrated the good news (εὐαγγέλια) and offered sacrifices on his behalf."[29]

My argument is not that the more "mundane" senses of the terms are entirely vacant, but that the political or military sense rises to the surface in the Greco-Roman literature. Philo uses the term in a more "mundane" sense when

---

19. Michael F. Bird, *The Gospel of the Lord: How the Early Church Wrote the Story of Jesus* (Grand Rapids: Eerdmans, 2014), 6.

20. *NIDNTT* 2:307.

21. Cf. Burrows, "The Origin of the Term 'Gospel,'" 21.

22. For the Greek text see Victor Ehrenberg and Arnold Hugh Martin Jones, eds., *Documents Illustrating the Reigns of Augustus and Tiberius*, 2nd ed. (Oxford: Clarendon, 1955), 84.

23. Burrows, "The Origin of the Term 'Gospel,'" 21.

24. See Alexandra Wilding, *Reinventing the Amphiareion at Oropos*, MSHACA 445 (Leiden: Brill, 2021), 249.

25. Plutarch, *Moralia* 347D.

26. Plutarch, *Sertorius* 11.4.

27. Plutarch, *Pompeius* 66.3.

28. Philo, *Ad Gaium* 231.

29. Josephus, *J. W.* 4.618.

he speaks of the patriarch Joseph who urges his brothers to return to his father and give him good news that they have found him,[30] and when the servant found a wife for Isaac he brought him back good news.[31] Josephus also uses the term in more expansive contexts than political power. He employs it in the angelic announcement of Samson's birth, and in the announcement of the discovery of Saul's donkeys.[32]

Thus, what readers find in the Greco-Roman literature and inscriptions, is that "gospel" is regularly associated with "news" and news more particularly of military victory and or with the news of an emperor's birth or their accession. Occasionally, the term can refer to a favorable report, but most of the time it has political connotations.[33] This matches how it was used in the Baal stories and the Old Testament. Readers should thus expect this sense to continue in the New Testament.

New Testament Usage

The term εὐαγγέλιον is quite important in the NT, but its distribution is haphazard. The noun form occurs 75 times, and Paul makes up a full 60 of these occurrences. On the other hand, the verbal form εὐαγγελίζω occurs over 55 times, but over half of these are found in Luke's literature, and most of the remaining instances (21x) in Paul's letters.[34] As Dickson states, "while the language of 'gospel' is not exclusively Pauline it is distinctively Pauline. Eighty-two of the New Testament's one hundred and thirty-four instances of εὐαγγ- are found in the Pauline corpus."[35] Mark and Matthew prefer the noun form, with Matthew usually modifying it with "of the kingdom."[36] Mark, on the other hand, is more prone to use it absolutely, though he does employ the genitive modifier "of Jesus Christ" and "of God."[37] Mark never uses the verbal form. Luke, as already noted, is fond of the verbal form (ten times in Luke and fifteen in Acts), while John doesn't employ the term at all.

---

30. Philo, *On the Life of Joseph* 245.
31. Philo, *QG* 4.144.
32. Josephus, *Ant.* 5.277; 5.282; 2.45.
33. Aristophanes employs the term in a more mundane sense when he announces the news of an all-time low in the price of anchovies at the local market (*Equites* 644–47). Bird's conclusion is similar. Bird, *The Gospel of the Lord*, 8.
34. *NIDNTT* 2:308.
35. Dickson, *Mission-Commitment in Ancient Judaism and in the Pauline Communities*, 86.
36. Matt 4:23; 9:35; 24:14; 26:13. The only verbal form is found in Matt 11:5 where Matthew is quoting from the LXX.
37. Mark 1:1, 14 use the genitive modifier. Mark 1:15, 8:35; 10:29; 13:10; 14:9; 16:15 all use it absolutely.

For all the Gospel writers, the εὐαγγελ- language is heavily indebted to the Isaianic news of the anointed one who brings about Yahweh's reign over the earth. Following Isaiah, the center of this message revolves around the Suffering Servant who marks a shift in the ages. Matthew only employs the term a few times, but in these instances, he argues, the term gains its meaning from the *past*, summarizes Jesus' *present* ministry, and will echo into the *future*. The "gospel of the kingdom" is the summary statement of Jesus' message in Matthew (4:23; 9:35), the fulfillment of the Messianic hopes found in Isa 35:5 and 61:1, and that which to be proclaimed to the nations until the end (Matt 24:14; 26:13).

Mark labels his entire work "a gospel" because it is about Jesus' life, death, and resurrection (Mark 1:1).[38] Like in Matthew, the message of Jesus concerns, "the gospel of God" that requires a response (Mark 1:14–15). Twice Mark has Jesus paralleling "the cause of Jesus" with "the gospel" (Mark 8:35; 10:29), and three times Jesus speaks of the "gospel" being proclaimed to all nations (13:10; 14:9; 16:15).

Luke is drawn to the verbal form, and at the beginning of his narrative his emphasis is on the gospel's heavenly origin. Angels bring the good news (Luke 1:19; 2:10) and the Spirit of the Lord anoints Jesus to proclaim the message (4:18). Luke employs the phrase as a summary of the teachings of Jesus (4:43; 7:22; 8:1; 20:1), John (3:18), and the disciples (9:6). Acts gives the sense that the Gospel was the content of the early church's preaching (Acts 5:42; 8:12, 25, 35, 40; 10:36; 11:20; 13:32; 14:7; 14:15, 21; 15:7, 35; 16:10; 17:18; 20:24). Interestingly, in Acts, there seems to be a slight shift in that previously the gospel was something Jesus proclaimed, and now its object is Jesus (5:42; 8:12, 25, 35; 10:36; 11:20; 17:18).

Therefore, in the Gospels and in Acts the "good news" 1) is prophesied by the prophets, 2) proclaimed by Jesus, 3) finds it object in the king and the kingdom, 4) is centered on Jesus' sacrifice for people, 5) is to be the same message of Jesus followers, and 6) is to be spread to the nations.

What is different in the Gospels from the historical use of the term is the way this good news is accomplished, to whom it is offered, and its expansive scope. Rather than conquering by military power, Christ is conquered. Rather than subduing his enemies, Christ allows himself to be subdued so that he might be declared the Lord of all. He offers his "gospel" to all, as the prophets had foretold, and therefore the victory is cosmic. This reshaping of the term becomes the message of Paul as he preaches the good news to Gentiles.

Paul employs εὐαγγέλιον as a central concept of his theology, using it 20 times without further qualification to describe the content of his preaching.[39]

---

38. See Bird's argument for how it could go from a more oral proclamation to a written one. Bird, *The Gospel of the Lord*, 5–20.

39. Some debate exists as to whether εὐαγγελ- language refers not only to Paul's initial proclamation but the whole process of building Christians toward this goal. Bowers and O'Brien argue this is the case, while Dickson argues to the contrary. Paul

The gospel is thus the oral proclamation concerning Jesus' life, death, and resurrection. Romans 1:1–4, 1 Cor 15:1–7, and 2 Tim 2:8 most clearly indicate the content of the gospel for Paul. In Rom 1:1–4 Paul says this gospel was promised beforehand in the OT. It is anchored in salvation history. The gospel's *content* is also centered on Jesus (David's son), who has become the Lord (cf. Ps 110:1 [LXX 109:1]).

Any summary of the gospel, including the phrase "the Lord reigns" without specific reference to Jesus is lacking in Paul's mind. Yahweh reigns *in* and *through* Jesus. This is confirmed in Rom 1:4, where Paul says Christ was appointed to be the powerful Son of God. The gospel therefore seems to be about the dual identity of Jesus both as the Messiah and his filial relationship to the Father.

In 1 Cor 15:1–7, this gospel is also in accordance with the Scriptures and centered on Jesus' death and resurrection. In 2 Tim 2:8 the gospel concerns Jesus Christ, risen from the dead, offspring of David. The good news for Paul concerns the story of Jesus, the son of David (king), who died and was raised (1 Cor 1:17). This story of King Jesus was predicted beforehand, and the death and resurrection made Jesus the political ruler of the entire world. Now he spreads the good news of Jesus' cosmic and eschatological kingship to the nations.

For Paul, "εὐαγγέλιον does not mean only the content of what is preached, but also the act, process, and execution of the proclamation."[40] Now Paul's task is to preach this gospel to the world.[41] This gospel is power (Rom 1:16), it has abolished death and brought life (2 Tim 1:10), it comes not only in word but with power in the Holy Spirit and full conviction (1 Thess 1:5), and its goal is to bring people the glory of Jesus (2 Thess 2:14). It is the word of truth (Eph 1:13; Col 1:5), it comes from God and belongs to God (Rom 1:1; 15:16; 2 Cor 11:7; Gal 1:11; 1 Thess 2:2, 8–9), but also belongs to Jesus and concerns him (Rom 15:19–20; 16:25; 1 Cor 9:12; 2 Cor 2:12; 4:3; 9:13; 10:14; Gal 1:7, 16; Eph 3:8; 1 Thess 3:2; 2 Thess 1:8), and Paul preaches it to please God (1 Thess 2:4). Paul is imprisoned for the gospel (Phil 1:7; 2 Tim 1:8; Phlm 13), he says there are enemies of the gospel (Rom 11:28), sometimes the gospel is veiled (2 Cor 4:3–4), and other times a different gospel is preached (Gal 1:9). Paul calls it his

Bowers, "Studies in Paul's Understanding of His Mission" (Cambridge University, PhD diss., 1976); Peter T. O'Brien, *Gospel and Mission in the Writings of Paul: An Exegetical and Theological Analysis* (Grand Rapids: Baker Books, 1995), 61–65; Dickson, "Gospel as News." A major part of this debate concerns Rom 1:15 and whether the clause should be taken as implying a past tense or present tense. If present tense, then Paul wants to proclaim the gospel to those in Rome who are already believers thereby implying the gospel has now taken on the sense of building up Christians.

40. *NIDNTT* 2:310.

41. Rom 1:1, 9, 15, 16; 10:15; 15:16, 19–20; 16:25; 1 Cor 1:17; 4:15; 9:12, 14, 16, 18; 9:23; 15:1; 2 Cor 2:12; 4:3–4; 10:14, 16; 11:4, 7; Gal 1:8–9, 11, 23; 2:7; 4:13; Eph 3:8; 6:19; Phil 1:7, 16; 2:22; 4:3; Col 1:5, 23; 1 Thess 1:5; 2:2, 4, 8–9; 2 Thess 2:14; 1 Tim 1:11; 2 Tim 2:8.

gospel (Rom 2:16; 2 Tim 2:8; Gal 2:2), the faith (Gal 1:23; Phil 1:27), peace (Eph 6:15), and the grace of Christ (Gal 1:6).

Diverse images and metaphors are used, but for Paul the gospel concerns Jesus and his ascent to the throne of God. If Paul is basing the meaning of this term even partially on its historical use, then it is political at its very core. The good news is the proclamation of Yahweh's reign through his suffering king. This good news can be rejected, but it is offered to all, and it is centered on Jesus' death and resurrection. It is for this message that Paul suffers and sacrifices everything.

However, if it is a political message, it is curious that Paul does not explicitly seek to reform society or install political leaders. To say that the political sense is still present is rather ambiguous. Does this mean Jesus and Paul challenged the Roman empire? Was he explicitly responding to the imperial cult in his use of the term? Is εὐαγγέλιον an implicit critique of the good news proclaimed by Rome?

Affirmations and Denials

There has been a flurry of arguments around the political nature of Paul's gospel in the past few decades with some confidently asserting that Paul's message had a hidden code or signals that challenged the imperial cult. Others voice their concern with this line of thinking, arguing we are reading too much background into this term and see things that are never made explicit in the text itself.[42] After all, words garner their meaning from their immediate context and

---

42. For some perspectives on the New Testament and the Roman Empire see the following books and articles. John M. G. Barclay, *Pauline Churches and Diaspora Jews* (Grand Rapids: Eerdmans, 2016); Bird, *The Gospel of the Lord*; Brian K. Blount, *Can I Get A Witness?: Reading Revelation Through African American Culture* (Louisville: Westminster John Knox, 2005); Christopher Bryan, *Render to Caesar: Jesus, the Early Church, and the Roman Superpower* (Oxford: Oxford University Press, 2005); Warren Carter, *The Roman Empire and the New Testament: An Essential Guide* (Nashville: Abingdon, 2006); Richard J. Cassidy, *Christians and Roman Rule in the New Testament: New Perspectives* (New York: Herder & Herder, 2001); John Dominic Crossan, *God and Empire: Jesus Against Rome, Then and Now* (San Francisco: Harper One, 2008); Judith A. Diehl, "Anti-Imperial Rhetoric in the New Testament," *CurBR* 10 (2011): 9–52; Judith A. Diehl, "Empire and Epistles: Anti-Roman Rhetoric in the New Testament Epistles," *CurBR* 10 (2012): 217–63; Judith A Diehl, " 'Babylon': Then, Now and 'Not yet': Anti-Roman Rhetoric in the Book of Revelation," *CurBR* 11 (2013): 168–95; Richard A. Horsley, ed., *Paul and Empire: Religion and Power in Roman Imperial Society* (Harrisburg, PA: Trinity Press International, 1997); Richard A. Horsley, ed., *Jesus and Empire: The Kingdom of God and the New World Disorder* (Minneapolis: Fortress, 2002); Richard A. Horsley, ed., *In the Shadow of Empire: Reclaiming the Bible as a History of Faithful Resistance* (Louisville: Westminster John Knox, 2008); Seyoon Kim, *Christ and Caesar: The Gospel and the Roman Empire in the Writings of Paul and Luke* (Grand Rapids: Eerdmans, 2008); Scot McKnight and Joseph B. Modica, eds., *Jesus Is Lord, Caesar Is Not: Evaluating Empire in New Testament Studies* (Downers Grove, IL: IVP Academic, 2013); Stanley E. Porter and Cynthia Long Westfall, eds., *Empire in the New*

can be quite removed from their history. But, for me, it is difficult to see how one can erase the political nature of the Isaianic background which Paul and Jesus both explicitly employ. Therefore, it is necessary to ask the harder question of what it means this is political term.

Politics are simply the activities associated with the people, especially regarding the ordering of a society. It comes from the Greek word πόλις, which simply means city. Therefore, when I say εὐαγγέλιον is a political term, I am stating it relates to things such as governance, cities, kings, kingdoms, peace, war, and how to allow flourishing among citizens of particular realms.

The political nature of εὐαγγέλιον is evidenced by the following.[43] First, the first century does not recognize a boundary between religion and politics. We cannot say it is a religious as opposed to the political term. Second, there is a suspicion of imperial power from Jesus and Paul. Third, neither Jesus nor Paul are private and apolitical individuals. Fourth, Jesus and Paul announce a new order that indirectly challenges all other power structures; this includes Rome. Fourth, as already stated, to say that the term is a political term does not mean it is not eschatological, cosmic, or spiritual. Rather, I am asserting that the lexical and historical studies indicate the political sense is the bedrock upon which these other senses are built. To assert these other meanings are added does not wash out its basic sense.

But I also want to clarify what I *don't* mean about the political nature of εὐαγγέλιον. First, in line with John Barclay, neither Jesus nor Paul seemed to view Rome as the central antagonist they were opposing. Rather, there was a deeper supernatural battle that manifested itself in human governments. The main powers are the Spirit, sin, flesh, and death, not Rome. In this way, Jesus and Paul demoted Rome and its power by not explicitly speaking of it.

Second, the term εὐαγγέλιον did not grow out of the imperial cult context, but it was employed in that context. Therefore, it is part of the picture used in constructing what the term means, but to take it as the only or central context is overstating the case.

Third, in disagreement with Barclay, some benefit exists in seeing Paul and Jesus speaking in code. Language regularly works in ways that associations are

---

Testament (Eugene, OR: Pickwick, 2011); C. Kavin Rowe, *World Upside Down: Reading Acts in the Graeco-Roman Age* (New York: Oxford University Press, 2010); R. Alan Streett, *Subversive Meals: An Analysis of the Lord's Supper under Roman Domination during the First Century* (Eugene, OR: Pickwick, 2013); R. Alan Streett, *Caesar and the Sacrament: Baptism: A Rite of Resistance* (Eugene, OR: Cascade Books, 2018); Robert Louis Wilken, *The Christians as the Romans Saw Them* (New Haven: Yale University Press, 2003); Adam Winn, ed., *An Introduction to Empire in the New Testament*, RBS 84 (Atlanta: SBL Press, 2016).

43. Many of these points largely follow John Barclay's argument. Barclay, *Pauline Churches and Diaspora Jews* (Grand Rapids: Eerdmans, 2016), 331–88.

implicit rather than explicit. In some sense, all language is code. While we don't want to overemphasize the "coded" nature of language, we also should not underplay it. With the background I have just outlined, it is hard to imagine that when Jesus announced the "good news of the kingdom," or when Paul spoke of his gospel concerning the son of David, that Jews didn't hear a challenge to Rome.

Fourth, it is mistaken to argue that Jesus and Paul didn't attempt to overthrow the current regime in any way. He wasn't seeking Caesar's throne, but he was seeking a throne. To be the King of kings is to subordinate every other king. The good news of the kingdom may not be an explicit challenge, but it is undoubtedly an implicit one.

The shocking thing about the "good news" is that the victory is obtained through sacrifice and submission, not by sword and spear. Neither Jesus nor Paul viewed their role as directly challenging the government, but rather submitting to the government. Yet even this submission was subversive because they were to do so as free people. The *means* of accomplishing this kingdom is different, and the *nature* of this kingdom is unique. However, these distinctions between God's kingdom does not mean that the political sense is washed out—it is merely reconfigured.

To put it most succinctly, I suggest, we can apply what Kavin Rowe asserted about Acts and Paul's encounter with the Greco-Roman world to the term εὐαγγέλιον.[44] The NT authors juxtapose a "yes" and "no" in their use of the term in relation to politics. The problem is when we lose one or the other, or even overemphasize one or the other.

As Kavin Rowe puts it, "Yes, Jesus came calling people to a new life. No, Christians are not guilty of insurrection. Yes, Caesar challenges the Lordship of King Jesus. No, Jesus is not after Caesar's throne. Yes, the resurrection and ascension of Jesus threatens the stability of Roman life. No, Christian's are not violent zealots."[45] Though Christians are accused of sedition in Acts, Luke makes clear they are innocent of these charges. It is almost as if the Roman world doesn't know what to do with the claim of the resurrected King. They lack the hermeneutical framework within which to put this message of "yes" and "no." Maybe we too have lost this hermeneutical framework.

Conclusion

So what is the εὐαγγέλιον? For the ancient world it was a "media" term, connoting the announcement of a message that was good news to its hearers.[46] However, the term belongs not to the arena of formal education, but most

---

44. Rowe, *World Upside Down*, 140.
45. Rowe, *World Upside Down*, 140.
46. Dickson, "Gospel as News," 213.

commonly to realm of military or political victory. In Greco-Roman literature it takes on this sense, as well as in the OT.

The Psalms and the Prophets (and more specifically Isaiah) speak of the gospel as the announcement of the reign of God for Israel's benefit through Yahweh's servant. Following Isaiah, Jesus and the NT authors reconfigure the term in terms of its scope, primary opposition, and means. The good news now is offered to all flesh. The main problem is not the military power of other nations, but the spiritual forces and sin residing in their heart, and Jesus has dealt with all of this by his death and resurrection. By dealing with main problem, people can then flourish under their new King. The gospel in the NT, in short, is *the announcement that Yahweh reigns through Jesus' sacrifice and exaltation.*

Bibliography

Barclay, John M. G. *Pauline Churches and Diaspora Jews.* Grand Rapids: Eerdmans, 2016.

Bird, Michael F. *An Anomalous Jew: Paul among Jews, Greeks, and Romans.* Grand Rapids: Eerdmans, 2016.

———. *The Gospel of the Lord: How the Early Church Wrote the Story of Jesus.* Grand Rapids: Eerdmans, 2014.

Blount, Brian K. *Can I Get A Witness? Reading Revelation Through African American Culture.* Louisville: Westminster John Knox, 2005.

Bowers, Paul. "Studies in Paul's Understanding of His Mission." PhD diss., Cambridge University, 1976.

Bryan, Christopher. *Render to Caesar: Jesus, the Early Church, and the Roman Superpower.* Oxford: Oxford University Press, 2005.

Burrows, Millar. "The Origin of the Term 'Gospel.'" *JBL* 44 (1925): 21–33.

Carson, D. A. *Exegetical Fallacies.* 2nd ed. Grand Rapids: Baker Academic, 1996.

Carter, Warren. *The Roman Empire and the New Testament: An Essential Guide.* Nashville: Abingdon Press, 2006.

Cassidy, Richard J. *Christians and Roman Rule in the New Testament: New Perspectives.* New York: Herder & Herder, 2001.

Crossan, John Dominic. *God and Empire: Jesus Against Rome, Then and Now.* San Francisco: Harper One, 2008.

Dickson, John P. "Gospel as News: εὐαγελλ- from Aristophanes to the Apostle Paul." *NTS* 51 (2005): 212–30.

———. *Mission-Commitment in Ancient Judaism and in the Pauline Communities: The Shape, Extent and Background of Early Christian Mission.* WUNT 2.159. Tübingen: Mohr Siebeck, 2003.

Diehl, Judith A. "Anti-Imperial Rhetoric in the New Testament." *CurBR* 10 (2011): 9–52.

———. " 'Babylon': Then, Now and 'Not yet': Anti-Roman Rhetoric in the Book of Revelation." *CurBR* 11 (2013): 168–95.

———. "Empire and Epistles: Anti-Roman Rhetoric in the New Testament Epistles." *CurBR* 10 (2012): 217–63.

Ehrenberg, Victor, and Arnold Hugh Martin Jones, eds. *Documents Illustrating the Reigns of Augustus and Tiberius.* 2nd ed. Oxford: Clarendon, 1955.

Horsley, Richard A., ed. *In the Shadow of Empire: Reclaiming the Bible as a History of Faithful Resistance.* Louisville: Westminster John Knox, 2008.

———. *Jesus and Empire: The Kingdom of God and the New World Disorder.* Minneapolis: Fortress, 2002.

———, ed. *Paul and Empire: Religion and Power in Roman Imperial Society.* Valley Forge, PA: Trinity Press International, 1997.

Kim, Seyoon. *Christ and Caesar: The Gospel and the Roman Empire in the Writings of Paul and Luke.* Grand Rapids: Eerdmans, 2008.

Leithart, Peter J. *Deep Exegesis: The Mystery of Reading Scripture.* Waco, TX: Baylor University Press, 2009.

McKnight, Scot, and Joseph B. Modica, eds. *Jesus Is Lord, Caesar Is Not: Evaluating Empire in New Testament Studies.* Downers Grove, IL: IVP Academic, 2013.

O'Brien, Peter T. *Gospel and Mission in the Writings of Paul: An Exegetical and Theological Analysis.* Grand Rapids: Baker Books, 1995.

Porter, Stanley E., and Cynthia Long Westfall, eds. *Empire in the New Testament.* Eugene, OR: Pickwick, 2011.

Rowe, C. Kavin. *World Upside Down: Reading Acts in the Graeco-Roman Age.* Oxford: Oxford University Press, 2010.

Streett, R. Alan. *Caesar and the Sacrament: Baptism: A Rite of Resistance.* Eugene, OR: Cascade Books, 2018.

———. *Subversive Meals: An Analysis of the Lord's Supper under Roman Domination during the First Century.* Eugene, OR: Pickwick, 2013.

Wilding, Alexandra. *Reinventing the Amphiareion at Oropos.* MSHACA 445. Leiden: Brill, 2021.

Wilken, Robert Louis. *The Christians as the Romans Saw Them.* New Haven: Yale University Press, 2003.

Winn, Adam, ed. *An Introduction to Empire in the New Testament.* RBS 84. Atlanta: SBL Press, 2016.

CHAPTER 6

God's Grace and Israel's Righteousness in Early Judaism and in Romans

Christopher Bruno

Over the last several decades, we have made great advancements in our understanding of "righteousness" in early Judaism and Christianity; with those advancements have come many new questions and debates. In recent years, John Barclay's research on the nature of grace and gifts in the ancient world has advanced our understanding of these concepts in a similar way. Barclay's work has certainly shined new light on grace in the first century, it has also uncovered new questions about the relationship between grace and righteousness.

In his book *Paul and the Gift*, John Barclay examines the variegated understanding of God's grace and gifts in early Judaism and Christianity. Noting the diverse ways gifts are understood, he suggests six "common perfections of the gift" found in Jewish and Christian literature: 1) superabundance, or extravagance; 2) singularity, or benevolence; 3) priority, or timing with respect to the recipient's action; 4) incongruity, "without regard to the worth of the recipient"; 5) efficacy, and 6) non-circularity, without reciprocity.[1]

I am happy to join the chorus that has applauded Barclay's work. He has both helped us move forward in many places and opened new avenues for exploration. However, as Douglas Moo has noted, Barclay's exclusive focus on χάρις as "gift" limits his study.[2] Of course, threading the needle between a narrow lexical study and an overly broad thematic study is a perpetual challenge in any study of a concept or theme in early Jewish and Christian literature. To be clear, Barclay's work is neither unhelpfully narrow nor undefinedly broad. Yet the necessary limitation of his study leaves his categories somewhat open-ended. Not to mention, only six perfections of the gift feels one short of perfection.[3]

In this paper we will consider Testament of Abraham 13–14 and Romans 3–4 in concert in order to observe how each text describes the nature of God's

---

1. John M. G. Barclay, *Paul and the Gift* (Grand Rapids: Eerdmans, 2015), 69–75.

2. Douglas J. Moo, "John Barclay's *Paul and the Gift* and the New Perspective on Paul," *Themelios* 41.2 (2016): 279–88.

3. To be fair, Barclay claims that "one may distinguish at least *six* common perfections of the gift" (*Paul and the Gift*, 69). Certainly, he does not imply that his six perfections are the only possibilities.

gift and grace and the righteousness of the recipient. From this, we will engage with Barclay's analysis in *Paul and the Gift* and make some concluding observations and suggest some theological implications for the presentation of God's grace and Israel's righteousness in these texts. We will see that in the Testament of Abraham, God's grace to Abraham—and perhaps by implication, to all of Israel—is congruous. However, through righteous Abraham, this grace can somehow benefit the unrighteous. In Romans, Abraham and all Israel, along with the Gentiles, are recipients of God's incongruent grace, which is mediated through the only true righteous and congruent recipient of God's gifts, the Messiah Jesus.

Testament of Abraham 13–14

The Testament of Abraham was likely written in the first or second century AD, though its origin and authorship are unknown.[4] In any case, it is roughly contemporary with the NT.[5] While this document by no means represents the unanimous (or perhaps even the majority) view of judgment in early Judaism, and may in fact be a satire of sorts, its portrayal of Abraham's righteousness provides a good window into one understanding of righteousness and judgment in the final judgment.[6] Therefore, in spite of some tensions within the text itself, we will read it more or less straightforwardly, at least within the "Testament" genre.

Nearly all extant versions of the Testament are found in one of two recensions and most scholars argue that the longer A recension is closer to the original edition and that the short B recension is a later edition.[7] Neither recension is without difficulty, and a case can be made for the consistency of the B

---

4. Our observations will larger come from the longer form of the Testament (the A recension; T. Ab. A). M. R. James, who produced what is still the only critical text of the Testament, suggests that an editor abridged an original longer version to produce the B recension. However, the original was not the A recension, but rather an edition from which the A recension was produced (Montague Rhodes James, *The Testament of Abraham: The Greek Text Now First Edited with an Introduction and Notes*, TS 2/2 [Cambridge: Cambridge University Press, 1892], 49). Therefore, James' critical text is largely based on A, but considers B as a possible witness to an earlier version than either recension.

5. E. P. Sanders dates the Testament to within twenty-five years of AD 100. On its lack of Christian insertions, he also observes, "Despite being repeatedly copied by Christian scribes, the Testament of Abraham in both recensions remains unmistakably Jewish" (*OTP* 1:875).

6. See Annette Yoshiko Reed, "The Construction and Subversion of Patriarchal Perfection: Abraham and Exemplarity in Philo, Josephus, and the *Testament of Abraham*," *JSJ* 40 (2009): 209.

7. Jan Dochhorn, "Zur Krise der Gerechtigkeit im frühen Judentum. Reflexionen über das Entstehungsmilieu des frühen Christentums," *BN* 155 (2012): 100.

recension.[8] Nevertheless, we will give primary attention here to the A recension while commenting on the B recension where most relevant.[9]

Both recensions describe Abraham's reaction when he sees the sins of the human race. As he witnesses various sins being committed, his response is to call for immediate and unmitigated judgment upon the sinners, and because he himself has not sinned, he does not pity sinners (A 10:13). He calls for wild beasts to devour murderers (A 10:5–7; B 12:9–11), for the earth to swallow up both a couple committing sexual immorality (A 10:8–9; B 12:2–4) and men who speak evil of each other (B 12:6–7), and for fire to fall from heaven to consume thieves as they burgle a house (A 10:10–11). In each of these cases, Abraham's request is granted. In the B recension, "the Lord said to Michael, 'Do whatever Abraham asks you to do for him'" (T. Ab. B 12:5; my translation). In fact, Abraham is so merciless that his tour is cut short so that he will not destroy the whole creation (A 10:13; B 12:12–13). Dale Allison suggests when Abraham's tour is cut short, the text "contrasts Abraham's judgmental piety with the indulgent mercy of the Creator."[10] However, the scene that follows is not exactly one of "indulgent mercy."

After this episode in the B recension, Abraham is immediately returned to his house, but the longer recension includes an extended account of Abraham's "tour of heaven" (had he lived in our day, he could have written a bestseller). The archangel Michael guides Abraham through the air to the gates of heaven. Abraham and his angelic guide eventually reach a courtroom-type scene, where human beings undergo the first of three judgments (T. Ab. A 11:10–14). In the first, described here, Abel, the son of Adam, functions as judge of the souls passing through judgment. Following this, Michael informs Abraham, they are judged by the twelve tribes of Israel and then finally by God himself (T. Ab. A 13:3–8). Thus, the principle of three witnesses is firmly established (T. Ab. A 13:8).

As the souls are brought forward, two angels sit on the right and the left of Abel, the judge. "The one on the right records righteous deeds, while the one on the left (records) sins" (T. Ab. A 13:9; cf. A 12:12). Their good and evil works are weighed on a balance, and the souls whose sins are more than their righteous deeds are "turned over to the torturers" (A 12:18); those souls with more righteous deeds are saved. Therefore, the normal pattern of salvation and

---

8. See Francoise Mirguet, "Attachment to the Body in the Greek *Testament of Abraham*: A Reappraisal of the Short Recension," *JSP* 19 (2010): 251–75. For more on the manuscript tradition, see also Silviu Bunta, "One Man (φως) in Heaven: Adam-Moses Polemics in the Romanian Versions of *The Testament of Abraham* and Ezekiel the Tragedian's *Exagoge*," *JSP* 16 (2007): 139–65.

9. Unless noted otherwise, translations of the Testament of Abraham are from E. P. Sanders in *OTP* 1:871–902.

10. Dale C. Allison, *Testament of Abraham*, CEJL (Berlin: de Gruyter, 2003), 219.

judgment seems to be based on the congruence of the life of the person to his reward in the afterlife. Yet it is not quite that simple, for there does not seem to be any gradation in the rewards given. In order to pass the test, one only needs to score a 51%. Anything beyond this does not merit extra credit. Therefore, many scholars assume that we find in the Testament of Abraham a simple pattern: righteous behavior makes one worthy of eternal salvation.[11] However, the text does hint at the possibility of a reward that is not entirely congruent.

As Abraham and Michael stood observing the proceedings, one poor soul happened to have an equal number of sins and righteous deeds, so he was left to wait in no-man's land until the last judgment, when God himself would make a final determination (A 14:2). The archangel informed Abraham that if this soul in limbo obtains "one act of righteousness" (μία δικαιοσύνην) beyond its sins it will be saved (A 14:4). In response, "righteous Abraham" intervened and prayed for this person, who needed only one more righteous deed to be saved (A 14:4).

Abraham's response here can be contrasted with his earlier call for sinners to receive immediate retribution; he later asks that those sinners who were consumed by fire, swallowed by the earth, and devoured by wild animals to be granted a second chance (A 14:12–14). This change of heart seems due to a desire that God might allow sinners to amend their ways and attain more righteous than wicked deeds, but it is unclear whether Abraham himself has mercy or a better understanding of the need for judgment on the basis of, to use a familiar phrase, "the whole life lived."[12] In any case, Abraham's request was granted, "because of [God's] exceeding kindness" (δι' ἄκραν ἀγαθότητα).[13]

Abraham's intercession for the soul in limbo is likely rooted in Gen 18, where Abraham intercedes on behalf of Lot in Sodom, making him "an effective and paradigmatic intercessor."[14] He also suggests that the text has a link to the "rabbinic notion of the salvific זכות = 'merit' of Abraham, Isaac, and Jacob."[15] He does not consider what that link is in any detail. In any case, the Testament introduces the possibility of a single act of righteousness tipping the scales of God's grace. This is one of the rare places in biblical and non-biblical Greek literature of this era that speaks of "one act of righteousness." We will consider another below.

---

11. See, for example, Simon Gathercole's discussion of this text alongside of t. Sanh. 13.3 and t. Qidd. 1.14 in *Where is Boasting? Early Jewish Soteriology and Paul's Response in Romans 1–5* (Grand Rapids: Eerdmans, 2002,) 153.

12. N. T. Wright, *Paul: A Biography* (New York: HarperOne, 2018), 57.

13. Sanders' translation in *OTP* is "by my great goodness" (1:891). The word ἄκρον could also mean "extreme end or limit" (BDAG 40), with the result that the phrase means something like "the extreme end of God's kindness." If this were the case, it may imply that the restoration of these sinners marked the furthest extent of God's mercy, so that any further grace would only be congruent grace.

14. Allison, *Testament of Abraham*, 299.

15. Allison, *Testament of Abraham*, 299.

Although the B recension does not include the lengthy tour that the A recension does, it does include a similar picture to what we observed above. After seeing the place where souls are judged (and damned), Michael tells Abraham to search among the souls to look for "even one righteous person" (κἂν μία δικαία; T. Ab. B 9:7). As in the A recension, one person was found whose good works and sins were equal (τὰς ἁμαρτίας ἰσοζυγούσας μετὰ τὰ ἔργα αὐτῆς ἅπαντα; T. Ab. B 9:8). However, in this account the woman is left in limbo, where her works were "neither in labor nor rest, but in a place in between" (καὶ οὐκ ἦσαν ἐν μόχθῳ οὐδὲ ἐν ἀναπαύσει, ἀλλ᾿ ἐν τόπῳ μεσότητος; T. Ab. B 9:8). To the question of whether there are any righteous Gentiles, the Testament seems to answer, "no, not one."

Many assume that the Testament portrays a "lowest-common-denominator universalism of its soteriology," as Sanders describes it.[16] It is true that the Testament initially portrays salvation and damnation as simply dependent on whether one's good works outweigh the bad, even by the slimmest of margins, but this is not exactly the whole picture. In the A recension, the turning point of Abraham's visit to heaven is not the weighing of good and bad deeds with the appropriate sentencing to follow. Rather, the heavenly vision emphasizes Abraham interceding on behalf of this soul who stands between life and death. Thus, Sanders' claim that the document makes "no distinction between Jew and gentile" is not entirely accurate.[17] Abraham, the Israelite *par excellence*, is distinguished quite sharply from those being judged. He himself has not sinned (T. Ab. 10:13). Moreover, the document earlier marked out both Abraham and Sarah as the progenitors of an elect people (see T. Ab. A 8:5–7).[18]

The OT itself sees the patriarchs as a paradigm while not shying away from the moral failures and foibles of Israel's fathers. A prime example would, of course, be the life of Abraham, which includes both significant failure in the incidents with Abimelech (Gen 20:1–16) and the birth of Ishmael (Gen 16) as well as stunning faith on display in the *Akedah* (Gen 22). However, as Annette Reed notes, "In Second Temple Jewish sources, stories about Israel's ancestors are not merely records that chronicle past events. Rather, patriarchs become paradigms."[19] In the Testament, Abraham is not only a paradigm of sinless obedience but, in the A recension, he is also a paradigm for intercession for the nations.[20]

---

16. *OTP* 1:877.

17. *OTP* 1:877.

18. Troy W. Martin, "The TestAbr and the Background of 1 Pet 3,6," *ZNW* 90 (1999): 142–43, notes a particular emphasis on Sarah as the mother of the elect.

19. Reed, "The Construction and Subversion of Patriarchal Perfection," 187.

20. While there is no direct textual evidence for this, a desire to exclude the Gentiles from salvation may explain the omission of Abraham's intercession in the B recension.

Therefore, we might suggest that the Testament presents Abraham as a paradigm or representative for Israel. It creates a pattern in which Israel was to be the means of salvation for the world. While many scholars note that there is no mention of the law or Israel as the souls are brought forward for judgment, it may be that the author(s) considers that the rest of the world was essentially *Gentile* in Abraham's era. Perhaps then the goal of the Testament was not to explain a universalistic model of salvation, but rather to indicate the decisive role that Abraham and Israel would have in the salvation of the world. Because of Abraham's intercession, the "neutral" soul was saved. Thus, while there is a distinction made between Jew and Gentile, Abraham's righteousness or a benefit of his righteous status becomes the means by which the Gentiles are saved.

This is different than the later medieval treasury of merits or the Reformed doctrine of imputation, for it is not an actual transferal of grace from one party to another or even a legal reckoning, but rather an incongruent grace that God chooses to pour out because of the intercession of a congruent recipient. Abraham's righteousness is not actually transferred to another individual, but instead, his righteousness wins him a hearing to intercede on behalf of a soul that teeters on the brink between salvation and damnation. Thus, Abraham's righteousness is the decisive factor for this "neutral" soul to be saved. If this soul represents the "righteous Gentile" and Abraham represents Israel, then the Testament is suggesting that the congruous grace given to Israel becomes the basis for an ever so slightly incongruous gift of grace. While the χάρις word group does not appear in either recension of the Testament of Abraham, we can see the concept here, for this soul receives the gift of salvation from God via Abraham/Israel.

Therefore, the Testament of Abraham is not a "lowest-common-denominator universalism" as Sanders and others suggest.[21] Rather, while recognizing the place of the righteous Gentile, the Testament still envisions Israel's righteousness, personified in the Patriarch Abraham, as the deciding factor in whether these poor souls who stand on the brink of salvation and damnation will be delivered. Thus, Abraham, and then perhaps Israel, becomes the agent through whom God's salvation is extended to the Gentile nations.

Romans

When we put the picture of grace and righteousness from T. Ab. in conversation with Romans, we find some unexpected overlap as well as some significant differences. Firstly, we should note that the genre of Romans is quite different from the Testament of Abraham, so in some ways it is unfair to compare the

---

21. *OTP* 1:876.

two. But this is true with almost any early Jewish document we put in conversation with Paul's letters. Therefore, while the genres are quite different, the reading of the Testament that I propose above may help us better understand the patterns that Paul was working with in interpreting the Abraham story while also distinguishing Paul's view of salvation through the Messiah Jesus.[22]

Romans 4

Regardless of how one interprets Rom 1–3, virtually all interpreters agree that Paul establishes the equality of Jew and Gentile in both salvation and judgment in these chapters. The argument climaxes at the end of Rom 3 with an emphasis on justification for both Jew and Gentile through the Messiah Jesus. As he turns to the Abraham example in chapter 4, we find ourselves in a different genre from the T. Ab., and while we will observe some interesting correspondences, Paul's understanding of God's grace moves in a different and Christological direction. In contrast to the Testament of Abraham, Paul clearly asserts that there is none righteous, not a single one (οὐκ ἔστιν δίκαιος οὐδὲ εἷς; Rom 3:10). Also, unlike Abraham's intervention in the A recension, the decisive figure for the salvation of this "neutral Gentile" is neither Abraham nor Israel.

Like Testament of Abraham, Paul's argument in Rom 4 has the salvation of the Gentiles in view. In both texts, there does not appear to be any hope for Gentiles to acquire salvation in their own power. There, the salvation of a neutral Gentile is dependent on the righteousness of Abraham as the representative of Israel. Here, the salvation of Abraham himself is dependent on his trust in God's promises, which are ultimately fulfilled through the Messiah. Unlike either recension of the T. Ab., in Romans both Jew and Gentile alike are unable to reach even this neutral point, let alone a state of positive righteousness.

I admittedly favor a more "traditional" reading of this chapter, seeing Abraham as the prime example of justification by faith alone apart from works. However, those who see Paul's emphasis as the father of a "covenant family" would likely not disagree with my observations here as well.[23] Regardless of how one understands Paul's argument, he presents Abraham as the paradigm of justification by faith alone. Therefore, we can affirm with Barclay that the "inclusion of Jews and Gentiles, united in faith, is the reflection of the fact that the Abrahamic family, from the beginning, has been created by the grace and

---

22. As Samuel Sandmel, "Philo's Place in Judaism: A Study of Conceptions of Abraham in Jewish Literature, Part I," *HUCA* 25 (1954): 237, observed over six decades ago: "To see what the writer makes of Abraham is often to see most clearly what the writer is trying to say."

23. For example, see N. T. Wright, *Paul and the Faithfulness of God*, COQG 4 (Minneapolis: Fortress, 2013), 849–50.

the calling of God, who has never paid regard to human criteria of capacity or worth. This incongruity between divine action and human status is the unifying theme of Paul's argument."[24]

Paul's point in Rom 4 is in tension with at least some early Jewish portrayals of Abraham, including the one seen above. Abraham, and every other recipient of God's covenant grace, receives an incongruent grace. As Barclay notes, Paul observes that "nothing Abraham did made him worthy of the favor of God."[25] This is admittedly different than the simple caricature of first-century Judaism as a religion of unabashed legalism. Barclay's categories are particularly helpful here, for he helps us to see that the perspective Paul argues against is not an unvarnished legalism but instead the expectation that God's grace is given only to congruent recipients. Nonetheless, whether this grace is "earned" by good works (OPP) or comes natural by means of ethnicity or covenant membership (NPP), the point stands. In contrast to T. Ab., God's grace to Abraham and every other recipient of it is always incongruous. Therefore, Jew and Gentile stand in the same place as unworthy recipients of God's grace.

Here Paul applies the category of a congruent recipient of God's grace in a different direction. This is only hinted at in the Abraham example at its very conclusion in Rom 4:25, as Paul refers to the resurrection of Jesus as the foundation for the justification of his people. In some way, the justification of Jesus in his resurrection belongs to those who are united to him. However, Rom 5:12–19 gives us a fuller picture of this dynamic. Here, Paul describes the Messiah's "one act of righteousness" as the foundation for the justification of all.

While I certainly would not argue for literary dependence in either direction, it is noteworthy that in the T. Ab. the angel told Abraham that the soul in limbo lacked only "one righteousness" (μία δικαιοσύνην; T. Ab. A 14:4). In Rom 5:18, Paul states that "one righteous deed" (ἑνὸς δικαιώματος) leads to justification and life for all. While these are different nuances of δικαιοσύνην, they communicate the same basic idea. In the T. Ab., Abraham's prayer becomes the "one righteousness" lacking to grant the soul in limbo to salvation. In Romans, the Messiah's obedience is far more than the extra push a soul in limbo needs. Rather, the Messiah's righteousness has a far greater efficacy, for it overcomes the judgment of sin that both Jew and Gentile receive and grants them the righteousness necessary for life.

Therefore, through his obedience, Jesus the Messiah becomes the only congruent recipient of God's grace. Romans 5:17 summarizes this dynamic: εἰ γὰρ τῷ τοῦ ἑνὸς παραπτώματι ὁ θάνατος ἐβασίλευσεν διὰ τοῦ ἑνός, πολλῷ μᾶλλον οἱ τὴν περισσείαν τῆς χάριτος καὶ τῆς δωρεᾶς τῆς δικαιοσύνης λαμβάνοντες ἐν ζωῇ βασιλεύσουσιν διὰ τοῦ ἑνὸς Ἰησοῦ Χριστοῦ.

---

24. Barclay, *Paul and the Gift*, 481.
25. Barclay, *Paul and the Gift*, 484.

By his one righteous deed, the Messiah enables human beings to receive the abundance of grace and of the gift of righteousness (τὴν περισσείαν τῆς χάριτος καὶ τῆς δωρεᾶς τῆς δικαιοσύνης). This gift is given to those who are its incongruous recipients through the Messiah (v. 17) who obeyed (v. 19) with the result that those who are united with him receive new life (Rom 6:1–5). Those incongruous recipients of God's gift of grace receive that gift on the basis of their union with the Messiah, who has provided the "one act of righteousness" necessary to overcome the sin that all inherit from Adam and provide "righteousness leading to eternal life (Rom 5:21).

Comparisons

In both the Testament of Abraham and in Romans, as in virtually all first-century Jewish perspectives, Abraham is clearly the fountain head of the covenant people of God. Moreover, in both texts Abraham has the status of "righteous" (T. Ab. A 14:2; Rom 4:1–3). And in both texts Abraham is presented as a paradigm for God's people thereafter. It is there that we can observe the first difference between the texts.

Despite these similarities, there are also a number of differences that help us see the different views of grace in Paul and in the T. Ab. Whereas Abraham's righteous status was granted because of his conduct in the Testament of Abraham, in Romans, Abraham's righteous status is granted because of his faith. Therefore, to return to Barclay's categories, in the Testament of Abraham, Abraham is the paradigm of the recipient of a congruous grace. In Romans, both Abraham and David are paradigmatic examples of incongruous grace (i.e., being justified by faith).

Building on these observations, Abraham's role as the recipient of congruous grace in T. Ab. may then position him as the foundation for the salvation of "neutral Gentiles." If he is paradigmatic of Israel, then the author may be assigning Israel a similar role. That is to say, as Abraham is to the neutral soul, so Israel is to the neutral Gentiles. This would then provide an apologetic for early Jewish acceptance of "virtuous pagans." Paul, on the other hand, will allow no such possibility. Abraham receives incongruous grace that is grounded in the congruous grace that is given to the Messiah, which then becomes the paradigm for all who will be justified, Jew and Gentile alike.

Thus, the difference between God's grace and Israel's righteousness in Romans and the T. Ab. is that the latter assumes Abraham (and Israel) to receive congruous grace while the latter assumes that any grace any sinner receives, from Abraham to David until the present, is always incongruous grace. While it would be a stretch to claim that the Testament of Abraham presents Abraham as a model of a sort of "sinless perfection," it does present him as the paradigmatic recipient of God's congruous grace, given to him and all of his descendants who follow in his pattern of faithfulness. Moreover, this grace is somehow able to benefit others. In Romans, the grace given to the Messiah Jesus is also congruent and able to benefit others. Abraham's congruous grace in T. Ab. benefits the nations; Jesus' congruous grace in Romans is foundation for justification.

In both T. Ab. and in Romans, it is assumed that a righteous representative can perform "one act of righteousness" which then becomes the basis for or the impetus of the salvation of another. That is, when a recipient of God's congruous grace chooses to intercede on behalf of an individual who lacks this congruity, God, on behalf of the congruent recipient, extends his grace in salvation to the one who lacks it. In T. Ab., Abraham himself is the recipient of this grace, which may create a paradigm by which Israel is the congruent recipient of God's grace who then, through "one act of righteousness," extends salvation to the Gentile nations. We might say that Paul's conception of Israel's role in salvation is somewhat similar; however, rather than Abraham or the Israel receiving congruent grace that becomes the basis for the salvation of neutral Gentiles, the Messiah Jesus, who is the corporate representative of Israel, through his "one act of righteousness," extends God's saving grace not just to neutral Gentiles, but instead to sinful and undeserving Jews and Gentiles alike.

Finally, based on the observations we've made here, I am suggesting a seventh perfection of God's grace: transference. Note that it is not the righteousness itself that is transferred, but rather the gift or grace of God on the basis of another's righteousness. This perfection, therefore, while not identical to the Reformational doctrine of imputation, may then lay a historical and exegetical foundation for this important theological concept. As John Calvin wrote in his exposition of Abraham's life in Genesis, "faith borrows a righteousness elsewhere, of which we, in ourselves are destitute."[26] While this could, to a limited degree, describe the neutral soul in T. Ab., it fits quite well with Paul's conception of God's grace and the righteousness of all human beings in Romans.

Bibliography

Allison, Dale C. *Testament of Abraham*. CEJL. Berlin: de Gruyter, 2003.

Barclay, John M. G. *Paul and the Gift*. Grand Rapids: Eerdmans, 2015.

Bunta, Silviu. "One Man (φως) in Heaven: Adam-Moses Polemics in the Romanian Versions of *The Testament of Abraham* and Ezekiel the Tragedian's *Exagoge*." *JSP* 16 (2007): 139–65.

Calvin, John. *Calvin's Commentaries: Commentary on the Book of Genesis*. Grand Rapids: Eerdmans, 1989.

---

26. John Calvin, *Calvin's Commentaries: Commentary on the Book of Genesis* (Grand Rapids: Eerdmans, 1989), 407.

Dochhorn, Jan. "Zur Krise der Gerechtigkeit im frühen Judentum. Reflexionen über das Entstehungsmilieu des frühen Christentums." *BN* 155 (2012): 77–111.

Gathercole, Simon. *Where is Boasting? Early Jewish Soteriology and Paul's Response in Romans 1–5.* Grand Rapids: Eerdmans, 2002.

James, Montague Rhodes. *The Testament of Abraham: The Greek Text Now First Edited with an Introduction and Notes.* TS 2/2. Cambridge: Cambridge University Press, 1892.

Martin, Troy W. "The TestAbr and the Background of 1 Pet 3,6." *ZNW* 90 (1999): 139–46.

Mirguet, Francoise. "Attachment to the Body in the Greek *Testament of Abraham*: A Reappraisal of the Short Recension." *JSP* 19 (2010): 251–75.

Moo, Douglas J. "John Barclay's *Paul and the Gift* and the New Perspective on Paul." *Themelios* 41.2 (2016): 279–88.

Reed, Annette Yoshiko. "The Construction and Subversion of Patriarchal Perfection: Abraham and Exemplarity in Philo, Josephus, and the *Testament of Abraham*." *JSJ* 40 (2009): 185–212.

Sanders, E. P. "Testament of Abraham (First to Second Century A.D.): A New Translation and Introduction." Pages 871–902 in vol. 1 of *The Old Testament Pseudepigrapha.* Edited by James H. Charlesworth. New York: Doubleday, 1983.

Sandmel, Samuel. "Philo's Place in Judaism: A Study of Conceptions of Abraham in Jewish Literature, Part I." *HUCA* 25 (1954): 209–37.

Wright, N. T. *Paul: A Biography.* New York: HarperOne, 2018.

———. *Paul and the Faithfulness of God.* COQG 4. Minneapolis: Fortress, 2013.

PART TWO

Adam, Abraham, and Jesus Messiah (ETS 2019)

CHAPTER 7

The Revelation of God's Saving Righteousness (Romans 3:21–31)

Brian S. Rosner

Introduction

Romans 3:21–31 is among the most studied passages in Paul's letters, if not in all of ancient literature. It is not so much a minefield that awaits the naïve interpreter, as a series of Tolkienesque bottomless pits in which menacing Balrogs lurk with fiery whips of many thongs at the ready. The mines of Moria in Rom 3:21–31 in which many interpreters have plunged include: the meaning of *dikaiosynē theou*, "the righteousness of God;" *hilastērion*, propitiation, expiation, the place of atonement, the mercy seat, etc.; *pistis Christou*, "the faith of Christ;" *pistis* itself, faith or allegiance; *erga nomou*, the works of the law; and *dikaioō*, justification. Multiple journal articles and monographs are devoted to these terms and phrases.

Given the complexities, this essay will not rehearse the history of interpretation of Rom 3:21–31, nor canvass and sort through every exegetical position. Instead, it aims to present a fresh and succinct exegesis, majoring on the contribution of 3:21–31 to the argument of Romans, which is where most gain is to be made in terms of a theology of Romans and the most accurate interpretation of 3:21–31 is found. Indeed, almost all interpreters agree that Romans has a sustained argument from beginning to end (or perhaps, end to beginning[1]). Driving our investigation is the question: What does 3:21–31 contribute to Romans and vice versa?

The first task is to delimit the passage. Specifically, why Rom 3:21–31 and not just vv. 21–26, a paragraph which many commentators treat on its own? However, if vv. 21 and 26 offer an inclusio with "righteousness" language, vv. 21 and 31 exhibit an inclusio with references to "the law." Furthermore, the questions of vv. 27–31 unpack some of the implications of the revelation of the saving righteousness of God in vv. 21–26, linking the two directly. The two paragraphs belong together and to treat them separately can skew the meaning of both.

Reading Rom 3:21–26 with vv. 27–31 highlights the importance of the law and Judaism in the whole unit, opening and closing as it does with references to the law. And it helps address a big interpretive issue related to Paul and Ju-

---

1. Cf. Scot McKnight, *Reading Romans Backwards: A Gospel of Peace in the Midst of Empire* (Waco, TX: Baylor University Press, 2019). See below on the purpose of Romans.

daism, namely the New Perspective. In broad terms, if the New Perspective on Paul insists on a horizontal meaning of justification (Gentiles becoming part of the people of God), and Reformed thinking sees justification primarily in vertical terms (a new legal status before God), Rom 3:21–31 has both elements.[2]

There is a horizontal dimension to justification, as 3:27–31 indicates: God is the God of both Jews and Gentiles. However, the horizontal does not negate the vertical. The blessing of justification is a new righteous status before God, as well as becoming part of a new people of God.[3] Romans 4 makes it clear that justification by grace also refers to the more general notion of God's generous kindness to the underserving (4:4: "Now to the one who works, wages are not credited as a gift but as an obligation"; cf. Eph 2:8–9; 2 Tim 1:9).[4] Romans 4 also has both aspects of grace, undeserved favour and Jews and Gentiles in the new family of God.

As it turns out, the horizontal in Rom 3:21–31 is not entirely postponed to vv. 27–31. In the context of Rom 1:18–3:20, the "all" who have sinned in Rom 3:23 and are justified by grace in v. 24 are both Jews and Gentiles. When Paul thinks of the grace of God given to someone, he often has in mind his apostolic ministry to Gentiles, as for example in Rom 12:3 and 15:15–21 (cf. Gal 2:9; 1 Cor 3:10; 2 Cor 6:1). Paul also uses "grace" to characterize himself as the preacher of a universal gospel, available to both Jews and Gentiles, in Rom 1:5 and 15:15 (cf. Gal 1:15–24; 2:7–9). The epitome of grace for Paul, God's ill-deserved favor, was the admission of Gentiles, people without God and without hope, including some Roman Christians, to the glorious privileges which had been exclusive to Israel.

A final preliminary matter requires our attention before expounding the passage in more detail. How does Rom 3:21–31 fit with the occasion and purpose of Romans? Douglas Moo points out, with reference to the key figures, that the history of the discussion of the theme of Romans, from which treatments of the purpose have in part arisen, can be seen "as a movement from a focus on the beginning of the epistle to its end."[5] The Reformers saw the center of the letter as chs. 1–4 with its focus on justification by grace through faith. Albert Schweitzer famously dismissed this emphasis as a mere battle doctrine (*Kampflehre*) and took chs. 5–8 and union with Christ and the work of the Spirit as the center of the letter. The next move, following Krister Stendahl, was to regard the incorporation of Gentiles into the people of God in chs. 9–11 as

---

2. The two halves of Eph 2 similarly expound the vertical and horizontal dimensions of salvation. If the early proponents of the New Perspective neglected Rom 4 and Phil 3 in their treatment of justification, Reformed exegesis has long focused on Rom 3:21–26 to the neglect of 3:27–31.

3. Cf. Michael F. Bird, "Progressive Reformed View," in *Justification: Five Views*, ed. James K. Beilby and Paul Rhodes Eddy (Downers Grove, IL: IVP Academic, 2011), 131–75.

4. Cf. I. Howard Marshall, "Salvation, Grace and Works in the Later Writings in the Pauline Corpus," *NTS* 42 (1996): 339–58.

5. Douglas J. Moo, *The Letter to the Romans*, 2nd ed., NICNT (Grand Rapids: Eerdmans, 2018), 21.

Paul's real interest. Finally, in the last thirty years most scholars have emphasized Romans as an occasional letter written in response to a split in the church
in Rome between Jewish and Gentile believers. Fittingly, Scot McKnight's recent book argues that "to read Romans well, we need *to read it backwards.*"[6]

The debates surrounding the reasons for Romans are of course too extensive
to consider here. In broad terms there are proponents of three purposes and
combinations thereof: theological, expounding Paul's gospel; missional, enlisting
support for Paul's proposed mission to Spain; and pastoral, healing divisions in
the church in Rome, which was divided roughly along Jewish and Gentile lines.

Scot McKnight's understanding of Rom 3:21–26 prioritizes the pastoral
purpose and follows it to its logical conclusion by reading our passage in light
of Rom 14 and 15. McKnight treats this section in light of the "weak" versus
"strong" dichotomy and concludes that Rom 3:21–26 is about destroying the
privilege of both and insisting that both are sinners and need redemption, thus
paving the way for Paul's healing of the divisions.[7]

However, to my mind, the epistolary frame of Romans in chs. 1 and 15–16
(1:9, 15–16; 15:15–21; 16:25) supplies the most explicit indications of Paul's purpose in writing and supports a missional purpose, which leads to a theological
one, the exposition of Paul's gospel. Each major section of Romans, including
chs. 14 and 15, coheres well with a missionary purpose and does not require a
concrete historical problem in Rome to account for it. Arguably, Paul deals with
hypothetical opponents throughout the letter using the style of diatribe, including chs. 14 and 15. Hence, I favor reading Rom 14 and 15 in light of Rom 3 instead
of the other way around, reading Romans forwards rather than backwards, if
you like. Doubtless, Paul's gospel has social implications for the church, just as
it has implications for dealing with persecution and government in Rom 12 and
13. However, such concerns are not the primary reason for Romans.

The Revelation of God's Saving Righteousness
Through Faith (3:21–31)

Marcus Mininger maintains that "the main point [of Romans 3:21–26] … is
in the strong, opening affirmation that God's righteousness has now been revealed (v. 21), which is reiterated in verses 22, 25 and 26."[8] Arguably, the same

---

6. McKnight, *Reading Romans Backwards*, 179.

7. McKnight, *Reading Romans Backwards,* 121: Paul "destroys the 'privilege' of both:
the weak are sinners, and the strong are sinners; both need redemption; that redemption will not come from Torah observance, and status in the church does not come
by way of Torah observance or Torah non-observance; and it does come from God's
gift – Christ on the cross, who secures atonement for all who believe, Jew or Greek."

8. Marcus A. Mininger, *Uncovering the Theme of Revelation in Romans 1:16–3:26,*
WUNT 2.445 (Tübingen: Mohr Siebeck, 2017), 357.

theme extends through to the end of ch. 3. The following exegesis of 3:21–31 underscores what each of the six subdivisions highlights about the revelation of God's saving righteousness.[9]

The Revelation of God's Saving Righteousness was

1. Manifested in the new age (21–22b)

Paul writes in Rom 3:21: "But now the righteousness of God has been manifested apart from the law, although the Law and the Prophets bear witness to it." As Cranfield notes, this "attestation of the gospel by the OT is of fundamental importance for Paul [which] is indicated by the solemn way in which he insists on it here in what is one of the great hinge sentences on which the argument of the epistle turns."[10] Indeed, along with its tone and placement, we may note the uncommon language it uses as underlining its significance; Paul nowhere else in his letters uses the phrase, "the Law and the Prophets," and this is the only time Paul uses the verb, *martyreō*, in reference to the witness of Scripture.[11]

Romans 3:21 sets up a contrast between the failure of the law of Moses to save and the testimony of the Law along with the Prophets to God's saving action in Christ. Many commentators take "apart from law" to mean, "apart from doing the law."[12] But, while it is true theologically that we are saved not by works, and Paul affirms this elsewhere, the point here seems to be something more than just this. Here it is not that righteousness is "received apart from law," but righteousness is "disclosed apart from law." Paul's "but now" signals a new stage of salvation history. As Moo puts it:

> In the new era inaugurated by Christ's death God has acted to deliver and vindicate his people "apart from" the law. It is not primarily the law as something for humans to do, but the law as a system, as a stage in God's unfolding plan, that is in view here. "Law" (*nomos*), then, refers to the Mosaic covenant, that (temporary) administration set up between God and his people to regulate their lives and reveal their sin until the establishment of the promise in Christ.[13]

---

9. The outline is adapted from John D. Harvey, *Romans*, EGGNT (Nashville: B&H Academic, 2017), 100–104.

10. C. E. B. Cranfield, *A Critical and Exegetical Commentary on the Epistle to the Romans*, 2 vols., ICC (Edinburgh: T&T Clark, 1975–79), 1:203.

11. The imagery of the law court, in the background of 1:18–3:18 and to the fore in 3:19–20, explains the use of "testimony" language, *martyreō*; the law and the prophets are summoned as witnesses to "the righteousness of God through faith in Jesus Christ for all who believe." Cf. James D. G. Dunn, *Romans 1–8*, WBC 38A (Dallas: Word, 1988), 165.

12. E.g., Calvin, Cranfield, and Murray.

13. Moo, *Romans*, 242.

In Rom 3:21 *nomos* has the same referent in both sides of the contrast. The righteousness of God has been disclosed apart from the law *as law-covenant*, but it is testified to by the Law (and the Prophets) *as prophecy*, a view I explain and defend elsewhere.[14] With this shift in salvation history, the law does not cease to be relevant. Rather, its function changes; even if the law-covenant did not disclose the saving righteousness of God, it does (along with the Prophets) bear witness to it. The same point is made in verse 31, where Paul insists that the saving righteousness of God upholds the law as prophecy of the gospel.

The contrast is between Rom 1:18–3:20 and 3:21–26 and a shift from the old era to the new era. But it is important to understand the nature of the temporal shift. It is not that we move from the wrath of God to the righteousness of God; Paul affirms that the old era displayed God's forbearance (3:26). Rather, as D. A. Carson puts it,

> the law-covenant could not effect righteousness or ensure that anyone be declared righteous . . . under the new era what is needed is righteousness that is manifested apart from the law. . . . According to Paul God gave the law not only to regulate the conduct of his people and to reveal their sin until the fulfillment of the promises in Christ. He also gave it because the law has *a prophetic function*, a witness function: it pointed in the right direction; it bore witness to the righteousness that is now being revealed.[15]

Paul in fact points to prophetic function of Jewish Scriptures at the very beginning and end of Romans, using the noun "prophets" and the adjective "prophetic" respectively. In Rom 1:2 the gospel of God was promised beforehand through his prophets (*dia tōn prophētōn*) in the holy Scriptures, which includes the Law. And in Rom 16:25–26 the revelation of the mystery, which is the gospel about Jesus Christ, is disclosed through the prophetic Scriptures (*graphōn prophētikōn*). Paul cites the Jewish Bible on four occasions in Romans using the title "Scripture"; significantly, two of the texts are from the Law and two are from the Prophets.

---

14. Brian S. Rosner, *Paul and the Law: Keeping the Commandments of God*, NSBT 31 (Downers Grove, IL: IVP Academic, 2013).

15. D. A. Carson, "Atonement in Romans 3:21–26" in *The Glory of the Atonement: Biblical, Historical, and Practical Perspectives: Essays in Honor of Roger R. Nicole*, ed. Charles E. Hill and Frank A. James III (Downers Grove, IL: IVP Academic, 2004), 122–23 (emphasis mine). Cf. Douglas A. Campbell, *The Rhetoric of Righteousness in Romans 3.21-26*, JSNTSup 65 (London: Bloomsbury, 1992), 180–81: "Paul's statements [in Rom 3:21–22a] amount to a deliberate contrast between different function of the same body of writings—a contrast made possible by wordplay on the signifier νόμος. As part of a soteriological condition or response, the Torah now seems defunct for Paul, but as an inspired and authoritative testimony to the acts of God, the writings still serve their appointed function."

The question of the law raises the issue of the relationship of Paul and his gospel to Judaism. In defining first-century Judaism, scholars sometimes refer to the pillars of Judaism, its core or defining beliefs or symbols. The three that are mentioned most often are Israel's election, the law of Moses, and the Temple. (The land and the Shema are also sometimes thrown into the mix.) The charge brought against Paul in Acts 21 by Jews in Jerusalem mentions these very three: according to his opponents, Paul was teaching against "our people, our law and this place [i.e., the Jewish Temple]" (Acts 21:28). How does Paul deal with the pillars of Judaism?

A pattern of rejection and re-appropriation emerges in Romans for all three, not least in Rom 3:21–31. The law here, rejected as law-covenant and re-appropriated as prophecy of the gospel. Paul opposed the law of Moses as not bringing life, but death, and insisted that believers in Christ are not under the law. In Romans Paul rejects *the law* as law-covenant and legal code, but also re-appropriates it as prophecy of the gospel and elsewhere as wisdom for living.[16] The same pattern emerges, I will argue, for election in Rom 3:23–24 and 29–30, and the temple in v. 26. With respect to the pillars of Judaism, in Romans Paul reconfigured them rather than just abandoned them.

But back in Rom 3:21, what exactly is the righteousness of God to which the Law and the Prophets testify? Is *dikaiosyne theou* an activity of God, an attribute of God or a status given to believers? In terms of usage of the phrase in the LXX, it is significant that God's righteousness and God's salvation often appear in poetic parallelism in Psalms and Isaiah (e.g., LXX Pss 39:11; 50:16; 70:15; 97:2; 118:123; Isa 33:6; 46:13; 51:5–6, 8; 62:1; 63:1). But more specifically, as Moo (see ch. 2 of the present volume) argues, in a few places in the LXX speak of the eschatological revelation of God's righteousness and seem to be referring to God acting righteously to save his people; for example, Ps 98:2: "The LORD has made his salvation known and revealed his righteousness to the nations" (cf. Isa 51:5–8).

Michael Bird combines activity and attribute, arguing that "God's righteousness is chiefly a way of designating his saving action as it is expressed in his feats of deliverance for his people. The righteousness of God then is the character of God embodied and enacted in his saving works."[17] On the other hand, the context of justification cautions against entirely ruling out the new righteous status of believers as at least part of the meaning of the phrase in Rom 3. Perhaps Peter Stuhlmacher is right that Paul includes "both poles of the event of justification . . . The gracious activity of God himself and

---

16. Rosner, *Paul and the Law*, passim.

17. Michael F. Bird, *The Saving Righteousness of God: Studies on Paul, Justification and the New Perspective* (Milton Keynes: Paternoster, 2006), 111.

the end result of the divine work in the form of the righteousness granted to the sinner."[18]

In Rom 3:22 this saving righteousness of God comes διὰ πίστεως Ἰησοῦ Χριστοῦ. The big question here of course is whether *pistis Christou* refers to faith in Christ or the faithfulness of Christ (see NRSV and CEB among English versions), an objective or a subjective genitive. Perhaps it is a deliberately ambiguous phrase, as Francis Watson argues, "pointing open-endedly, to the faith that pertains to God's saving action in Christ – originating it, participating in it, and oriented towards it."[19] The arguments are ongoing.

Paul's unambiguously uses *pistis* and *pisteuō* in contexts of salvation, both here in Romans and elsewhere, to refer to human belief and trust. The question is then is whether the ambiguous one, *pistis Christou,* is meant to reinforce these or supplement them with a reference to Christ's faithfulness. Teresa Morgan's important study of *Roman Faith and Christian Faith* argues that when πίστις refers to people it should not be thought of the semantic domain of interpersonal relationships (often or typically asymmetrical interpersonal relationships), where it refers to "a nexus of faithfulness, trustworthiness, and trust which runs in all directions."[20] However, Roy Ciampa notes that in the LXX and NT it is common to describe love on God's side and faith on the side of humans in the reciprocal relationship.[21] We see this pattern in Gal 2:20, where Paul says he now lives by faith in the Son of God (ἐν πίστει ζῶ τῇ τοῦ υἱοῦ τοῦ θεοῦ), who loved him and gave himself up for him (τοῦ ἀγαπήσαντός με καὶ παραδόντος ἑαυτὸν ὑπὲρ ἐμοῦ).[22] Hence, on balance I favor taking *pistis Christou* as an objective genitive in Rom 3:22.

Either way, little is at stake theologically, for Paul underscores the critical part played by the obedience of Christ to our salvation in Rom 5:12–21 and Phil 2:5–11 and the need for faith in Christ is common in Paul, not least in the following words in Rom 3:22. The argument that the following reference to human faith makes the objective genitive interpretation of *pistis*

---

18. Peter Stuhlmacher, "The Theme of Romans," in *The Romans Debate*, ed. Karl P. Donfried, rev. ed. (Peabody, MA: Hendrickson, 1991), 339.

19. Francis Watson, *Paul, Judaism and the Gentiles: Beyond the New Perspective* (Grand Rapids: Eerdmans, 2007), 255.

20. Teresa Morgan, *Roman Faith and Christian Faith: Pistis and Fides in the Early Roman Empire and Early Churches* (Oxford: Oxford University Press, 2015), 281.

21. See, e.g., Deut 7:9; Pss. Sol. 14:1; John 3:16; 1 Cor 4:17; Gal 2:20; 5:6; Eph 1:15; 3:17; 6:21; Col 1:4, 7; 4:7, 9; 1 Thess 3:6; 2 Thess 1:3; 1 Tim 1:14; 6:2; 2 Tim 1:13; 2:22; Titus 2:2; Phlm 5; James 2:5; 1 Pet 1:8; 1 John 3:23; 4:16; 5:1; 3 John 5; Jude 20; Rev 1:5; 2:19. Cf. 1 Macc 7:8; 3 Macc 3:10; 5:44; Sir 6:14–16; 27:16–17; John 16:27; Tit 3:15; James 2:23.

22. See the discussion of Gal 2:20 in Roy E. Ciampa, *The Presence and Function of Scripture in Galatians 1 and 2*, WUNT 2.102 (Tübingen: Mohr Siebeck, 1998), 210–12, where it is argued that there Paul may be playing with the possibilities of both a messianic and an ecclesiocentric interpretation of Hab 2:4.

Christou redundant can cut both ways; one person's redundancy is another person's emphasis.

The Revelation of God's Saving Righteousness is

2. Available to all (22c–24)

Paul goes on to say that the saving righteousness of God is to the advantage (εἰς + the accusative) of all who exercise faith in Christ. As mentioned earlier, the "all" in context here is both believing Jews and believing Gentiles; there is no διαστολὴ, no distinction or difference. The only other place in Romans where this term occurs, in 10:12, is a virtual commentary on its use here: "For there is no difference between Jew and Gentile—the same Lord is Lord of all and richly blesses all who call on him."

Here in vv. 23–24 and in vv. 29–30 we catch a glimpse of Paul repudiating and re-purposing the second pillar of Judaism, namely, election. With respect to the election of Israel, in Romans Paul opposes the notion that the Jews, Abraham's sons, constitute the people of God: "For not all who are descended from Israel are Israel" (Rom 9:6). In its place Paul identifies believers in Christ as the new people of God, whom he describes in Romans as the elect (8:33); called (1:6–7; 8:28, 30; 9:7, 12, 24–28); beloved (1:7; 9:25), saints (1:7), beloved children of Abraham (4:11–12,16–17), and the true circumcision (2:28–29), all designations that one would expect a Jew to apply strictly to Jews.

Paul's explanation for God's impartiality (note the explanatory γάρ) is given in 3:23 in terms of the universality of human sin. It recalls Paul's argument in 1:18–3:20 and the concluding verdict in 3:9 that "Jews and Gentiles alike are all under sin."

The consequence of human sin, taking the connective καὶ in the sense of "and so,"[23] are that human beings "lack"[24] τῆς δόξης τοῦ θεοῦ, probably a reference to the glory Adam lost when he transgressed in the Garden, which applies to all people, since all according to Rom 5 were in Adam when he fell. The next reference in Romans to "the glory of God" is in 5:2 (cf. 8:30: "those he justified, he also glorified"), indicating that the blessings of salvation include a joyous restoration of that glory.

Paul goes on in 3:24 to describe those who exercise faith in Christ and benefit from the saving righteousness of God; δικαιούμενοι is an adjectival participle modifying πάντες in v. 23. Using the terms δωρεάν and χάρις Paul indicates that the saving righteousness of God has the character of a gift. More

---

23. Harvey, *Romans*, 92.
24. BDAG s.v. ὑστερέω 2 (1043).

controversially, Paul describes the salvation that God's saving righteousness brings is described in terms of justification, a term repeated in 26 and 28, and redemption, drawing on lawcourt and slave market imagery respectively.

Both usage in the LXX and Paul's letters and context in Romans points to justification as a forensic term meaning God's declaration in the present of a verdict of acquittal and forgiveness, effectively a declaration of righteousness. In the LXX, God commands judges in Israel to uphold justice and not to "acquit," δικαιόω, the "ungodly," ἀσεβής (Exod 23:7 and Isa 5:22–23). The fact that the verbs to justify and to condemn are frequently set in opposition to each other in the LXX (e.g., Deut 25:1; cf. Prov 17:15), a contrast that also appears in Rom 8:33–34, is worth noting.

The agency (διὰ + the genitive) through which justification is made possible is redemption, ἀπολύτρωσις. The notion of redemption is common in Paul and is associated with the forgiveness of sins, release from captivity and the payment of a ransom in various contexts. While committing the fallacy of totality transfer is to be avoided, there are good grounds to take redemption in the broadest sense in Rom 3:24. The Old Testament background has both freedom from slavery and the payment of a price in view and this fits well in the context of Rom 3:23–24. As Schreiner notes: "The contrast between "freely" and the redemption provided by God suggest that the latter includes the idea of a price being paid."[25] Additionally, sacrificial overtones are present in the terms *hilastērion* and "blood" in v. 26.

The redemption takes place "in Christ Jesus," pointing either to its location, spatially, or its source,[26] or best, as Campbell argues, in association with Christ Jesus.[27] All three are true elsewhere according to Paul. As it often the case in exegesis of Rom 3:21–26, the question is not whether Paul says something, but rather whether that is what he says here.

The Revelation of God's Saving Righteousness is

3. Displayed in the death of Jesus Christ (25–26)

In Rom 3:25–26 an extended relative clause "describes the details of how God is able to declare sinners righteous without violating his own righteousness."[28] Taking it bit by bit, first, God publicly displayed Christ as a ἱλαστήριον, that

---

25. Schreiner, *Romans,* 198.

26. Richard N. Longenecker, *The Epistle to the Romans: A Commentary on the Greek Text,* NIGTC (Grand Rapids: Eerdmans, 2016), 424.

27. Constantine R. Campbell, *Paul and Union with Christ: An Exegetical and Theological Study* (Grand Rapids: Zondervan Academic, 2012), 74.

28. Harvey, *Romans,* 93.

is, as a propitiation, or expiation, or sacrifice of atonement, or place of atonement, or mercy seat. The meaning of ἱλαστήριον in Rom 3:25 has generated a great deal of discussion. Along with the question of the meaning of ἱλαστήριον, there is the question of whether the phrase "in his blood" modifies it or is the object of "faith." On that question, while word order might be thought to favor the latter, the cultic associations of blood suggest that it was by his blood that Jesus became the ἱλαστήριον.

As to the meaning of ἱλαστήριον, the tide is turning in favor of "mercy seat" or "place of atonement," and that is my understanding. Stephen Hultgren's two *JTS* articles, building in part on Dan Bailey's work, lay out the evidence convincingly. He argues that:

> Biblical "atonement" is multifaceted, comprehending expiation and forgiveness, as well as removal of divine wrath. In the LXX the ἱλάσκομαι word group is also complex, retaining propitiatory overtones from classical usage (although it is often better to speak of God removing his own wrath), while taking on the additional meaning of expiation and forgiveness. The Pentateuchal ἱλαστήριον is a "place" for such "atonement." Amidst many proposals, "the place of atonement" with allusion to the כַּפֹּרֶת remains the most likely meaning for ἱλαστήριον in Rom. 3:25. Christ is the "place" where divine justice and mercy meet. His death is the visible manifestation of divine justice, the consequence of humanity's collective sin, which was "building up" towards a permanent breach in the relationship between God and humanity. Christ's death is also a ransom and the means by which God objectively removes sin and so frees humanity from death."[29]

My only quibble is that whereas Hultgren marginally favors "place of atonement" over "mercy seat" as the best English translation, I prefer "mercy seat," which is the most frequent meaning of ἱλαστήριον in the LXX, where it takes that meaning in as many as 21 of 26 occurrences.[30]

Sadly, most of the proposals for translating ἱλαστήριον are obscure in English. "Propitiation" and "expiation" are not modern English, "atonement" is a good novel, but also not in common usage. "Mercy seat" has the benefit of an established use in the OT and is used in Heb 9:5, with the NIV an outlier, rendering the word in Rom 3:25 and elsewhere as "atonement cover."

The mercy seat interpretation connects directly to the temple theme in Romans and thereby the third pillar of Judaism. Although Paul never explicitly rejects the Jewish Temple and its priesthood and sacrifices, he implies as much

---

29. Stephen Hultgren, "*Hilastērion* (Rom 3:25) and the Union of Divine Justice and Mercy. Part II: Atonement in the Old Testament and in Romans 1–5," *JTS* 70.2 (2019): 546.

30. Harvey, *Romans,* 93.

in his use of cultic imagery to refer to the work of Christ. With respect to the temple in Romans Paul identifies Christ as the mercy seat (3:21–26), calls on believers to offer their bodies as living sacrifices with cultic terminology in 12:1–2, and Paul characterizes his mission in terms of "priestly service" in 15:17, but not, it must be said, in the Jerusalem Temple. Once again, we observe a pattern of rejection, though in this case implicit, and elaborate reappropriation of a central symbol of Judaism.

The purpose (εἰς + the accusative) of God displaying Jesus as the mercy seat by his blood is to demonstrate his righteousness. How does it do this? God's righteous character might have been called into question since he had passed over sins prior to the sacrifice of Christ without punishing them. But the death of Christ vindicates God's righteous character in the present era "showing that the forgiveness granted did not compromise his justice"[31]; thus God remains righteous when declaring righteous those who believe in Jesus.

A possible weakness with this interpretation of 3:25b-26 is that the demonstration of God's righteousness here is his judging righteousness rather than his saving righteousness. However, δικαιοσύνη θεοῦ appears in Rom 3:5 as God's judging righteousness and the cognate term, δικαιοκρισία, in Rom 2:5 refers to God's "just verdict" in punishing sinners.[32] And as Schreiner points out, "the presence of δίκαιον [in 3:26] indicates that God's righteousness can't be confined to his saving righteousness."[33] In other words, not only God's saving righteousness but also his judging righteousness are displayed in the death of Christ.

The Revelation of God's Saving Righteousness

1. Excludes boasting (27–28)

Paul's exposition of the saving righteousness of God in 3:21–26 as manifested in the new age, available to all without distinction, and displayed in the death of Christ raises questions concerning the role of the law of Moses, something he mentioned back in v. 21. The revelation of the saving righteousness of God has implications (οὖν) for the role of the law. In short, Rom 3:27–31 picks up on the critical nature of faith in the justification of both Jews and Gentiles, a theme introduced in 3:22, 26. Paul makes three points in 3:27–31 (in vv. 27–28, 29–30, and 31). Once again, taking full account of this passage's contribution to the ongoing argument of Romans is key to its interpretation.

---

31. Schreiner, *Romans*, 204.
32. BDAG s.v. δικαιοκρισία (246).
33. Schreiner, *Romans*, 206.

First, in vv. 27–28 the revelation of God's saving righteousness excludes boasting. It does this in two ways, through the law of faith in v. 27 and because God justifies people by faith apart from works in v. 28.

In v. 27 boasting is excluded not by a ποίου νόμου but by a νόμου πίστεως. Some interpreters understand "the law of faith" and "the law of works" as two different ways of using the law of Moses. Understood in terms of works, the law leads to boasting; understood in terms of faith, it does not.[34] However, as Moo argues, at this point in Romans Paul has made the law and faith mutually exclusive; 3:21–26 and 3:28 are what lead Paul to ask in 3:31, "do we then nullify the law through faith?" "This question does not make sense unless Paul has, in this context, separated "faith" from the law of Moses."[35] Indeed, the distinction between doing and believing, with the former aligned with the law, is maintained throughout Romans (see 2:25–29; 3:2; 4:2–8; 9:31–10:8).

It is better to understand Paul contrasting two different "laws" in Rom 3:27. The referent to "law of works," as Moo puts it, "would naturally bring to mind *the* law, the torah."[36] Paul has forged such a link between the law and works in Romans (see 2:6–16, 25–27; 3:20) that the connection may be assumed. Thus, with the contrast between "the law of faith" and "the law of works" Paul asserts that "the characteristic demand of the Mosaic covenant—works—is contrasted with the basic demand of the New Covenant—faith."[37] The "law of faith," as Thielman suggests, may even refer to the new covenant.[38]

Similar expressions to "law of works" and "law of faith" are found in Rom 8:1–2:

> There is therefore now no condemnation for those who are in Christ Jesus. *For the law of the Spirit of life in Christ Jesus (ho gar nomos tou pneumatos tēs zōēs en Christō Iēsou)* has set you free from the law of sin and of death.

As Schreiner puts it, "it is hard to conceive of Paul that the law in conjunction with the Spirit frees people from sin, since elsewhere Paul emphasizes that those who are 'under the law' are under sin."[39] The law promised life but proved to be death (7:10). It is better to take "the law of the Spirit of life" in contrast to "the law of sin and death."

---

34. See Moo, *Romans*, 268n834, for a list of proponents, including Cranfield, Wright, and Dunn.

35. Moo, *Romans*, 269.

36. Moo, *Romans*, 270.

37. Moo, *Romans*, 270.

38. Frank Thielman, *Paul and the Law: A Contextual Approach* (Downers Grove, IL: InterVarsity Press, 1994), 183.

39. Thomas R. Schreiner, *40 Questions about Christians and the Biblical Law* (Grand Rapids: Kregel, 2010), 22.

A second reason boasting is excluded is in v. 28: "a person is declared righteous by faith apart from the works of the law," repeating a point Paul made in 3:20. Jumping over another mine in Moria, I take *erga nomou* to be Paul's shorthand for "doing what the law requires,"[40] which can take on different nuances in different contexts.[41]

But what sort of boasting is excluded? Set in the broader context of Romans, it emerges that Paul opposes both the idea of salvation by good works and Jewish privilege. In Rom 2:17, 23 Paul mentions Israel's boast in the law and in the knowledge of God, knowledge they take to be a status above the Gentiles.[42] And in 4:2 Paul pits faith and doing in the more general sense as ways of obtaining the righteousness of God.

Moving further into Romans, in a surprising move, Paul engages in semantic wordplay using the verb *kauchaomai* in a positive sense, declaring a "resurrection of boasting," to use Gathercole's turn of phrase, in which believers in Christ boast in hope, hardship and "in God through our Lord Jesus Christ, through whom we have received reconciliation" (vv. 2, 3, 11 respectively).[43] Romans 15:17 connects Christian "boasting" directly to Jesus Christ via Paul's personal example: "Therefore I glory [or "take pride in"; *kauchēsis*] in Christ Jesus in my service to God."

The Revelation of God's Saving Righteousness also

2. Establishes God as the God of both Jews and Gentiles (29–30)

Verse 29 opens with the particle, ἤ, "or," introducing a second implication of the revelation of the saving righteousness of God—namely, it establishes God as the God of both Jews and Gentiles. In short, the fact that there is one God means that there is one way of salvation for all people.

The words "God is one" is an allusion to the Shema. Christopher Bruno correctly observes that the oneness of God is connected in the Old Testament

---

40. See Thomas R. Schreiner, *New Testament Theology: Magnifying God in Christ* (Grand Rapids: Baker Academic, 2008), 526–27, for a recent survey of the interpretation of "works of law." Bird, *The Saving Righteousness of God*, 96–99, offers a convincing critique of Dunn's and Wright's attempt to limit the phrase to those laws which functioned as boundary markers between Jews and Gentiles (i.e., circumcision, Sabbath keeping, and dietary regulations).

41. Cf. Bird, *The Saving Righteousness of God*, 98, who defines the phrase as "a metonym for the stipulations of the entire Mosaic code" and note that such works are "just as much *ethical* as they are *ethnic*" (italics original).

42. Simon J. Gathercole, *Where Is Boasting? Early Jewish Soteriology and Paul's Response in Romans 1–5* (Grand Rapids: Eerdmans, 2002), 225.

43. Most English versions translate *kauchaomai* in Rom 5:2, 3, 11 as "rejoice," obscuring the connection with 2:17 and 23.

to God's covenant with Israel. But Paul subverts this association by also alluding to Zech 14:9: "The LORD will be king over the whole earth. On that day there will be one LORD."[44]

In describing Jews as "circumcised" and Gentiles as "the uncircumcised" Paul hints that faith and not Jewish privilege or performance is critical for being part of God's family. Both Jews and Gentiles are justified by faith.

The Revelation of God's Saving Righteousness

3. Confirms the prophetic role of the law (31)

Paul climaxes Rom 3:21–31 by answering the objection that his emphasis on faith in the new era of universal salvation, when righteousness is manifested apart from the law-covenant for both Jews and Gentiles, abolishes the law altogether: "Do we then overthrow (*katargeō*) the law by this faith? By no means! On the contrary, we uphold the law (*alla nomon histanomen*)" (Rom 3:31).

Paul's positive approval of the law represents a formal contradiction to his negative critique of the law in Eph 2:15, where he says that Christ has in fact overthrown, abolished or set aside the law, using the same verb as in Rom 3:31, *katargeō*.[45] But the contradiction is only apparent, for in Ephesians Christ abolishes the law as law-covenant, "with its commands and regulations." Whereas, in Romans the revelation of God's saving righteousness does not abolish but upholds the law as prophecy of the gospel.

Paul denies that the new thing that God has done in the sacrificial death of Christ (3:25) does away with the law. It is not that Christians end up "under the law" after all; Paul, as Carson puts it, "does not uphold *nomos* ("law") as *lex*, as ongoing legal demand."[46] Rather, the law is upheld, that is "validated" and its "validity reinforced,"[47] but not *as commandments in the new age*, but *as prophecy of the new age* in which both Jews and Gentiles will be justified by

---

44. Christopher R. Bruno, *"God is One": The Function of* Eis ho Theos *as a Ground for Gentile Inclusion in the Pauline Epistles*, LNTS 497 (London: T&T Clark, 2013), 139–51.

45. The verb "to abolish," *katargeō*, is equally unambiguous. BDAG's glosses include "abolish, wipe out, set aside" (s.v. καταργέω 3 [525]). A survey of Pauline usage confirms the strength of the term, along with frequent apocalyptic overtones. The following translations appear in the NRSV: "nullify" (Rom 3:3; 4:14; Gal 3:17); "discharge" (Rom 7:2, 6); "reduce to nothing" (1 Cor 1:28); "doom to perish" (1 Cor 2:6); "destroy" (1 Cor 6:13; 15:24, 26); "come to an end" (1 Cor 13:8[2x], 10, 11); "set aside" (2 Cor 3:7, 11, 13, 14); "cut off" (Gal 5:4); "remove" (Gal 5:11); "annihilate" (2 Thess 2:8); and "abolish" (Eph 2:15; 2 Tim 1:10). To paraphrase Eph 2:15, using Louw & Nida's definition of *katargeō* (13.100), "Christ has put an end to the law in its entirety."

46. Carson, "Atonement," 139.

47. BDAG s.v. ἵστημι 4 (482).

grace through faith. Paul abolishes the law as law-covenant, but upholds it as prophecy.[48]

The upholding of the law (3:31b) is in effect "the unpacking of the last clause of Romans 3:21: the Law and the Prophets testify to this new 'righteousness from God' that has come in Christ Jesus, and thus their valid continuity is sustained in that to which they point. . . . The law is upheld precisely because the redemptive-historical purposes and anticipations of the law are upheld."[49] The connection of 3:31 with 3:21 is given more credence when it is recognized that 4:1–25 is effectively an exposition to Gen 15:6 from the Law and Ps 32:1–2 from the Prophets.[50]

But to what in particular do the Law and the Prophets testify? Most commentators, if they answer this question, do so in general ways with little attempt at validating their opinion from the rest of Romans. Fitzmyer and Dunn are exceptions. Fitzmyer suggests that Rom 4:23–24 "illustrate" the Old Testament bearing witness to the gospel.[51] And Dunn points in the same direction, to the rest of the epistle: "The testimony he will subsequently elaborate, particularly in chaps. 4 and 9–11, is of a community in the character of God's saving purpose through Israel, with is not to be confused with a national or ethnic continuity as such."[52]

As it turns out, in Romans Paul regularly cites the Law as a prophecy of the gospel in tandem with the Prophets, something not unexpected in the light of Rom 1:2, 3:21 and 16:25–26. Six times in the letter Paul quotes the Law in its prophetic capacity and in every case there is in the same context a quotation or quotations from the Prophets. Despite the thicket of exegetical issues that typically slow progress in the interpretation of Romans, the following brief summary affirms little that is controversial. There is solid evidence that Paul cites the Law and the Prophets together in Romans as a witness to his gospel:

- In Rom 4 the Law and the Prophets testify to righteousness by faith apart from the law: in connection with Abraham's faith in Gen 15:6, 22 (Rom 4:1–4, 9ff); and David's forgiveness in Ps 32:1–2 (Rom 4:6–8).

---

48. See Rosner, *Paul and the Law*, passim. Cf. Joseph A. Fitzmyer, *Romans: A New Translation with Introduction and Commentary*, AB 33 (New York: Doubleday, 1993), 367: "In insisting on faith as the one principle of salvation, and in linking it to the one God, Paul affirms the basic message of the OT, and in particular that of the Mosaic law itself, rightly understood."

49. Carson, "Atonement," 139.

50. Cf. John Murray, *The Epistle to the Romans*, 2 vols., NICNT (Grand Rapids: Eerdmans, 1959–65), 1:124: "By appeal to Abraham and David (4:1–8) the apostle shows that the doctrine of justification by faith was imbedded in the Old Testament itself, and that it was at the centre of the revelation which had been entrusted to the Jews and in possession of which they boasted."

51. Fitzmyer, *Romans*, 344.

52. Dunn, *Romans 1–8*, 166.

- In Rom 9 the Law and the Prophets testify to the partial hardening of Israel that has accompanied the gospel: in Gen 21:12; 18:10, 14; 25:23 and Exod 33:19; 9:16 (Rom 9:6–18); and in Mal 1:2–3, Isa 29:16; 45:9, 10:22–23; 1:9, and Hos 2:23; 1:10 (Rom 9:25–29).[53]

- In Rom 10 the Law and the Prophets testify to righteousness by faith: in Deut 9:4 and 30:11–14 (Rom 10:6–9); and in Isa 28:16; 53:1 and Joel 2:32 (Rom 10:11–15).

- In Rom 10 the Law and the Prophets testify to not all Israelites accepting the gospel: in Deut 32:21 (Rom 10:19); and in Ps 19:4 and Isa 65:1–2 (Rom 10:18, 20–21).

- In Rom 11 the Law and the Prophets testify to the hardening of Israel; "As it is written" in Deut 29:4//Isa 29:10; "And David says" in Ps 69:22–23 (Rom 11:8–10).

- In Rom 15 the Law and the Prophets testify to Gentiles glorifying God; in Deut 32:43; and in 2 Sam 22:50//Ps 18:49, Ps 117:1 and Isa 11:10.

The six examples illustrate Paul's conviction that the gospel of salvation through faith in Christ for all who believe does not overthrow the law, but rather upholds the law as prophecy (3:31), that the Law and the Prophets testify to the manifestation of the righteousness of God in the new era.

The issue of Jews and Gentiles in the people of God is a recurring theme in Paul's reading of the law as prophecy in Romans; it occurs in five of the examples, with only the first from Rom 10 as an exception. However, it would be unwise to conclude that according to Paul the witness of the prophetic scriptures is limited to or even focused on this question. Paul tends to cite Scripture explicitly more often when dealing with questions with which his Jewish readers and opponents took issue. The concentration of quotations in Rom 9–11, which deals with the election of Israel and the inclusion of the Gentiles, bears this out.[54]

It is also noteworthy that in citing the Law and the Prophets as testimony to the gospel in the six examples that Paul has chosen to cite texts drawn first from the Law and then from the Prophets; this sequence is clearly discernible. The only partial exception is the quotation of Ps 19:4 in Rom 10:18, which is

---

53. Cf. Mark A. Seifrid, "Romans," in *Commentary on the New Testament use of the Old Testament,* ed. G. K. Beale and D. A. Carson (Grand Rapids: Baker Academic, 2007), 639: "The law itself defines the children of Abraham and of Israel as those created by the word of promise."

54. According to UBS4, there are 62 OT quotations in Romans, with 32 in Rom 9–11. In fact, up to a third of all of the quotations of Scripture in all of Paul's letters, depending on how you count them, occur in Rom 9–11. Cf. Seifrid, "Romans", 638: "The long drought of direct citation of the Scriptures in chapters 5–8, which Paul breaks in 8:36, is followed by a flood of citations in chapters 9–11."

followed by a quotation from Deuteronomy and then Isaiah in that order. I am not suggesting that this pattern of citing the Law and then the Prophets is contrived or even conscious on Paul's part. However, it is striking that the only place in his letters where he refers to Scripture as "the Law and the Prophets" is in Rom 3:21, which (along with 1:2 and 3:31) sets up his appeal to the Law and the Prophets as a witness to the gospel in the rest of the letter.

Conclusion

To sum up, in Rom 3:21–31 Paul asserts that the revelation of God's saving righteousness:[55]

1. Is manifested in the new age (21–22b)

2. Available to all (22c–24)

3. Displayed in the death of Jesus Christ (25–26)

4. Excludes boasting (27–28)

5. Establishes God as the God of both Jews and Gentiles (29–30); and

6. Confirms the prophetic role of the law (31)

Bibliography

Bird, Michael F. "Progressive Reformed View." Pages 131–57 in *Justification: Five Views*. Edited by James K. Beilby and Paul Rhodes Eddy. Downers Grove, IL: IVP Academic, 2011.

———. *The Saving Righteousness of God: Studies on Paul, Justification and the New Perspective*. Milton Keynes: Paternoster, 2006.

Bruno, Christopher R. *"God is One": The Function of* Eis ho Theos *as a Ground for Gentile Inclusion in the Pauline Epistles*. LNTS 497. London: T&T Clark, 2013.

Campbell, Constantine R. *Paul and Union with Christ: An Exegetical and Theological Study*. Grand Rapids: Zondervan Academic, 2012.

Campbell, Douglas A. *The Deliverance of God: An Apocalyptic Rereading of Justification in Paul*. Grand Rapids: Eerdmans, 2013.

———. *The Rhetoric of Righteousness in Romans 3.21–26*. JSNTSup 65. London: Bloomsbury, 1992.

Carson, D. A. "Atonement in Romans 3:21–26." Pages 119–39 in *The Glory of the Atonement: Biblical, Historical and Practical Perspectives: Essays in Honor*

---

55. This outline adapted from Harvey, *Romans*, 100–104.

of Roger Nicole. Edited by Charles E. Hill and Frank A. James III. Downers Grove, IL: InterVarsity Press, 2004.

Ciampa, Roy E. *The Presence and Function of Scripture in Galatians 1 and 2.* WUNT 2.102. Tübingen: Mohr Siebeck, 1998.

Cranfield, C. E. B. *A Critical and Exegetical Commentary on the Epistle to the Romans.* 2 vols. ICC. Edinburgh: T&T Clark, 1975–79.

Dunn, James D. G. *Romans 1–8.* WBC 38A. Dallas: Word, 1988.

Fitzmyer, Joseph A. *Romans: A New Translation with Introduction and Commentary.* AB 33. New York: Doubleday, 1993.

Gathercole, Simon J. *Where Is Boasting? Early Jewish Soteriology and Paul's Response in Romans 1–5.* Grand Rapids: Eerdmans, 2002.

Harvey, John D. *Romans.* EGGNT. Nashville: B&H Academic, 2017.

Hultgren, Stephen. "*Hilastērion* (Rom 3:25) and the Union of Divine Justice and Mercy. Part I: The Convergence of Temple and Martyrdom Theologies." *JTS* 70.1 (2019): 69–109.

———. "*Hilastērion* (Rom 3:25) and the Union of Divine Justice and Mercy. Part II: Atonement in the Old Testament and in Romans 1–5." *JTS* 70.2 (2019): 546–99.

Longenecker, Richard N. *The Epistle to the Romans: A Commentary on the Greek Text.* NIGTC. Grand Rapids: Eerdmans, 2016.

Marshall, I. Howard. "Salvation, Grace and Works in the Later Writings in the Pauline Corpus." *NTS* 42 (1996): 339–58.

McKnight, Scot. *Reading Romans Backwards: A Gospel of Peace in the Midst of Empire.* Waco, TX: Baylor University Press, 2019.

Mininger, Marcus A. *Uncovering the Theme of Revelation in Romans 1:16–3:26.* WUNT 2.445. Tübingen: Mohr Siebeck, 2017.

Moo, Douglas J. *The Letter to the Romans.* 2nd ed. NICNT. Grand Rapids: Eerdmans, 2018.

Morgan, Teresa. *Roman Faith and Christian Faith: Pistis and Fides in the Early Roman Empire and Early Churches.* Oxford: Oxford University Press, 2015.

Murray, John. *The Epistle to the Romans.* 2 vols. NICNT. Grand Rapids: Eerdmans, 1959–65.

O'Brien, Peter T. *Introductory Thanksgivings in the Letters of Paul.* Eugene, OR: Wipf & Stock, 2009.

Rosner, Brian S. *Paul and the Law: Keeping the Commandments of God.* NSBT 31. Downers Grove, IL: IVP Academic, 2013.

Schreiner, Thomas R. *New Testament Theology: Magnifying God in Christ.* Grand Rapids: Baker Academic, 2008.

———. *40 Questions about Christians and the Biblical Law.* Grand Rapids: Kregel, 2010.

———. *Romans.* 2nd ed. BECNT. Grand Rapids: Baker Academic, 2018.

Seifrid, Mark A. "Romans." Pages 607–94 in *Commentary on the New Testament use of the Old Testament*. Edited by G. K. Beale and D. A. Carson. Grand Rapids: Baker Academic, 2007.

Stuhlmacher, Peter. "The Theme of Romans." Pages 333–45 in *The Romans Debate*. Rev. ed. Edited by Karl P. Donfried. Peabody, MA: Hendrickson, 1991.

Thielman, Frank. *Paul and the Law: A Contextual Approach*. Downers Grove, IL: InterVarsity Press, 1994.

Watson, Francis. *Paul, Judaism and the Gentiles: Beyond the New Perspective*. Grand Rapids: Eerdmans, 2007.

CHAPTER 8

Believing without Hope: Abraham and Justification by Faith (Romans 4)

Kevin McFadden

Faith is a highly debated topic among those who study Pauline theology. Does Paul teach that we are justified by our faith or by the faith of Jesus Christ? Does the word πίστις in his letters mean "belief," "trust," "faithfulness," "allegiance," or what?

At the very least, I think we can all agree that faith is an important topic in the apostle's theology, and especially in his letter to the Romans. The opening thanksgiving sections of Paul's letters often indicate important themes in the letter.[1] And in the long opening of this letter Paul highlights the theme of faith. He first greets the saints in Rome as an apostle, set apart to proclaim the gospel in order "to bring about the obedience of *faith* . . . among all the nations" (Rom 1:5, my emphasis).[2] He then gives thanks to God through Jesus Christ "because your *faith* is proclaimed in all the world" (1:8, my emphasis). He says he longs to see these believers in order "that we may be mutually encouraged by each other's *faith*, both yours and mine" (1:12, my emphasis). And finally, faith is one of the most prominent topics in Rom 1:16–17, which most interpreters view as a statement of the fundamental theme of the letter: "For I am not ashamed of the gospel, for it is the power of God for salvation to everyone who *believes*, to the Jew first and also to the Greek. For in it the righteousness of God is revealed from *faith* for *faith*, as it is written, 'the righteous shall live by *faith*'" (my emphasis). So whether one takes Rom 1:17 as a reference to our faith or to Jesus' faith or God's faithfulness, we can all at least acknowledge the centrality of the topic of faith in this letter, a topic which is especially highlighted in chs. 3, 4, 9, 10, 11, and 14.

But what does Paul mean when he talks about faith? This is the question, isn't it? Space does not permit me to fully answer this question here.[3] But I can take one step toward answering it by explaining Rom 4, a chapter in which, according to Dunn, "Paul gives his clearest and most powerful exposition of

---

1. Thomas R. Schreiner, *Interpreting the Pauline Epistles*, 2nd ed. (Grand Rapids: Baker Academic, 2011).

2. All citations of Scripture are from the ESV.

3. See my book, *Faith in the Son of God: The Place of Christ-Oriented Faith within Pauline Theology* (Wheaton, IL: Crossway, 2021).

what he understood by πίστις, 'faith.'"[4] However, even attempting to explain Rom 4 in such a short space is a daunting task. Many contributors to this book have thought deeply and written carefully about Rom 4, and the definitive monograph on the chapter, by Schliesser, is over four hundred pages long.[5] Thus even here my claims must be modest. My goal in this essay is to explain how Paul describes Abraham's faith as a faith without works (4:1–8), a faith without circumcision (4:9–12), a faith without the law (4:13–16a), and a faith without hope (4:16b–22).[6] Then, in the conclusion of the essay, I will reflect on how this description of Abraham's faith should inform our faith (4:23–25) and our understanding of faith in Paul's theology.

Faith without Works (4:1–8)

Paul opens the chapter by describing Abraham's faith in God as a faith without works.[7] This description was as controversial in the first century as it is today. James famously protests that a faith without works is dead.[8] And modern scholars who have forged a new perspective on Paul argue that this description in Rom 4:1–8 does not represent Paul's real concern in the chapter or its broader context. In Hays' words, "Paul's concern focuses not on the mechanics of justification but on the relation of Jews and Gentiles in light of the message of justification."[9] A more balanced approach is that of Barclay and Schreiner

---

4. James D. G. Dunn, *The Theology of Paul the Apostle* (Grand Rapids: Eerdmans, 1998), 377. Dunn is referring specifically to Rom 4:13–22.

5. Benjamin Schliesser, *Abraham's Faith in Romans 4*, WUNT 2.224 (Tübingen: Mohr Siebeck, 2007).

6. After writing the first draft of this essay, I found that Moo describes faith in Rom 4 with very similar categories: "a faith that is *apart from works, apart from circumcision, apart from the law, apart from sight.*" Douglas J. Moo, *The Letter to the Romans*, 2nd ed., NICNT (Grand Rapids: Eerdmans, 2018), 313, cf. 298.

7. Note especially the phrase "apart from [without] works" (χωρὶς ἔργων) in Rom 4:6. Cf. Rom 3:28: "For we hold that one is justified by faith apart from [without] works of the law (χωρὶς ἔργων νόμου)."

8. "For as the body apart from the spirit is dead, so also faith apart from [without] works (χωρὶς ἔργων) is dead" (James 2:26). It is likely that James was protesting against a misrepresentation or overstatement of Paul's teaching that claimed believers could continue to live in sin. Paul himself must counter this same misrepresentation of his teaching in Rom 3:8 and 6:1ff.

9. Richard B. Hays, *The Conversion of the Imagination: Paul as Interpreter of Israel's Scripture* (Grand Rapids: Eerdmans, 2005), 75, cf. 79, 83. Corresponding with this claim, Hays argues for a new translation of the question that opens the chapter: "*What then shall we say? Have we found Abraham (to be) our forefather according to the flesh*" (67, cf. 62–69; he is followed by N. T. Wright, *Pauline Perspectives: Essays on Paul, 1978–2013* (Minneapolis: Fortress, 2013), 579–84). Grammatically, however, this translation is unlikely: "forefather" (τὸν προπάτορα) is not in predicate position, and more importantly the infinitive "found" (εὑρηκέναι) after a verb of saying (ἐροῦμεν)

who argue that Paul is concerned with both the mechanics of justification and the inclusion of the Gentiles in this chapter.[10] In fact, one cannot understand how Abraham is the father of believing Gentiles without first understanding the mechanics of his justification.

Rhetorically the chapter opens with a question that addresses a potential objection which follows from what the apostle has just argued:[11] "What then shall we say that Abraham, our forefather according to the flesh, has found?" (Rom 4:1, my translation).[12] Paul's identification of Abraham as "our forefather according to the flesh,"[13] that is, the founder of the Jewish nation, shows that he is addressing a Jewish objection to his argument, an objection he begins to explain and answer in the next verse: "For if Abraham was justified by works, he has something to boast about . . ." (4:2). Here Paul's language of "works" and "boasting" recalls his previous argument that boasting is excluded because "one is justified by faith apart from [without] works of the law" (Rom 3:28). In other words, here we see the mechanics of justification at issue in the objection. But what about Abraham? Was he not justified by his works?[14]

This objection fits with what we know of some of Paul's Jewish contemporaries whose writings highlight Abraham's exemplary obedience and his faithfulness in testing as the reason for his justification.[15] Paul concedes that

---

surely introduces the discourse of what is said. This means that Rom 4:1 is one sentence, not two, and that "Abraham" is the accusative subject of the infinitive "found": "What then shall we say that Abraham, our forefather according to the flesh, has found?" (my translation).

10. John M. G. Barclay, *Paul and the Gift* (Grand Rapids: Eerdmans, 2015), 482; see his interaction with Hays on this point, 488n105; Thomas R. Schreiner, *Romans*, 2nd ed., BECNT (Grand Rapids: Baker Academic, 2018), 217, 231, 237. *Pace* Moo who sees Gentile inclusion as very important but still an implication of the more fundamental concern of Abraham as an exemplar of justification by faith (*Romans*, 277n881).

11. "As so often in Romans, Paul uses a rhetorical question to introduce the next stage of his argument." Moo, *Romans*, 281. Cf. Rom 3:8; 6:1; 7:7; 9:14; 9:30; 11:1. The conjunction "then" (οὖν) in Rom 4:1 shows that the chapter begins a new section in Paul's argument (Schreiner, *Romans*, 217).

12. I have given my own translation since the ESV translates εὑρηκέναι with the gloss "gained" rather than the more literal "has found" or "has discovered."

13. The word order of Paul's question shows that "according to the flesh" (κατὰ σάρκα) modifies "forefather" (προπάτορα) (cf. "my kinsmen according to the flesh" in Rom 9:5). *Pace* Schliesser, who makes the interesting suggestion that "according to the flesh" modifies "we say" (ἐροῦμεν) and speaks of the human standard in contrast with the divine standard of "before God" (*Romans 4*, 325–26).

14. Barclay observes that "there are good reasons why Paul could not speak of 'works of the Law' in the case of Abraham (whom he dates before the arrival of the law, 5:13–14). His point is to exclude from God's reckoning not only one but *any* form of symbolic capital that might be taken to constitute a source of worth before God (cf. 9:6–13)" (*Gift*, 484n92).

15. E.g., 1 Macc 2:52: "Was not Abraham found faithful when tested, and it was reckoned to him as righteousness?" (NRSVue). See Simon J. Gathercole, *Where is Boasting?*

if Abraham was justified by his works, then he does have a reason to boast. However, Paul's concession can only go so far. Abraham may have a reason to boast because of his works before men, "but not before God."[16] In fact, this is the teaching of Scripture, since Gen 15:6 is the ground of the apostle's argument: "For what does the Scripture say? 'Abraham believed God, and it was counted to him as righteousness'" (Rom 4:3).

In the next two verses, Paul explains the meaning of Gen 15:6 and its language of "believing," "counting," and "righteousness." Perhaps he also alludes to Abraham's great reward in Gen 15:1 with the word "wages" (μισθὸς) in v. 4, as Wright now suggests.[17] Certainly Abraham's reward would include the worldwide family which he was promised, since the question of offspring is so pronounced in Gen 15:1–6 and is discussed by Paul as well in Rom 4:9–17. But does it follow from this possible allusion, as Wright argues, that Paul is "primarily mounting an argument about the worldwide meaning of the covenant?"[18] This reading seems to skip to Rom 4:9 without considering what Paul says in Rom 4:4–5. For when we read these verses, we see that Paul is still concerned with the mechanics of justification in Gen 15:6. And he continues to dialogue with the Jewish objection he has just anticipated. Gathercole observes that it was common in Jewish soteriological discussions to use economic or commercial metaphors, and this is what Paul does here by contrasting the worker with the believer.[19]

The apostle first asks his readers to consider by what means the reward or wage is counted "to the one who works." It is "not counted as a gift but as his due" (v. 4). The metaphor is simple: The worker earns wages as what is due and not as a gift. Paul then contrasts this image with that of the believer. In fact, worker and believer are not only contrasted in vv. 4 and 5; this contrast is also reinforced in the language of v. 5: "to the one who does not work but believes . . ."

Early Jewish Soteriology and Paul's Response in Romans 1–5 (Grand Rapids: Eerdmans, 2002), 235–36.

16. The phrase "but not before God" in Rom 4:2 seems to deny that Abraham is qualified to boast specifically before God rather than denying that Abraham has any reason to boast at all, contra most English commentators but following many German commentators (Gathercole, *Boasting*, 241–42; e.g., Eckhard J. Schnabel, *Der Brief des Paulus an die Römer: Kapitel 1–5*, HTA [Witten/Gießen: Brockhaus/Brunnen, 2015], 449–50). Gathercole observes that Jesus criticized the Pharisees for justifying themselves in the eyes of men rather than God (Luke 16:15) and that Sirach speaks of Israel's glorious ancestors as the "boast" (καύχημα) of their times (Sir 44:7), including Abraham who "kept the law of the Most High" and "when he was tested he proved faithful" (Sir 44:20 NRSVue).

17. Wright, *Perspectives*, 562.

18. Wright, *Perspectives*, 563, 591–92.

19. Gathercole, *Boasting*, 244 (e.g., "The one who does what is right saves up life for himself with the Lord"; Pss. Sol. 9:5 [translation from R. B. Wright in *OTP* 2:660]). *Pace* Barclay, who argues that "4:4–5 serves an exegetical but not a polemical purpose" (*Gift*, 424n93).

Clearly Paul understands works and faith as antithetical means of obtaining the reward or obtaining righteousness. Abraham's faith was a faith without works because working accords with what is due, whereas believing accords with gift or grace.

Paul then elucidates the gracious character of believing with his striking and memorable description of the God who was the object of Abraham's faith: "him who justifies the ungodly." Barclay observes that Paul could have contrasted the pay of the worker with the gracious gift given to the deserving recipient. But instead, Paul highlights the incongruity of God's grace in justifying the ungodly.[20] God justifies the one who deserves his wrath according to Rom 1:18.[21] Thus Abraham's faith accords with grace because the object of his faith was the God of grace.[22]

And this was not only true of Abraham, Paul says, "David also speaks of the blessing of the one to whom God counts righteousness apart from works: 'Blessed are those whose lawless deeds are forgiven, and whose sins are covered; blessed is the man against whom the Lord will not count his sin" (Rom 4:6–8). Paul speaks of this blessing of forgiveness as basically the equivalent of justification by faith, seeing a pattern in the law and the prophets: David like Abraham before him believed in the God of grace who forgave his sin.[23] They were both justified by a faith without works.

Faith without Circumcision (4:9–12)

It follows, then, that this blessing of forgiveness can be had by anyone, because Abraham was justified by faith before and without circumcision. Rom 4:9–12 is not a digression in Paul's argument but a conclusion from it, introduced by the inferential particle "then" (οὖν). Here Paul anticipates another potential Jewish objection—namely that the blessing of forgiveness about which David speaks about is only for the Jews not the Gentiles: "Is this blessing then only for the circumcised, or also for the uncircumcised?" (Rom 4:9a). David, after all, was circumcised. But the apostle quickly reminds us again of the centrality

---

20. Barclay, *Gift*, 485.

21. It is very unlikely that "ungodly" refers not to Abraham but to the Gentiles from different ethnic and moral backgrounds (contra Wright, *Perspectives*, 564, 586), just as it is very unlikely that the "sinner" spoken of in 4:6–8 refers not to David but to the Gentiles (contra Wright, *Perspectives*, 588). Are we to believe that Paul did not think David was referring to his own sin in Ps 32?

22. Frank Thielman, *Romans*, ZECNT 6 (Grand Rapids: Zondervan Academic, 2018), 224, similarly observes that God justified Abraham because "he trusted God to be gracious to him."

23. Gathercole, *Boasting*, 247, observes that "contra K. Stendahl, forgiveness is seen as a vital component of justification."

of Abraham and Gen 15:6 in this discussion: "we say that faith was counted to Abraham as righteousness" (Rom 4:9b).[24] This is the foundational text on which the apostle will again rely to argue that the blessing of forgiveness extends to all believers.

Paul's argument in v. 10 considers the state Abraham was in when he was justified by faith: "How then was it counted to him? Was it before or after he had been circumcised? It was not after, but before he was circumcised." Here Paul appeals to the chronology of the Abraham narratives. In Gen 15 Abraham was not yet circumcised. So his faith was counted to him as righteousness when he was still in the state of uncircumcision. Paul emphasizes the patriarch's reception of this blessing in an uncircumcised state again in v. 11: "He received the sign of circumcision as a seal of the righteousness that he had by faith while he was still uncircumcised." More literally, Paul speaks of Abraham's "faith-in-uncircumcision" (τῆς πίστεως τῆς ἐν τῇ ἀκροβυστίᾳ). This in-uncircumcision-faith was then sealed by Abraham's later circumcision, the "sign of the covenant" between God, Abraham, and his offspring. [25]

Wright again argues that the worldwide nature of this covenant is the whole point of Paul's argument and that in Rom 4:11 we can see that "righteousness" in fact refers to the status of covenant membership. Where Gen 17:11 has "sign of the covenant," Rom 4:11 has "seal of the righteousness of faith."[26] But if Paul wanted to emphasize the covenant here, why does he not use the word "covenant" or perhaps the word "promise" as he does in his discussion of the Abrahamic covenant in Gal 3:15–18?[27] I suggest that the apostle's focus is not yet on the covenant God made in Gen 15:7–21, when his fiery presence walked between the parts to guarantee his promise. Rather, Paul is once again drawing us back to Gen 15:6 and keeping our focus on the "righteousness that he [Abraham] had by faith while he was still uncircumcised." The sign of circumcision, which Abraham received years later, was a seal which authenticated or confirmed that righteousness.[28] Just as the wedding ring authenticates the pre-existing

---

24. Moo helpfully observes that Paul's allusion to Gen 15:6 in Rom 9:6b "does not explain the opening question, nor does it gives [sic] its answer. Rather, Paul here sets the stage for his answer by reminding his readers of the OT text that speaks authoritatively about these matters" (*Romans*, 293).

25. Paul alludes specifically to Gen 17:11: "You shall be circumcised in the flesh of your foreskins, and it shall be a sign of the covenant between me and you." The "you" is plural in the MT and LXX, referring to both Abraham and his offspring.

26. Wright, *Perspectives*, 565–66. Here Wright incorrectly says that Paul speaks of the "sign of *dikaiosynē*" and thus makes Gen 17:11 and Rom 4:11 sound more parallel than they actually are. Instead, Paul says, "He received the sign of circumcision as a *seal* of the righteousness that he had by faith" (my emphasis).

27. Schliesser observes that Paul omits "covenant" in his allusion to Gen 17:11 (*Romans 4*, 357, 360).

28. See BDAG s.v. σφραγίς 4a (980).

love between husband and wife, so circumcision authenticated the pre-existing "righteousness of faith" which Abraham already possessed "in uncircumcision." Abraham's faith was a faith before and thus without circumcision.

Two results follow from Abraham's "faith-in-uncircumcision" in Gen 15:6: First, he is father of *all* those who believe; and second, he is the father of *only* those who believe. Here Paul probably sees divine intention in the way that Scripture was written.[29] "The purpose was to make him the father of all who believe without being circumcised, so that righteousness would be counted to them" (Rom 4:11).[30] This seems to be typological reasoning, viewing Gen 15:6 as an intended foreshadowing of "the obedience of faith . . . among all the nations" or Gentiles (Rom 1:5). But Gen 15:6 was also foreshadowing the call for Jews to believe the gospel, for the second purpose was "to make him the father of the circumcised who are not merely circumcised but who also walk in the footsteps of the faith that our father Abraham had before he was circumcised" (Rom 4:12).[31] More literally, Paul again speaks of "the in-uncircumcision-faith" (τῆς ἐν ἀκροβυστίᾳ πίστεως) of our father Abraham. The implication of Abraham's faith in this state for the Jews is that circumcision is not enough to be counted as a child of Abraham (Rom 2:25–29; cf. 9:6). The children must also walk in their father's footsteps—namely, his footsteps of faith without circumcision.

In conclusion, we should consider the significance of Abraham's fatherhood in Rom 4:9–12. In what sense for Paul is Abraham the father of all Gentile and Jewish believers? Hays suggests that Paul considers Abraham a representative figure who affects the destinies of others.[32] Christians are "vicariously" included in the reckoning of righteousness to Abraham,[33] and thus Abraham's faith is a "prefiguration of the faith of Jesus Christ (cf. Rom 3:22), whose faith/obedience now has vicarious soteriological consequences for those who know

---

29. The clause εἰς τὸ εἶναι could refer simply to result (NIV) or to the divine purpose (ESV). It seems more likely that it speaks of God's purpose because this is the same kind of reasoning we will see in the end of the chapter (Rom 4:23–25).

30. I have left out the ESV's "as well" since this represents the word *kai*, which is textually uncertain. The NA28 has it in brackets, and the Tyndale House GNT does not include it as part of the original text.

31. The grammar of Rom 4:12 is a classic conundrum: Paul uses the article τοῖς two times, which would seem to indicate two different groups (Jews and Gentiles), but the flow of the argument seems to refer to one group (Jews) since he has already mentioned the Gentiles. Thielman sees the grammar clarified by the placement of "only" or "merely" (μόνον): "He does not say "not only for those who . . ." (οὐκ μόνον τοῖς . . .) but "for those who are only . . ." (τοῖς οὐκ . . . μόνον)" (*Romans*, 235). Thus Paul is referring to one group (Jews), and the second article should just be considered infelicitous or "intrusive" (C. F. D. Moule, *An Idiom Book of New Testament Greek*, 2nd ed. [Cambridge: Cambridge University Press, 1959], 110).

32. Hays, *Conversion*, 76.

33. Hays, *Conversion*, 80.

him as Lord."[34] But Paul never says this.[35] He never presents Abraham as a vicarious representative like he does Adam and Christ in Rom 5:12–21. He does not say, for example, that Abraham's one act of faith brought justification for the many.[36] Our father Abraham is not presented in Rom 4:9–12 as a vicarious representative of his children, but as a representative pattern or example for his children. Paul presents his fatherhood as the type of faith or pattern of faith or "footsteps of faith" in which his children must now walk.[37] Thus Abraham is not a prefiguration of Christ but a prefiguration of us—of uncircumcised Gentiles who believe and are justified as Abraham was, and of Jews who are not only circumcised but who themselves walk down the path of faith which their uncircumcised forefather trod millennia ago.

Faith without the Law (4:13–16a)

In Rom 4:13–22, Paul begins to weave together his arguments about the fatherhood of Abraham and the mechanics of his justification.[38] Rom 4:13 also introduces two words not yet seen in this chapter: "promise" and "law." Promise is a theme developed throughout all of 4:13–22, indicating that it is really one paragraph.[39] But the Mosaic law is a theme unique to 4:13–16a with Paul using the word "law" five times in these verses and nowhere else in the chapter. Moreover, Rom 4:16b–22 is structured around two parallel relative clauses in v. 16b and v. 18 that speak respectively of Abraham's fatherhood and of his faith.[40] For these reasons I will discuss 4:13–16a and 4:16b–22 as distinct units within the paragraph, the first describing Abraham's faith without the law and the second describing his faith without hope.

The category of promise introduced in v. 13 explains a further significance of Abraham's fatherhood. Abraham is not only the representative pattern or example of faith; he is also the one to whom God made the promise to bless the whole world. The word "promise" in Paul refers to the covenant God had made with Abraham since he uses "promise" and "covenant" interchangeably in

---

34. Hays, *Conversion*, 84.

35. So, Schliesser, *Romans 4*, 341–42, 387n1204.

36. And he certainly does not say his one act of "obedience" (!) brought justification for the many, for he has just argued that Abraham's faith was a faith without works.

37. Walking in someone's "footsteps" is a way of referring to following their example (cf. 2 Cor 12:18; 1 Pet 2:21).

38. Cf. Barclay: "If 4:1–8 has described the characteristic trait of the Abrahamic family as faith despite the absence of worth, and 4:9–12 its intended inclusion of Gentile and Jewish believers, the following section of this chapter, 4:13–18, joins the themes of 4:1–8 and 9–12 together" (*Gift*, 488).

39. "[T]he theme of the promise runs throughout vv. 13–22, binding them together in an overall unity." Moo, *Romans*, 298.

40. Hays also observes these two parallel relative clauses (*Conversion*, 76–77n45).

Gal 3:15–18. Here Paul spells out the substance of this covenant as the promise "that he [Abraham] would be heir of the world" (Rom 4:13). Wright suggests that Paul is thinking primarily of Abraham's descendants here, that he would be the father of many nations, "indeed of the whole world."[41] But since Paul says that this promised inheritance is made to both Abraham *and* to his offspring, it seems more likely that he is thinking about the land promise.[42] Like most Jews of his day Paul speaks of this promise as encompassing the entire earth.[43] And since God had made this promise to Abraham and his offspring, it really matters to Paul whether uncircumcised, believing Gentiles belong to Abraham's offspring, as Wright has observed.[44]

But it also matters *how* the inheritance comes to Abraham and his offspring. In other words, Paul is also concerned with the mechanics: "For the promise to Abraham and his offspring that he would be heir of the world did not come through the law but through the righteousness of faith" (Rom 4:13). Here we see a contrast between the law and the righteousness of faith much like Paul's earlier contrast between the worker and the believer. The difference is that Paul's discussion has moved into the realm of Israel's salvation history.

Why did the promise made to Abraham and his offspring not come about by means of Israel's law? Paul answers this question with a chain of reasoning beginning with a conditional statement: "For if it is the adherents of the law who are to be the heirs, faith is null and the promise is void" (Rom 4:14). But why? Paul gives the reason in next verse: "For the law brings wrath, but where there is no law there is no transgression" (Rom 4:15). The reference to Israel's transgression reveals that Paul is thinking about human inability to obey the law. The law does not bring about the inheritance of Abraham but rather brings about transgression and the wrath of God.[45] Thus, if the promise to Abraham rested on human ability to obey the law it would never be fulfilled. Interestingly, Paul says that in this case even Abraham's faith itself would be "null" or literally "have become vain." His point is similar to his argument in 1 Corinthians 15 that the Corinthians' faith would be in vain if the object of their faith, the resurrection, did not truly happen (cf. 1 Cor 15:3, 14, 17). We begin to see, then, that Abraham's faith was not only in the person of God but in the promise of God.

---

41. Wright, *Perspectives*, 560.

42. Note also that the "heirs" of the promise is plural in Rom 4:14.

43. E.g., in the book of Jubilees, Abraham blesses Jacob with these words: "May he strengthen you and bless you, and may you inherit all of the earth" (Jub. 22:14). Translation from O. S. Wintermute in *OTP* 2:98.

44. Wright, *Perspectives*, 573.

45. Cf. Moo: "The first clause of this verses [v. 15] substantiates the conclusion drawn in v. 14 by showing what the law *does*—"produces wrath"—as opposed to what it *cannot do*—secure the inheritance" (*Romans*, 301). Paul is probably thinking about how the giving of the law resulted in the exile, Israel's experience of God's wrath because of their transgression, rather than the securing of the Abrahamic inheritance.

If the object of Abraham's faith—the promise—was voided out or invalidated by the wrath-bringing law, then even the patriarch's faith would be in vain.

"That is why," Paul concludes in v. 16, "it depends on faith." In light of the ground that leads to this conclusion, the apostle is implicitly saying that it depends on faith *and not the law* or on a faith without the law.[46] His reasoning is similar to Rom 4:4–5. The inheritance of the world depends on faith "in order that the promise may rest on grace."[47] Once again, faith as the means by which one inherits the promise accords with grace because the object of Abraham's faith and the object of our faith is the gift of God, the inheritance of the world given freely by God in fulfillment of his promise. His reasoning in v. 16 is also similar to Rom 4:11–12. The promise comes by faith and accords with grace ultimately in order that it might "be guaranteed to all his offspring—not only to the adherent of the law but also to the one who shares the faith of Abraham." Thus, the result of the promised inheritance of the world resting on faith and grace is that it is secure or "guaranteed" (βεβαίαν) for every single one of Abraham's offspring, including both Jews *and* Gentile who share in Abraham's faith.[48]

Faith without Hope (4:16b–22)

Finally, in Rom 4:16b–22 Paul describes Abraham's faith as a faith without hope, a faith that relies on God to raise the dead. Here we come to the two parallel relative clauses which describe Abraham's universal fatherhood (4:16b–17) and his faith and subsequent justification (4:18–22). Wright argues that Rom 4:16–17 is the climax of this entire chapter and that Paul's main point is about the worldwide significance of the covenant God made with Abraham.[49] But this reading seems to miss the fact that Paul follows up these verses with an even longer description of Abraham's faith in Rom 4:18–22.[50]

---

46. Cf. Rom 3:21: "But now the righteousness of God has been manifested apart from [without] the law (χωρὶς νόμου)."

47. Paul uses the same phrase "according to grace" (κατὰ χάριν) in Rom 4:4 and 4:16 which is translated by the ESV with "as a gift" in v. 4 and with the more dynamic "the promise may rest on grace" in v. 16.

48. On a first reading of Rom 4:16 it might sound like Paul saying that the promise comes based on law adherence for some and faith for others. But this would contradict what Paul has been arguing in the previous verses. Thus it is better to see Paul using "of the law" (ἐκ τοῦ νόμου) in v. 16 in a different way than he uses it in v. 14. In v. 14 it indicates the means by which one inherits the promise. But in v. 16 it is simply a designation of a Jew as opposed to a Gentile like the similar designation "of the circumcision" (ἐκ περιτομῆς) in v. 12. Paul's language is compact, but he is surely distinguishing Jewish believers from Gentile believers who do not have the law but have the same faith as Abraham (so most commentators, e.g., Schreiner, *Romans,* 240).

49. Wright, *Perspectives,* 563, 583, 591–92.

50. This final description of Abraham's faith reads like a mini-commentary on Gen 15:6: Vv. 18–21 describe the statement "Abraham believed God," and v. 22 describes the statement "and it was counted to him as righteousness."

In the first relative clause Paul describes Abraham as "the father of us all" (4:16b). He supports this point by quoting Gen 17:5 where God gives Abram the new name "Abraham": "as it is written, 'I have made you the father of many nations'" (Rom 4:17a). This means that according to the word of God, and as Paul says, "in the presence of God," Abraham is the father of us all.[51] Paul began the chapter by conceding that Abraham might have a reason to boast before men, but he does not have a reason to boast before God. Here we see similar reasoning: Gentile believers might not be considered Abraham's offspring according to human considerations of fleshly descent, but they are considered Abraham's offspring by the God in whom Abraham believed. Paul's vivid description of Abraham's God explains how this can be: He is the one "who gives life to the dead and calls into existence the things that do not exist" (Rom 4:17b). Thus he can raise up and call those who were not his people to be Abraham's offspring who will inherit the world (cf. Rom 9:24–26).[52]

The second relative clause describes Abraham's faith in this God who raises the dead: "In hope he believed against hope, that he should become the father of many nations, as he had been told, 'So shall your offspring be'" (Rom 4:18). Here we see more clearly that the object of Abraham's faith was not only the person of God but also the promise or word of God.[53] Paul is reading Gen 15:6 in its immediate context because he quotes from Gen 15:5, God's promise to Abraham that his offspring would be like the stars. This divine promise was the hopeful basis of Abraham's faith, which is why Paul says that he believed "in hope."

---

51. The phrase "in the presence of God" probably modifies "the father of us all" with the intervening citation of Gen 17:5 supporting this idea (the majority view, according to Moo, *Romans*, 305). Or "in the presence of God" could modify the citation which immediately precedes it (so, Thielman, *Romans*, 248). In either case the meaning is that Abraham is the father "of us all" or "of many nations" in the presence of God.

52. I am taking "calls into existence the things that do not exist" in Rom 4:17 as a description of God's creative power which calls or chooses literally "the things that are not" so that (ὡς) they now "are" (so, Schreiner, *Romans*, 244–25; Schnabel, *Der Brief des Paulus an die Römer: Kapitel 1–5*, 479; cf. 1 Cor 1:26–28 which uses the same phrase "things that are not," τὰ μὴ ὄντα; cf. also the similar language in Herm. Mand. 1.1). Thielman and Moo think it is unlikely that ὡς in Rom 4:17 refers to the purpose of God's call so they conclude that "call" refers to God speaking of things "as though" they already exist, referring to the certainty of God's promise (Thielman, *Romans*, 249; Moo, *Romans*, 307–8). Wright has a fascinating reading of 4:17, suggesting that those whom God raises from the dead are Jewish believers and those whom he calls into existence from nothing are Gentile believers (e.g., *Perspectives*, 561). Unfortunately, this is not clear in the immediate context (although cf. 11:15).

53. The clause "that he should become the father of many nations" in Rom 4:18 probably indicates the object of the verb "believed" (cf. Gal 2:16 for πιστεύω with εἰς indicating the object of faith). It could also indicate the purpose or result of Abraham's faith (Thielman, *Romans*, 249). In either case, Abraham's belief was in what "he had been told" by God.

But paradoxically, Paul says that Abraham also believed "against hope" or without hope. Here Paul is thinking of Abraham's own human circumstances over many years. He describes Abraham's faith from the perspective of Gen 17, noting that "he was about a hundred years old," an allusion to Gen 17:17. This was many years after the promise that Abraham's offspring would be like the stars. The elephant in the room in the years between Gen 15–17 was the cold hard fact that Sarah was barren. Paul describes these circumstances as a state of death: Abraham's body had already died (ἤδη νενεκρωμένον) and Sarah's womb was characterized by "barrenness" or literally "deadness" (τὴν νέκρωσιν). But Paul says that Abraham did not ignore his circumstances but "considered" or contemplated them.[54] He considered that his human circumstances were without hope (cf. Heb 11:1–12).

And yet Abraham still believed God. He "did not weaken in faith . . . but he grew strong in his faith" (Rom 4:19–20). Again Paul speaks about Abraham's faith in the promise of God: "No unbelief made him waver concerning the promise of God."[55] But further, Paul speaks about Abraham's faith in the *power* of God to accomplish his promise: Abraham "gave glory to God, fully convinced that God was able to do what he had promised."[56] Abraham's faith grew strong over those many years without hope in his own power to bring about offspring but with hope in the promise that his offspring would be like the stars and in the power of God to raise the dead.[57] "That is why," Paul says, "his faith was 'counted to him as righteousness'" (Rom 4:22).

Conclusion: Abraham's Faith and Our Faith (4:23–25)

The apostle concludes this remarkable chapter by drawing our attention again to the divine purpose behind the writing of Gen 15:6: "[T]he words 'it was counted to him' were not written for his sake alone, but for ours also" (Rom 4:23–24a). These words were written to instruct and encourage us (cf. Rom 15:4) that God will count our faith as righteousness as well. We now follow

---

54. Interestingly, some manuscripts say that Abraham "did *not* consider" these circumstances (having the negative particle οὐ) (see KJV). But this seems to be an addition to the text in the Western text family.

55. There is some question about how to translate "waver" (ἐνεδυναμώθη). Many have translated it "doubt" because it is often contrasted with πίστις in the NT (e.g., Jeremias, from Benjamin Schliesser, "'Abraham Did Not "Doubt" in Unbelief' (Rom. 4:20): Faith, Doubt, and Dispute in Paul's Letter to the Romans," *JTS* 63.2 [2012]: 499). But this meaning is unknown before the NT and Schliesser now argues that it means Abraham did not "dispute" the promise.

56. Perhaps "glory" here refers to Abraham acknowledging God's power to raise the dead. Cf. "Christ was raised from the dead by the glory of the Father" (Rom 6:4).

57. Cf. Schlatter's point that Abraham's inability led him to trust in God's ability (from Schreiner, *Romans*, 244n2).

in the footsteps of Abraham and share in the same faith and justification as Abraham because we believe in the same God, the one who raises the dead: "It will be counted to us who believe in him who raised from the dead Jesus our Lord, who was delivered up for our trespasses and raised for our justification" (Rom 4:24b–25). Here it is striking that in the only place Paul speaks about Jesus Christ in this chapter he speaks about his death and resurrection as a part of the object of our faith. In the death and resurrection of Christ God's work of justifying the ungodly and giving life to the dead has become concrete: God has delivered up his own Son for our trespasses and raised him from the dead for our justification.[58] Paul refers immediately to the justification secured already by Jesus' resurrection since the next verse begins with the premise that "we have been justified by faith" (Rom 5:1). Our faith relies on the promise of God which has already been fulfilled through the death and resurrection of our Lord Jesus Christ. But Paul also implies our future justification in Rom 4:23–25, for as he says in 5:9, if "we have now been justified by his blood, much more shall we be saved by him from the wrath of God" (Rom 5:9). Thus, like Abraham, our faith relies on the promise of God which has not yet been fulfilled as well as the power of God to accomplish that promise.[59] Like Abraham, we believe "in hope against hope" over the course of many years. When we contemplate ourselves and our bodies and our circumstances, we find no reason for hope. Our faith in God is by definition "empty-handed," to use the words of Schliesser,[60] or "without," to use the words of this essay. How then can it be correct to say that the Pauline concept of faith must include in its very definition embodied works of human faithfulness?[61] Certainly Paul says in many places that our faith must result in love and good works (e.g., Eph 2:10). But these things are not a part of justifying faith any more than circumcision is. By definition, our faith does not find hope in our mortal bodies but rather believes and trusts in the God of grace who justifies the ungodly, raises the dead, and gives hope to the hopeless.

---

58. Rom 8:32 uses the same verb "gave him up" (παρέδωκεν) as "delivered up" (παρεδόθη) in Rom 4:23. Note also the allusion to Isa 53:12.

59. Wright suggests that the traditional reading of Rom 4:5 wrongly says that "Abraham is justified by faith because he believes in justification by faith" (*Perspectives*, 564). But while Paul clearly says that Abraham was justified because he believed in *God*, he also defines this God in whom Abraham believed as "him who justifies the ungodly." Thus, there must be some sense in which Abraham's faith in God included the truth that this God justifies the ungodly by faith.

60. Schliesser, *Romans 4*, 341, 386.

61. See Timmins' critique on Bates at this point, noting Paul's focus on Abraham's inability and bodily impotence in Rom 4 in response to Bates' argument that πίστις must include works of "embodied allegiance." Will N. Timmins, "A Faith Unlike Abraham's: Matthew Bates on Salvation by Allegiance Alone," *JETS* 61.3 (2018): 613.

Bibliography

Barclay, John M. G. *Paul and the Gift.* Grand Rapids: Eerdmans, 2015.

Dunn, James D. G. *The Theology of Paul the Apostle.* Grand Rapids: Eerdmans, 1998.

Gathercole, Simon J. *Where is Boasting? Early Jewish Soteriology and Paul's Response in Romans 1–5.* Grand Rapids: Eerdmans, 2002.

Hays, Richard B. *The Conversion of the Imagination: Paul as Interpreter of Israel's Scripture.* Grand Rapids: Eerdmans, 2005.

McFadden, Kevin. *Faith in the Son of God: The Place of Christ-Oriented Faith within Pauline Theology.* Wheaton, IL: Crossway, 2021.

Moo, Douglas J. *The Letter to the Romans.* 2nd ed. NICNT. Grand Rapids: Eerdmans, 2018.

Moule, C. F. D. *An Idiom Book of New Testament Greek.* 2nd ed. Cambridge: Cambridge University Press, 1959.

Schliesser, Benjamin. "'Abraham Did Not "Doubt" in Unbelief' (Rom. 4:20): Faith, Doubt, and Dispute in Paul's Letter to the Romans." *JTS* 63.2 (2012): 492–522.

———. *Abraham's Faith in Romans 4.* WUNT 2.224. Tübingen: Mohr Siebeck, 2007.

Schnabel, Eckhard J. *Der Brief des Paulus an die Römer: Kapitel 1–5.* HTA. Witten/Gießen: Brockhaus/Brunnen, 2015.

Schreiner, Thomas R. *Interpreting the Pauline Epistles.* 2nd ed. Grand Rapids: Baker Academic, 2011.

———. *Romans.* 2nd ed. BECNT. Grand Rapids: Baker Academic, 2018.

Thielman, Frank. *Romans.* ZECNT 6. Grand Rapids: Zondervan Academic, 2018.

Timmins, Will N. "A Faith Unlike Abraham's: Matthew Bates on Salvation by Allegiance Alone." *JETS* 61.3 (2018): 595–615.

Wintermute, O. S. "Jubilees (Second Century B.C.): A New Translation and Introduction." Pages 35–142 in vol. 2 of *The Old Testament Pseudepigrapha.* Edited by James H. Charlesworth. New York: Doubleday, 1985.

Wright, N. T. *Pauline Perspectives: Essays on Paul, 1978–2013.* Minneapolis: Fortress, 2013.

Wright, R. B. "Psalms of Solomon (First Century B.C.): A New Translation and Introduction." Pages 639–70 in vol. 2 of *The Old Testament Pseudepigrapha.* Edited by James H. Charlesworth. New York: Doubleday, 1985.

CHAPTER 9

Adam's Sin and Jesus' Death in Romans 5:12–21

Frank Thielman

In this chapter, I will argue that in Rom 5:12–21 Paul has two great concerns, each of them equally important, and each of them closely connected to the other. Paul's first concern is to show the overwhelmingly gracious nature of the death of Christ. Interpreters often recognize this first concern and sometimes comment on how important it is not to miss the significance of this theme by becoming bogged down in the difficult syntactical, rhetorical, and theological problems of v. 12.

Logically subordinate to this first concern, but no less important for Paul's argument, is his second concern. Paul wants to show that the amazing grace of Christ's death should give those who have received it the confidence that they are capable of living apart from sin's domination. The passage, therefore, points forward to chapter six, and Paul intends for it to assure his listeners that God's gracious justification and reconciliation of his people was an act of such power that it has established a new realm in which sin and death no longer hold sway over their lives.

This second concern is more controversial than the first concern. Interpreters typically take 5:12–21 as pointing mainly backwards to 5:1–11, to 3:21–5:11, or to all of 1:18–5:11. In one view, 5:12–21 illustrates by reference to Adam and Christ the doctrine of justification by faith that Paul has just finished explaining in the first part of the epistle.[1] In another view, 5:12–21 universalizes the reconciliation with God that Paul described in 5:1–11.[2] Yet another reading understands the passage as part of Paul's attempt in 5:1–8:39 to make more intelligible to non-Jews the ideas of universal sin and reconciliation to God that Paul expressed in Jewish terms in 1:18–4:25.[3] Still another interpretation claims the

---

1. See, e.g., Charles Hodge, *Commentary on the Epistle to the Romans* (Grand Rapids: Eerdmans, 1950 [orig. 1886]), 142–43; Eckhard J. Schnabel, *Der Brief des Paulus an die Römer: Kapitel 1–5*, 2nd ed., HTA (Witten/Gießen: Brockhaus/Brunnen, 2018), 545.

2. John Murray, *The Epistle to the Romans*, 2 vols., NICNT (Grand Rapids: Eerdmans, 1959–65), 1:179–80; Otto Michel, *Der Brief an die Römer*, 14th ed., KEK 4 (Göttingen: Vandenhoeck & Ruprecht, 1978), 185; Ernst Käsemann, *Commentary on Romans*, trans. and ed. Geoffrey W. Bromiley (Grand Rapids: Eerdmans, 1980), 141; Schnabel, *Der Brief des Paulus an die Römer: Kapitel 1–5*, 551.

3. Richard N. Longenecker, *The Epistle to the Romans: A Commentary on the Greek Text*, NIGTC (Grand Rapids: Eerdmans, 2016), 581–82.

passage provides further assurance to believers of the hope of reconciliation with God that Paul has just described in 5:1–11.[4]

Only very rarely have interpreters understood Paul's focus on the overwhelming nature of God's grace in 5:12–21 as purposefully laying the foundation for Paul's discourse on freedom from the power of sin in chapter six. They sometimes view chapter six as arising out of the contrast between Adam and Christ and the two ages they represent in 5:12–21. Ernst Käsemann, for example, says that in chapter six Paul issues a summons to Christians "to confirm in their personal life the change of aeons that has been effected" according to the Adam/Christ contrast of 5:12–21.[5] N. T. Wright similarly says that 5:12–21 is "the thematic statement out of which chaps. 6–8 are quarried," and that in chapter six Paul is answering the question, "Where do Christians live on the map of 5:12–21?"[6] Theodor Zahn comes close to the emphasis on God's grace that I would like to argue is the thread that connects 5:12–21 to chapter six. He understood 5:12 as the beginning of the third great section of the letter, stretching from 5:12 to 8:39, and labeled this large section, "The Royal Reign of the Grace of God in Christ over Christians."[7]

In the argument that follows, I do not intend to imply that the only function of 5:12–21 is to portray grace as an overwhelming power that gives believers the ability to live righteous lives. The passage probably has more than one function. My case is simply that 5:12–21 is foundational for what Paul says about believers refusing to let sin reign in their mortal bodies (6:12), and that providing this foundation is an important, and somewhat neglected, purpose for 5:12–21.

Despite the danger of getting carried away with the difficulties of 5:12, it is important to begin with this much contested verse. If the problems of the Greek are resolved according to the most likely interpretation of the grammar, and without allowing rhetorical and theological questions to overwhelm the discussion, Paul's primary concerns in the rest of the passage also become dominant in 5:12.

Difficulty begins immediately with Paul's opening διὰ τοῦτο. This phrase appears four other times in Romans, three times in the course of Paul's own

---

4. C. K. Barrett, *The Epistle to the Romans*, 2nd ed., BNTC 6 (Grand Rapids: Baker Academic, 1991), 102.

5. Käsemann, *Romans*, 159. His idea of God's righteousness as both gift and power also moves in this direction, although I want to be somewhat clearer than Käsemann that justification and sanctification do not merge together in Paul's thought. See Ernst Käsemann, *New Testament Questions of Today*, trans. W. J. Montague (Philadelphia: Fortress, 1969), 170; Käsemann, *Romans*, 175–76.

6. N. T. Wright, "The Letter to the Romans: Introduction, Commentary, and Reflections" in *The New Interpreter's Bible*, ed. Leander E. Keck (Nashville: Abingdon, 2002), 10:525, 533.

7. Theodor Zahn, *Der Brief des Paulus an die Römer*, 3rd ed., KNT 6 (Leipzig/Erlangen: A. Deichertsche/Werner Scholl, 1925), 261.

argument (1:26; 4:16; 5:12; 13:6), and a fourth time in a quotation from Scripture (15:9). If we discount this use of the phrase in a quotation, all of Paul's other uses point backward and draw a conclusion from something that he has previously said. It is likely, then, that Paul uses the phrase in the same way here. The phrase points backward to indicate that Paul is about to draw a conclusion from something he has said prior to 5:12.

This normal meaning for the phrase is controversial in this particular case, however, because, as Douglas Moo puts it, 5:12–21 makes "better sense when viewed as the *basis* for what has just been said" (italics mine).[8] The confidence Paul expresses in 5:1–11 that God will rescue believers from his future wrath seems more likely to be the result of the great reversal that Paul describes in 5:12–21 than the cause of that great reversal. To put it another way, Christ's reversal of the sin and death that Adam introduced into the world makes better sense as the foundation for Paul's boast in the hope of God's glory than as somehow the result of Paul's hope. Accordingly, interpreters sometimes give διὰ τοῦτο an unusual meaning: they read it simply as a transitional phrase or as pointing forward to the fulfillment of the hope that Paul expresses in 5:9–11.[9]

To understand the flow of Paul's argument this way, however, does not take sufficiently into account the transitional role that 5:12–21 plays in Paul's argument. This paragraph is a bridge between Paul's expression of confidence in God's love because of Christ's death (and resurrection) in 5:1–11 and the more admonitory tone of chapter six. The most straightforward way of taking Paul's discourse at this point is to view the διὰ τοῦτο as pointing back to v. 11 where Paul says that believers boast in God through the Lord Jesus Christ because of the reconciliation they have received with God through him. Paul will now say in 5:12–21 that this reconciliation with God, achieved by Christ, is the starting point and foundation for the believer's transition from the kingdom of sin and death into the kingdom of righteousness and life.

In order to make this point, Paul will continue to dwell on the death of Christ, just as he did in 5:6–10, but with two differences. First, he changes the way that he describes the benefit that believers receive from Christ's death. In 5:6–10 the benefit they received was a peaceful relationship with God, or, to put

---

8. Douglas J. Moo, *The Letter to the Romans*, 2nd ed., NICOT (Grand Rapids: Eerdmans, 2018), 345. See also Thomas R. Schreiner, *Romans*, 2nd ed., BECNT (Grand Rapids: Baker Academic, 2018), 277, who notes that "it is difficult to see how the preceding context functions as the basis or reason for the effect of Christ's work being greater than Adam's."

9. See, e.g., M. J. Lagrange, *Saint Paul: Épitre aux Romains*, 3rd ed. Ébib (Paris: Librairie Victor Lecoffre, 1925), 105 ("une simple liaison"); Michael Wolter, *Der Brief an die Römer (Teilband 1: Röm 1–8)*, EKK 6/1 (Neukirchen-Vluyn/Ostfildern: Neukirchener/Patmos, 2014), 341 ("Übergangswendung" [quoting Bultmann]); Moo, *Romans*, 345–46, the events described in 5:12–19 happened "for the sake of" the salvation described in vv. 9–11.

it another way, freedom from the wrath of his judgment. In 5:12–21 the benefit that believers receive from Christ's death is both freedom from the wrath of his judgment (δικαίωμα, v. 16) and freedom from the reign of sin and death (v. 21). Second, in order to make this change, Paul brings an additional figure into his argument, namely Adam, who introduced the powerful, reigning forces of sin and death into the world.

Even more contested than Paul's opening διὰ τοῦτο is the question of what Paul means by ἐφ' ᾧ in 5:12. When Paul uses this phrase, what exactly is he saying about the relationship between sin and death in Adam's experience and the relationship between sin and death in the experience of all subsequent human beings? Again, a straightforward reading of the Greek helps to solve the problem.

In a carefully researched study that, in my opinion, no one has successfully refuted after more than a quarter century, Joseph Fitzmyer argued that despite the modern tendency to translate this phrase "because" in RomO 5:12, it is very unlikely to have this meaning.[10] The phrase most naturally means "with the result that" or "whereupon." It is sometimes said that Paul himself uses the phrase to mean "because" in 2 Cor 5:4, Phil 3:12, and Phil 4:10, and so it likely has the same meaning here.[11] The phrase seems to have different meanings in each of these other passages, however, and in none of them is "because" an obvious choice. If we then take the phrase with its more common meaning in Greek generally, Paul is saying four things in 5:12:

1. that sin entered the world through Adam's disobedience,

2. that death entered the world through sin,

3. that the entrance of sin and death through Adam's disobedience affected all human beings, and

4. when these three events happened, or as a result of these three events, all people sinned.

To put it succinctly, Rom 5:12 is about the beginning of the reign of sin and death over the world. It makes the point that this reign began with one human being and has held within its power all human beings who have ever lived since that time. Paul will not use the verb βασιλεύω until 5:14, but, already in 5:12, he has set the stage for portraying sin and death as co-regents over God's rebellious creation.[12]

---

10. Joseph A. Fitzmyer, "The Consecutive Meaning of ἐφ' ᾧ in Romans 5.12," NTS 39 (1993): 321–39.

11. See, e.g., Arland J. Hultgren, Paul's Letter to the Romans: A Commentary (Grand Rapids: Eerdmans, 2011), 222.

12. As Robert Jewett, Romans: A Commentary, Hermeneia (Minneapolis: Fortress, 2007), 370, says, "The verb 'rule over' is . . . a key to the passage, employed for Adam,

The point of vv. 13–14 is to put the finishing touches on this important part of the argument. These verses explain the extent to which sin and death affected all of humanity. Even before the law appeared on the scene to provide an explicit description of sin and its penalty, sin and death reigned over the world like kings. Paul had already said that the law produces God's wrath and that where there is no law there is no transgression (4:15). His readers might therefore assume that in the absence of the law the reign of sin and death over humanity was less secure. In vv. 13–14, Paul makes clear that sin and death reigned just as securely in the absence of the law as in its presence. Those who sinned without a specific commandment from God to transgress, still sinned, and both spiritual and physical death justly came upon them as the penalty for their sin.

In a commentary on Romans that appeared in 2018, I followed the view that 5:13–14 are an interruption to the main flow of Paul's thought and that the main line of Paul's argument, which he started in 5:12, did not get back on track until v. 18.[13] I am now beginning to think, however, that although vv. 13–14 are a grammatical interruption to the syntax of 5:12, they are not at all an interruption to the main idea that Paul is developing in 5:12. Paul intended to say something like what he says in vv. 13–14 when he started the section. He just had trouble expressing all that he wanted to say in a single, long sentence.

Just as in 1:18–3:20, then, Paul emphasizes in 5:12–14 the depth of the human plight before turning to God's solution to that plight in the death of Christ. Here in 5:12–14, however, sin and death move from simply being transgression and its penalty, as they were in 1:18–3:20 (1:32; 2:12–13; 3:9, 20, 23; 4:7–8), into being powers that reign over the world. Here Paul depicts the human plight in even darker terms than he had portrayed it in 1:18–3:20. We now learn that the irresponsible conduct Paul described in 1:18–3:20 was not simply the product of a series of bad choices to which God handed people over (1:24, 26, 28), but was also the product of an original bad choice. Adam's decision to disobey God damaged the rest of humanity to the extent that they would inevitably make his same mistake and suffer the same penalty.

Paul deepens the somber colors of his portrayal of human sin in 5:12–14 because he intends to demonstrate the lavish nature of God's grace revealed in the death of Christ. This, in turn, will prove that God's grace is powerful enough fully to overcome the domination of sin. Just as Paul follows his lengthy, depressing description of human sin in 1:18–3:20 with the good news of God's

---

Christ, and finally for believers reigning through Christ in the fivefold paronomasia of vv. 14, 17, 21."

13. Frank Thielman, *Romans*, ZECNT 6 (Grand Rapids: Zondervan Academic, 2018), 285. Wolter, *Der Brief an die Römer (Teilband 1: Röm 1–8)*, 362, says that Paul lost control of a sentence that he intended as a short appendix to 5:1–11 and produced instead a weighty discourse on the relationship between sin and grace.

grace in 3:21–26, so he follows his even more depressing statement about the universal domination of sin and death in 5:12–14 with a description of God's overwhelming grace. This emphasis on grace comes not only through the "how much more" phrases in 5:15 and 17, but through Paul's recollection and intensification of the language of free grace that he used in 3:24 to describe the gracious nature of God's redemption in Christ's death. In 3:24, Paul had spoken of "being justified freely by [God's] grace" (δικαιούμενοι δωρεὰν τῇ αὐτοῦ χάριτι), using the noun δωρεά in the accusative singular as an adverb together with the noun χάρις to emphasize the enormous generosity God displayed in justifying those who have sinned and fallen short of God's glory.[14]

Now, Paul repeats that combination of terms in a way that echoes 3:24 but emphasizes the overpowering grace of God even more fully than he had done in that passage. Once again, he uses δωρεά, and words closely related to it, in combination with χάρις and its cognates, but now he uses this combination repeatedly. In v. 15 he speaks of "the grace (χάρις) of God and the free gift (δωρεὰ) in grace (χάριτι)." In v. 16 he speaks of "the gift"—the δώρημα—then the "gracious gift"—the χάρισμα. In v. 17, he describes people who "receive the abundance of grace (χάριτος) and the gift (δωρεᾶς) of righteousness." Paul articulates the point of this emphasis clearly in v. 17: "If, by the transgression of the one man, death reigned (ἐβασίλευσεν) through that one man, how much more will those who receive the abundance of grace and the gift of righteousness reign (βασιλεύσουσιν) in life through Jesus Christ." As Paul's use of the term "reign" for the first time since v. 14 shows, he is saying here that God's overpowering grace through the death of Christ has toppled the reign of sin and death that began with Adam and affected everyone according to vv. 12–14.

It is also important for understanding the development of Paul's argument in chapter six, with its emphasis on Christ's death, that the death of Christ lies behind Paul's use of "gift" and "grace" language in 5:15–17. That language recalls Paul's statement in 3:24 that believers were justified freely by God's grace in the sacrificial death of Christ. This is also something that the explicit reference to Christ's death as a sign of God's love just a few sentences earlier, in 5:6–10, should make clear. Later, then, when Paul speaks of the "righteous deed" (δικαίωμα) of Christ in 5:18 and the "obedience" (ὑπακοή) of Christ in 5:19 he is not speaking of the obedience that Christ gave to God throughout his whole life as Charles Cranfield thought.[15] He is instead speaking specifically of Christ's obedient death.

14. See also Ulrich Wilckens, *Der Brief an die Römer (Röm 1–5)*, EKK 6/1 (Zürich/Neukirchener-Vluyn: Benziger/Neukirchener, 1978), 307.

15. C. E. B. Cranfield, *A Critical and Exegetical Commentary on the Epistle to the Romans*, 2 vols., ICC (Edinburgh: T&T Clark, 1975–79), 1:289, cf. 291.

In 5:20–21 Paul summarizes the theme of the whole passage but now uses the law as the means of proving his point. He picks up the story of humanity where 5:14 left off and answers the question of whether the entrance of the law onto the scene somehow improved the human condition. Quite the opposite, Paul insists, it only made the situation worse and confirmed the co-regency of sin and death over human beings. As we already expect from the preceding argument, however, Paul maintains with equal conviction that in the very place where sin increased, "grace immeasurably exceeded it" (as the REB translates ὑπερεπερίσσευσεν ἡ χάρις). Here, it seems to me, Cranfield is precisely right when he says that the very place where sin increased was in the human hard-heartedness and injustice that led to Christ's crucifixion.[16] In this place, where sin did its worst, God revealed his grace to a superlative degree.

To summarize our argument so far, in 5:12–21 Paul describes the human plight under sin and death in emphatically bleak terms. This plight extends chronologically all the way back to the first man, Adam, and extends universally to every human being, even to those that had received no specific revelation of God's law. Paul describes the human plight this way because he wants to stress the overwhelming greatness of God's grace, which did not merely overcome this plight in all its profundity but did so in a way that "vastly exceeded" its effects (v. 15, REB). Paul describes all this without referring explicitly to the death of Christ, but he uses language that also makes clear how critical Christ's death was in effecting this massively gracious reversal.

If we think of the argument of 5:12–21 in this way, then the nature of the opening rhetorical questions of chapter six becomes clear: "What, then, shall we say? Should we remain in sin in order that grace may abound?" These questions probably reflect a charge that has been levelled at Paul, and in 5:12–21 he has laid a firm theological foundation for refuting this charge.[17] As with his effort to refute the similar charge in 3:8, Paul is flabbergasted that anyone could conclude from what he actually teaches about God's grace that remaining in sin is an option. God's grace, shown most perfectly in the death of Christ, is a powerful force, not merely just as powerful as sin and death, but more so. According to 5:21, grace is a king that reigns over God's people because it won a massive victory over the co-regents sin and death. The idea of combining this understanding of God's grace with the claim that God's people are free to sin was therefore ludicrous. In chapter six, Paul will show how absurd this idea is by building on the foundation he has laid in 5:12–21 with its description of the greatness of God's grace in the death of Christ.

---

16. Cranfield, *Romans*, 1:293–94.

17. For the idea that Paul responds to opponents in 6:1, see Peter Stuhlmacher, *Paul's Letter to the Romans: A Commentary*, trans. Scott J. Hafemann (Louisville: Westminster John Knox, 1994), 90.

First, in 6:2–11, Paul will describe the importance of the death of Christ in releasing God's people from living within the sphere of sin's control. Just as Jesus died on the cross, so believers have "died to sin" (6:2), have been "baptized into his death" (6:3–4), have been "united in the likeness of his death" (6:5), have been "crucified together" with him (6:6), and have "died with" him (6:8). That Paul is thinking of death here as a power that once ruled over humanity, but whose rule is now broken because of Christ's death, becomes clear in 6:9. Here, Paul again uses the language of political domination to show that death's reign over humanity has been broken by the death of Christ. "We know that Christ, having been raised from the dead," Paul says, "no longer dies; death no longer rules over him." The verb Paul uses for "rules over" here is κυριεύω rather than the βασιλεύω of chapter five, but the concept is the same.[18] The power of death to rule over all humanity has, through the death of Christ, been broken for the first time since Adam sinned, and believers are united with Christ's death in precisely this sense. For them, too, the power of death has been broken.

If the power of death has been broken for them, however, so has the power of sin, for we know from 5:12–21 that sin and death are co-regents. They rule over humanity together and work in tandem. Thus, throughout 6:1–11, Paul insists that to die with Christ on the cross, and in this way to defeat the power of death, also entails a release from the power of sin. Then, in 6:12–14, Paul uses the language of dominion to recall even more explicitly the argument of 5:12–21 and to make the case that believers are under the reign of the powerful grace that Paul described in that passage, and not under the reign of sin. He uses the verb βασιλεύω in 6:12, for the first time since its fivefold use in 5:14–21. He also refers to ὅπλα twice in 6:13, and he uses this word in a context thick with metaphors drawn from the world of political domination. This term, then, should probably be translated "weapons" rather than the usual "instruments."[19] He concludes the first part of chapter six in v. 14 with the summary statement, "sin will not rule over (κυριεύσει) you, for you are not under law, but under grace." This summary clearly recalls the implication of 5:12–21 that God's grace is a powerful force that has conquered the ability of sin and death to hold sway over humanity.

---

18. Commentators occasionally recognize this. See, e.g., James D. G. Dunn, *Romans 1–8*, WBC 38A (Dallas: Word, 1988), 323 ("κυριεύω is used synonymously with βασιλεύω, as the parallel with 5:14, 17 shows"); Jewett, *Romans*, 407 ("The power of death referred to in 5:14 and 17 has been broken by Christ"); Wolter, *An die Römer (Teilband 1: Röm 1–8)*, 382 ("Mit V. 9 wiederholt Paulus denselben Gedanken in den Kategorien von Röm 5,14.17"). Eckhard J. Schnabel, *Der Brief des Paulus an die Römer: Kapitel 6–16*, HTA (Witten/Gießen: Brockhaus/Brunnen, 2016), 50 ("Jesus hat durch seinen Sündetod am Kreuz und seine Auferstehung die seit Adam bestehende Herrschaft beendet, die der Tod [θάνατος] infolge der Sünde über die Menschen ausübte [5,14.17]").

19. Jewett, *Romans*, 410; Wolter, *An die Römer (Teilband 1: Röm 1–8)*, 390; Schnabel, *Der Brief des Paulus an die Römer: Kapitel 6–16*, 58.

In 6:1–14, then, Paul draws an ethical conclusion from his argument in 5:12–21 that the death of Christ and the grace of God has defeated the co-regency of sin and death over humanity. The great power of God's grace on display there, and the effect of Christ's death on the power of sin, has broken the rule of sin and death over God's people and made righteous living and eternal life more of a possibility for them than for any set of human beings since Adam's transgression.

Bibliography

Barrett, C. K. *The Epistle to the Romans*. 2nd ed. BNTC 6. Grand Rapids: Baker Academic, 1991.

Cranfield, C. E. B. *A Critical and Exegetical Commentary on the Epistle to the Romans*. 2 vols. ICC. Edinburgh: T&T Clark, 1975–79.

Dunn, James D. G. *Romans 1–8*. WBC 38A. Dallas: Word, 1988.

Fitzmyer, Joseph A. "The Consecutive Meaning of ἐφ᾽ ᾧ in Romans 5.12." *NTS* 39 (1993): 321–39.

Hodge, Charles. *Commentary on the Epistle to the Romans*. Grand Rapids: Eerdmans, 1950 [orig. 1886].

Hultgren, Arland J. *Paul's Letter to the Romans: A Commentary*. Grand Rapids: Eerdmans, 2011.

Jewett, Robert. *Romans: A Commentary*. Hermeneia. Minneapolis: Fortress, 2007.

Käsemann, Ernst. *Commentary on Romans*. Translated and edited by Geoffrey W. Bromiley. Grand Rapids: Eerdmans, 1980.

———. *New Testament Questions of Today*. Translated by W. J. Montague. Philadelphia: Fortress, 1969.

Lagrange, M. J. *Saint Paul: Épitre aux Romains*. 3rd ed. *Ébib*. Paris: Librairie Victor Lecoffre, 1925.

Longenecker, Richard N. *The Epistle to the Romans: A Commentary on the Greek Text*. NIGTC. Grand Rapids: Eerdmans, 2016.

Michel, Otto. *Der Brief an die Römer*. 14th ed. KEK 4. Göttingen: Vandenhoeck & Ruprecht, 1978.

Moo, Douglas J. *The Letter to the Romans*. 2nd ed. NICNT. Grand Rapids: Eerdmans, 2018.

Murray, John. *The Epistle to the Romans*. 2 vols. NICNT. Grand Rapids: Eerdmans, 1959–65.

Schnabel, Eckhard J. *Der Brief des Paulus an die Römer: Kapitel 1–5*. 2nd ed. HTA. Witten/Gießen: Brockhaus/Brunnen, 2018.

———. *Der Brief des Paulus an die Römer: Kapitel 6–16*. HTA. Witten/Gießen: Brockhaus/Brunnen, 2016.

Schreiner, Thomas R. *Romans.* 2nd ed. BECNT. Grand Rapids: Baker Academic, 2018.

Stuhlmacher, Peter. *Paul's Letter to the Romans: A Commentary.* Translated by Scott J. Hafemann. Louisville: Westminster John Knox, 1994.

Thielman, Frank. *Romans.* ZECNT 6. Grand Rapids: Zondervan Academic, 2018.

Wilckens, Ulrich. *Der Brief an die Römer (Röm 1–5).* EKK 6/1. Zürich/Neukirchener-Vluyn: Benziger/Neukirchener, 1978.

Wolter, Michael. *Der Brief an die Römer (Teilband 1: Röm 1–8).* EKK 6/1. Neukirchener-Vluyn/Ostfildern: Neukirchener/Patmos, 2014.

Wright, N. T. "The Letter to the Romans: Introduction, Commentary, and Reflections." Pages 395–770 in vol. 10 of *The New Interpreter's Bible.* Edited by Leander E. Keck. Nashville: Abingdon, 2002.

Zahn, Theodor. *Der Brief des Paulus an die Römer.* 3rd ed. KNT 6. Leipzig/Erlangen: A. Deichertsche/Werner Scholl, 1925.

CHAPTER 10

Terms for Sin in Romans

Benjamin Gladd

This essay attempts to evaluate a handful of prominent terms for sin in the book of Romans. Any attempt to study specific terms is, however, beset with a host of methodological issues: the word-concept fallacy, the etymological fallacy, and so on. Our best defense against word fallacies is to examine these sin terms in the immediate and broad context of Romans. Further, what constitutes a "sin term"? Some words, such as "desire" (ἐπιθυμία), can refer to a sin (e.g., Rom 1:24) but not always (e.g., Phil 1:23). So, our brief investigation will focus on the more prominent terms that Paul invokes at key junctures in his epistle. We are also on the hunt for patterns within Romans that reveal redemptive-historical clues about how the apostle conceives of sin. Since Paul establishes the major theological planks of his argument in the first half of the letter, we will confine our investigation there.

Unbelieving Gentiles (1:18–32)

Scholars interpret Paul's target audience in 1:18–32 as primarily (but not exclusively) Gentiles. Verse 18, perhaps functioning as the heading of the entire section of 1:18–3:20,[1] is critical. According to 1:18, God pours out his wrath upon "all godlessness and wickedness of people" (ἐπὶ πᾶσαν ἀσέβειαν καὶ ἀδικίαν ἀνθρώπων).[2] The two important terms ἀσέβεια and ἀδικία are coupled in several OT (LXX Ps 72:6; Prov 11:5; Job 36:18; Hos 10:13; Mic 7:18; Ezek 18:30; 21:24) and Jewish texts (e.g., *Deus* 112; *Sacr.* 22; *Spec.* 1.215; *J. W.* 7.260; *Ag. Ap.* 2.217, 2.291; 1 En. 10:20; 13:2). And many of these texts use the two terms as a general reference to wickedness. For example, LXX Ps 72:2b–8 reads:

> My steps nearly slipped,
> because I was envious of *the lawless* [τοῖς ἀνόμοις],
>   as I observed *sinners'* [ἁμαρτωλῶν] peace,
> because there is nothing negative to their death
>   and no firmness in their scourge.

---

1. Douglas J. Moo, *The Letter to the Romans*, 2nd ed., NICNT (Grand Rapids: Eerdmans, 2018), 108.

2. Unless otherwise noted, all English translations are based upon the NIV (2011).

They are not in trouble of human beings,
and with human beings they will not be scourged.
Therefore pride seized them;
they clothed themselves with *injustice* [ἀδικίαν] and their
impiety [ἀσέβειαν].
Their *injustice* [ἡ ἀδικία] will go forth as though from fat;
they progressed according to their heart's disposition.
They schemed and spoke with malice;
injustice [ἀδικίαν] they spoke against the height.[3]

In the immediate context of Rom 1, the two terms ἀσέβεια and ἀδικία may be an umbrella that covers all the particular sins mentioned in 1:21–32. The term ἀσέβεια and its cognates (e.g., ἀσεβέω, ἀσεβής, σέβω) highlight one's devotion or worship to a deity (e.g., Josh 4:24; 1 Macc 1:3), whereas ἀδικία and its cognates (e.g., ἀδικέω, ἀδίκημα, ἄδικος, ἀδίκως, δίκαιος, δικαιοσύνη, δικαιόω, δικαίωμα, δικαίως) are broader and often found in contexts referring to one's relationship to God's personal attributes, his law/covenant, or to the natural order of the cosmos (e.g., Exod 9:27; Deut 32:43). Therefore, any act that is antithetical to exclusive worship of God or any behavior that violates God's character and law can be deemed ἀσέβεια or ἀδικία.

In Rom 1, Paul explains *why* Gentiles are guilty of both ἀσέβεια and ἀδικία and thus deserving of God's wrath. He anchors his indictment of them in 1:18b–20 and 1:21–23. Although the Gentiles are not privy to Mosaic legislation, knowledge of God is still evident. Further, according to 1:23, unbelieving Gentiles "exchanged the glory of the immortal God for images made to look like a mortal human being and birds and animals and reptiles." Paul alludes here to Ps 106:20 and Jer 2:11. According to Ps 106 and Jer 2, the first generation of Israelites committed idolatry, and subsequent generations of Israelites repeat the same form of idolatry. Paul's language of "image," "man," "birds," "animals," and "reptiles" also recalls Gen 1–3. Romans 1:21–32 is brimming with idolatry, then, and 1:25 makes this connection explicit: "They exchanged the truth about God for a lie, and *worshiped and served created things rather than the Creator* [ἐσεβάσθησαν καὶ ἐλάτρευσαν τῇ κτίσει παρὰ τὸν κτίσαντα]."

So, unbelieving Gentiles bear God's wrath, *because* they commit ἀσέβεια and ἀδικία. Why are they in a state of ἀσέβεια and ἀδικία? They, like the first generation of Israelites and, ultimately, Adam and Eve, reject God's law and choose to worship creation instead of the Creator.

---

3. Paul's wording in 1:18 also resembles Ezekiel's oracle of judgment against the nation of Israel: "Because you recalled your *injustices* [ἀδικίας] *when your impieties were uncovered* [ἐν τῷ ἀποκαλυφθῆναι τὰς ἀσεβείας], that your sins be seen in all your *impieties* [ἀσεβείαις] and in your practices—because you recalled, you shall be captured by means of them" (LXX Ezek 21:29 [Eng. 21:24]). *If* Paul alludes to Ezek 21, then he sees the Gentiles mimicking the same behavior that incurred God's judgment in sending the nation to Babylonian captivity (Ezek 21:19–23).

Unbelieving Jews (2:1–3:8)

The Jewish dialogue partner in ch. 2, while probably hypothetical, embodies a real, historical viewpoint. Unbelieving, idolatrous first-century Jews find themselves in the same predicament as unbelieving Gentiles (1:18–32). God's "wrath" also comes upon unbelieving Jews; they stand condemned because of their "stubbornness and . . . unrepentant heart" (τὴν σκληρότητά σου καὶ ἀμετανόητον καρδίαν; 2:5). Just as pagan Gentiles are in a state of ἀδικία (1:18), so are unbelieving Jews, explaining why Paul applies the same key term ἀδικία to Jews (2:8; 3:5).

Why do many Jews commit ἀδικία? They stand condemned for two reasons: First, instead of fashioning physical idols out of gold and silver, they manufacture figurative ones out of God's law. They worship the law instead of the Lawgiver and "boast" in their covenantal identity rather than the one who cut that covenant with them (2:17, 23). The sin of idolatry may elucidate why Paul weds "stubbornness" (σκληρότητά) and "heart" (καρδία) in 2:5. The same terms or cognates thereof are littered throughout the exodus narrative referring to the "hardness" of Pharaoh's "heart" (e.g., Exod 4:21; 7:3; 10:1; 11:10). Elsewhere in the OT, the nation of Israel possesses a "hardened heart" on account of unbelief and idolatry (Deut 10:16; Ps 94:8 [Eng. 95:8]; Isa 63:17; Jer 4:4; cf. Bar 2:30). Second, in addition to worshiping the law, Jews are also guilty before God because they "steal," "commit adultery," and "rob temples" (2:21–22). These three activities correspond to the second, seventh, and eighth commandments (Exod 20:4–5, 14, 15; Deut 5:8, 18, 19). Paul then labels this form of treason as "breaking the law" (παραβάσεως τοῦ νόμου; 2:23; see 4:15; 5:14) and considers first-century Jews as "lawbreakers" (παραβάτης; 2:25, 27). Note that Paul does not use the term "lawbreaker" in his previous indictment of Gentiles in ch. 1; he reserves this special term for the Jews and their relationship to the Mosaic covenant. In broaching the issue of "lawbreaking," he also prepares his audience for a fuller exposition of sin, transgression, and lawbreaking in ch. 5.

Therefore, the Jewish people, like the Gentiles, commit ἀδικία. Like the Gentiles, unbelieving Jews commit a form of idolatry by worshiping the law and breaking the very law they pledged to obey. They are lawbreakers (παραβάτης). First-century Jews too repeat the sins of the first generation of Israelites. Paul describes the Gentiles as committing ἀσέβεια in ch. 1, but that term does not occur in ch. 2; instead, Paul puts his finger on the Jews' relationship to the Torah in his use of παράβασις/παραβάτης.

All Humanity (3:9–20)

In ch. 3, Paul concludes that both groups "are all under the power of sin" (πάντας ὑφ᾽ ἁμαρτίαν εἶναι; 3:9). The unique phrase ὑπό ἁμαρτία or ὑπὸ τὴν ἁμαρτίαν does not occur in the LXX but only in Rom 3:9, 7:14, and Gal 3:22. By employing this unusual expression, Paul personifies sin as a controlling power[4] that subjects all of humanity under its tyranny. No one is "righteous" (δίκαιος; 3:10) before God, and the string of texts from the OT in 3:10–18 demonstrate that the "whole world is *accountable* [ὑπόδικος] to God" (3:19).

The Fall of Adam (5:12–21)

Paul deems all humanity as "ungodly" (ἀσεβῶν; 5:6) and "sinners" (ἁμαρτωλῶν; 5:8). He argues in ch. 1–2 that Gentiles and Jews commit idolatry and break God's law, but here in ch. 5 we learn *why* ἀδικία is unavoidable and *why* sin imprisons humanity. Before we get into the why, let's examine Paul's unique portrayal of sin.

The personification of sin, first broached in 3:9, continues into ch. 5: "sin entered the world through one man" (5:12a);[5] "sin was in the world before the law was given" (5:13a). While "sin" (ἁμαρτία) is rarely personified in the LXX (see Sir 27:10; Wis 3:6), Paul appears to personify it in Rom 5:20–21, 6:12, 6:14, 7:8–9, 11, 13, 17, 20 and once in 1 Cor 15:56 (see also James 1:15). Paul doesn't explain here in ch. 5 where sin originated, but he does describe how it penetrated the cosmos and infected the created order.

All are sinners and ungodly because of the first Adam's "transgression": "death reigned from Adam to Moses, even over those who did not sin in the likeness of Adam's *transgression* [παραβάσεως]" (5:14). We first encountered παράβασις/παραβάτης in 2:23–27, where Paul condemns Jews for breaking the law of Moses. Here, though, Paul forces his audience to read between the lines. Did Adam, like Israel, break a *covenant*, or did he simply break God's *law*? Both terms (παράβασις/παραβάτης) are elsewhere in the NT connected to violating specific commands of the Mosaic covenant (e.g., James 2:11) and the covenant itself (e.g., Heb 9:15). In the LXX, παραβαίνω/παράβασις often entails Israel's breaking of the Mosaic covenant:[6]

---

4. Murray J. Harris, *Prepositions and Theology in the Greek New Testament* (Grand Rapids: Zondervan, 2012), 221.

5. As far as I can tell and with the exception of 7:9, Rom 5:12 is the only place in Jewish and Christian literature where ἁμαρτία is the subject of ἔρχομαι and its cognates.

6. Jubilees 3.32 likewise pairs παραβαίνω/παράβασις with Adam's failure in the garden, "In the seventh year *he transgressed* [παρέβη] and in the eighth they had cast (them) from Paradise . . . after forty-five days since *the transgression* [τῆς παραβάσεως], in the rising of Pleiades. Adam made in Paradise a calendar (consisting of) three hundred sixty-five days. And he was cast out with the woman Eve, on account of *the transgression* [τὴν παράβασιν] on the tenth (day) of the month of May." Translation from Craig A. Evans, *The Pseudepigrapha* (Oak Tree Software, 2009).

The people have sinned and *transgressed the covenant* [παρέβη τὴν διαθήκην] that I made with them. (Josh 7:11)[7]

They did not obey the voice of the Lord, their God, but *transgressed his covenant* [παρέβησαν τὴν διαθήκην αὐτοῦ]—all that Moyses the slave of the Lord had commanded. (2 Kgs 18:12)

You were transgressing my covenant [παρεβαίνετε τὴν διαθήκην μου] in all your lawless acts. (Ezek 44:7)[8]

On the other hand, παραβαίνω/παράβασις is found in conjunction with God's commandments on a few occasions:

So that his heart may not be exalted above his brothers so that he not *turn aside from the commandments* [παραβῇ ἀπὸ τῶν ἐντολῶν]. (Deut 17:20)

We have sinned, acted wickedly, done wrong and rebelled and *passed over your commandments* [παρέβημεν τὰς ἐντολάς σου]. (Dan 9:5)

Do not desire to sin or *to transgress his commandments* [παραβῆναι τὰς ἐντολὰς αὐτοῦ]. (Tob 4:5)[9]

The scales may tilt in favor of viewing Adam's failure as a covenantal breach in light of Paul's contrast with the last Adam's faithfulness that produces "the gift of righteousness" (5:17; see also 5:19). According to Gen 1–2, God promised the first Adam end-time righteousness upon perfect obedience to the covenant of works. Adam breaks that covenant by disobeying God's law (Gen 1:28; 2:15–17; 2:24). Even if Paul is not describing the first Adam's relationship to the covenant here in ch. 5, but the specific prohibition in Gen 2:17, my overall point remains the same: Adam's idolatrous behavior in the garden continues to manifest itself within his offspring. In other words, history repeats itself.

The switch from παράβασις in 5:14 to παράπτωμα in 5:15–18, 20 is perplexing:

Nevertheless, death reigned from the time of Adam to the time of Moses, even over those who did not sin by *breaking a command* [παραβάσεως]. (v. 14)

But the gift is not like *the trespass* [ὁ παράπτωμα]. For if the many died by *the trespass* [παραπτώματι] of the one man . . . (v. 15)

The gift followed many *trespasses* [παραπτωμάτων] and brought justification. (v. 16)

---

7. Unless otherwise noted, all English translations of the LXX are adapted from the NETS.

8. See also Josh 7:15; 23:16; Hos 6:7; 8;1; Isa 24:5; Ezek 17:15–16, 18–19.

9. See also Ps 100:3; 4 Macc 9:1; 13:15; 16:24; Sir 10:19; 39:31.

Just as one *trespass* [παραπτώματος] resulted in condemnation for all people
... (v. 18)

The law was brought in so that *the trespass* [παράπτωμα] might increase (v. 20)

Why the shift? The term παράπτωμα invokes the image of taking a wrong
step,[10] while παράβασις means to overstep a boundary.[11] According to the LXX,
παραπίπτω/παράπτωμα broadly refers to any behavior that lacks conformity
to God's perfect standard. Ezekiel 18:24 reads, for example,

> After the *righteous one* [δίκαιον] turns back *from his righteousness* [ἐκ τῆς
> δικαιοσύνης αὐτοῦ] and commits *injustice* [ἀδικίαν] *like all the lawless acts
> that the lawless commits* [κατὰ πάσας τὰς ἀνομίας, ἃς ἐποίησεν ὁ ἄνομος],
> none of *his righteous acts* [αἱ δικαιοσύναι αὐτοῦ] that he performed shall be
> remembered, for his *transgression* [ἐν τῷ παραπτώματι] by which *he trans-
> gressed* [παρέπεσεν] and *in his sins that he committed* [αἷς ἁμαρτίαις αὐτοῦ,
> αἷς ἥμαρτεν] in these he shall die.[12]

The two terms, παράβασις and παράπτωμα, then, appear to be nearly identical
in meaning.

In summary, on account of Adam breaking God's covenant, all of humanity is subjected to the tyranny of sin and powerless to breaks its bonds. Adam's
transgression/trespass generates humanity's ungodliness (ἀδικία) and, subsequently, God's wrath. Synthesizing our previous conclusions, we discover
that Adam's conduct in the garden (5:12–21) produced offspring that mirror
his idolatrous actions. According to 1:22–25, Gentiles commit the same form
of idolatry by worshiping "created things" rather than the "Creator." While
Paul doesn't explicitly connect Jewish idolatry to Adam in 2:1–3:8, it lurks in
the background through his use of παράβασις/παραβάτης (2:23–27) and then
comes into the foreground in his personal relationship to the law in 7:7–12. Not
only is sin itself passed down from Adam to his descendants—the form of sin,
namely, idolatry—rears its ugly head in every succeeding generation.

Romans 7: Sin and the Serpent

Paul's explanation of sin reaches a highpoint in ch. 7 when he discusses the relationship between sin and the law. His personification of sin first appears in 3:9
and then continues in ch. 5 and 6 (5:12, 13, 20–21, 6:12, 14). Here in 7:7b–11 Paul
virtually equates sin with the serpent itself:

---

10. Louw and Nida 88.297.
11. *LSJ*, 1305; BDAG s.v. παράβασις (758).
12. See also Ps 18:13; 21:2; Ezek 3:20; 14:11, 13; 15:8; 18:24; 20:27; Zech 9:5.

For I would not have known what coveting really was if the law had not said, "You shall not covet." But *sin, seizing the opportunity afforded by the commandment, produced in me every kind of coveting.* For apart from the law, sin was dead. Once I was alive apart from the law; but when the commandment came, *sin sprang to life* and I died. I found that the very commandment that was intended to bring life actually brought death. For *sin,* seizing the opportunity afforded by the commandment, *deceived me,* and through the commandment *put me to death.*

As some commentators argue, Paul brilliantly blends Adam and Israel's conduct. Both parties fail, succumbing to idolatry and breaking God's law. The Adamic dimension is worth contemplating.

Paul states that sin "deceived" (ἐξηπάτησέν)[13] him and "put" him "to death" (ἀπέκτεινεν). The Serpent is now the very source of sin that enslaves humanity: "For sin [ἁμαρτία], seizing an opportunity through the commandment, deceived me, and through it killed me" (7:11). Up to this point, Paul characterized sin as a power that infested the cosmos and enslaves all of humanity (3:9; 5:20–21, 6:12, 14). He finally unmasks the power as Satan himself. Notice the progression in Paul's personification of sin from a domain of rule to the ruler himself:

Jews and Gentiles alike are all under the power of sin. (Rom 3:9)

Sin *reigned* [ἐβασίλευσεν] in death. (Rom 5:21)

Do not let sin *reign* [βασιλευέτω] in your mortal body. (Rom 6:12)

For sin . . . *put me to death* [ἀπέκτεινεν]. (Rom 7:11)

It appears that the next explicit reference to Satan is in 16:20 when God promises to "soon crush Satan" under the church's "feet"—a clear allusion to Gen 3:15.

Paul's progression from sin to the serpent reinforces the importance of Gen 1–3 in the story line of the Bible. The serpent's victory in the idolatrous fall of Adam and Eve in the paradise of Eden repeated itself throughout every generation of humanity—Jews and Gentiles. But Jesus' life, death, and resurrection broke the chain. On the cross, Jesus identifies with sinners and bears God's just wrath. But Jesus not only functions as a substitutionary sacrifice, he also, as Israel's king, defeats the devil. He conquers the cause (the serpent) and the effect (sin). This explains why Paul opens his letter with a description of Christ as a "descendant of David" (1:3), who has come to conquer humanity's greatest enemy. It may also explain why Paul sounds off with a reference to the

---

13. Josephus also uses the same word in the context of the serpent's deception of Eve: "she persuaded Adam with the same arguments wherewith the serpent *had persuaded* [ἐξηπάτησε] her" (*Ant.* 1.49; see also *QG* 1.31; *Sib. Or.* 1:40; *LAE* 16:5).

church's "already but not yet" defeat of Satan. With the battle now won, the church actively "crushes" under its "feet" (16:20) by obeying the gospel and proclaiming it to the nations.

Conclusion

In ch. 1 Paul condemns the Gentiles because they, like Adam, worship idols—the creature instead of the Creator. They commit ἀσέβεια and ἀδικία. Jews, too, remain guilty before God and commit ἀδικία. Like the Gentiles in ch. 1, unbelieving Jews commit idolatry by worshiping the law and breaking the very law they pledged to obey. They are, like the first generation of Israelites, lawbreakers (παραβάτης). Both groups, then, are now "under the power of sin" (ὑφ᾽ ἁμαρτίαν; 3:9). Sin has imprisoned them. Paul discloses why both groups unavoidably commit idolatry—Adam, the father of all humanity, broke God's covenant (or law) and committed a transgression (παράπτωμα). Adam's conduct in the garden produced offspring that mirror his idolatrous actions. Paul waits until ch. 7 to reveal the figure behind sin itself—the serpent. The coming of Christ, then, not only liberates Jews and Gentiles from the domain of sin but also conquers the serpent. Both must be defeated.

Bibliography

Evans, Craig A. *The Pseudepigrapha*. Oak Tree Software, 2009.
Harris, Murray J. *Prepositions and Theology in the Greek New Testament*. Grand Rapids: Zondervan, 2012.
Moo, Douglas J. *The Letter to the Romans*. 2nd ed. NICNT. Grand Rapids: Eerdmans, 2018.

CHAPTER 11

Jesus' Identity in Romans

Charles L. Quarles

If asked to rank documents from the Pauline corpus that clearly exhibit a high Christology, most scholars would likely place the Prison letters Philippians and Colossians at the top of the list. One can hardly imagine how Paul could possibly affirm Jesus' deity more explicitly than he does by identifying Jesus as the embodiment of all the fullness of Deity (Col 2:9) or one who existed in the form of God, bears the name that is above every other name (a circumlocution for the divine name), and who is worshiped by all creatures in fulfillment of Isaiah's description of the eschatological worship of Yahweh (Isa 45:23) as he does in Phil 2:5–11.

Surprisingly, this high Christology is sometimes seen as either strikingly absent or, at the least, far less prominent in what Philip Melanchthon described as a "compendium of Christian doctrine."[1] In this paper, I will argue that Paul's Christology in Romans is higher and much more pervasive than some contemporary scholars acknowledge. The paper will take a Christological tour through Romans from beginning to end, pausing to examine important Christological highlights, and then summarizing Paul's various ways of affirming the deity of Christ.

Paul's introduction to Romans shows that his primary agenda is to clearly articulate the gospel which he proclaims in fulfillment of his commission as an apostle. He insists that this is the gospel of God, the message of salvation that God revealed through the OT prophets. This gospel is thoroughly Christo-centric due to the triadic confession of Rom 1:3–4 at its core. Jesus is the promised seed of David, the fulfillment of the Davidic covenant, the Messiah who reigns forever over God's people. He is the Son of God who at his resurrection was endowed with the power to save sinners.[2] The climactic confession in the summary of the gospel is the declaration that Jesus is "our Lord."[3]

---

1. Charles L. Hill, trans., *The Loci Communes of Philip Melanchthon* (Boston: Meador, 1944), 69. For a helpful discussion of Melanchthon's often-misunderstood description of the epistle, see Robert L. Plummer, "Melanchthon as Interpreter of the New Testament," *WTJ* 62.2 (2000): 257–65.

2. Douglas J. Moo, *The Letter to the Romans*, 2nd ed., NICNT (Grand Rapids: Eerdmans, 2018), 45–49. Moo helpfully cites Heb 7:25 in support of this interpretation.

3. Gordon Fee did not discuss the use of κύριος in his treatment of Romans 1:3–4. Even more surprisingly, he later states that "Paul's Κύριος Christology emerges first in this letter in 8:34" even though "the actual use of κύριος as a Christological title" does

This confession is appropriately described as climactic not only because of the order of clauses in 1:3–4 which appears to crescendo, but also because of the prominence of this confession later in the epistle. Romans 10:9 identifies Jesus' identity as Lord as the essential Christian confession. Accurately and precisely defining the meaning of "Lord" in this confession is crucial. Is this a mere title of royal authority or something more?

In her recent book, *Paul: The Pagans' Apostle*, Paula Fredriksen has urged that Paul's Christology and the Christology of Romans in particular be interpreted "in innocence of the imperial church's later creedal formulas."[4] When read with this innocence, Paul's descriptions of Jesus as Son of David, Son of God, and Lord will be recognized as presenting Jesus solely as the "final Davidic, royal Messiah," and certainly not as a reference to Jesus' "unique divinity."[5] Consequently, Fredriksen's translation of Rom 10:9 attempts to express the meaning of the Greek κύριος as "lord," using a lowercase "l" to indicate that the title merely expresses Messianic authority. She emphasizes that "The point is that Kurios here does not function primarily as a special title for a metaphysical divine entity ("Jesus as Lord," the "lordship of Jesus"), but as an indicator of Jesus' royal, Davidic, messianic role—thus, his status as God's eschatological champion."[6] This interpretation overlooks the close parallelism between Rom 10:9 and the quotation of Joel 2:32 in Rom 10:13. Confessing with your mouth that Jesus is Lord corresponds to Joel's reference to calling on the name of the Lord.[7] Paul's promise "will be saved" corresponds to Joel's assurance "will be saved." Joel 2:32 serves as Paul's prooftext confirming the promise of Rom 10:9. The κύριος of Joel 2:32 in the Septuagint which Paul precisely quotes in Rom 10:13 translates the Hebrew divine name. Fee observed that this citation of Joel 2:32 "is the only certain instance in this letter where ὁ κύριος = Yahweh of a Septuagint text is applied directly to Christ."[8] The parallels between Rom 10:9 and 10:13 suggest that Paul intended κύριος in 10:9 to serve as a reference to the divine name. This seems confirmed by the statement in 10:12 that Jesus is Lord of all, that is, both Jew and Greek. This statement parallels 3:29 in which God is God of both Jew and Gentile.

---

not begin until 10:9. Fee regarded 1:4 as an example of the "threefold combination 'Lord Jesus Christ'" which he apparently does not view as Christologically significant. See Gordon D. Fee, *Pauline Christology: An Exegetical-Theological Study* (Peabody, MA: Hendrickson, 2007), 240–44, 254.

4. Paula Fredriksen, *Paul: The Pagans' Apostle* (New Haven: Yale University Press, 2017), 144.

5. Fredriksen, *Paul*, 144–45.

6. Fredriksen, *Paul*, 145.

7. For the use of the expression "call upon the name of the LORD" in the Hebrew Bible, see Carl Judson Davis, *The Name and Way of the Lord: Old Testament Themes, New Testament Christology*, JSNTSup 129 (Sheffield: Sheffield Academic Press, 1996), 106.

8. Fee, *Pauline Christology*, 258. Fee regarded Rom 14:11 as an example that was probable, but not certain.

Romans 1:3–4 seems to imply Jesus' divine sonship preceded his birth through the line of David.[9] This implication will be explicit in Rom 8:3, which says that God sent "his own Son in the likeness of sinful flesh as a sin offering."[10] Thus Jesus existed as Son of God prior to his incarnation. Not surprisingly, Michael Gorman lists Rom 8:3 as one of three passages in which it is "virtually certain" that "Paul affirms the preexistence and divine status of Jesus" despite that fact that some scholars object.[11]

In Rom 8:9, Paul refers to the Spirit of God that resides in believers. In the very next sentence of the same verse this indwelling Spirit is referred to as the Spirit of Christ. By using "God" and "Christ" interchangeably, Paul strongly implies the deity of the Messiah. Paul has also affirmed the deity of Christ quite explicitly in 9:5. This claim depends on how one punctuates the Greek text of the verse. The proper punctuation of the verse has long been the subject of debate among New Testament scholars and has been the focus of extensive treatment by a number of scholars. The most thorough treatments have consistently, and I believe accurately, concluded that Paul identified Jesus as God. This conclusion has been affirmed in detailed studies by Timothy Dwight,[12] William Sanday and A. C. Headlam,[13] Bruce Metzger,[14] Murray Harris,[15] and Hans-Christian Kammler.[16] The most recent extensive analysis is the book appropriately titled *Christ is God over All: Romans 9:5 in the context of Romans 9–11* by George Carraway.[17] Most evangelical and Catholic commentators affirm this position.

Several lines of evidence support this punctuation. First, Paul's doxologies are normally dependent (Rom 1:25; 11:36; 2 Cor 11:31; Gal 1:15; Eph 3:21; Phil 4:20; 1 Tim 1:17; 2 Tim 4:18). Second, every single instance of the ninety-eight occurrences of the adjective εὐλογητός in the Septuagint and New Testament

---

9. Thomas R. Schreiner, *Romans*, 2nd ed., BECNT (Grand Rapids: Baker Academic, 2018), 42–43.

10. Moo suggests that the "sending" in 8:3 refers primarily to Jesus' redemptive death "without eliminating allusion to the incarnation" (*Romans*, 501–2).

11. Michael J. Gorman, *Apostle of the Crucified Lord: A Theological Introduction to Paul and His Letters* (Grand Rapids: Eerdmans, 2004), 138. James D. G. Dunn has argued against this view. See his *Romans 1–8*, WBC 38A (Dallas: Word, 1988), 420–21.

12. Timothy Dwight, "On Romans ix.5," *Journal of the Society of Biblical Literature and Exegesis* 1 (1881): 22–55.

13. William Sanday and Arthur C. Headlam, *A Critical and Exegetical Commentary on the Epistle to the Romans*, 5th ed., ICC (New York: Scribner's Sons, 1902), 233–38.

14. Bruce M. Metzger, "The Punctuation of Romans 9:5," in *Christ and Spirit in the New Testament: Studies in Honour of Charles Francis Digby Moule*, ed. B. Lindars and S. S. Smalley (Cambridge: Cambridge University Press, 1973), 95–112.

15. Murray J. Harris, *Jesus as God: The New Testament Use of Theos in Reference to Jesus* (Grand Rapids: Baker Books, 1992), 143–72.

16. Hans-Christian Kammler, "Die Prädikation Jesu Christi als 'Gott' und die paulinische Christologie: Erwägen zur Exegese von Röm 9,5b," *ZNW* 94 (2003): 164–80.

17. George Carraway, *Christ Is God over All: Romans 9:5 in the Context of Romans 9–11*, LNTS 489 (London: T&T Clark, 2013).

places the adjective before the noun referring to God when independent. Although Ps 67:19–20 may appear to be a single exception to this pattern, this passage is also consistent with it when properly punctuated. Third, Paul's construction in Rom 9:5 most closely parallels 2 Cor 11:31 which is clearly dependent (ὁ θεὸς καὶ πατὴρ τοῦ κυρίου Ἰησοῦ οἶδεν, ὁ ὢν εὐλογητὸς εἰς τοὺς αἰῶνας, ὅτι οὐ ψεύδομαι). This interpretation also suits the context well. The reference to Jesus' deity carefully balances the reference to his humanity. Jesus is from the Israelites as far as his human nature is concerned. Yet he is also God over all. The pattern is similar to the one that appears in the gospel summary in Rom 1:2–4, in which Jesus is identified as a descendant of David as far as his human nature is concerned and then immediately identified as Son of God and Lord. It also resembles 8:3 in which the Son of God comes in the likeness of sinful flesh.

In Rom 9:33, Paul conflates two texts from Isaiah, Isa 28:16 and 8:14, based on the shared word "stone" and the shared references to faith or trust in the LXX. The context in Romans demonstrates that Paul interprets the "stone" in both texts as a reference to the Messiah. In Rom 10:11 Paul supports his claim that confession of Jesus' identity as Lord and belief in his resurrection result in salvation by citing Isa 28:16 again: "Everyone who believes on him will not be put to shame." Although the referent of the stone in Isa 28:16 is not entirely clear, the referent of the stone in 8:14 is definitely Yahweh. Isaiah 8:13–14 says, "You are to regard only the Lord of hosts as holy. Only he should be feared; only he should be held in awe. He will be a sanctuary; but for the two houses of Israel, he will be a stone to stumble over and a rock to trip over . . ." David Capes rightly concludes: "Paul takes Isaiah's oracle describing YHWH as the stumbling stone for both houses of Israel and transfers those words to Christ."[18]

In Rom 11:25–26, Paul seeks to demonstrate that all Israel will be saved by appealing to a conflation of OT texts, Isa 59:20, Ps 14:7, and Isa 27:9 with a probable allusion to Jer 31:33 as well. The string of quotations portrays Jesus as the deliverer who will come from Zion and will remove ungodliness from Jacob. Paul's reference to Jesus here is supported by Paul's adaptation of Isa 59:20 in which he, possibly influenced by Ps 14:7 (LXX 13:7), substitutes the phrase ἐκ Σιών for the original LXX phrase ἕνεκεν Σιων. Although a number of commentators hold that Zion refers to the heavenly Jerusalem along the lines of Paul's allegory in Gal 4:26,[19] a reference to Jerusalem is more likely since 1) Paul has not prepared the reader to understand the reference allegorically as he did in Gal 4:24,

---

18. David Capes, *The Divine Christ: Paul, The Lord Jesus, and the Scriptures of Israel* (Grand Rapids: Baker Academic, 2018), 112.

19. For the view that Zion refers to heaven, see Dunn, *Romans*, 682; Schreiner, *Romans*, 603. For the view that Zion refers to Jerusalem, see N. T. Wright, "The Letter to the Romans: Introduction, Commentary, and Reflections," in *The New Interpreter's Bible*, ed. Leander E. Keck (Nashville: Abingdon, 2002), 10:692–93; A. Andrew Das, *Paul and the Jews*, LPS (Peabody, MA: Hendrickson, 2003), 109–11; Eckhard J. Schnabel,

2) Paul's only other reference to Zion in this epistle (9:33 quoting Isa 28:16) refers to Jerusalem, and 3) this was the meaning intended by Isaiah and the Psalmist.[20] The most likely motive for changing the preposition in the quotation is to clarify that the deliverer is Jesus. Furthermore, the expression "the deliverer from Zion" parallels the reference to the Messiah from Israel in Rom 9:5.

In its original context, the deliverer of Isa 59:20 is clearly Yahweh. Yahweh's arm has power to save (Isa 59:1). Yahweh's own arm brought salvation (Isa 59:16). Most importantly, Isa 59:19 (MT) promises that "he [Yahweh] will come like a rushing stream driven by the wind of the LORD." In the LXX, three uses of ἥξει (he will come) appear in rapid succession and Yahweh is the one who comes like a mighty river and the one who comes with wrath in v. 19 as well as the one who brings deliverance in v. 20. Thus, as David Capes has helpfully demonstrated, Rom 11:25–26 is a clear example of Paul's application of an OT Yahweh text to Jesus.[21]

A similar phenomenon occurs in Rom 14:11. Paul merges a portion of Isa 49:18 with Isa 45:23: "As I live, says the LORD, every knee will bow to me and every tongue will confess to God." Although most commentators have argued that the quotation refers to God (the Father) as LORD, Gordon Fee joined Matthew Black and David Capes in arguing that Paul intends κύριος here to refer specifically to Christ. Fee presents six reasons supporting this view.[22] First, Paul likely added the brief phrase from Isa 45:23, "As I live, says the LORD," as a reference to the statement two verses earlier that Christ died and came to life (ἔζησεν). Second, this interpretation places both Christ, the Lord, and God the Father at eschatological judgment. This explains why Paul can describe final judgment as occurring before the judgment seat of God as he did in 2 Cor 5:10 but can describe this same judgment as occurring before the judgment seat of Christ as he does in Rom 14:10. Third, this interpretation matches Paul's later usage of Isa 45:23 in Phil 2:10–11, in which Paul unambiguously applies this text to Jesus. Fourth, Paul has consistently used the title "Lord" as a reference

Der Brief des Paulus an die Römer: Kapitel 6–16, HTA (Witten/Gießen: Brockhaus/Brunnen, 2016), 510–14; Moo, *Romans*, 742–43.

20. The argument that the future tenses in Paul's quotations support a reference to the Second Coming from the heavenly Jerusalem (Schreiner, *Romans*, 604) is unpersuasive since Paul has simply preserved the grammatical forms from the LXX in each case. From Isaiah's temporal vantage point, the coming of the deliverer was in the future whether the reference is to Jesus' first or second coming. Paul does not regularly adjust the tenses used in the quotation of OT prophecies to demonstrate past fulfillment. Carraway helpfully points to 15:12 as an example (*Christ is God over All*, 180). Paul preserved the future tense of Isa 11:10 even though he likely understood the prophecy to be fulfilled already.

21. For a helpful study of this feature of Paul's letters and its implications for Pauline Christology, see David Capes, *Old Testament Yahweh Texts in Paul's Christology*, WUNT 2.47 (Tübingen: Mohr Siebeck, 1992), esp. 102.

22. Fee, *Pauline Christology*, 264–65.

to Jesus. Fifth and sixth, this interpretation helps explain why scribes produced both of the important textual variants in this section. Thus, this passage constitutes another application of an OT Yahweh text to Jesus. Fee rightly concludes that Paul's use of Isaiah reflects a "very high Christology" in which Jesus' lordship extends to both the living and the dead and adds: "Under any circumstances, in Jewish thought this is the prerogative of God alone."[23]

The references to the deity of Jesus appear at critical junctures in this letter. Richard Longenecker has argued that Romans contains a " 'mother lode' of early Christian confessional material" and that this confessional material "has a strategic place in the overall argument of Romans."[24] Romans 1:3–4 appears at the beginning of the letter and highlights several themes which Paul treats later in the letter. Romans 10:9 "appears at the heart of Paul's discussion of the Christian Gospel and the hope of Israel in chs. 9–11."[25] Although he admits that scholars continue to debate this, he recognizes that the distinct section 9–11 begins with a subsection that concludes with a confessional doxology. In addition, this confessional doxology is mirrored by a description of Jesus as the divine deliverer in the final subsection immediately before the concluding doxology.[26]

In conclusion, Paul's epistle to the Romans highlights the deity of Jesus in at least five ways:

1. describing Jesus as Lord in contexts that strongly suggest that κύριος functions as the Greek translation of the Hebrew divine name

2. explicitly identifying Jesus as the God who is over all

3. referring interchangeably to the Spirit of God and the Spirit of Christ

4. referring to Jesus as the preexistent Son of God

5. repeatedly using the YHWH texts of the OT to describe Jesus

Thus, the Jesus of Romans is, in the very highest sense, Paul's LORD.

Bibliography

Capes, David. *The Divine Christ: Paul, The Lord Jesus, and the Scriptures of Israel*. Grand Rapids: Baker Academic, 2018.
———. *Old Testament Yahweh Texts in Paul's Christology*. WUNT 2.47. Tübingen: Mohr Siebeck, 1992.

23. Fee, *Pauline Christology*, 266. See also Capes, *The Divine Christ*, 117–23.
24. Richard N. Longenecker, *The Epistle to the Romans: A Commentary on the Greek Text*, NIGTC (Grand Rapids: Eerdmans, 2016), 96.
25. Longenecker, *Romans*, 96.
26. Longenecker, *Romans*, 97.

Carraway, George. *Christ Is God over All: Romans 9:5 in the Context of Romans 9–11.* LNTS 489. London: T&T Clark, 2013.

Das, A. Andrew. *Paul and the Jews.* LPS. Peabody, MA: Hendrickson, 2003.

Davis, Carl Judson. *The Name and Way of the Lord: Old Testament Themes, New Testament Christology.* JSNTSup 129. Sheffield: Sheffield Academic Press, 1996.

Dunn, James D. G. *Romans 1–8.* WBC 38A. Dallas: Word, 1988.

Dwight, Timothy. "On Romans ix.5." *Journal of the Society of Biblical Literature and Exegesis* 1 (1881): 22–55.

Fee, Gordon D. *Pauline Christology: An Exegetical-Theological Study.* Peabody, MA: Hendrickson, 2007.

Fredriksen, Paula. *Paul: The Pagans' Apostle.* New Haven: Yale University Press, 2017.

Gorman, Michael J. *Apostle of the Crucified Lord: A Theological Introduction to Paul and His Letters.* Grand Rapids: Eerdmans, 2004.

Harris, Murray J. *Jesus as God: The New Testament Use of Theos in Reference to Jesus.* Grand Rapids: Baker Books, 1992.

Hill, Charles L., trans. *The* Loci Communes *of Philip Melanchthon.* Boston: Meador, 1944.

Kammler, Hans-Christian. "Die Prädikation Jesu Christi als 'Gott' und die paulinische Christologie: Erwägen zur Exegese von Röm 9,5b." *ZNW* 94 (2003): 164–80.

Longenecker, Richard N. *The Epistle to the Romans: A Commentary on the Greek Text.* NIGTC. Grand Rapids: Eerdmans, 2016.

Metzger, Bruce M. "The Punctuation of Romans 9:5." Pages 95–112 in *Christ and Spirit in the New Testament: Studies in Honour of Charles Francis Digby Moule.* Edited by B. Lindars and S. S. Smalley. Cambridge: Cambridge University Press, 1973.

Moo, Douglas J. *The Letter to the Romans.* 2nd ed. NICNT. Grand Rapids: Eerdmans, 2018.

Plummer, Robert L. "Melanchthon as Interpreter of the New Testament." *WTJ* 62.2 (2000): 257–65.

Sanday, William, and Arthur C. Headlam. *A Critical and Exegetical Commentary on the Epistle to the Romans.* 5th ed. ICC. New York: Scribner's Sons, 1902.

Schnabel, Eckhard J. *Der Brief des Paulus an die Römer: Kapitel 6–16.* HTA. Witten/Gießen: Brockhaus/Brunnen, 2016.

Schreiner, Thomas R. *Romans.* 2nd ed. BECNT. Grand Rapids: Baker Academic, 2018.

Wright, N. T. "The Letter to the Romans: Introduction, Commentary, and Reflections." Pages 395–770 in vol. 10 of *The New Interpreter's Bible.* Edited by Leander E. Keck. Nashville: Abingdon, 2002.

PART THREE

TRUE RIGHTEOUSNESS
(ETS 2021)

CHAPTER 12

Jesus Messiah and the New Life of True Righteousness (Romans 6)

Eckhard J. Schnabel

Romans 6 belongs to the central section of Paul's letter to the believers in the city of Rome, in which he explains the reality of God's justification of sinners proclaimed in the gospel of Jesus, the crucified Messiah and risen Lord (Rom 1:3–4, 16–17), in the life of the believers (Rom 6–8) and in the life of the Jewish people (Rom 9–11).

Context

Understanding the *skopos*, or "frame" of Rom 6 is of crucial significance. A host of interpreters regard the chapter as the *locus classicus* of Paul's view of baptism, or indeed of the NT's view of baptism. Note the following headings in major commentaries: "Dead to Sin by Baptism;"[1] "Die Befreiung von der Sündenmacht in der Taufe" (The liberation from the power of sin in baptism);[2] "Die Wirklichkeit der Taufe im christlichen Leben" (The reality of baptism in Christian life);[3] "Der Herrschaftswechsel in der Taufe" (The change of control in baptism);[4] "Freedom from Sin and Self Through Baptism;"[5] "L'inserimento in Cristo, mediato dal battesimo" (Insertion, or absorption into Christ, mediated by baptism).[6] Monographs and essays often make the same point,

---

1. Ernst Käsemann, *An die Römer*, 4th ed., HNT 8a (Tübingen: Mohr Siebeck, 1980), 151; Ernst Käsemann, *Commentary on Romans*, trans. and ed. Geoffrey W. Bromiley (Grand Rapids: Eerdmans, 1980), 160.
2. Heinrich Schlier, *Der Römerbrief*, 3rd ed., HThK 6 (Freiburg: Herder, 1987), 190.
3. Ulrich Wilckens, *Der Brief an die Römer*, EKK 6 (Neukirchen-Vluyn/Einsiedeln: Neukirchener Verlag/Benzinger, 1978–82), 2:6.
4. Peter Stuhlmacher, *Der Brief an die Römer*, NTD 6 (Göttingen: Vandenhoeck & Ruprecht, 1989), 83; Peter Stuhlmacher, *Paul's Letter to the Romans* (Louisville: Westminster John Knox, 1994), 89.
5. Joseph A. Fitzmyer, *Romans: A New Translation with Introduction and Commentary*, AB 33 (New York: Doubleday, 1993), 429.
6. Romano Penna, *Lettera ai Romani*, SDOC 6 (Bologna: Dehoniane, 2010), 413 (for the section covering 6:1–7:6).

not infrequently without making the case that Paul wrote about Christian water baptism.[7]

Many commentators recognize that Paul neither quotes a baptismal tradition nor speaks primarily about baptism, as again headings in many commentaries indicate, such as: "Die Auferweckung der für die Sünde Gestorbenen" (Resurrection of those who died to sin);[8] "Death to Sin, Alive to God;"[9] "Das neue Leben als Tod und Auferstehung" (The new life as death and resurrection);[10] "Mit Christus der Sünde gestorben dienen wir Gott" (Died to sin with Christ, we serve God);[11] "The Believer Has Died to Sin;"[12] "'Death to Sin' Through Union with Christ;"[13] "Freedom from Sin's Tyranny;"[14] "La grâce n'autorise pas le péché" (Grace does not authorize sin);[15] "Die Befreiung von der Gewalt der Sünde" (Liberation from the power of sin);[16] "Kein fauler Friede im Kampf mit der Sünde" (No sell-out peace in the struggle against sin);[17] "Das neue Leben als Anschluss an Tod und Auferstehung Jesu" (The new life as at-

---

7. Cf. Friedrich Wilhelm Horn, *Das Angeld des Geistes. Studien zur paulinischen Pneumatologie*, FRLANT 154 (Göttingen: Vandenhoeck & Ruprecht, 1992), 176; Petra von Gemünden, "Die urchristliche Taufe und der Umgang mit den Affekten," in *Transformations of the Inner Self in Ancient Religions*, ed. J. Assmann and G. G. Stroumsa, SHR 83 (Leiden: Brill, 1999), 115–36, esp. 129; Günter Röhser, *Stellvertretung im Neuen Testament*, SBS 195 (Stuttgart: Verlag Katholisches Bibelwerk, 2002), 241; Michael J. Gorman, *Inhabiting the Cruciform God: Kenosis, Justification, and Theosis in Paul's Narrative Soteriology* (Grand Rapids: Eerdmans, 2009), 63–86; David Hellholm, "Vorgeformte Tauftradition und deren Benutzung in den Paulusbriefen," in *Ablution, Initiation, and Baptism: Late Antiquity, Early Judaism, and Early Christianity*, ed. D. Hellholm et al., BZAW 176 (Berlin: de Gruyter, 2011), 415–95, 469; Grant Macaskill, *Union with Christ in the New Testament* (Oxford: Oxford University Press, 2013), 192–96; Isaac Augustine Morales, "Baptism and Union with Christ," in *"In Christ" in Paul: Explorations of Paul's Theology of Union and Participation*, ed. Michael J. Thate, Kevin J. Vanhoozer, and Constantine R. Campbell (Grand Rapids: Eerdmans, 2018), 151–79.

8. Adolf Schlatter, *Gottes Gerechtigkeit: Ein Kommentar zum Römerbrief* (Stuttgart: Calwer, 1975 [repr. 1935]), 194; Adolf Schlatter, *Romans: The Righteousness of God*, trans. S. S. Schatzmann (Peabody, MA: Hendrickson, 1995), 132.

9. C. E. B. Cranfield, *A Critical and Exegetical Commentary on the Epistle to the Romans*, 2 vols., ICC, (Edinburgh: T&T Clark, 1975–79), 1:296.

10. Otto Michel, *Der Brief an die Römer,* 5th rev. ed., KEK 4 (Göttingen: Vandenhoeck & Ruprecht, 1978), 199.

11. Dieter Zeller, *Der Brief an die Römer*, RNT (Regensburg: Pustet, 1985), 122.

12. James D. G. Dunn, *Romans 1–8*, WBC 38A (Dallas: Word, 1988), 303.

13. Douglas J. Moo, *The Letter to the Romans*, 2nd ed., NICNT (Grand Rapids: Eerdmans, 2018), 378.

14. Thomas R. Schreiner, *Romans*, 2nd ed., BECNT (Grand Rapids: Baker Academic, 2018), 305.

15. Simon Légasse, *L'épître de Paul aux Romains*, LD 10 (Paris: Cerf, 2002), 389.

16. Eduard Lohse, *Der Brief an die Römer*, KEK 4 (Göttingen: Vandenhoeck & Ruprecht, 2003), 184.

17. Klaus Haacker, *Der Brief des Paulus an die Römer,* 4th rev. ed., ThHKNT 6 (Leipzig: Evangelische Verlagsanstalt, 2012), 149.

tachment to the death and resurrection of Jesus);[18] "Union with Christ as the Source of Righteous Living."[19]

It is noteworthy that while editions of Luther's German translation usually have headings such as "Taufe und neues Leben" (Baptism and the New Life),[20] Luther, in his lectures on Romans, does not mention baptism in his succinct summary of chapter 6, when he writes, "Casus summarius. Declarat Apostolus in peccatis non esse menendum, et quod sit virtuose operandum" (Summary: The apostle declares that one may not remain in sin but act with virtue).[21]

Michael Wolter has "Die Taufe bringt Tod und Leben" (Baptism brings Death and Life) as heading for 6:1–11; but then he goes on to emphasize that baptism is not the object of Paul's interpretation but the means of his interpretation: Paul does not intend to explain baptism but he uses baptism to explain why Christian believers have died to sin and no longer live in sin; Wolter explains the plausibility of Paul's interpretation with reference to the fact that there is no Christian who has not been baptized, and with reference to the fact that baptism was, in Paul's time, always *Bekehrungstaufe*, i.e., baptism following conversion.[22]

The context of Rom 6 is established, quite obviously, by the content of Rom 1–5 or, more accurately, by the content of 1:18–5:21. Most commentators agree that the first main section of Romans is 1:18–3:20 where Paul explains the nature and the consequences of human sin which is God's condemnation of sinners on the day of judgment in the future and in the plight of human living in the present (1:18–32), a reality from which the Jewish people are not exempt (2:1–3:8), providing biblical evidence for the charge that Jews are sinners deserving judgment (3:9–20). In the second main section, Paul explains God's initiative in Jesus Messiah to solve the sin problem once and for all (3:21–5:21) which is proclaimed in the gospel, as defined in 1:3–4, 16–17:[23] he outlines the

---

18. Eckhard J. Schnabel, *Der Brief des Paulus an die Römer: Kapitel 6–16*, HTA (Witten/Gießen: Brockhaus/Brunnen, 2016), 17.

19. Frank Thielman, *Romans*, ZECNT 6 (Grand Rapids: Zondervan Academic, 2018), 299.

20. *Die Bibel nach der Übersetzung Martin Luthers, mit Apokryphen* (Bibeltext in der revidierten Fassung von 1983. Herausgegeben von der Evangelischen Kirche in Deutschland; Stuttgart: Deutsche Bibelgesellschaft, 1999; *The Bible according to the translation of Martin Luther, with Apocrypha,* Biblical Text of the 1983 revision, ed. Evangelische Kirche in Deutschland [Stuttgart: Deutsche Bibelgesellschaft, 1999]).

21. Martin Luther, *Vorlesung über den Römerbrief 1915/1916*, Lateinisch-deutsche Ausgabe (Darmstadt: Wissenschaftliche Buchgesellschaft, 1915–16), 1:362 (Inhaltsangabe: Der Apostel legt dar, daß man nicht in Sünden verharren dürfe und tugendhaft handeln müsse). Martin Luther, *Lectures on Romans: Glosses and Scholia*, ed. H. C. Oswald, Luther's Works 25 (St. Louis: Concordia, 1972), 50.

22. Michael Wolter, *Der Brief an die Römer: Teilband 1: Röm 1–8*, EKK VI (Neukirchen-Vluyn/Mannheim: Neukirchener/Patmos, 2014), 364, 370.

23. Cf. Robert M. Calhoun, *Paul's Definitions of the Gospel in Romans 1*, WUNT 2.316 (Tübingen: Mohr Siebeck, 2011).

possibility and reality of justification of sinners by faith on the basis of God's act of atonement in the death of Jesus Messiah (3:21–26); he explains the universality of justification by faith (3:27–31); he details nature of faith and the creation of the universal people of God as present fulfillment of the promises God gave to Abraham as Gentiles come to faith in God's promise of the forgiveness of sins through Jesus Messiah (4:1–25); he describes the hope and the peace of the justified sinners (5:1–11); he concludes with a summary description of the rule of God's grace that has become a reality through the death and resurrection of Jesus Messiah and that triumphs over the rule of sin and death that had become a reality through the sin of Adam (5:12–21). The context of Rom 6 is thus the defeat of the power of sin and the cancellation of the consequences of sin—the death of the sinner, condemnation in God's judgment—on account of the death and resurrection of Jesus Messiah.[24]

In 5:21 Paul makes three assertions. First, sin reigns in death: sin is in control of sinners, evidenced in the fact that people die, as death is the consequence of sin (1:32; 5:12). Second, grace reigns through Jesus Messiah our Lord: grace, the gift of divine forgiveness, controls sinners who have come to faith in the crucified and risen Jesus Messiah. Third, sinners who have received God's grace have received in the present the gift of righteousness (cf. 5:15, 17; 3:24) and will receive in the future the gift of eternal life.

The fact that sinners who believe in Jesus, the crucified Messiah and risen Lord, have been transferred from the dominion of sin to the domain of righteousness raises the question of 6:1: "Shall we go on sinning so that grace may increase?" (NIV). Since Paul had argued in 1:18–5:21 that God justifies the ungodly sinner (5:6, 8) on account of the death of Jesus Messiah, a critic might argue that believers in Jesus can persist in sinning, as this will increase the amount of grace that God can then demonstrate in forgiving these sins. The objection of 6:1 seeks to demonstrate the absurdity of the statement in 5:20 where Paul had asserted that where sin increased as a result of the coming of the law, God's grace increased all the more. If indeed God reacted to the many sins of sinners with the fullness of his grace, people can continue to sin without any reservation since God forgives every sin all the time, including sins committed deliberately.

---

24. A comment on the phrase "Jesus Messiah" is in order: despite what many NT scholars have been and are writing, Χριστός, for Paul, was not a personal name. When he prayed in Hebrew—which he presumably did every day, not only when he was in Jerusalem—he would have used the phrase יֵשׁוּעַ הַמָּשִׁיחַ—yēšûaʿ hammāšîaḥ, "Jesus Messiah"; when he prayed in Aramaic, he addressed him as יֵשׁוּעַ מְשִׁיחָא—yēšûaʿ məšîḥāʾ, "Jesus Messiah"; and when he prayed in Greek, he used the phrase Χριστός Ἰησοῦς, Christos Iēsous, or Ἰησοῦς Χριστός, Iēsous Christos, "Jesus Messiah." Schnabel, Der Brief des Paulus an die Römer: Kapitel 1–5, 84–85; Eckhard J. Schnabel, Jesus in Jerusalem: The Last Days (Grand Rapids: Eerdmans, 2018), 379.

This is precisely the question that Paul answers in Rom 6: the question of the reality of grace, the question of the permissibility of sinning. Paul demonstrates in Rom 6 that the critic confuses two irreconcilable perspectives: the perspective of the sinner who does not understand the grace of God, and the perspective of the followers of Jesus who have experienced God's grace, who have been liberated from the control of sin, and who thus cannot and will not consciously and deliberately tolerate acts of rebellion against the will of God.

The *skopos* of sin and of the reality of God's grace through the death and resurrection of Jesus Messiah is confirmed by word statistics. The noun ἁμαρτία occurs ten times in Rom 1–5, and sixteen times in 6:1, 2, 6[2x], 7, 10, 11, 12, 13, 14, 16, 17, 18, 20, 22, 23; the verb ἁμαρτάνω occurs six times in chs. 1–5, once in 6:15. Death (θάνατος) is mentioned seven times in Romans 6: the death of Jesus Messiah (6:3, 4, 5), and the eternal death of sinners (6:9, 16, 21, 23). God (θεός) is specifically mentioned seven times (6:10, 11, 13[2x], 17, 22, 23), and he is the implied subject of ten passive verbal forms: ἐβαπτίσθημεν (6:3 [2x]), συνετάφημεν (6:4), ἠγέρθη (6:4), συνεσταυρώθη (6:6), καταργηθῇ (6:6), δεδικαίωται (6:7), ἐγερθείς (6:9), ἐλευθερωθέντες (6:18, 22), ἐδουλώθητε (6:18), δουλωθέντες (6:22), i.e., God's action is referenced a total of nineteen times. Jesus Messiah is explicitly referred to as Χριστός Ἰησοῦς (6:3, 11, 23) and Χριστός (6:4, 8, 9), and he is mentioned in 6:5 [2x], 6, 10 [4x], i.e., Jesus is referenced a total of twelve times.

Paul's Statements about God, Jesus Messiah, and Believers

Discourse analysis is an important tool for analyzing the statements of a text before one ventures a translation into a language that may not share even basic grammatical features of the source language. While my goal here is not to provide a full discourse analysis of Rom 6, the itemization of Paul's syntactically interconnected statements in independent sentences should prove helpful in understanding the contours of Paul's argument.

Statements about God

God immersed us into Messiah Jesus (ἐβαπτίσθημεν εἰς Χριστὸν Ἰησοῦν, 6:3);

he immersed us into the death of Jesus (εἰς τὸν θάνατον αὐτοῦ ἐβαπτίσθημεν, 6:3);

he buried us together with Jesus into death (συνετάφημεν αὐτῷ . . . εἰς τὸν θάνατον, 6:4);

he raised the Messiah from the dead (ἠγέρθη Χριστὸς ἐκ νεκρῶν, 6:4, 9);

he crucified our old self with Jesus Messiah (ὁ παλαιὸς ἡμῶν ἄνθρωπος συνεσταυρώθη, 6:6);

he destroyed the body ruled by sin (καταργηθῇ τὸ σῶμα τῆς ἁμαρτίας, 6:6);

he sets free from sin all whose death happened when Jesus died (ὁ ἀποθανὼν δεδικαίωται ἀπὸ τῆς ἁμαρτίας, 6:7);

his glory and his will are the content and purpose of the new life of the believer who has died to sin (ζῇ τῷ θεῷ, 6:10);

he set us free from sin (ἐλευθερωθέντες ἀπὸ τῆς ἁμαρτίας, 6:18, 22);

he made us slaves to righteousness (ἐδουλώθητε τῇ δικαιοσύνῃ, 6:18);

he made us slaves of himself (δουλωθέντες δὲ τῷ θεῷ, 6:22).

Statements about Jesus Messiah

Jesus Messiah is the reality into which we have been immersed (ἐβαπτίσθημεν εἰς Χριστὸν Ἰησοῦν, 6:3);

his death is the reality which has become our reality (εἰς τὸν θάνατον αὐτοῦ ἐβαπτίσθημεν, 6:3);

his burial has become our own reality (συνετάφημεν αὐτῷ, 6:4);

he was raised from the dead (ἠγέρθη Χριστὸς ἐκ νεκρῶν, 6:4);

his death constitutes a union with those who believe in him (σύμφυτοι γεγόναμεν τῷ ὁμοιώματι τοῦ θανάτου αὐτοῦ, 6:5);

his resurrection will be shared by those who believe in him ([σύμφυτοι τῷ ὁμοιώματι] τῆς ἀναστάσεως ἐσόμεθα, 6:5);

when he was crucified, the old self of those who believe in him was crucified with him (ὁ παλαιὸς ἡμῶν ἄνθρωπος συνεσταυρώθη, 6:6);

when he died, those who believe in him died (ἀπεθάνομεν σὺν Χριστῷ, 6:8);

since he lives, we will live (συζήσομεν αὐτῷ, 6:8);

he was raised from the dead (Χριστὸς ἐγερθεὶς ἐκ νεκρῶν, 6:9);

he will not die again (οὐκέτι ἀποθνῄσκει, 6:9);

he is not controlled by death (θάνατος αὐτοῦ οὐκέτι κυριεύει, 6:9);

when he died, he was freed from the rule of sin once and for all (ὃ ἀπέθανεν, τῇ ἁμαρτίᾳ ἀπέθανεν ἐφάπαξ, 6:10);

he lives for the glory and the will of God (ὃ ζῇ, ζῇ τῷ θεῷ, 6:10);

he is the reason why sinners are freed from sin (ὑμεῖς λογίζεσθε ἑαυτοὺς εἶναι νεκροὺς μὲν τῇ ἁμαρτίᾳ, 6:11);

he is the reason why sinners live for God (ζῶντας δὲ τῷ θεῷ ἐν Χριστῷ Ἰησοῦ, 6:11);

he is the reason why God grants the gift of eternal life to sinners (τὸ χάρισμα τοῦ θεοῦ ζωὴ αἰώνιος ἐν Χριστῷ Ἰησοῦ τῷ κυρίῳ ἡμῶν, 6:23).

Statements about Believers

Believers in Jesus Messiah will certainly not go on sinning (ἐπιμένωμεν τῇ ἁμαρτίᾳ, ἵνα ἡ χάρις πλεονάσῃ; μὴ γένοιτο, 6:1–2);

we have died with respect to sin (ἀπεθάνομεν τῇ ἁμαρτίᾳ, 6:2);

we can no longer live in sin (πῶς ἔτι ζήσομεν ἐν αὐτῇ, 6:2);

we have been incorporated into Jesus Messiah by God (ἐβαπτίσθημεν εἰς Χριστὸν Ἰησοῦν, 6:3);

we have been incorporated into the death of Jesus Messiah (εἰς τὸν θάνατον αὐτοῦ ἐβαπτίσθημεν, 6:3);

we have been buried by incorporation into his death (συνετάφημεν οὖν αὐτῷ διὰ τοῦ βαπτίσματος εἰς τὸν θάνατον, 6:4);

we live a new life in consequence of the resurrection of Jesus from the dead (ὥσπερ ἠγέρθη Χριστὸς ἐκ νεκρῶν διὰ τῆς δόξης τοῦ πατρός, οὕτως καὶ ἡμεῖς ἐν καινότητι ζωῆς περιπατήσωμεν, 6:4);

we have been united with Jesus Messiah in the likeness of his death (σύμφυτοι γεγόναμεν τῷ ὁμοιώματι τοῦ θανάτου αὐτοῦ, 6:5);

we will be united with Jesus Messiah with the likeness of his resurrection (καὶ τῆς ἀναστάσεως ἐσόμεθα, 6:5);

our old self was crucified when Jesus was crucified (ὁ παλαιὸς ἡμῶν ἄνθρωπος συνεσταυρώθη, 6:6);

our existence controlled by sin came to an end when Jesus was crucified (ἵνα καταργηθῇ τὸ σῶμα τῆς ἁμαρτίας, 6:6);

we are no longer slaves to sin (τοῦ μηκέτι δουλεύειν ἡμᾶς τῇ ἁμαρτίᾳ, 6:6);

we died when Jesus died (ἀπεθάνομεν σὺν Χριστῷ, 6:8);

we will live with Jesus (συζήσομεν αὐτῷ, 6:8);

we must draw the conclusion that we are dead with respect to sin (ὑμεῖς λογίζεσθε ἑαυτοὺς εἶναι νεκροὺς μὲν τῇ ἁμαρτίᾳ, 6:11);

we must draw the conclusion that we are alive with respect to God on account of our union with Jesus Messiah ([λογίζεσθε ἑαυτοὺς εἶναι] ζῶντας δὲ τῷ θεῷ ἐν Χριστῷ Ἰησοῦ, 6:11);

we must not allow sin to regain control in our earthly existence (μὴ βασιλευέτω ἡ ἁμαρτία ἐν τῷ θνητῷ ὑμῶν σώματι, 6:12);

we must not obey human lusts ([μὴ] εἰς τὸ ὑπακούειν ταῖς ἐπιθυμίαις αὐτοῦ, 6:12);

we must not offer any member of our bodies to sin as weapons fighting in support of unrighteousness (μηδὲ παριστάνετε τὰ μέλη ὑμῶν ὅπλα ἀδικίας τῇ ἁμαρτίᾳ, 6:13);

we must offer ourselves to God as people who have been brought from death to life (παραστήσατε ἑαυτοὺς τῷ θεῷ ὡσεὶ ἐκ νεκρῶν ζῶντας, 6:13);

we must offer every member of our body to God as weapons fighting in support of righteousness (παραστήσατε ἑαυτοὺς τῷ θεῷ ὡσεὶ ἐκ νεκρῶν ζῶντας καὶ τὰ μέλη ὑμῶν ὅπλα δικαιοσύνης τῷ θεῷ, 6:13);

we will not have sin as our master (ἁμαρτία ὑμῶν οὐ κυριεύσει, 6:14);

we are not under the control of the law but under the control of grace (οὐ ἐστε ὑπὸ νόμον ἀλλὰ ὑπὸ χάριν, 6:14);

we shall certainly not sin (ἁμαρτήσωμεν … μὴ γένοιτο, 6:15);

we used to be slaves to sin (ἦτε δοῦλοι τῆς ἁμαρτίας, 6:17);

we have become obedient from the heart to the teaching of the gospel (ὑπηκούσατε δὲ ἐκ καρδίας εἰς ὃν παρεδόθητε τύπον διδαχῆς, 6:17);

we have been set free from sin (ἐλευθερωθέντες ἀπὸ τῆς ἁμαρτίας, 6:18);

we have been made slaves of righteousness (ἐδουλώθητε τῇ δικαιοσύνῃ, 6:18);

we used to offer ourselves as slaves to impurity and wickedness (παρεστήσατε τὰ μέλη ὑμῶν δοῦλα τῇ ἀκαθαρσίᾳ καὶ τῇ ἀνομίᾳ εἰς τὴν ἀνομίαν, 6:19);

we shall now offer ourselves as slaves to righteousness leading to holiness (νῦν παραστήσατε τὰ μέλη ὑμῶν δοῦλα τῇ δικαιοσύνῃ εἰς ἁγιασμόν, 6:19);

we were slaves to sin (δοῦλοι ἦτε τῆς ἁμαρτίας, 6:20);

we were freed from the control of righteousness (ἐλεύθεροι ἦτε τῇ δικαιοσύνῃ, 6:20);

we had shame as fruit of our deeds (τίνα οὖν καρπὸν εἴχετε τότε ἐφ᾽ οἷς νῦν ἐπαισχύνεσθε, 6:21);

we suffered death as consequence of our sinful behavior (τὸ γὰρ τέλος ἐκείνων θάνατος, 6:21);

we now have been set free from sin (νυνὶ δέ, ἐλευθερωθέντες ἀπὸ τῆς ἁμαρτίας, 6:22);

we now have been made slaves of God (δουλωθέντες δὲ τῷ θεῷ, 6:22);

we now have holiness as fruit (ἔχετε τὸν καρπὸν ὑμῶν εἰς ἁγιασμόν, 6:22);

we will have eternal life as the consequence of holiness (τὸ δὲ τέλος ζωὴν αἰώνιον, 6:22).

It is quite obvious: Paul explains in Rom 6 what God is doing when sinners come to faith in him as the one true, just, and holy God; when they come to faith in Jesus, the crucified Messiah and risen Lord.

The Past Life of the Believer: Slavery to Sin Resulting in Death

Paul had described the past of believers in 1:18–3:20, as summarized in 3:23: "all have sinned and fall short of the glory of God." The main metaphor that Paul uses to describe the reality and the effect of sin is derived from slavery.[25] Slaves belong to their master who has full control over what they do in the present and what they can hope for in the future. Paul asserts that people who have not experienced the power of God for salvation through faith in Jesus Messiah (1:3–4, 16–17) are "slaves" to sin: they obey sin, they sin as a matter of course; their future is controlled by sin, both in terms of further acts of sin and in terms of the death of condemnation in God's judgment.[26] Paul asserts in 6:6 that in the past, believers were "enslaved to sin" (δουλεύειν ἡμᾶς τῇ ἁμαρτίᾳ). In line with the definition of δουλεύειν here as "to act or conduct oneself as one in total service to another,"[27] Paul describes "sin" metaphorically as a person whom believers rendered services as slaves. The genitive τῆς ἁμαρτίας in the phrase τὸ σῶμα τῆς ἁμαρτίας ("the body of sin") can be interpreted as posses-sive genitive: the body of sinners belongs to sin—as sin controls what the body does, and as sin thus controls the future of the body on the day of the body's death and on the day of God's judgment, the body of the sinner "belongs" to sin. Similarly, in 6:17 Paul asserts that before they came to faith in Jesus Mes-siah, they used to be slaves to sin (ἦτε δοῦλοι τῆς ἁμαρτίας). In 6:19 Paul says that believers, before coming to faith in Jesus Messiah, offered themselves,

---

25. On the metaphor of slavery see Dale B. Martin, *Slavery as Salvation: The Metaphor of Slavery in Pauline Christianity* (New Haven: Yale University Press, 1990); John Byron, *Slavery Metaphors in Early Judaism and Pauline Christianity: A Traditio-Historical and Exegetical Examination*, WUNT 2.162 (Tübingen: Mohr Siebeck, 2003); John K. Goodrich, "From Slaves of Sin to Slaves of God: Reconsidering the Origin of Paul's Slavery Metaphor in Romans 6," *BBR* 23.4 (2013): 509–30.

26. On sin in Paul's theology, see more recently Udo Schnelle, *The Human Condi-tion: Anthropology in the Teachings of Jesus, Paul, and John*, trans. O. C. Dean (Edin-burgh/Minneapolis: T&T Clark/Fortress, 1996); James D. G. Dunn, *The Theology of Paul the Apostle* (Grand Rapids: Eerdmans, 1998), 51–78; Udo Schnelle, *Apostle Paul: His Life and Theology*, trans. M. Eugene Boring (Grand Rapids: Baker Academic, 2005), 499–505; Matthias Klinghardt, "Sünde und Gericht bei Paulus," *ZNW* 88 (1997): 56–80; Eun-Geol Lyu, *Sünde und Rechtfertigung bei Paulus. Eine exegetische Untersuchung zum paulinischen Sündenverständnis aus soteriologischer Sicht*, WUNT 2.318 (Tübingen: Mohr Siebeck, 2011); Matthew Croasmun, *The Emergence of Sin: The Cosmic Tyrant in Romans* (Oxford: Oxford University Press, 2017); Peter Stuhlmacher, *Biblical Theology of the New Testament*, trans. Daniel P. Bailey (Grand Rapids: Eerdmans, 2018), 302–16.

27. BDAG s.v. δουλέω 2 (259).

in their specific daily behavior, as slaves to impurity and wickedness (δοῦλα τῇ ἀκαθαρσίᾳ καὶ τῇ ἀνομίᾳ εἰς τὴν ἀνομίαν). In 6:20 he again states that believers, in their past lives, were slaves to sin (δοῦλοι ἦτε τῆς ἁμαρτίας). The metaphor of slavery is also implied in 6:18, 22 when Paul states that believers have been set free from sin (ἐλευθερωθέντες ἀπὸ τῆς ἁμαρτίας . . . νυνὶ δέ, ἐλευθερωθέντες ἀπὸ τῆς ἁμαρτίας): they were slaves to sin before God liberated them from sin.

In 6:12, Paul asserts that sin exercised control (βασιλευέτω ἡ ἁμαρτία); sin determined the behavior of the human body. The same verb is used in 5:14 where Paul had explained the effects of sin on the people who are sinning: as sin came into the world, death came, with the result that "death exercised dominion" (ἐβασίλευσεν ὁ θάνατος). The inescapability of death shows the effectiveness of sin's established control over human beings. We do not need Martin Heidegger to know that human existence is "being toward death": the sequence of twenty-four-hour days that continues incessantly from the present into future will one day come to an end. The only exception seems to have been Elijah (and Enoch), although the chariot of fire pulled by horses of fire and the whirlwind that took the prophet into heaven (2 Kgs 2:11)—dramatically put to music by Felix Mendelssohn-Bartholdy—also stopped the clock of his earthly life. In 6:12, Paul asserts that sinful lusts (ἐπιθυμίαι) demanded obedience (ὑπακούειν). In 6:13 he uses the military image of weapons: sin wants to use the members of our body as weapons fighting in support of unrighteousness (ὅπλα ἀδικίας τῇ ἁμαρτίᾳ)—sin produces more sin. Sin is like an avalanche: once snow starts moving down a slope, the moving mass becomes bigger and heavier and more compressed and thus more deadly. In 6:14 Paul asserts that sin is the master of unbelievers (ἁμαρτία κυριεύσει).

Note again the verbs that Paul uses in Romans 6 to describe the reality of sin: sin is a master that enslaves (δουλεύειν, 6:6, 17, 19, 20; also 6:18, 22); it is a ruler demanding absolute control (βασιλεύειν, 6:12); its triggers sinful lusts demanding obedience (ὑπακούειν, 6:12); it exercises control as the superior authority (κυριεύειν, 6:14).

The effect of sin is *more* sin. Sin triggers sinful lusts that lead to more sinful actions (6:12). In so doing, it uses the members of the human body—feet, hands, arms, eyes, ears, mouth—as weapons (6:13). The main consequence is the death of the sinner (6:9, 16, 21, 23), as Paul says in 6:12: "the wages of sin is death" (τὰ ὀψώνια τῆς ἁμαρτίας θάνατος). It has been suggested that ὀψώνιον has the meaning "victuals bought," identified with wages in the sense of remuneration for work (μισθός), with the meaning "provisions" always present.[28] Even when the ὀψώνιον was increasingly paid out in money, it continued to

---

28. Chrys C. Caragounis, "ΟΨΩΝΙΟΝ: A Reconsideration of its Meaning," *NovT* 16 (1974): 35–57.

constitute wages that provided for room and board.[29] The term is often used in a military context in terms of provisions/wages paid to soldiers, mainly wheat, wine, and fodder for the horses, but it occurs in many other contexts as well, e.g., for provisions/wages given to guards, officials, and priests. It is not a technical military term, and it seems preferable not to introduce a military connotation here.[30] If Paul wanted to refer to remuneration in the sense of "pay, wages" he could have used the term μισθός, as he does in Rom 4:4; 1 Cor 3:8, 14; 9:17, 18; 1 Tim 5:18. The thought that sin offers death as wages is difficult, unless one assumes the presence of irony. Also, the context does not refer to workers who have earned the right to receive wages, but to slaves who are forced to work and who have no rights, even though they do receive provisions.[31] The use of the word ὀψώνιον (also in 1 Cor 9:7; 2 Cor 11:8) seems deliberate. Sin offers provisions sustaining life but then doles out death, tricking the sinner, which is what Paul will describe in 7:11. Sinners think that sin benefits them. In reality, and in God's judgment, they are forced to realize that sin results not in life, but in death. Irrespective of the meaning of ὀψώνιον, the intended meaning of Paul's statement has no doubt: sin brings about the death of the sinner.

The Transfer of the Believer from the Sphere of Sin to the Sphere of Life

As Paul explains in Rom 6, faith in God and in his power to bring salvation through Jesus moves the sinner from the sphere of sin, resulting in death, to the sphere of life in the presence of God and Jesus Messiah, resulting in eternal life (1:3–4, 16–17). This transfer from sin and death to righteousness and life is succinctly formulated in the phrase "those who have been brought from death to life" (ἐκ νεκρῶν ζῶντας) in 6:13. The rhetorical question in 6:2—"How can we who died to sin go on living in it?" (NRSVue)—is the answer to the objection of the critic in 6:1: "we who have died to sin" cannot go on living in sin. Paul explains what he means in 6:3–10.

We begin with 6:5. Paul asserts that believers have been "united" with the death of Jesus Messiah. He uses an agricultural metaphor: the verbal adjective σύμφυτος is used in the LXX only for agricultural matters, which is also the context in the papyri; the meaning of the verb συμφύειν, "to be attached

---

29. R. Kritzer, *1. Korinther*, ed. Peter Arzt-Grabner et al., PKNT 2 (Göttingen: Vandenhoeck & Ruprecht, 2006), 342; 341n440 for the following comment.

30. Differently Moo, *Romans*, 434n622, who relies on *MM* and *LSJ*. The military metaphor of "weapons" in 6:13 is too far removed to suggest a military connotation in 6:23. Note that Wolter, *Römer 1–8*, 404, is also determined to avoid military connotations.

31. Thus Caragounis, "ΟΨΩΝΙΟΝ", 55–56 (here and for the following point).

or united to or combined with" fits both agricultural contexts and other uses of the term.[32] If one takes the term as an agricultural metaphor, one should not interpret Paul as saying that faith in Jesus leads to a process of growth,[33] which may be implied but which is not Paul's point here. It seems best to translate σύμφυτος with "fused" or "united." The entity with which believers have been "fused" is "the likeness of his death" (τῷ ὁμοιώματι τοῦ θανάτου αὐτοῦ). Paul's basic assertion is that believers have been fused with the death of Jesus Messiah. Instead of "fusion," one can speak of "union," "incorporation," or "participation."[34] The term ὁμοίωμα, which is most plausibly interpreted in the context of its use in 5:14, implies commonality and difference.[35] When sinners come to faith in Jesus Messiah, they are fused with his death: they died when Jesus died on Friday, Nisan 14, April 8, AD 30, while it is also true that this death occurs as they come to faith in Jesus, i.e., in their conversion. The commonality of ὁμοίωμα is the fact of the experience of death, the difference is the timing: the believer experiences the reality of Jesus' death in his conversion. The perfect tense of γεγόναμεν describes the state of affairs that was started in the past and pertains in the present: believers were fused with the death of Jesus Messiah when Jesus died on the cross and in their conversion, a fusion that continues to mark the reality of their existence. The second half of v. 5, introduced with ἀλλὰ καί, which introduces an additional point in an emphatic manner,[36] is an ellipsis, with σύμφυτοι τῷ ὁμοιώματι to be supplied; the apodosis of the first-class conditional sentence reads: [σύμφυτοι τῷ ὁμοιώματι] τῆς ἀναστάσεως ἐσόμεθα, "we will certainly be fused with the likeness of his resurrection." The future tense of ἐσόμεθα is most plausibly taken as referring to the future (rather than as a logical or gnomic future tense), given the fact that participation in salvation in the present is already stated in the perfect tense of the first half of the verse. Paul asserts that believers who have been fused with the death of Jesus Messiah in whose death God forgives the sins of sinners (3:24–25) will certainly participate in his resurrection in terms of participating in the glory of God (5:2). The commonality with the resurrection of Jesus is the visible realization of resurrection as the resur-

---

32. *TLNT* 3:321.

33. Thus Heinrich Schwarzmann, *Zur Tauftheologie des heiligen Paulus in Röm 6* (Heidelberg: Kerle, 1950), 28–29; justly criticized by Hubert Frankemölle, *Das Taufverständnis des Paulus. Taufe, Tod und Auferstehung nach Röm 6*, SBS 47 (Stuttgart: Katholisches Bibelwerk, 1970), 63.

34. Cf. Constantine R. Campbell, *Paul and Union with Christ: An Exegetical and Theological Study* (Grand Rapids: Zondervan, 2012); Macaskill, *Union with Christ in the New Testament*; cf. Michael J. Gorman, *Cruciformity: Paul's Narrative Spirituality of the Cross* (Grand Rapids: Eerdmans, 2001).

35. Wolter, *Römer 1–8*, 376.

36. BDF 448 (6); cf. BDAG s.v. ἀλλά 4a (45): "for strong alternative/additional consideration," here in the apodosis of conditional sentences, with reference to Rom 6:5.

rection from the dead; the difference from the resurrection of Jesus is again chronological: Jesus rose from the dead on the third day after his death on the cross, while the resurrection of the believer will happen on an unknown day in the future, on the day of Jesus' return and the inauguration of the new heavens and the new earth. The certainty of future participation in Jesus' resurrection from the dead is, as explained in vv. 11–14, a powerful and effective motivation for believers to make sure that the fusion with the death and resurrection of Jesus becomes a reality in their present way of living. Believers in the crucified and risen Messiah will not regard acts of sin as inconsequential or trivial, as the critic of 6:1 insinuated. They know that their future resurrection guaranteed by their union with Jesus Messiah will be a demonstration of the power of God for salvation (1:16), which is also the power of God active in their present life as people fused with Jesus Messiah.[37]

In 6:6 Paul explains the union of believers with the death and the resurrection of Jesus using the metaphor of crucifixion: we were "crucified with him" (συνεσταυρώθη). The fusion with the death of Jesus Messiah connects believers with his death on the cross. The prefix συν emphasizes the union of the death of the believing sinner with the death of Jesus. Paul had used this formulation, employing the first-person singular of the verb, in his letter to the believers in Galatia, written eight years earlier: "I have been crucified with the Messiah" (Χριστῷ συνεσταύρωμαι; Gal 2:19). This is what Paul taught the believers in the churches that he established; this is what Paul's coworkers would have taught, including Aquila and Priscilla who are back in Rome; this is why Paul can refer in v. 6 to the knowledge that believers have in this regard. Sinners who have come to faith in the gospel were crucified, metaphorically, when Jesus was crucified; the crucifixion of Jesus Messiah is their personal crucifixion, as they were fused with him when they came to faith in him as their Savior. Death by crucifixion is final, nobody returns from such a death.[38] This is Paul's point: the death that believing sinners have experienced on account of their fusion with Jesus Messiah is beyond recall, is it final, irrevocable, which makes unthinkable the notion expressed in 6:1 that believers may cheerfully considering the possibility of committing acts of sin because God in his grace forgives all sin. The reality of the grace of God on account of Jesus Messiah is fundamentally linked with the sinners' fusion with the death of Jesus Messiah, which was death by crucifixion. The crucifixion on Nisan 14 in AD 30 ended the earthly life of Jesus.

---

37. Cf. Lohse, *Römer*, 191.

38. On crucifixion, see Martin Hengel, *Crucifixion in the Ancient World and the Folly of the Message of the Cross*, trans. J. Bowden (Philadelphia: Fortress, 1977); John Granger Cook, *Crucifixion in the Mediterranean World*, WUNT 327 (Tübingen: Mohr Siebeck, 2014); David W. Chapman, "Crucifixion," in *The Trial and Crucifixion of Jesus: Texts and Commentary*, ed. David W. Chapman and Eckhard J. Schnabel, WUNT 344 (Tübingen: Mohr Siebeck, 2015), 299–754.

The believers' fusion with the crucifixion of Jesus Messiah, put into effect by God (note the passive voice of συνεσταύρωμαι) ended their life in the sphere of human existence in which sin was normal, accepted, and enjoyed, a past reality described by Paul as "our old self" (ὁ παλαιὸς ἡμῶν ἄνθρωπος). Paul explains further that when our "old self" was crucified, God "destroyed the body of sin" (καταργηθῇ τὸ σῶμα τῆς ἁμαρτίας), which is identical with the "body of death" (σῶμα τοῦ θανάτου) mentioned in 7:24. God eliminates the predicament of our existence controlled by sin issuing in death through our fusion with Jesus' death. The body of the "old self" controlled by the power of sin, refusing to honor God, consumed by ungodliness and wickedness (1:18), has been set free for a life of obedience to God the creator. The consecutive clause at the end of v. 6 underscores the point that God's salvific intervention results in a new life in which believers no longer do the bidding of sin: we are "no longer enslaved to sin," we no longer serve sin—we serve God and Jesus Messiah.

In 6:8 Paul reiterates the assertion of v. 5: we have died with Jesus Messiah, with the result that we will also live with him. In 6:9–10 Paul affirms that Jesus' resurrection from the dead guarantees that he will never die again: "death no longer exercises authority over him" because the death he died "he died to sin." His death brought the rule of death to an end, "once and for all" (ἐφάπαξ). His death and resurrection are unique in that their effects are universal—applicable to both Jews and Gentiles—and final: the forgiveness of sins and eternal life after physical death depend, exclusively, on the death and resurrection of Jesus Messiah. The life Jesus lives as the risen Lord "he lives to God," i.e., in the presence of God and for the glory of God, doing his will. The language of death is the vehicle of Paul's metaphors as he answers the critique voiced in 6:1.[39]

Immersion into the Reality of Jesus Messiah

We now turn to 6:3–4. In these two verses, Paul uses two metaphors in his explanation why believers in Jesus Messiah who have experienced the power of God for salvation will not willingly contemplate acts of sin.

First, in order to describe our fusion with the death of Jesus, Paul uses the term βαπτίζειν: "Do you not know that all of us who have been baptized into Christ Jesus were baptized into his death?" (6:3 NRSVue). The English versions render ἐβαπτίσθημεν as "baptized" which is, of course, not a translation but a transliteration that connotes Christian water baptism. To say that βαπτίζειν means "to baptize" is the same as saying "Gesundheit means Gesundheit" after people sneeze and you cheer them on with the exclamation "Gesundheit!" To render βαπτίζειν with "baptize" is traditional, but not helpful because it does not convey the lexical meaning of the term. I have explained

39. Sorin Sabou, *Between Horror and Hope: Paul's Metaphorical Language of Death in Romans 6:1–11*, PBM (Milton Keynes: Paternoster, 2005), 57–93.

the meaning of βαπτίζειν elsewhere in some detail, based on a study of the use of the term in Greek literature and documentary texts.[40] One should note that the entry in BDAG separates the evidence for βαπτίζειν in NT texts from the everyday language of NT authors and their audiences; the readers of Paul's letter in Rome would have been utterly perplexed had they read BDAG on βαπτίζω, which does not present the everyday usage of the term. The verb has physical uses and metaphorical uses. The physical uses describe objects being inserted into a yielding substance, such as liquid (e.g., water or dyes), or the body of an animal, or a human being. The objects inserted range from ships that sink in the ocean,[41] people who drown in water,[42] people who wash themselves with water,[43] cloth dyed in liquid containing color pigments,[44] a knife plunged into a sacrificial animal,[45] the finger of a physician thrust into a wound,[46] and a drinking vessel dipped into a well.[47] In all these cases the term βαπτίζειν is used. When Paul stayed in the house of Aquila and Priscilla in Corinth, and when he volunteered to help wash the dishes after a meeting of the believers, Priscilla would have used βαπτίζειν for her suggestion that he place the dirty dishes into a basin filled with water. Luke the physician would have used βαπτίζειν when suggesting that he should explore with his index finger an open sore Paul contracted as a result of forty days of walking. It is implausible to assume that, since βαπτίζειν was used for the act of immersion in water as an expression of the cleansing from sin that faith in the crucified and risen Jesus Messiah and Lord provides, believers would stop using the term in everyday living. Besides the physical uses of the term there are metaphorical uses, with the meaning "to be overpowered by an abstract reality, such as debts, arguments, or thoughts,"[48] and "to become intoxicated, submerged in the effects of an intoxicating liquid."[49] The early church fathers continued to use βαπτίζειν in the various physical and metaphorical senses,[50] which conclusively demonstrates that the verb had not become a technical term used exclusively for Christian water baptism.

---

40. Eckhard J. Schnabel, "The Meaning of βαπτίζειν in Greek, Jewish, and Patristic Literature [2011]," in *Jesus, Paul, and the Early Church: Missionary Realities in Historical Contexts: Collected Essays*, WUNT 406 (Tübingen: Mohr Siebeck, 2018), 225–57.

41. Polybius, *Histories* 1.51.6; Josephus, *Ant.* 9.212.

42. Diodorus, *Library* 16.80.4; Plutarch, *Caesar* 49.4; Josephus, *J. W.* 1.437.

43. Aristotle, *Politica* 1336a.

44. Aristophanes, *Ecclesiazusae* 216–19; Josephus, *J. W.* 1.490.

45. Euripides, *Phoenissae* 1577–78; Josephus, *J. W.* 2.476.

46. John Chrysostom, *Homiliae 5.3 in 1 Thess* (PG 62.427).

47. Euripides, *Hippolytus* 121–24.

48. Plutarch, *Galba* 21.2; LXX Isa 21:4; Philo, *Leg.* 3.18.

49. Plato, *Symposium* 176A–B; Josephus, *Ant.* 10.169.

50. Cf. Justin Martyr, *Dial.* 46.2; 86.6; Clement of Alexandria, *Quis. div.* 34.3; *Protr.* 1.4; John Chrysostom, *Homiliae 33.1 in Joh.* (PG 59.187); *Homiliae 1.3 in Eph.* (PG 62.20); *Homiliae 40.5 in Matt* (PG 57.438).

Two examples documenting the first metaphorical meaning ("to be overwhelmed, immersed") shall suffice. Justin Martyr writes in *Dialogue with Trypho* 86.6: "Just as our Christ, by being crucified on the wood of the cross and by purifying us with water, redeemed us who had been immersed in the grievous sins which we have committed and made us a house of prayer and worship"; trans. T. B. Falls, modified. This text is instructive: Justin speaks of Christian water baptism using the verb ἁγνίσαι ("treat as holy, purify, sanctify"), while using the verb βαπτίζειν to describe the sinful past of believers before they became Christians: we were "immersed in the grievous sins which we have committed" (βεβαπτισμένους ταῖς βαρυτάταις ἁμαρτίαις ἃς ἐπράξαμεν), a state of affairs from which Christ saved us. Clement of Alexandria writes in *Protrepticus* 1.4: "The silly are stocks and stones, and still more senseless than stones is a man who is steeped in ignorance (ἀγνοίᾳ βεβαπτισμένος)"; trans. P. Schaff.

In the phrase ἐβαπτίσθημεν εἰς Χριστὸν Ἰησοῦν in Rom 6:3, the verb βαπτίζειν clearly has a non-physical sense: believers are not described as being immersed into a substance, such as water; they are immersed εἰς Χριστὸν Ἰησοῦν, i.e., they are immersed into a person.[51] It seems obvious that the first of the two metaphorical meanings is present: Paul speaks of being "immersed" in a reality that overwhelms the person being immersed. The preposition εἰς indicates movement into this reality. We can translate "we have been immersed into the reality of the Messiah Jesus."[52] Or, marking the passive voice as *passivum divinum*, we could translate "we have been overwhelmed by God toward the Messiah Jesus," or "God overwhelmed us, placing us into the reality of the Messiah Jesus."[53] The acknowledgement of a metaphorical meaning of βαπτίζειν in 6:3 is sometimes linked with "the imagery of immersion as a drowning to reinforce the point: their death by drowning was a sharing in Christ's death—as Jesus himself had hinted."[54] The reference to drowning is unnecessary, since the metaphorical meaning of the verb does not refer to drowning—the physical

---

51. For the meaning of βαπτίζειν in Rom 6:3–4 cf. Eckhard J. Schnabel, "The Language of Baptism: The Meaning of βαπτίζειν in the New Testament [2011]," in *Jesus, Paul, and the Early Church: Missionary Realities in Historical Contexts: Collected Essays*, WUNT 406 (Tübingen: Mohr Siebeck, 2018), 259–87, esp. 274–78.

52. Cf. Frédéric Godet, *Commentaire sur l'Épître aux Romains*, 3rd ed. (Geneva: Labor et Fides, 1879 [repr. 1968]), 2:17: "être plongé en lui, en sa mort"; Alphonse Maillot, *L'Épître aux Romains* (Paris: Centurion/Labor et Fides, 1984), 155: "nous tous qui avons été immergés dans le Christ-Jésus, nous avons aussi été immergés dans sa mort." See the discussion in Dunn, *Romans 1–8*, 311, who acknowledges the metaphorical meaning, referring to Maillot, but thinks that βαπτίζειν "has already attained the status of a Christian technical term."

53. Cf. Sabou, *Death*, 101–9.

54. James D. G. Dunn, "'Baptized' as Metaphor," in *Baptism, the New Testament and the Church: Historical and Contemporary Studies in Honour of R. E. O. White*, ed. Stanley E. Porter and Anthony R. Cross, JSNTSup 171 (Sheffield: Sheffield Academic Press, 1999), 294–310, esp. 307.

uses of the verb do not always connote water—but to the immersion into an abstract reality.

The second half of v. 6 uses the metaphor of being united with the death of Jesus: "we have been immersed into his death" (εἰς τὸν θάνατον αὐτοῦ ἐβαπτίσθημεν). Again, the entity into which believers are immersed is not a physical object, such as water, or a wound, but θάνατος, specifically the death of Jesus Messiah. This is Paul's main thought, as our exploration of 6:5–10 has shown: Paul refers to the death and resurrection of Jesus Messiah with which believers have been fused, as the first part of his answer to the objection of the critic in 6:1. Believers cannot cheerfully contemplate to commit acts of sin because they have been united with the death of Jesus Messiah "whom God displayed publicly as the mercy seat, through faith, by his blood."[55] Incorporation into Jesus Messiah (v. 3a) is incorporation into his death (v. 3b).

Second, following the metaphor of death, Paul uses the metaphor of burial: "we have been buried with him by our immersion into his death" (συνετάφημεν οὖν αὐτῷ διὰ τοῦ βαπτίσματος εἰς τὸν θάνατον; 6:4). The noun βάπτισμα occurs here for the first time in the history of the Greek language. It is not a technical term for physical water baptism: in Mark 10:38–39 and Luke 12:50 the term is used as a metaphor for being "immersed" into suffering and death: "Are you able to drink the cup that I drink, or be overwhelmed by the submersion by which I am overwhelmed?" (τὸ βάπτισμα ὃ ἐγὼ βαπτίζομαι βαπτισθῆναι, Mark 10:38).[56] Commentaries recognize the metaphorical meaning of both the noun βάπτισμα and the verb βαπτίζειν, and sometimes suggest the meaning "being overwhelmed,"[57] although they usually follow the English versions and translate "baptism" and "baptized" with the connotation of John's baptism and, in the minds of later readers, Christian water baptism.[58] The editors of BDAG are closer to the mark when they write, "perhaps the stark metaphor of impending personal disaster is to be rendered, 'are you prepared to be drowned the way I'm going to be drowned?'"[59] The assumption of an implicit connotation of water is not present in the meaning of βαπτίζειν, however; the metaphorical meaning of both noun and verb translated "being overwhelmed" captures what

---

55. Translation from Thielman, *Romans*, 207.

56. Translation from Schnabel, "The Meaning of βαπτίζειν in Greek, Jewish, and Patristic Literature [2011]," 282.

57. Cf. R. T. France, *The Gospel of Mark: A Commentary on the Greek Text*, NIGTC (Eerdmans: Grand Rapids, 2002), 416; Joel Marcus, *Mark 1–8: A New Translation with Introduction and Commentary*, AB 27 (New York: Doubleday, 2000), 747; I. Howard Marshall, *The Gospel of Luke: A Commentary on the Greek Text*, NIGTC (Grand Rapids: Eerdmans, 1978), 547, who explains that βαπτίζειν is used "in the metaphorical sense of being overwhelmed by catastrophe."

58. Thus Marcus, *Mark*, 754, for the "Markan community." The addiction to tradition and the translation "baptism" is strong.

59. BDAG s.v. βαπτίζω 3c (165).

Jesus is saying: he will be "completely overwhelmed in suffering and death"[60] and he announces that his followers will also be overwhelmed with the "immersion into death" which Jesus will soon experience.

Paul emphasizes in v. 4a that believers in Jesus, who belong to Jesus and who have been fused into the reality of Jesus, are really and completely "dead" when it comes to willingly committing acts of sin. They are definitely, conclusively separated from the reality in which disobedience to the will of God was normal, in which acts of sin were tolerated, even enjoyed. In antiquity, a great many deceased were buried in the same tomb, which leads to another thought: being fused with the burial of Jesus establishes a close fellowship with Jesus.

In v. 4b Paul moves from the death and burial of Jesus Messiah with which the believers have been united to Jesus' resurrection from the dead, with the result that "we too might walk in newness of life." As the resurrection of Jesus was an act of God (ἠγέρθη, *passivum divinum*), demonstrating the reality of the glory of God the Father, so the new reality of the everyday existence and behavior of the believers is the result of God's intervention. What is implicit here is explicit in 2 Cor 13:4: "For to be sure, he was crucified in weakness, yet he lives by God's power. Likewise, we are weak in him, yet by God's power we will live with him in our dealing with you (ζήσομεν σὺν αὐτῷ ἐκ δυνάμεως θεοῦ εἰς ὑμᾶς)" (NIV; cf. Eph 1:19–20). The phrase "newness of life" (καινότης ζωῆς) is best understood in terms of an epexegetical genitive.[61] Sinners who are fused with the reality of Jesus are transferred into a new reality, a "novelty" which is described as a life no longer lived under the shadow of the wrath of God (1:18) and the foreboding control of death which has ruled human beings since the sin of Adam (5:12, 17, 21). The newness of life means that God declares us sinners righteous; it means redemption and forgiveness of sins (3:24–25), peace with God, and the certain hope of eternal life in which we share the glory of God (5:1–2). It also means a new way of life that reflects the reality of the "newness" that the fusion with the death and resurrection of Jesus brings about as they share the resurrection life of Jesus Messiah who "lives to God" (6:10).

The Present Life of the Believer

Having explained why believers in Jesus, the crucified Messiah and risen Lord, cannot trivialize the seriousness of sinful actions, Paul explains in 6:11–14 the consequences that arise. The explanation is formulated with a series of impera-

---

60. Everett Ferguson, *Baptism in the Early Church: History, Theology, and Liturgy in the First Five Centuries* (Grand Rapids: Eerdmans, 2008), 130, although he also uses the terms "baptized," "drowned," and "submerged" as translation options.
61. Heinrich von Siebenthal, *Griechische Grammatik zum Neuen Testament* (Gießen/Basel: Brunnen, 2011), §162c.

tives (in the previous chapters, the only imperative occurred in 3:4, addressed to people in general).

In 6:11, Paul calls on the believers to draw the consequences from their fusion with the death of Jesus Messiah, making sure that they live for God (ζῶντας τῷ θεῷ). The present imperative λογίζεσθε signals that believers must evaluate their status as people whom God has fused with the death and resurrection of Jesus constantly, throughout their lives. Paul does not describe the believers as sinners who have been resurrected from the dead and who will never die again, in the manner that he described Jesus in v. 9 as having been raised from the dead never to die again. Their death on account of their fusion with Jesus is a metaphorical death, and their resurrection together with Jesus is in the future as far as their bodies are concerned. They will be raised from the dead in the future, but they are called upon to live their present lives in the presence of God, a reality of committed faith that precludes a willingness to tolerate sin.

In 6:12, Paul calls on the believers to not allow sin to resume control (μὴ βασιλευέτω ἡ ἁμαρτία), a control sin exercises through unbridled passions. The imperative is formally addressed to sin but is meant for the believers who read and hear Paul's letter. The fact that believers continue to have a "mortal body" (θνητὸν σῶμα) explains why the temptation to commit acts of sin, and the weakness to give in to temptation, are still very real possibilities. The mortal body will be made alive only in the future, as Paul will explain in 8:11, 21–23 (cf. 1 Cor 15:53–54). The expression θνητὸν σῶμα is not identical with the "body of sin" (v. 6) or the "body of death" (7:24), both of which have been eliminated on account of the believers' fusion with Jesus' atoning death. The expression θνητὸν σῶμα describes the believers' earthly existence in terms of their bodily existence in the world which continues to be a world in rebellion against God. Believers live in the reality of a world dominated by sin and death, and at the same time they live, with their bodies, in the reality marked by the death and resurrection of Jesus Messiah and thus in the reality distinguished by the power of God who makes living for his glory possible.

In 6:13, Paul reformulates v. 12 with two imperatives: "Do not offer (μηδὲ παριστάνετε) any part of yourself to sin as an instrument of wickedness, but rather offer yourselves (παραστήσατε ἑαυτούς) to God as those who have been brought from death to life; and offer every part of yourself to him as an instrument of righteousness" (NIV). Paul speaks, specifically, of "your members" (τὰ μέλη ὑμῶν), i.e., the members and organs of the human body—feet, hands, arms, eyes, ears, mouth, sexual organs—that can be "instruments" (ὅπλα), or weapons, promoting wickedness. Believers do not allow their bodies to expedite sinful actions. Rather, on account of their transfer "from death to life" (ἐκ νεκρῶν ζῶντας), they advance God (παραστήσατε ἑαυτοὺς τῷ θεῷ) and righteousness in the service of God (ὅπλα δικαιοσύνης τῷ θεῷ). The verb παρίστημι implies that it is God who enables believers to promote righteousness. The reference to military weapons implies the believers' deliberate, voluntary, but totally committed service to God.[62]

In 6:14, Paul grounds the imperatives of vv. 12–13 in a promise: "sin will not exercise control over you because you are not under the law but under grace." The law controls sinners on account of the death sentence it pronounces against them. This is true not only for Gentiles (1:18–32) but also for Jews (2:1–3:20), since atonement and forgiveness of sins are granted by God now, in the messianic era of the crucified and risen Lord Jesus, not on account of circumcision and the law with its stipulated sacrifices and other means of maintaining covenant faithfulness, but by faith in the revelation of the power of God bringing salvation through the death and resurrection of Jesus Messiah (1:16–17; 3:21–5:21). Because believers in Jesus belong to Jesus Messiah who died on the cross and who was raised from the dead, they belong to the realm of grace which exercises "dominion through justification leading to eternal life through Jesus Christ our Lord" (5:21 NRSV). The future tense of οὐ κυριεύσει describes the *status quo* of resurrection life, which is still in the future, secured in consequence of the resurrection of Jesus (cf. 8:31–39), but which is effective in the present, given their fusion with the death and resurrection of Jesus Messiah.

In 6:15–23, Paul describes the new life of the believers in terms of freedom and obedience. Paul repeats the objection of v. 1: some might argue that being controlled by grace rather than by the law gives believers in Jesus permission to sin; he again emphatically rejects such a conclusion (v. 15).

Paul then presents two mutually exclusive options of commitment: a person is committed either to sin or to righteousness (vv. 16–18). Paul uses the metaphor of slavery when he describes the different realities that exercise control in the world. Believers must know that they are slaves of the master whom they obey. People whose master is sin, the result is death. People whose master is God, the result is righteousness. Before they came to faith in Jesus Messiah, the believers were enslaved to sin. When they accepted the teaching of the apostles, God liberated them from the power of sin and its concomitant death sentence, which means that they are now controlled by God, committed to righteousness.

Paul proceeds to explain again what happens in conversion (vv. 19–23). Once, before they came to faith in Jesus Messiah, the believers were controlled by impurity and lawlessness. Now, in their present new life, believers are, and must be, controlled by righteousness which results in holiness. People who are subject to the tyranny of sin lack righteousness: the result of their shameful ac-

---

62. Cf. Christine Gerber, "Vom Waffendienst des Christenmenschen (Röm 6,12–14.23)," in "... *was ihr auf dem Weg verhandelt habt*": *Beiträge zur Exegese und Theologie des Neuen Testaments: Festschrift für Ferdinand Hahn zum 75. Geburtstag*, ed. P. Müller, C. Gerber, and T. Knöppler (Neukirchen-Vluyn: Neukirchener Verlag, 2001), 129–42, esp. 138; Hanna Stettler, *Heiligung bei Paulus. Ein Beitrag aus biblisch-theologischer Sicht*, WUNT 2.368 (Tübingen: Mohr Siebeck, 2014), 442.

tions is God's death sentence. Believers in Jesus Messiah have been liberated by God from the power of sin; they have become subject to the lordship of God, resulting in a holy life (ἔχετε τὸν καρπὸν ὑμῶν εἰς ἁγιασμόν) and eventually in eternal life (τὸ δὲ τέλος ζωὴν αἰώνιον), which is God's free gift on account of Jesus, our Messiah and Lord (ἐν Χριστῷ Ἰησοῦ τῷ κυρίῳ ἡμῶν, v. 22).

Conclusion

The critical question of 6:1 arose in the context of Paul's teaching that when sinners come to faith in Jesus, the crucified Messiah and risen Lord, God forgives all of their sins—the sins they committed before their conversion and the sins they have committed and will commit after their conversion. Paul addresses the question whether Christians can accept sinful actions, and he does so with theological stringency and existential urgency. This question was a most relevant question for the churches. Jude knows intruders "who pervert the grace of our God into licentiousness and deny our only Master and Lord, Jesus Christ" (Jude 4). James knows Christians who understand faith as intellectual acceptance of some tenets of Christian doctrine and who claim that they are justified by faith without living out the consequences of faith in God and in Jesus Messiah in their everyday lives (James 2:18–26). John warns of a group called the Nicolaitans who promote integration in pagan society including eating food sacrificed to idols and fornication (Rev 2:14–15). Paul argues that the reality and the glory of the grace of God cannot be an excuse for sin. Believers in Jesus whom God has declared righteous, whose sins were atoned when Jesus died on the cross, whose sins are forgiven, who have peace with God, have no choice except commit themselves to God, to the risen Messiah Jesus, to the Holy Spirit as Paul will argue in Romans 8, and thus to obedience to the will of God, to righteousness and holiness.

The *Wirkungsgeschichte* of Rom 6 includes discussions of the role of sinful passions (Lat. *concupiscentia*; cf. "concupiscence" in KJV), Luther's *simul iustus et peccator*, and baptism, practiced for centuries as baptism of newly born infants. Discussions of conversion in the context of missionary work are rare.[63] The vast majority of commentators on Paul's letter to the believers in the city of Rome wrote in the social context of so-called Christian countries in which just about everybody had been baptized as an infant, where everybody was regarded as a Christian, and where conversion and discipleship had largely disappeared as subjects of theological discussion or ecclesial concern—a situation that Dietrich Bonhoeffer famously analyzed in terms of "cheap grace."[64]

Paul writes in the context of his mission to Jews and Gentiles, waiting in Corinth for the spring which would allow him to travel by ship to Jerusalem and

---

63. But see the comments of Wilckens, *Römer*, 2:27; Wolter, *Römer 1–8*, 370, 383.

64. Chapter 1 of Dietrich Bonhoeffer, *The Cost of Discipleship* (New York: Macmillan, 1959). The first German edition was published in 1937.

then to Spain where he wanted to preach the gospel in cities that presumably no other missionaries had reached. The fact that Paul writes about the effects of the gospel in the lives of believers with indicatives and with imperatives has been described as paradoxical juxtaposition[65] or as dialectic,[66] which seems to say more about the interpreter than about Paul.[67] The indicatives and the imperatives make sense when we acknowledge the fundamental significance of conversion: the indicatives describe what happens in conversion, the imperatives refer to the consequences of conversion.[68] The indicatives describe the believers' identity: they came to faith in Jesus Messiah, with the effect that God fused them with the death and resurrection of Jesus, which means they are dead to sin and alive for God. Identity is always connected with a particular ethos. This was true for Israel: the "indicative" of salvation—"I am the LORD your God, who brought you out of the land of Egypt, out of the house of slavery" (Exod 20:2)—is followed by a description of the ethos of Israel which follows from their liberation from slavery and the covenant that God granted them. The imperatives in Rom 6 have a dual purpose. First, the imperatives call on the believers to live out their identity as the messianic covenant people of God who are united with Jesus Messiah and who are thus people "who have been brought from death to life" (ἐκ νεκρῶν ζῶντες, 6:13). Second, the imperatives serve to foster the transformation of the cognitive identity of the believers—comprised of believing Jews, Gentiles, freeborn, slaves, men, and women—into the social identity of the messianic community of believers in Jesus, committed to the will of God, fused with the death and resurrection of Jesus Messiah, empowered by the Spirit, to live for the glory of God.

Bibliography

The Bible according to the translation of Martin Luther, with Apocrypha. Biblical Text of the 1983 revision. Edited by the Evangelische Kirche in Deutschland. Stuttgart: Deutsche Bibelgesellschaft, 1999.
Bonhoeffer, Dietrich. *The Cost of Discipleship.* New York: Macmillan, 1959.

---

65. Rudolf Bultmann, "Jesus Christus und die Mythologie [1958/1964]," in *Glauben und Verstehen IV* (Tübingen: Mohr Siebeck, 1965), 141–89, esp. 183.

66. Wolfgang Schrage, *Ethik des Neuen Testaments,* 2nd rev. ed., GzNT 4 (Göttingen: Vandenhoeck & Ruprecht, 1989), 161.

67. Note Käsemann, *Römer,* 175, who speaks of the "so-called imperatives."

68. Wolter, *Römer 1–8,* 406; Michael Wolter, "Identität und Ethos bei Paulus," in *Theologie und Ethos im frühen Christentum. Studien zu Jesus, Paulus und Lukas,* WUNT 236 (Tübingen: Mohr Siebeck, 2009), 121–69, esp. 136–139, with reference to Wiard Popkes, *Paränese und Neues Testament,* SBS 168 (Stuttgart: Katholisches Bibelwerk, 1996). See Eckhard J. Schnabel, "How Paul Developed His Ethics [1994]," in *Jesus, Paul, and the Early Church: Missionary Realities in Historical Contexts: Collected Essays,* WUNT 406 (Tübingen: Mohr Siebeck, 2018), 193–222.

Bultmann, Rudolf. "Jesus Christus und die Mythologie [1958/1964]." Pages 141–89 in *Glauben und Verstehen IV*. Tübingen: Mohr Siebeck, 1965.

Byron, John. *Slavery Metaphors in Early Judaism and Pauline Christianity: A Traditio-Historical and Exegetical Examination*. WUNT 2.162. Tübingen: Mohr Siebeck, 2003.

Calhoun, Robert M. *Paul's Definitions of the Gospel in Romans 1*. WUNT 2.316. Tübingen: Mohr Siebeck, 2011.

Campbell, Constantine R. *Paul and Union with Christ: An Exegetical and Theological Study*. Grand Rapids: Zondervan, 2012.

Caragounis, Chrys C. "ΟΨΩΝΙΟΝ: A Reconsideration of its Meaning." *NovT* 16 (1974): 35–57.

Chapman, David W. "Crucifixion." Pages 299–754 in *The Trial and Crucifixion of Jesus: Texts and Commentary*. Edited by David W. Chapman and Eckhard J. Schnabel. WUNT 344. Tübingen: Mohr Siebeck, 2015.

Cook, John Granger. *Crucifixion in the Mediterranean World*. WUNT 327. Tübingen: Mohr Siebeck, 2014.

Cranfield, C. E. B. *A Critical and Exegetical Commentary on the Epistle to the Romans*. 2 vols. ICC. Edinburgh: T&T Clark, 1975–79.

Croasmun, Matthew. *The Emergence of Sin: The Cosmic Tyrant in Romans*. Oxford: Oxford University Press, 2017.

Dunn, James D. G. "'Baptized' as Metaphor." Pages 294–310 in *Baptism, the New Testament and the Church: Historical and Contemporary Studies in Honour of R. E. O. White*. Edited by Stanley E. Porter and Anthony R. Cross. JSNTSup 171. Sheffield: Sheffield Academic Press, 1999.

———. *Romans 1–8*. WBC 38A. Dallas: Word, 1988.

———. *The Theology of Paul the Apostle*. Grand Rapids: Eerdmans, 1998.

Ferguson, Everett. *Baptism in the Early Church: History, Theology, and Liturgy in the First Five Centuries*. Grand Rapids: Eerdmans, 2008.

Fitzmyer, Joseph A. *Romans: A New Translation with Introduction and Commentary*. AB 33. New York: Doubleday, 1993.

France, R. T. *The Gospel of Mark: A Commentary on the Greek Text*. NIGTC. Eerdmans: Grand Rapids, 2002.

Frankemölle, Hubert. *Das Taufverständnis des Paulus: Taufe, Tod und Auferstehung nach Röm 6*. SBS 47. Stuttgart: Katholisches Bibelwerk, 1970.

Gemünden, Petra von. "Die urchristliche Taufe und der Umgang mit den Affekten." Pages 115–36 in *Transformations of the Inner Self in Ancient Religions*. Edited by J. Assmann and G. G. Stroumsa. SHR 83. Leiden: Brill, 1999.

Gerber, Christine. "Vom Waffendienst des Christenmenschen (Röm 6,12–14.23)." Pages 129–42 in *". . . was ihr auf dem Weg verhandelt habt": Beiträge zur Exegese und Theologie des Neuen Testaments: Festschrift für Ferdinand Hahn zum 75. Geburtstag*. Edited by P. Müller, C. Gerber, and T. Knöppler. Neukirchen-Vluyn: Neukirchener Verlag, 2001.

Godet, Frédéric. *Commentaire sur l'Épître aux Romains.* 3rd ed. Geneva: Labor et Fides, 1879 [repr. 1968].

Goodrich, John K. "From Slaves of Sin to Slaves of God: Reconsidering the Origin of Paul's Slavery Metaphor in Romans 6." *BBR* 23.4 (2013): 509–30.

Gorman, Michael J. *Cruciformity: Paul's Narrative Spirituality of the Cross.* Grand Rapids: Eerdmans, 2001.

———. *Inhabiting the Cruciform God: Kenosis, Justification, and Theosis in Paul's Narrative Soteriology.* Grand Rapids: Eerdmans, 2009.

Haacker, Klaus. *Der Brief des Paulus an die Römer.* 4th rev. ed. ThHKNT 6. Leipzig: Evangelische Verlagsanstalt, 2012.

Hellholm, David. "Vorgeformte Tauftradition und deren Benutzung in den Paulusbriefen." Pages 415–95 in *Ablution, Initiation, and Baptism: Late Antiquity, Early Judaism, and Early Christianity.* Edited by D. Hellholm et al. BZAW 176. Berlin: de Gruyter, 2011.

Hengel, Martin. *Crucifixion in the Ancient World and the Folly of the Message of the Cross.* Translated by J. Bowden. Philadelphia: Fortress, 1977.

Horn, Friedrich Wilhelm. *Das Angeld des Geistes. Studien zur paulinischen Pneumatologie.* FRLANT 154. Göttingen: Vandenhoeck & Ruprecht, 1992.

Käsemann, Ernst. *An die Römer.* 4th ed. HNT 8a. Tübingen: Mohr Siebeck, 1980.

———. *Commentary on Romans.* Translated and edited by Geoffrey W. Bromiley. Grand Rapids: Eerdmans, 1980.

Klinghardt, Matthias. "Sünde und Gericht bei Paulus." *ZNW* 88 (1997): 56–80.

Kritzer, R. *1. Korinther.* Edited by Peter Arzt-Grabner et al. PKNT 2. Göttingen: Vandenhoeck & Ruprecht, 2006.

Légasse, Simon. *L'épître de Paul aux Romains.* LD 10. Paris: Cerf, 2002.

Lohse, Eduard. *Der Brief an die Römer.* KEK 4. Göttingen: Vandenhoeck & Ruprecht, 2003.

Luther, Martin. *Lectures on Romans: Glosses and Scholia.* Edited by H. C. Oswald. Luther's Works 25. St. Louis: Concordia, 1972.

———. *Vorlesung über den Römerbrief 1915/1916.* 2 vols. Lateinisch-deutsche Ausgabe. Darmstadt: Wissenschaftliche Buchgesellschaft, 1915–16.

Lyu, Eun-Geol. *Sünde und Rechtfertigung bei Paulus. Eine exegetische Untersuchung zum paulinischen Sündenverständnis aus soteriologischer Sicht.* WUNT 2.318. Tübingen: Mohr Siebeck, 2011.

Macaskill, Grant. *Union with Christ in the New Testament.* Oxford: Oxford University Press, 2013.

Maillot, Alphonse. *L'Épître aux Romains.* Paris: Centurion/Labor et Fides, 1984.

Marcus, Joel. *Mark 1–8: A New Translation with Introduction and Commentary.* AB 27. New York: Doubleday, 2000.

Marshall, I. Howard. *The Gospel of Luke: A Commentary on the Greek Text.* NIGTC. Grand Rapids: Eerdmans, 1978.

Martin, Dale B. *Slavery as Salvation: The Metaphor of Slavery in Pauline Christianity.* New Haven: Yale University Press, 1990.

Moo, Douglas J. *The Letter to the Romans.* 2nd ed. NICNT. Grand Rapids: Eerdmans, 2018.

Morales, Isaac Augustine. "Baptism and Union with Christ." Pages 151–79 in *"In Christ" in Paul: Explorations of Paul's Theology of Union and Participation.* Edited by Michael J. Thate, Kevin J. Vanhoozer, and Constantine R. Campbell. Grand Rapids: Eerdmans, 2018.

Penna, Romano. *Lettera ai Romani.* SDOC 6. Bologna: Dehoniane, 2010.

Popkes, Wiard. *Paränese und Neues Testament.* SBS 168. Stuttgart: Katholisches Bibelwerk, 1996.

Röhser, Günter. *Stellvertretung im Neuen Testament.* SBS 195. Stuttgart: Verlag Katholisches Bibelwerk, 2002.

Sabou, Sorin. *Between Horror and Hope: Paul's Metaphorical Language of Death in Romans 6:1–11.* PBM. Milton Keynes: Paternoster, 2005.

Schlatter Adolf. *Gottes Gerechtigkeit: Ein Kommentar zum Römerbrief.* Stuttgart: Calwer, 1975 [repr. 1935].

———. *Romans: The Righteousness of God.* Translated by S. S. Schatzmann. Peabody, MA: Hendrickson, 1995.

Schlier, Heinrich. *Der Römerbrief.* 3rd ed. HThK 6. Freiburg: Herder, 1987.

Schnabel, Eckhard J. *Der Brief des Paulus an die Römer: Kapitel 1–5.* 2nd ed. HTA. Witten/Gießen: Brockhaus/Brunnen, 2018.

———. *Der Brief des Paulus an die Römer: Kapitel 6–16.* HTA. Witten/Gießen: Brockhaus/Brunnen, 2016.

———. "How Paul Developed His Ethics [1994]." Pages 193–222 in *Jesus, Paul, and the Early Church: Missionary Realities in Historical Contexts: Collected Essays.* WUNT 406. Tübingen: Mohr Siebeck, 2018.

———. *Jesus in Jerusalem: The Last Days.* Grand Rapids: Eerdmans, 2018.

———. "The Language of Baptism: The Meaning of βαπτίζειν in the New Testament [2011]." Pages 259–87 in *Jesus, Paul, and the Early Church: Missionary Realities in Historical Contexts: Collected Essays.* WUNT 406. Tübingen: Mohr Siebeck, 2018.

———. "The Meaning of βαπτίζειν in Greek, Jewish, and Patristic Literature [2011]." Pages 225–57 in *Jesus, Paul, and the Early Church: Missionary Realities in Historical Contexts: Collected Essays.* WUNT 406. Tübingen: Mohr Siebeck, 2018.

Schnelle, Udo. *Apostle Paul: His Life and Theology.* Translated M. Eugene Boring. Grand Rapids: Baker Academic, 2005.

———. *The Human Condition: Anthropology in the Teachings of Jesus, Paul, and John.* Translated by O. C. Dean. Edinburgh/Minneapolis: T&T Clark/Fortress, 1996.

Schrage, Wolfgang. *Ethik des Neuen Testaments*. 2nd ed. GzNT 4. Göttingen: Vandenhoeck & Ruprecht, 1989.

Schreiner, Thomas R. *Romans*. 2nd ed. BECNT. Grand Rapids: Baker Academic, 2018.

Schwarzmann, Heinrich. *Zur Tauftheologie des heiligen Paulus in Röm 6*. Heidelberg: Kerle, 1950.

Siebenthal, Heinrich von. *Griechische Grammatik zum Neuen Testament*. Gießen/Basel: Brunnen, 2011.

Stettler, Hanna. *Heiligung bei Paulus. Ein Beitrag aus biblisch-theologischer Sicht*. WUNT 2.368. Tübingen: Mohr Siebeck, 2014.

Stuhlmacher, Peter. *Biblical Theology of the New Testament*. Translated by Daniel P. Bailey. Grand Rapids: Eerdmans, 2018.

———. *Der Brief an die Römer*. NTD 6. Göttingen: Vandenhoeck & Ruprecht, 1989.

———. *Paul's Letter to the Romans*. Louisville: Westminster John Knox, 1994.

Thielman, Frank. *Romans*. ZECNT 6. Grand Rapids: Zondervan Academic, 2018.

Wilckens, Ulrich. *Der Brief an die Römer*. EKK 6. Neukirchen-Vluyn/Einsiedeln: Neukirchener Verlag/Benzinger, 1978–82.

Wolter, Michael. *Der Brief an die Römer: Teilband 1: Röm 1–8*. EKK 6. Neukirchen-Vluyn/Mannheim: Neukirchener/Patmos, 2014.

———. *Der Brief an die Römer: Teilband 2: Röm 9–16*. EKK 6. Neukirchen-Vluyn/Mannheim: Neukirchener/Patmos, 2019.

———. "Identität und Ethos bei Paulus." Pages 121–69 in *Theologie und Ethos im frühen Christentum: Studien zu Jesus, Paulus und Lukas*. WUNT 236. Tübingen: Mohr Siebeck, 2009.

Zeller, Dieter. *Der Brief an die Römer*. RNT. Regensburg: Pustet, 1985.

CHAPTER 13

"Ego-bashing" or Autobiography? The Revelatory Purpose of the Law in Romans 7

Ben C. Dunson

Introduction

It has become common in Pauline scholarship to argue that Paul is not writing about himself in Rom 7 in any way, whether past, present, or future. I believe this understanding to be incorrect. To show this I will begin by addressing two of the common arguments against an autobiographical reading of Rom 7. The first argument claims that Paul's use of ἐγώ, although utilizing the present tense, cannot be harmonized with his autobiographical statements in Phil 3:4–11, and thus that Paul must be speaking "in character" as Adam or Israel in Rom 7. The second argument claims that Paul could never have said of himself that there was a time when he "was alive apart from the law" (7:9).

My central argument, however, is positive. I will attempt to show how the cognitive language throughout Rom 7 (which continues a train of thought Paul began earlier in Romans) shows God's purpose in promulgating the law to be a revelatory one: it was given in order to reveal the true condition of the human heart, a condition clarified by Paul's recounting of his own past existential encounter with the full force of the demands inscribed in God's law. The cognitive language in Rom 7 is nonsensical if we posit merely speech-in-character or some other device so as to excise the individual from Paul's argument. Of course, Paul did not need to employ the first person singular to make the argument he makes in Rom 7, but I will argue that it contributes to the persuasiveness and power of his argument.

Against Ego-Bashing

The speech-in-character (προσωποποιία) argument against Paul referring to himself takes two main forms: Paul is writing as Adam, or Paul is writing as Israel. There are two main textual details put forward in defense of Paul's ἐγώ being Adam.[1] First, the general sense of God's commandment against coveting

---

1. For a recent treatment of ἐγώ in Romans 7, with bibliographical entries for additional related studies, see Monika E. Götte, "Adam und Christus – Christus und Adam. Römer 7 im Licht von Genesis 3," in *Perspektiven auf Römer 7*, ed. Stefan Krauter

being the very occasion for covetousness to arise in the heart seems to corre-spond with Adam and Eve's situation in the garden. The serpent twists God's prohibition against eating of the tree of the knowledge of good and evil so as to tempt Eve. He falsely expands the prohibition to include all trees in the garden and, contrary to God's word, denies that death will result from eating from the tree of the knowledge of good and evil. Satan's temptation, then, stirs up a desire on Eve's part for what God prohibited: "when the woman saw that the tree was good for food, and that it was a delight to the eyes, and that the tree was to be desired to make one wise, she took of its fruit and ate, and she also gave some to her husband who was with her, and he ate" (Gen 3:6 ESV).[2]

The second textual detail is that Paul describes in 7:10 how sin took an (illegitimate) opportunity through God's commandment, deceived him, and thereby killed him. Paul uses the verb ἐξαπατάω, which is a nearly synonymous cognate verb with ἀπατάω, which itself is the verb on Eve's lips in LXX Gen 3:13 used to shift the blame for her eating onto the serpent: "The serpent deceived me [ἠπάτησέν], and I ate." Both allusions are indeed possible, maybe even likely, but should not be overstated. The speech-in-character, for that matter, if present at all, is not Adam's, but Eve's.[3]

Alternatively, it has been argued that Paul is writing of himself as Israel.[4] One argument in support of this claim is that Paul quotes an abbreviated form of the tenth commandment, which was taken by some contemporary Jews as a summary of the whole of God's law. Another supporting argument is the focus on how the law enflames covetous desire, just as it did for Israel in the wilder-ness (as recounted throughout the book of Numbers).[5] All of this is plausible

---

(Neukirchener-Vluyn: Neurkirchener, 2016), 49–82. See also the literatuere cited in Thomas R. Schreiner, *Romans*, BECNT, 2nd ed. (Grand Rapids: Baker Academic, 2018), 357n7. Cf. Hermann Lichtenberger, *Das Ich Adams und das Ich der Menschheit*, WUNT 164 (Tübingen: Mohr Siebeck, 2004), 125–86; Otfried Hofius, "Der Mensch im Shatten Adams. Römer 7,7–25a," in *Paulusstudien II*, WUNT 143 (Tübingen: Mohr Siebeck, 2002), 110–21, 134–35.

2. All English translations are from the ESV unless otherwise noted.

3. Cf. Schreiner, *Romans*, 358n9. On the speech-in-character view see especially Stanley K. Stowers, *A Rereading of Romans: Justice, Jews, and Gentiles* (New Haven: Yale University Press, 1997), 16–21, 264–69; cf. Werner G. Kümmel, *Römer 7 und das Bild des Menschen in Neuen Testament* (Munich: Kaiser, 1974 [orig. 1929]); Robert Jewett, *Romans: A Commentary*, Hermeneia (Minneapolis: Fortress, 2007), 441–45.

4. See, e.g., Frank Thielman, "The Story of Israel and the Theology of Romans 5–8," in *Pauline Theology: Volume 3: Romans*, ed. David M. Hay and E. Elizabeth Johnson (Minneapolis: Fortress, 1995), 190–94; N. T. Wright, "Romans and the Theology of Paul," in *Pauline Theology: Volume 3: Romans*, ed. David M. Hay and E. Elizabeth John-son (Minneapolis: Fortress, 1995), 49–54; Douglas J. Moo, "Israel and Paul in Romans 7.7–12," *NTS* 32.1 (1986): 122–35.

5. See Francis Watson, *Paul and the Hermeneutics of Faith* (London: T&T Clark, 2004), 354–80.

too, but a realistic assessment of Rom 7:7–12 should surely recognize that these echoes, like those alluding to Adam or Eve, are faint. If anything, it would seem better to argue that Paul understands his own experience with God's law as a kind of recapitulation of Adam and Eve's experience in the garden, and that he writes, not as Israel, but as what he really is, an Israel*ite*, even a representative Israelite. The general sense then, far from pushing us to cut Paul's own experience out of 7:7–12, is that Paul's existential encounter with the demands of God's law is by no means unique to him. It is the experience of his primeval parents (although we must account for the differences in the pre-fall situation). It is also the experience of all Israelites. Law, as all parents of small children know, creates a desire for what is prohibited.

In 7:13 we arrive at Paul's question: "Did that which is good, then, bring death to me?" If sin, seizing an opportunity through God's commandment, deceived Paul and killed him, is it not obviously the case that God's good law (see 7:12) is to blame for spiritual death? Paul answers: "By no means!" He then proceeds to explain throughout the rest of chapter 7 why this is a false inference.

It is especially in Rom 7:14–25 that scholars have insisted that Paul cannot be writing about his own experience as a believer. The main reasons, in brief, are as follows. First, it is said that Paul's statements about his desires and actions conflict with what he has already said in chapter 6, and what he will say in chapter 8 about the nature of life in union with Christ. Second, the Holy Spirit is not mentioned once in 7:14–25, a perplexing omission if this is describing the normal Christian life. Finally, it is asked whether a believer could utter the cry of total despair found in 7:24: "Wretched man that I am! Who will deliver me from this body of death?"

Stephen Chester, attempting to retain the autobiographical focus, argues that all of these difficulties can be explained if we simply shift the referent from Paul's present life to his past.[6] The Spirit-less agony of 7:14–25, Chester argues, took place prior to Paul's conversion. In line with much writing on Greek verbal aspect, Chester rightly notes that the present tense verbs in this section need not refer to present time. They could be a form of the "historical present," meant to give a sense of vividness and urgency to what Paul says, even though the real-world time-referent is to the past.

The present tense verb forms certainly do not *have* to refer to Paul's present experience, but Chester's contention introduces an even greater dilemma for interpreters: if everything in 7:7–24 took place in Paul's past, why shift to present tense verbs midway through the discussion? Would not the rhetorical power

---

6. Stephen J. Chester, "The Retrospective View of Romans 7: Paul's Past in Present Perspective," in *Perspectives on Our Struggle with Sin: Three Views of Romans 7*, ed. T. L. Wilder (Nashville: Broadman & Holman, 2011), 57–103; Stephen J. Chester, *Conversion at Corinth: Perspectives on Conversion in Paul's Theology and the Corinthian Church*, SNTW (London: T&T Clark, 2003), 183–90.

of vv. 7–12 have been heightened with the historical present as well? Chester inadvertently introduces a new interpretive difficulty: explaining the shift to the present tense when it doesn't actually convey a shift in temporal perspective at all. What is *possible* according to verbal aspect appears to have become an easy way out of a different difficulty: the seeming conflict of the material in chapter 7 with the nature of the Christian life as Paul writes of it in chapters 6 and 8.

Furthermore, Richard Longenecker rightly notes that οἴδαμεν ὅτι ("we know that") in 7:14 is one of Paul's standard "disclosure formulas" indicating "the beginning of a new section of material."[7] Thus, as Longenecker puts it, the "difference between 7:7–13 in its use of past tenses and 7:14–25 in its use of present tenses," along with the concluding "inferential expression ἄρα οὖν" in 7:25b, "should have alerted all previous commentators to the differing purposes and functions of these two passages."[8]

The most natural reading of the shift to the present tense in 7:14, then, barring obvious contextual indications of a continuation in topic and perspective, is that Paul has intentionally shifted the temporal focus from past (in 7:7–12) to the present.[9]

Even more importantly: 7:14–25 is the answer to the fourth (of four) rhetorical questions in chapters 6–7. These questions provide the structural undergirding that moves Paul's argument forward in these chapters. In particular they answer specific challenges that Paul anticipates in light of what he writes in 5:20–21,[10] since these two verses might seem to indicate that God gave his law because he *desires* people to sin. It came "in order to [ἵνα] increase the trespass," after all.

Here I can merely summarize Paul's purpose in posing these questions: the law itself can do nothing to rescue those who are outside of Christ from spiritual bondage. It is not the law that is the problem, however—it is sinful flesh. As flesh encounters God's good law, it is not perfected, but rather enslaved. Romans 7:14–25, as the answer to the last of these rhetorical questions, is an integral part of Paul's treatment of the salvation of the individual believer, namely by answering whether the law itself was responsible for Paul's own spiritual death.[11] All four rhetorical questions together reveal Paul's understanding

---

7. Richard N. Longenecker, *The Epistle to the Romans: A Commentary on the Greek Text*, NIGTC (Grand Rapids: Eerdmans, 2016), 659.

8. Longenecker, *Romans*, 659, 671.

9. Furthermore, according to the pre-Christian view, even within Rom 7:14–25 itself, "as Seifrid observes (1992: 230–31; see also Timmins 2017: 6), the text alternates awkwardly . . . between Paul's present experience (7:14, 21–24, 25b) and his past perspective (7:15, 18b–19)" (Schreiner, *Romans*, 372n6).

10. Generally recognized by commentators. See Longenecker, *Romans*, 638–39, 643–44.

11. Against anti-individual interpretations of Paul in general see Ben C. Dunson, *Individual and Community in Paul's Letter to the Romans*, WUNT 2.332 (Tübingen: Mohr Siebeck, 2012).

of what the law can and cannot do with regard to God's saving work in the life of the individual believer. Autobiography cannot be excised without destroying the logic of this section of text.

The Positive Function of Paul's Autobiography

This brief examination of the main objections to an autobiographical reading of chapter 7 does not explain why Paul *does* speak in the first person throughout. I would suggest he does so for two main reasons: first, to show the revelatory function of the law in his past experience (7:7–13), and second, to show the inability of the law itself to enable Christian obedience (7:14–25).

The Revelatory Function of the Law

First, Paul writes in the first person to describe the revelatory function of the law. Paul has already written of this function of the law in his statement of the absolute contrast between justification by works of the law (Rom 3:19–20) or by faith in Jesus Christ (3:21–26). In particular: "through the law comes knowledge of sin" (Rom 3:20).[12] Paul then prefaces his discussion of his past experience in 7:7 with an unmistakable reference to how the law reveals sin: he would not even have "known sin" if "it had not been for the law," referring specifically to the tenth commandment.[13] It is clearly nonsensical to insist that Paul, zealous defender of the law that he was before his conversion (see Phil 3:6), literally did not know what sin was. Paul's statement is intelligible, however, as a statement recounting the progression in his *experience*: sin was there in his heart, but he was not fully aware of its power and pervasiveness. Paul's existential encounter with the law, as he has already said in Rom 5:20–21, had the effect of stirring up sinful desires, rather than bringing them under control. This, then, is what Paul means when he says that "apart from the law sin lies dead" (Rom 7:8): his true condition was hidden from him on account of his own willful suppression of the truth. Paul certainly *perceived* himself to be alive apart from this existential, experiential encounter with the demands of God's law, but was in fact dead, something that manifested itself to him "when the commandment came and sin came alive" (Rom 7:9)—that is, when his inability to keep the law brought about a dawning awareness of how things really stood

---

12. On connection between chapter 7 and revelatory function of law in Rom 3:20 (and Gal 3:19–25) see Longenecker, *Romans*, 643. On this theme in general see Marcus Mininger, *Uncovering the Theme of Revelation in Romans 1:16–3:26: Discovering a New Approach to Paul's Argument*, WUNT 2.445 (Tübingen: Mohr Siebeck, 2017).

13. Watson (*Hermeneutics of Faith*, 374) notes that in Rom 7:7–10 "Paul sees the whole law as summarized in the tenth commandment, which he cites in abbreviated form."

in his life. This, then, is an answer to those who argue that Paul could not at any point in his life say that he was "alive apart from the law."

The commandment, which "promised life" upon faithful keeping of it, "proved death" to him because of his failure to actually obey (Rom 7:10). The epistemological focus is reinforced in 7:11: sin deceived Paul because he thought he could keep it. Paul's "death" is his emerging *recognition* that he is, in fact, spiritually dead. Paul attributes this to his having been deceived by sin, which used the commandment to kill him, or bring him into spiritual bondage. The law in this way served its holy, righteous, and good purpose (7:12). In fact, the law is seen to be holy, righteous, and good precisely in revealing the true state of things, "in order that sin might be shown to be sin, and through the commandment might become sinful beyond measure" (7:13).

All of this could have been stated in non-autobiographical terms, but Paul deliberately frames it in terms of his own past experience. Why? I would argue that what one literary critic has said about nineteenth century Russian novelists like Tolstoy and Dostoevsky applies to Paul here: they "test theories not by logic, evidence, or counter-argument, as philosophical treatises do, but by examining what it means to live by them."[14]

How does this square with what Paul writes in Phil 3:3–6, which has been consistently put forward as one of the main reasons Paul could not be writing about himself in Rom 7:7–12? In Phil 3:3–6 we read that Paul had "confidence in his flesh" because of his pristine pedigree in Judaism, his zeal for maintaining pure religion, and his blameless conduct as defined by the law. Keeping the revelatory function of the law in view gives us the answer, at least partially. In Philippians Paul clearly describes how he perceived himself at the time. He lists his persecution of the church as a manifestation of zeal and blamelessness under the law, after all (3:6).

Some scholars think it impossible that Paul could write in Rom 7:7–12 about how things actually stood prior to his conversion.[15] Many features of this section, however, show that this is indeed the case. Paul says that at that time he thought he was alive apart from the law having done its work to reveal his true condition. He sought life through the law, although he was in bondage to spiritual death. In all of this he was deceived, as 7:11 says. The difference between Phil 3:3–6 and Rom 7:7–12 is that in Philippians Paul focuses on how confident he felt at the time, while in Romans he writes about the experiential knowledge

---

14. Gary Saul Morson, "Turgenev's liberal sensibility." *New Criterion.* September 2021, 37, https://newcriterion.com/issues/2021/9/turgenevs-liberal-sensibility. In so arguing I am not saying that Paul *never* uses "logic, evidence, or counter-argument," all of which is evident throughout Romans and the rest of his letters.

15. For example (and exercising a significant influence on subsequent interpretations): Kümmel, *Römer 7,* 52–53.

he was in the process of acquiring, which he only came to understand in its full significance *after* his conversion.

The Law Cannot Produce Obedience

The second reason Paul writes in the first person, this time in 7:13–25, is to make vivid the law's role in Christian obedience, whether positive or negative. And here "the temptation the interpreter faces," as Will Timmins puts it, "is to disregard those parts of the text that stubbornly refuse to fit the proposed paradigm."[16] The history of interpretation amply bears this out.

Thomas Schreiner and Timmins (among others) point to what I believe is the only solution that can hold together both Paul's negative and positive statements about the law and his relationship to it: Paul is neither describing his pre-conversion state, nor the totality of the normal Christian life, but rather (as Schreiner puts it) the "inherent capacities of human beings."[17] Those inherent capacities, it turns out, are non-existent.

What can and can't the law do? Positively, it "shows sin to be sin." That is, it reveals the full force of sin, that it is "sinful beyond measure," stirring up Paul's covetous desires, rather than suppressing them (7:13). It also reveals what is good (7:16). Negatively, it neither provides deliverance from the things Paul hates (7:15–16) nor the ability to do the good he desires (7:18–23). But Paul does not stop there, as if that exhaustively defines the existence of the believer. No, as he writes in 8:2: "the law of the Spirit of life has set you free in Christ Jesus from the law of sin and death." The law alone could do nothing for Paul, but the Holy Spirit has rescued him from bondage to sin. Paul relates this explicitly to the law's inability in 8:3–4: "God has done what the law, weakened by the flesh, could not do. By sending his own Son in the likeness of sinful flesh and for sin, he condemned sin in the flesh, in order that the righteous requirement of the law might be fulfilled in us, who walk not according to the flesh but according to the Spirit."

The condemnation deserved for sin has been taken by Christ, while the righteous requirement of the law has been fulfilled in us. The latter phrase ("fulfilled in us") is not a reference to Christ's work merely external to ourselves (as is his taking the condemnation we deserve), which would rather have been indicated by a phrase like "fulfilled for us," or "fulfilled in him," or "by him," or some such thing. What can "the righteous requirement of the law" is "fulfilled *in us*" mean apart from a manifestation of obedience to it in our own lives? The key distinction in chapter 8 is that even this working of obedience is enabled by

---

16. Will N. Timmins, *Romans 7 and Christian Identity: A Study of the 'I' in its Literary Context*, SNTSMS 170 (Cambridge: Cambridge University Press, 2017), 9.

17. Schreiner, *Romans*, 387.

God's Spirit, whereas all of Paul's vain attempts at obedience in chapter 7 were according to the power inherent in his flesh, without reference to the Spirit's work at all. The believer is not stuck in Rom 7, but certainly can temporarily revert back to that miserable state through self-reliant striving, or simply a failure to live life in humble, prayerful dependence on the Spirit's power.

Certain aspects of what Paul writes in chapter 7 make more sense when read as the experience of an *Israelite* with explicit knowledge of God's written law: his statements of the way that the law stirred up his sinful desires (7:7–11), of the goodness of the law (7:12), of his desire to keep it (7:15–21), and especially of his delight in it (7:22). That said, all of these must be understood within the broader argument that began in 6:1 and comes to a close in 8:12–14 where Paul writes about how our freedom in Christ is related to our adoption into God's family.

Conclusion

The whole sweep of Paul's lengthy argument in chapters 6–7 (with all its twists and turns) is Paul's way of dealing with several expected misunderstandings of his claim in 5:20 that "the law came in to increase the trespass." The wrong implication was that believers should "sin that grace may abound" (6:1). Every-thing else, all the way to the middle of chapter 8, demonstrates how believers have been rescued from bondage to sin through the death and resurrection of Christ (chapter 6) and by the power of the Holy Spirit (chapter 8), with the interlude about the inherent capacities of the flesh in chapter 7. This life of resurrection and Spirit-empowered obedience is the life of every believer. As Patrick Reardon aptly summarizes, "The 'I' in these verses . . . is the whole human race coming to grips with sin, death, and the Law."[18]

All of this would lose its force if Paul somehow extracted himself from the "I" he describes in these verses. This is nowhere more clearly seen than in 8:2, where the redemption found in Christ is described in intensely personal terms as indicated by σε: the law has set "you" (singular) free.[19] Thus, Paul reaches the

---

18. Patrick Henry Reardon, *Romans: An Orthodox Commentary* (Yonkers, NY: St. Vladimir's Seminary Press, 2018), 90. "On Paul's use of the 'I' to designate either believers or men in general, cf. Rom 13.21; 1 Cor 8.13; 13.1–3, 11–12; 14:6–19" (Reardon, *Romans*, 90n2).

19. Galatians 5:16–18, a text from which no one (to my knowledge) would argue excludes Paul himself, says much the same thing as Rom 7:13–25 in a much briefer space. Longenecker (*Romans*, 655–66), relying on Luke Timothy Johnson (*Reading Romans: A Literary and Theological Commentary* [Macon, GA: Smyth & Helwys, 2013], 115), is correct that Paul often uses the first person singular in a generic fashion to refer to the experience of all men (e.g., Rom 3:7; 1 Cor 6:15; 13:1–13; 14:11, 14–15; Gal 2:19–21; etc.). It would be exceedingly odd, however, if Paul excluded *himself* from such universal statements.

culmination of what he began in 5:20, and shows that, despite all the scholarly ink spilled attempting to prove the contrary, he has had himself in view all along, not in order merely to talk about himself, but rather, in order vividly to portray through his own experience the powerlessness of the law in and of itself to effect the change that has been brought about in his life through union with Jesus Christ, by the working of the Holy Spirit.

Bibliography

Chester, Stephen J. *Conversion at Corinth: Perspectives on Conversion in Paul's Theology and the Corinthian Church*. SNTW. London: T&T Clark, 2003.

———. "The Retrospective View of Romans 7: Paul's Past in Present Perspective." Pages 57–103 in *Perspectives on Our Struggle with Sin: Three Views of Romans 7*. Edited by T. L. Wilder. Nashville: Broadman & Holman, 2011.

Dunson, Ben C. *Individual and Community in Paul's Letter to the Romans*. WUNT 2.332. Tübingen, Mohr Siebeck, 2012.

Götte, Monika E. "Adam und Christus – Christus und Adam. Römer 7 im Licht von Genesis 3." Pages 49–82 in *Perskpektiven auf Römer 7*. Edited by Stefan Krauter. Neukirchener-Vluyn: Neurkirchener, 2016.

Hofius, Otfried. "Der Mensch im Shatten Adams. Römer 7,7–25a." Pages 104–54 in *Paulusstudien II*. WUNT 143. Tübingen: Mohr Siebeck, 2002.

Jewett, Robert. *Romans: A Commentary*. Hermeneia. Minneapolis: Fortress, 2007.

Johnson, Luke Timothy. *Reading Romans: A Literary and Theological Commentary*. Macon, GA: Smyth & Helwys, 2013.

Kümmel, Werner G. *Römer 7 und das Bild des Menschen in Neuen Testament*. Munich: Kaiser, 1974 [orig. 1929].

Lichtenberger, Hermann. *Das Ich Adams und das Ich der Menschheit*. WUNT 164. Tübingen: Mohr Siebeck, 2004.

Longenecker, Richard N. *The Epistle to the Romans: A Commentary on the Greek Text*. NIGTC. Grand Rapids: Eerdmans, 2016.

Mininger, Marcus. *Uncovering the Theme of Revelation in Romans 1:16–3:26: Discovering a New Approach to Paul's Argument*. WUNT 2.445. Tübingen: Mohr Siebeck, 2017.

Morson, Gary Saul. "Turgenev's liberal sensibility." *New Criterion*. September 2021. https://newcriterion.com/issues/2021/9/turgenevs-liberal -sensibility.

Reardon, Patrick Henry. *Romans: An Orthodox Commentary*. Yonkers, NY: St. Vladimir's Seminary Press, 2018.

Schreiner, Thomas R. *Romans*. BECNT. 2nd ed. Grand Rapids: Baker Academic, 2018.

Stowers, Stanley K. *A Rereading of Romans: Justice, Jews, and Gentiles.* New Haven: Yale University Press, 1997.

Thielman, Frank. "The Story of Israel and the Theology of Romans 5–8." Pages 169–95 in *Pauline Theology: Volume 3: Romans.* Edited by David M. Hay and E. Elizabeth Johnson. Minneapolis: Fortress, 1995.

Timmins, Will N. *Romans 7 and Christian Identity: A Study of the 'I' in its Literary Context.* SNTSMS 170. Cambridge: Cambridge University Press, 2017.

Watson, Francis. *Paul and the Hermeneutics of Faith.* London: T&T Clark, 2004.

Wright, N. T. "Romans and the Theology of Paul." Pages 49–54 in *Pauline Theology: Volume 3: Romans.* Edited by David M. Hay and E. Elizabeth Johnson. Minneapolis: Fortress, 1995.

CHAPTER 14

Multifarious Agency in the Textured World of Romans 8

Kyle B. Wells

Romans 8, with its exposition of life in the Spirit and its declaration of a believer's assurance, is fertile ground for exploring the relationship Paul posits
between divine and human agency. A surprising feature of Romans 8, however,
is that the chapter's agency discourse begins and ends with neither a divine nor
a human agent. Grammatically speaking, the first agent mentioned is the law
(ὁ νόμος): "For the law of the Spirit of life has liberated you" (8:2). The chapter
closes with a list of various non-human agents that threaten, but are ultimately
unable, to separate the believer from God's love: death, life, angels, principalities, things present, things to come, powers, height, depth, and everything
else that makes up creation (8:38–39). Interpreters have wrestled with Paul's
language. Does Paul really attribute causative action to non-human entities or
is this metaphoric hyperbole? If the latter, should we follow Rudolf Bultmann's
assumption that Paul's agency discourse is ultimately reducible to God and the
individual?[1]

Recent work on Pauline anthropology suggests that Paul's discourse is not
so reducible. Over the last decade a number of studies have come out decidedly
against reading into Paul substantialist notions of the self: a self that exists complete, apart from the acts and relations which make up human existence. Emmanuel Rehfeld, for instance, argues that human ontology is relational in Paul's
letters.[2] Susan Eastman goes a step further, specifying how "persons are constituted by participation in realities larger than the self or than merely human
relations," so much so that "the structure of human beings cannot be disassociated from the structure of the cosmos."[3] Samuel Ferguson's work emphasizes

---

1. See, e.g., Rudolf Bultmann, *The New Testament and Mythology and Other Basic
Writings,* trans. Schubert M. Ogden (Philadelphia: Fortress, 1984), 1–11; Rudolf Karl
Bultmann, *Theology of the New Testament,* trans. Kendrick Grobel (London: SCM
Press, 1952), 244–46, 251–53, 256–59.

2. Emmanuel L. Rehfeld, *Relationale Ontologie bei Paulus: die ontische Wirksamkeit der Christusbezogenheit im Denken des Heidenapostels,* WUNT 2.326, (Tübingen:
Mohr Siebeck, 2012).

3. Susan Grove Eastman, *Paul and the Person: Reframing Paul's Anthropology*
(Grand Rapids: Eerdmans, 2017), 177, 180.

the Spirit's role in generating and sustaining such relationships.[4] Somewhat independent, but supportive, of these conclusions are those older studies by Dale Martin and Michelle Lee-Barnwell that situate Paul's understanding of *soma* in its Hellenistic context, where the body was thought to be porous, fluid, and an actual instantiation of the world to which it belongs.[5] For all these writers, Paul's notion of personhood is participatory in some fundamental manner.

Relational and participatory approaches to Pauline anthropology converge in fresh and interesting ways in Matthew Croasmun's *The Emergence of Sin*.[6] Croasmun analyzes Paul's hamartiology through the framework of Emergence Theory. In an emergence account, human anthropology is relational and participatory precisely because that is the structure of the cosmos.[7] "Life," Croasmun observes, "is fundamentally combinatorial," and "organisms are systems all the way down."[8] The individual human is a "higher-level entity" composed of various parts—organelles, cells, tissues, organs—and this higher-level entity "exercises downward causation" by setting boundary conditions on its lower parts.[9] It is the various parts' relationship to this higher level entity that determines how they function and relate to one another. Moreover, each of those parts are themselves higher level entities that are similarly structured. Emergence theory, then, offers yet another participatory account of human nature. Humans are both "internally composite" and "integrated externally with their environments."[10]

What becomes particularly relevant for Croasmun's study of sin in Romans is that this dynamic does not just happen within individual human bodies, but beyond them. Biology gives rise to psychology, which gives rise to sociology, which gives rise to what, for want of a better term, Croasmun calls mythology.[11] The human self is not the highest-level entity. Families, institutions, nations, and all manner of complex composites emerge from human persons. Significantly, these entities share many of the same attributes ascribed to human personhood. Like human persons, these are higher-level, composite entities that exercise downward causation, organizing and putting boundary conditions

---

4. Samuel D. Ferguson, *The Spirit and Relational Anthropology in Paul*, WUNT 2.520 (Tübingen: Mohr Siebeck, 2020).

5. Dale B. Martin, *The Corinthian Body* (New Haven: Yale University Press, 1995); Michelle V. Lee, *Paul, the Stoics, and the Body of Christ*, SNTSMS 137 (Cambridge: Cambridge University Press, 2006).

6. Matthew Croasmun, *The Emergence of Sin: The Cosmic Tyrant in Romans* (Oxford: Oxford University Press, 2017).

7. For an introduction and overview of the history of emergence theory, see Philip Clayton and P. C. W. Davies, eds., *The Re-emergence of Emergence: The Emergentist Hypothesis from Science to Religion* (Oxford: Oxford University Press, 2006), 1–34.

8. Croasmun, *Emergence of Sin*, 79.

9. Croasmun, *Emergence of Sin*, 79.

10. Croasmun, *Emergence of Sin*, 43, 59.

11. Croasmun, *Emergence of Sin*, 22, 55.

on their constituent parts (which includes individuals). Like human persons, these entities wield causative influence on the surrounding world. Thus, human existence is intrinsically connected to and inevitably shaped by these higher level entities that humans themselves constitute.

Such an ontology holds direct implications for how we think about human agency. For if these studies are correct, then humans are never "free" agents, if "freedom" implies an autonomous self.[12] Rather, human agency is always formed and specified in relationship to entities and agencies beyond the self. We cannot address the matter of human agency then without at the same time giving due consideration to the overlapping and complex network of agencies and environments in which all human life is entangled. Simply put, to think "emergently" about human agency necessitates that we think "environmentally."[13]

So, taking our cue from emergence theory, how might thinking environmentally illuminate Paul's agency discourse in Rom 8? The remainder of this chapter attempts to provide an initial answer to that question. First, we will look at how the drama of divine and human agency play out in relation to the nexus of Law, Sin, and death (Rom 8:1–17). Then we will look at how this divine and human drama plays out in the context of a corruption-enmeshed creation (8:17–39).

Divine and Human Agency in Relation to Law, Sin, and Death

In Rom 8:1–2 Paul issues an emancipation proclamation that is as bewildering as it is definitive. The self that cries out for deliverance in Rom 7:24 is decisively liberated. Surprisingly, the agent that emancipates is none other than ὁ νόμος. Significantly, νόμος here is qualified by the genitive construction: it is the νόμος of the life-giving Spirit in Jesus, the Messiah (τοῦ πνεύματος τῆς ζωῆς ἐν Χριστῷ Ἰησοῦ). Equally significant and perhaps equally puzzling is that this emancipating νόμος liberates from ὁ νόμος. The enslaving νόμος is also qualified by a genitive construction: it is the νόμος of sin and of death (τῆς ἁμαρτίας καὶ τοῦ θανάτου).

---

12. Eastman, *Paul and the Person*, 177. So also Udo Schnelle, *Apostle Paul: His Life and Theology* (Grand Rapids: Baker Academic, 2005), 294: "for Paul human life by nature exist within a comprehensive set of connections. And thus people cannot live out of themselves, on their own resources, for they always find themselves in a previously existing force field where various powers already hold sway." Significantly this means that "the human being is not autonomous but is exposed to the powers that prevail in creation: God, and evil in the form of sin."

13. In one way or another, all these studies confirm, revise, or build upon the instincts of Ernst Käsemann. Against Bultmann, Käsemann insisted that for Paul embodied humans are neither bounded nor self-determined. Rather, Käsemann claimed, the body sets persons within "a structure of solidarity"; it concretely binds persons to their larger environments, environments which in turn influence human existence. See, e.g., Ernst Käsemann, *Perspectives on Paul* (London: SCM Press, 1971), 22.

Interpreters have struggled with what to make of these verses and especially of Paul's νόμος plus genitive constructions. The majority of Pauline interpreters sympathize with Heikki Räisänen, for whom it is unthinkable that Paul would attribute saving agency to the law.[14] As such, most interpreters assume we are dealing with an atypical use of νόμος in Rom 8:2: Paul speaks more generally, perhaps metaphorically, of a norm, principle, or power.[15] Whatever the case, these scholars assume νόμος could not reference Israel's Torah, especially when paired with Spirit and life.[16]

In support of this interpretation is verse 3, where Paul explains himself (γάρ) by quickly attributing divine agency to human emancipation: "God . . . consigned Sin to destruction" (ὁ θεὸς . . . κατέκρινεν τὴν ἁμαρτίαν). Does this not confirm that ὁ νόμος τοῦ πνεύματος τῆς ζωῆς is circumlocution for God? Moreover, Paul sets the efficacy of God's action in direct contrast to the incompetence (ἀδύνατος) of what interpreters readily take to be the Mosaic Torah. As Michael Bird maintains: "to make the Torah the liberating agent in 8:2 would flat out contradict 8:3, where God sends his son precisely because of Torah's inability to save."[17] How could an incompetent Torah perform an efficacious act? To be sure, an increasing minority of scholars have objected to rendering νόμος as anything other than Torah, but most still attribute Paul's use of νόμος in 8:2 to his polemics or to a play on words.[18]

---

14. Heikki Räisänen, "Sprachliches zum Spiel des Paulus mit *nomos*," in *Glaube und Gerechtigkeit: in memoriam Rafael Gyllenberg (18.6.1893–29.7.1982)*, ed. Jarmo Kiilunen, Wille Riekkinen, and Heikki Räisänen, SFEG 38 (Helsinki: Finnische Exegetische Gesellschaft, 1983), 154: "Eine derart aktive Rolle ist für die wie auch immer verstandene Tora im Denken des Paulus unvorstellbar." Similarly, see Douglas J. Moo, *The Letter to the Romans*, 2nd ed., NICNT (Grand Rapids: Eerdmans, 2018), 497.

15. So, e.g., Heikki Räisänen, *Paul and the Law* (Tübingen: Mohr Siebeck, 1987), 52: Paul "is speaking of the 'order' of the Spirit," which he takes to be "a rhetorical paraphrase" for the Spirit.

16. For commentaries and major monographs published within the last 15 years that interpret νόμος more generally in 8:2, see: Arland J. Hultgren, *Paul's Letter to the Romans: A Commentary* (Grand Rapids: Eerdmans, 2011), 297; Tom Holland, *Romans: The Divine Marriage* (Eugene, OR: Pickwick, 2011), 256; Brian S. Rosner, *Paul and the Law: Keeping the Commandments of God* (Downers Grove, IL: IVP Academic, 2013), 119–21; David Peterson, *Commentary on Romans* (Nashville: Holman Reference, 2017), 306; Frank Thielman, *Romans*, ZECNT 6 (Grand Rapids: Zondervan Academic, 2018), 379; Richard N. Longenecker, *The Epistle to the Romans: A Commentary on the Greek Text*, NIGTC (Grand Rapids: Eerdmans, 2016), 685; Moo, *Romans*, 498; Thomas R. Schreiner, *Romans*, 2nd ed., BECNT (Grand Rapids: Baker Academic, 2018), 396. These works are conflicted on whether "the law of sin and death" refers to Torah.

17. Michael F. Bird, *Romans,* SGBC (Grand Rapids: Zondervan, 2016), 259. See also Moo, *Romans*, 497; Schreiner, *Romans*, 396.

18. For those interpreters that take νόμος to reference Torah, see, e.g., Hans Hübner, *Law in Paul's Thought: A Contribution to the Development of Pauline Theology*, trans. James C. G. Greig (Edinburgh: T&T Clark, 1984), 144–49; James D. G. Dunn, *Romans 1–8*, WBC 38A (Dallas: Word, 1988), 416–17; Ulrich Wilckens, *Der Brief an*

But if Paul does not want to assign Torah a role in the economy of salvation, then why, as J. Louis Martyn has asked, does Paul even use the word νόμος at all?[19] Why not say, "For the Spirit of life has liberated you"? Can polemics or wordplay really account for Paul's language, especially given how liable he would be to misunderstanding? Paul certainly contrasts the respective abilities of God and Torah here, but that is not the same as saying that Torah is intrinsically impotent, or antithetical to God's saving agency. Might there be a better explanation for these curious νόμος plus genitive constructions?

It is noteworthy that Paul explicitly attributes the incompetence of Torah to Torah's relationship with the Flesh: Torah was "weakened through the Flesh" (ἠσθένει διὰ τῆς σαρκός). Conceivably, then, Torah could be disassociated from the flesh, wherein it was not so weakened.[20] What if we start from the assumption that Paul held to a participatory ontology and that all creation and creative agency, including that of Torah, is relational by nature? What if Torah itself has a participatory agency?

Torah's Participatory Agency

For the last two chapters in Romans, Paul has explained how Torah is intimately, but not inevitably, related to Sin. That is: while the Torah is emphatically not Sin (7:7), Torah and Sin have taken on a mutually causative relationship. Torah arouses Sin (7:5) and is Sin's power (1 Cor 15:56). Sin works through Torah (7:8, 11, 13). The relationship is not symmetrical. Sin's influence on Torah is not the same in force or kind as Torah's influence on Sin. This asymmetry is especially clear in Rom 7:13, where Paul rhetorically asks: "Did the good [Torah] generate death in me? Not in the least, it was Sin accomplishing death in me through the good [Torah]."

---

die Römer, EKK 6 (Neukirchen-Vluyn/Einsiedeln: Neukirchener Verlag/Benzinger, 1978–82), 1:122–23; Anthony C. Thiselton, *Discovering Romans: Content, Interpretation, Reception* (Grand Rapids: Eerdmans, 2016), 165; Sigve K. Tonstad, *The Letter to the Romans: Paul Among the Ecologists*, The Earth Bible Commentary (Sheffield: Sheffield Phoenix Press, 2016), 231–32; Eckhard J. Schnabel, *Der Brief des Paulus an die Römer: Kapitel 6–16*, HTA (Witten/Gießen: Brockhaus/Brunnen, 2016), 193–95.

19. J. Louis Martyn, "Nomos Plus Genitive Noun in Paul: The History of God's Law," in *Early Christianity and Classical Culture: Comparative Studies in Honor of Abraham J. Malherbe*, ed. John T. Fitzgerald, Thomas H. Olbricht, and L. Michael White, NovTSup 110 (Leiden: Brill, 2003), 580.

20. Bryan Blazosky, *The Law's Universal Condemning and Enslaving Power: Reading Paul, the Old Testament, and Second Temple Jewish Literature*, BBRSup 24 (University Park: The Pennsylvania State University Press, 2019), 161, makes the suggestive statement that "Paul is equally clear that ἁμαρτία, θάνατος, and νόμος are only able to enslave people who are ἐν σαρκί." The implications for those who are not "in flesh" is not developed.

What Paul says in verse 13 about Torah bears a striking similarity to Paul's curious "I, yet not I" statements in verses 16–17, and verse 20. In each, we have an accomplishment considered (accomplishing what I do not will/Torah generating death), followed by a denial of agency (not I; Did the good Torah . . . by no means), followed by an affirmation of Sin's agency (but Sin).

7:13	Τὸ οὖν ἀγαθὸν ἐμοὶ ἐγένετο θάνατος;	(Accomplishment by Agent 1 considered)
	μὴ γένοιτο	(Agency of Agent 1 Denied)
	ἀλλ' ἡ ἁμαρτία . . . κατεργαζομένη θάνατον	(Agency of Agent 2 affirmed)
7:16–17	εἰ δὲ ὃ οὐ θέλω τοῦτο ποιῶ . . .	(Accomplishment by Agent 1 considered)
	νυνὶ δὲ οὐκέτι ἐγὼ κατεργάζομαι αὐτὸ	(Agency of Agent 1 Denied)
	ἀλλὰ ἡ οἰκοῦσα ἐν ἐμοὶ ἁμαρτία	(Agency of Agent 2 affirmed)
7:20	εἰ δὲ ὃ οὐ θέλω [ἐγὼ] τοῦτο ποιῶ	(Accomplishment by Agent 1 considered)
	οὐκέτι ἐγὼ κατεργάζομαι αὐτὸ	(Agency of Agent 1 Denied)
	ἀλλ' ἡ οἰκοῦσα ἐν ἐμοὶ ἁμαρτία	(Agency of Agent 2 affirmed)

Sin's relationship to Torah and to the self appear to share an analogous structure. In an earlier work I argued that Paul's "I, yet not I" statements do not deny the efficacy of human agency so much as qualify it by showing how human agency is substantially formed by and dependent on the self's relationship to other powers (like Christ, Grace, and Sin).[21] While the self still wills and lives and works, these powers set the potential and the limits for human agency's expression. The self exists in an asymmetrical, yet co-inherent relationship to these other agents. This asymmetrical co-inherence is so strong that human accomplishment can be attributed without reservation or qualification to the higher networks of power.

What Paul says about Torah bears similar marks. Paul clearly believes that an intimate relationship exists between Torah, Sin, and Death (1 Cor 15:56). Thus, he can infer from the fact that believers are no longer under Torah that Sin no longer masters them (κυριεύω, Rom 6:14; cf. Gal 3:23–4:3). Significantly, the only subjects of the verb κυριεύω in Romans are Death (6:9), Sin (6:14), Law (7:1), and Jesus (14:9).[22] The rule of Jesus stands out in stark, antithetical contrast to the rules of Sin, Death, and Law, which elide in the book of Romans. To be sure, Sin and Death can rule where there is no Torah (5:13), but when Torah is present Sin rules through it (διὰ τῆς ἐντολῆς), producing death (7:8–11). In such an environment, to be under Torah is to be under the respective dominions of Sin and Death. Just like human agency, Torah's agency is substantially formed by and is dependent on its relationship to other powers.

---

21. Kyle B. Wells, *Grace and agency in Paul and Second Temple Judaism: Interpreting the Transformation of the Heart*, NovTSup 157 (Leiden: Brill, 2015), 303. So Paul says: It is no longer I who live, but Christ in me (Gal 2:20). It is no longer I who work, but grace in me (1 Cor 15:10). It is no longer I who accomplish evil, but Sin in me (Rom 7:17, 20).
22. English translations obscure the repetition of κυριεύω in 7:1.

We are now in a position to return to Rom 8:2–3 and Paul's νόμος plus genitive constructions. When read in light of a participatory ontology, the νόμος of
Sin and Death most likely refers to the Torah as it is embedded in the environment of Sin and Death. Amongst those interpreters who refuse to demystify
Paul's personifications, it is notoriously difficult to explicate the agencies of Sin
and Death concretely. Matthew Croasmun has proposed the principle of "marginal control" as a promising place to start. The principle of marginal control
comes from the work of emergent theorists like Michael Polanyi and describes
a type of causation that happens when higher level entities impose a "structural
constraint within which they restrict" the operations of lower level mechanisms.[23]
These higher level entities "provide the context within which lower-level entities
indeed follow the laws relevant to their level of scale and complexity."[24] In the
case of biological systems, the biological structures shape "the boundaries of the
lower level which is relied on to obey the laws of inanimate nature, i.e., physics
and chemistry."[25] In our case, Sin sets the boundary conditions through which
humans interact with Torah—conditions in which human action necessarily
brings forth sin and death instead of righteousness and life (cf. 8:6–7). Something like this is perhaps what Paul means when he says that Torah was weakened through the Flesh (8:3). Flesh denotes existence outside of a relationship
to God and God's life-giving, righteous agency. Flesh is another environmental
condition of this complex system in which Torah is embedded and operates.

It is this Torah, the Torah embedded in the nexus of Flesh and Sin and
Death, which rules over humanity and from which humans need emancipation. Conversely, I suggest that the νόμος of the life-giving Spirit is Torah as it
is embedded in the generative environment of God's Spirit. One of the crucial
questions that interpreters must face is whether Paul is talking about the same
νόμος or two distinct νόμοι in Rom 8:2. When read through the lens of a participatory ontology the answer is yes and yes. On the one hand, we can say that
in both instances Paul is talking about the Torah. But, on the other hand, it is
Torah as it has been reconstituted through its embeddedness in a completely
different, indeed antithetical, relational network. In this sense the continuity
and discontinuity of the Torah is not altogether different from the continuity and discontinuity of the crucified, yet miraculously existing self that has
been reconstituted in Christ (cf. Gal 2:20).[26] Perhaps, then, it is not too much
of a stretch to say that for Paul the Torah has been effected by the crucifixion

23. See further, Michael Polanyi, *The Tacit Dimension* (London: Routledge & K.
Paul, 1967), 38–44.

24. Croasmun, *Emergence of Sin*, 39.

25. Croasmun, *Emergence of Sin*, 68.

26. On the continuity and discontinuity of self in Paul, see Jonathan A. Linebaugh,
"'The Speech of the Dead': Identifying the No Longer and Now Living 'I' of Galatians
2.20,'" *NTS* 66.1 (2020): 87–105.

of Christ. It is no longer Torah that governs in the eschaton, but the Spirit of
resurrection life in Torah.

But what would it mean for the Spirit-embedded Torah to liberate one
from the Sin-embedded Torah? And why does Paul immediately attribute this
to God in verse 3? Our exposition thus far provides some potential answers to
these questions. Above I noted how the realities of Sin and Death set boundary
conditions on how humans interact with Torah. No matter what lawful actions
humans take, their lawful actions will be constrained by Sin and result in Death
(Rom 8:6–7; cf. Gal 3:21–23). Because Sin and Torah's agencies co-inhere in
a non-competitive fashion, Paul conceives of humans as under both the rule
of Sin and the rule of the Sin-embedded Torah. But if Paul can describe the
νόμος as having mastery, then it should not be difficult for us to conceive of
how the νόμος could liberate those under its mastery, even if this is as simple
as relinquishing control. To cease to hold a formerly held hand is to release that
hand. Similarly, if Torah itself has been placed in a new set of relationships,
relationships distinct from the rule of Sin, then Torah would cease to impose
its Sin-embedded governor on humans, thus releasing humans from its own
Sin-infected dominion.

This liberation can also and ultimately be attributed to God and God's
Spirit; for this reordering of relationships is more fundamentally a death *of* and
a death *to* the present evil age, along with the inauguration of a new creation
(Gal 1:4, 6:16; 2 Cor 5:17). Both realities (death and new creation) are predicated upon God's preemptive sending of his Son in identification with sinful
Flesh and as a sin-offering (Rom 8:3). Through this act, God consigned Sin to
destruction and initiates a transfer wherein believers pass from the old world
that is governed by Sin and Death into the new creation that is governed by
the life-producing agency of the Spirit. It is only as Torah is embedded in the
Spirit's own life-giving agency that those humans who relate to it find emancipation from the Sin-embedded Torah (8:2). This is the structure in which to
understand the drama of divine and human agency in Rom 8.

Believer's Participatory Agency

If the self that has been emancipated from Sin and Death is relational all the
way down, then emancipation must include a change of environmental factors
and relationships. As verses 5–9 make clear, human existence (ὄντες) always
has a location ἐν σαρκὶ or ἐν πνεύματι. This location puts persons squarely in
a nexus of relationships that set boundary conditions on human action. So,
for instance, humans perceive the world (φρονέω, 8:5), but they do so from
a perception (φρόνημα, 8:6–7). What Paul has in mind, as his turn to the
nominal, singular form makes clear, is a higher order collective mentality, a

zeitgeist that delimits an individual's behavior. The φρόνημα of the Flesh or the φρόνημα of the Spirit are the respective presuppositions and plausibility structures that set the boundary conditions on what kind of thoughts are likely or even possible. The φρόνημα of the Flesh sets conditions which are opposed to God and submission to Torah. Thus, those who reason from the location of the Flesh cannot please God (8:8). Paul's return to the plural here in verse 8 (οἱ . . . ὄντες) is yet another illustration of how human action asymmetrically and non-competitively participates in higher level entities—in this case the φρόνημα of the Flesh.

Contrariwise, when believers exercise agency in the sphere of the Spirit— that is, when they "carry on according to the Spirit"—they have a new relationship to Torah wherein its righteous requirement is passively fulfilled in them (8:4). Here we see Paul's non-competitive, yet asymmetrical agency dynamics on full display. It is important to remember that Paul is alluding to LXX Ezek 36–37.[27] In Ezekiel's prophecy it is precisely the agency of the Spirit reconstituting human wills in a resurrection state that brings about their keeping of Torah. Similarly in Rom 8:4 the Spirit fulfills the requirement of Torah by vivifying and animating those who participate in the resurrected Christ.[28]

Throughout the first half of this chapter, Paul will highlight how the believer now acts in dynamic dependence upon the Spirit's agency. "By the Spirit" believers put to death the deeds of the body (8:13) and cry Abba Father (8:15), both forms of being led by the Spirit (8:14). Moreover, in union with the Spirit's agency believers co-witness to their own Sonship (8:16). All these examples show how believers have been brought into a new network of life-giving relationships, which are founded upon what God has done in Christ and by the Spirit. And yet, as the second half of the chapter attests, other relationships remain.

---

27. To summarize: Though uses of the terms vary, both texts reference δικαίωμα ("righteous requirement/s"), σάρξ ("flesh") and πνεῦμα ("Spirit"). A less exact parallel is that while Ezekiel speaks of κρίματα ("decrees"), Paul has just declared that there is no "decree against" (κατάκριμα) those in Christ (8:1). Furthermore, both texts denote lifestyle with "walking" terminology (περιπατέω/πορεύομαι). The broader contexts of both passages strengthen the link. While Ezekiel says that God will place his Spirit in people (τὸ πνεῦμά μου δώσω ἐν ὑμῖν), Paul tells believers, "the Spirit of God dwells in you" (πνεῦμα θεοῦ οἰκεῖ ἐν ὑμῖν, 8:9). Ezekiel dramatizes this divine act in ch. 37, where God pledges to the dead exiles: "I will bring to you the Spirit of life" (πνεῦμα ζωῆς, 37:5). Strikingly similar is Rom 8:10: "though the body is dead (νεκρόν) on account of sin, the Spirit is life (πνεῦμα ζωή) on account of righteousness." In both texts, this life-Spirit refers to God's Spirit (πνεῦμα μου, LXX Ezek 37:6 / πνεῦμα θεοῦ, Rom 8:9), and the Spirit's indwelling leads to life. See further Wells, *Grace and agency in Paul*, 260–62.

28. For an alternative interpretation of Rom 8:4 along forensic lines, see Jonathan A. Linebaugh, *God, Grace, and Righteousness in Wisdom of Solomon and Paul's Letter to the Romans: Texts in Conversation*, NovTSup 152 (Leiden: Brill, 2013), 147–48. Paul's scriptural allusion makes the forensic interpretation of 8:4 unlikely, however.

Divine and Human Agency in a Corruption-enmeshed Creation

Up to verse 17, Paul's focus has been on how human agency has been recalibrated in light of its new relationship to Christ and the Spirit. The focus changes after verse 17. Talk of active human agency dissipates into human passivity. There is no putting to death, thinking, walking, or bearing witness. Rather believers suffer, groan, and wait (8:18, 23, 25). Viewed from the perspective of ancient philosophical reflection, such "actions" would be seen as the antithesis to a robust expression of human agency. Not even Rom 8:19–23, which has been taken as an environmental mantra, provides us with a positive view of human agency. Contrary to popular assumption, humans play no explicit role in creation's degradation or liberation in Rom 8.[29] The one exception to these verses' passive portrait is Paul's declaration that believers are more than conquerors (8:37). But this statement is exceptional and feels curiously out of place, coming just after a comparison between believers and butchered sheep (8:36). This focus on human passivity is striking when compared to the first 17 verses. What accounts for such an abrupt shift from believers' active agency in the first half of the chapter to their passive suffering in the second half?

Paul's participatory ontology provides an answer. Note that in these verses Paul again speaks of a liberation, not of one that happened to believers through God's sending of the Son but of one that will happen at the resurrection of the body (8:21, 23). In verse 19, Paul writes that κτίσις is held in suspense, waiting for the unveiling of God's children. This unveiling is specified in verse 23 as adoption, the redemption of our (singular!) body (τοῦ σώματος ἡμῶν). The reason (γάρ) κτίσις eagerly waits for this body's resurrection is that κτίσις itself will be liberated from its bondage to corruption (φθορά) and share in the children's glorious future (8:21). Believers and all creation are longing to be liberated from a corrupt environment.

Romans 8 is not the only place where Paul associates freedom from corruption (φθορά) with bodily resurrection. In the midst of an extended discussion on the resurrection of the dead, Paul notes how the body is sown ἐν φθορᾷ (1 Cor 15:42) and thus disqualified from God's eschatological inheritance: "I declare to you, brothers, that flesh and blood cannot inherit the kingdom of God, nor does the corruptible (φθορᾷ) inherit the incorruptible (ἀφθαρσία; 1 Cor 15:50)."[30] Resurrection resolves this dilemma: "What is sown in corruptibility (ἐν φθορᾷ) is raised in incorruptibility (ἐν ἀφθαρσίᾳ, 1 Cor

---

29. On this point, see Kyle B. Wells, "'The Liberation of the Body of Creation: Towards a Pauline Environmental Ethic," *JTS* 73.1 (2022): 92–103, esp. 92–99.

30. Compare Gal 6:8, the only other time Paul uses the word.

15:42). Κτίσις and σῶμα are thus closely related in Paul's mind: both κτίσις and σῶμα are subject to φθορά, and the predicament of both is resolved in a body's resurrection.

If Paul has a participatory anthropology, then his rationale becomes immediately clear. The fluidity of σῶμα makes σῶμα the intersection between the human person, other humans, and the rest of creation. Paul conceives of the interconnectedness of resurrected bodies as a singular "body" in Rom 8:23. But the fluidity of that body also means that those somatically revealed as God's eschatological children must inhabit an environment that is no longer enslaved to corruption. Paul's statement in 1 Cor 15:42 that "What is sown in corruptibility (ἐν φθορᾷ) is raised in incorruptibility (ἐν ἀφθαρσίᾳ)" applies not to a bounded body but to a fluid one. The body's incorruptibility is tied to everything that makes up somatic existence. In other words, incorruptibility must entail πᾶσα ἡ κτίσις ("the whole creation," Rom 8:22).[31]

But this is currently not the state of things. At present, believers are somatically embedded into a larger body of creation that is in bondage to corruption (8:21). This puts the believer in a peculiar and precarious place. Peculiar because the believer is both alive and dead, free and slave. Alive by the Spirit they put to death the deeds of the body, but they do so in an existence that is irreducibly embodied, entangled in a corrupted creation, and thus enslaved. Having been released from the rule of sin, they do not actively collude with φθορά—that is, with death. But, having a mortal body (8:10-11), they are also vulnerable to death and all the other powers into which κτίσις is embedded. In certain respect then, this situation renders them especially passive. And so they suffer, groan, are killed, and are slaughtered (8:18, 23, 36).

But the vulnerability into which somatic existence has plunged believers has its limits. Believers are not just acted upon by tribulation, distress, persecution, famine, nakedness, peril (8:35); they are also subject to the loving action of God—who helps in weakness, intercedes with groans (8:26), works out all things for good (8:28), foreknows, predestines, calls, justifies, glorifies (8:29-30), and freely handed over his Son for them (8:32), who intercedes at the Father's right hand (8:34). Paul is confident that the loving agency of God is stronger than the agency of anything in all creation, whether death, life, angels, principalities, things present or things to come (8:39). And it is for this reason that Paul can say that believers are more than conquerors "in all these sufferings" (8:37)—because they are embedded in the strong and sure love of God (the inviable agent)—and his crucified, yet conquering Messiah.

---

31. Cf. Joseph A. Fitzmyer, *Romans: A New Translation with Introduction and Commentary*, AB 33 (New York: Doubleday, 1993), 505-6, who sees creation as distinct from humanity.

Bibliography

Bird, Michael F. *Romans*. SGBC. Grand Rapids: Zondervan, 2016.

Blazosky, Bryan. *The Law's Universal Condemning and Enslaving Power: Reading Paul, the Old Testament, and Second Temple Jewish Literature*. BBRSup 24. University Park: The Pennsylvania State University Press, 2019.

Bultmann, Rudolf. *The New Testament and Mythology and Other Basic Writings*. Translated by Schubert M. Ogden. Philadelphia: Fortress, 1984.

———. *Theology of the New Testament*. Translated by Kendrick Grobel. London: SCM Press, 1952.

Clayton, Philip, and P. C. W. Davies, eds. *The Re-emergence of Emergence: The Emergentist Hypothesis from Science to Religion*. Oxford: Oxford University Press, 2006.

Croasmun, Matthew. *The Emergence of Sin: The Cosmic Tyrant in Romans*. Oxford: Oxford University Press, 2017.

Dunn, James D. G. *Romans 1–8*. WBC 38A. Dallas: Word, 1988.

Eastman, Susan Grove. *Paul and the Person: Reframing Paul's Anthropology*. Grand Rapids: Eerdmans, 2017.

Ferguson, Samuel D. *The Spirit and Relational Anthropology in Paul*. WUNT 2.520. Tübingen: Mohr Siebeck, 2020.

Fitzmyer, Joseph A. *Romans: A New Translation with Introduction and Commentary*. AB 33. New York: Doubleday, 1993.

Holland, Tom. *Romans: The Divine Marriage*. Eugene, OR: Pickwick, 2011.

Hübner, Hans. *Law in Paul's Thought: A Contribution to the Development of Pauline Theology*. Translated by James C. G. Greig. Edinburgh: T&T Clark, 1984.

Hultgren, Arland J. *Paul's Letter to the Romans: A Commentary*. Grand Rapids: Eerdmans, 2011.

Käsemann, Ernst. *Perspectives on Paul*. London: SCM Press, 1971.

Lee, Michelle V. *Paul, the Stoics, and the Body of Christ*. SNTSMS 137. Cambridge: Cambridge University Press, 2006.

Linebaugh, Jonathan A. *God, Grace, and Righteousness in Wisdom of Solomon and Paul's Letter to the Romans: Texts in Conversation*. NovTSup 152. Leiden: Brill, 2013.

———. "'The Speech of the Dead': Identifying the No Longer and Now Living 'I' of Galatians 2.20." *NTS* 66.1 (2020): 87–105.

Longenecker, Richard N. *The Epistle to the Romans: A Commentary on the Greek Text*. NIGTC. Grand Rapids: Eerdmans, 2016.

Martin, Dale B. *The Corinthian Body*. New Haven: Yale University Press, 1995.

Martyn, J. Louis. "Nomos Plus Genitive Noun in Paul: The History of God's Law." Pages 575–88 in *Early Christianity and Classical Culture: Comparative Studies in Honor of Abraham J. Malherbe*. Edited by John T. Fitzgerald, Thomas H. Olbricht, and L. Michael White. NovTSup 110. Leiden: Brill, 2003.

Moo, Douglas J. *The Letter to the Romans.* 2nd ed. NICNT. Grand Rapids: Eerdmans, 2018.

Peterson, David. *Commentary on Romans.* Nashville: Holman Reference, 2017.

Polanyi, Michael. *The Tacit Dimension.* London: Routledge & K. Paul, 1967.

Räisänen, Heikki. *Paul and the Law.* Tübingen: Mohr Siebeck, 1987.

———. "Sprachliches zum Spiel des Paulus mit nomos." Pages 134–49 in *Glaube und Gerechtigkeit: in memoriam Rafael Gyllenberg (18.6.1893–29.7.1982).* SFEG 38. Edited by Jarmo Kiilunen, Wille Riekkinen, and Heikki Räisänen. Helsinki: Finnische Exegetische Gesellschaft, 1983.

Rehfeld, Emmanuel L. *Relationale Ontologie bei Paulus: die ontische Wirksamkeit der Christusbezogenheit im Denken des Heidenapostels.* WUNT 2.326. Tübingen: Mohr Siebeck, 2012.

Rosner, Brian S. *Paul and the Law: Keeping the Commandments of God.* Downers Grove, IL: IVP Academic, 2013.

Schnabel, Eckhard J. *Der Brief des Paulus an die Römer: Kapitel 6–16.* HTA. Witten/Gießen: Brockhaus/Brunnen, 2016.

Schnelle, Udo. *Apostle Paul: His Life and Theology.* Translated by M. Eugene Boring. Grand Rapids: Baker Academic, 2005.

Schreiner, Thomas R. *Romans.* 2nd ed. BECNT. Grand Rapids: Baker Academic, 2018.

Thielman, Frank. *Romans.* ZECNT 6. Grand Rapids: Zondervan Academic, 2018.

Thiselton, Anthony C. *Discovering Romans: Content, Interpretation, Reception.* Grand Rapids: Eerdmans, 2016.

Tonstad, Sigve K. *The Letter to the Romans: Paul Among the Ecologists.* The Earth Bible Commentary. Sheffield: Sheffield Phoenix Press, 2016.

Wells, Kyle B. *Grace and Agency in Paul and Second Temple Judaism: Interpreting the Transformation of the Heart.* NovTSup 157. Leiden: Brill, 2015.

———. "The Liberation of the Body of Creation: Towards a Pauline Environmental Ethic." *JTS* 73.1 (2022): 92–103.

Wilckens, Ulrich. *Der Brief an die Römer.* EKK 6. Neukirchen-Vluyn/Einsiedeln: Neukirchener Verlag/Benzinger, 1978–82.

CHAPTER 15

The Assurance of Divine Favor in Romans 8: Historical and Theological Reflections

Michael F. Bird

Introduction

One can legitimately argue that the root of the Reformation's protest against the medieval magisterium was not opposition to justification as a process of sanctification. The debate over an infused versus forensic righteousness (i.e., justification) was the presenting issue, but not the underlying issue. The real object of protest was against the dominant view that it was impossible for anyone to have assurance of salvation.[1] Accordingly, to be justified by faith was to have complete assurance that one was elect, called, justified, and would assuredly attain eternal life. Sinclair Ferguson elegantly sums up the Reformed emphasis of assurance:

> Assurance of salvation is the fruit of faith in Christ. Christ is able to and does, in fact, save all those who come to him through faith. Since faith is trust in Christ as the one who is able to save, there is a certain confidence and assurance seminally inherent in faith. The act of faith, therefore, contains within it the seed of assurance. Indeed, faith in its first exercise is an assurance about Christ."[2]

So emphatic was the Reformed emphasis on assurance that the Reformers sometimes reduced faith to a sense of assurance. While this meant that assurance of God's love and salvation were attainable, it also created a pastoral dilemma, whereby if one lacked assurance, it may have entailed that one did not have true faith. Thus, Reformed teaching required extended instruction in having assurance about one's assurance!

One place in Scripture to expound assurance as medicine for spiritual anxieties has quite understandably been Paul's epistle to the Romans. The letter is suffused with Paul's bold affirmations that God is for believers, Christ died

---

1. Assurance of salvation was part of thesis 16 of Luther's famous 95 Theses.

2. Sinclair B. Ferguson, *The Whole Christ: Legalism, Antinomianism, and Gospel Assurance—Why the Marrow Controversy Still Matters* (Wheaton, IL: Crossway, 2016), 197.

for them, and the Spirit is with them. Although we could mention several sections or verses in Romans that lend themselves towards providing a sense of assurance, I think it uncontroversial to state that Rom 8 has provided a word of solace to those despondent or anxious about their spiritual state. Yung Suk Kim comments that: "Overall, in Rom 8, Paul emphasizes the power and role of the Spirit, which sustains God's on-going work of salvation through Christ, and at the same time empowers Christians to stay in the faith. . . . The Spirit sustains Christian life until the end. It also helps them in their weakness and intercedes for them in all situations."[3]

Be that as it may, we need to take into account two further things: (1) While Rom 8 is certainly conducive to comforting the introspective soul concerned with their eternal state, we need to avoid anachronism, since Paul's purposes in Rom 8 are not directed towards how to console the spiritual anxieties of Christians amidst debates between Roman Catholics, Reformers, and Remonstrant about the nature of saving faith and its benefits. Rather, Paul is expounding his gospel to a (mostly?) Gentile Christ-believing audience to assure them that they, as Gentiles, as Christ-believers, truly belong to God's people. Before we prosecute Paul's theological utility and pastoral relevance on assurance, we need to first grasp its historical particularity.[4] (2) We need to remember that across Paul's letters, throughout Romans, and even in Rom 8, Paul ties together both stern admonitions on the necessity of perseverance as well as promises of God's enduring faithfulness. As Howard Marshall put it, sober exegesis means that we must admit and wrestle with the fact that the New Testament, especially Paul's letters, presents a two-fold emphasis on the possibility of failure to persevere as well as resting in confidence in God's grace to sustain believers.[5]

Therefore, it is the aim of this short study to briefly expound the meaning of assurance in Rom 8 with respect to the historical setting and literary context in which Paul constructs it.

Anxiety and Assurance in its Social and Literary Contexts

We can imagine the potential unease that Gentile Christ-believers may have had concerning their relationship with God and the divine world and how this called for a response by Paul.

---

3. Yung Suk Kim, *Rereading Romans from the Perspective of Paul's Gospel: A Literary and Theological Commentary* (Eugene, OR: Wipf & Stock, 2019), 63.

4. On the attempt to theologically appropriate and expound biblical teaching on assurance, see Michael F. Bird, *Evangelical Theology: A Biblical and Systematic Introduction*, 2nd ed. (Grand Rapids: Zondervan, 2020), 651–61.

5. I. Howard Marshall, *Kept by the Power of God: A Study in Perseverance and Falling Away* (Minneapolis: Bethany, 1969), 208–10.

First, these Gentile Christ-believers, during their former time as "pagans," arguably knew the precarious nature of their fate in the hands of the traditional deities. In the ancient world, *religio* was the attempt through ritual, prayers, and sacrifices to fulfill one's obligation to the gods and to secure their blessings, favor, and fortune. But one never really knew for certain if one had pleased the gods or could rely on their favor at any given time. The gods oscillated between fidelity and fickleness, they had favorites, and they were thought to reward virtue and piety and punish avarice and impiety. The scrupulous performance of religious duties by the individual, the household, a city, province, and entire empire were paramount if the *pax deorum* was to be maintained. But it was never a given, never to be assumed—precisely why temples, altars, and shrines had to be carefully curated, otherwise one risked incurring divine disfavor through illness or some other misfortune. There is the possibility that Gentile converts to Christian faith may have carried with them an expectation that God the Father needed to be constantly placated if divine pleasure was to be maintained.

Second, we have to appreciate the ambiguous space that Gentile Christ-believers occupied as devotees to Jesus within socio-religious networks of first-century Rome. Gentile observance of Jewish rites and conversion to Judaism met with the ire of Roman elites so much so that several expulsions of Jews from Rome took place whenever adherence to Jewish ways were perceived to be threatening traditional Roman-ness.[6] Gentile Christians did Judaize, in a sense, by adopting Jewish monotheism, adopting an aversion to idolatry, and rejecting Roman sexual mores.[7] Thus, Gentile Christ-believers who adopted Jewish habits could be accused of playing the part of the Jew (Epictetus, *Diatr.* 2.9.20) or drifting into Jewish ways (Dio Cassius, *Hist. Rom.* 67.14.1–2), either could be labelled as social deviancy.[8] In addition, Gentile allegiance to and veneration of a crucified, risen, and exalted messiah, even in association with devotion to Israel's God, could also result in Gentile Christ-believers being alienated from the Jewish communities of Rome. Accordingly, Gentile Christ-believers were in a peculiar place, claiming devotion to Israel's God and his messianic son, identified by Jewish Christ-believers as former Gentiles/pagans (1 Cor 12:2), told that Israel's sacred history is their own (1 Cor 10:11), yet they were still distinguishable from Jews (1 Cor 10:32). They were, argues Joshua Garroway, "Gentile Jews."[9]

---

6. See Michael F. Bird, *Crossing Over Sea and Land: Jewish Proselytizing Activity in the Second-Temple Period* (Peabody, MA: Hendrickson, 2010), 127–32.

7. Paula Fredriksen, "Paul's Letter to the Romans, the Ten Commandments, and Pagan 'Justification by faith,'" *JBL* 133.4 (2014): 801–8.

8. Bird, *Crossing Over Sea and Land*, 121–32.

9. Joshua D. Garroway, *Paul's Gentile-Jews: Neither Jew Nor Gentile, But Both* (New York: Palgrave-Macmillan, 2012).

The Gentile Christ-believers in Rome could reflect on their defection from devotion to Roman deities, lament their estrangement from Jewish synagogues, and become anxious as to whether they were truly pleasing God with their allegiance to Jesus the Messiah. It surely must have entered their minds that maybe their neglect of rites honoring the Capitoline Triad would incur divine wrath or even social reprisal from their neighbors if they were found out. Or, perhaps they wondered if they had been duped by Jewish sectarians into venerating a crucified sophist and needlessly antagonized the Jewish community that once considered them guests as "God-fearers."[10]

The assurance that the Christ-believers in Rome pined for was not Luther's longing for a merciful God or even Kierkegaard's escape from dread, but to know that God was pleased with them, would protect them, would receive them into paradise, and that they belonged to his people. It is this type of anxiety, or something analogous to it, that sets the scene for Paul's discourse on the assurance of divine favor.

Assurance through the Spirit (Rom 8:1–17)

Paul begins a new section by recapitulating his primary thesis (Rom 1:16; 3:21–31; 5:1) that believers are "righteoused" by faith, God has no condemnation in store for them (8:1), because Christ and the Spirit have redeemed them from the triumvirate tyranny of Torah-Sin-Death (8:2–3). Paul next expounds what it means to live "in the new life of the Spirit" (7:6). Much like he has said before (6:1), life in the reign of grace is not a license to yield to the former Oberführer of sin, since it requires walking according to the Spirit and not according to the flesh (8:4). The subsequent contrast between Spirit and flesh in vv. 5–8 is meant, says Moo, "to highlight the radical differences between the flesh and the Spirit as a means of showing why only those who 'walk/think/are' after the Spirit can have eschatological life."[11] This is life that the Israelite prophets promised would be the great act of covenant renewal and this, Paul declares, has been poured out upon Gentile Christ-believers. Thus, to escape the anxiety about divine enmity (ἔχθρα) and to attain assurance that one pleases God (θεῷ ἀρέσαι), requires faith in Christ and walking in the Spirit.

The substance of vv. 9–11 is that believers, by possessing the Spirit, belong to and are bonded to Christ. Without the Spirit there is no participation in Christ and concomitantly no rescue from sin and no hope for resurrection

---

10. On "God-fearers" (θεοσεβής) in Roman synagogues, see Peter Lampe, *From Paul to Valentinus: Christians at Rome in the First Two Centuries* (Minneapolis: Fortress, 2003), 69–70.
11. Douglas J. Moo, *The Epistle to the Romans*, NICNT (Grand Rapids: Eerdmans, 1996), 486.

in the future. Then, in vv. 12–17, Paul sets out a complex blend of conditions, assertions, promises, and exhortations. Paul assumes something analogous to a Jewish two-ways to live ethical paradigm (e.g., Deut 30:15, 19) expressed in v. 13 with a juxtaposition of fleshly existence leading to death and Spirit-animated existence leading to eschatological life. The conditional clause of v. 13 is not intended to manufacture doubt as to the Christ-believer's position before God, but describes the cause and effect of a theocentric universe in which divine judgment is an inevitable reality. Paul's driving point in vv. 12–17 is that *if* Christ lives in them and *if* the Spirit enlivens them, *then* it is unimaginable for the Christ-believer to walk according to pattern of the flesh. The evidence for new life *within* believers is the fact that it is demonstrably acted out *by* them.[12]

Beyond that, what Paul stresses is not the precarity of their status before God, but rather, their deliverance from servile fear and freedom from concern that they are alienated from God. Paul deploys the language of spiritual testimony, adoption, sonship, household children, paternal affection, inheritance, and union with Christ. Irrespective of the two-ways leading to death and life, Paul's expectation for Christ-believers is that they believe, behave, and belong to God as his children, are led by the Spirit, and are united with Christ. In effect, those led by the Spirit are adopted as sons of God, this sonship brings a new status, it provides an intimate relationship with God, and it secures a glorious future as co-heirs with Christ in glory. [13]

Assurance through Patient Endurance (Rom 8:18–30)

Life in the city of Rome was a daily battle for survival, poor sanitation, fragile food security, prevalence of diseases, periodic plagues, little to no medicine, violent crime, shoddy housing, tenuous nature of employment, high rates of women dying in childbirth, high infant mortality, low life expectancy, scorching summers, and bitter winters. As Valerie Hope notes: "[I]n Rome, and probably much of its empire, life was often short. Death was a present danger. . . . Death, of others, and ultimately of the self, was something that people had to live with, cope with and to some extent accept. Death, by its frequent presence, could be a matter-of-fact part of life."[14] This was a world where, when you woke up in the morning, you could not be sure if you would still be alive at the end of the day.

---

12. John M. G. Barclay, *Paul and the Gift* (Grand Rapids: Eerdmans, 2015), 503.
13. Expounded further in Michael F. Bird, *Romans*, SGBC (Grand Rapids: Zondervan, 2016), 254–68.
14. Valerie M. Hope, *Roman Death: The Dying and the Dead in Ancient Rome* (London: Continuum, 2009), 43.

In vv. 18–30, Paul writes to show that the travails of Roman urban life are part of the slavery of creation to the forces of chaos and death; a slavery that will be ended with the resurrection of the dead and the renewal of creation. Until then, Paul urges Christ-believers to patiently persevere in hope, knowing that the Spirit leads them in their prayers, God works all things for the good of those who love him, and they are destined to be conformed to the image of the divine Son. In which case, the final goal is what Ben Blackwell calls *Christification* or *Christosis*, which means, "Being glorified, or experiencing the resurrection life of Christ through the agency of the Spirit, is the pinnacle of being conformed to Christ's image."[15] But this is more than a destiny, it is also a privilege and mission. As Haley Goranson Jacob puts it, "to be conformed to the image of his Son" (συμμόρφους τῆς εἰκόνος τοῦ υἱοῦ αὐτοῦ) means "the vocational participation of believers in the Firstborn Son's honorable status of power and authority over creation as adopted members of God's family and as renewed humanity."[16] It is an honor better than adoption into a senatorial household or even membership in any of the priestly collegia of Rome.

Paul tells them, that in this Messiah-shaped family, that they can rest in the hope for the redemption of their bodies, the revelation of their sonship of a cosmic stage, and the eschatological consummation with Christ Jesus. In the meantime, however, Christ-believers need to exhibit "patient fortitude"[17] and rely on the Spirit's intercession to assist them in their struggles. They are to persevere knowing that the golden chain of salvation, from God's eternal decision to eschatological deliverance, is immutable and it will bring them into "eternal life" (6:23) which is nothing other than a creation liberated from the anti-god forces of death and corruption (8:21).

Assurance through God's Inexhaustible Love (Rom 8:31–39)

Paul's exhortation in vv. 31–39 constitute a dramatic crescendo as he weaves together the motifs of divine favor, atonement, resurrection, grace, justification, the exaltation of Christ, the priesthood of Christ, suffering, triumph, and divine love. Paul waxes eloquently about the majestic span of God's favor for believers in Christ Jesus despite the precarious nature of life, pejorative taunts from rivals, and the danger of incurring the wrath of heavenly powers. Indeed, Paul is hymn-like in his reflection of how God's love in Christ Jesus wins a victory for believers over all things that might conceivably oppose them.[18]

---

15. Ben Blackwell, *Christosis: Pauline Soteriology in Light of Deification in Irenaeus and Cyril of Alexandria*, WUNT 2.134 (Tübingen: Mohr Siebeck, 2011), 167.

16. Haley Goranson Jacob, *Conformed to the Image of His Son: Reconsidering Paul's Theology of Glory in Romans* (Downers Grove, IL: IVP Academic, 2018), 263.

17. Moo, *Romans*, 510.

18. Bird, *Romans*, 290–91.

Paul consoles his audience that amidst hardship, despair, persecution, hunger, shame, daily threats, and injustice, that God is for them. Paul tells them not to fear the condemnation of the magistrate or their own conscience, for the only one who condemns is Christ, and he stands as their advocate and intercessor. Paul wants them to know that while Seneca said, "Most men ebb and flow in wretchedness between the fear of death and the hardships of life; they are unwilling to live, and yet do not know how to die,"[19] they can know that even death cannot separate them from the love of God. Paul's thought is elegantly captured by N. T. Wright: "Those who follow their Messiah into the valley of the shadow of death will find that they need fear no evil. Though they sometimes seem sheep for the slaughter, yet they may trust the Shepherd, whose love will follow them all the days of their life."[20] Or else, in the words of David Garland:

> From a human vantage point, life seems so fragile. All will be touched by the pain of losing loved ones and must face the reality of their own deaths and the anguish of suffering. Paul responds to this reality from God's vantage point. God's love and power over-come death and will glorify believers with Christ whom he raised from death. Therefore, he assures Christ-followers that they have a sure hope even in the thick of suffering when others might think all is hopeless. Paul does not dismiss suffering as a mere trifle compared with the glory to come. The afflictions are not trifling. Paul argues instead that God has not promised believers immunity from suffering in this age, and when they suffer for their faith in Christ they should not let the shadows of world-weariness darken their hope in God.[21]

In sum, the Roman believers can be assured of divine favor, because of divine faithfulness, which meets them in Christ, and is experienced by them in the Spirit's guidance.

Conclusion

In summary, in Rom 8, we need to appreciate how Paul's words would be a consoling message for the Gentile-majority house churches in Rome, meeting in tenements and shops, some of whom had associations with Jewish communities and may have continued to observe some Jewish rites and customs. These Gentile Christ-believers consisted mostly of slaves and freedmen, labor-

---

19. Seneca, *Letters* 4.6.

20. N. T. Wright, "The Letter to the Romans: Introduction, Commentary, and Reflections," in *The New Interpreter's Bible*, ed. Leander E. Keck (Nashville: Abingdon, 2002), 10:615.

21. David E. Garland, *Romans: An Introduction and Commentary*, TNTC 6 (Downers Grove, IL: IVP Academic, 2021), 295.

ers and artisans, living on or beneath the poverty line, where death filled the streets, poverty was only one illness away, a dense urban life that was cut-throat, and full of rivalries. These believers very probably faced opposition on several fronts, perhaps chastised by family for neglecting the household *lares*, ejected from professional guilds for failing to honor the emperor, neighbors gossiping that they had drifted into Jewish ways, or had been ostracized by former Jewish friends for association with a rogue messianic cult. Paul writes to Gentile Christ-believers in a world where no-one was ever certain of divine favor, where good fortune was desperately pursued but never guaranteed, and Paul assures them of divine favor. God is for them, Christ died for them, and the Spirit intercedes for them. Paul assures them of divine patronage, and more than that, declares that they are part of God's holy people, and they can take solace in God's love for them as they welcome each other in the Messiah's name.

Paul discourses on assurance but not without some conditions or agency. The Christ-believers are instructed to not allow sin to reign over their bodies, to obey its desires (6:12–14), they are told to fulfill the law (8:4) by walking in the Spirit and giving no quarter to the flesh (8:12–14), and by loving their neighbor (13:8–10). Paul himself can make grave warnings about the dangers of falling away (Rom 11:21–22) and he can warn of dire consequences if the Christ-believers in Rome yield to the desires of the flesh (Rom 8:13). Yet Paul brings together both divine promises of deliverance with exhortations towards faithful perseverance. Paul knows that salvation, eschatological salvation, is certainly conditional. However, Paul always anchors salvation not in human action as the decisive condition, but rather, in God's constant faithfulness, scandalous mercy, and enduring love.

Bibliography

Barclay, John M. G. *Paul and the Gift*. Grand Rapids: Eerdmans, 2015.

Bird, Michael F. *Crossing Over Sea and Land: Jewish Proselytizing Activity in the Second-Temple Period*. Peabody, MA: Hendrickson, 2010.

———. *Evangelical Theology: A Biblical and Systematic Introduction*. 2nd ed. Grand Rapids: Zondervan, 2020.

———. *Romans*. SGBC. Grand Rapids: Zondervan, 2016.

Blackwell, Ben. *Christosis: Pauline Soteriology in Light of Deification in Irenaeus and Cyril of Alexandria*. WUNT 2.134. Tübingen: Mohr Siebeck, 2011.

Ferguson, Sinclair B. *The Whole Christ: Legalism, Antinomianism, and Gospel Assurance—Why the Marrow Controversy Still Matters*. Wheaton, IL: Crossway, 2016.

Fredriksen, Paula. "Paul's Letter to the Romans, the Ten Commandments, and Pagan 'Justification by faith.'" *JBL* 133.4 (2014): 801–8.

Garland, David E. *Romans: An Introduction and Commentary.* TNTC 6. Downers Grove, IL: IVP Academic, 2021.

Garroway, Joshua D. *Paul's Gentile-Jews: Neither Jew Nor Gentile, But Both.* New York: Palgrave-Macmillan, 2012.

Hope, Valerie M. *Roman Death: The Dying and the Dead in Ancient Rome.* London: Continuum, 2009.

Jacob, Haley Goranson. *Conformed to the Image of His Son: Reconsidering Paul's Theology of Glory in Romans.* Downers Grove, IL: IVP Academic, 2018.

Kim, Yung Suk. *Rereading Romans from the Perspective of Paul's Gospel: A Literary and Theological Commentary.* Eugene, OR: Wipf & Stock, 2019.

Lampe, Peter. *From Paul to Valentinus: Christians at Rome in the First Two Centuries.* Minneapolis: Fortress, 2003.

Marshall, I. Howard. *Kept by the Power of God: A Study in Perseverance and Falling Away.* Minneapolis: Bethany, 1969.

Moo, Douglas J. *The Epistle to the Romans.* NICNT. Grand Rapids: Eerdmans, 1996.

Wright, N. T. "The Letter to the Romans: Introduction, Commentary, and Reflections." Pages 395–770 in vol. 10 of *The New Interpreter's Bible.* Edited by Leander E. Keck. Nashville: Abingdon, 2002.

CHAPTER 16

Paul's Indictment of Israel in Romans 9:31–10:10

Joshua M. Greever

In this chapter, I will seek to shed light on the coherence of Paul's indictment of Israel in Rom 9:31–10:10. I will contend that the substance of this indictment was that Israel had fundamentally failed to trust God as the source of their righteousness and salvation. Israel's failure was a rejection of God and thus was a form of idolatry; as a result, their plight was vertical (directed towards God), not mainly horizontal (directed towards other humans). In order to demonstrate this, I will briefly analyze the structure of 9:31–10:10, from which I will make several observations regarding the nature of Paul's indictment of Israel.

The Structure of Romans 9:31–10:10

The passage divides into three subsections: 9:31–33; 10:1–4; and 10:5–10. In three subsections Paul makes, as it were, three passes on the same topic—namely, why Israel failed to obtain righteousness and salvation. All three passes, while different in the details, are mutually interpretive and provide a holistic, kaleidoscopic portrayal of Israel's failure. In Table 1, I have put the parallel components of Paul's indictment of Israel in bold font.

Table 1: The Structure of Romans 9:31–10:10

FIRST PASS (9:31–33)
Israel failed to arrive at the law of righteousness (9:31)
Because (διὰ τί) not by faith, but (ἀλλά) as though **by works** (9:32a; *reason for 9:31*)

Israel **stumbled** (9:32b–33; *explanation/result of 9:32a*)

SECOND PASS (10:1–4)
Paul's desire for Israel's salvation (10:1)
Because (γάρ) despite Israel's zeal, yet (ἀλλά) **without knowledge** (10:2; *reason for 10:1*)

Israel's attempt to establish **their own righteousness** (10:3; *explanation/result of 10:2*)

TRANSITION (10:4)
> Israel's misguided pursuit of νόμος, Israel's lack of knowledge (*summarizes 9:31–10:3*)
> Anticipates the witness of the law (*anticipates 10:5–10*)
> Anticipates the witness of the prophets (*anticipates 10:11–13*)

THIRD PASS (10:5–10; *explains 10:4*)
> The righteousness of the law: ***doing*** as the means to life (10:5)
> The righteousness of faith:
>> What it does not say (10:6–7)
>>> ***Ascending*** to heaven (10:6)
>>> ***Descending*** to the abyss (10:7)
>> What it says (10:8–10)

The first two passes are especially parallel. In both 9:31–33 and 10:1–3 Paul states the plight of Israel: they failed to obtain what they were pursuing (the law for righteousness, 9:31), and they were not saved (10:1). After stating the plight, Paul gives the reason or the ground for that plight: they pursued the law of righteousness not by faith but as though (ὡς) it could be obtained by works (9:32), and despite their zeal, they lacked knowledge (10:2). Finally, after stating the reason for Israel's plight, Paul explains that reason in greater detail, emphasizing its result. Israel's works resulted in their stumbling (9:32–33), and Israel's lack of knowledge led them to a failed attempt to establish their own righteousness instead of the righteousness of God (10:3). The parallel structure of these sections is a strong indicator that they are mutually interpretive.[1]

Romans 10:4 serves to transition from the second pass to the third. On the one hand, 10:4 draws together the motifs of 9:31–10:3. Key words from 9:31–10:3 such as νόμος (9:31), δικαιοσύνη (9:30–31; 10:3), and πιστεύω (9:30, 32–33) reappear in 10:4. Specifically, τέλος in 10:4 concludes the race metaphor of 9:30–32.[2] On the other hand, 10:4 anticipates Rom 10:5–13. Specifically, it anticipates the witness of the law in 10:5–10, as Paul quotes from Leviticus and Deuteronomy to point to the righteousness of faith. Further, the phrase παντὶ τῷ πιστεύοντι anticipates the witness of the prophets and the universalizing motif in 10:11–13.

The third pass (10:5–10) is related to the first two but differs in some significant ways. Paul shifts away from using plural verbs—with which he recounts

---

1. This does not suggest that all the terms are synonymous and mean the same thing; rather, there is a close link between them.

2. Rightly Robert Badenas, *Christ the End of the Law: Romans 10:4 in Pauline Perspective*, JSNTSup 10 (Sheffield: JSOT Press, 1985), 101–2.

Israel's story in 9:31–10:3—to using singular verbs. This shift indicates that the third pass does not recount Israel's story so much as it clarifies Israel's failure by commenting on the relationship between the law, righteousness, and faith. In this third pass, Paul contrasts (δέ, 10:5) two kinds of righteousness, which receive their witness from the Torah: the righteousness of the law and the righteousness of faith.[3] The righteousness of the law (10:5) is aptly stated by Lev 18:5—the person who does the commandments will live by them. The righteousness of faith (10:6–10) is divided into what that righteousness does *not* say and what it *does* say. It does *not* say a person must ascend to heaven to bring Christ down or descend to the abyss to raise Christ from the dead (10:6–7). What it *does* say is that God has brought the word of faith so near that it is in the mouth and in the heart (10:8–10). If indeed the righteousness of the law is set in contrast to the righteousness of faith, then the righteousness of the law—*doing* as a means to life (10:5)—corresponds to the attempt to ascend and descend in order to obtain Christ (10:6–7).

Hence, in 9:31–10:10 Paul presents a holistic depiction of Israel's failure by means of three passes. Because each pass analyzes or interprets Israel's failure, the result is a kaleidoscopic portrayal of the story of Israel; each pass builds on the previous one, and collectively they show that Israel's fundamental sin was a failure to trust God as the source of their righteousness and salvation. Based on this structural analysis of 9:31–10:10, we are now equipped to make a few observations regarding the nature of Paul's indictment. Specifically, we will focus on Israel's works and stumbling (9:32–33), Israel's spiritual ignorance and failed attempt to establish their own righteousness (10:2–3), and Paul's attention to the witness of the law (10:5–7).

Israel's "Works" and "Stumbling" (9:32–33)

Romans 9:31 states that Israel, in contrast with the Gentiles (9:30), did not achieve the law of righteousness that they pursued. The phrase "law of righteousness" (νόμον δικαιοσύνης) expresses the goal Israel hoped to obtain (that is, righteousness through adherence to the law's demands), and it probably connotes the close association between the law of Moses and

---

3. The attempt to deny an antithesis in between the two kinds of righteousness (10:5–6) flies in the face of Paul's consistent antithesis between law/works and faith, as well as the parallel passage in Phil 3:9. Rightly, James D. G. Dunn, *Romans 9–16*, WBC 38B (Dallas: Word, 1988), 602; Jason C. Meyer, *The End of the Law: Mosaic Covenant in Pauline Theology*, NACSBT (Nashville: Broadman & Holman, 2009), 222–23; Thomas R. Schreiner, *Romans*, 2nd ed., BECNT (Grand Rapids: Baker Academic, 2018), 536–38; contra Robert Jewett, *Romans: A Commentary*, Hermeneia (Minneapolis: Fortress, 2007), 624–25.

righteousness.[4] In 9:30 Paul had spoken of the Gentiles not pursuing the goal of "righteousness"—and yet they obtained it—but in 9:31 the goal becomes not simply "righteousness" but that kind of righteousness associated with law-keeping since the law was the peculiar possession of the Jews for which they were zealous.

In 9:32, Paul grounds (διὰ τί) Israel's failure in the wrong means by which they sought to obtain their goal.[5] They pursued righteousness "not by faith" but as if (ὡς) they could obtain it "by works." With the adverb ὡς ("as if") Paul distances himself from the notion that Israel actually could have obtained righteousness by works, since Israel was under the dominion of sin and therefore was unable to accomplish the requisite obedience. Hence, the problem was not the goal of righteousness but the means Israel used to obtain it ("by works").

In 9:32b–33 Paul explains the nature of "works" through Israel's story of "stumbling" in Isaiah; that is, Israel's stumbling in the time of Isaiah illustrates what Paul means by "works" and its necessary outcome. The quote in 9:33 is a composite of Isa 8:14 and 28:16.[6] In both texts Judah and the inhabitants of Jerusalem faced the threat of invasion and desolation. In Isa 7–8 the Southern Kingdom of Judah was threatened by a coalition of Syria and the Northern Kingdom of Israel. In response to the threat King Ahaz was to trust Yahweh by being "firm in faith" (Isa 7:9). Additionally, Yahweh warned Isaiah not to "walk in the way of this people" but to trust in the LORD. Isaiah committed himself to "wait for Yahweh . . . and hope in him" (8:17). For the inhabitants of Jerusalem who failed to trust Yahweh, Yahweh would become "a stone of offense and a rock of stumbling" (8:14).[7] Israel's stumbling would be the consequence of their failure to walk in faith. Thus, as shown in Table 2, Israel's failure to trust in Yahweh corresponds to Paul's conception of "works" in Rom 9:32, since the consequence of both is Israel's "stumbling."

---

4. It is possible δικαιοσύνης is a genitive of result or an objective genitive, and it expresses either the law's demand for righteousness or Israel's attempt to obtain righteousness through it. For a good discussion of the options, see J. Ross Wagner, *Heralds of the Good News: Isaiah and Paul in Concert in the Letter to the Romans*, NovTSup 101 (Leiden: Brill, 2003), 152; Douglas J. Moo, *The Letter to the Romans*, 2nd ed., NICNT (Grand Rapids: Eerdmans, 2018), 642–46; Schreiner, *Romans*, 525.

5. Moo, *Romans*, 645–46, suggests Paul indicts Israel for both the goal and the manner of obtaining it. Even if this is true, the use of ὡς suggests Paul has in view primarily the manner of Israel's pursuit.

6. LXX Isa 28:16 appears to be the primary text in view, though the metaphor of stumbling (πρόσκομμα) over a rock (πέτρα) derives from LXX Isa 8:14. For an analysis of Paul's citation of the Isaianic text, see Wagner, *Heralds of the Good News*, 126–31.

7. Wagner (*Heralds of the Good News*, 141) suggests that the insertion of the phrase ἐὰν ἐπ᾽ αὐτῷ πεποιθὼς ᾖς in LXX Isa 8:14 "makes trust in God the thematic center of gravity of the passage."

Table 2: The Relationship Between "Works" and "Stumbling"

Rom 9:32	"Works"	➤	"Stumbling"
Isa 8:14	Failure to Trust Yahweh	➤	"Stumbling"

Similarly, in Isa 28 the rulers of Jerusalem had refused to trust in Yahweh. Instead they had "made a covenant with death, and with Sheol ... an agreement" (28:15). This is probably a reference to placing their trust in Egypt for safety and security from the Assyrian threat.[8] They trusted in falsehood and not in Yahweh, to which Yahweh responded that he was laying a stone in Zion based on the sure foundation that "whoever believes will not be in haste" (28:16).[9]

In both Isa 8 and 28 the inhabitants of Jerusalem chose not to trust in Yahweh when faced with threats from without and fears within. They chose to look elsewhere for safety, security, and salvation; they chose to make a covenant with Egypt instead of keep their covenant with Yahweh. In a word, they "stumbled" on the stone of Yahweh himself, who became to them not a source of salvation but of judgment. Hence, in Isaiah "stumbling" refers to the consequence of not trusting in Yahweh for deliverance. It is judgment resulting from an attempt to obtain deliverance ("salvation") by means of human effort—in the case of Israel, through a coalition with neighboring peoples.

For Paul, Israel's failure to trust and take refuge in Yahweh in the time of Isaiah aptly illustrates Paul's conception of Israel's "works." As in Isaiah's prophecy, Israel's "works" were simply human efforts to find safety and security in people and places other than Yahweh. And as in Isaiah, the sure consequence of this failure for Israel was "stumbling"—this time, not over Yahweh's temporal deliverance of Jerusalem from Assyrian aggression, but over Yahweh's provision of final salvation through the righteousness of the Messiah. In this sense, Israel's "works" were simply a form of idolatry.

Israel's Spiritual Ignorance and Attempt to Establish Their Own Righteousness (10:2–3)

The second observation regarding Paul's indictment of Israel is that Israel's spiritual ignorance led to their failed attempt to establish their own righteousness (10:2–3). As the structural analysis indicates, Israel's ignorance of God (10:2–3a) corresponds to their "works" (9:32a), and their attempt to establish their own

---

8. J. Alec Motyer, *The Prophecy of Isaiah: An Introduction and Commentary* (Downers Grove, IL: IVP Academic, 1993), 233.

9. See Wagner, *Heralds of the Good News*, 142–45, for a discussion of whether the stone is a maxim or an individual, as well as the possible referents for the object of one's hope (LXX Isa 28:16: ἐπ' αὐτῷ).

righteousness (10:3b) corresponds to their experience of stumbling (9:32b–33). That is, the former elements give rise to the latter. In Israel's experience, they had a zeal for God—Paul himself possessed such zeal prior to his conversion (cf. Phil 3:6).[10] But their zeal, which in Rom 10:2 refers to *"Jewish ardency to discharge the injunctions of Torah holistically conceived, with an eye towards God,"*[11] was insufficient because it did not coincide with a true knowledge of God.

In his Pauline theology, James Dunn claims that in Rom 10:3 Paul indicted Israel for failing to accept God's inclusion of the Gentiles into the plan of salvation. He does so on the basis of the word ἰδίαν ("their own"), claiming that it "properly denotes" one's own possession in the sense of "belonging to them and not to others." He says this to uphold his view that Paul indicts Israel not for legalism but for attempting to exclude the Gentiles *as Gentiles* from the people of God. Israel's attempt to establish "their own righteousness," according to Dunn, was Israel's attempt to preserve their national and Jewish identity. This is what Israel was zealous for (10:2), and this is why Paul speaks of a righteousness that belongs to them and not to others—namely, the Gentiles.[12]

Dunn's interpretation of ἰδίαν fails to convince, not because the word does not refer to one's own private, peculiar possession—it does.[13] The question, though, concerns *in what sense* Israel sought their own private, peculiar righteousness. In the context, "one's own righteousness" (τὴν ἰδίαν δικαιοσύνην) is set in contrast to "the righteousness of God" (τῇ δικαιοσύνῃ τοῦ θεοῦ), which suggests that ἰδίαν and θεοῦ are antonyms. Hence, an analysis of the genitive θεοῦ will help to determine the sense of ἰδίαν.

Emerging from the immediate context are at least two reasons why θεοῦ is a genitive of source—that is, righteousness that comes "from God." First, the structure of the passage shows that 10:3 corresponds to Israel's stumbling in 9:32b–33. As observed above, Israel's stumbling in Isaiah's prophecy was the consequence of their failure to trust Yahweh as the *source* of salvation. They failed to recognize Yahweh as the provider of deliverance from their enemies. This observation suggests that in the Rom 10:3 parallel, the genitive θεοῦ refers to God as the *source* of Israel's righteousness. Second, as the structural analysis indicates, Paul's citation of Deut 30:12–14 in his third pass (Rom 10:6–8) comments further on the nature of "works" as well as the righteousness that saves. In Deuteronomy, Israel was told not to seek far and wide for the commandment since God had already brought it to them. God was not only the Lawgiver but

---

10. In the construction ζῆλον θεοῦ, θεοῦ is an objective genitive. Dane C. Ortlund, *Zeal Without Knowledge: The Concept of Zeal in Romans 10, Galatians 1, and Philippians 3*, LNTS 472 (New York: T&T Clark, 2021), 126, comments that this interpretation of the syntax accords with similar constructions in the Hebrew Bible (קנא) and LXX (ζῆλ-).

11. Ortlund, *Zeal Without Knowledge*, 134 (emphasis original).

12. James D. G. Dunn, *The Theology of Paul the Apostle* (Grand Rapids: Eerdmans, 1998), 368.

13. *LSJ*, 818; BDAG s.v. ἴδιος (466).

he was also the *source* of Israel's ability to hear and do the commandment. Thus, bracketing the genitive θεοῦ in Rom 10:3 are Paul's citations of Isaiah and Deuteronomy, in which the law and prophets collectively bear witness to God as the source of Israel's life. These observations from the immediate context of Rom 10:3 commend θεοῦ as a genitive of source—the righteousness "of God" refers to the righteousness that comes "from God."[14]

If this analysis is on the right track, then in Rom 10:3 Paul indicted Israel not for the possession of righteousness *per se* but for seeking to be the *source* of its accomplishment.[15] Paul indicted Israel for seeking to establish a righteousness that comes from themselves and, in this sense, is a righteousness peculiar to them. It is only a righteousness that is "belonging to them and not to others" precisely because they, and not others, sought to be the source of "their own righteousness." This clarifies the vertical dimension of Israel's failure, for even though they had a kind of zeal for God (10:2a), it was misguided in the sense that they actually rejected God as the source of righteousness and instead sought it from within themselves.[16]

Doing the Law, and Ascending and Descending to Obtain Christ (10:5–7)

The last observation that relates to Paul's indictment of Israel is his citation of Lev 18:5 and Deut 30:12–13 (and Deut 9:4) in Rom 10:5–7. In these verses Paul does not directly indict Israel but, using the law as witness, comments on that which is antithetical to the righteousness of faith. Given the immediately preceding context, there is a conceptual parallel between the story of Israel (9:31–10:4) and the witness of the law (10:5–10). Specifically, Israel's "works," "stumbling," spiritual ignorance, and attempt to establish their own righteousness correspond to what the righteousness of the law *says* (10:5) and what the righteousness of faith does *not* say (10:6–7). To put the matter positively, 10:5–7 reveals the outlook of the Jew who pursued righteousness by works, ignorant of the righteousness of God.[17]

---

14. For a substantial defense of this interpretation of δικαιοσύνη θεοῦ in Paul, see Charles Lee Irons, *The Righteousness of God: A Lexical Examination of the Covenant-Faithfulness Interpretation*, WUNT 2.386 (Tübingen: Mohr Siebeck, 2015).

15. Cf. Phil 3:9, where Paul speaks autobiographically of "my own righteousness from the law" (ἐμὴν δικαιοσύνην τὴν ἐκ νόμου) set in contrast with "righteousness from God" (τὴν ἐκ θεοῦ δικαιοσύνην).

16. If Paul had wanted to contrast exclusively Jewish identity with the identity of the new people of God (Jews and Gentiles in Christ by faith), one would have expected a contrast between "one's own righteousness" (i.e., Jewish righteousness) with Gentile righteousness (or lack thereof).

17. Francis Watson, *Paul and the Hermeneutics of Faith*, 2nd ed. (New York: T&T Clark, 2016), 313, similarly suggests the individual commanded in Rom 10:6—"do not say in your heart"—is the ἄνθρωπος of Rom 10:5.

Paul cites Lev 18:5 in Rom 10:5 as a summary of the righteousness of the law (τὴν δικαιοσύνην τὴν ἐκ τοῦ νόμου). For Paul, Lev 18:5 was an especially apt summary because it evinced a close relationship between obedience and life (עָשָׂה/ποιέω; חָיָה/ζάω). To be sure, in its original context Lev 18:5 was not antithetical to faith, nor was the Sinai covenant legalistic since its existence owed to God's prior and gracious redemption from Egypt. Nevertheless, the promise of life in the land was contingent on Israel's obedience, a conditionality that Lev 18:5 powerfully expressed (cf. Exod 19:45; Lev 26:3–45).[18] This covenantal contingency, which was written into the very fabric of the old covenant, called for a new and better covenant, one not subject to the dominion of sin (cf. Rom 8:3; Heb 8:6). Paul's citation of Lev 18:5 highlights the weakness of the old covenant.[19] Even more, now that the new covenant had arrived through God's climactic redemption in Christ, to return to life under the old covenant—along with its covenantal contingency as expressed in Lev 18:5—would be tantamount to a rejection of Christ and an attempt to establish one's own righteousness before God.[20] Thus, when viewed from the lens of the arrival of the new covenant, Lev 18:5 is an apt summary of the "righteousness of the law" that corresponds to Israel's failure to trust God for righteousness and life.

What the righteousness of faith does *not* say (Rom 10:6–7) corresponds to the righteousness of the law (Rom 10:5). Romans 10:6–7 forms a composite quote of Deut 9:4 and 30:12–13.[21] In LXX Deut 9:4–6 Yahweh commands Israel not to say in their heart (μὴ εἴπῃς ἐν τῇ καρδίᾳ σου) that their righteousness is the basis (διὰ τὴν δικαιοσύνην μου) for entering the promised land (LXX Deut 9:4). In fact, Yahweh emphatically negates (οὐχί, LXX Deut 9:5) their righteousness as the basis for their entrance into theland, precisely because Israel was not righteous but a "stiff-necked people" (Deut 9:6; cf. Deut 8:17).[22]

Similarly, in Deut 30:11–14 Yahweh tells Israel that his command is not too hard for them, neither is it far off from them, but it is as near as can be, even

---

18. Meyer, *End of the Law*, 217–19, rightly notes that Moses didn't teach legalism since life in Lev 18:5 referred to life in the land, not eternal life. Nevertheless, within the scope of the biblical metanarrative, Israel's life in the land pointed beyond itself to eternal life, an interpretive move found often in later Old Testament texts or in Second Temple Judaism (Simon J. Gathercole, "Torah, Life, and Salvation: Leviticus 18:5 in Early Judaism and the New Testament," in *From Prophecy to Testament: The Function of the Old Testament the New Testament*, ed. Craig A. Evans [Peabody, MA: Hendrickson, 2004], 126–45; Preston M. Sprinkle, *Law and Life: The Interpretation of Leviticus 18:5 in Early Judaism and in Paul*, WUNT 2.241 [Tübingen: Mohr Siebeck, 2008]).

19. Similarly Sprinkle, *Law and Life*, 196–99. Dunn, *Romans 9–16*, 600, adds that Paul explicitly named Moses "to characterize the old epoch now superseded by Christ."

20. Rightly, Schreiner, *Romans*, 540–42.

21. There are other possible texts he had in mind, such as Deut 8:17 and Prov 30:4; however, Deut 9:4 and 30:12–13 seem to be primary.

22. Cf. Frank Thielman, *Romans*, ZECNT 6 (Grand Rapids: Zondervan Academic, 2018), 491–92.

in their mouth and heart. Therefore, they need not go to great extremes to find the command; they need not search for it in heaven or go across the sea to access it, for Yahweh has already brought it near. The point of this is to remind Israel, very much like Deut 9, that Israel must not think of their relationship with Yahweh as one based on their own efforts. Yahweh is the Giver, and they are the receivers; God does it all for them, so to speak. And if their relationship with Yahweh was to remain, they would have to depend on Yahweh in faith. This point is strongly underscored when we note that the preceding passage (Deut 30:1–10) stresses that Israel's only hope is Yahweh, who would one day circumcise Israel's hearts so that Israel would love and obey Yahweh. Even if Deut 30:11–14 shifts back in focus to Israel's status on the plains of Moab, the near proximity of Israel's eschatological hope casts an eschatological shadow over 30:11–14.[23] That is, on the plains of Moab Moses was calling Israel to hope in God as the Giver and source of their life, both then and at the eschaton.

This analysis of Deut 9:4 and 30:12–13 explains the appearance of the composite quote in Rom 10:6–7. In both texts God is portrayed as the source of his people's life and righteousness. If it was not Israel's righteousness that brought them into the promised land (Deut 9:4), then how much more should Jews and Gentiles alike who are "under sin" (Rom 3:9) trust in God as the source of their righteousness? If Israel was charged not to cross sky and sea to obtain Yahweh's commandment but to hope in Yahweh as the Giver of all good things, how much more should Israel in Paul's day look in faith to God as the one who *has given* all good things in the Messiah?[24] Indeed, in Paul's quote the Deuteronomic "commandment" that Yahweh brought near to Israel has given way to the incarnation and resurrection of the Christ. One need not ascend to heaven to bring Christ down (Rom 10:6b) since God sent his own son in the incarnation, quite apart from the effort of humanity (cf. Rom 5:6–8; 8:3, 32).[25] Further, one need not descend to the abyss to raise Christ from the dead (Rom 10:7) since

---

23. Similarly Frank Thielman, *Paul and the Law: A Contextual Approach* (Downers Grove, IL: InterVarsity Press, 1994), 210; Meyer, *End of the Law*, 226–27. For this reason, despite the numerous ways in which Paul modifies the Deuteronomic text, I am not convinced that Paul's interpretation of Deut 30 runs against the grain of its logic and is thus a Pauline invention (contra Watson, *Hermeneutics of Faith*, 401; David Lincicum, *Paul and the Early Jewish Encounter with Deuteronomy*, WUNT 2.284 [Tübingen: Mohr Siebeck, 2010], 155–58).

24. Similarly Brian S. Rosner, *Paul and the Law: Keeping the Commandments of God*, NSBT 31 (Downers Grove, IL: IVP Academic, 2013), 141.

25. Wagner, *Heralds of the Good News*, 167–68n47, thinks the notion of bringing Christ down refers to the attempt to bring him back from his exalted state (as though his work on earth were incomplete), since this coheres better with the confession of Jesus as Lord in Rom 10:9. While this does not appear to be the likeliest interpretation, even if Wagner is correct, my point still stands, for the point is that God has finished the work for his people such that there is nothing they can add to it.

God raised him from the dead apart from any human effort (cf. Rom 4:25; 6:4). The Christ-event, from beginning to end, is entirely the work of God and the sole basis for Israel's life. On the basis of God's work in Christ, the word of the gospel has come near, as promised in the new covenant, in our mouths and hearts (Rom 10:8; cf. Deut 30:6; Jer 31:33–34). This saving event Israel could neither add to nor improve upon, and the only proper response was confession and faith, a laying hold of the righteousness and salvation that comes from God in Christ (Rom 10:9–10).[26]

Paul's indictment of Israel in Rom 10:6–7, therefore, takes shape as a commentary on Israel's attempt to establish their own righteousness due to their "works" and spiritual ignorance. Moses' warning had come to pass in Paul's day with Israel's rejection of Christ. Israel had failed to see God in Christ as the source of their righteousness and salvation, and thus they "stumbled" and were placed under the judgment of God.

Conclusion

The structure of Rom 9:31–10:10 indicates that Paul presents a holistic, kaleidoscopic depiction of Israel's failure to obtain righteousness and salvation. The phrases "by works," "stumbled," "not according to knowledge," "their own righteousness," "doing" the commandments as a means to life, and "ascending to heaven . . . descending to the abyss" collectively show that Israel's fundamental failure was that they did not trust God as the source of their righteousness and salvation. Israel's failure is explained in terms of their rejection of God; their plight was a form of idolatry and was primarily vertical, not horizontal.[27]

A concluding ramification of this study concerns the nature of Israel's "works," a hotly debated topic among Pauline scholars.[28] Due to the structure of Rom 9:31–10:10, Israel's "works" refers to Israel's attempts—through obedience to the Torah or otherwise—to trust in themselves for righteousness, security, and salvation. Israel had a history of "works," which they manifested in different

---

26. Similarly, Wagner, *Heralds of the Good News*, 168, who stresses the necessity of simply believing and confessing since God has accomplished his redemptive work in Christ.

27. Thus, as Ortlund, *Zeal Without Knowledge*, 135–36, has rightly suggested, Israel's plight in Rom 9:31–10:10 was the manner by which they pursued the law, not primarily their failure to obey it (as in Rom 2:17–29).

28. For a discussion of the major interpretive options of the phrase "works of the law" (ἔργα νόμου) in Paul, see Thomas R. Schreiner, "'Works of the Law' in Paul," *NovT* 33.3 (1991): 217–44. "Works" as human attempts or human "doing" are not intrinsically evil, for in other contexts Paul can speak highly of keeping the commandments (1 Cor 7:19). But in soteriological contexts, the notion of "works" as a means of obtaining righteousness and salvation is condemned, the underlying assumption being the power of sin and the necessity of salvation from outside oneself (cf. Deut 9:4–6).

ways. In Moses' day, Israel's "works" would have been evident by an attempt to cross sky and sea to bring Yahweh and his word to them, or by a claim to have entered the promised land on the basis of their own righteousness. In Isaiah's day, Israel's "works" took shape as a covenant with Egypt for protection against the threat of the Assyrian invasion. Finally—and climactically—in Paul's day, it looked like Israel seeking to establish their own righteousness instead of looking to God in Christ as the source of righteousness. In all these manifestations of Israel's "works," the common thread is self-reliance, the effort to obtain righteousness, safety, refuge, or salvation in anyone or anything other than God. Thus, Israel's "works" fall under the vertical category of idolatry, not fundamentally under the horizontal category of Gentile exclusion.

Bibliography

Badenas, Robert. *Christ the End of the Law: Romans 10:4 in Pauline Perspective.* JSNTSup 10. Sheffield: JSOT Press, 1985.

Dunn, James D. G. *Romans 9–16.* WBC 38B. Dallas: Word, 1988.

———. *The Theology of Paul the Apostle.* Grand Rapids: Eerdmans, 1998.

Gathercole, Simon J. "Torah, Life, and Salvation: Leviticus 18:5 in Early Judaism and the New Testament." Pages 126–45 in *From Prophecy to Testament: The Function of the Old Testament the New Testament.* Edited by Craig A. Evans. Peabody, MA: Hendrickson, 2004.

Irons, Charles Lee. *The Righteousness of God: A Lexical Examination of the Covenant-Faithfulness Interpretation.* WUNT 2.386. Tübingen: Mohr Siebeck, 2015.

Jewett, Robert. *Romans: A Commentary.* Hermeneia. Minneapolis: Fortress, 2007.

Lincicum, David. *Paul and the Early Jewish Encounter with Deuteronomy.* WUNT 2.284. Tübingen: Mohr Siebeck, 2010.

Meyer, Jason C. *The End of the Law: Mosaic Covenant in Pauline Theology.* NACSBT. Nashville: Broadman & Holman, 2009.

Moo, Douglas J. *The Letter to the Romans.* 2nd ed. NICNT. Grand Rapids: Eerdmans, 2018.

Motyer, J. Alec. *The Prophecy of Isaiah: An Introduction and Commentary.* Downers Grove, IL: IVP Academic, 1993.

Ortlund, Dane C. *Zeal Without Knowledge: The Concept of Zeal in Romans 10, Galatians 1, and Philippians 3.* LNTS 472. New York: T&T Clark, 2021.

Rosner, Brian S. *Paul and the Law: Keeping the Commandments of God.* NSBT 31. Downers Grove, IL: IVP Academic, 2013.

Schreiner, Thomas R. *Romans.* 2nd ed. BECNT. Grand Rapids: Baker Academic, 2018.

———. "'Works of the Law' in Paul." *NovT* 33.3 (1991): 217–44.

Sprinkle, Preston M. *Law and Life: The Interpretation of Leviticus 18:5 in Early Judaism and in Paul.* WUNT 2.241. Tübingen: Mohr Siebeck, 2008.

Thielman, Frank. *Paul and the Law: A Contextual Approach.* Downers Grove, IL: InterVarsity Press, 1994.

———. *Romans.* ZECNT 6. Grand Rapids: Zondervan Academic, 2018.

Wagner, J. Ross. *Heralds of the Good News: Isaiah and Paul in Concert in the Letter to the Romans.* NovTSup 101. Leiden: Brill, 2003.

Watson, Francis. *Paul and the Hermeneutics of Faith.* 2nd ed. New York: T&T Clark, 2016.

CHAPTER 17

Revisiting Romans 11:26: The Salvation of the Elect of Ethnic Israel

Benjamin L. Merkle

This chapter is titled "Revisiting Romans 11:26" because this is not the first time I have addressed this topic. In 2000 I published "Romans 11 and the Future of Ethnic Israel"[1] and more than a decade and a half later, I was asked to contribute to a *Three Views* book on the same topic. My chapter was titled, "A Typological, Non-Future–Mass-Conversion View."[2] My purpose here is to summarize my position, offering ten reasons why I still hold to this view. But first I will briefly state my position in relation to other positions.

In contrast to the views that affirm either a future mass-conversion of ethnic Israel or that by "Israel" Paul is referring to all the elect, both Jew and Gentile, my view is that "all Israel" represents the elect of ethnic Israel throughout history. That is, when Paul writes that "all Israel will be saved" (Rom 11:26), he is not predicting a future time when the majority of ethnic Jews will embrace Jesus as the Messiah and be saved. Instead, Paul's point is that God will never completely forsake the nation of Israel but that there will always be a remnant of believing Jews throughout history. Israel will experience only a *partial* hardening until the end of time (i.e., until the fullness of the Gentiles comes in). They will never be *fully* hardened and rejected from the salvation offered in the Messiah. Thus, the sum-total of all the elect remnant throughout history represents the salvation of "all Israel." Although not the majority view, there continues to be a (growing) remnant who embrace it.[3]

---

1. Ben L. Merkle, "Romans 11 and the Future of Ethnic Israel," *JETS* 43 (2000): 709–21.

2. Benjamin L. Merkle, "A Typological, Non-Future–Mass-Conversion View," in *Three Views on Israel and the Church: Perspectives on Romans 9–11*, ed. Jared Compton and Andrew David Naselli (Grand Rapids: Kregel, 2018), 161–208 (see also pages 85–96, 151–60). Although unique in its arrangement, this current essay is heavily dependent on the two essays listed above.

3. Those who hold this view include Herman Bavinck, *The Last Things*, trans. John Vriend (Grand Rapids: Baker Books, 1996), 104–7; G. K. Beale, *A New Testament Biblical Theology: The Unfolding of the Old Testament in the New* (Grand Rapids: Baker Academic, 2011), 710; Louis Berkhof, *Systematic Theology* (Grand Rapids: Eerdmans, 1994), 699–700; Christopher R. Bruno, "The Deliverer from Zion: The Source(s) and Function of Paul's Citation in Romans 11:26–27," *TynBul* 59 (2008): 119–34; William

Romans 9–11 Should Be Taken as a
Consistent and Coherent Whole.

All acknowledge that Rom 9–11 forms a unit in Paul's thought. Therefore, any interpretation of Rom 11 must also be consistent with Romans 9 and 10. Whether these three chapters function as an excursus, the climax,[4] or, as I prefer, an integral step that continues Paul's argument, it is crucial to honor the unity and consistency of this passage.

At the end of Rom 8, Paul unequivocally affirms God's sovereignty and benevolence in the life of the believer. But all these grandiose promises are called into question if God is not able or willing to deliver on them. Andrew Das rightly identifies the problem: "If God is so faithful to the elect in Christ, of what value is God's prior election to ethnic Israel? Were not all these blessings originally Israel's? . . . How can Christians find solace in their special place of election by God when God's historic, elect people are not benefiting from their blessings?"[5]

Thus, beginning in chapter 9 Paul addresses the question of God's faithfulness to his promises. If God made promises to the people of Israel but did not deliver on those promises, what kind of assurance do believers have regarding his promises to them? Romans 9–11, then, vindicates God's righteousness and faithfulness regarding his covenantal promises to Israel.[6] I agree with Hafemann that God's faithfulness is the central theme of Romans 9–11.[7] But Paul's

---

Hendriksen, *Exposition of Paul's Letter to the Romans* (Grand Rapids: Baker Academic, 1981), 359–85; Anthony A. Hoekema, *The Bible and the Future* (Grand Rapids: Eerdmans, 1979), 139–47; Charles Horne, "The Meaning of the Phrase 'And Thus All Israel Will Be Saved' (Romans 11:26)," *JETS* 21.4 (1978): 329–34; Colin G. Kruse, *Paul's Letter to the Romans*, Pillar New Testament Commentary (Grand Rapids: Eerdmans, 2012), 441–44, 448–51; Robert L. Reymond, *Paul: Missionary Theologian* (Fearn, Scotland: Mentor, 2000), 539–48; Herman Ridderbos, *Paul: An Outline of His Theology*, trans. John R. De Witt (Grand Rapids: Eerdmans, 1975), 354–61; O. Palmer Robertson, *The Israel of God: Yesterday, Today, and Tomorrow* (Phillipsburg, NJ: P&R Publishing, 2000), 167–92; Sam Storms, *Kingdom Come: An Amillennial Alternative* (Fearn, Scotland: Mentor, 2013), 303–34.

4. Excursus: C. H. Dodd, *The Epistle of Paul to the Romans* (London: Hodder & Stoughton, 1949), 148–50. Climax: James D. G. Dunn, *Romans 1–8*, WBC 38A (Dallas: Word, 1988), lxii; N. T. Wright, *The Climax of the Covenant* (Minneapolis: Fortress, 1991), 246; A. Andrew Das, *Paul and the Jews*, LPS (Peabody, MA: Hendrickson, 2003), 86.

5. Das, *Paul and the Jews*, 82. See also Paul J. Achtemeier, *Romans*, IBC (Louisville: Westminster John Knox, 1985), 153–54; James D. G. Dunn, *Romans 9–16*, WBC 38B (Dallas: Word, 1988), 530.

6. See Wright, *The Climax of the Covenant*, 234, 236; Joseph A. Fitzmyer, *Romans*, AB (New York: Doubleday, 1993), 559; David E. Holwerda, *Jesus and Israel: One Covenant or Two?* (Grand Rapids: Eerdmans, 1995), 153.

7. Scott Hafemann states, "The central issue in Romans 9–11 is whether God's faithfulness to himself and to his promised redemptive, saving activity can be maintained in spite of Israel's rejection of Jesus" (Scott Hafemann, "The Salvation of Israel in Romans

answer to the question of God's faithfulness should be seen as consistently answered through the entire passage.

Romans 9–11 Consistently Refers to Ethnic Jews.

I have no theological problem with a typological correlation between Israel and the church. In fact, in Gal 6:16, I think Gentile Christians are included in Paul's reference to the "Israel of God." Furthermore, I think that the 144,000 from the twelve tribes of Israel in Revelation are symbolic of the church (Rev 7:4–8; 14:1–5). But I do not believe that Paul uses the term "Israel" to represent the church in 11:26. Just because Paul *can* use the term "Israel" (or terms associated with Israel) as a designation for the church, this does not mean he *always* uses the term in this way.

So, I want to distinguish my view from those who maintain that "all Israel" refers to all of God's people, Jews and Gentiles.[8] I disagree with them that when Paul states, "And in this way all Israel will be saved," he is offering a "polemical redefinition" of the term so that "Israel" also includes believing Gentiles (i.e., the church).[9]

In Rom 9–11 the term "Israel" is used 11 times (9:6 [2x], 27 [2x], 31; 10:19, 21; 11:2, 7, 25) and the term "Israelite(s)" is used twice (9:4; 11:1). In every use it consistently refers to an ethnic group. Furthermore, Paul wishes he could be accursed for the sake of his "brothers," his "kinsmen according to the flesh" (9:3). Israel is "beloved for the sake of their forefathers" (11:28). Thus, the entire

---

11:25–32: A Response to Krister Stendahl," *ExAud* 4 [1988]: 43; see also Thomas R. Schreiner, *Romans*, BECNT [Grand Rapids: Baker Academic, 1998], 471).

8. See John Calvin, *Commentary on the Epistle to the Romans*, trans. John King (Grand Rapids: Baker Books, 1993), 437; Wright, *The Climax of the Covenant*, 249–50; N. T. Wright, "The Letter to the Romans: Introduction, Commentary, and Reflections," in *The New Interpreter's Bible*, ed. Leander E. Keck (Nashville: Abingdon, 2002), 10:689; N. T. Wright, *Paul and the Faithfulness of God*, COQG 4 (Minneapolis: Fortress, 2013), 1242–43; Charles Lee Irons, "Paul's Theology of Israel's Future: A Nonmillennial Interpretation of Romans 11," *Reformation and Revival* 6.2 (1997): 101–26. See also Philip E. Hughes, "The Olive Tree of Romans XI," *EvQ* 20 (1948): 44–45; Karl Barth, *The Epistle to the Romans*, trans. Edwyn C. Hoskyns (London: Oxford University Press, 1968), 415–16; Ralph P. Martin, *Reconciliation: A Study of Paul's Theology* (Atlanta: John Knox, 1981), 134; Hervé Ponsot, "Et Ainsi Tout Israel Sera Sauvé: Rom., XI, 26a," *RB* 89 (1982): 406–17. Robertson later endorsed this view in *The Israel of God*, 187–92.

9. Wright calls Paul's use of "Israel" a "polemical redefinition" consistent with Paul's redefinition of "Jew" (Rom 2:29), "circumcision" (Rom 2:29; Phil 3:3), and "seed of Abraham" (Rom 4; 9:6–9; Gal 3) ("Romans," 690; Wright, *Paul and the Faithfulness of God*, 1242–43). Irons similarly maintains that "the reference in verse 26 to 'all Israel' should be interpreted as a Pauline redefinition of the concept of 'Israel' in light of the great mystery that has been revealed in the person and work of the Lord Jesus Christ" ("Paul's Theology of Israel's Future," 102).

purpose of Paul's discussion centers on the fate of his fellow Jews. It would be altogether unexpected at the end of Rom 9–11 for Paul to introduce the same term with a different referent.[10] Thus, the context of Rom 9–11 strongly argues *against* the view that "Israel" is a designation for the church. Rather, throughout Rom 9–11, Paul is referring to ethnic Jews.

Romans 9–11 Paradigmatically Uses 9:6 and the Concept of Two Israels.

Correctly understanding the meaning of 9:6 is the key to correctly interpreting 11:26. God is not unfaithful to his promises to Israel regarding their salvation. Why? "For not all Israel is Israel" (9:6). That is, not every physical Israelite receives God's promises. Notice that Paul uses the term "Israel" with two different, yet overlapping, referents. The first group refers to all physical Israelites (Israel[A]), whereas the second group denotes a smaller sub-group of Israelites who are heirs of God's promises (Israel[B]). God never promised Abraham that all his descendants would be saved based on their ethnic identity. True Israel consists of those who are the children of promise, not the children of the flesh. God never promised that every individual Jew would be saved but only those he unconditionally elected within Israel. In Isaac, not in Ishmael, Abraham's descendants were named (9:7); and it was Jacob, not Esau, in whom the covenant promises were to be fulfilled (9:10–13).

God is not unfaithful to his promises. Why? God never promised to save every ethnic Jew but only an elect remnant.[11] Charles Horne comments, "If Paul is speaking in 11:26 of a future mass-conversion of the nation of Israel, then he is destroying the entire development of his argument in chaps. 9–11. For the one important point that he is trying to establish constantly is exactly this: that God's promises attain fulfillment not in the nation as such (that

---

10. Additionally, one wonders if Gentiles would misuse such a redefinition. As Moo put it, "For Paul in this context to call the church 'Israel' would be to fuel the fire of the Gentiles' arrogance by giving them grounds to brag that 'we are the true Israel'" (Douglas J. Moo, *The Letter to the Romans*, 2nd ed., NICNT [Grand Rapids: Eerdmans, 2018], 721).

11. But if that is the answer to this apparent dilemma, then why do some feel that such an answer is insufficient? If God never promised to save all ethnic Jews or at least all ethnic Jews living at one time, then why would Paul change his initial response and state that God will indeed save all ethnic Jews in the future (even though such an approach has never been God's *modus operandi*)? E.g., Das maintains that Rom 9:6 is only Paul's "first attempt" at resolving the problem of God's elect people not benefiting from their elect status, and that in Rom 11:25–32 Paul "reaches a very different conclusion" (*Paul and the Jews*, 88–89). He later calls Paul's conclusion a "sudden and powerful reversal of the course of [his] argument" (96).

is, all of ethnic Israel) but rather in the remnant according to the election of grace."[12]

In 11:7 Paul uses different terms to make the same division: "The elect [Israel[B]] obtained it, but the rest [Israel[A]] were hardened." Those who are described as "the rest" represent the majority (Israel[A]) whereas "the elect" represent the faithful "remnant" (Israel[B]) (11:5). In 11:25–26, this same pattern is repeated (nation and the elect within the nation): "a partial hardening has come upon Israel . . . And in this way all Israel will be saved." Some, however, are convinced that it is not probable that Paul uses "Israel" with two different referents in the space of two sentences.[13]

But there is no reason why Paul could not shift the meaning, especially when we consider the key text, 9:6. In the *same sentence*, Paul undoubtedly uses the term "Israel" with two different (but overlapping) referents: "Not all Israel (the nation) is Israel (the elect within the nation)." This is precisely the pattern in 11:25–26. N. T. Wright explains: "It is impermissible to argue that 'Israel' cannot change its referent within the space of two verses, so that 'Israel' in v.25 must mean the same as 'Israel' in v.26: Paul actually began the whole section (9.6) with just such a programmatic distinction of two 'Israels.'"[14]

Romans 9–11 Declares That Israel Stumbled But Did Not Fall.

Paul opens chapter 11 with a question: "Has God rejected his people?" (11:1). This question *in no way* anticipates a future restoration of Israel. Rather, Paul is asking whether God has *completely* rejected his covenant people. His answer, of course, is "By no means!" (μὴ γένοιτο, 11:1). God has not totally rejected his people because God always has an elect remnant, even when it appears that all have forsaken him. Thus, Paul uses himself (11:1b) and Elijah (11: 2–4) as examples. In verse 11 Paul rephrases the question found in verse 1: "So I ask,

---

12. Charles Horne, "The Meaning of the Phrase 'And Thus All Israel Will Be Saved,'" 333; see also Bavinck, *The Last Things*, 105. Wright addresses the same dilemma: "The problem about the content of Romans 9–11 then becomes one of *integration*. Put simply, the issue is this: if Paul rejects the possibility of a status of special privilege for Jews in chs. 9 and 10, how does he manage, apparently, to reinstate such a position in ch. 11?" (*The Climax of the Covenant*, 236).

13. C. E. B. Cranfield comments, "It is not feasible to understand [Israel] in v. 26 in a different sense from that which it has in v. 25" (*A Critical and Exegetical Commentary on the Epistle to the Romans*, 2 vols., ICC [Edinburgh: T&T Clark, 1975–79], 2:576). See also Moo, *Romans*, 722; and Schreiner, *Romans*, 615.

14. Wright, *The Climax of the Covenant*, 250; Robertson likewise states, "The fact that in this view the term *Israel* is used in two different ways in consecutive verses (Rom 11:25–26) should not be disturbing. When Paul says in Romans 9:6 that 'they are not all Israel that are Israel,' he is using the term *Israel* with two different meanings in a single verse" (*The Israel of God*, 186).

did they stumble in order that they might fall?" His answer is the same, "By no means!" Again, this question does not presuppose the reversal of Israel's fortune in the future. Paul is asking if God has *completely* and *utterly* rejected his covenant people.

Some wrongly read v. 11 as if Israel has fallen (now) but that their fallen state is only temporary and not permanent. Michael Vlach states, "Paul's emphatic 'May it never be!' (11:11b) emphatically reveals that Israel's stumbling is not a permanent fall. A reversal is coming."[15] Zaspel and Hamilton declare, "Israel has fallen, but not forever."[16]

But Paul clearly and emphatically states that Israel has *not* fallen: "did they stumble so as to fall? May it never be!" (11:11). Paul asks whether Israel's refusal of the Messiah (their "stumbling") constitutes a complete rejection from God's saving purposes ("fall"). His answer is emphatically "No!" (μὴ γένοιτο). In other words, Israel did *not* stumble so as to fall. They did stumble, but their stumbling did not result in them falling. Although the majority of Israel has stumbled and has not embraced God's Messiah, they did not fall from God's saving purposes. Paul is asking whether Israel is completely out, and the answer he provides is "absolutely not." They are not out of the race. God has not completely rejected them. There is no hint of a reversal of Israel's fortunes since Paul's answer is that they did not fall.

Romans 9–11 Is Speaking Primarily about Paul's Present, Not the Future.

Romans 9–11 (especially ch. 11) focuses on the present, not the future. In answer to the question in 11:1, Paul offers himself as proof that God has not rejected his people: "For I myself am an Israelite, a descendant of Abraham, a member of the tribe of Benjamin" (11:1). Hendriksen paraphrases: "Does anyone need proof that God fulfills his promise and has not rejected Israel? Well, then look at me. God did not reject me, and I am an Israelite."[17]

Verse 5 gives further evidence that the present is at the forefront of Paul's reasoning: "So too *at the present time* there is a remnant, chosen by grace" (emphasis added). In the preceding verses Paul illustrates his point with the example

---

15. Michael J. Vlach, "A Non-Typological Future-Mass-Conversion view," in *Three Views on Israel and the Church: Perspectives on Romans 9–11*, ed. Jared Compton and Andrew David Naselli (Grand Rapids: Kregel, 2018), 40.

16. Fred G. Zaspel and James M. Hamilton, Jr., "A Typological Future-Mass-Conversion View," in *Three Views on Israel and the Church: Perspectives on Romans 9–11*, ed. Jared Compton and Andrew David Naselli (Grand Rapids: Kregel, 2018), 108. They continue, "Israel has fallen, but God's ultimate purpose for it is not its fall but its recovery" (112).

17. Hendriksen, *Romans*, 361.

of Elijah. Just as in Elijah's day there was a remnant, so now there is a remnant within Israel. God did not reject his people during the days of Elijah and has not done so now. Paul's point is *not* that God has rejected his people temporarily, and in the future will once again show mercy to them. Rather, his point is that just as God did not reject Israel in the past (but preserved a faithful remnant as in the days of Elijah), so too God has not rejected his people during Paul's day.

Verses 13–14 further support this conclusion: "Now I am speaking to you Gentiles. Inasmuch then as I am an apostle to the Gentiles, *I magnify my ministry* in order somehow to make my fellow Jews jealous, and thus save some of them" (emphasis added). Paul's hope of provoking the Jews to jealousy does not imply a future mass-conversion since he uses his own ministry as the means of provocation. That is, Paul's hope for the salvation of "some of them" comes through his own ministry. The principle that a "remnant" will remain throughout every age is the basis for Paul's hope that "some" would be saved during his ministry.

Finally, verses 30–31 support the thesis that Paul is concerned with the present more than with the future: The Gentiles "now" receive mercy whereas Israel "now" is disobedient although some of Israel "now" receives mercy. Although the final "now" is textually debated, most commentators favor its inclusion.[18] Romans 11 focuses on the present, not the future.

Romans 9–11 Does Not Imply a Reversal of Israel's Fate.

In 11:12 Paul declares, "Now if their [Israel^A] trespass means riches for the world, and if their [Israel^A] failure means riches for the Gentiles, how much more will their [Israel^B] full inclusion mean!" Verse 15 parallels v. 12: "For if their [Israel^A] rejection means the reconciliation of the world, what will their [Israel^B] acceptance mean but life from the dead?" Those who interpret 11:26 as referring to a future mass-conversion of ethnic Israel state that Israel's "trespass," "failure," and "rejection" refer to the present time, whereas their "full inclusion" and "acceptance" refer to a time yet to come. Currently, Israel is rejecting Christ, but the time will come when they accept Christ and will be saved.[19]

The above interpretation is not without its difficulties. First, it is often assumed that Paul is speaking temporally: Israel's trespass, failure, and rejection are happening now, but their acceptance is in the future. Instead, I would

---

18. See Robert Jewett, *Romans: A Commentary*, Hermeneia (Minneapolis: Fortress, 2007), 694; and Richard Bell, *Provoked to Jealousy: The Origin and Purpose of the Jealousy Motif in Romans 9–11* (Tübingen: Mohr Siebeck, 1994), 149n233, who cites various scholars who include the third νῦν as authentic. See also Bruce M. Metzger, *A Textual Commentary on the Greek New Testament*, 2nd ed. (Stuttgart: United Bible Societies, 1994), 465.

19. See Cranfield, *Romans*, 2:577; Dunn, *Romans 9–16*, 668; Schreiner, *Romans*, 597–99.

propose that we understand Paul's statement to coincide with 9:6 and the paradigmatic use of the two Israels: Israel[A] (the nation) is rejecting now, but Israel[B] (the elect remnant within the nation) is accepting now. Second, the ESV cited above is interpretive when it translates πλήρωμα as "full inclusion" (v. 12).[20] A more form-based translation of v. 12 is "how much more their fullness [πλήρωμα]." To translate πλήρωμα as "full inclusion" biases one to the future mass-conversion view. Third, there is no clear evidence in this passage that "fullness" refers to a future event when Israel returns to their God. One clue to the meaning of "fullness" is in v. 25 where Paul speaks of the "fullness" of the Gentiles. Since virtually every scholar interprets "the fullness of the Gentiles" as the full number of elect Gentiles throughout history,[21] is it not also likely that the "fullness" of Israel refers to the full number of elect Jews throughout history? Colin Kruse writes, "In light of the use of 'fullness' in respect to the Gentiles in 11:25 we are justified in concluding that Israel's 'full inclusion' means the full number of believing Jews, which will be made up when those yet to believe are added to the remnant that already believe."[22]

Romans 9–11 Does Not Promise a Future Ingrafting of the Nation of Israel.

Paul states in 11:23, "And even they [Israel[B]], if [ἐάν] they do not continue in their [Israel[B]] unbelief, will be grafted in." Those who affirm a special future for Israel claim that Paul teaches that a great majority of ethnic Israelites will be grafted into the tree of salvation.[23] This interpretation has a couple of fatal errors. First, Paul's primary purpose for using this metaphor is to warn the Gentiles of pride; they are not the natural branches. In other words, this metaphor does not demonstrate that in the future Israel will be grafted back into the olive tree; it cautions the Gentiles not to become arrogant. Second, nowhere does Paul state or even imply that God is going to graft *all* unbelieving Jews back into the tree. Rather, he states that *those who believe* will be grafted into

---

20. Cf. NLT: "how much greater a blessing the world will share when they finally accept it [i.e., God's offer of salvation]."

21. For example, Cranfield comments that the phrase *fullness of the Gentiles* "is probably to be explained as the meaning of the full number of the elect from among the Gentiles" (*Romans*, 2:575). See also Moo, *Romans*, 719; Schreiner, *Romans*, 598–99; Kruse, *Romans*, 428, 443.

22. Kruse, *Romans*, 428–29. Wright maintains, "There is no reason to suppose that 'the fullness' of Israel will mean anything more than this: the complete number of Jews, many more than at present, who likewise come to faith in the gospel" ("Romans," 681).

23. See John M. G. Barclay, *Paul and the Gift* (Grand Rapids: Eerdmans, 2015), 554; Cranfield, *Romans*, 2:577; Das, *Paul and the Jews*, 109; Jason C. Meyer, *The End of the Law: Mosaic Covenant in Pauline Theology*, NACSBT (Nashville: Broadman & Holman, 2009), 175, 179; Schreiner, *Romans*, 617.

the olive tree. In fact, Paul prefaces his statement with a third-class conditional clause. If God can graft in the wild branches, certainly he can do the same with the natural branches. Paul does not prophesy or predict that God will graft the unbelieving nation *as a whole* back into the tree of salvation. Rather, he is stating that whenever individual Jews have genuine faith in Jesus the Messiah, they will be grafted back in.

Romans 9–11 Demonstrates a Redemptive-Historical Relationship between Jews and Gentiles.

Those who reject my position often state that the mystery that Paul speaks of is no longer a mystery if Paul is only declaring that all the elect Jews will be saved.[24] But Paul is not simply asserting *that* all elect Israel will be saved; he is speaking of the *manner* ("and in this way/manner") in which God will save them. What then is the nature of this mystery? It likely involves the interdependence of the salvation of the Gentiles and Israel. Ridderbos explains that this mystery involves "the strange interdependence of the salvation of Israel and that of the gentiles. . . . God grants no mercy to Israel without the gentiles, but neither does he do so to the gentiles without Israel." [25]

I shall address two other questions related to 11:25. First, what does Paul mean when he states that Israel is experiencing a "partial hardening" (πώρωσις ἀπὸ μέρους)? The noun "hardening" (πώρωσις) is a cognate of the verb "were hardened" (from πωρόω) in 11:7, where Paul contrasts "the elect" of Israel who obtain salvation with "the rest" who were hardened (ἐπωρώθησαν). As in v. 7, in v. 25 Paul is speaking quantitatively ("in part") and not temporally ("for a while"). In other words, this verse does *not* mean "for a while hardening has happened to Israel," but "part of Israel is hardened." By a "partial hardening" Paul does not mean that all of Israel is only partially hardened, but that some are fully hardened while the elect remnant is being saved. In no way does the phrase suggest that God intends to initiate a special dispensation for Israel in the future.

---

24. E.g., John Murray argues, "That all the elect will be saved does not have the particularity that 'mystery' in this instance involves" (*The Epistle to the Romans*, 2 vols., NICNT [Grand Rapids: Eerdmans, 1959–65], 2:97). Michael Vanlaningham argues, "If 'all Israel' is simply the elect from ethnic Israel who are saved along with the Gentiles throughout the age, special revelation to Paul in the form of a *mysterion* (v. 25) is pointless" ("Romans 11:25–27 and the Future of Israel in Paul's Thought," *MSJ* 3 [1992]: 160). See also Cranfield, *Romans*, 2:576; Schreiner, *Romans*, 617.

25. Ridderbos, *Paul*, 359–60. See also Hendriksen, *Romans*, 378; Robertson, *The Israel of God*, 182n9; Wright, *The Climax of the Covenant*, 249; Storms, *Kingdom Come*, 329–30). Beale and Gladd argue that the mystery is the reversal of the order of salvation from Jew first, then Gentile to Gentile first, then Jew (G. K. Beale and Benjamin L. Gladd, *Hidden but Now Revealed: A Biblical Theology of Mystery* [Downers Grove, IL: InterVarsity Press, 2014], 89).

Second, what is the meaning of "until the fullness of the Gentiles has come in"? Those who affirm a future mass-conversion of Jews interpret this phrase to mean that Israel is currently hardened, but their hardened status will change when God turns from saving the Gentiles to saving Israel. When this shift takes place, an unprecedented number of Jews will put their faith in Christ. But is that the most natural way to read this phrase ("until," ἄχρις οὗ)?

This phrase is essentially terminative in its significance, implying the end of something. Yet only the context can determine where the emphasis lies after the termination. Often the phrase occurs in an eschatological context where the termination implies eschatological fulfillment and not an eschatological reversal.[26] In 1 Cor 11:26 Paul states that the church is to partake of the Lord's Supper and thus proclaim the Lord's death "until" (ἄχρις οὗ) he comes. Paul's purpose is not to stress that one day the church will not celebrate the Lord's Supper. Instead, his point is that this celebration will continue "until" the end of time. First Corinthians 15:25 states that Christ must reign "until" (ἄχρις οὗ) he has put all enemies under his feet. The intended stress is not that a time will come when Christ will no longer reign, but that he must continue to reign until the last enemy is conquered at the final judgment.[27]

Likewise, the partial hardening of Israel that will occur "until" the fullness of the Gentiles comes in refers to an eschatological termination.[28] Paul is not suggesting a time when the hardening will be reversed but a time when the hardening will be eschatologically fulfilled.

Romans 9–11 Demonstrates That the Mystery Does Not Include a Future Mass-Conversion.

The climax of the mystery is v. 26a: "And in this way all Israel will be saved." What is the meaning of οὕτως ("thus, so")? Although a temporal ("and *then* all Israel will be saved")[29] or logical ("and *in consequence of this process* [v. 25b]

---

26. So Robertson, *The Israel of God*, 178–80; Reymond, *Paul*, 546; Marten H. Woudstra, "Israel and the Church: A Case for Continuity," in *Continuity and Discontinuity: Perspectives on the Relationship between the Old and New Testaments*, ed. John S. Feinberg (Wheaton, IL: Crossway, 1988), 236.

27. See also Luke 21:44; Acts 7:18; 27:33; Gal 3:19; Heb 3:13; and Rev 2:25, where ἄχρι(ς) οὗ) occurs, and Matt 24:38; Acts 22:4; and Heb 4:12, where only ἄχρι occurs.

28. Joachim Jeremias states, "Actually, in the New Testament ἄχρι οὗ with the aorist subjunctive without ἄν regularly introduces a reference to reaching the eschatological goal, Rom 11.25; 1 Cor 15.25; Luke 21.24." *The Eucharistic Words of Jesus* (New York: Scribner's Sons, 1966), 253.

29. *Temporal:* Hardening has happened to part of Israel "until" the fullness of the Gentiles has come in; but *then after that*, all Israel will be saved. The NEB apparently follows this popular, but little supported, rendering by translating it, "when that has happened, all Israel will be saved." But οὕτως rarely, if ever, has temporal significance (BDAG does not even list a temporal use). For an attempt to justify the temporal mean-

all Israel will be saved")[30] meaning might be possible, most scholars opt for the modal usage (*"in this manner*, all Israel will be saved").

But this reading does not settle the interpretive debate since the "manner" comes from the context (vv. 11–24, which v. 25 summarizes).[31] Although argued by some,[32] the context does not support a temporal reference for οὕτως. If οὕτως has a (future) temporal reference, then Paul is claiming that the salvation of "all Israel" takes place after the salvation of every elect Gentile. Presumably, there are Gentile nations in that period, but not a single person from among them turns to the Lord.[33] Furthermore, if "all" means a great number of Jews at the end of time, does that interpretation do justice to the meaning of "all"? It would in fact include only a small fraction of Jews, which is not as climactic as it might first appear.[34] Finally, a future mass-conversion of Israel is completely absent, not only in the rest of Paul's writings,[35] but in the rest of the New Testament.

Romans 9–11 Focuses on the First Coming, Not the Second Coming.

After Paul states "And in this way all Israel will be saved," he quotes Isa 59:20–21a in 11:26–27a and Isa 27:9 in 11:27b: "The Deliverer will come from Zion, he

---

ing, see Pieter W. van der Horst, "'Only Then Will All Israel Be Saved': A Short Note on the Meaning of καὶ οὕτως in Romans 11:26," *JBL* 119 (2000): 521–39. He suggests that Acts 7:8; 20:11; 27:17; and 1 Thess 4:16–17 support the temporal usage of οὕτως. Those four examples are debated (see Wright, *Paul and the Faithfulness of God*, 1240n677). In addition, the term οὕτως occurs 208 times in the NT, and therefore, his four debated examples are far from convincing. Thus, Das incorrectly claims that the temporal interpretation "is equally plausible" as the modal interpretation (*Paul and the Jews*, 117).

30. *Logical:* There are a few cases in Paul where οὕτως has a logical sense (Rom 1:15; 6:11; 1 Cor 14:25; 1 Thess 4:17). See Otfried Hofius, "'All Israel Will Be Saved': Divine Salvation in Romans 9–11," *PSB 11*, Suppl 1 (1990): 35.

31. Although it is possible that the manner is found in what follows (i.e., the quote from Isa 59:20–21), this interpretation is not likely because the pairing of οὕτως with "as it is written" (καθὼς γέγραπται) is never found in Paul (see Moo, *Romans*, 720). The position that οὕτως refers to what follows is held by BDAG s.v. οὕτως (742); Peter Stuhlmacher, *Paul's Letter to the Romans: A Commentary*, trans. Scott J. Hafemann (Louisville: Westminster John Knox, 1994), 172.

32. Moo, *Romans*, 720; see also Bell, *Provoked to Jealousy*, 136; Cranfield, *Romans*, 2:576; Schreiner, *Romans*, 621.

33. Bavinck clarifies the difficulty of the position: "Is there, then a lapse of time between the coming of the *plērōma* from the Gentile world and the end of the ages? If so, are there still Gentile nations in that period and is there not a single person from among them that turns to the Lord?" (*The Last Things*, 107).

34. See Kruse, *Romans*, 443; Robertson, *The Israel of God*, 183; Wright, "Romans," 689; Irons, "Paul's Theology of Israel's Future," 121. Schreiner rightly notes that a future mass-conversion of Jews "is still the salvation of only a remnant of Israel throughout history" (*Romans*, 622).

35. Moo comments, "Paul's teaching about a final ingathering of Jewish people has no parallel elsewhere in his writings" (*Romans*, 739).

will banish ungodliness from Jacob; and this will be my covenant with them when I take away their sins."[36] Some argue that Paul is referring to the second coming of Christ because he uses the future tense: "The Deliverer *will come* [ἥξει] from Zion."[37] But the question is whether or not *Paul* understood it as future. Certainly, it was future from the perspective of Isaiah, but when Paul quotes the passage, he is quoting it because he sees it as past.[38]

Those who maintain that Paul is referring to the second coming often insist that "Zion" means "heavenly Zion."[39] But in Isaiah's context, Zion is earthly, not heavenly.[40] It is also assumed that Paul's reference to Christ as the "Deliverer" (ὁ ῥυόμενος) presupposes the second coming since that term is associated with Christ's return in 1 Thess 1:10 ("Jesus who delivers [τὸν ῥυόμενον] us from the wrath to come"). But this connection is not convincing since the term "deliverer" appears in a number of Pauline texts that do not refer to the second coming (Rom 7:24; 15:31; 2 Cor 1:10; Col 1:13). It is better to see Rom 11:26 as referring to Christ's first coming.[41]

The climax of redemptive history is the cross and resurrection of Christ. Chris Bruno states,

---

36. Paul's citation of Isaiah does not exactly follow the Septuagint. The most notable difference is that in Isaiah the Deliverer will come "for the sake of" Zion (ἕνεκεν; Heb. "to Zion"), but Paul writes that the Deliverer will come "out of" or "from" (ἐκ) Zion. Bruno suggests that Paul is intentionally alluding to Isa 2:3 ("For out of Zion [ἐκ Σιων, LXX] shall go the law, and the word of the LORD from Jerusalem") together with Isa 59:20–21 and Isa 27:9 ("The Deliverer from Zion," 119–34).

37. See Cranfield, *Romans*, 2:578; Dunn, *Romans 9–16*, 682–83, 692; Meyer, *The End of the Law*, 179, 183; Moo, *Romans*, 724, 728; Schreiner, *Romans*, 619–20; Stuhlmacher, *Romans*, 172–73; Hofius, "'All Israel Will Be Saved,'" 36; George Eldon Ladd, "Israel and the Church," *EvQ* 36 (1964): 212–13 (tentatively).

38. Bruno notes, "For Paul, the [first] coming of Christ marked the beginning of the eschatological era" ("The Deliverer from Zion," 127).

39. See, e.g., Barry E. Horner, *Future Israel: Why Christian Anti-Judaism Must Be Challenged*, NACSBT (Nashville: Broadman & Holman, 2007), 261; Meyer, *The End of the Law*, 183.

40. Bruno comments, "Throughout the book of Isaiah, Zion, although transformed from an immoral city, is consistently an *earthly* location. Paul's quotation reflects the original Isaiah context, and the original context of Zion in Isaiah 59 is clearly not an ethereal heavenly city, but a more tangible earthly location" ("The Deliverer from Zion," 127 [emphasis original]).

41. See Bruno, "The Deliverer from Zion," 119–34; Das, *Paul and the Jews*, 110; Hendriksen, *Romans*, 383; Hoekema, *The Bible and the Future*, 146; Holwerda, *Jesus and Israel*, 172–73; Reidar Hvalvik, "A 'Sonderweg' for Israel: A Critical Examination of a Current Interpretation of Romans 11.25–27," *JSNT* 38 (1990): 92–95; Marten, "Israel and the Church," 236; Kim Riddlebarger, *A Case for Amillennialism: Understanding the End Times* (Grand Rapids: Baker Books, 2003), 220–21; Reymond, *Paul*, 547; Robertson, "Is There a Distinctive Future for Ethnic Israel in Romans 11?," 226; Storms, *Kingdom Come*, 331; Wright, *The Climax of the Covenant*, 250–51.

The OT promises of salvation have been fulfilled through Christ; therefore, Paul views Isaiah 59 as an already fulfilled prophecy that is continuing to be applied to the people of God during his ministry (and beyond). Furthermore, the decisive removal of sin in Pauline theology was clearly accomplished in the death and resurrection of Christ.[42]

Andrew Das further explains,

Nowhere in Romans 11 does Paul connect the salvation of all Israel to Christ's Parousia or second coming. Paul does not even refer to the Parousia of Christ in Romans 9–11. In 11:26–27 he certainly speaks of a Deliverer who 'will come' out of Zion . . . but for Paul those prophecies have already been fulfilled. Christ came from Zion as the Jewish Messiah (9:5). God has already placed in Zion the stumbling stone (9:33). . . . The prophecies Paul cites in 11:26–27 were therefore fulfilled in Christ's *first* coming.[43]

Conclusion

Romans 9–11 does not teach or imply a future mass-conversion but that there will always be a remnant of believing Jews throughout history. God has not rejected or forsaken Israel; they have not fallen. But God has never promised to save all, only those who are children of the promise. Whenever individual Jews believe in the Messiah, they are grafted back into God's olive tree of salvation. But God's salvation of Israel is connected to the salvation of the Gentiles. And this is the mystery: God has not forsaken Israel since only part of them is hardened until the last Gentile has been saved. And that is how "all Israel" will be saved.

Bibliography

Achtemeier, Paul J. *Romans*. IBC. Louisville: Westminster John Knox, 1985.

Barclay, John M. G. *Paul and the Gift*. Grand Rapids: Eerdmans, 2015.

Barth, Karl. *The Epistle to the Romans*. Translated by Edwyn C. Hoskyns. London: Oxford University Press, 1968.

Bavinck, Herman. *The Last Things*. Translated by John Vriend. Grand Rapids: Baker Books, 1996.

Beale, G. K. *A New Testament Biblical Theology: The Unfolding of the Old Testament in the New*. Grand Rapids: Baker Academic, 2011.

Beale, G. K., and Benjamin L. Gladd. *Hidden but Now Revealed: A Biblical Theology of Mystery*. Downers Grove, IL: InterVarsity Press, 2014.

---

42. Bruno, "The Deliverer from Zion," 128.
43. Das, *Paul and the Jews*, 110.

Bell, Richard. *Provoked to Jealousy: The Origin and Purpose of the Jealousy Motif in Romans 9–11*. Tübingen: Mohr Siebeck, 1994.

Berkhof, Louis. *Systematic Theology*. Grand Rapids: Eerdmans, 1994.

Bruno, Christopher R. "The Deliverer from Zion: The Source(s) and Function of Paul's Citation in Romans 11:26–27." *TynBul* 59 (2008): 119–34.

Calvin, John. *Commentary on the Epistle to the Romans*. Translated by John King. Grand Rapids: Baker Books, 1993.

Cranfield, C. E. B. *A Critical and Exegetical Commentary on the Epistle to the Romans*. 2 vols. ICC. Edinburgh: T&T Clark, 1975–79.

Das, A. Andrew. *Paul and the Jews*. LPS. Peabody, MA: Hendrickson, 2003.

Dodd, C. H. *The Epistle of Paul to the Romans*. London: Hodder & Stoughton, 1949.

Dunn, James D. G. *Romans 1–8*, WBC 38A. Dallas: Word, 1988.

———. *Romans 9–16*. WBC 38B. Dallas: Word, 1988.

Fitzmyer, Joseph A. *Romans*. AB 33. New York: Doubleday, 1993.

Hafemann, Scott. "The Salvation of Israel in Romans 11:25–32: A Response to Krister Stendahl." *ExAud* 4 (1988): 38–58.

Hendriksen, William. *Exposition of Paul's Letter to the Romans*. Grand Rapids: Baker Academic, 1981.

Hoekema, Anthony A. *The Bible and the Future*. Grand Rapids: Eerdmans, 1979.

Hofius, Otfried. "'All Israel Will Be Saved': Divine Salvation in Romans 9–11." *PSB 11*, Suppl 1 (1990): 19–39.

Holwerda, David E. *Jesus and Israel: One Covenant or Two?* Grand Rapids: Eerdmans, 1995.

Horne, Charles. "The Meaning of the Phrase 'And Thus All Israel Will Be Saved' (Romans 11:26)." *JETS* 21.4 (1978): 329–34.

Horner, Barry E. *Future Israel: Why Christian Anti-Judaism Must Be Challenged*. NACSBT. Nashville: Broadman & Holman, 2007.

Hughes, Philip E. "The Olive Tree of Romans XI." *EvQ* 20 (1948): 44–45.

Hvalvik, Reidar. "A 'Sonderweg' for Israel: A Critical Examination of a Current Interpretation of Romans 11.25–27." *JSNT* 38 (1990): 87–107.

Irons, Charles Lee. "Paul's Theology of Israel's Future: A Nonmillennial Interpretation of Romans 11." *Reformation and Revival* 6.2 (1997): 101–26.

Jeremias, Joachim. *The Eucharistic Words of Jesus*. New York: Scribner's Sons, 1966.

Jewett, Robert. *Romans: A Commentary*. Hermeneia. Minneapolis: Fortress, 2007.

Kruse, Colin G. *Paul's Letter to the Romans*. PNTC. Grand Rapids: Eerdmans, 2012.

Ladd, George Eldon. "Israel and the Church." *EvQ* 36 (1964): 206–13.

Martin, Ralph P. *Reconciliation: A Study of Paul's Theology*. Atlanta: John Knox, 1981.

Merkle, Benjamin L. "Romans 11 and the Future of Ethnic Israel." *JETS* 43 (2000): 709–21.

———. "A Typological, Non-Future–Mass-Conversion View." Pages 161–208 in *Three Views on Israel and the Church: Perspectives on Romans 9–11.* Edited by Jared Compton and Andrew David Naselli. Grand Rapids: Kregel, 2018.

Metzger, Bruce M. *A Textual Commentary on the Greek New Testament.* 2nd ed. Stuttgart: United Bible Societies, 1994.

Meyer, Jason C. *The End of the Law: Mosaic Covenant in Pauline Theology*, NACSBT. Nashville: Broadman & Holman, 2009.

Moo, Douglas J. *The Letter to the Romans.* 2nd ed. NICNT. Grand Rapids: Eerdmans, 2018.

Murray, John. *The Epistle to the Romans.* 2 vols. NICNT. Grand Rapids: Eerdmans, 1959–65.

Ponsot, Hervé. "Et Ainsi Tout Israel Sera Sauvé: Rom., XI, 26a," *RB* 89 (1982): 406–17.

Reymond, Robert L. *Paul: Missionary Theologian.* Fearn, Scotland: Mentor, 2000.

Ridderbos, Herman. *Paul: An Outline of His Theology.* Translated by John R. De Witt. Grand Rapids: Eerdmans, 1975.

Riddlebarger, Kim. *A Case for Amillennialism: Understanding the End Times.* Grand Rapids: Baker Books, 2003.

Robertson, O. Palmer. *The Israel of God: Yesterday, Today, and Tomorrow.* Phillipsburg, NJ: P&R Publishing, 2000.

Schreiner, Thomas R. *Romans.* BECNT. Grand Rapids: Baker Academic, 1998.

Storms, Sam. *Kingdom Come: An Amillennial Alternative.* Fearn, Scotland: Mentor, 2013.

Stuhlmacher, Peter. *Paul's Letter to the Romans: A Commentary.* Translated by Scott J. Hafemann. NTL. Louisville: Westminster John Knox, 1994.

Van der Horst, Pieter W. "'Only Then Will All Israel Be Saved': A Short Note on the Meaning of καὶ οὕτως in Romans 11:26." *JBL* 119 (2000): 521–39.

Vanlaningham, Michael. "Romans 11:25–27 and the Future of Israel in Paul's Thought." *MSJ* 3 (1992): 141–74.

Vlach, Michael J. "A Non-Typological Future-Mass-Conversion view." Pages 21–74 in *Three Views on Israel and the Church: Perspectives on Romans 9–11.* Edited by Jared Compton and Andrew David Naselli. Grand Rapids: Kregel, 2018.

Woudstra, Marten H. "Israel and the Church: A Case for Continuity." Pages 221–38 in *Continuity and Discontinuity: Perspectives on the Relationship between the Old and New Testaments: Essays in Honor of S. Lewis Johnson, Jr.* Edited by John S. Feinberg. Wheaton, IL: Crossway, 1988.

Wright, N. T. *The Climax of the Covenant.* Minneapolis: Fortress, 1991.

—————. "The Letter to the Romans: Introduction, Commentary, and Reflections." Pages 395–770 in vol. 10 of *The New Interpreter's Bible*. Edited by Leander E. Keck. Nashville: Abingdon, 2002.

—————. *Paul and the Faithfulness of God*. COQG 4. Minneapolis: Fortress, 2013.

Zaspel, Fred G., and James M. Hamilton, Jr. "A Typological Future-Mass-Conversion View." Pages 97–140 in *Three Views on Israel and the Church: Perspectives on Romans 9–11*. Edited by Jared Compton and Andrew David Naselli. Grand Rapids: Kregel, 2018.

CHAPTER 18

Wrath and Justification: Proleptic Visitations of Last Day Judgment

Ardel B. Caneday

If the apostle Paul's proposition of Rom 1:16–17 entails a reference to God's righteous character in ἡ δικαιοσύνη τοῦ θεοῦ, it is no surprise that in 1:18, the law court imagery immediately begins to dominate his argument.[1] Also unsurprising is the dual role the apostle fills, comparable to Israel's prophets as he adjudicates his thesis concerning God's righteousness. First, he functions as God's *prosecuting attorney* and then as God's *defense attorney*, defending both God's character and his act of justifying sinners.

During initial readings of the Letter to the Romans, the significance of Paul's expression in 1:18 may elude notice. However, multiple readings prompt one to observe that Paul subtly employs linguistic conventions when he writes, "The wrath of God *is being revealed from heaven* against all human godlessness and unrighteousness" (Rom 1:18; ἀσέβεια, ἀδικία 2x). First, the passive voice, "God's wrath *is being revealed*," prepares readers to recognize that God displays his anger not only by actively pouring out his punitive wrath, as in the Day of Wrath, but also by retributively withdrawing his common grace.[2] Second, that Paul states, "God's wrath is being revealed *from heaven*," seems to convey two

---

1. If Rom 1:16–17 constitute the apostle Paul's thesis statement that he develops throughout his Letter to the Romans, surely, his assigned meaning of δικαιοσύνη θεοῦ depends for its reference upon his uses of the phrase throughout the letter. Thus, I contend that the decisive uses of δικαιοσύνη θεοῦ, which provide the meaning of the expression in Rom 1:17, are the apostle's uses of the phrases θεοῦ δικαιοσύνη and δικαιοσύνη αὐτοῦ in Rom 3, the first and concentrated uses of the phrase following his thesis statement. Paul's use of θεοῦ δικαιοσύνη in 3:5, juxtaposed with ἡ πίστις τοῦ θεοῦ (God's faithfulness) and ἡ ἀλήθεια τοῦ θεοῦ (God's truthfulness), unambiguously refers to God's character as righteous, "God's righteousness." Likewise, his two uses of ἡ δικαιοσύνη αὐτοῦ (his righteousness) in 3:25, 26, where αὐτοῦ stands in for θεοῦ, the reference unambiguously is to God's character. Hence, it is a mistake to insist that Paul uses δικαιοσύνη θεοῦ in 1:17 and 3:21–22 "to describe the activity by which God justifies people" but his uses in 3:5 and 3:25–26 "must mean something different than it does in vv. 21–22, where the process by which God justifies sinful people is designated" (Douglas J. Moo, *The Epistle to the Romans*, NICNT [Grand Rapids: Eerdmans, 1996], 190, 240).

2. The theme of divine revelation in Paul's Letter to the Romans is much too expansive to linger over within this brief presentation. On the theme of revelation in Romans, see Marcus A. Mininger, *Uncovering the Theme of Revelation in Romans 1:16–3:26:*

corollary implications concerning God's wrath: (1) the Day of God's wrath will be *inescapable*, but it is *not yet*, and (2) the Day of God's wrath *already* invades the present age but *obliquely*.

God "hands over" people to founder in their own pursuit of unreality as the consequence of their idolatrous rejection of him. He retributively withdraws from people to whom he has bequeathed knowledge of himself through all things he has made. Consequently, because they exchange the glory of the immortal God for images that resemble mortal humans, birds, animals, and creeping things, God exacerbates their idolatrous worship of the creature. Thus, three times God's prosecuting attorney announces, "God gave them over" (Διὸ παρέδωκεν αὐτοὺς ὁ θεὸς): first "in the lusts of their hearts to impurity" (1:24), (2) then "to dishonorable passions" (1:26), and finally "to a debased mind to do what ought not to be done" (1:28).[3] These three uses of παραδίδωμι, signaling divine judgment, anticipate three additional uses as Paul develops his thesis concerning God's righteousness, twice concerning Christ (4:25–5:1; 8:32) and once concerning God's redeemed people (6:17). Each bears implications concerning divine judgment but with the verdict of justification, not wrath.

Throughout his Letter to the Romans, Paul pivots between functioning as God's prosecuting and defense attorney. Initially, like Israel's prophets, he prosecutes God's stinging indictment, first against Gentiles who are "filled with all unrighteousness" and therefore worthy of death under God's wrath (1:29, 32). Jews do not escape this prophetic arraignment before God's "righteous judgment."[4] The apostle indicts them for presuming that mere possession of the law covenant and of circumcision assures their footing before God, apart from being "doers of the law" (2:1–29). Their pedigree, their possession of the law covenant, and their ritual circumcision will not avert God's inviolable criterion of judgment: "He will recompense every person according to one's deeds" (Rom 2:6). Incidental distinguishing features, including ethnicity, will protect no one because God's judgment is impartial.[5]

As he brings charges against Jews, Paul echoes Isaiah's indictment of Israel: "God's name is blasphemed among the Gentiles on account of you" (Rom 2:24; cf. Isa 52:5). As in the days of the prophet, Jews who blaspheme God's name remain exiled and alienated from God. While glorying in possessing ritual

---

Discovering a New Approach to Paul's Argument, WUNT 2.445 (Tübingen: Mohr Siebeck, 2017).

3. See A. B. Caneday, "'They Exchanged the Glory of God for the Likeness of an Image': Idolatrous Adam and Israel as Representatives in Paul's Letter to the Romans," *SBJT* 11.3 (2007): 34–45.

4. Cf. ἀποκαλύψεως δικαιοκρισίας τοῦ θεοῦ (2:5) with ἀποκαλύπτεται ὀργὴ θεοῦ ἀπ᾽ οὐρανοῦ (1:18).

5. See A. B. Caneday, "Judgment, Behavior, and Justification according to Paul's Gospel in Romans 2," *JSPL* 1.2 (2011), 153–92.

circumcision and the law of Moses, from uncircumcised hearts they disobey the law and bring reproach upon the Lord's name among the Gentiles.[6]

Paul realizes that his arraignment of Jews prompts questions about God's justice. Thus, before completing his opening arraignment of sinful humanity, he momentarily foreshadows his more dominant role in his Letter to the Romans as God's defense attorney to argue that God is justified in his words of condemnation and he prevails when he judges (cf. Ps 51:4: "that you might be justified in your words and might prevail when you judge"). Thus, Paul engages his interlocutor's questions: "What advantage has the Jew? Or what benefit is circumcision?" (Rom 3:1). His initial response to the question—"much in every way"—leads one to expect a list of advantages. However, Paul suspends the list until he resumes it much later in his letter, at Rom 9:4–5, when he functions as God's defense attorney more extensively. At this early point in his argument (Rom 3:2), concerning his question about advantage or benefit, Paul offers a response that reinforces his indictment of Jews: "They were entrusted with the words of God" (τὰ λογία τοῦ θεοῦ, 3:2; cf. ἐν τοῖς λόγοις σου, 3:4), an expression that likely refers to the OT as a whole, including God's stipulations and promises, especially beginning with the promise of a seed to Abraham which Paul expounds in chapter 4.[7] To the Jews, the Lord had given the adoption, the glory, the covenants, the law covenant, the priestly service, the promises, and the patriarchs from whom the Christ comes according to the flesh (9:4–5). Nevertheless, so richly *entrusted*, Israel proved *unfaithful* (*untrustworthy*), *unrighteous*, and *untruthful*.

Against the interlocutor's charge that God is unrighteous as though he is failing to keep his promises (3:1–5; cf. 9:1–6), Paul insists that Israel's *unfaithfulness* has not nullified God's *faithfulness* (*trustworthiness*). Instead, circumcised Israel's *unrighteousness* highlights God's *righteousness* because, through Israel's *untruthfulness*, God's *truthfulness* abounds to his own glory. Paul concludes his opening indictment of humanity and then gets to the heart of his thesis, that the gospel discloses God's righteousness (i.e., God's righteous character), which entails the justification of God's character even as he justifies the ungodly.

Because God is righteous, he publicly set forth his Son, Jesus Christ, as the ἱλαστήριον, the place where divine justice and mercy converge to demonstrate his righteousness in the present time that he might simultaneously be righteous and declare righteous those who belong to God's Son, with no distinction between Jew or Gentile (3:21–26). Hence, the gospel proclaims Christ's propitiating

---

6. N. T. Wright, "The Letter to the Romans: Introduction, Commentary, and Reflections," in *The New Interpreter's Bible*, ed. Leander Keck (Nashville: Abingdon, 2002), 10:447–48.

7. Some take Paul's use of τὰ λογία τοῦ θεοῦ with a narrow referent. For example, Sam K. Williams takes it as referring to God's promises to the patriarchs ("'The Righteousness of God' in Romans," *JBL* 99 [1980]: 266–67). Most scholars see a more general reference to Paul's expression. See Moo, *Romans*, 192–93.

of God's wrath as decisive, bringing forward the two sharply contrasting verdicts of the Last Day into the midst of history: one justification, and the other condemnation. Thus, one's response to the crucified and risen Christ is determinative.

Earlier I briefly mentioned that the three uses of παραδίδωμι in ch. 1, signaling divine judgment, anticipate three additional uses as Paul develops his thesis concerning God's righteousness, twice concerning Christ (4:25–5:1; 8:32) and once concerning God's redeemed people (6:17). The latter of these depicts the transaction of being freed from sin's enslavement to become slaves to righteousness, being "handed over" to the gospel, grounded in Christ's being "handed over on account of our trespasses" (4:25).[8]

Paul copiously mines allusions from Isaiah that provide scriptural warrants for both his prosecution of God's wrath against unfaithful Jews and his defense of God's righteousness revealed in the present satisfaction of his wrath in the sacrificial death of Jesus Christ.

In Rom 4:23–25, Paul seems deliberate to allude to Isaiah's fourth "servant song" when his unusual phrasing resembles Isaiah's use in 53:6, 12.[9] Like Isaiah, Paul uses "being handed over" (παρεδόθη), "not the most natural word," to speak of Christ's sacrificial death.[10] As Paul brings his argument from 3:21–8:39 to its zenith, the law court imagery returns with a reprisal of his use of παραδίδωμι from Isaiah's Servant Song.

Once again, as he does in 2:1–16, Paul projects readers to the Day of Judgment; this time, however, not as God's attorney prosecuting sinful humans but as God's appointed defense attorney on behalf of his chosen ones. He begins, "What then shall we say to these things? If God is for us, who is against us?"[11] He responds: "For, since he did not spare his own Son, but handed him over for us all, how shall he not also with him graciously give us all things?"[12] Paul's

---

8. See Moo, *Romans*, 401. Cf. Thomas R. Schreiner, *Romans*, 2nd ed., BECNT, (Grand Rapids: Baker Academic, 2018), 334. Schreiner agrees with Moo that εἰς ὃν παρεδόθητε "is not speaking of tradition being delivered to believers but of believers being handed over to the imprint or stamp of teaching." Schreiner rightly sees τύπον διδαχῆς, "the imprint of teaching" to which believers are handed over, as "the gospel." (χάρις δὲ τῷ θεῷ ὅτι ἦτε δοῦλοι τῆς ἁμαρτίας ὑπηκούσατε δὲ ἐκ καρδίας εἰς ὃν παρεδόθητε τύπον διδαχῆς, ἐλευθερωθέντες δὲ ἀπὸ τῆς ἁμαρτίας ἐδουλώθητε τῇ δικαιοσύνῃ. But thanks be to God that although you were slaves of sin, from the heart you became obedient to the pattern of teaching unto which you were handed over, and having been set free from sin, you were enslaved to righteousness. 6:17, 18).

9. In the LXX Isa 53:5, παρεδόθη occurs once, and in 53:12, it occurs twice. Also, Paul's expression, "who was raised because of our justification," may also allude to LXX Isa 53:11 which depicts the servant as "justifying the righteous." This allusion is not entirely clear because the LXX diverges from the Hebrew text.

10. Wright, "Romans," 503n164.

11. The principal question may allude to Ps 118:6.

12. Paul alludes to LXX Gen 22:16, "You did not spare your beloved son" (οὐκ ἐφείσω τοῦ υἱοῦ σου τοῦ ἀγαπητοῦ) when he writes, "Who did not spare his own Son" (ὅς γε τοῦ ἰδίου υἱοῦ οὐκ ἐφείσατο). See Schreiner, *Romans*, 451.

phrase, "but handed him over for us" (8:32), reprises his appeal to Isa 53:6, 11–12 in Rom 4:23–25.[13] God handed over the "Servant of the Lord" on behalf of us all. Paul's juxtaposition of Isa 53:6 with Isa 50:8–9 is subtle, but those with eyes to see will recognize the apostle's argument.[14] The Lord handed over the "Servant of the Lord" "on behalf of us" (ὑπὲρ ἡμῶν πάντων). The allusion correctly positions the law court summation against the backdrop of the whole fourth "Servant Song." Thus, as one proceeds with Paul's closing argument, Isaiah's words ring out: "By his knowledge [covenant loyalty] the Righteous One, my servant, will vindicate many" (53:11). How will he vindicate many? Isaiah 50:8–9 warrants Paul's confident assertions.

LXX Isa 50:8–9	Rom 8:31–36
ὅτι ἐγγίζει ὁ **δικαιώσας** με, τίς ὁ κρινόμενός μοι	τίς ἐγκαλέσει κατὰ ἐκλεκτῶν θεοῦ θεὸς ὁ **δικαιῶν**: Who shall accuse God's elect?
ἀντιστήτω μοι ἅμα, καὶ τίς ὁ κρινόμενός μοι ἐγγισάτω μοι	τίς ὁ κατακρινῶν Χριστὸς Ἰησοῦς ὁ ἀποθανών, μᾶλλον δὲ ἐγερθείς, Who shall condemn us?
ἰδοὺ κύριος βοηθεῖ μοι, τίς κακώσει μὲ;	τίς ἡμᾶς χωρίσει ἀπὸ τῆς ἀγάπης τοῦ Χριστοῦ Who shall separate us from Christ's love?

13. καὶ κύριος **παρέδωκεν** αὐτὸν ταῖς ἁμαρτίαις ἡμῶν (LXX Isa 53:6). ἀλλὰ ὑπὲρ ἡμῶν πάντων **παρέδωκεν αὐτὸν** (Rom 8:32).

14. Hays well states: "The letter to the Romans is salted with numerous quotations of and allusions to Isaiah 40–55, including several passages that seem to echo the Suffering Servant motif of Isa 53 (e.g., Rom 4:24–25, 5:15–19, 10:16, 15:21). Why, then, does Paul not draw this prophecy into the open and use the servant figure as an explicit basis for his interpretation of Israel, or of the church, or of Jesus? Paul's motive for this evasion or reticence, whichever it is, remains forever lost to us, but the effect of his rhetorical strategy can be readily described. He hints and whispers all around Isaiah 53 but never mentions the prophetic typology that would supremely integrate his interpretation of Christ and Israel. The result is a compelling example of metalepsis: Paul's transumptive silence cries out for the reader to complete the trope. Those who have ears to hear will hear and understand that the people of God, reckoned as sheep to be slaughtered, are suffering with Christ (Rom 8:17: *sympaschomen*) and thus living out the vocation prophesied for them according to the Scriptures" (*Echoes of Scripture in the Letters of Paul* [New Haven: Yale University Press, 1989], 63). Also see, A. B. Caneday, "'Christ has become a servant of the circumcision on behalf of God's truthfulness'—Jesus as Isaiah's Servant of the Lord in Romans 15:8?" (Unpublished essay presented at the Upper Midwest Meeting of the SBL, Luther Theological Seminary, St. Paul, MN, 2004).

The Lord's Servant taunts:

He who vindicates me is nearby. *Who will contend with me?* Let us stand up together. *Who is my adversary?* Let him come near to me. Behold, the Lord God helps me; *who will declare me guilty?* Behold, all of them will wear out like a garment; the moth will eat them up. (Isa 50:8–9)

These questions seem to inform and structure Paul's framing of his queries in Rom 8. He tauntingly beckons accusers to come forward against God's elect, fully convinced, as he is, that no one can successfully indict God's elect whom he vindicates in Christ.

Who shall bring an accusation against God's elect? God is the one who justifies. *Who shall condemn us?* Christ Jesus is the one who died and even more has been raised, who is also at the right hand of God, who also intercedes for us. *Who shall separate us from Christ's love?* Shall affliction or distress or persecution or famine or nakedness or danger or the sword? Just as it is written, "For your sake we suffer death all day long; we are considered as sheep to be slaughtered." (Rom 8:31–36)

Thus, the Lord's Servant vindicates many because God vindicates his Servant (ὁ δικαιώσας με, Isa 50:8). By acting on behalf of others, God's verdict pronounced over his Servant becomes God's verdict declared in the proclaimed gospel over everyone for whom Christ intercedes. As the Lord's Servant is justified, so all for whom he sacrifices himself are justified. Thus, having argued at length that God is righteous to keep his promises to the patriarchs, which entails setting right those who belong to Christ, Paul stands against every accuser, defending God's people for whom God handed over Jesus as the sin offering. God has confirmed his promises in Christ Jesus. Therefore, everything that belongs to Christ Jesus also belongs to those for whom he acts. Paul's courtroom defense of God's people who are in Christ depends upon his developed argument throughout Rom 3:21–8:30. Because Jesus Christ acts on behalf of others, Paul contends that the Lord's justifying verdict pronounced over Christ belongs to all for whom God handed him over. Any accuser who dares charge God's chosen people will have to reverse God's verdict, for he is the judge who has justified all who are in Christ by faith.[15]

---

15. Wright, "Romans," 613, observes: "And that verdict—that those in the Messiah, marked out by faith, are already to be seen as 'righteous,' even ahead of the final vindication—is precisely what the lawcourt dimension of 'justification' is all about. We should note that at this point Paul is once again speaking of the *final* day of judgment, as in 2:1–6 and 8:1."

Bibliography

Caneday, A. B. "'Christ has become a servant of the circumcision on behalf of God's truthfulness'—Jesus as Isaiah's Servant of the Lord in Romans 15:8?" Unpublished essay presented at the Upper Midwest Meeting of the SBL. Luther Theological Seminary, St. Paul, MN, 2004.

————. "Judgment, Behavior, and Justification according to Paul's Gospel in Romans 2." *JSPL* 1.2 (2011): 153–92.

————. "'They Exchanged the Glory of God for the Likeness of an Image': Idolatrous Adam and Israel as Representatives in Paul's Letter to the Romans." *SBJT* 11.3 (2007): 34–45.

Hays, Richard B. *Echoes of Scripture in the Pauline Letters.* New Haven: Yale University Press, 1989.

Mininger, Marcus A. *Uncovering the Theme of Revelation in Romans 1:16–3:26: Discovering a New Approach to Paul's Argument.* WUNT 2.445. Tübingen: Mohr Siebeck, 2017.

Moo, Douglas J. *The Epistle to the Romans.* NICNT. Grand Rapids: Eerdmans, 1996.

Schreiner, Thomas R. *Romans.* 2nd ed. BECNT. Grand Rapids: Baker Academic, 2018.

Williams, Sam K. "'The Righteousness of God' in Romans." *JBL* 99 (1980): 241–90.

Wright, N. T. "The Letter to the Romans: Introduction, Commentary, and Reflections." Pages 395–770 in vol. 10 of *The New Interpreter's Bible.* Edited by Leander E. Keck. Nashville: Abingdon, 2002.

PART FOUR

CHURCH, STATE, WORSHIP, AND MISSION (ETS 2022)

CHAPTER 19

The Function of Romans 12 in the Argument and Purpose of Romans

Sigurd Grindheim

Introduction

When commentators reach chapter 12 of Paul's letter to the Romans, they frequently make reference to Martin Dibelius. He famously claimed that the ethical exhortations in the New Testament were merely conventional ethical advice strung together without any connection to the gospel message.[1] It is difficult to find anyone who agrees with Dibelius, however. The current consensus is that chapters 12–15 are necessary to complete the argument of the letter. Without them, Paul's discussion on God's righteousness would have lacked a practical and ethical application. Typically categorized as paraenesis or as Paul's discussion of ethics, the content of these chapters is considered to be an incontrovertible consequence of Paul's proclamation of God's righteousness.[2]

In this paper, I will argue that the integration of these chapters with the rest of the letter is even tighter. They do not merely contain the ethical teaching that follows as a natural consequence of Paul's proclamation of the gospel. Rather, in these chapters, Paul continues to explain how God's righteousness is revealed. He does not change topic or proceed to ethics, but he shows how the revelation of God's righteousness manifests itself in believers' life in community.

---

1. Martin Dibelius, *A Fresh Approach to the New Testament and Early Christian Literature*, International Library of Christian Knowledge (New York: Scribner's Sons, 1936), 217–19.

2. Joseph A. Fitzmyer, *Romans: A New Translation with Introduction and Commentary*, AB 33 (New York: Doubleday, 1993), 637, calls chapters 12–15 "a paraenetic development of the consequences of justification." James D. G. Dunn, *Romans 9–16*, WBC 38B (Dallas: Word, 1988), 705, observes that "chaps. 12–15 follow naturally from and constitute a necessary corollary to the overall argument of chaps. 1–11." For similar positions, see Carl J. Bjerkelund, *Parakalô: Form, Funktion und Sinn der parakalô-Sätze in den paulinischen Briefen*, Bibliotheca Theologica Norvegica 1 (Oslo: Universitetsforlaget, 1967), 161; Heinrich Schlier, *Der Römerbrief*, HThK 6 (Freiburg: Herder, 1977), 349; George Smiga, "Romans 12:1–2 and 15:30–32 and the Occasion of the Letter to the Romans," *CBQ* 53.2 (1991): 266–67; Richard N. Longenecker, *The Epistle to the Romans: A Commentary on the Greek Text*, NIGTC (Grand Rapids: Eerdmans, 2016), 911–12.

My argument is twofold. I will begin by highlighting some of the many verbal links between chapters 12–15 and the preceding discussion, showing how Paul's exhortations continue to unpack many of the ideas he has mentioned earlier. Second, based on the many connections between these chapters and the teaching and example of Jesus Christ, I will argue that Paul's vision for the Christian life represents the manifestation of Christ's own obedience, death, and resurrection. My primary focus will be on Rom 12, but the topic at hand necessitates a constant view to the succeeding chapters as well.

Verbal Links

Paul begins this section with a set of powerful exhortations:

> Therefore, I urge you, brothers and sisters, in view of God's mercy, to offer your bodies as a living sacrifice, holy and pleasing to God—this is your true and proper worship. Do not conform to the pattern of this world, but be transformed by the renewing of your mind. Then you will be able to test and approve what God's will is—his good, pleasing and perfect will. (Rom 12:1–2)[3]

Already the particle that is translated "therefore" (οὖν) signals that what follows is closely related to the foregoing and draws out the implications.[4] Likewise, the reference to God's mercy (τῶν οἰκτιρμῶν τοῦ θεοῦ), which is offered as the basis for the exhortation, connects it with the preceding discussion. The specific term that is used (οἰκτιρμός) is a *hapax legomenon* in the New Testament, but Paul has employed a cognate term before in his letter to the Romans. In his discussion on the predestination of Jacob, he has quoted from LXX Exod 33:19, where God says to Moses: "I will have mercy on whom I have mercy, and I will have compassion (οἰκτιρήσω) on whom I have compassion (οἰκτίρω)." The original context for this quotation is God's revelation to Moses following the plague that resulted from the golden calf incident. While Moses was not allowed to see God's face, the LORD assured him of his continued mercy. The broader associations are to be spared from God's punishment and wrath, as it is in most other occurrences of this terminology in the Greek Old Testament.[5] Paul's use of this language refers most directly

---

3. All English translations of Scripture are from the NIV unless otherwise noted.
4. C. E. B. Cranfield, *A Critical and Exegetical Commentary on the Epistle to the Romans*, 2 vols., ICC (Edinburgh: T&T Clark, 1979), 2:595; *pace* Hans Lietzmann, *An die Römer*, 3rd ed., HNT 8 (Tübingen: Mohr Siebeck, 1933), 107; Ernst Käsemann, *Commentary on Romans*, trans. and ed. Geoffrey W. Bromiley (Grand Rapids: Eerdmans, 1980), 326.
5. Nijay K. Gupta, "What 'Mercies of God'? *Oiktirmos* in Romans 12:1 Against Its Septuagintal Background," *BBR* 22.1 (2012): 84, observes that the majority of

to God's mercy in election, as it is outlined in Rom 9–11, but when he repeats the terminology in 12:1, he probably also recalls the main theme of the entire epistle: the revelation of God's righteousness that brings deliverance from God's judgment (1:16–17).[6]

Paul's reference to the mercy of God serves to express the authority behind his appeal, and it may be paraphrased "in the name of God's mercy."[7] The exhortation is not simply offered in light of God's mercy; it is as if God's mercy is issuing the exhortation. In other words, the exhortation represents the effects of God's mercy in deliverance, the same mercy that Paul has described in the preceding chapters.

Paul's exhortation aims at establishing true and proper worship, a form of worship that represents a reversal of the judgment that was described in the letter's first major section, stretching from 1:18 to 3:20, the discussion of God's judgment.[8] The recurrence of several key terms, such as "body" (σῶμα), "service" (λατρεία, λατρεύω), "mind" (νοῦς), and "approval" (δοκιμάζω), shows that Paul probably intended for his audience to notice this contrast between existence under God's judgment and existence dominated by his mercy.[9]

According to 1:24, God's judgment consisted in God giving people over to "the degrading of their bodies (σώματα) with one another." In the following exposition, the term "body" (σῶμα) is consistently associated with sin and death.[10]

Apart from the reference to Christ's body in 7:4, it is not until chapter 12 that the term "body" is used in a positive way. Now, believers are called to offer their "bodies as a living sacrifice, holy and pleasing to God" (12:1). With this note, Paul turns from a negative to a positive description of God's righteousness, from explaining what believers have been delivered from to portraying

---

occurrences of the words οἰκτιρμός and οἰκτίρω are found with reference to God's promise to deliver his people.

6. Scholars have reached different conclusions regarding what part of the letter Paul has in mind with this mention of God's mercy, some favoring chs. 1–11, others chs. 9–11, and others again ch. 11. Yet others see a general reference to God's mercy. For an overview, cf. Gupta, "'Mercies of God,'" 82.

7. Carl J. Bjerkelund compares the expression to Jewish invocation formulas and concludes that an appeal to the attributes of God is the most binding form of appeal (*Parakalô*, 164–65). Quoting Alexandros Pallis, Ernst Käsemann suggests the paraphrase "in the name of God's mercy" (*Romans*, 326).

8. Cf. Christopher Evans, "Rom 12:1–2: The True Worship," in *Dimensions de la vie chrétienne (Rm 12–13)*, ed. Lorenzo De Lorenzi, SMBen (Rome: Abbaye de St. Paul, 1979), 30–31.

9. Michael Thompson, *Clothed with Christ: The Example and Teaching of Jesus in Romans 12.11–15.13*, JSNTSup 59 (Sheffield: JSOT Press, 1991), 79–82; Matteo Crimella, "Λογικὴ λατρεία (Rom 12:1): The Pauline Idea of Worship Between the Hebrew and Hellenistic Worlds," *Verbum Vitae* 39.3 (2021): 794.

10. Cf. 4:19; 6:6, 12; 7:25; 8:10, 11, 13, 23. In 7:4, it refers to Christ's body, which is the means by which the audience "also died to the law."

what they have been delivered to. As the body is delivered from God's wrath, it has become the means of worshiping him. From being identified with sin, it has become pleasing to God.[11]

As it is portrayed in chapter 1, people's situation under God's judgment is caused by misplaced worship. According to 1:25, they "worshiped and served (ἐλάτρευσαν) created things rather than the Creator." A noun from the same root as the verb that is here translated "served" occurs in 12:1 as well, when Paul maintains that the offering of their bodies is their "true and proper worship (τὴν λογικὴν λατρείαν)."

The expression he uses is notoriously difficult to translate. Besides "true and proper worship," translations such as "true worship" (CSB), "reasonable service" (KJV), "worship offered by mind and heart" (NEB, REB), and "spiritual worship" (ESV, NAB, NRSV) are found in major English versions. The Greek term λογικός is frequently used in philosophical writings with the meaning "possessed of reason" (LSJ). In Paul's usage, it probably denotes the kind of worship that is appropriate for humans to render to God.[12] Against the background of grossly inappropriate worship described in chapter 1, appropriate worship has now been restored.

The former, misplaced worship was related to the fact that the people "did not think it worthwhile (ἐδοκίμασαν) to retain the knowledge of God" (1:28a). The result was that God gave them over "to a depraved mind (νοῦν)" (1:28b). In chapter 12, this plight is also reversed. The verb that the NIV translates "did not think it worthwhile" (δοκιμάζω) recurs in chapter 12 as well, as Paul expects the audience to "be able to test and approve (δοκιμάζειν) what God's will is" (12:2; cf. 14:22) following "the renewing of your mind (τοῦ νοὸς)" (12:2).

Paul's reference to true and proper worship in 12:1 is not the first time he has alluded to this theme. In his exhortations not to continue in sin in 6:11–23, he repeatedly employed the key term "to offer" (παρίστημι), as he urged the believers not to "offer (παριστάνετε) any part of yourself to sin," "but rather offer (παραστήσατε) yourselves to God" (6:13; cf. v. 19b).[13] In chapter 12, he

---

11. Haritsima Razanadrakoto, "Sans la loi mais par la foi . . . et dans l'unique corps: Exégèse de Romains 12,1–15,13," *ETL* 93.1 (2018): 135. The above observations, as well as the fact that the term is used in the plural in 12:1, militate against the interpretation of Smiga, that Paul is calling for the community, consisting of Jews and Gentiles, to be presented as a sacrifice to God ("Romans 12:1–2 and 15:30–32," 269–70).

12. Similarly, Otto Michel, *Der Brief an die Römer*, 5th ed., KEK (Göttingen: Vandenhoeck & Ruprecht, 1966), 370; Dunn, *Romans 9–16*, 711–12; Longenecker, *Romans*, 921; Douglas J. Moo, *The Letter to the Romans*, 2nd ed., NICNT (Grand Rapids: Eerdmans, 2018), 771–72.

13. Victor Paul Furnish, *Theology and Ethics in Paul* (Nashville: Abingdon, 1968), 105–6; Ulrich Wilckens, *Der Brief an die Römer (Röm 12–16)*, EKK 6/3 (Zürich/Neukirchener-Vluyn: Benziger/Neukirchener, 1982), 3; Morna D. Hooker, "Interchange in Christ and Ethics," *JSNT* 25 (1985): 4; Thompson, *Clothed with Christ*, 79; Eckhard

describes the antithesis to the slavery under sin from which believers have been delivered and calls on them "to offer (παραστῆσαι) your bodies as a living sacrifice" (12:1).[14] That this offer is "living" recalls Paul's affirmations that believers "live a new life" (6:4; cf. vv. 11, 13).[15]

The corollary to such a sacrifice is a transformed mind, as Paul in Rom 12:2 urges his audience not to "conform to the pattern of this world, but be transformed by the renewing of your mind." The language of renewal (ἀνακαινώσει) also picks up an idea from the preceding chapters.[16] In 6:4, Paul outlined the effects of Christ's resurrection and maintained that "we too may live a new (καινότητι) life" (cf. 7:6). The content of his exhortation in 12:2 is nothing other than the effect of Christ's work, the effect Paul has already mentioned: the new life of believers.

According to 7:6, living this new life means being led by the Spirit, a theme Paul returns to in 12:11, when he urges his audience not to "lack diligence in zeal," but "be fervent in the Spirit" (CSB; cf. 14:17; 15:13).[17] The call to such fervor is immediately coupled by the exhortation to serve the Lord (12:11). With this terminology, Paul recalls another important concept from his explanation of the gospel in Rom 6.[18] Unfortunately, English translations obscure the connection, as they alternate between the language of service and slavery, even though the same term is used in both places in Greek, a term most aptly translated as slavery (δουλεύω). The service or slavery to which Paul encourages his audience is the slavery he has previously described as the positive contrast to slavery to sin (6:6, 16, 17, 19a), namely slavery to righteousness (6:18, 19b; cf. 6:22; 7:6, 25). To be delivered from slavery under sin in order to be slaves to righteousness is the direct result of believers' union with Christ in his crucifixion (6:6;

J. Schnabel, *Der Brief des Paulus an die Römer: Kapitel 6–16*, HTA (Witten/Gießen: Brockhaus/Brunnen, 2016), 561–62; Michael Wolter, *Der Brief an die Römer (Teilband 2: Röm 9–16)*, EKK 6/2 (Neukirchener-Vluyn/Ostfildern: Neukirchener/Patmos, 2019), 244.

14. See also the correspondence between the offering that leads to holiness (ἁγιασμον) in 6:19b and the sacrifice that is called "holy (ἁγιάν) and pleasing to God" in 12:1.

15. Schnabel, *Römer, Kapitel 6–16*, 567.

16. Wolter, *Röm 9–16*, 244.

17. Cf. Wolter, *Röm 9–16*, 244. Unfortunately, the NIV renders the expression as "keep your spiritual fervor," taking πνεῦμα as a reference to the human spirit, rather than the Holy Spirit (cf. ESV, KJV, NAB, NEB, NJB, NLT, NRSV). However, the parallel expression "serving the Lord" indicates that the reference is to the Holy Spirit. Cf. CEB, REB; Cranfield, *Romans*, 2:633–34; Dunn, *Romans 9–16*, 742; Thomas R. Schreiner, *Romans*, BECNT (Grand Rapids: Baker Academic, 1998), 665; Robert Jewett, *Romans: A Commentary*, Hermeneia (Minneapolis: Fortress, 2007), 763; Moo, *Romans*, 796; *pace* Fitzmyer, *Romans*, 654; Frank Thielman, *Romans*, ZECNT 6 (Grand Rapids: Zondervan, 2018), 591.

18. Wolter, *Röm 9–16*, 245.

cf. 6:17). Therefore, Paul's subsequent exhortations take the form of a call to behave in accordance with their new status. Since they are no longer slaves to sin, but slaves to righteousness, they are reminded to "offer yourselves as slaves to righteousness leading to holiness" (6:19b). In Rom 12–15, Paul unpacks this exhortation further.[19]

This new life manifests itself through transformation "by the renewing of your mind" (12:2). What it means to be transformed in this way is explained in the following paragraph, as Paul insists that believers "[d]o not think of yourself more highly (ὑπερφρονεῖν) than you ought, but rather think (φρονεῖν) of yourself with sober judgment (σωφρονεῖν)" (12:3). The two verbs that are translated "think" as well as the verb that in the NIV is rendered "sober judgment" are all from the same root, namely φρήν, from which the philosophical term φρόνησις, is also formed. This term is used for practical wisdom, for the prudence required to live ethically.[20]

Employing three different verbs formed from this root (φρήν), Paul resumes the thought he expressed in 8:5–7, where words from the same root occur four times. As he was hailing the work of the Holy Spirit, Paul warned his audience that

[t]hose who live according to the flesh have their minds set (φρονοῦσιν) on what the flesh desires, but those who live in accordance with the Spirit have their minds set on what the Spirit desires. The mind (φρόνημα) governed by the flesh is death, but the mind (φρόνημα) governed by the Spirit is life and peace. The mind (φρόνημα) governed by the flesh is hostile to God; it does not submit to God's law, nor can it do so.

By returning to this terminology, Paul now continues to show how his gospel brings about the reversal of the sinfulness that results in God's judgment. He will now describe the positive counterpart to the mind that is governed by the flesh, namely the mind governed by the Spirit. In a word, such a mind is a mind of humility. It is a mind that does not cause one to think of oneself more highly than one ought (12:3).[21] The verb σωφρονέω is related to the noun σωφροσύνη, a term denoting the ethical quality that stands in opposition to

---

19. Wolter, *Röm 9–16*, 245.

20. *TDNT* 9:221–22.

21. One may compare 1 John 2:16, which defines "everything in the world" as "the lust of the flesh, the lust of the eyes, and the pride of life." The last of these phrases Î(ἡ ἀλαζονεία τοῦ βίου) is difficult to interpret, but probably refers to "[o]verconfidence stemming from the security of one's life" (Raymond E. Brown, *The Epistles of John: Translated with Introduction, Notes, and Commentary*, AB 30 [New York: Doubleday, 1982], 312). Cf. Rudolf Schnackenburg, *The Johannine Epistles: A Commentary*, trans. Reginald and Ilse Fuller (New York: Crossroad, 1992), 122–23; Karen H. Jobes, *1–3 John*, ZECNT 19 (Grand Rapids: Zondervan Academic, 2014), 113.

hubris (Plato, *Republic* 399b).[22] In Paul's usage, it contrasts with the socially destructive attitude of claiming too much for oneself.[23] More specifically, what Paul calls for is a mindset that is characterized by a consideration of the body of Christ and the ways in which different members have different functions in his body (12:4–8).[24]

The topic of right thinking will recur throughout chapters 12–15. When Paul in chapters 14–15 addresses the question of which holy days to be observed he explains that the believers' mind and their convictions should guide their conduct (14:5–6).[25] To solve the conflict, he prays that God will "give you the same attitude of mind (φρονεῖν) toward each other that Christ Jesus had" (15:5). The attitude to which he refers is described more explicitly in 12:9–21, where Paul admonishes the audience to show sincere love. Such love manifests itself in right thinking, as Paul urges them to "live in harmony with one another," or, in a more literal translation, "think (φρονοῦντες) the same thing toward one another; do not think (φρονοῦντες) arrogantly, but associate with the lowly. Do not be wise (φρόνιμοι) in your own sight" (12:16 LEB).

Even though there are no obvious allusions to the Jesus tradition, it is reasonable to assume that the example of Jesus serves as the blueprint for Paul's admonishment.[26] Jesus' association with those of low status is a stock theme in the Synoptic Gospels (e.g., Matt 11:19//Luke 7:34), and it is congenial with Paul's portrait of Jesus as the one who "though he was rich, yet for your sake . . . became poor" (2 Cor 8:9) and who "made himself nothing by taking the very nature of a servant, being made in human likeness" (Phil 2:7).

---

22. *TDNT* 7:1098.

23. John Elliott, *1 Peter: A New Translation with Introduction and Commentary*, AB 37B (New York: Doubleday, 2000), 748; Philip F. Esler, "Paul and Stoicism: Romans 12 as a Test Case," *NTS* 50.1 (2004): 116.

24. Razanadrakoto, "Sans la loi," 136.

25. Note the repeated use of the verb φρονέω ("think") (14:6; 15:5). Cf. Käsemann, *Romans*, 370–71; A. J. M. Wedderburn, *The Reasons for Romans*, SNTW (Edinburgh: T&T Clark, 1988), 75–77; Kuo-Wei Peng, *Hate the Evil, Hold Fast to the Good: Structuring Romans 12:1–15:1*, LNTS 300 (London: T&T Clark, 2006), 190.

26. Thompson, *Clothed with Christ*, 106–7. Noting the contrast with the ethics outlined in Arius Didymus's *Epitome of Stoic Ethics*, Esler suggests that Paul may also have intended the exhortations to associate with those of low status and not think highly of oneself as an ethical ideal that is in direct contradiction to Stoicism ("Paul and Stoicism," 121–22). Runar M. Thorsteinsson, "Paul and Roman Stoicism: Romans 12 and Contemporary Stoic Ethics," *JSNT* 29.2 (2006): 159, has responded to Esler's study and maintains that "nothing could be further from the truth than the claim that Paul's moral teaching in Rom. 12 was 'radically different' from Stoic ethics." However, even Thorsteinsson concedes that Paul's exhortation to "weep with those who weep" differs from the Stoics, provided that he meant that they should "make their grief their own" ("Paul and Roman Stoicism," 156).

Conformation to the Image of Christ

The transformation (μεταμορφοῦσθε) that results from the renewing of the mind, therefore, is conformation to the image of Christ.[27] What Paul unpacks on these lines is the powerful idea he has introduced in Rom 8:29, where he used another term that is formed from the same root, μορφή: "For those God foreknew he also predestined to be conformed (συμμόρφους) to the image of his Son."

The aim of the renewing of the mind is nothing other than the mindset of Christ, the mindset Paul has memorably portrayed in Phil 2:5–8, also there with terminology from the φρήν-root:

> In your relationships with one another, have the same mindset (φρονεῖτε) as Christ Jesus: who, being in very nature God, did not consider equality with God something to be used to his own advantage; rather, he made himself nothing by taking the very nature of a servant, being made in human likeness. And being found in appearance as a man, he humbled himself by becoming obedient to death—even death on a cross.

As he concludes his more general exhortations and prepares to address the situation in Rome more directly, Paul invokes the character of Jesus once again and urges the audience to "clothe yourselves with the Lord Jesus Christ" (13:14). He does not repeat the language he used in 8:29 (of conformity to the image of the Son), but the image of Christ serves as the blueprint for his exhortations.

The vision for Christian life that Paul develops in Rom 12 may very well be read as another portrait of the mindset of Christ as it is outlined it in Phil 2:5–8. In Rom 12:10b, Paul calls the Romans to "honor one another above yourselves," and in 12:16 not to "be proud, but be willing to associate with people of low position. Do not be conceited."

A negative observation corroborates this interpretation, namely the dearth of references to the Mosaic law. One might have expected that Paul's exhortations would be based on God's commandments as they had been revealed to Moses. After all, throughout the letter, Paul has been at pains to dismiss the accusation that his gospel represented an abolishment of the law. He begins his account of God's righteousness in 3:21 by affirming that this righteousness is attested by the law and the prophets. Indeed, the gospel not only complies with the law; it fulfills the law. "We uphold the law," Paul insists in 3:31 (cf. 8:4).

One gets the impression that these affirmations at least partly serve to address some of the accusations that have been launched against the apostle. He

---

27. Gupta, "'Mercies of God,'" 94–95; cf. also Scot McKnight, *Reading Romans Backwards: A Gospel of Peace in the Midst of Empire* (Waco, TX: Baylor University Press, 2019), 27–28.

refers to some people who "slanderously claim that we say—'Let us do evil that good may result'" (3:8), and he raises the question "Shall we go on sinning so that grace may increase?" only to dismiss it emphatically (6:1–2).

As Paul in 12:1 turns to developing the implications of his gospel for believers' life in community, one might expect him to explain more precisely how he upholds the law and ensures its fulfillment. It seems it would now be the time for Paul to discuss how the Mosaic commandments may truly be fulfilled.

With his introductory exhortation, Paul appears to meet this expectation. He invokes a cultic image, well-known from the Mosaic legislation, and calls the audience to offer their bodies as a living sacrifice (12:1). In the tradition of the Old Testament prophets, Paul apparently envisions a spiritual fulfillment of the legal requirements of the Mosaic revelation (cf. Heb 13:15; 1 Pet 2:5).[28]

Somewhat surprisingly, however, he does not develop this concept of a spiritual law fulfillment with additional references to the law. Indeed, he does not make any clear allusions to the law until 13:9, when he lists some of the ten commandments, only to add that these and all the other commandments "are summed up in this one command: 'Love your neighbor as yourself.'" His conclusion is that "love is the fulfillment of the law" (13:10). Even there, he does not actually call for the obedience of these specific commandments, but he insists that they are all fulfilled by fulfilling the love commandment, echoing the words of Jesus, who summarized the law in a similar way (Matt 22:37–40//Mark 12:29–31).[29]

Instead of developing his ethical vision with references to the Mosaic law, Paul draws upon the teaching and example of Jesus. The Pauline letters contain surprisingly few references to the earthly career of Jesus, but this section of Romans boasts the highest concentration of possible allusions and echoes.[30] His exhortations to sincere love (12:9–21) have obvious connections with the Sermon on the Mount. Jesus' command to "love your enemies and pray for those who persecute you" (Matt 5:44) is echoed in the apostle's exhortation to "bless those who persecute you" (12:14).[31] When the apostle urges his audience not to "repay anyone evil for evil" (12:17a), one recalls Jesus' words not to

---

28. 1 Sam 15:22; Isa 1:11–17; Jer 7:22–23; Hos 6:6; Amos 5:21–25; Mic 6:6–8; cf. Deut 30:6; Ps 50:8–15.

29. Dale C. Allison, Jr., "The Pauline Epistles and the Synoptic Gospels: The Pattern of the Parallels," *NTS* 28.1 (1982): 20; Thompson, *Clothed with Christ*, 121–40; Jewett, *Romans*, 813; Schnabel, *Der Brief des Paulus an die Römer: Kapitel 6–16*, 708; Moo, *Romans*, 832.

30. Michael Thompson finds "one probable allusion" in 14:14, "virtually certain echoes" in 12:14 and 13:8–10, a "highly probable echo" in 14:13a, "probable echoes" in 12:9, 17–19; 13:7, 11–12; 14:13a, 13b, 17, and possible influences in 12:3–8, 10, 11, 18; 14:18, 19 (*Clothed with Christ*, 237). But see Walter Wilson, *Love Without Pretense: Romans 12.9–21 and Hellenistic-Jewish Wisdom Literature*, WUNT 2.46 (Tübingen: Mohr Siebeck, 1991), 165–71, who even thinks an allusion to Jesus' teaching in 12:14 is unlikely.

31. Furnish, *Theology and Ethics*, 53; Schlier, *Römerbrief*, 379; Cranfield, *Romans*, 2:640; Allison, "The Pauline Epistles," 20; Dunn, *Romans 9–16*, 745; Fitzmyer,

"resist an evil person. If anyone slaps you on the right cheek, turn to them the other cheek also" (Matt 5:39).[32] Paul's injunction not to "be overcome by evil, but overcome evil with good" (12:21) may be inspired by the same tradition.[33]

The apparent dependence upon the words of Jesus continues in Rom 13–15. Paul's exhortation to pay taxes (Rom 13:6–7) seems to echo Jesus' words about giving "back to Caesar what is Caesar's and to God what is God's" (Mark 12:17).[34] His summary of the commandments (Rom 13:9) resembles a similar summary offered by Jesus (Mark 12:31).[35] When he prompts the audience to wake from their slumber (Rom 13:11) he may be echoing Jesus' words to the disciples in Gethsemane (Mark 14:41).[36] The question "why do you judge your brother or sister?" (Rom 14:10) is possibly also inspired by Jesus' words on judging others (Matt 7:1–2), as is the warning against putting a stumbling block in the way of fellow believers (Rom 14:13–14; cf. Mark 9:42).[37] Turning to the issue of food, Paul most likely alludes to the words of Jesus himself (Mark 7:15), when he affirms that "nothing is unclean in itself" (Rom 14:14) and that "all food is clean" (Rom 14:20).[38]

Even more important to Paul's argument are his appeals to the example of Jesus.[39] His call to watchfulness in 13:11–14 is concluded by the exhortation to "clothe yourselves with the Lord Jesus Christ" (13:14). The advice concerning

---

Romans, 655; Schreiner, *Romans*, 667; Schnabel, *Der Brief des Paulus an die Römer: Kapitel 6–16*, 632; Moo, *Romans*, 799; Thielman, *Romans*, 593.

32. Furnish, *Theology and Ethics*, 53; Schlier, *Römerbrief*, 381; Allison, "The Pauline Epistles," 20; Fitzmyer, *Romans*, 656; Schreiner, *Romans*, 672; Craig L. Blomberg, "Quotations, Allusions, and Echoes of Jesus in Paul," in *Studies in the Pauline Epistles: Essays in Honor of Douglas J. Moo*, ed. Matthew S. Harmon and Jay E. Smith (Grand Rapids: Zondervan, 2014), 134; Schnabel, *Der Brief des Paulus an die Römer: Kapitel 6–16*, 640; Moo, *Romans*, 802.

33. One may also compare Rom 12:18 and Mark 9:50 (cf. Matt 5:9). See also David Wenham, *Paul: Follower of Jesus or Founder of Christianity?* (Grand Rapids: Eerdmans, 1995), 73. For a maximalist approach to Pauline dependence upon the historical Jesus, see Seyoon Kim, "Jesus, Sayings Of," in *Dictionary of Paul and His Letters*, ed. Gerald F. Hawthorne, Ralph P. Martin, and Daniel G. Reid (Downers Grove, IL: IVP Academic, 1993), 474–91.

34. Furnish, *Theology and Ethics*, 53; Allison, "The Pauline Epistles," 20; Dunn, *Romans 9–16*, 768; Blomberg, "Quotations, Allusions, and Echoes of Jesus in Paul," 134; Schnabel, *Der Brief des Paulus an die Römer: Kapitel 6–16*, 696.

35. Cf. footnote 29 above.

36. Schnabel, *Der Brief des Paulus an die Römer: Kapitel 6–16*, 717.

37. Furnish, *Theology and Ethics*, 53; Allison, "The Pauline Epistles," 20.

38. Furnish, *Theology and Ethics*, 53; Schlier, *Römerbrief*, 413; Allison, "The Pauline Epistles," 20; Roger P. Booth, *Jesus and the Laws of Purity: Tradition History and Legal History in Mark 7*, JSNTSup 13 (Sheffield: JSOT Press, 1986), 99–100; Dunn, *Romans 9–16*, 819; Schreiner, *Romans*, 731; Jewett, *Romans*, 859; Blomberg, "Quotations, Allusions, and Echoes of Jesus in Paul," 135; Longenecker, *Romans*, 1006; Schnabel, *Der Brief des Paulus an die Römer: Kapitel 6–16*, 759, 773; Sigurd Grindheim, "Jesus and the Food Laws Revisited," *JSHJ* 18.1 (2020): 64–65.

39. Cf. Thompson, *Clothed with Christ*, 240.

unity between the weak and the strong is motivated by the observation that "Christ died and returned to life so that he might be the Lord of both the dead and the living" (14:9). When Paul calls the strong "to bear with the failings of the weak" (15:1), he argues based on the example of Jesus, who "did not please himself but, as it is written: 'The insults of those who insult you have fallen on me'" (15:3; cf. LXX Ps 68:10). Finally, in his concluding exhortation on the matter, he returns to the idea of Jesus as a role model: "Accept one another, then, just as Christ accepted you, in order to bring praise to God. For I tell you that Christ has become a servant of the Jews on behalf of God's truth, so that the promises made to the patriarchs might be confirmed and, moreover, that the Gentiles might glorify God for his mercy" (15:7b–9a).

In other words, where one might expect to find a development of the Mosaic commandments, Paul offers a selective summary of Jesus' teaching and example. It would appear that he understands the fulfillment of the law as a fulfillment that is taking place through the personal union with Christ.

Indeed, the vision Paul has for the fulfillment of the law corresponds relatively poorly to the picture provided in the Mosaic legislation. Paul's appeal to the concept of sacrifice demonstrates this clearly. Whereas the Levitical laws prescribe a certain share of one's possessions and harvest to be sacrificed to the Lord, Paul envisions an all-encompassing sacrifice. The object of sacrifice is "your bodies," a reference to the whole person with a view to their interaction with the world.[40]

Earlier in the letter, Paul has exhibited a similar kind of freedom with respect to the specific commandments of the law. In 2:26, he refers to an uncircumcised person who obeys the law. As the law requires circumcision, Paul apparently has a different kind of law-observance in mind, a fulfillment of God's law without observing the Mosaic commandments. To Paul, genuine law-fulfillment does not require adherence to the Mosaic code.[41]

In light of Rom 12, it becomes clear why Paul is able to think in this way. His blueprint for law-fulfillment is not found in the law of Moses, but in the life, ministry, and teaching of Jesus.

The ultimate form of obedience, as Paul sees it, is the ministry of Jesus. The obedience of this one man (Rom 5:19) constituted the "one righteous act" that "resulted in justification and life for all people" (5:18). This act of obedience is at the same time "God's abundant provision of grace and of the gift of righteousness" (5:17).

While this obedience is a once-for-all act, it is also a gift that keeps on giving. Following his account of its once-for-all character, Paul proceeds to explain

---

40. Similarly, Moo, *Romans*, 769.
41. C. K. Barrett, *The Epistle to the Romans*, 2nd ed., BNTC (Grand Rapids: Baker Academic, 1991), 56; Moo, *Romans*, 181.

that Christ's act of obedience and the gift of righteousness that he provides result in the transformation of believers' life. Through baptism, they have been united with Christ in his death and burial (Rom 6:3–4), with the promise also to be "united with him in a resurrection like his" (6:5). Therefore, their status as slaves to sin has been terminated.

In chs. 5 and 6, Paul has offered a negative description of this gift of righteousness: it has brought deliverance from sin. As mentioned above, the positive description follows in chs. 12–15: Christ's obedience manifests itself in the community of believers, when they display the mindset of Christ by loving their enemies and honoring one another above themselves.[42] As Leander Keck observes, "chapters 12–13 make concrete the righteousness/rectitude that results from God's rectifying the ungodly (4:5)."[43]

This is not to say that believers' ethical conduct follows automatically from their acceptance of the gospel. Paul's frequent use of imperatives shows that believers need to be encouraged to live this new life. However, their new life is a life that is lived in union with Christ. Their obedience, therefore, is not achieved autonomously, but by the agency of Christ.

God's Punitive Righteousness

The implication of these observations is that the community of believers represents the positive revelation of God's righteousness. If that is so, one might wonder whether this community also would serve as a manifestation of God's punitive justice.[44] Perhaps Paul anticipates this inference, as he turns to the topic of God's punitive justice in 12:17–21. In any case, he rejects the idea that believers should view themselves as instruments of God's punishment. The appropriate response to the evil that continues to exist in the world is still to imitate the life of Jesus. Echoing his commandments, Paul urges his audience to "bless those who persecute you" (v. 14; cf. Matt 5:44) and "not repay anyone evil for evil" (v. 17; cf. Matt 5:39).

---

42. Razanadrakoto calls it an "ethic of interdependence" ("Sans la loi," 142).

43. Leander E. Keck, *Romans*, ANTC (Nashville: Abingdon, 2005), 291. Similarly, Ernst Käsemann observes in a comment on ch. 6, that "justification is manifested as the grasping of our lives by Christ's lordship" (*Romans*, 323).

44. On the punitive aspects of God's righteousness, see especially Mark A. Seifrid, "Righteousness Language in the Hebrew Scriptures and Early Judaism," in *Justification and Variegated Nomism: Complexities of Second Temple Judaism*, ed. D. A. Carson, Peter T. O'Brien, and Mark A. Seifrid, WUNT 2.140 (Tübingen: Mohr Siebeck, 2001), 415–42; Mark A. Seifrid, "Paul's Use of Righteousness Language Against Its Hellenistic Background," in *Justification and Variegated Nomism: The Paradoxes of Paul*, ed. D. A. Carson, Peter T. O'Brien, and Mark A. Seifrid, WUNT 2.181 (Tübingen: Mohr Siebeck, 2004), 39–74.

With a quotation from LXX Deut 32:35, the apostle returns to the idea of God's punitive justice in v. 19. Apparently, the revelation of God's righteousness apart from the law (3:21) does not mean that the punitive aspects of this justice have been eliminated. With the words of Moses, God promises to execute his judgment: "Vengeance is mine, I will repay, says the Lord." Paul reverts to this terminology in 13:14, reminding the Romans that the secular government functions as God's agent in executing vengeance.[45]

In the immediate context, however, Paul quickly returns to the theme of restorative justice. His next quotation, from LXX Prov 25:21–22, probably functions as a reminder that good deeds done towards one's enemies will bring them to repentance: "if your enemies are hungry, feed them; if they are thirsty, give them something to drink; for by doing this you will heap burning coals on their heads." There is considerable discussion regarding the connotations of "burning coals," whether it refers to *judgment* or to *shame* leading to repentance.[46] The context favors the latter understanding, as Paul concludes this paragraph with the exhortation not to "be overcome by evil, but overcome evil with good" (v. 21). In the spirit of Jesus' Sermon on the Mount, the audience is urged to show kindness to all, especially to their enemies. By following his instructions, believers are instruments of God's restorative justice and bring peace where there was discord, friendship where there was enmity.

Conclusion

Romans 12–15 is tightly integrated with the preceding argument, so tightly that it is misleading to understand this section as introducing a new topic, such as

---

45. Similarly, Erwin Ochsenmeier, "Romans 12,17–13,7 and the Justice of God: Two Neglected Features of Paul's Argument," *ETL* 89.4 (2013): 381.

46. In favor of the former interpretation speak the connection with the preceding quotation as well as the use of "coal" (ἄνθραξ) as a metaphor of wrath in the LXX (2 Kgdms [2 Sam] 22:9, 12; Pss 17:9, 13; 139:11; Job 41:12, 13; Sir 8:10; Isa 5:24; 2 Esd 16:53). On this interpretation, the second quotation functions as a renewed exhortation not to preempt God's punishment. Cf. Schreiner, *Romans*, 675; Ochsenmeier, "Romans 12,17–13,7," 371; Wolter, *Röm 9–16*, 301–2. On the other hand, comparison has been made with an Egyptian ritual, attested in the third century BCE, in which penitents placed burning coals on their head, in order to demonstrate the genuineness of their repentance (Siegfried Morenz, "Feurige Kohlen auf dem Haupt," *TLZ* 7 [1953]: 187–92). It is impossible to know whether this ritual was known to Paul or to his Roman audience, but in light of the extensive communication within the Roman Empire and the Egyptian influence on Roman society, it is not unlikely. At least a general knowledge of the positive connotations of the metaphor may plausibly be assumed. In any case, the overall context tips the balance in favor of the latter interpretation, as most commentators acknowledge (e.g., Wilckens, *Römer*, 26; Dunn, *Romans 9–16*, 751; Longenecker, *Romans*, 941; Moo, *Romans*, 806; more cautiously, Jewett, *Romans*, 777; Thielman, *Romans*, 596). For both meanings, see Mark A. Seifrid, "Romans," in *Commentary on the New Testament Use of the Old Testament*, ed. G. K. Beale and D. A. Carson (Grand Rapids: Baker Academic, 2007), 681.

Paul's ethical teaching, even if this new topic is understood as the necessary implication of what has gone before.[47] Instead, these chapters continue to describe the revelation of God's righteousness as it manifests itself in the deliverance of God's people.[48] Broadly speaking, Paul turns from a negative to a positive description, moving from explaining what God has delivered his people from, to explaining what they have been delivered to.

Accordingly, it would be more appropriate to understand Rom 12–15 as the flip side of the coin, rather than the second step of a process.[49] Rather than reading the exhortations as an implication of the preceding, they continue to describe how God's righteousness manifests itself within the community. Logically, the gift of Christ precedes the exhortations, as it does in Rom 6:1–14. The fact that believers are united with Christ in his death and resurrection serves as the presupposition for the exhortation to "count yourselves dead to sin but alive to God in Christ Jesus" (v. 12).

At the same time, the metaphor of deliverance illustrates the futility of isolating the one from the other. Even though, logically, the liberation precedes the exhortation to walk free, the two cannot be separated. Israel's deliverance from Egypt may serve as an illustration. While the people of Israel were in Egypt, it would be meaningless to say that they had experienced deliverance, but that they still needed to experience the implications of their deliverance and leave Egypt. If they were delivered from Egypt, they were no longer in Egypt; they were somewhere else. Likewise, when God's people are delivered from sin, they are no longer slaves to sin, but their lives are fundamentally different.

---

47. Cf. Philip Esler, who demonstrates the untenability of the categories "ethics" and "paraenesis" for understanding Paul's purposes in Rom 12–15. Noting that Ambrosiaster in his commentary explains Rom 12 as an exhortation to lead a good life (*ac bonam vitam agendam hortatur*) (PL 17:164), Esler maintains that the scope of this section is wider than merely advice on right actions. Instead, he proposes to read this section in light of the ancient philosophical understanding of "the good life" as well as modern social identity theory. Read in this light, Paul is developing his vision for believers' new identity, transforming their self-understanding in its "evaluative, emotional, and cognitive dimensions" as well as the resulting patterns of behavior. Philip F. Esler, "Social Identity, the Virtues and the Good Life: A New Approach to Romans 12:1–15:13," *BTB* 33.2 (2003): 51–63; similarly, Wolter, *Röm 9–16*, 244.

48. Cf. Haritsima Razanadrakoto, who argues that the purpose of the section is to make the gospel effective (*effectuer*) in the audience's life ("Sans la loi," 134). On "righteousness" and "justification" entailing an act of deliverance, see especially Seifrid, "Paul's Use."

49. Moo observes that " '[i]ndicative' and 'imperative' do not succeed each other as two distinct stages in Christian experience, but are two sides of the same coin" (*Romans*, 764).

Bibliography

Allison, Dale C., Jr. "The Pauline Epistles and the Synoptic Gospels: The Pattern of the Parallels." *NTS* 28.1 (1982): 1–32.

Barrett, C. K. *The Epistle to the Romans.* 2nd ed. BNTC. Grand Rapids: Baker Academic, 1991.

Bjerkelund, Carl J. *Parakalô: Form, Funktion und Sinn der parakalô-Sätze in den paulinischen Briefen.* Bibliotheca Theologica Norvegica 1. Oslo: Universitetsforlaget, 1967.

Blomberg, Craig L. "Quotations, Allusions, and Echoes of Jesus in Paul." Pages 129–43 in *Studies in the Pauline Epistles: Essays in Honor of Douglas J. Moo.* Edited by Matthew S. Harmon and Jay E. Smith. Grand Rapids: Zondervan, 2014.

Booth, Roger P. *Jesus and the Laws of Purity: Tradition History and Legal History in Mark 7.* JSNTSup 13. Sheffield: JSOT Press, 1986.

Brown, Raymond E. *The Epistles of John: Translated with Introduction, Notes, and Commentary.* AB 30. New York: Doubleday, 1982.

Cranfield, C. E. B. *A Critical and Exegetical Commentary on the Epistle to the Romans.* 2 vols. ICC. Edinburgh: T&T Clark, 1975–79.

Crimella, Matteo. "Λογικὴ λατρεία (Rom 12:1): The Pauline Idea of Worship Between the Hebrew and Hellenistic Worlds." *Verbum Vitae* 39.3 (2021): 791–806.

Dibelius, Martin. *A Fresh Approach to the New Testament and Early Christian Literature.* International Library of Christian Knowledge. New York: Scribner's Sons, 1936.

Dunn, James D. G. *Romans 9–16.* WBC 38B. Dallas: Word, 1988.

Elliott, John. *1 Peter: A New Translation with Introduction and Commentary.* AB 37B. New York: Doubleday, 2000.

Esler, Philip F. "Paul and Stoicism: Romans 12 as a Test Case." *NTS* 50.1 (2004): 106–24.

———. "Social Identity, the Virtues and the Good Life: A New Approach to Romans 12:1–15:13." *BTB* 33.2 (2003): 51–63.

Evans, Christopher. "Rom 12:1–2: The True Worship." Pages 7–49 in *Dimensions de la vie chrétienne (Rm 12–13).* Edited by Lorenzo De Lorenzi. SMBen. Rome: Abbaye de St. Paul, 1979.

Fitzmyer, Joseph A. *Romans: A New Translation with Introduction and Commentary.* AB 33. New York: Doubleday, 1993.

Furnish, Victor Paul. *Theology and Ethics in Paul.* Nashville: Abingdon, 1968.

Grindheim, Sigurd. "Jesus and the Food Laws Revisited." *JSHJ* 18.1 (2020): 61–76.

Gupta, Nijay K. "What 'Mercies of God'? *Oiktirmos* in Romans 12:1 Against Its Septuagintal Background." *BBR* 22.1 (2012): 81–96.

Hooker, Morna D. "Interchange in Christ and Ethics." *JSNT* 25 (1985): 3–17.

Jewett, Robert. *Romans: A Commentary*. Hermeneia. Minneapolis: Fortress, 2007.

Jobes, Karen H. *1–3 John*. ZECNT 19. Grand Rapids: Zondervan Academic, 2014.

Käsemann, Ernst. *Commentary on Romans*. Translated and edited by Geoffrey W. Bromiley. Grand Rapids: Eerdmans, 1980.

Keck, Leander E. *Romans*. ANTC. Nashville: Abingdon, 2005.

Kim, Seyoon. "Jesus, Sayings Of." Pages 474–91 in *Dictionary of Paul and His Letters*. Edited by Gerald F. Hawthorne, Ralph P. Martin, and Daniel G. Reid. Downers Grove, IL: IVP Academic, 1993.

Lietzmann, Hans. *An die Römer*. 3rd ed. HNT 8. Tübingen: Mohr Siebeck, 1933.

Longenecker, Richard N. *The Epistle to the Romans: A Commentary on the Greek Text*. NIGTC. Grand Rapids: Eerdmans, 2016.

McKnight, Scot. *Reading Romans Backwards: A Gospel of Peace in the Midst of Empire*. Waco, TX: Baylor University Press, 2019.

Michel, Otto. *Der Brief an die Römer*. 5th ed. KEK. Göttingen: Vandenhoeck & Ruprecht, 1966.

Moo, Douglas J. *The Letter to the Romans*. 2nd ed. NICNT. Grand Rapids: Eerdmans, 2018.

Morenz, Siegfried. "Feurige Kohlen auf dem Haupt." *TLZ* 7 (1953): 187–92.

Ochsenmeier, Erwin. "Romans 12,17–13,7 and the Justice of God: Two Neglected Features of Paul's Argument." *ETL* 89.4 (2013): 361–82.

Peng, Kuo-Wei. *Hate the Evil, Hold Fast to the Good: Structuring Romans 12:1–15:1*. LNTS 300. London: T&T Clark, 2006.

Razanadrakoto, Haritsima. "Sans la loi mais par la foi . . . et dans l'unique corps: Exégèse de Romains 12,1–15,13." *ETL* 93.1 (2018): 133–43.

Schlier, Heinrich. *Der Römerbrief*. HThK 6. Freiburg: Herder, 1977.

Schnabel, Eckhard J. *Der Brief des Paulus an die Römer: Kapitel 6–16*. HTA. Witten/Gießen: Brockhaus/Brunnen, 2016.

Schnackenburg, Rudolf. *The Johannine Epistles: A Commentary*. Translated by Reginald and Ilse Fuller. New York: Crossroad, 1992.

Schreiner, Thomas R. *Romans*. BECNT. Grand Rapids: Baker Academic, 1998.

Seifrid, Mark A. "Paul's Use of Righteousness Language Against Its Hellenistic Background." Pages 39–74 in *Justification and Variegated Nomism: The Paradoxes of Paul*. Edited by D. A. Carson, Peter T. O'Brien, and Mark A. Seifrid. WUNT 2.181. Tübingen: Mohr Siebeck, 2004.

———. "Righteousness Language in the Hebrew Scriptures and Early Judaism." Pages 415–42 in *Justification and Variegated Nomism: Complexities of Second Temple Judaism*. Edited by D. A. Carson, Peter T. O'Brien, and Mark A. Seifrid. WUNT 2.140. Tübingen: Mohr Siebeck, 2001.

———. "Romans." Pages 607–94 in *Commentary on the New Testament Use of the Old Testament*. Edited by G. K. Beale and D. A. Carson. Grand Rapids: Baker Academic, 2007.

Smiga, George. "Romans 12:1–2 and 15:30–32 and the Occasion of the Letter to the Romans." *CBQ* 53.2 (1991): 257–73.

Thielman, Frank. *Romans.* ZECNT 6. Grand Rapids: Zondervan Academic, 2018.

Thompson, Michael. *Clothed with Christ: The Example and Teaching of Jesus in Romans 12.11–15.13.* JSNTSup 59. Sheffield: JSOT Press, 1991.

Thorsteinsson, Runar M. "Paul and Roman Stoicism: Romans 12 and Contemporary Stoic Ethics." *JSNT* 29.2 (2006): 139–61.

Wedderburn, A. J. M. *The Reasons for Romans.* SNTW. Edinburgh: T&T Clark, 1988.

Wenham, David. *Paul: Follower of Jesus or Founder of Christianity?* Grand Rapids: Eerdmans, 1995.

Wilckens, Ulrich. *Der Brief an die Römer (Röm 12–16).* EKK 6/3. Zürich/Neukirchener-Vluyn: Benziger/Neukirchener, 1982.

Wilson, Walter. *Love Without Pretense: Romans 12.9–21 and Hellenistic-Jewish Wisdom Literature.* WUNT 2.46. Tübingen: Mohr Siebeck, 1991.

Wolter, Michael. *Der Brief an die Römer (Teilband 2: Röm 9–16).* EKK 6/2. Neukirchener-Vluyn/Ostfildern: Neukirchener/Patmos, 2019.

CHAPTER 20

Church and State in Romans 13: How Universally Applicable Are Paul's Exhortations?

Thomas R. Schreiner

Introduction

The question before us centers on the normative status of Rom 13:1–7. Are Paul's words universally applicable or restricted to a particular situation? I define universally applicable as what is normally the case, as what we should usually or typically do. My answer is yes: Paul's admonition isn't restricted to the situation in Rome in the first century but applies to all Christians everywhere and for all time. Still, it does not follow from this that governing authorities should always be obeyed in every situation, and the reason for this limitation is that Paul did not intend for his instructions to be understood that way in the first place. So, yes, these words are normative for all times and places, but that does not mean that governments have absolute and ultimate authority. This essay will proceed in three parts. First, I will provide textual evidence for the universality of the admonitions. Second, I will critique various attempts (which I find rather unconvincing) to qualify the admonition in Rom 13:1–7. Third, I will explain why the universal applicability of the call to submit to rulers and authorities should be qualified to some extent.

Textual Evidence for the Universality of the Admonitions

We must first consider the context in which Rom 13:1–7 occurs. Romans 12:1–2 commences the exhortation section of the letter, encouraging readers to give themselves entirely to God as living sacrifices. Their minds are to be transformed and renewed so that they discern the will of God. Paul's instructions on the governing authorities accords with this larger purpose, and thus those who submit to governing authorities demonstrate that their minds are being renewed and that they are giving themselves wholly to God. Jean-Noël Aletti observes an illuminating chiasm.[1]

---

1. Jean-Noël Aletti, "La soumission des chrétiens aux autorités en Rm 13,1–7: Validité des arguments pauliniens?" *Bib* 89 (2008): 465. The outline paraphrases Aletti's chiasm.

A Love in the Church (12:9–16)

    B Relation with the world (12:17–21)

    B¹ Relation with political authorities in the world (13:1–7)

A¹ Love in the Church (13:8–10)

The chiasm is helpful because it gives us a picture of the larger framework for interpreting Rom 13:1–7. No one would claim that the exhortations that call upon believers to love one another—the outer elements of the chiasm—are limited to the situation in Rome. The admonition to love one another as believers is universally applicable in all times and in all places. I suggest that the inner elements of the chiasm also convey what believers are regularly called upon to do. The admonition to pursue peace with all, to abjure vengeance, and to overcome evil with good (12:17–21) are transcendent moral norms that apply to all people everywhere. We have every reason to expect, therefore, that the summons to submit to governing authorities (13:1–7)—the second element in the chiasm—would represent a general norm as well. I do not wish to press this point unduly since there is a sense in which the admonition to submit to authorities is qualified in a way that the call to love one another is not. Still, I will contend that the command to submit to rulers is a general norm.

It is also important to see that the two inner elements of the chiasm (relation with the world in 12:17–21 and relation with political authorities in the world) are closely tied to one another. A number of words link the two sections together. The words "evil" (κακός) and "good" (ἀγαθός) are found in both Rom 12:17, 21, and 13:3–4. "Wrath" (ὀργή) is mentioned in 12:19 and 13:4–5. The concept of vengeance appears in 12:19 (ἐκδικοῦντες, ἐκδίκησις) and in 13:4 (ἔκδικος). Romans 12:17 says not to repay (ἀποδιδόντες) evil with evil, while 13:7 says believers are to repay (ἀπόδοτε) what is owed to others, namely, taxes. The verbal links between the two sections and the chiastic pattern suggest we should read these two texts together, pointing to the universal validity of Paul's instructions in Rom 13:1–7. In other words, individuals are not to take vengeance, nor should they attempt to instantiate justice in this world when they are personally mistreated. However, this does not mean that evil in the world is allowed to run wild, for governing authorities are summoned to enact justice and to inflict punishment on those who commit crimes, on those who disrupt the public order by engaging in violence or other forms of corruption. Evil should not be permitted to run rampant or unchecked in society. The responsibility of believers is traced in the three imperatives structuring the passage: "submit" in vv. 1 and 5 (ὑποτασσέσθω and ὑποτάσσεσθαι[2]) and

---

2. The infinitive here has an imperatival sense.

"pay" (ἀπόδοτε) taxes in v. 5. The fundamental emphasis in the text is on the paying of taxes since paying taxes is the typical way of submitting to governmental authority.[3]

The transcendent character of the exhortations is also supported by the Pauline emphasis on divine ordination. The call to submit to governing powers in v. 1 is grounded in God's sovereign rule over the world. The civil authorities (ἐξουσίαι) exercise their rule by virtue of the will of God. Paul goes on to say that they are ordained (τεταγμέναι)—appointed and commissioned by God himself. We find the same notion in the OT. Daniel 2:21 says that the Lord "removes kings and sets up kings." The same sentiment is expressed elsewhere in Daniel (Dan 2:37; 5:18, 21). If the authorities are ordained by God and appointed by him, then the command to submit is a general norm.

Further support for the universal viability of the admonition comes from comparing the admonition here to other NT texts that address the relation of believers to governing authorities. The command to submit to rulers and authorities accords with Titus 3:1 where believers are taught to "submit to rulers and authorities." Similarly, in 1 Pet 2:12–13 believers are called upon to submit to the emperor or to governors appointed by him. The Petrine parallel is particularly interesting since Peter often emphasizes members of society who suffer under the authority of those who have more power (e.g., 1 Pet 2:18–3:6). Nevertheless, Peter admonishes believers to submit to those in authority. I have noted that submission manifests itself particularly in the command to pay taxes and to render honor since their rulers are ministers (λειτουργοί) of God (Rom 13:6–7). In saying that one should pay taxes Paul reflects the teaching of Jesus who enjoined the paying of taxes when confronted with this controversial question (Matt 22:15–22; Mark 12:13–17; Luke 20:20–26). Similarly, the Pauline injunction to grant honor (τιμήν) to whom honor is due (Rom 13:7) matches 1 Pet 2:17 where believers are instructed to "honor the emperor" (τὸν βασιλέα τιμᾶτε). These various admonitions suggest that submitting to authorities, paying taxes, and honoring rulers is the normal pattern for believers. Since we have exhortations to submit and to follow rulers in several texts, it seems that it was part of the common paraenetical tradition that was mediated to churches so that they would live in a way that befits those who are called Christians. In other words, the inclination of believers should be one where they are disposed to obey and carry out the laws and policies mandated by secular authority. All of this points to the universal applicability of the instructions here.

---

3. Douglas J. Moo, *The Epistle to the Romans*, NICNT (Grand Rapids: Eerdmans, 1996), 793; Stanley E. Porter, "Romans 13:1–7 as Pauline Political Rhetoric," *Filología Neotestamentaria* 3 (1990): 116.

Challenges to the Universal Applicability of Paul's Instructions

The applicability of the text relative to the government is called into question by Mark Nanos' interpretation,[4] for he argues that the authorities here are not governing authorities at all but represent rulers and authorities in synagogues. This novel reading of the text is almost certainly wrong. First, it is difficult to see why believers in Christ would be told to submit to synagogue authorities, especially since the latter were often opposed to Christians. We don't find a similar injunction anywhere else, but we saw above in several texts that submission to governing authorities was a common Christian topos (Matt 22:15–22; Mark 12:13–17; Luke 20:20–26; Titus 3:1: 1 Pet 2:13–17). Second, the paying of taxes fits with a reference to Rome instead of the synagogues. Nanos understands the word τέλος as a reference to Jewish "customs" or "behavior." But the term τέλος refers to taxes or tolls, and this is strengthened by the word φόρος which refers to paying taxes in Luke (20:22; 23:2) Josephus (*J.W.* 2.403), and 1 Maccabees (8:2, 4), and in many other instances as well. The clear references to payment of tax and tributes certifies that payment of taxes to governing authorities is intended. Finally, the reference to the sword in Rom 13:4 points to the punishments by the state,[5] not to penalties meted out by synagogal authorities.[6]

Some might say, however, that there are other indications that Paul's instructions are limited to the specific situation addressed in Rome. The older notion that Romans represents a Pauline treatise—a complete summation of his theology—is no longer the consensus. Most agree that the letter was written concerning particular circumstances facing the churches in Rome. When we recognize the situational nature of the letter, we have reasons to think that the admonition to submit to governing authorities is directed to a particular problem in Rome. We can be even more specific. The historian Suetonius (*Nero* 6.10 §1) tells us that taxes were exorbitant in Rome, and Tacitus (*Annals* 13.50–51) records complaints that were voiced over the extortion practiced by tax collectors in AD 57–58. As a consequence, Nero thought about repealing indirect taxes, but the senate advised against such a move, counseling moderation and prudence since repealing indirect taxes would probably lead the populace to call for the repeal of direct taxes as well. The incident described may have occurred after Romans was written, but we can be fairly confident that the matter was fermenting and causing controversy before it came to a head in AD 57–58.[7]

---

4. Mark D. Nanos, *The Mystery of Romans: The Jewish Context of Paul's Letter* (Minneapolis: Fortress, 1996), 289–336.

5. See Eckhard J. Schnabel, *Der Brief des Paulus an die Römer: Kapitel 6–16*, HTA (Witten/Gießen: Brockhaus/Brunnen, 2016), 686.

6. Leander E. Keck, *Romans*, ANTC (Nashville: Abingdon, 2005), 313, is correct in saying that Nanos' reading is "wholly fanciful."

7. For this reading, see Johannes Friedrich, Wolfgang Pöhlmann, and Peter Stuhlmacher, "Zur historischen Situation und Intention von Röm 13,1–7," *ZTK* 73 (1976): 131–66.

Several things can be said in response. First, some scholars think the matter of excessive taxation accounts for the matter being introduced here, and that is certainly possible. On the other hand, it is really impossible to know if this is the case since Paul says nothing about local circumstances. The admonition to pay taxes and to honor those who should be honored (Rom 13:6–7) is rather general.[8] We have no indication in the context, then, that the instructions relative to government were precipitated by the circumstances in the Roman church. Second, let's grant for the sake of argument that the matter of taxes is addressed because onerous taxes were becoming an issue in Rome, that the tax burden on the people was brewing discontent. Such a state of affairs is certainly possible. I have never heard people rejoicing over taxes that are levied, and generally people think taxes are too high. We can go even further. Let's stipulate that Paul addresses the Romans because they were feeling particularly oppressed by the tax structure. But even if this is true, it doesn't remove the universal applicability of the admonition since the readers are instructed to pay taxes. If the church was grumbling about paying taxes, Paul tells the readers to pay taxes anyway. Actually, we would have some reason to conclude that the instructions were limited by the specific situation Paul addressed if he said that in this particular instance they did not have to pay taxes since the taxes imposed were grinding the face of the people into the dirt. But Paul says nothing of the kind. Instead, the Roman Christians are to pay their taxes, and this seems to reflect the common Christian stance on the matter. This leads me to the third point. Most scholars agree today that Romans was written to address a specific situation, and we need not linger here on what that situation was. It is imperative to see, however, that Pauline letters addressed to particular circumstances in the churches may communicate universal norms and transcendent instructions. We must eschew the logic that a specific circumstance necessarily means that the exhortations do not (or cannot) apply more broadly. Often when a specific ethical question is asked, the answer to that question reflects a larger and transcendental norm, and that is the case here as well.

Another circumstantial reading is suggested by Stanley Porter, who argues that obedience should only be rendered to "just" rulers and governments.[9] The admonition does not bear universal applicability if some rulers (i.e., evil rulers) can be exempted from what Paul commands. Perhaps what Porter means at the end of the day is no different from my understanding of the text. But the way he frames his argument suggests that citizens do not have to obey the

---

8. Cf. Eduard Lohse, *Der Brief an die Römer*, KEK 4 (Göttingen: Vandenhoeck & Ruprecht, 2003), 358; Arland J. Hultgren, *Paul's Letter to the Romans: A Commentary* (Grand Rapids: Eerdmans, 2011), 468–69.

9. Porter, "Romans 13:1–7 as Pauline Political Rhetoric," 122–24; Stanley E. Porter, *The Letter to the Romans: A Linguistic and Literary Commentary*, NTM 37 (Sheffield: Sheffield Phoenix Press, 2015), 244–50.

prescriptions of unjust rulers and unjust governments. As I noted, in one sense this could be interpreted in a way that conforms with the thesis advanced here, but we need to be careful. Given the level of corruption in the world, it is easy to imagine that almost every government and every ruler could be considered corrupt. As Käsemann notes, corruption and petty despotism are exceedingly common, and it is hard to believe Paul would not be acquainted with such.[10] Porter's thesis runs into heavy weather when we apply it to Paul's day since it is difficult to believe that Paul would have thought that the emperor Nero was a just ruler. Some scholars have suggested, however, that Paul gave this advice about submitting to rulers during the good part of Nero's reign so that he had not yet considered how oppressive and evil governments can be.[11] Such naïveté on Paul's part is unconvincing. After all, Paul knew that Jesus of Nazareth was put to death unjustly by the Roman procurator Pontius Pilate (cf. 1 Tim 6:13). Furthermore, from childhood he had heard the stories about Pharaoh enslaving and oppressing Israel. He had read the accounts in Daniel of Nebuchadnezzar and Belteshazzar who were both judged for the evil they perpetrated. Furthermore, Paul himself had been mistreated by imperial authority, as is evident from the beating inflicted upon him and Silas when they were in Philippi (Acts 16:19–40). The instructions found here cannot be attributed to inexperience nor can they be limited to good rulers. As Leander Keck says, "Nor is there a word suggesting that Christians are to submit to authorities with whose 'politics' they agree or whose moral integrity they respect."[12]

An interesting appropriation of the text is suggested by Philip Towner, who says that the text must be interpreted in a missiological framework.[13] Such an observation does not necessarily undercut the universality of the admonition since the missiological context could fit with the notion that the commands given here are universal. On the other hand, a missiological framework could suggest that the Pauline instructions are limited situationally to a cutting-edge missions situation so that they do not represent what believers should do when

---

10. Ernst Käsemann, *Commentary on Romans*, trans. and ed. by Geoffrey W. Bromiley (Grand Rapids: Eerdmans, 1980), 356. But Käsemann also goes astray in saying that Paul wrote the text because the Roman churches had contempt for or indifference to leaders (357). Nor can we accept J. C. Miller's (*The Obedience of Faith, the Eschatological People of God, and the Purpose of Romans*, SBLDS 177 [Atlanta: SBL Press, 2000], 169–72) assertion that there was division in Rome over whether to pay taxes. Such claims are not warranted by the evidence.

11. Cf. Richard N. Longenecker, *The Epistle to the Romans: A Commentary on the Greek Text*, NIGTC (Grand Rapids: Eerdmans, 2016), 964.

12. Keck, *Romans*, 325.

13. Philip H. Towner, "Romans 13:1–7 and Paul's Missiological Perspective: A Call to Political Quietism or Transformation?" in *Romans and the People of God: Essays in Honor of Gordon D. Fee on the Occasion of His 65th Birthday*, ed. Sven K. Soderlund and N. T. Wright (Grand Rapids: Eerdmans, 1999), 149–69.

they are settled down in the world. Certainly, there is a missionary cast to Romans since Paul desires to travel to Spain and wants the Romans to support him in that mission (Rom 15:20–24). Such a general observation, however, does not lead us to the conclusion that the call to submit to rulers and authorities can be traced to Paul's missionary impulse. We need more compelling evidence than Towner provides to support the notion that the admonition is given fundamentally because of the missional situation of the churches, particularly because Paul says nothing about missions in this paragraph.

A fascinating reading of the text sees the command to submit to authorities as subversive. This reading is advanced in various ways. Robert Jewett claims that if the Roman Christians grasped what Paul wrote it would undercut and undermine Roman authority.[14] Christoph Stenschke says that the text can be read as counter-imperial, even if it was not Paul's explicit intention to propound a counter-imperial theme.[15] Many scholars see an anti-imperial message in Paul's writings generally, claiming that there is a hidden code that is unearthed by a careful reading.[16] Still, I agree with Seyoon Kim who says that "Rom 13:1–7 is the Achilles' heel for all anti-imperial readings of Paul."[17] John Barclay argues that seeing a hidden agenda in the writings of Paul fails to persuade.[18] Seeing this text as subversive or as raising questions about imperial authority is difficult to defend. We need clear contextual clues and evidence to support the notion that there is a code in the text that leads us to read the text contrary to the wording that we actually have in the text. Indeed, as noted previously, Paul grounds the call to submit to rulers in God sovereignly appointing such rulers (Rom 13:1). Further, those who disobey are threatened with judgment and punishment (Rom 13:2–4), which I take primarily as judgment meted out by

---

14. Robert Jewett, *Romans: A Commentary,* Hermeneia (Minneapolis: Fortress, 2007), 790.

15. Christoph W. Stenschke, "Paul's Jewish Gospel and the Claims of Rome in Paul's Epistle to the Romans," *Neot* 46 (2012): 338–78.

16. Cf. Neil Elliott "Romans 13:1–7 in the Context of Imperial Propaganda," in *Paul and Empire: Religion and Power in Roman Imperial Society,* ed. Richard A. Horsley (Harrisburg, PA: Trinity, 1997), 184–204; Neil Elliott, *The Arrogance of Nations: Reading Romans in the Shadow of Empire* (Minneapolis: Fortress, 2008); Richard A. Horsley, ed., *Paul and Empire: Religion and Power in Roman Imperial Society* (Harrisburg, PA: Trinity, 1997); Richard A. Horsley, *Paul and Politics: Ekklesia, Israel, Imperium, Interpretation: Essays in Honor of Krister Stendahl* (Harrisburg, PA: Trinity, 2000); Richard A. Horsley, *Paul and the Roman Imperial Order* (Harrisburg, PA: Trinity, 2004); N. T. Wright, *Paul: In Fresh Perspective* (Minneapolis: Fortress, 2005), 59–79; James R. Harrison, *Paul and the Imperial Authorities at Thessalonica and Rome: A Study in the Conflict of Ideology,* WUNT 273 (Tübingen: Mohr Siebeck, 2011).

17. Seyoon Kim, *Christ and Caesar: The Gospel and the Roman Empire in the Writings of Paul and Luke* (Grand Rapids: Eerdmans, 2008), 36.

18. John M. G. Barclay, *Pauline Churches and Diaspora Jews,* WUNT 275 (Tübingen: Mohr Siebeck, 2011), 379, cf. his discussion on pages 345–62.

government authority, though perhaps the judgment of the government previews and anticipates the judgment of God on the final day. Since the governing authorities are described as God's servant (διάκονός, Rom 13:4)[19] and as his ministers (λειτουργοί, Rom 13:6), they are not criticized but commended. Such designations, however, do remind readers that Roman rule is not ultimate, that God is the supreme ruler, even over Rome. In that sense Paul reminds readers that the emperor should not be worshiped or esteemed as divine. In that sense, the rule of Rome is relativized. In any case, believers are to submit for the sake of their consciences (συνείδησιν, 13:5), and it seems quite strange that Paul would appeal to the conscience of believers if he actually intended to undercut governing authority. In fact, it is hard to imagine a more positive defense for submitting to governing authority than is given here.

An inner canonical argument can also be raised against the universality of the admonitions in Rom 13. We read in Rev 13 about the beast from the sea, the beast that is summoned by the dragon—by the devil—out of the sea. The imagery comes from Dan 7 where four evil empires arise out of the sea. It seems in Revelation that the beast described represents the fourth beast of Dan 7, a beast that combines all the terrible qualities of the first three beasts and is terrifying in its ferocity and implacability. Most commentators agree that the beast in Rev 13 represents Rome. John's writing about government seems to stand in contrast to Paul since he does not see the Roman imperial power as a servant of God, as God's minister. Instead, the beast represents the antichrist, imperial power that is totalitarian, oppressive, and dehumanizing. The Roman empire does not foster goodness and righteousness. Instead, the beast demands of all human beings total allegiance, and those who do not worship the beast are slain. The beast arrogates to itself godlike qualities, resisting the command given to all people everywhere that they are to submit to God's lordship. The perspective of Rev 13 about the government needs to be integrated with Rom 13. The government is meant to restrain evil, but governing powers can become authoritarian—the state may become an antichrist. We think of some of the terrible regimes of the twentieth century where millions upon millions were killed by governing authorities, as in the slaying of millions in Nazi Germany or the slaughter and starvation precipitated by Joseph Stalin in the former Soviet Union.

But there is a sense, even in these evil regimes, in which the admonitions of Rom 13:1–7 still stand. For instance, we are told twice in Rev 13 that beast's ability to perpetrate evil "was given" (ἐδόθη, Rev 13:5, 7). Most commentators agree that the passive ἐδόθη is a divine passive, so that the beast's authority ultimately comes from God himself. The active verb "he gave" (ἔδωκεν, Rev 13:4) is used to describe the dragon giving authority and power to the beast, while the passive verb denotes the Lord granting authority to the beast. The passive verb, communicating God's sovereign appointment of the beast, demonstrates that John's understanding of God's sovereignty is nuanced. The passive verb absolves God from the evil the beast does. The beast does not reign and rule apart from God's sovereign will, and yet the Lord himself is not stained by evil. The Lord is sovereign but does not stand directly behind the evil carried out by the beast. There is a mystery here in that God rules over evil without himself being contaminated by evil, but we should see that Rev 13 agrees with Rom 13 in claiming that the rulers that exist are ordained by God. Even the reign of the beast cannot take place without God's permissive will. As N. T. Wright says, "There may be a certain sense here . . . that even when they are grievously deceived and almost demonic, ruling authorities still have a certain level of divine authorization."[20]

There is another sense in which Rev 13 accords with Rom 13. Even the most oppressive governments typically practice some form of law and order that prevents society from spinning into absolute anarchy. In other words, governments may be responsible for great evils but may also at the same time play a key role in restraining murder, stealing, rape, etc. Robert Stein remarks, "Governments, even oppressive governments, by their very nature seek to prevent the evils of indiscriminate murder, riot, thievery, as well as the general instability and chaos, and good acts do at times meet with approval and praise."[21] To put it another way: Rev 13 and Rom 13 at first glance seem to contradict one another. But when we put them together we receive a nuanced and fuller picture of governing authorities. Rulers occupy their office or position because of the will of God, and they restrain to some extent rampant evil in society. At the same time, however, these same authorities may perpetrate horrific evils, evils that are the height of injustice, evils that are sometimes unspeakable in their horror and savagery.

Qualifications to the Admonitions in Romans 13

Are the commands in Rom 13:1–7 universally applicable? Yes, they are a general norm, but we need to explain this further and introduce some qualifications. The universal applicability of the admonitions does not mean that there are no exceptions to the call to submit. What Paul writes here represents the typical and normal response to governing authorities, but at the same time what Paul writes here should not be thought of as a treatise where he gives a comprehensive answer to how believers relate to government. We cannot ask this passage

---

20. N. T. Wright, "The Letter to the Romans: Introduction, Commentary, and Reflections," in *The New Interpreter's Bible*, ed. Leander E. Keck (Nashville: Abingdon, 2002), 10:718.

21. Robert H. Stein, "The Argument of Romans 13:1–7." *NovT* 31.4 (1989): 334.

to do more than is warranted. What we see from the New Testament and this text specifically is that believers were expected to submit to governing authorities and to pay their taxes. That is the ordinary and everyday requirement for those who confess Jesus Christ as Lord. It will not do to say that the text does not speak to us today on the grounds that Paul did not know there would be modern nation states, as Franz Leenhardt and Joseph Fitzmyer allege.[22] Still, this text is misunderstood if it is taken to be a full reflection on the relationship believers have to government, and some have made the mistake of interpreting these verses as if in every conceivable situation believers should submit to whatever the governing authorities say. Paul focuses here on rulers doing what they are appointed and commissioned to do: punishing evil and rewarding what is good.

In contemporary application, it is crucial we recognize that the admonitions to submit to governmental authority in this text are applicable while also maintaining that there are exceptions to the rule; the details of such exceptions do not further Paul's authorial purpose in Romans and, therefore, are not elucidated in this text. We need to consult the entire scriptural witness to work out fully the relationship of believers to governing authority. It is evident in Rev 13 that believers are not to submit to the beast when it demands that all people everywhere worship him. Similarly, there are circumstances where government officials have used their position to extort those under them, but John the Baptist clearly says that no one serving in the government should participate in such activities (Luke 3:14). The Hebrew midwives resisted the dictates of Pharaoh (Exod 1:15–21), and Rahab defied the orders of Jericho's king (Josh 2:1–21; 6:22–25). Similarly, Daniel resisted the decree that forbade him to pray (Dan 6:10), and the apostles famously said to Jewish authorities who outlawed the preaching of the gospel that "it is necessary to obey God instead of people" (Acts 5:29). In both the OT and NT there is not an uncritical subservience to governing authorities. There are many examples where prophets challenged kings. When Asa depended on military strength instead of the LORD, the prophet Hanani reproved him (2 Chr 16:1–10). Unfortunately, Asa responded with rage, imprisoned the prophet, and was guilty of other human rights abuses.

The admonition in Rom 13 to submit to governing authorities and to pay taxes is universal in that it represents what believers are to do normally. Even though the Roman imperium often exercised power unjustly, believers were still asked to pay taxes under an unjust regime. Nor is space granted to citizens to pay only some taxes, the taxes that accord with our sense of justice and

---

22. Franz J. Leenhardt, *The Epistle to the Romans: A Commentary*, trans. H. Knight (London: Lutterworth, 1961), 328; Joseph A. Fitzmyer, *Romans: A New Translation with Introduction and Commentary*, AB 33 (New York: Doubleday, 1993), 662.

righteousness. And yet we recognize that the word about submission to governing authorities and the payment of taxes does not represent an exhaustive and complete discussion on the relationship to rulers. There are times when ruling authorities should be disobeyed and resisted. Paul sketches in what is generally true, but there are complexities and difficulties that have to be worked out by consulting the entire canonical witness and by exercising wisdom and prudence. Sometimes believers are compelled to disobey government orders, but when and where that should not happen is beyond what can be discussed here. That is not the purpose of my paper, and it was not Paul's purpose in Rom 13 either.

Bibliography

Aletti, Jean-Noël. "La soumission des chrétiens aux autorités en Rm 13,1–7: Validité des arguments pauliniens?" *Bib* 89 (2008): 457–76.

Barclay, John M. G. *Pauline Churches and Diaspora Jews.* WUNT 275. Tübingen: Mohr Siebeck, 2011.

Elliott, Neil. *The Arrogance of Nations: Reading Romans in the Shadow of Empire.* Minneapolis: Fortress, 2008.

———. "Romans 13:1–7 in the Context of Imperial Propaganda." Pages 184–204 in *Paul and Empire: Religion and Power in Roman Imperial Society.* Edited by Richard A. Horsley. Harrisburg, PA: Trinity, 1997.

Fitzmyer, Joseph A. *Romans: A New Translation with Introduction and Commentary.* AB 33. New York: Doubleday, 1993.

Friedrich, Johannes, Wolfgang Pöhlmann, and Peter Stuhlmacher. "Zur historischen Situation und Intention von Röm 13,1–7." *ZTK* 73 (1976): 131–66.

Harrison, James R. *Paul and the Imperial Authorities at Thessalonica and Rome: A Study in the Conflict of Ideology.* WUNT 273. Tübingen: Mohr Siebeck, 2011.

Horsley, Richard A., ed. *Paul and Empire: Religion and Power in Roman Imperial Society.* Harrisburg, PA: Trinity, 1997.

———. *Paul and Politics: Ekklesia, Israel, Imperium, Interpretation: Essays in Honor of Krister Stendahl.* Harrisburg, PA: Trinity, 2000.

———. *Paul and the Roman Imperial Order.* Harrisburg, PA: Trinity, 2004.

Hultgren, Arland J. *Paul's Letter to the Romans: A Commentary.* Grand Rapids: Eerdmans, 2011.

Jewett, Robert. *Romans: A Commentary.* Hermeneia. Minneapolis: Fortress, 2007.

Käsemann, Ernst. *Commentary on Romans.* Translated and edited by Geoffrey W. Bromiley. Grand Rapids: Eerdmans, 1980.

Keck, Leander E. *Romans.* ANTC. Nashville: Abingdon, 2005.

Kim, Seyoon. *Christ and Caesar: The Gospel and the Roman Empire in the Writings of Paul and Luke*. Grand Rapids: Eerdmans, 2008.

Leenhardt, Franz J. *The Epistle to the Romans: A Commentary*. Translated by H. Knight. London: Lutterworth, 1961.

Lohse, Eduard. *Der Brief an die Römer*. KEK 4. Göttingen: Vandenhoeck & Ruprecht, 2003.

Longenecker, Richard N. *The Epistle to the Romans: A Commentary on the Greek Text*. NIGTC. Grand Rapids: Eerdmans, 2016.

Miller, J. C. *The Obedience of Faith, the Eschatological People of God, and the Purpose of Romans*. SBLDS 177. Atlanta: SBL Press, 2000.

Moo, Douglas J. *The Epistle to the Romans*. NICNT. Grand Rapids: Eerdmans, 1996.

Nanos, Mark D. *The Mystery of Romans: The Jewish Context of Paul's Letter*. Minneapolis: Fortress, 1996.

Porter, Stanley E. *The Letter to the Romans: A Linguistic and Literary Commentary*. NTM 37. Sheffield: Sheffield Phoenix Press, 2015.

———. "Romans 13:1–7 as Pauline Political Rhetoric." *Filología Neotestamentaria* 3 (1990): 115–39.

Schnabel, Eckhard J. *Der Brief des Paulus an die Römer: Kapitel 6–16*. HTA. Witten/Gießen: Brockhaus/Brunnen, 2016.

Stein, Robert H. "The Argument of Romans 13:1–7." *NovT* 31.4 (1989): 325–43.

Stenschke, Christoph W. "Paul's Jewish Gospel and the Claims of Rome in Paul's Epistle to the Romans." *Neot* 46 (2012): 338–78.

Towner, Philip H. "Romans 13:1–7 and Paul's Missiological Perspective: A Call to Political Quietism or Transformation?" Pages 149–69 in *Romans and the People of God: Essays in Honor of Gordon D. Fee on the Occasion of His 65th Birthday*. Edited by Sven K. Soderlund and N. T. Wright. Grand Rapids: Eerdmans, 1999.

Wright, N. T. "The Letter to the Romans: Introduction, Commentary, and Reflections." Pages 395–770 in vol. 10 of *The New Interpreter's Bible*. Edited by Leander E. Keck. Nashville: Abingdon, 2002.

———. *Paul: In Fresh Perspective*. Minneapolis: Fortress, 2005.

CHAPTER 21

What Does Romans 14:1–15:13 Tell Us about Jewish Christianity in Rome?

A. Andrew Das

Introduction

In the footsteps of Walter Bauer and Ernst Käsemann, J. Louis Martyn stressed that the interpretative task is never complete until the reader has taken an imagined seat within the original congregation(s).[1] Paul wrote to specific audiences to address specific concerns. Unfortunately, two long millennia separate the modern interpreter from the Pauline churches. Interpreters hunt for clues that might unravel the occasioning situation and contextualize the letter. The data is incomplete, and competing reconstructions lead to dramatically differing "original" settings.[2] Book titles bear witness to the frustration: *The Romans Debate* or *The Mystery of Romans*. One book was daringly called *Solving the Romans Debate*.[3] A key puzzle piece is Rom 14:1–15:13 with its glimpse of an apparent dispute taking place in the Roman congregations. Given the attention to Rom 15:7–13 in a *JSNT* article years ago, this paper will be weighted toward the front end of that body of text: Rom 14:1–15:6.[4]

A Concrete Situation?

Romans 14:1–3 and 14:20–23 frame the chapter with the language of disputing in vv. 1 and 23 (διακρίσις, διακρίνομαι), judging in vv. 3, 4, 22, and 23 (κρίνω, κατακρίνω), believing or trusting in vv. 1–2, 22–23 (πίστις/πιστεύω, 14:1, 2, 22, 23), and eating in vv. 2, 3, 20, 21, and 23 (ἐσθίω, 14:2, 3, 20, 21, 23).[5]

---

1. J. Louis Martyn, *Galatians: A New Translation with Introduction and Commentary*, AB 33A (New York: Doubleday, 1997), 42.

2. A. Andrew Das, "The Pauline Letters in Contemporary Research," in *The Oxford Handbook of Pauline Studies*, ed. Matthew Novenson and R. Barry Matlock (Oxford: Oxford University Press, 2022), 237–57.

3. At least the author did not claim to have "solved" it; A. Andrew Das, *Solving the Romans Debate* (Minneapolis: Fortress, 2007).

4. A. Andrew Das, "'Praise the Lord, All You Gentiles': The Encoded Audience of Romans 15.7–13," *JSNT* 34.1 (2011): 90–110.

5. The parallels with 14:20–23 occasionally extend to 15:7; note the parallel imperatives in 14:1 and 15:7.

Brothers and sisters in the faith are improperly judging and disputing with their peers in the context of eating and drinking.[6] The household vocabulary ("lord" [κύριος], "slave" [οἰκέτης], "building" [οἰκοδομή], "brother [or sister]" [ἀδελφός], "neighbor" [πλησίον], "eating" [ἐσθίω], "serving" [δουλεύω], and "welcoming" [προσλάμβανω]) indicates that these Christ-believing gatherings and meals were taking place in homes. The Romans are to practice hospitality. Hosts welcome their guests into their homes and social spaces.[7] Judging or disputing disrupts their relationships and gatherings for meals and worship. They are to be accepting of each other's dietary practices. The question is whether these instructions go beyond the mutual acceptance of Christ-believers and concern also the relationship between Jews and Gentiles, or between circumcised and uncircumcised.

Romans 14:1–15:6 introduces the "weak" in 14:1–2 as eating only vegetables. Jews would adopt this approach when they did not have control over their diet to avoid gentile idolatry. In Dan 1, Daniel and his friends ate only vegetables in a series of tests involving idolatry (Dan 1–6; here 1:5, 8, 10, 12, 16; cf. 10:3). Tobit (1:11) would not eat the food of gentiles. Joseph sought to avoid the idolatry associated with the bread of strangulation and the wine of libation at the home of his future in-laws (Jos. Asen. 7:1; 8:5–7; 10:1).[8] Indeed, Rom 14:21 mentions the avoidance of wine. Gentiles sought to accommodate Jewish sensibilities regarding meat and drink in Let. Aris. 142, 181.[9] Josephus relates how Jewish

---

6. Wayne A. Meeks, "Judgment and the Brother: Romans 14:1–15:13" in *Tradition and Interpretation in the New Testament: Essays in Honor of E. Earle Ellis for His 60th Birthday,* ed. Gerald F. Hawthorne and Otto Betz (Grand Rapids: Eerdmans, 1987), 291; Peter Spitaler, "Household Disputes in Rome (Romans 14:1–15:13)," *RB* 116 (2009): 50. David Rudolph: "A more broad-ranging approach would make room for the possibility that *the issue was not purity but people who were purists about purity*" (emphasis his); "Paul and the Food Laws: A Reassessment of Romans 14:14, 20," in *Paul the Jew: Rereading the Apostle as a Figure of Second Temple Judaism,* ed. Gabriele Boccaccini and Carlos A. Segovia (Minneapolis: Fortress, 2016), 162. Peter J. Tomson calls the "weak" "hyper-halakhic" and "oversensitive" individuals; *Paul and the Jewish Law: Halakha in the Letters of the Apostle to the Gentiles,* CRINT 3.1 (Assen/Minneapolis: Van Gorcum/ Fortress, 1990), 244–45. He adds: "In Rome as in Antioch, Jews could not maintain ritual purity because of the decree of impurity on gentile lands" (243); cf. 153–54n12, 228–29 (noting Talmudic citations of early second century CE figures). Purity rules would be, for Tomson, irrelevant to the interpretation of Rom 14.

7. Robert Jewett, *Romans: A Commentary,* Hermeneia (Minneapolis: Fortress, 2007), 835; James D. G. Dunn, *Romans 9–16,* WBC 38B (Dallas: Word, 1988), 798; Spitaler, "Household Disputes," 46n4.

8. On Jews' avoiding the wine of libation, see Add Esth C 14:17 and m. 'Abod. Zar. 5:3–7; cf. 2:3–4; 4:10–5:12. On Jews' avoiding meat and wine, see also T. Reub. 1.10 and T. Jud. 15.4.

9. Philip F. Esler, *Galatians,* NTR (London: Routledge, 1998), 102–16, although he reduces the issue to concerns about gentile idolatry. Jews could also be concerned with the immorality of gentiles or gentile uncleanness in general.

priests on their way to Rome during the reign of Nero ate only figs and nuts to avoid contact with meat offered to pagan idols (*Life* 3 §§13–14).[10]

Confirming that Jewish customs are at issue for the "weak," Rom 14:20 refers to their preference for food that is "clean" (καθαρά), a Septuagintal and Second Temple word for the ritual cleanliness required by the Torah (e.g., LXX Gen 7:2–3, 9; 8:20; Lev 4:12; 6:11; 7:19; Ezra 6:20; Mal 1:11; Jdt 10:5; 12:9; 1 Macc 1:48).[11] Conversely, in Rom 14:14 Paul contrasts his own view with those who see certain foods as "common" or "unclean" (κοινός; three times!).[12] The use of this Greek word for matters of ritual impurity is unique to the Jews.[13] Finally, in 14:5 some judge one day as more important than another. Could this be a nod to a Jewish calendar? Most commentators have concluded that the vegetarian diet, the avoidance of unclean food in favor of the clean, the avoidance of wine, and the observance of days cumulatively provide evidence that the "weak" Christ-believers of 14:1–3 are Jewish.[14]

Others in Rom 14 are comfortable eating all things, and in Rom 15:1 Paul overtly refers to the "strong." Most commentators conflate those who "eat everything" in 14:3 with the "strong" of 15:1 and identify them as Gentile. Thus for many commentators Paul is addressing a conflict at Rome between a Gentile Christ-believing "strong" group and a Jewish Christ-believing "weak." Romans 15:7's "therefore" concludes in view of this situation that the Romans are to welcome one another even as Christ has welcomed both Jews and Gentiles.[15] Christ's welcoming Jews and Gentiles presumably serves as a model for the Jews and Gentiles in the Roman congregations.[16]

---

10. Peter Lampe, *From Paul to Valentinus: Christians at Rome in the First Two Centuries* (Minneapolis: Fortress, 2003), 73, commented: "They were not far in a time and place from the people presupposed in the letter to the Romans!"

11. Dunn, *Romans 9–16*, 825–26.

12. Cf. 1 Macc 1:47, 62; *Ant.* 3.7.7 §181; 11.8.7 §346; 12.7.6 §320; 13.1.1 §4; Mark 7:15–23; Acts 10:14, 28; 11:8.

13. Dunn, *Romans 9–16*, 818–19.

14. John M. G. Barclay, " 'Do We Undermine the Law?': A Study on Romans 14.1–15.6," in *Paul and the Mosaic Law,* ed. James D. G. Dunn (Grand Rapids: Eerdmans, 1996), 294–99.

15. With Michael Thompson, *Clothed With Christ: The Example and Teaching of Jesus in Romans 12.1–15.13,* JSNTSup 59 (Sheffield: Sheffield Academic Press, 1991), 230n3: "A comparative καθώς, however, better explains the addition of the preposition [εἰς], since Paul has just prayed that his readers will *glorify* God [15:6] by finding unity in their emulation of Christ"; so also Franz J. Leenhardt, *The Epistle to the Romans: A Commentary* (London: Lutterworth, 1961), 364. Note the "κατὰ Χριστόν in 15:3, 5 that suggests that καθώς should be taken with its normal comparative force; rightly J. Ross Wagner, "The Christ, Servant of Jew and Gentile: A Fresh Approach to Romans 15:8–9," *JBL* 116.3 (1997): 474–75n11.

16. Representative are Scott J. Hafemann, "Eschatology and Ethics: The Future of Israel and the Nations in Romans 15:1–13," *TynBul* 51.2 (2000): 161–92, here 187–88, 190; Dunn, *Romans 9–16*, 845; Ernst Käsemann, *Commentary on Romans,* trans. and

Always a cautious interpreter of texts, Wayne Meeks sounded a warning about this reconstruction decades ago. First, Meeks cautioned that the key term εἰδωλόθυτα in 1 Cor 8–10 is missing in Rom 14:[17] "Indeed the whole question of idolatry is unmentioned in this context," even though the Jews, when avoiding idolatry, would resort to vegetables and avoid wine—two practices that *are* mentioned in Rom 14:1–15:6.[18] Mention of a vegetarian diet in a context where idolatry is not at issue is puzzling.

Second, Meeks noted how Paul never actually identifies the "weak" of Rom 14:1–3 as Jewish nor the "strong" of Rom 15:1 as Gentile, as if a Gentile Christ-believing "strong" were being juxtaposed with a Jewish Christ-believing "weak."[19] This omission is even more acute when one considers that Paul has not shied away from explicitly discussing Jews and Gentiles all throughout the letter to this point. For that matter, Paul does not identify the "weak" as circumcised or the "strong" as uncircumcised, even though those categories have figured prominently earlier in the letter. These omissions are glaring. Often overlooked, Paul does not identify a corresponding "strong" at the point when he introduces the "weak" early in Rom 14.[20]

Third, while the "weak" esteem one day over another, Paul conspicuously avoids any mention of the Sabbath. Paul's description is stated generally enough that *any* sacred day, even a Gentile's, would match the description.[21] The general nature of Paul's language in this section calls into question the nature and level of discord most interpreters assume in the Roman congregations.[22]

---

ed. Geoffrey W. Bromiley (Grand Rapids: Eerdmans 1980), 384; C. E. B. Cranfield, *A Critical and Exegetical Commentary on the Epistle to the Romans,* 2 vols., ICC (Edinburgh: T&T Clark 1979), 2:740–41; Thomas R. Schreiner, *Romans,* BECNT (Grand Rapids: Baker Academic, 1998), 753–54: "[T]he reference to Jews and Gentiles confirms the suspicion that the "weak" consist primarily of Jewish Christians, while the "strong" come primarily from Gentiles."

17. Meeks, "Judgment and the Brother," 292.

18. Wayne A. Meeks, "The Polyphonic Ethics of the Apostle Paul," *Annual of the Society of Christian Ethics* 8 (1988): 25. Strangely, Kevin B. McCruden, "Judgment and Life for the Lord: Occasion and Theology of Romans 14,1–15,13," *Bib* 86.2 (2005): 229–44, cites Meeks but overlooks the omission of this key term in Rom 14 in suggesting the possibility of pagan sacrifices.

19. Meeks, "Polyphonic Effects," 25.

20. That he does not identify the "strong" until 15:1 should be granted more consideration than is usually the case, and the "strong" of 15:1 are not identified as eating everything; with Neil Elliott, "Asceticism Among the 'Weak' and 'Strong' in Romans 14–15," in *Asceticism and the New Testament,* ed. Leif E. Vaage and Vincent L. Wimbush (London: Routledge, 1999), 231–51, here 238; Beverly Roberts Gaventa, "Reading for the Subject: The Paradox of Power in Romans 14:1–15:6," *JTI* 5 (2011): 7–10, esp. 7–8: They are to use their power not to please themselves but, like Christ, to build others up.

21. Meeks, "Polyphonic Effects," 25–26.

22. McCruden, "Judgment," 229–44.

Fourth, in addition to Meeks' qualms, Rom 14 employs elements of diatribe. The diatribal style functioned primarily for the sake of instruction and not necessarily to address a specific situation.[23] Like the diatribe in Rom 2:1–11 and 2:17–29, Paul is again addressing the individual who arrogantly, presumptuously judges another. Note the judgment vocabulary throughout Rom 14.[24] Confrontational questions characterize the style even as Paul questions the hearer in 14:10: "Why are you judging?" (cf. the direct address in 14:4).[25] To what extent, then, is Paul addressing a specific problem among contending parties?[26] As McCruden observed, "The entire passage has a distinctly general and indefinite tone, just as Rom 2,1–11 does."[27] Paul is warning against assuming the role of God in their relationships by judging a brother or sister, whether for food customs or calendrical observances.

Nevertheless, those criticizing a situational reading of Rom 14:1–15:6 still see it is as situational to *some* extent. For McCruden, Paul is offering the Romans instructions on food and sabbath observances. Even if not a conflict between separate parties of weak and strong, Paul is still reflecting on "the relationship between Jew and Gentile in the eyes of God."[28] Meeks concedes that there may be tensions between Jews and Gentiles in the Roman communities, even as that relationship figures prominently in the letter.[29]

Judgment language remains central. The Romans are not to pass judgment on each other since doing so causes the brother or sister to stumble (14:13). By judging and grieving someone with respect to food choices, the Romans will destroy one for whom Christ died (14:15). A judgment without love (12:9–10) is destructive (14:23).[30] Rather, each must give an account to the God who judges

---

23. Robert J. Karris, "Romans 14:1–15:13 and the Occasion of Romans," in *The Romans Debate: Revised and Expanded Edition*, ed. Karl P. Donfried (Peabody, MA: Hendrickson, 1991), 70n32.

24. κρινέτω in 14:3; κρίνων in 14:3; κρίνει in 14:5; κρίνεις in 14:10; κρίνωμεν in 14:13; κρίννων 14:22; and κατακέκριται in 14:23.

25. Abraham J. Malherbe, *Moral Exhortation: A Greco-Roman Sourcebook* (Philadelphia: Westminster, 1986), 129–34, esp. 129–30.

26. McCruden, "Judgment," 233–36.

27. McCruden, "Judgment," 233. Paul in Rom 14 is building on his reminders throughout the letter of the coming judgment before God's throne (3:4, 6; 5:16, 18; 8:1, 3; 13:2; 14:10–12) but especially the extended discussion in Rom 2:1–16. Since all will be judged by God according to their works, what rationale could any of the Romans have to be judging another? Romans 14 is potent rhetoric in light of all that Paul has written. Cf. Klaus-Michael Bull, "'Wir Werden Alle vor den Richterstuhl Gottes Gestellt Werden' (Röm 14, 10): Zur Funktion des Motivs vom Endgericht in den Argumentationen des Römerbriefes," in *Apokalyptik als Herausforderung Neutestamentlicher Theologie*, ed. Michael Becker and Markus Öhler, WUNT 2.214 (Tübingen: Mohr Siebeck, 2006), 125–43; Meeks, "Judgment," 293–98.

28. McCruden, "Judgment," 243, cf. 244.

29. Meeks, "Polyphonic Effects," 25.

30. In the one body of brothers and sisters (Rom 12–13).

rightly at the Last Day (14:10, 12) with Christ as Lord of the living and the dead (14:9). Paul contrasts the destructive power of the Romans' judging with the transformative power of God (1:16) that builds up.[31] "However, it must be emphasized that Paul invariably couches this relationship in generalized terms, reflecting on the relationship between Jews and Gentiles as a whole and seldom in terms of individual Jews and Gentiles."[32]

Christ-Believers in the Context of the Synagogues?

Paul regularly draws on the Jewish Scriptures in addressing the Romans. In Rom 14:11 he cites Isa 45:23 and 49:19, but Gentile authors from this period appear entirely unaware of the content of the Jewish Scriptures beyond Gen 1 (Longinus, [*Subl.*] 9.9 and Ocellus Lucanus). Gentile knowledge of the Scriptures is not attested in the Roman world apart from the synagogues. Whereas Paul responds to the rivals' use of Scripture at Galatia and cites little of the Scriptures to the Thessalonians, by way of contrast he regularly employs Scripture with the Romans in a manner that assumes at least their appreciation of the ancient sacred texts.[33] The Roman Gentiles have apparently interacted with synagogue Jews.

One model for accounting for the Romans' appreciation of the Jewish Scriptures, Mark Nanos' pioneering Paul-within-Judaism proposal, is that the Gentile Christ-believers of Rome were meeting as subgroups *within* the larger synagogue gatherings.[34] As Paul addressed the Christ-believing Romans, he lamented that the synagogue Jews had not recognized the full significance of Jesus as Israel's Savior and Messiah (Rom 9:1–5). For Nanos, the non-Christ-believing Jews were still "brothers (and sisters)" of "faith," even if "weak" in that faith (Rom 14:1, 10; cf. Rom 9:3).[35] Although an intra-synagogal context would account for the Roman Christ-believers' appreciation of the Scriptures, at least five factors eliminate the possibility.

31. McCruden, "Judgment," 238.
32. McCruden, "Judgment," 231, following Meeks, "Polyphonic Effects," 25
33. On the responsive use of Scripture at Galatia, see A. Andrew Das, "Israel's Scriptures in Galatians," in *Israel's Scriptures in Early Christian Writings: The Use of the Old Testament in the New*, ed. Matthias Henze and David Lincicum (Grand Rapids: Eerdmans, 2023), 388–406. On the level of biblical literacy at Rome, see Christopher D. Stanley, *Arguing with Scripture: The Rhetoric of Quotations in the Letters of Paul* (New York: T&T Clark, 2004), 136–70, esp. 139–42; Christopher D. Stanley, "'Pearls Before Swine': Did Paul's Audiences Understand His Biblical Quotations," *NovT* 41.2 (1999): 124–44; also A. Andrew Das, *Paul and the Stories of Israel: Grand Thematic Narratives in Galatians* (Minneapolis: Fortress, 2016), 22–23.
34. Mark D. Nanos, *The Mystery of Romans: The Jewish Context of Paul's Letter* (Minneapolis: Fortress, 1996).
35. In Rom 9:3 his own ethnic people are "brothers (and sisters)."

First, Paul's instructions to and admonitions of the strong assume that they bear responsibility and control over the relationship with the weak. That would not be the case were they gathering under the auspices of the non-Christ-believing synagogue leadership.[36] Those who eat everything are not to *judge* the weak (Rom 14:1–3).[37] Even as the weak should not judge the strong in vv. 3 and 10, in 14:13 the strong are also not to judge the weak.[38]

Second, on what basis could Paul admonish the weak not to judge the strong if they were non-Christ-believing Jews? Paul repeatedly identifies himself as the apostle to the Roman *Gentiles* (11:13; cf. 1:5–6, 13–15; 15:15–17; Gal 2:7–9). As he addresses and admonishes the "weak" in Rom 14, he thereby includes them in the implied audience of Romans, which he has already identified as *Christ-believing* (e.g., Rom 1:1–8).

Third, Paul identifies his own ethnic people as brothers and sisters in Rom 9:3, but he also heavily qualifies the appellation, indicating that it is unusual: "*my*" brothers and sisters who are "*according to the flesh*." Apart from such unusual qualifications, "brothers (and sisters)" elsewhere in Romans refers to *Christ-believers*, members of the one body of Christ (12:1, 3–8), recipients of Christ's Spirit (8:12), who have died to the law through the body of Christ (7:4, 6). In fact, Paul *distinguishes* the "brothers (and sisters)" in 10:1 from "them"/ Israel. Apart from Rom 9:3 with its qualifiers signaling a *departure*, no clear instance of "brother" is used for non-Christ-believing Jews.

Fourth, the "faith" Paul describes is *Christ*-centered, which is incomprehensible if the "weak in faith" are non-Christ-believing. In Rom 14:6 one eats or does not eat "to the Lord." In 14:8 one lives or dies "to the Lord," for "we are the Lord's." In Rom 14:9 that Lord is defined as *Christ* who lived and died that he might be "Lord" of both the dead and the living. Therefore, when a person lives or dies "for the Lord" in 14:8, that person is living for Christ. The weak and the strong must be Christ-believers.

Fifth, whereas those who resort to vegetables are "*weak* in faith" (14:1–2), Paul describes his own non-Christ-believing peers as in "unbelief" (τῇ ἀπιστίᾳ, 11:20, 23; cf. 3:3). Paul simply does not offer any obvious indication that the Romans were gathering in non-Christ-believing larger settings. Nanos' intra-synagogal context for Romans should be rejected.[39] These considerations shift

---

36. The critique of Nanos' thesis here is drawn from a more comprehensive critique in Das, *Solving the Romans Debate*, 115–48.

37. In view of the κριν- vocabulary in this passage, διακρίσεις would mean passing judgment; LXX Job 37:16; 1 Cor 12:10; Heb 5:14; cf. the cognate verb "passing judgment" in Acts 10:20; 11:2; Jude 9.

38. They should decide ("judge") not to put a stumbling block in the way of a brother (14:21).

39. William S. Campbell's rhetoric betrays the weakness of the intra-synagogal perspective. He argues at length for the *possibility* of a synagogue context for the Roman

the locus of the tensions to independent Roman Christ-believing gatherings. Such a "decisive split" from the synagogues for worship gatherings does not mean that many Christ-believers did not remain sympathetic to or frequent also the synagogues.[40]

A Jewish Christ-Believing Weak?

Since the customs at issue in Rom 14:1–15:6 are largely Jewish, the usual assumption is that the "weak" who practice them must be Jewish.[41] This assumption is problematic: Jews would eat vegetables where they had no control over their diet. Josephus describes Jewish priests as prisoners sent "in bonds" to Rome by the governor Felix. In Roman custody they had to resort to figs and nuts since they were not free to purchase their own food (*Life* 3 §§13–14). Jewish kosher markets in Rome, of all places, would have been plentiful (*Ant.* 14.10.1–26 §§185–267). Synagogue Jews in Rome were among the least likely to be lacking kosher meat and wine, a fact militating against a Jewish identity of the practitioners. A vegetarian diet may be more likely for a Gentile Christ-believer, sympathetic to Jewish customs but without regular access to those markets.[42] Gentiles who avoided meat tainted with idolatry would also have been concerned by the attitude of their peers who ate everything, especially if they might not have been scrupulous in avoiding idolatrous food and drink for the shared meals.[43]

The observance of Jewish customs does not require the presence of Jews in Paul's audience. Josephus brags: "The masses have long since shown a keen

---

Christ-believing assemblies but does not respond to the longstanding problems posed for such a thesis; "The Addressees of Paul's Letter to the Romans: Assemblies of God in House Churches and Synagogues?" in *Between Gospel and Election: Explorations in the Interpretation of Romans 9–11*, ed. Florian Wilk and J. Ross Wagner, with the assistance of Frank Schleritt, WUNT 257 (Tübingen: Mohr Siebeck, 2010), 187–88, 194n77.

40. Contra Campbell's misunderstanding ("Addressees," 187) in his critique of my *Solving the Romans Debate*. For a critique of Paul-within-Judaism readings of Paul more generally, see A. Andrew Das, "Traditional Protestant Perspective Response to Zetterholm," in *Perspectives on Paul: Five Views*, ed. Scot McKnight and B. J. Oropeza (Grand Rapids: Baker Academic, 2020), 201–6.

41. Lampe, *From Paul to Valentinus*, 73.

42. Melito of Sardis (in Eusebius, *Historia ecclesiastica* 4.26.9–10 [NPNF[2] 1:205–6]) and Clement of Rome (1 Clem. 5.2, 4, 5) both attribute the persecution that broke out under Nero (cf. Tacitus) to jealousy and envy. The Jews lived, worked, and gathered nearby in the same sections of Rome; Lampe, *From Paul to Valentinus*, 19–47 esp. 38–40. Apparently, some degree of separation had taken place between the two communities to the extent that Nero blamed the Christ-believers (cf. Claudius and the "Chrestus" incident in the synagogues). Gentile sympathizers of Judaism may not have enjoyed the same access to Jewish vendors as in the less tense years of the relationship.

43. Barclay, "'Do We Undermine the Law?'" 291–92.

desire to adopt our religious observances; and there is not one city, Greek or barbarian, nor a single nation, to which our custom of abstaining from work on the seventh day has not spread, . . . and [where] many of our prohibitions in the matter of food are not observed" (*Ag. Ap.* 2.39 §282 [Thackeray, LCL]).[44] Food and Sabbath observances, Josephus claims, have become popular among the Gentiles. Louis Feldman notes how Josephus refers here to Sabbath observance and *many* of the Jewish food customs as popular among non-Jews: "[W]e are dealing not with full proselytes but with 'sympathizers.'"[45] Similarly for Philo: "[Jewish customs] attract and win the attention of all, of barbarians, of Greeks, of dwellers on the mainland and islands, of nations of the east and the west, of Europe and Asia, of the whole inhabited world from end to end" (*Mos.* 2.4 §20).

Among Gentile authors, Juvenal writes of uncircumcised Gentiles rigidly observing the Sabbath and food prescriptions, including abstention from pork (*Sat.* 14.96–106). Horace relates a conversation with one of his friends (*Satires* 1.9.68–72 [Fairclough, LCL]), who claims he cannot converse since "to-day is the thirtieth Sabbath. Would you affront the circumcised Jews?" When Horace responds that he does not observe such customs, Fuscus jokes that he is "a somewhat weaker brother, one of the many" (note the language of "weakness" in connection with Gentile observance of Jewish customs). Fuscus' humor depends on the general perception that the Sabbath was a superstition common in the populace, especially among the ordinary and less educated.[46] Ovid frequently mentions the Sabbath (*Am.* 219–20), even observing how shops and businesses throughout the general populace were closing on the Sabbath (*Ars* 1.413–16).[47] Seneca (*Ep.* 95.47) and Persius (*Satirae* 5.180–84) both lament how some Romans are lighting lamps on the Jewish Sabbath, a practice Josephus proudly mentioned along with the cessation of work in *Ag. Ap.* 2.282.[48] Seneca the Younger (4 BCE – 65 CE) laments: "The customs of that most accursed nation [the Jews] have gained such strength that they have been now received

---

44. See also *Ag. Ap.* 2.10 §§121–24 (and *Ant.* 3.8.9 §217, 3.15.3 §§318–319, 20.2.3 §34, 20.2.4 §41, 20.8.11 §195; *J. W.* 2.7.10 §454; 2.8.2 §463 and Tertullian, *Nat.* 1.13).

45. Louis H. Feldman, *Jew and Gentile in the Ancient World: Attitudes and Interactions from Alexander to Justinian* (Princeton: Princeton University Press, 2021), 352.

46. John M. G. Barclay, *Jews in the Mediterranean Diaspora: From Alexander to Trajan (323 BCE – 117 CE)* (Berkeley: University of California Press, 1996), 296–97; Barclay, "'Do we undermine the Law?'" 297. For further examples of Gentiles observing Jewish customs, see Shaye J. D. Cohen "Crossing the Boundary and Becoming a Jew," *HTR* 82.1 (1989): 20–21. Ovid assumed a general familiarity with the Jews' Sabbath in *Ars* 1.75–76.

47. Barclay, "'Do we undermine the Law?'" 297; Barclay, *Jews in the Mediterranean Diaspora*, 296–97.

48. Barclay, "'Do we undermine the Law?'" 298. For observers' perception of the Jewish Sabbath practice, see Erich S. Gruen, *Diaspora: Jews Amidst Greeks and Romans* (Cambridge: Harvard University Press, 2002), 48–50.

in all lands. The conquered have given laws to the conquerors" (as cited by Augustine, *Civ.* 6.11 [*NPNF*¹ 2:120–21]).

The Jewish customs identified in Rom 14:1–15:13 are precisely the sort observed by Gentiles attracted to the Jewish faith. Again, Paul does not mention circumcision in Rom 14 but rather food laws and the honoring of the day. He does not call the "weak" Jewish even as he repeatedly identifies the Romans elsewhere in the letter as Gentiles (1:5–6, 13; 15:15–16, 18).

Gentiles and Jewish Purity Rules

David Rudolph complains: "Studies on Romans 14 often do not make a distinction between the Torah's dietary laws that define clean/unclean animals (Lev 11; Deut 14:3–20) and purity legislation (e.g., Lev 11–15; Num 19)."[49] Neither the Torah nor Jews in the Second Temple and rabbinic periods required unconverted Gentiles to observe Jewish purity laws.[50] Jonathan Klawans is categoric: "[I]t is an error to assume that Jews in ancient times generally considered Gentiles to be ritually defiling, and it is even more of an error to assume that such a conception would have been an impediment to Jewish-Gentile interaction."[51] "[N]owhere is the Gentile identified as a source or possible conveyor of ritual impurity."[52] Such matters immediately raise questions about the Roman audience. If the weak's avoidance of contaminated food is for the sake of purity laws, why are only contaminated foods mentioned and not other potential sources of contamination for Jews? For instance, in m. Neg. 11:1 a non-Jew's clothes do not become impure; but clothes from non-Jews may become impure for Jews if the

---

49. Rudolph, "Paul and the Food Laws," 172n3.

50. E.g., Christine E. Hayes, *Gentile Impurities and Jewish Identities: Intermarriage and Conversion from the Bible to the Talmud* (Oxford: Oxford University Press, 2002), 20. As Doosuk Kim documents, several mishnaic passages illustrate how purity laws are simply irrelevant to Gentiles; "Romans 14 and Impurity in the Mishnah," *JGRChJ* 16 (2020): 79–104. In m. 'Abod. Zar. 2:1 contact between Gentiles and Jews is possible in limited circumstances, and impurity is possible only in one direction. A Jew cannot be a midwife to a Gentile because of the danger of being rendered impure by idolatry, but the non-Jew could serve as a midwife in the home of a Jewish woman. The danger of impurity is for the Jew but not the Gentile. In m. 'Abod. Zar. 5:4–5 the Gentile's entering, staying, and eating in the house of a Jew is not prohibited. In m. Neg. 3:1 everyone is made impure but *not* the Gentile or resident alien. In m. Zabim 2:1 the Gentile does not become impure because of a genital discharge. If a Gentile woman discharges semen from a Jew, it is impure for Jews. If a Jewish woman discharges semen from a Gentile, she is pure (m. Miqw. 8:4). In m. Nid. 7:3 menstrual blood from a Gentile is pure, but not from an Israelite or Samaritan. Thus, ritual impurity regulations do not pertain to Gentiles. Only Jews are affected.

51. Jonathan Klawans, "Notions of Gentile Impurity in Ancient Judaism," *AJSR* 20.2 (1995): 288.

52. Klawans, "Notions of Gentile Impurity," 290.

Jew does not upon purchase inspect them for blemishes. Absent such concerns, the practices of the "weak" correspond more closely to Jewish customs adopted by Gentile sympathizers. Note that Paul does not identify the sorts of potential purity concerns one sees in Acts 15:29 (cf. Jub. 7).[53] Second, the "weak" are judging and despising those who eat everything in Rom 14:10, a two-way issue between the weak and the strong, even though purity rules would not apply to Gentiles who are eating everything. This stance is difficult to understand from the perspective of ritual purity rules.

Paul, for his part, stresses *moral* and *not* ritual purity throughout Romans, and moral purity laws *are* required of Gentiles in the Old Testament (e.g., Lev 18:26—required of the resident alien).[54] Leviticus 19 begins in v. 2: "You shall be holy, for I the LORD your God am holy." Paul draws on the holiness of Leviticus in Rom 12–15. In Rom 12:1: "I appeal to you therefore, brothers and sisters, to present your bodies as a living sacrifice, *holy* and acceptable to God." This holy and acceptable sacrifice takes place in the verses that follow in the love the Romans express for one another in their "holy" communities (12:9, 13). Paul explicitly quotes Lev 19:18 in Rom 13:9: "Love your neighbor as yourself," which he expresses as what the law of Moses had always admonished.[55] That love for neighbor is rendered concrete through the fulfillment of the moral precepts of the second table of the Ten Commandments in 13:8–10. This appears to be Paul's response to qualms of many Second Temple Jews toward *morally* impure Gentiles.[56] Note that Paul does not stress any cultic aspects of purity within the Roman communities in Rom 12–13. Paul is demonstrating in these chapters how the Romans' moral purity and holiness contrasts with the idolatry and immorality highlighted in Rom 1. The exclusive stress on moral purity throughout Romans would be fitting for a Gentile Christ-believing audience that had abandoned the idolatry and immorality that had characterized their pagan pasts.

If Paul is addressing a non-Jewish audience at Rome, then when he declares that everything in pure in Rom 14:20, this would not be a blanket statement against Jewish ritual purity laws. As Kathy Ehrensperger stressed: "Thus what Paul formulates here is not a general statement about the perception of food,

53. Cana Werman, "The Concept of Holiness and the Requirements of Purity in Second Temple and Tannaitic Literature," in *Purity and Holiness: The Heritage of Leviticus*, ed. Marcel Poorthuis and Joshua J. Schwartz, JCPS 2 (Leiden: Brill, 2000), 169–74.

54. Klawans, "Notions of Gentile Impurity."

55. Kathy Ehrensperger, "'Called to be saints' – the Identity-shaping Dimension of Paul's Priestly Discourse in Romans," in *Reading Paul in Context: Explorations in Identity Formation: Essays in Honour of William S. Campbell*, ed. Kathy Ehrensperger and J. Brian Tucker, LNTS 428 (London: T&T Clark, 2010), 102.

56. Jonathan Klawans has stressed how Second Temple Jews frequently viewed the Gentiles as guilty of *moral* impurity (idolatry, murder, sexual sin, as opposed to ritual impurity such as defiled food, contact with dead bodies or bodily discharges); Klawans, "Notions of Gentile Impurity in Ancient Judaism," 293–96.

but a specific statement addressed to specific people in a specific context. . . . Non-adherence to these laws does not render Gentiles impure or sinners, because they are irrelevant for them from a Jewish perspective."[57] In short, Paul's comment in Rom 14:20 would make sense were Paul addressing a Gentile audience. He could not have made such a claim to Jewish Christ-believers. For that matter, concerns about meat *and wine* are typical in interactions with the Gentiles since there was the danger of meals tainted by idolatry.[58]

Varying Views of Impurity

Regarding ritual impurity, Jewish understandings varied. Many Second Temple Jews attest a physical conception. Leviticus 11:34a, 38 describes liquids transferring impurities. Based on this, 11QT 49:6–8 describes water poured on food in a house where a man has died rendering the food and liquid there unclean.[59] The liquid bears the power to transfer and even attract impurity. In 4Q274 frag. 3 cols. i and iii, water falling on or moistening herbs, fruit, or food can render them unclean.[60] Rabbinic sources claim that the Pharisaic House of Hillel contended for a radically different understanding of impurity, one based on human intention, over against the House of Shammai.[61] Whether falling liquids defile would depend on the intention of the person involved.[62] The Hillelite stress

---

57. Ehrensperger, " 'Called to Be Saints,' " 106.

58. Esler, *Galatians*, 94–116, although see Charles H. Cosgrove's caveats about idol wine at Greco-Roman banquets; "Banquet Ceremonies Involving Wine in the Greco-Roman World and Early Christianity," *CBQ* 79.2 (2017): 299–316: A banquet may or may not include a libation to the gods. It was not a regular feature, unlike the meat of sacrifice.

59. Numbers 19 on corpse impurity interpreted in view of Lev 11.

60. Moral impurity is defiling as well; Eric Ottenheijm, "Impurity Between Intention and Deed: Purity Disputes in First Century Judaism and in the New Testament," in *Purity and Holiness: The Heritage of Leviticus*, ed. Marcel Poorthuis and Joshua J. Schwartz, JCPS 2 (Leiden: Brill, 2000), 132–34, following Jonathan Klawans, "The Impurity of Immorality in Ancient Judaism," *JJS* 48 (1997): 1–16; Jonathan Klawans, "Idolatry, Incest, and Impurity: Moral Defilement in Ancient Judaism," *JSJ* 29.4 (1998): 391–415. Intention plays no role in this conception of impurity, and moral impurity in Second Temple texts is regularly ritually defiling as well.

61. Ottehheijm, "Impurity," 131, 131n8.

62. For the Hillelites impurity is not an external, objective force. In m. Mak. 1:2–3 (Lev 11:34, 37–38) a person shaking a tree to loosen food from it does not render the food unclean, only when one intends to release fluids while shaking the tree—and this is limited to the initial act and not later fluids falling from the tree (Ottenheijm, "Impurity," 135). The Tosefta explains that Hillel and Shammai had differed in this instance over whether shaking a tree for food and not just liquid could cause impurity since Hillel emphasized the lack of intention with food, but Shammai emphasized liquid physically falling in both instances (t. Mak. 1:2). For Shammai, if one does something intentionally, then it is unclean, but if it fails to produce result, Hillel says it is *not* unclean since the

on intention reflects a shift in emphasis to the individual and human will.[63] Human intention and will thus are key factors in determining what is rendered contaminated.[64]

In agreement with the Hillelite perspective described by the rabbis, Paul claims in Rom 14:14 that nothing is contaminated in itself but rather it is contaminated to the one who *thinks* it is contaminated. The apostle distinguishes foods *perceived* to be contaminated from intrinsically contaminated foods. In m. Ḥag. 2:5–7 an individual may choose or intend to take on ritual purity obligations personally.[65] The rabbis report that the Houses of Hillel and Shammai differed over whether human intention is a factor in determining the halakhic status of actions or vessels. Conversely, "nothing is contaminated in itself" (Rom 14:14) from the Hillelite point of view—but this is a view attested even earlier. In Let. Aris. 147 animals originally designated by God in Creation as "good" became unclean and forbidden to the Jews.[66]

David Rudolph concluded that Paul is having to explain to the weak as *non-Jews* seeking to honor Jewish food customs that they have misunderstood those laws. They are not aware that no food is contaminated in itself when they consider certain foods unclean (Paul's Hillelite approach). Rudolph thought that *Gentiles* oriented toward Judaism, after previously associating with magic and superstition, would have taken an objective ontological approach to the Jewish food laws.[67] Others at Rome, however, did not view anything as contaminated "in itself" and ate everything (Rom 14:14, 20; 15:1). Rudolph, however, does not account for varying Jewish conceptions of purity at this time, and thus his argument for the "weak" being composed of Gentiles is not decisive.

Although there is no evidence that the "weak" of Rom 14 had gone beyond those Jewish customs popular among Gentiles, their rationale for adopting

---

intent was for the result. According to m. Makš. 1:2 since the intention is *not* to bring water but food down from the tree, then the water falling does not produce impurity for Hillel, but does for Shammai, despite intention otherwise. See also t. Ṭehar. 5:8 for intention. Human intention and not the food itself renders impure. Kim, "Romans 14," 95: "For these rabbis, there is no normative or fixed law in terms of the impurity of food."

After discussing additional instances from the Mishnah and Tosefta, Ottenheijm concludes ("Impurity," 141): "According to Beth Shammai any action sets into motion autonomous processes of moistening. The Hillelites note only whether the application of the fluids was done willfully or not, i.e., whether the fluids have to be consciously classified for moistening. . . . One could say that this was a dispute between susceptibility by moistening (Beth Shammai) versus susceptibility by will power (Beth Hillel)."

63. Ottenheijm, "Impurity," 142–43.

64. Ottenheijm, "Impurity," 141–43; see the additional sources in Rudolph, "Paul and the Food Laws," 174n25.

65. Rudolph, "Paul and the Food Laws," 156–67, citing Yair Fursternberg.

66. Rudolph, "Paul and the Food Laws," 160–61; Ehrensperger, "'Called to Be Saints,'" 101, 105–6; Nanos, *Mystery*, 199–200.

67. Rudolph, "Paul and the Food Laws," 168.

them may have reflected, for Paul, a popular view of ritual purity in the Second Temple period—and one with which Paul disagreed. Paul could be correcting other Second Temple Jews, albeit Christ-believers, with a Hillelite conception of purity. In other words, an emphasis on human intention could be directed at *either* Gentiles or Jews in the audience.

One Last Angle on This Discussion

One final factor in the interpretation of Rom 14:14, 20 remains and attests to the cloudy picture regarding purity concerns. J. Duncan M. Derrett years ago stressed the distinction between κοινός and ἀκάθαρτος. Κοινός always meant "contaminated" whereas ἀκάθαρτος meant (intrinsically) "unclean."[68] In the Septuagint, Lev 11 and Deut 14 both describe essentially unclean foods that are strictly forbidden (always ἀκάθαρτος). Κοινός as a ritual term is unattested in non-Jewish Greek literature and is absent in the LXX Pentateuch. This use of the word first appears in relation to food in 1 Macc 1:47, 62 and 4 Macc 7:6 and does not function as a synonym for ἀκάθαρτος, as has often been assumed.

First Maccabees 1:47 distinguishes a *second* category, "*contaminated* creatures" that one is not to eat (κτήνη κοινά), from pig parts that are *intrinsically* unclean (ὕεια).[69] In view of that distinction, Paul would be declaring *contaminated* or κοινός foods to be cleansed by faith in Rom 14:14, 20. He would not be making any claim about *intrinsically* unclean foods that are ἀκάθαρτος. Thus, in Acts 10:15 what God cleanses is no longer κοινός. Neither Luke in Acts nor Paul in Romans is declaring essentially unclean food clean. These declarations would be in response to those who consider the food of Gentiles or certain Jews to be defiling (κοινά), if not those people themselves, even if they are not intrinsically unclean from the point of view of the Torah.[70]

To return to the audience of Romans: pork is intrinsically unclean for the law-observant Jew, but not for the non-Jew. For the *non-Jew* choosing to be respectful of Jewish customs, pork would not be intrinsically unclean but could, as a matter of conscience, be viewed as *contaminated*. In other words, a concern with κοινός foods may suggest a Gentile audience. Were Jews in the Roman audience, the concern would not just be with κοινός, or contaminated,

---

68. J. Duncan M. Derrett, "Κοινός, κοινόω," *Filología Neotestamentaria* 5 (1992): 69–78.

69. With David J. Bolton, perhaps the intrinsically unclean pig parts, mixed with other creatures, had rendered *them* contaminated; "Who Are You Calling 'Weak'? A Short Critique on James Dunn's Reading of Rom 14,1–15,6," in *The Letter to the Romans*, ed. Udo Schnelle, BETL 226 (Leuven: Peeters, 2009), 621n27.

70. E.g., LXX Esth 5:1 [6]; Ehrensperger, "'Called to Be Saints,'" 98–103; Rudolph, "Paul and the Food Laws," 155.

foods but also with those that are intrinsically unclean or ἀκάθαρτος. Ritual purity matters, obviously, beg for further clarity.

Romans 15:1–13

In Rom 15:1 Paul finally turns to the "strong," among whom he numbers himself, confounding the reflexive identification of the strong with Gentiles and the weak with Jews.[71] What characterizes the "strong" is not the food they eat. The strong may or may not be identified or overlap with those who eat everything in Rom 14. What characterizes the "strong" is that they are to bear the weaknesses of the weak and not please themselves. They are to act in a Christ-like manner, selflessly bearing the needs of others. The apostle, again, does not offer any indication of the ethnic make-up of the Roman congregations.

Many have taken Rom 15:7–9 as clear evidence that Paul is attempting to resolve a situation in which Gentile Christ-believers are at odds with Jewish Christ-believers.[72] The verses make no such claim: "To conclude the presence of Jews in 15:7–9 would be analogous to concluding that Jews had to be in the audience of Romans because Paul spoke *about* Israel in Romans 9–11."[73] Paul in 15:7 never specifies the Roman recipients of Christ's welcome as Jewish. The verses indicate an *interest* in Judaism, but that would equally be the case with Gentiles sympathetic toward Judaism. In the midst of Gentiles less predisposed toward Judaism, they are to welcome one another.

Some have appealed beyond Rom 14:1–15:6 to Rom 16 where Paul identifies some who are likely Jewish Christ-believers. First, it is not clear that Paul is identifying people in the Roman congregations. Paul is asking the Romans to greet this third-person group. Requesting a second-person group to greet a third-person party, in ancient letters, is always a request for the addressees to greet someone *outside* their group.[74] These outsiders could well be Paul's associates arriving in Rome as Paul contemplates using Rome as a launching point for a mission to Spain (Rom 15:23, 28). Second, the Jewish Christ-believers Paul mentions in Rom 16 tend to confirm that the Romans themselves are Gentiles. Paul names Prisca and Aquila, who were his coworkers in his Gentile ministry

---

71. E.g., Meeks, "Judgement and the Brother," 292.

72. Frank Thielman (*Romans*, ZECNT 6 [Grand Rapids: Zondervan Academic, 2018], 630), for instance, considers these verses decisive in demonstrating that at least some of the weak are Jewish. That confidence is difficult to understand.

73. Das, *Solving the Romans Debate*, 105.

74. Das, *Solving the Romans Debate*, 101–3; see, e.g., Terence Y. Mullins, "Greetings as a New Testament Form," *JBL* 87.4 (1968): 418–26; John L. White, *Light from Ancient Letters* (Philadelphia: Fortress, 1986), 202; Hans-Josef Klauck, *Ancient Letters and the New Testament: A Guide to Content and Exegesis* (Waco, TX: Baylor University Press, 2006), 24–25.

(16:3; 1 Cor 16:19; cf. Acts 18:1–3). Andronicus and Junia were in Christ *before* Paul and were imprisoned *with* Paul, which suggests that they were laboring and suffering alongside Paul as he worked to take the message of Christ to Gentiles (16:7). The presence of a handful of Jewish Christian missionaries to the Gentiles would affirm the Gentile identity of the Roman congregations.[75] Thus the encoded audience of Paul's letter to the Romans remains Gentile—and the actual audience consists of a few Jewish Christ-believers who were laboring in Gentile ministry.[76]

Conclusion

In conclusion, Rom 14 does not paint a particularly concrete picture. While some at Rome were avoiding contaminated food and wine, observing days, and eating vegetables, Paul does not describe them as Jews or as circumcised, despite the letter's extensive discussion of the Jews and the circumcised to this point. The apostle does not identify the observed day as a Sabbath (σάββατον) or Levitical feast (ἑορτή). Paul resorts to oblique identifications, which would make sense if in the context of Gentiles sympathetic to Judaism.[77] Romans 14:1–15:13 unfortunately offers little or no help in reconstructing the situation of Jews or Jewish Christ-believers in the Roman congregations at the time of Paul's letter.

Bibliography

Barclay, John M. G. "'Do We Undermine the Law?': A Study on Romans 14.1–15.6." Pages 287–308 in *Paul and the Mosaic Law*. Edited by James D. G. Dunn. Grand Rapids: Eerdmans, 1996.

———. *Jews in the Mediterranean Diaspora: From Alexander to Trajan (323 BCE – 117 CE)*. Berkeley: University of California Press, 1996.

Bolton, David J. "Who Are You Calling 'Weak'? A Short Critique on James Dunn's Reading of Rom 14,1—15,6." Pages 617–29 in *The Letter to the Romans*. Edited by Udo Schnelle. BETL 226. Leuven: Peeters, 2009.

---

75. Das, *Solving the Romans Debate*, 101. Carl N. Toney does not address the evidence from ancient letters regarding the recipients' greeting a third-person group; *Paul's Inclusive Ethic: Resolving Community Conflict and Promoting Mission in Romans 14–15*, WUNT 2.252 (Tübingen: Mohr Siebeck, 2008), 38. To posit the "you" group greeting "each other" in Rom 16:16 is not a useful counterargument since that remains clearly in terms of the "you" group. Greeting "each other" may even be contrasted with greeting those *not among* them in the other admonitions to greet.

76. Campbell ("Addressees," 182n38) again inexplicably misunderstands the case made for a Gentile audience in Rome, as if the presence of Paul's Jewish Christ-believing missionary associates to the Gentiles had been denied.

77. "One of the major conundrums in the interpretation of this section of the letter is thus resolved." Das, *Solving the Romans Debate*, 109.

Bull, Klaus-Michael. "'Wir Werden Alle vor den Richterstuhl Gottes Gestellt Werden' (Röm 14, 10): Zur Funktion des Motivs vom Endgericht in den Argumentationen des Römerbriefes." Pages 125–43 in *Apokalyptik als Herausforerung Neutestamentlicher Theologie.* Edited by Michael Becker and Markus Öhler. WUNT 2.214. Tübingen: Mohr Siebeck, 2006.

Campbell, William S. "The Addressees of Paul's Letter to the Romans: Assemblies of God in House Churches and Synagogues?" Pages 171–95 in *Between Gospel and Election: Explorations in the Interpretation of Romans 9–11.* Edited by Florian Wilk and J. Ross Wagner, with the assistance of Frank Schleritt. WUNT 257. Tübingen: Mohr Siebeck, 2010.

Cohen, Shaye J. D. "Crossing the Boundary and Becoming a Jew." *HTR* 82.1 (1989): 13–33.

Cosgrove, Charles H. "Banquet Ceremonies Involving Wine in the Greco-Roman World and Early Christianity." *CBQ* 79.2 (2017): 299–316.

Cranfield, C. E. B. *A Critical and Exegetical Commentary on the Epistle to the Romans.* 2 vols. ICC. Edinburgh: T&T Clark, 1979.

Das, A. Andrew. "Israel's Scriptures in Galatians." Pages 388–406 in *Israel's Scriptures in Early Christian Writings: The Use of the Old Testament in the New.* Edited by Matthias Henze and David Lincinum. Grand Rapids: Eerdmans, 2023.

———. *Paul and the Stories of Israel: Grand Thematic Narratives in Galatians.* Minneapolis: Fortress, 2016.

———. "The Pauline Letters in Contemporary Research." Pages 237–57 in *The Oxford Handbook of Pauline Studies.* Edited by Matthew Novenson and R. Barry Matlock. Oxford: Oxford University Press, 2022.

———. "'Praise the Lord, All You Gentiles': The Encoded Audience of Romans 15.7–13." *JSNT* 34.1 (2011): 90–110.

———. *Solving the Romans Debate.* Minneapolis: Fortress, 2007.

———. "Traditional Protestant Perspective Response to Zetterholm." Pages 201–6 in *Perspectives on Paul: Five Views.* Edited by Scot McKnight and B. J. Oropeza. Grand Rapids: Baker Academic, 2020.

Derrett, J. Duncan M. "Κοινός, κοινόω." *Filología Neotestamentaria* 5 (1992): 69–78.

Dunn, James D. G. *Romans 9–16.* WBC 38B. Dallas: Word, 1988.

Ehrensperger, Kathy. "'Called to be saints' – the Identity-shaping Dimension of Paul's Priestly Discourse in Romans." Pages 90–109 in *Reading Paul in Context: Explorations in Identity Formation: Essays in Honour of William S. Campbell.* Edited by Kathy Ehrensperger and J. Brian Tucker. LNTS 428. London: T&T Clark, 2010.

Elliott, Neil. "Asceticism Among the 'Weak' and 'Strong' in Romans 14–15." Pages 231–51 in *Asceticism and the New Testament.* Edited by Leif E. Vaage and Vincent L. Wimbush. London: Routledge, 1999.

Esler, Philip F. *Galatians*. NTR. London: Routledge, 1998.

Feldman, Louis H. *Jew and Gentile in the Ancient World: Attitudes and Interactions from Alexander to Justinian*. Princeton: Princeton University Press, 2021.

Gaventa, Beverly Roberts. "Reading for the Subject: The Paradox of Power in Romans 14:1–15:6." *JTI* 5 (2011): 1–12.

Gruen, Erich S. *Diaspora: Jews Amidst Greeks and Romans*. Cambridge: Harvard University Press, 2002.

Hafemann, Scott J. "Eschatology and Ethics: The Future of Israel and the Nations in Romans 15:1–13." *TynBul* 51.2 (2000): 161–92.

Hayes, Christine E. *Gentile Impurities and Jewish Identities: Intermarriage and Conversion from the Bible to the Talmud*. Oxford: Oxford University Press, 2002.

Jewett, Robert. *Romans: A Commentary*. Hermeneia. Minneapolis: Fortress, 2007.

Karris, Robert J. "Romans 14:1–15:13 and the Occasion of Romans." Pages 65–84 in *The Romans Debate: Revised and Expanded Edition*. Edited by Karl P. Donfried. Peabody, MA: Hendrickson, 1991.

Käsemann, Ernst. *Commentary on Romans*. Translated and edited by Geoffrey W. Bromiley. Grand Rapids: Eerdmans, 1980.

Kim, Doosuk. "Romans 14 and Impurity in the Mishnah." *JGRChJ* 16 (2020): 79–104.

Klauck, Hans-Josef. *Ancient Letters and the New Testament: A Guide to Content and Exegesis*. Waco, TX: Baylor University Press, 2006.

Klawans, Jonathan. "Idolatry, Incest, and Impurity: Moral Defilement in Ancient Judaism." *JSJ* 29.4 (1998): 391–415.

———. "The Impurity of Immorality in Ancient Judaism." *JJS* 48 (1997): 1–16.

———. "Notions of Gentile Impurity in Ancient Judaism." *AJSR* 20.2 (1995): 285–312.

Lampe, Peter. *From Paul to Valentinus: Christians at Rome in the First Two Centuries*. Minneapolis: Fortress, 2003.

Leenhardt, Franz J. *The Epistle to the Romans: A Commentary*. London: Lutterworth, 1961.

Malherbe, Abraham J. *Moral Exhortation: A Greco-Roman Sourcebook*. Philadelphia: Westminster, 1986.

Martyn, J. Louis. *Galatians: A New Translation with Introduction and Commentary*. AB 33A. New York: Doubleday, 1997.

McCruden, Kevin B. "Judgment and Life for the Lord: Occasion and Theology of Romans 14,1–15,13." *Bib* 86.2 (2005): 229–44.

Meeks, Wayne A. "Judgment and the Brother: Romans 14:1–15:13." Pages 290–98 in *Tradition and Interpretation in the New Testament: Essays in Honor of E. Earle Ellis for His 60th Birthday*. Edited by Gerald F. Hawthorne and Otto Betz. Grand Rapids: Eerdmans, 1987.

————. "The Polyphonic Ethics of the Apostle Paul." *Annual of the Society of Christian Ethics* 8 (1988): 17–29.

Mullins, Terence Y. "Greetings as a New Testament Form." *JBL* 87.4 (1968): 418–26.

Nanos, Mark D. *The Mystery of Romans: The Jewish Context of Paul's Letter.* Minneapolis: Fortress, 1996.

Ottenheijm, Eric. "Impurity Between Intention and Deed: Purity Disputes in First Century Judaism and in the New Testament." Pages 129–47 in *Purity and Holiness: The Heritage of Leviticus.* Edited by Marcel Poorthuis and Joshua J. Schwartz. JCPS 2. Leiden: Brill, 2000.

Rudolph, David. "Paul and the Food Laws: A Reassessment of Romans 14:14, 20." Pages 151–81 in *Paul the Jew: Rereading the Apostle as a Figure of Second Temple Judaism.* Edited by Gabriele Boccaccini and Carlos A. Segovia. Minneapolis: Fortress, 2016.

Schreiner, Thomas R. *Romans.* BECNT. Grand Rapids: Baker Academic, 1998.

Spitaler, Peter. "Household Disputes in Rome (Romans 14:1–15:13)." *RB* 116.1 (2009): 44–69.

Stanley, Christopher D. *Arguing with Scripture: The Rhetoric of Quotations in the Letters of Paul.* New York: T&T Clark, 2004.

————. "'Pearls Before Swine': Did Paul's Audiences Understand His Biblical Quotations?" *NovT* 41.2 (1999): 124–44.

Thielman, Frank. *Romans.* ZECNT 6. Grand Rapids: Zondervan Academic, 2018.

Thompson, Michael. *Clothed With Christ: The Example and Teaching of Jesus in Romans 12.1–15.13.* JSNTSup 59. Sheffield: Sheffield Academic Press, 1991.

Tomson, Peter J. *Paul and the Jewish Law: Halakha in the Letters of the Apostle to the Gentiles.* CRINT 3.1. Assen/Minneapolis: Van Gorcum/Fortress, 1990.

Toney, Carl N. *Paul's Inclusive Ethic: Resolving Community Conflict and Promoting Mission in Romans 14–15.* WUNT 2.252. Tübingen: Mohr Siebeck, 2008.

Wagner, J. Ross. "The Christ, Servant of Jew and Gentile: A Fresh Approach to Romans 15:8–9." *JBL* 116.3 (1997): 473–85.

Werman, Cana. "The Concept of Holiness and the Requirements of Purity in Second Temple and Tannaitic Literature." Pages 162–79 in *Purity and Holiness: The Heritage of Leviticus.* Edited by Marcel Poorthuis and Joshua J. Schwartz. JCPS 2. Leiden: Brill, 2000.

White, John L. *Light from Ancient Letters.* Philadelphia: Fortress, 1986.

CHAPTER 22

What Do Paul's Travels (Romans 15:14–32) and Letter Closing (Romans 15:33–16:27) Say about His Mission?

Jeffrey A. D. Weima

Introduction

The body section of Paul's long letter to the Romans reaches a discernable climax in 15:13, signaled by no less than four OT quotations given immediately after each other (15:9–12) and by a concluding prayer (15:13).[1] The remaining material of the letter consists of two distinct units: the first unit of 15:14–32, which deals generally with the topic of Paul's travels, both past and future; and the second unit of 15:33–16:27, which formally constitutes the letter closing. These two units at the *end* of the letter to the Romans are intended by Paul to parallel the two units at the *beginning* of the letter—the letter opening (1:1–7) and the thanksgiving (1:8–15)—so that these four units serve as the epistolary framework for the body of the letter (1:16–15:13). Paul skillfully adapts each of these epistolary units that surround the letter body so that they emphasize his divine calling to preach the gospel to the Roman Christians.[2] As the apostle to the Gentiles, Paul felt not only uniquely qualified but also divinely obligated to share with the believers in Rome *his* gospel in the conviction that this would

---

1. Many leading Roman commentators recognize that 15:13 marks the end of the letter body and beginning of the letter's conclusion or letter closing. For example, Joseph A. Fitzmyer (*Romans: A New Translation with Introduction and Commentary*, AB 33 [New York: Doubleday, 1993], 709) begins his treatment of 15:14–33 by stating: "Now that Paul has finished his exposé of the gospel and set forth its implication for upright Christian life, he adds the epistolary conclusion to his letter to the Romans." Douglas J. Moo, *The Epistle to the Romans*, NICNT (Grand Rapids: Eerdmans, 1996), 884, similarly opens his comments on 15:14–16:27 by claiming that "Paul's sustained argument about the nature and implications of the gospel is at an end" and by identifying the remaining material in the correspondence as "The Letter Closing." Thomas R. Schreiner, *Romans*, BECNT (Grand Rapids: Baker Academic, 1998), 76, likewise prefaces his comments about 15:14–16:23 with the assertion: "The substance of Paul's exhortation to the Romans is completed."

2. "But it is exactly the theme of the gospel and Paul's responsibility for carrying it out in Rome which connect the letter's opening, body and closing." Günter Klein, "Paul's Purpose in Writing the Epistle to the Romans," in *The Romans Debate: Revised and Expanded Edition*, ed. Karl P. Donfried (Peabody, MA: Hendrickson, 1991), 34n22.

strengthen their faith in the face of Jewish-Gentile tensions within the Roman house churches. Before presenting his gospel in the body of the letter, however, Paul expands and shapes both the letter opening and the thanksgiving in order to induce these readers in Rome—whom he has neither converted nor even visited and who have heard some questionable things about the content of his preaching (Rom 3:8; see also 6:1)—nevertheless to recognize his apostleship and to accept the gospel that he proclaims.[3] Now that Paul has finished "preaching" his gospel to them in the letter body,[4] he deftly shapes in a similar manner the final two sections of the letter—the report of his travels (15:14–32) and the letter closing (15:33–16:27)—to confirm and clarify his position as the Roman Christians' divinely appointed apostle whose gospel ought to be accepted and whose evangelistic mission ought to be supported.

I. Paul's Travels (15:14–32)

Since the content of 15:14–32 deals generally with Paul's travels[5]—both his past travels in the east (vv. 14–22) and his future travels in the west (vv. 23–32), this section and passages like it in Paul's other letters are often formally labelled as a "travelogue." The problem with this label, however, is that the term is typically understood as Paul simply informing his readers about his travels in a pro forma manner at the end of the letter merely to satisfy their curiosity or to provide details about his personal life for their general interest, and thus the important function that this unit has in the overall argument of the letter is all too often missed. It is better, therefore, to identify 15:14–32 as an "apostolic parousia."[6]

---

3. See the full examination of the letter opening and the thanksgiving in Jeffrey A. D. Weima, "Preaching the Gospel in Rome: A Study of the Epistolary Framework of Romans," in *Gospel in Paul: Studies on Corinthians, Galatians and Romans for Richard N. Longenecker*, ed. L. Ann Jervis and Peter Richardson, JSNTSup 108 (Sheffield: Sheffield Academic Press, 1994), 337–66; also Jeffrey A. D. Weima, *Paul the Ancient Letter Writer: An Introduction to Epistolary Analysis* (Grand Rapids: Baker Academic, 2016), 14–19.

4. The first to suggest that Paul in the letter of Romans is preaching his gospel apparently was Nils A. Dahl, *Studies in Paul* (Minneapolis: Augsburg, 1977), 77: "What Paul does in his letter is what he had for a long time hoped to do in person: he preached the gospel to those in Rome (see 1.15)." This position has been subsequently advocated by several others: e.g., Paul Bowers, "Fulfilling the Gospel: The Scope of the Pauline Mission," *JETS* 30.2 (1987): 195–96; Neil Elliott, *The Rhetoric of Romans: Argumentative Constraint and Strategy and Paul's Dialogue with Judaism*, JSNTSup 45 (Sheffield: JSOT Press, 1990), 69–97, esp. 84, 87; L. Ann Jervis, *The Purpose of Romans: A Comparative Letter Structure Investigation*, JSNTSup 55 (Sheffield: JSOT Press, 1991); Jeffrey A. D. Weima, "The Reason for Romans: The Evidence of Its Epistolary Framework (1:1–15; 15:14–16:27)," *RevExp* 100 (2003): 17–33.

5. "Paul's travels are the leitmotif of this section [15:14–33] and identify it as a discrete literary unit." Moo, *Romans*, 885.

6. This epistolary convention was first identified and defined by Robert W. Funk, "The Apostolic *Parousia*: Form and Significance," in *Christian History and*

The Greek word *parousia* has not only the sense of "coming, arrival" but also "presence."[7] The term "apostolic parousia" thus refers to a section of the letter where an apostle, in this case Paul, is particularly concerned to make his "presence" felt by his readers. Paul, of course, is already present in some sense with the recipients through the reading of the letter, which is a substitute for his actual presence. Yet the apostle's letters often contain a distinct section where he tries to make his presence more fully felt by the recipients. The most effective way he accomplishes this is by referring to a future visit that he plans to make to his readers. When such a visit is not possible, however, Paul makes his presence more powerfully experienced through two alternative means: he refers either to the sending of one of his representatives for a visit or to the act of writing the letter itself. Paul employs two of these three means in 15:14–32 to make his presence more powerfully felt among his audience in Rome: he refers briefly to the act of writing the letter in vv. 15–16 but speaks extensively about his future travel plans to personally visit the recipients of the letter in vv. 23–32.

The purpose of all this "writing and travel talk" is to exert his authority over his Roman readers. As Robert Funk observes more generally about the apostolic parousia: "All of these [i.e., references to either Paul's impending visit, the sending of his emissary, or his writing of the letter] are media by which Paul makes his apostolic authority effective in his churches. The underlying theme is therefore the apostolic parousia—the presence of apostolic authority and power."[8] This authoritative function of the apostolic parousia at work in 15:14–32, however, should not be interpreted as a power-hungry ego trip by the apostle. Rather, it is better understood as an effective literary means of placing his largely unknown and somewhat skeptical readers in Rome under his authority such that they will not only accept the gospel that he has just preached to them in the body of the letter but also support his evangelistic mission.

A proper interpretation of 15:14–32 requires not only the right identification of this passage's form and function but also a recognition of its close relationship to the two opening units with which it frames the letter body.[9] This

---

Interpretation: Studies Presented to John Knox, ed. W. R. Farmer, C. F. D. Moule, and R. R. Niebuhr (Cambridge: Cambridge University Press, 1967), 249–68. For further comments on the form and function of the apostolic parousia in three other Pauline letters (1 Cor 4:14–21; 1 Thess 2:17–3:10; Phlm 22), see Weima, *Paul the Ancient Letter Writer*, 113–19. For a recent major commentary of Romans that identifies 15:14–32 as an apostolic parousia, see Richard N. Longenecker, *The Epistle to the Romans: A Commentary on the Greek Text*, NIGTC (Grand Rapids: Eerdmans, 2016), 1023–52, esp. 1032–36.

7. The Greek word *parousia* is a compound noun made up of the feminine participle of the verb "to be" and the preposition *para* meaning "near, beside, with." See BDAG s.v. παρουσία 1 (780): "the state of being present at a place, *presence*."

8. Funk, "Apostolic *Parousia*," 249.

9. James D. G. Dunn, *Romans 9–16*, WBC 38B (Dallas: Word, 1988), 857: "The restatement [in 15:14–33] of themes covered in 1:8–15 is ... intended to reinforce the

close relationship is signaled by the high number of verbal and thematic links between the apostolic parousia and both the letter opening (1:1–7) and also especially the thanksgiving (1:8–15).

Verbal/Thematic Link	Opening & Thanksgiving	Apostolic Parousia
1. Praise of Roman Christians	1:8 (see also 1:7)	15:14
2. Paul's Apostleship		
a. An act of grace	1:5 (χάρις)	15:15 (χάρις δοθεῖσα)
b. Its "service" character	1:9 ("whom I serve")	15:15 ("in the priestly service")
c. Directed to the Gentiles	1:5, 13 (τὰ ἔθνη) 1:14 (Ἕλλησές τε καὶ βαρβάροι)	15:16 [2x], 27 (τὰ ἔθνη)
d. To win obedience	1:5 (εἰς ὑπακοήν)	15:18 (εἰς ὑπακοήν)
3. Paul's Gospel		
a. References to the gospel	1:1, 9, 15	15:16, 19, 20
b. His service to the gospel	1:9 (εὐαγγέλιον)	15:16 (εὐαγγέλιον)
c. His task to preach the gospel	1:15 (οὕτως . . . εὐαγγελίσασθαι)	15:19 (πεπληρωκέναι τὸ εὐαγγέλιον) 15:20 (οὕτως . . . εὐαγγελίζεσθαι)
4. Visit the Christians in Rome		
a. Desire/intention to come	1:10, 11, 13, 15	15:22, 23, 24, 29, 32
b. Inability to come	1:10 (implied); 1:13	15:22
c. Submissive to God's will	1:10 (ἐν τῷ θελήματι τοῦ θεοῦ)	15:32 (διὰ θελήματος θεοῦ)
d. Mutual benefit of visit	1:12	15:23–24, 28–29, 32
5. Obligation	1:14 (ὀφειλέτης εἰμί)	15:25–27 (ὀφείλω [2x])
6. Reference to prayer	1:9–10 (Paul)	15:30–32 (Believers in Rome)

These impressive links serve not just to create a formal framework of introductory and concluding units that surround the body of the letter but also to strengthen the purpose at work in these bracketing units. Just as Paul has skillfully shaped the opening and thanksgiving units to win the acceptance of his apostleship and his gospel among the believers in Rome, so he has similarly constructed the apostolic parousia to emphasize these same key themes.

---

bracketing effect of the two sections on the main body of the letter." Similarly, Moo (*Romans*, 885–86): "The way in which the letter opening and closing "frame" the body of Romans is seen all the more clearly when we note the way in which the contents of 15:14–33 match those of 1:1–15, and especially 1:8–15." Moo additionally notes that these parallels have been long observed by commentators, ever since the time of John Chrysostom in his *Homilies on the Epistle to the Romans*, Homily 29.

1. The First Half of the Apostolic Parousia:
Paul's Past Travels (15:14–22)

Paul opens the first half of the apostolic parousia with a strategically placed confidence formula[10] which both further wins over the audience by saying positive things about them but also implicitly puts pressure on them to live up to that positive description: "I myself have confidence about you, my brothers and sisters, that you yourselves are full of goodness, filled with all knowledge, and able to admonish one another" (15:14).[11] The first two references to the readers as those who are "full of goodness" and "filled with all knowledge" echo Paul's praise of the Roman Christians in the opening thanksgiving (1:8: "First, I thank my God through Jesus Christ for all of you because your faith is being reported all over the world") and reveal again that his purpose in writing this letter is not to convert them but to strengthen their already existing faith (1:11: "For I long to see you, that I may impart to you some spiritual gift to strengthen you"). The third and final reference to the readers' ability "to admonish one another" likely has in view the tensions that exist between the Jewish and Gentile members of the Roman house churches and how the gospel that Paul has just finished preaching to them in the body of the letter ought to help them resolve those tensions.

Paul's confidence in the spiritual condition and abilities of the Roman readers, however, does not mean that the apostle did not have any pressing need to write to them. The immediately following words by Paul, in fact, contains the clearest statement anywhere in the letter as to why he felt compelled to write them:

> But on some points I have written to you very boldly by way of reminder, because of the grace given me by God to be a minister of Christ Jesus to the Gentiles in the priestly service of the gospel of God, so that the offering of the Gentiles may be acceptable, sanctified by the Holy Spirit (15:15–16).

What Paul has been claiming in a somewhat veiled way in the letter opening and the thanksgiving is now stated explicitly. For here is the "smoking gun" that directly links what Paul has written to the Roman Christians in the body of the letter with his apostolic responsibility to preach the gospel to the Gentiles. Paul claims that he has received grace from God to be "a minister of Christ Jesus"—a claim to authority that echoes his assertion of apostleship in the letter opening (1:5: "through whom we have received grace and apostleship"). Furthermore, this authoritative ministry divinely given to Paul is specifically directed "to the Gentiles" (τὰ ἔθνη occurs twice in v. 16) and involved "the gospel of God." Therefore, the Roman Christians should view Paul's action of boldly preaching

---

10. For an introduction to the form and function of this epistolary convention, see Weima, *Paul the Ancient Letter Writer*, 119–23.

11. The translation here and elsewhere, unless otherwise noted, is mine.

his gospel in the body of the letter as a fulfillment of his God-given responsibility to the Gentiles.

It is striking and at first glance surprising that Paul here describes his apostolic calling to the *Gentiles* by means of no less than five cultic terms that all have a strong *Jewish* background: his evangelistic mission to the Gentiles was (1) "a priestly ministry" (λειτουργόν) that (2) involved "the priestly service (ἱερουργοῦντα) of the gospel of God," motivated out of his desire that through this service (3) "the offering (ἡ προσφορά) of the Gentiles" would be (4) "acceptable" (εὐπρόσδεκτος) to God, having been (5) "sanctified" (ἡγιασμένη) by the Holy Spirit. This "piling up of cultic terms,"[12] however, does make sense, if Paul is writing to Christians at Rome—both Jew and Gentile—who were well-trained and knowledgeable about the vocabulary and theology of the OT.[13] In fact, such readers would not only appreciate Paul's use of such cultic terms to describe his ministry but this would further win over the trust and confidence of those Christians in Rome who still harbored suspicions about the apostle's faithfulness to the sacred writings of the Jewish faith.

The remaining verses in the first half of the apostolic parousia continue to emphasize the authoritative nature of Paul's relationship with his readers in Rome in at least five ways.

First, Paul issues an expression of self-confidence:[14] "Therefore, I have boasting in Christ Jesus with reference to the things of God" (15:17). Although Paul avoids the charge of false pride by explicitly locating his boasting "in Christ Jesus," he nevertheless implicitly commends himself and his apostolic ministry to the Roman readers as one whose priestly ministry to the Gentiles can be justly judged as a cause for boasting. As Frank Thielman notes, "the boast is only possible because Paul possessed a certain role and competence that qualified him to speak boldly, even to gentile believers in a city that he had never visited."[15]

Second, Paul states his refusal to speak of anything "except what Christ has worked through me to win the obedience of the Gentiles by word or deed" (15:18). While the apostle diplomatically acknowledges that Christ is the primary actor in his apostolic ministry, he simultaneously emphasizes his own important role as the one through whom Christ is working to bring about

---

12. Schreiner, *Romans*, 766.

13 "If, however, we understand Paul to be writing to Christians at Rome who had been extensively influenced by the theology, language, and ways of thinking of Jewish Christianity (whatever their own particular ethnicities), it should come as no surprise that he would speak of the nature of his God-given ministry using religious expressions that they would understand and religious imagery that they would appreciate." Longenecker, *Romans*, 1039.

14. See Stanley N. Olsen, "Epistolary Uses of Expressions of Self-Confidence," *JBL* 103.4 (1984): 585–97.

15. Frank Thielman, *Romans*, ZECNT 6 (Grand Rapids: Zondervan Academic, 2018), 683.

obedience from the Gentiles: this happened "through me" and "by [my] word or [my] deed." Consequently, if the Roman readers do not wish to reject Christ, they must accept Paul (and his gospel) as the one through whom Christ is working to bring about their obedience of faith.

Third, Paul draws his readers' attention not only broadly to his own "word or deed" but also more narrowly to those miraculous signs that have accompanied his preaching ministry: "in the power of signs and wonders, in the power of the Holy Spirit" (15:19a). Paul presents himself as a miracle worker whose "signs and wonders" are persuasive evidence that testify to the divine origin of his apostleship and the genuineness of his gospel.[16]

Fourth, Paul spells out the results of his preaching ministry: "so that from Jerusalem and as far round as Illyricum I have fulfilled the gospel of Christ" (15:19b). Paul's success in making the gospel effective in Gentile churches throughout the eastern half of the Mediterranean testifies to the power and legitimacy of his gospel. This proven "track record" of the effectiveness of Paul's gospel places further pressure on the Roman readers to accept it despite their likely discomfort with the bold way he has preached to them in the body of the letter.

Fifth, Paul spells out his evangelistic strategy of preaching the gospel only in places where Christ has not yet been proclaimed (15:20) and then defends that strategy by citing an OT text from the prophet Isaiah (Rom 15:21; cf. Isa 52:15). No one in the house churches of Rome, therefore, can fault Paul for not visiting them up to this point, since he was following God's will in this mission strategy as evidenced by not only the OT citation from Isaiah but also the use of the divine passive in the closing statement, "This is why I was hindered many times from coming to you" (15:22). Paul's statements here also prepare his Roman readers to accept what he will do in the next section, namely, solicit their support for his future missionary activity in the new region of Spain.

2. The Second Half of the Apostolic Parousia: Paul's Future Travels (15:23–32)

There is a clear shift in the second half of the apostolic parousia (15:23–32) from Paul's *past* travels in the east to his *future* travels in the west. This shift is signaled by the emphatic temporal marker "but now" (νυνὶ δέ) that opens 15:23 and is confirmed by the content of the subsequent verses that speak of

---

16. See esp. 2 Cor 12:12: "I persevered in demonstrating among you the marks of a true apostle, including signs, wonders and miracles." See further Acts 2:43; 4:30; 5:12; 6:8; 14:3; 15:12; Heb 2:4. Note also the observation of Moo (*Romans*, 893): "Paul may then choose to illustrate his apostolic work with this phrase ['signs and wonders'] in order to suggest the salvation-historical significance of his own ministry. For Paul is not just another apostle; he is *the* apostle to the Gentiles, the one chosen to have a unique role in opening up the Gentile world to the gospel."

the apostle's plans for his future journeys. These future journeys involve a visit to the Roman house churches as part of a new missionary initiative in Spain: "But now, since I no longer have a place for ministry in these regions, and since I have a longing for many years to come to you, I hope to see you while I am traveling to Spain" (15:23–24a). Paul's reference that his strong desire to visit the believers in Rome goes back "many years" echoes his earlier statement in the thanksgiving (1:11: "I want you to know, brothers and sisters, that I have many times wanted to come to you") and involves "diplomatic flattery"[17] that both further elicits the warm feelings of the Roman readers towards the apostle and also wins their support for his future missionary activity in Spain.[18]

Paul's planned travels to Rome and Spain, however, are currently on hold until the apostle can first complete another journey—this one to Jerusalem in order to deliver to the needy Jewish Christians there a financial gift from the predominantly Gentile churches that Paul has founded. Here too the apostle's extended comments about his trip to Jerusalem should be understood not as a mere travelogue but as an additional way that Paul makes his parousia—his presence and power—felt among the Roman readers. The apostle accomplishes this in at least three ways.

First, Paul's comments about the collection provide more evidence to the believers in Rome of the success and thus the legitimacy of his gospel. For the financial support that Paul has won from the churches in Macedonia and Achaia is powerful proof that these believers have done what Paul hopes the Roman readers will also do, namely, recognize the legitimacy of Paul's apostleship and his gospel.

Second, the collection itself is a tangible illustration of the gospel that Paul has been preaching in the body of the letter—a gospel that has important implications for solving the all-too-common division that existed in the early church between Jew and Gentile (see, e.g., 1:16; 3:22–23, 29–30; 4:11–12; 9:4–5; 11:11–12, 13–18; 14:1–15:13). Just as Paul's gospel motivated Gentile Christians from churches he founded to give money to needy Jewish Christians in Jerusalem as a public sign of their unity in Christ, so also the apostle hopes that his gospel preached in this letter will result in solving the problematic tensions that exist between Jewish and Gentile Christians in Rome.[19]

---

17. Thielman, *Romans*, 688n50.

18. "There is an element of *captatio benevolentiae* in this statement that prepares the way for the missional collaboration suggested in the subsequent verses." Robert Jewett, *Romans: A Commentary*, Hermeneia (Minneapolis: Fortress, 2007), 923.

19. "Paul's ministry to 'the poor among the saints in Jerusalem,' then, was hardly just a pesky delay in his effort to get to Rome and on to Spain. It was a practical expression of a primary theme of the gospel as Paul has explained it in the letter (e.g., 1:16; 3:22–23; 29–30; 4:11–12; 9:4–5; 11:17–18). This same theme also needed appropriation among the believers in Rome in the midst of their own divisions over the relationship between gentile and Jewish Christianity (14:1–15:13)." Thielman, *Romans*, 694.

Third, Paul does not command but diplomatically appeals[20] for the Roman readers to join forces with him in the life-threatening battle that the apostle will face in Jerusalem. Instead of simply asking the Christians in Rome to pray for him, Paul uses a rare verb that presents the situation he faces as a military conflict in which he needs the Roman readers to do battle alongside of him: "Now I appeal to you, brothers and sisters, through our Lord Jesus Christ and through the love of the Spirit *to fight along with me*[21] in prayers to God for my behalf" (15:30). Paul's request for the readers in Rome to partner with him in his dangerous mission through their prayers for him strengthens the solidarity between the apostle and his readers that he has been developing throughout the letter. Paul's request also highlights the very real danger that he would be facing in Jerusalem, which in turn further demonstrates the genuineness of his apostolic calling and gospel: Paul is willing to suffer and even die in carrying out his divinely appointed mission.

II. The Letter Closing (15:33–16:27)

The excessive length of the letter closing of Romans—the longest among all of Paul's existing letter closings—as well as the presence of several unique features has led many scholars to question the authenticity and integrity of this final section of the apostle's letter. All the distinctive aspects of the Roman's letter closing, however, are better explained as serving Paul's overall purposes in this letter's epistolary framework, namely, to confirm and clarify his position as the Roman Christians' divinely appointed apostle whose gospel ought to be accepted and whose evangelistic mission ought to be supported. The formal features of the Romans letter closing can be outlined as follows:

> Peace Benediction (15:33)
> Commendation of the Letter Carrier (16:1–2)
> Greetings (16:3–16)
> > second-person greetings (vv. 3–15)
> > kiss greeting (v. 16a)
> > third-person greeting (v. 16b)
> Hortatory (Autograph) Section (16:17–20a)
> Grace Benediction (16:20b)
> Additional (Non-autograph) Greetings (16:21–23)
> Doxology (16:25–27)

---

20. On the form and function of the appeal formula, especially to convey a friendly, less heavy-handed request, see Weima, *Paul the Ancient Letter Writer*, 92–94.

21. BDAG s.v. συναγωνίζομαι (963–64): "to join w. someone in a common effort, *fight/contend along with* τινί, *someone*, w. focus on a supportive role." This is the only occurrence of the verb in the NT.

1. Peace Benediction (15:33)

Modern readers should not be misled by the chapter break in their Bible: the start of the letter closing occurs not in the opening verse of ch. 16 but in the final verse of ch. 15, which contains a peace benediction: "May the God of peace be with all of you!" (15:33).[22] The peace benediction occurs seven times in Paul's letters (see also Rom 16:20a; 2 Cor 13:11b; Gal 6:16; Phil 4:9b; 1 Thess 5:23; 2 Thess 3:16) and every one of them not only clearly belongs to the letter closing, they also, as is the case here, typically mark the beginning of the letter closing.[23]

Although this epistolary convention is a common occurrence at the start of Paul's letter closings, his prayer for the Roman audience that "the God of peace" be with them almost certainly has in view the existing conflict between "the Strong" and "the Weak" that has preoccupied the apostle's attention in the preceding material of 14:1–15:13. That Paul has the specific Roman situation in mind when issuing this prayer for peace gains support from four observations. First, there is the subtle but significant addition of "all" to the expected form of the prayer ("May the God of peace be with *all* of you"), an addition not found in any of the other peace benedictions, with the result that it comprehensively includes both "the Strong" and "the Weak." Second, the upcoming command in 16:16a to "Greet each other with a holy kiss" is issued by Paul only in contexts where there is internal division within the church.[24] Third, Paul makes an explicit reference to the tensions that exist between the Roman believers in his upcoming closing exhortation to "take note of those who create divisions and difficulties" (16:17), indicating that the tensions among the Roman house churches addressed in 14:1–15:13 are still very much in his mind. Fourth, the apostle feels the need to add yet a second peace benediction to this letter closing (16:20a: "But the God of peace will soon crush Satan under your feet"), thereby emphasizing the peace that ought to characterize relationships between the various Roman house churches.

---

22. Virtually all translations add to this peace benediction a concluding "Amen." Nevertheless, the oldest extant manuscript of Romans ($\mathfrak{P}^{46}$) omits the word, as do a number of other important manuscripts (the uncials A F G, several minuscules [330 436 451 630 1739 1998], and Latin versions) with the result that the external textual evidence is equally divided. When one considers the internal textual evidence, two important facts support the omission of "Amen" here: first, none of the other peace benedictions in Paul's letter closings end with a concluding "Amen" (Rom 16:20a; 2 Cor 13:11b; Gal 6:16; Phil 4:9b; 1 Thess 5:23; 2 Thess 3:16); second, "copyists would have been tempted to add it to such a quasi-liturgical statement as is ver. 33." Bruce M. Metzger, *A Textual Commentary on the Greek New Testament* (Stuttgart: United Bible Societies, 1971), 538.

23. The location of the peace benediction as typically the first item in the letter closing (in contrast to the grace benediction that typically occurs in the last position) stems from the chiasm that Paul creates between the opening greeting ("Grace to you and peace") and the closing peace and grace benedictions.

24. See the discussion of the kiss-greeting in Weima, *Paul the Ancient Letter Writer*, 187–88.

2. Commendation of the Letter Carrier (16:1–2)

Paul continues his letter closing to the Romans by including a formal commendation of the person carrying the letter on his behalf to the capital city—a woman named Phoebe from Cenchreae, the port city of Corinth. Since delivery service for non-governmental or non-military mail did not exist in that day, all other letters needed to be hand delivered. It was common for the letter writer to include at the end of the correspondence a commendation of the person delivering the document, asking the recipient to show hospitality and help to the letter carrier.[25] Paul includes a commendation of the letter carrier in the closings of his later letters to the Ephesians and the Colossians (Eph 6:21–22; Col 4:7–8), where he not only introduces Tychicus ("Mr. Lucky") to the recipients as the deliverer of the letter but also authorizes him to supplement the contents of the correspondence. It was, in fact, a frequent practice in that day for a letter carrier to expand upon the contents of the document that they were delivering.[26] This suggests that Phoebe is not only delivering Paul's lengthy letter to the Romans, but the apostle's commendation authorizes her to supplement or explain the contents of the document on the apostle's behalf.[27]

Paul stresses the high status of Phoebe by means of two terms: she is a "deacon" (διάκονον) of the church in Cenchreae and she is also a "benefactor" (προστάτις) of many Christians but especially of Paul. The most natural way to interpret these two terms is to view Phoebe as a woman of wealth and high social status who allowed the church of Cenchreae to meet in her home for worship and who provided important financial and logistical support for Paul as well as other Christian missionaries. What ought not to be missed is the fact that Paul's strong commendation of Phoebe also ultimately involves a strong commendation of himself, since she is his representative in Rome, and her reading and/or interpretation of Paul's letter is an effective means by which the apostle makes his parousia or presence more powerfully felt among the Roman readers.[28]

---

25. See Chan-Hie Kim, *Form and Structure of the Familiar Greek Letter of Recommendation*, SBLDS 4 (Missoula, MT: Scholars Press, 1972).

26. Peter M. Head, "Named Letter-Carriers among the Oxyrhynchus Papyri," *JSNT* 31.3 (2009): 288–89, 293, 295–98. Head concludes his study by stating: "The papyrological evidence surveyed here supports the further idea that in the Pauline tradition the accredited letter-carriers functioned not only as personal private postmen, but as personal mediators of Paul's authoritative instruction to his churches, and *as the earliest interpreters of the individual letters*" (298, emphasis added).

27. Thus, for example, Longenecker (*Romans*, 1064) states: "Probably Phoebe should be viewed as the first commentator to others on Paul's letter to Rome."

28. Note in this regard the observation of M. Luther Stirewalt, Jr., *Paul, the Letter Writer* (Grand Rapids: Eerdmans, 2003), 5, that "the living voice of the reader [i.e., the oral report of the letter carrier] underscored the sense of the writer's personal presence, thereby strengthening the relationship between sender and receiver."

3. Greetings (16:3–16)

The third item in Paul's letter closing to the Romans consists of greetings. Greetings, of course, are a common epistolary convention of Paul's letter closings but these greetings are unusual in two ways. First, there are a lot of greetings, far more than in any other Pauline letter closing, as the apostle uses the greeting formula seventeen times to identify twenty-four individuals by name, three households by name, two unnamed individuals, and two unnamed groups. Many commentators have found this extensive greeting list problematic, as they question the likelihood that Paul would know so many Jesus-followers in a city where he had not yet ever visited in person.

Second, the greetings are also distinctive for the strong commendatory manner in which those being greeted are described—a feature not found in any of Paul's other closing greetings. This laudable aspect of the greetings is often accomplished by means of a simple term of endearment or praise: "my beloved" (16:5b, 8, 9, 12b), "esteemed in Christ" (16:10a), "chosen in the Lord" (16:8, 11, 12 [2x], 13). This laudable aspect is frequently further stressed by means of a relative clause: "who risked their necks for my life" (16:4a), "to whom not only I but also all the church of Gentiles give thanks" (16:4b), "who is the first convert of Asia for Christ" (16:5b), "who has worked hard among you" (16:6), "who are outstanding among the apostles" (16:7b), "who were in Christ before me" (16:7c), and "who has worked hard in the Lord" (16:12b).

These two unique features of the greetings in the closing of Romans—their frequency and their commendatory character—both serve Paul's overall purposes in this letter's epistolary framework, namely, to confirm and clarify his position as the Roman Christians' divinely appointed apostle whose gospel ought to be accepted and whose evangelistic mission ought to be supported. The reason why Paul included such laudatory descriptions is obviously not to help the house churches in Rome identify the person being greeted, since such persons would have been well known to the Christian communities there. These seemingly superfluous additions rather emphasize the close relations that Paul enjoys with key people in the Roman house churches. In colloquial terms, one might say that the apostle is "name dropping." The situation is somewhat similar to a political advertisement in a newspaper where the candidate lists the names of leading people within the local community who support his or her candidacy. Paul builds up his own standing in the Roman churches by not merely greeting a great number of respected people in Rome but also associating himself so closely with such persons that he himself shares in the commendation that they receive.[29]

---

29. Harry Y. Gamble, *The Textual History of the Letter to the Romans*, SD 42 (Grand Rapids: Eerdmans, 1977), 92: "It is especially striking how, in the descriptive phrases,

That Paul uses the greetings to commend himself more fully to the Roman Christians can also be seen in the order in which he greets specific people.[30] The first persons greeted are Prisca and Aquila whose stature among "all the churches of the Gentiles" (16:4) and whose missionary partnership with Paul (16:3: "my fellow workers") in Corinth and Ephesus (Acts 18:1–2, 18; 1 Cor 16:19) means that they are influential leaders who can testify to the Roman Christians from first-hand experience as to Paul's apostleship as well as the orthodoxy and success of his gospel. The second person greeted is Epaenetus who, as "the first convert [of Paul] in Asia" (16:5b), is living proof of the genuineness and effectiveness of Paul's gospel. Similarly, the identification of Mariam in the third greeting as someone "who has worked very hard among you" (16:6), and Andronicus and Junia(s) in the fourth greeting as "those who are outstanding among the apostles" (16:7), means that these individuals can function as weighty "character references" for the legitimacy of Paul's apostolic status and his gospel.

The unique aspect of the final greeting should not be overlooked: "All the churches of Christ greet you" (16:16b). Nowhere else does Paul speak so broadly ("*all* the churches") in conveying the greetings of others. This comprehensive greeting implies that the apostle enjoys the official backing of all the churches in Achaia, Macedonia, Asia, Galatia, Syria and elsewhere. As James Dunn observes: "The greeting thus has a 'political' overtone: Paul speaks for all these churches, and they are behind him in his mission."[31] The implicit challenge in this final greeting is that the churches in Rome ought to join all these worldwide churches in recognizing Paul's apostleship and gospel.

4. Hortatory (autograph) Section (16:17–20a)

After the lengthy and commendatory greetings, Paul includes in the letter closing a hortatory section (16:17–20a) in which he issues some final commands. A few commentators have found this section to be problematic as well, interpreting the apostle's closing commands as a harsh rebuke of the Roman Christians that does not fit his positive tone in the rest of the letter and that creates "an egregious break" between the warm greetings of the preceding verses of

---

a heavy emphasis is placed on the relationship between the individuals and Paul himself. He ties them to himself, and himself to them. From these features it can be seen that Paul's commendatory greetings to specific individuals serve to place those individuals in a position of respect vis-à-vis the community, but also, by linking the Apostle so closely to them, place Paul in the same position." So also Longenecker, *Romans*, 1066, 1070.

30. Jervis, *Purpose of Romans*, 151–52. Contra Jewett (*Romans*, 952) who states: "The perception that the greetings are in a rather random sequence is correct."

31. Dunn, *Romans 9–16*, 899.

3–16 and the greetings of the subsequent verses of 21–23.[32] This interpretation, however, is undermined by a number of important facts.

First, Paul here is following his regular pattern of including in the letter closing some final exhortations and commands (cf. 1 Cor 16:13–16, 22; 2 Cor 13:11a; Gal 6:17; Phil 4:8–9a; 1 Thess 5:25, 27; Phlm 20).

Second, the apparent shift in tone in this section likely is due from Paul here taking over the quill and ink from the secretary Tertius and writing this material in his own hand, as the apostle does in his other letter closings, often in order to issue a strong command or word of warning (cf. Gal 6:11–18; 1 Cor 16:22; 1 Thess 5:27).[33]

Third, Paul in this hortatory section actually speaks positively of the believers in Rome as he continues to strengthen his good relations with them: he opens this section not with a heavy-handed command but with the user-friendly appeal formula, just as he did earlier in 15:30; he refers affectionately to them as "brothers and sisters" (16:17); he affirms that they have learned proper teaching; he places them in an entirely different category from those divisive persons "who do not serve our Lord Jesus Christ but their own selfish desires" (16:18); he includes a joy expression that praises the Roman Christians for the fact that "your obedience is known to all" (16:19); and he concludes this hortatory section with a modified peace benediction by which he assures his Roman readers that "the God of peace will soon crush Satan under your feet" (16:20a).[34]

Fourth, this hortatory section fits the specific Roman situation. Paul's exhortation for his Roman readers to watch out for those who create "divisions and stumbling blocks" by advocating things "contrary to the teaching that you have learned" most likely looks back to the apostle's earlier exhortations in 14:1–15:13 dealing with the division that existed in the Roman house churches

---

32. See esp. the extended discussion of Jewett, *Romans*, 986–88, who argues that 16:17–20a is a non-Pauline interpolation.

33. Several Roman commentators believe that this hortatory section was written in Paul's own hand: H. Lietzmann, *An die Römer*, 4th ed., HNT 8 (Tübingen: Mohr, 1933), 121–22; K. H. Schelke, *The Epistle to the Romans* (Freiburg: Herder, 1964), 262; Gordon P. Wiles, *Paul's Intercessory Prayers: The Significance of the Intercessory Prayer Passages in the Letters of Paul*, SNTSMS 24 (Cambridge: Cambridge University Press, 2007), 93; Leon Morris, *The Epistle to the Romans*, PNTC (Grand Rapids: Eerdmans, 1988), 538; Dunn, *Romans 9–16*, 902, 906; Fitzmyer, *Romans*, 745; Schreiner, *Romans*, 801; Longenecker, *Romans*, 1079, 1081.

34. See Brian S. Rosner, "Romans 16:20a as a Summary of Central Themes of Romans," in *The Seed of the Promise: The Sufferings and Glory of the Messiah: Essays in Honor of T. Desmond Alexander*, ed. Paul R. Williamson and Rita F. Cefalu, GFS 3 (Wilmore, KY: GlossaHouse, 2020), 314, who argues that "Paul's words in Rom. 16:20a, his second peace benediction in the Romans letter closing, strike the notes of joy and hope, recalling key texts in Romans that summarize several major themes in the letter."

between "the Strong" and "the Weak."[35] Some have questioned the link between this hortatory section and that earlier material, claiming: "Paul's strong denunciation in this text is completely different from anything we find in the earlier passage."[36] But as we have observed above, Paul's supposedly harsh words are not aimed at the Roman readers generally but more narrowly at those who are creating the internal divisions. Furthermore, the situation here is very similar to that of the letter closing of Galatians where Paul takes over from his secretary and in quite strong and pointed words issues final warnings and exhortations to the readers before bringing the letter to a definitive close (Gal 6:11–18).[37]

5. Grace Benediction (16:20b)

The fifth item in the letter closing of Romans is the grace benediction. Secular letters of Paul's day typically ended with the "farewell wish," expressed either in the form of "Be strong!" (ἔρρωσθε: Acts 15:29; 23:30 v.l.) or, less commonly, "Prosper!" (εὐτύχει). This fixed formula served to signal the end of a letter somewhat like the expression "sincerely" or "yours truly" is used to close our modern correspondence.[38] Paul, however, indicates the end of his letters by replacing this secular closing formula with a distinctively Christian one: "May the grace of our Lord Jesus Christ be with you." This wish for grace and its divine source, the Lord Jesus Christ, along with the preceding peace benediction (15:33) and its divine source, God, which is also part of the letter closing, form an inverted or chiastic inclusio with the greeting of the letter opening: "Grace to you and peace from God our Father and from the Lord Jesus Christ" (1:7b). This is Paul's literary way of marking the boundaries of the letter opening and the letter closing.

---

35. So Matthew Black, *Romans*, NCB (London: Oliphants, 1973), 212–13; Francis Watson, *Paul, Judaism, and the Gentiles: A Sociological Approach*, SNTSMS 56 (Cambridge: Cambridge University Press, 1986), 102; Karl P. Donfried, "A Short Note on Romans 16," in *The Romans Debate: Revised and Expanded Edition*, ed. Karl P. Donfried (Peabody, MA: Hendrickson, 1991), 51–52; C. K. Barrett, *The Epistle to the Romans*, 2nd ed., BNTC 6 (Grand Rapids: Baker Academic, 1991), 285; Longenecker, *Romans*, 1081.

36. Moo, *Romans*, 929. Most commentators, in fact, do not view the hortatory section of 16:17–20a as referring back to the divisions between "the Strong" and "the Weak" taken up in 14:1–15:13: see, e.g., John Murray, *The Epistle to the Romans*, 2 vols., NICNT (Grand Rapids: Eerdmans, 1959–65), 2:235–36; Ernst Käsemann, *Commentary on Romans*, trans. and ed. Geoffrey W. Bromiley (Grand Rapids: Eerdmans, 1980), 417; Dunn, *Romans 9–16*, 901; Fitzmyer, *Romans*, 745; Schreiner, *Romans*, 801.

37. Note also the point raised by Donfried ("Short Note on Romans 16," 52): "Is the break [at 16:17] in Romans any more 'abrupt' than the transition from 1 Cor. 16:20b, 'Greet one another with a holy kiss,' to v. 22a, 'If anyone has no love for the Lord, let him be accursed'?"

38. For examples and further discussion of the farewell wish, see Jeffrey A. D. Weima, *Neglected Endings: The Significance of the Pauline Letter Closings*, JSNTSup 101 (Sheffield: JSOT Press, 1994), 29–34.

6. Additional (Non-Autograph) Greetings (16:21–23)

Although the grace benediction typically marks the definitive end of Paul's letters, here in the letter closing of Romans the apostle includes two more epistolary conventions: additional greetings and a doxology. These two added sections should not be labeled a "postscript"[39] or "afterthought,"[40] as if Paul had forgotten to include a couple of things and thus simply tacked them on to the end of the letter.[41] Rather, both the additional greetings and the doxology strengthen in important ways the persuasive purposes of the apostle.

The additional greetings of vv. 21–23 differ in *form* from the previous greetings of vv. 3–16. Whereas the earlier greetings are second-person greetings by which Paul exhorts his readers to pass on his greetings to many key individuals in the house churches of Rome to whom he is connected, here we have third-person greetings by which Paul passes on to the Roman readers the greetings of eight named individuals who are with him in Corinth.[42] The additional greetings of vv. 21–23, however, have the same *function* as the previous greetings of vv. 3–16. Here too Paul uses the greetings to strengthen the credibility of his apostleship and his gospel among the Christians in Rome.

This can be seen most clearly in the greeting from Erastus who is identified as "the treasurer of the city" (v. 23b). Paul presents himself and his gospel ministry as enjoying the support of this person of great wealth and prestige.[43] Similarly, the greeting from Gaius whom Paul describes as "host to me and to the whole church" (v. 23a) is another person of financial means and high social standing who backs the apostle and his missionary activity. There are greetings from three individuals—Lucius, Jason, and Sosipater—whom Paul identifies as "my fellow countrymen" (v. 21b), that is, fellow Jewish Christians. Paul may have highlighted their Jewish ethnicity in order to show that his gospel—despite what detractors in Rome were saying about its opposition to the OT Scriptures—was accepted by Jewish Christians elsewhere in the Roman world and thus ought to be confidently embraced by Jewish Christians in the

---

39. "They [the greetings of 16:21–23] form a postscript and have really nothing to do with the theme or subject of chaps. 1–15." Fitzmyer, *Romans*, 748.

40. Thielman, *Romans*, 735.

41. Dunn (*Romans 9–16*, 908) observes in his discussion of the additional greetings of 16:21–23 that Ernst Käsemann, an important Romans commentator, "is clearly irritated that such a powerful letter should tail off in such a lame fashion."

42. To be precise the previous greetings of vv. 3–16 consist of sixteen second-person greetings which are concluded by a single third-person greeting (v. 16: "All the churches of Christ greet you") that is unique for how broadly Paul speaks on behalf of "all the churches."

43. As Jewett (*Romans*, 983) rightly notes: "The preceding reference to Erastus was intended to lend maximum public prestige to Paul's project."

capital city of the empire too.[44] The additional greetings of vv. 21–23, therefore, ought to be viewed not as a last-minute addition awkwardly tacked on to the ending of the Roman letter but rather, as Richard Longenecker observes, "as having been included primarily to support his [Paul's] apostolic authority and to enhance the acceptability of his contextualization of the gospel among the Christians at Rome."[45]

7. Doxology (16:25–27)

The final element in the letter closing of Romans is the doxology (16:25–27). The authenticity of this passage has been strongly questioned on two grounds: first, the doxology occurs among the extant manuscripts in several different locations, thus causing some to refer to this passage as the "wandering" doxology;[46] second, the passage's style and vocabulary are judged by many to be non-Pauline.

This is not the place to examine in detail the complex issue of the doxology's authenticity. Nevertheless, a brief comment is warranted. In response to the first ground, compelling text critical reasons exist for concluding that the doxology was the final item in the letter closing of a sixteen-chapter letter to the Romans.[47] In response to the second ground, the claimed problems of style and vocabulary can be resolved by the possibility that Paul has taken a pre-existing doxology that was part of the liturgy of the early church and skillfully revised it so that it echoes many of the key ideas that the apostle has shared with his Roman readers earlier in the letter.[48] This possibility gains greater likelihood in

---

44. Jewett (*Romans*, 978) believes that Paul's reference to these three individuals as being fellow Jews "is part of his campaign to grant equal honor to the Jewish Christian minority in Rome."

45. Longenecker, *Romans*, 1083.

46. R. F. Collins, "The Case of a Wandering Doxology (Rom 16,25–27)," in *New Testament Textual Criticism and Exegesis: Festschrift J. Delobel*, ed. A. Denaux, BETL 161 (Leuven: Leuven University Press, 2002), 293–303.

47. See esp. Larry W. Hurtado, "The Doxology at the End of Romans," in *New Testament Textual Criticism: Its Significance for Exegesis: Essays in Honour of Bruce M. Metzger*, ed. Eldon J. Epp and Gordon D. Fee (Oxford: Clarendon Press, 1981), 185–99. Fitzmyer (*Romans*, 44–51) ends his lengthy examination of the Greek text of Romans by stating that "the quality of the ancient witnesses supporting the positioning of it [the doxology] at 16:25–27, the geographical spread of their testimony, and the diversity of the textual traditions represented are decisive for reading it after 16:23" (50).

48. For a fulsome presentation and defense of this possibility, see J. B. Brewer, "The Origins of the Romans 16 Doxology: Reconsidering Its Form and Provenance," *BBR* 32.2 (2022): 141–64. Note also the earlier comment of John A. Ziesler, *Paul's Letter to the Romans* (London: SCM Press, 1989), 356–57, that "there is nothing in the passage [16:25–27] that is at odds with his [Paul's] thought or indeed that he might not have adapted from liturgical tradition."

light of Paul's demonstrated ability and practice of adapting epistolary conventions in his letter closings so that they more clearly and directly relate to main ideas taken up previously in the body of the letter.[49]

The doxology, in fact, is striking for the way it recapitulates the primary concern of Paul in the epistolary framework of the letter.[50] The reference to *"my* gospel" recalls well Paul's concern in the letter opening, the thanksgiving, the apostolic parousia, and the letter body to share his gospel with the Roman readers. The doxology claims that Paul's gospel will be used by God "to strengthen" (στηρίξαι) the believers in Rome—the same point that was made in the thanksgiving section (1:11: "in order that you might be strengthened" [εἰς τὸ στηριχθῆναι ὑμᾶς]). The doxology further highlights the continuity of Paul's gospel with the message of the OT—a matter also stressed in the letter opening (1:2–4). More specifically the phrase "through the prophetic writings" (16:26: διά τε γραφῶν προφητικῶν) is a deliberate allusion to the opening words of the letter, "through his prophets in the holy Scriptures" (1:2: διὰ τῶν προφητῶν αὐτοῦ ἐν γραφαῖς ἁγίαις). The goal or purpose of making the mystery of the gospel known is "to bring about the obedience of faith for all the Gentiles" (16:26: εἰς ὑπακοὴν πίστεως εἰς πάντα τὰ ἔθνη). This phrase from the doxology provides yet another direct verbal link with the letter opening: "to bring about the obedience of faith for all the Gentiles" (1:5: εἰς ὑπακοὴν πίστεως ἐν πᾶσιν τοῖς ἔθνεσιν). It also recalls Paul's point in the apostolic parousia that Christ is working through him "to bring about the obedience of the Gentiles" (15:18: εἰς ὑπακοὴν ἐθνῶν).

The strong recapitulating character of the doxology is not only evidence of the literary skill of Paul as a letter writer but more importantly functions as a further means by which Paul establishes the authority and acceptability of his gospel ministry among the Roman believers. And if Paul is, in fact, borrowing and adapting a doxology from the liturgy of the early church, then ending the Romans letter in this fashion would further win the confidence of any readers with lingering skepticism about the orthodoxy of Paul's gospel and the goal of his apostolic mission.

Conclusion

I have attempted to show that the two units at the *end* of the letter to the Romans—the report of his travels, or as it is better identified formally, his apostolic parousia (15:14–32), and the letter closing (15:33–16:27)—are intended

---

49. Weima, *Neglected Endings*; Jeffrey A. D. Weima, "Sincerely, Paul: The Significance of the Pauline Letter Closings," in *Paul and the Ancient Letter Form*, ed. Stanley E. Porter and Sean A. Adams, PAST 6 (Leiden: Brill, 2010), 307–45.

50. "Paul deliberately echoes in these verses [16:25–27] the language and themes of the letter, and particularly its opening section." Moo, *Romans*, 937.

by the apostle to parallel the two units at the *beginning* of the letter—the letter opening (1:1–7) and the thanksgiving (1:8–15)—so that these four units serve as the epistolary framework for the body of the letter (1:16–15:13). Paul skillfully adapts each of these epistolary units that surround the letter body so that they emphasize his divine calling to preach the gospel to the Roman Christians—readers whom he has neither converted nor even visited and who harbor some suspicion about the content of his gospel message. As the apostle to the Gentiles, Paul felt not only uniquely qualified but also divinely obligated to share with the believers in Rome *his* gospel in the conviction that this would strengthen their faith in face of Jewish-Gentile tensions within the Roman house churches. After Paul has finished "preaching" his gospel to them in the letter body, he deftly shapes in a similar manner the final two sections of the letter to confirm and clarify his position as the Roman Christians' divinely appointed apostle whose gospel ought to be accepted and whose evangelistic mission ought to be supported.

Bibliography

Barrett, C. K. *The Epistle to the Romans.* 2nd ed. BNTC 6. Grand Rapids: Baker Academic, 1991.

Black, Matthew. *Romans.* NCB. London: Oliphants, 1973.

Bowers, Paul. "Fulfilling the Gospel: The Scope of the Pauline Mission." *JETS* 30.2 (1987): 185–98.

Brewer, J. B. "The Origins of the Romans 16 Doxology: Reconsidering Its Form and Provenance." *BBR* 32.2 (2022): 141–64.

Collins, R. F. "The Case of a Wandering Doxology (Rom 16,25–27)." Pages 293–303 in *New Testament Textual Criticism and Exegesis: Festschrift J. Delobel.* Edited by A. Denaux. BETL 161. Leuven: Leuven University Press, 2002.

Dahl, Nils A. *Studies in Paul.* Minneapolis: Augsburg, 1977.

Donfried, Karl P. "A Short Note on Romans 16." Pages 44–52 in *The Romans Debate: Revised and Expanded Edition.* Edited by Karl P. Donfried. Peabody, MA: Hendrickson, 1991.

Dunn, James D. G. *Romans 9–16.* WBC 38B. Dallas: Word, 1988.

Elliott, Neil. *The Rhetoric of Romans: Argumentative Constraint and Strategy and Paul's Dialogue with Judaism.* JSNTSup 45. Sheffield: JSOT Press, 1990.

Fitzmyer, Joseph A. *Romans: A New Translation with Introduction and Commentary.* AB 33. New York: Doubleday, 1993.

Funk, Robert W. "The Apostolic *Parousia*: Form and Significance." Pages 249–68 in *Christian History and Interpretation: Studies Presented to John Knox.* Edited by W. R. Farmer, C. F. D. Moule, and R. R. Niebuhr. Cambridge: Cambridge University Press, 1967.

Gamble, Harry Y. *The Textual History of the Letter to the Romans*. SD 42. Grand Rapids: Eerdmans, 1977.

Head, Peter M. "Named Letter-Carriers among the Oxyrhynchus Papyri." *JSNT* 31.3 (2009): 279–99.

Hurtado, Larry W. "The Doxology at the End of Romans." Pages 185–99 in *New Testament Textual Criticism: Its Significance for Exegesis: Essays in Honour of Bruce M. Metzger*. Edited by Eldon J. Epp and Gordon D. Fee. Oxford: Clarendon Press, 1981.

Jervis, L. Ann. *The Purpose of Romans: A Comparative Letter Structure Investigation*. JSNTSup 55. Sheffield: JSOT Press, 1991.

Jewett, Robert. *Romans: A Commentary*. Hermeneia. Minneapolis: Fortress, 2007.

Käsemann, Ernst. *Commentary on Romans*. Translated and edited by Geoffrey W. Bromiley. Grand Rapids: Eerdmans, 1980.

Kim, Chan-Hie. *Form and Structure of the Familiar Greek Letter of Recommendation*. SBLDS 4. Missoula, MT: Scholars Press, 1972.

Klein, Günter. "Paul's Purpose in Writing the Epistle to the Romans." Pages 29–43 in *The Romans Debate: Revised and Expanded Edition*. Edited by Karl P. Donfried. Peabody, MA: Hendrickson, 1991.

Lietzmann, H. *An die Römer*. 4th ed. HNT 8. Tübingen: Mohr, 1933.

Longenecker, Richard N. *The Epistle to the Romans: A Commentary on the Greek Text*. NIGTC. Grand Rapids: Eerdmans, 2016.

Metzger, Bruce M. *A Textual Commentary on the Greek New Testament*. Stuttgart: United Bible Societies, 1971.

Moo, Douglas J. *The Epistle to the Romans*. NICNT. Grand Rapids: Eerdmans, 1996.

Morris, Leon. *The Epistle to the Romans*. PNTC. Grand Rapids: Eerdmans, 1988.

Murray, John. *The Epistle to the Romans*. 2 vols. NICNT. Grand Rapids: Eerdmans, 1959–65.

Olsen, Stanley N. "Epistolary Uses of Expressions of Self-Confidence." *JBL* 103.4 (1984): 585–97.

Rosner, Brian S. "Romans 16:20a as a Summary of Central Themes of Romans." Pages 299–314 in *The Seed of the Promise: The Sufferings and Glory of the Messiah: Essays in Honor of T. Desmond Alexander*. Edited by Paul R. Williamson and Rita F. Cefalu. GFS 3. Wilmore, KY: GlossaHouse, 2020.

Schelke, K. H. *The Epistle to the Romans*. Freiburg: Herder, 1964.

Schreiner, Thomas R. *Romans*. BECNT. Grand Rapids: Baker Academic, 1998.

Stirewalt, M. Luther, Jr. *Paul, the Letter Writer*. Grand Rapids: Eerdmans, 2003.

Thielman, Frank. *Romans*. ZECNT 6. Grand Rapids: Zondervan Academic, 2018.

Watson, Francis. *Paul, Judaism, and the Gentiles: A Sociological Approach*. SNTSMS 56. Cambridge: Cambridge University Press, 1986.

Weima, Jeffrey A. D. *Neglected Endings: The Significance of the Pauline Letter Closings.* JSNTSup 101. Sheffield: JSOT Press, 1994.

———. *Paul the Ancient Letter Writer: An Introduction to Epistolary Analysis.* Grand Rapids: Baker Academic, 2016.

———. "Preaching the Gospel in Rome: A Study of the Epistolary Framework of Romans." Pages 337–66 in *Gospel in Paul: Studies on Corinthians, Galatians and Romans for Richard N. Longenecker.* Edited by L. Ann Jervis and Peter Richardson. JSNTSup 108. Sheffield: Sheffield Academic Press, 1994.

———. "The Reason for Romans: The Evidence of Its Epistolary Framework (1:1–15; 15:14–16:27)." *RevExp* 100 (2003): 17–33.

———. "Sincerely, Paul: The Significance of the Pauline Letter Closings." Pages 307–45 in *Paul and the Ancient Letter Form.* Edited by Stanley E. Porter and Sean A. Adams. PAST 6. Leiden: Brill, 2010.

Wiles, Gordon P. *Paul's Intercessory Prayers: The Significance of the Intercessory Prayer Passages in the Letters of Paul.* SNTSMS 24. Cambridge: Cambridge University Press, 2007.

Ziesler, John A. *Paul's Letter to the Romans.* London: SCM Press, 1989.

CHAPTER 23

Love and Ethics in Romans

Mateus F. de Campos

Introduction

It is an easily observable fact that Rom 12–16 betrays a significant shift in the overall discourse of Romans. The heavily theological rhetoric of Rom 1–11, with its prominent themes of sin, justification by faith, sanctification, and the relationship between Jews and Gentiles in the history of salvation, gives way to a more ethical and pragmatic set of instructions, focusing on various aspects of Christian behavior. Given this shift, it may be tempting to see Rom 12–16 as a kind of appendix—a series of practical commands only marginally related to Paul's breathtaking theological argument.[1] However, this so-called "ethical section" of Romans should not be seen as an afterthought but the very "landing zone" of the apostle's treatment—the place where his theological argument finds its practical expression. The passage draws on several threads of the letter as a whole to express in practical terms the results of the theological reality portrayed thus far. At the center of this "landing zone" is a paraenesis framed by a love command (12:9) and a statement about the nomic fulfillment function of ἀγάπη (13:8–10), which effectively portrays love as a tangible expression of Paul's gospel.

That Paul's theological discourse lands in ethics should not come as a surprise. The apostle is part of a larger cultural environment where ethics occupy a prominent role in philosophical discourse. The apostle's use of love in his ethics, however, stands out in comparison to contemporary ethical treatments for its unique features. In this study, I aim at exploring the role of love in Paul's ethical paraenesis in Rom 12–13, first by situating Paul's love ethics within philosophical discussions of his time as well as within the larger theological argument of the letter, and then by assessing Paul's use of the concept of love in his ethics in the letter. It will be argued that the unique features of Paul's love ethics are drawn from a grammar of love developed in his theological argument—a

---

1. There seems to be a tendency in Pauline scholarship to focus more on Paul's theology than his ethics. Barclay calls attention to the fact that the history of scholarship on Paul's understanding of the law, for example, is heavily imbalanced towards the more theoretical rather than the practical. John M. G. Barclay, *Pauline Churches and Diaspora Jews* (Tübingen: Mohr Siebeck, 2011), 37.

grammar established by Paul's understanding of the display of God's love in Christ Jesus, which in turn shapes the ethical life of the believer.[2]

Theology and Ethics in Romans

The relationship between theology and ethics in Paul's theology is noticeable throughout the Pauline corpus. It is clear in the way that Paul develops his argument that his theological elaborations almost always land on practical ethical commands and appeals. As Morna Hooker states:

> It is not simply that, in writing to the congregations in his care, [Paul] tends to deal first with theological questions and then with ethical problems; rather, the one leads inevitably into the other. It is not that ethical questions are less important, and can therefore be dealt with in the tail-end of a letter, the truth is that ethical judgments can only be made on the basis of theological understanding. . . . belief and behaviour belong together.[3]

The interweaving of theology and ethics is not simply a rhetorical strategy; rather it is both an expression of Paul's immediate pastoral concerns and of a broader theological understanding of reality. In the case of Romans, as tempting as it is to see it as Paul's most systematic argument, it is clear that he writes as an apostle and a pastor who has in view the real issues of ethics and behavior which were part of the daily life of the early Christian communities.[4] This practical orientation notwithstanding, Paul approaches these issues within a robust theological framework, for Paul does not treat ethics from the point of view of some philosophical notion of moral duty, but based on his perception of the new reality inaugurated by the Christ event. Christ's redemptive work is not a mere theological subject for Paul, but an event with concrete implications.[5] For this reason, the pragmatic commands flow naturally from his theological understanding of God's work in Christ.

---

2. "Grammar" is used here conceptually, referring to the way words are used in a given linguistic context following certain conceptual rules. For a similar approach see Matthew V. Novenson, *The Grammar of Messianism: An Ancient Jewish Political Idiom and Its Users* (Oxford: Oxford University Press, 2017), 11–21.

3. Morna D. Hooker, "Interchange in Christ and Ethics," *JSNT* 25 (1985): 3.

4. Wolfgang Schrage, *The Ethics of the New Testament* (London: T&T Clark, 1988), 5, refers to this as "contextual ethics." According to Hays, Paul "responds ad hoc to the contingent pastoral problems that arise in his churches. . . . The constant aim of his theological reflection is to shape the behavior of his churches." Richard B. Hays, *The Moral Vision of the New Testament: Community, Cross, New Creation: A Contemporary Introduction to New Testament Ethic* (New York: Harper Collins, 1996), 17–18.

5. See Victor Paul Furnish, *Theology and Ethics in Paul* (Nashville: Abingdon, 1968), 67.

Since the nature of Paul's ethical treatments is largely occasional, it comes as no surprise that it is not uniform. In some of his letters, such as 1 Corinthians and Galatians, the practical issues are fronted, leading to Paul's weaving of theological arguments seamlessly into his exhortations and vice-versa. In other letters, such as Romans and Ephesians, theological exposition and paraenesis are more or less articulated in separate sections, with theology as the foundation of ethics, although the two categories are never hermetically isolated. It is possible that the two different approaches—one shaped around ethical issues and the other around theological argument—follows the nature of Paul's relationship with his audiences. In the case of Romans, more specifically, since Paul lacks the kind of relational capital with the audience that he has with the congregations he founded, he builds an extensive theological argument first, which serves both to commend his apostolic authority and to establish the reliability of his theology, which then allows him to move to the paraenesis of chs. 12–16.[6]

However, one should not discard the possibility that the kinds of issues that Paul deals with in the ethical section—more poignantly the divisions between the "weak" and the "strong" around matters such as food laws and observance of days (14:1–23)—are very much in Paul's mind from the beginning of the letter, and might have played a part in prompting its writing.[7] This seems to be reflected in the end of the longer paraenesis of 14:1–15:13, where Paul summarizes his admonition with an ethical appeal for the believers, presumably Jews and Gentiles, to "receive one another as Christ received them" (15:7). The appeal moves seamlessly to a short midrashic exposition on how Christ became a "servant to the circumcised" in order to open up the covenant to Gentiles (15:8–12)—which harks back to the argument developed in chs. 1–11. This subtle transition from ethics back to the theology that he develops earlier in the letter might serve as an indication that the practical issues have played a part in informing Paul's earlier theological exposition in Romans.[8]

Another important hint that the ethical section is more than an afterthought or an appendix in Romans is the pregnant inferential οὖν that introduces the section in 12:1. This conjunction is characteristic of Paul's rhetoric in Romans, appearing 47 times.[9] In most cases, οὖν is used either to move the argument further along—many times in conjunction with a rhetorical

---

6. As Barclay states, "Because he did not found the believer-communities in Rome, his approach toward them is delicately nonintrusive (1:11–12; 15:14–15)." John M. G. Barclay, *Paul and the Gift* (Grand Rapids: Eerdmans, 2015), 457.

7. On the centrality of this issue for the writing of Romans see Barclay, "'Do We Undermine the Law?'" 37–60; David G. Horrell, *Solidarity and Difference: A Contemporary Reading of Paul's Ethics* (London: T&T Clark, 2016), 201.

8. On the influence of the situation in Rome on Paul's argument in Rom 1–11, see A. J. M. Wedderburn, *The Reasons for Romans* (London: T&T Clark, 2004).

9. Rom 2:21, 26; 3:1, 9, 27, 31; 4:1, 9–10; 5:1, 9, 18; 6:1, 4, 12, 15, 21; 7:3, 7, 13, 25; 8:12, 31; 9:14, 16, 18–19, 30; 10:14; 11:1, 5, 7, 11, 13, 19, 22; 12:1; 13:10, 12; 14:8, 12–13, 16, 19; 15:17, 28; 16:19.

question—or inferentially, to present a conclusion or summary statement. In 12:1, however, the conjunction appears after a doxology that concludes the extended theological section (9–11). Given the formal closure of the doxology (cf. ἀμήν), it is better to see the inference as connecting the ethical section with the larger argument of chs. 1–11, which gives the sense that what follows in chs. 12–16 is the necessary inference of Paul's theological discussion as a whole.

Furthermore, as some have suggested, Paul's discourse in chs. 12–16 draws heavily on his theological argument.[10] Examples of shared themes include: the mercies of God (12:1; cf. 11:31–32), presenting the body (12:1; cf. 6:13–19), the wrath of God (12:19; cf. 1:18; 2:5, 8; 3:5; 4:15; 5:9; 9:22), doing good (12:9, 21; 13:3–4; cf. 2:7, 10; 3:8; 7:18–19), the role of the law (13:8–10; cf. 2:12–15, 17–18, 20, 23, 25–27; 3:19–21; 4:13–16; 5:13, 20; 6:14–15; 7:1–9, 12, 14, 16, 21–23, 25; 8:2–4, 7; 9:31; 10:4–5); the eschatological "day" (13:12–13; cf. 2:5, 16); Christ's death and resurrection (14:8–9; cf. 1:4; 4:24; 6:4, 9, 13; 7:4; 8:11; 10:9); and judging others (14:3, 10, 13, 22; cf. 2:1, 3, 27). It is likely that the reason for such an overlap is that, in Paul's mind, the ethical issues are integrated with his theological argument in a symbiotic relationship. The ethics of chs. 12–16 stand in the background of the theology of 1–11 as its unstated necessity. Conversely, the theological argument provides the grammar that the ethical section requires.

Therefore, Rom 12–16 does not work as a mere afterthought in Romans, as if Paul, having finished his main task, now sets himself to deal with a couple of housekeeping issues before concluding the letter. Rather, this section is the natural landing zone of his theological argument, a description of the real–life implications of his gospel, or, in other words, the important and inevitable "so what" of his theology.

Love Shaping Ethics

At the center of this landing zone is the emblematic phrase "Let love be genuine," which inaugurates the subsequent ethical paraenesis of 12:9–13:10. Love, in the passage, is not to be understood as a feeling or an internal disposition of the soul towards the object of one's love. Rather, love is described in strict ethical terms. Genuine love is expressed in "abhorring what is evil and holding fast to what is good" (12:9), in "living peaceably with all men" (12:18), and "overcoming evil with good" (12:21). Love is the operative catalyst of ethics and that which gives shape to it.

The idea of love informing ethics is present in philosophical discussions in antiquity. For our purposes, it will suffice to survey Plato, Aristotle, and Epicte-

---

10. See James D. G. Dunn, *Romans 9–16*, WBC 38B (Dallas: Word, 1988), 706; Robert Jewett, *Romans: A Commentary*, Hermeneia (Minneapolis: Fortress, 2007), 724–25; Michael D. Barram, "Romans 12:9–21," *Int* 57.4 (2003): 423.

tus, whose discussions on the relationship of love with the pursuit of the good can be used as a point of comparison to Paul's argument. Admittedly, the word for love used in these discussions is not typically ἀγάπη, which is likely due to the distinctive nature of the early Christian understanding of love. Nevertheless, the philosophical discussions provide fruitful comparison to Paul's paraenesis on a conceptual level, especially when it comes to their relationship to ethics.[11]

Plato, in *Symposium,* discusses the nature of love in an account of a fictional banquet attended by prominent Athenian figures. The discussion is comprised of five *encomia* culminating with Socrates' dialectic speech. The discussion is prompted by a perceived need to sing Eros' praises, who is, according to one of the participants, the most neglected among the gods when it comes to eulogies—an unfitting situation for the god who "has sovereign power to provide all virtue and happiness for men" (Plato, *Symp.* 180b [Fowler, LCL]). The ensuing debate goes in many directions, but it is Socrates' speech and his account of his interaction with the wise Diotima that reveals Plato's understanding of the relationship between love and the good. Socrates draws attention to the fact that the nature of love is to desire (199e–200b) and that the immediate object of love's desire is the beautiful. However, the desire for beauty is never actualized, for it is not clear what one obtains when they come to possess the beautiful (204c–d). But when the object of love is the good (τῶν ἀγαθῶν, 204e) the acquired value is unquestionable—the one who acquires the good is happy, or to quote Diotima: "the happy are happy because of the good" (205a). Therefore, for Plato, the love of good is the pathway to happiness. Tied to the earlier affirmation that "love provides all virtue and happiness for men," it may be said that the ultimate goal of love is happiness itself, which is attained when love has as its object the good. Love, therefore, is self-oriented.

A similar orientation exists in Aristotle's teachings. In his *Nicomachean Ethics*, Aristotle discusses the role of love (φιλία) in friendship. The larger context of the discussion is the pursuit of the good (ἀγαθός) and happiness (εὐδαιμονία) (Aristotle, *Eth. nic.* I, 4 [Rackham]), which is obtained through the acquisition of virtues (I, 10).[12] Friendship is understood as an indispensable

---

11. The distinction between ἔρος and ἀγάπη is the subject of Anders Nygren's seminal study, *Agape and Eros* (New York: Harper & Row, 1969). Nygren highlights a distinction between New Testament ἀγάπη and Platonic ἔρος. Danaher offers a critical assessment of Nygren's thesis, highlighting that although there is a unique way Christians spoke of love in relation to Plato, the distinction was less a matter of semantics than theology. The fact that different words for love are employed in relationship to ethics in the various treatments is an indication that despite the different usage, the words have a significant semantic overlap. James P. Danaher, "Love in Plato and the New Testament," *European Journal of Theology* 7.2 (1998): 119–26.

12. See Robert J. Fitterer, *Love and Objectivity in Virtue Ethics: Aristotle, Lonergan, and Nussbaum on Emotions and Moral Insight* (Toronto: University of Toronto Press, 2008), 10–15.

virtue for living (VIII, 1); and love is the "stuff" of friendship—that which ultimately makes it possible. For Aristotle, love is oriented towards the good, useful, or pleasant (VIII, 2); and in this rubric, love is also, for the most part, self-oriented—namely, when one loves others for being useful or pleasant for themselves. At best, love is something to be shared among people who are good "without qualifications" and are useful to each other as equals. In this context, love is only ideally shared between two equally good and mutually benefit- ing individuals—which Aristotle himself admits is a rare situation (VIII, 3–4). For Aristotle, therefore, love promotes the good of friendship only insofar as it serves as a path to one's own happiness. In this context, Aristotle defends self-love as the basis for all good actions (IX, 8). For him, the common good is achieved when good men pursue that which is good for themselves, and even the most altruistic of acts is ultimately self-centered.

This motivation for love is also present in the Stoic writings of Epictetus. According to him, what a man loves (φιλεῖ) is that which he applies himself earnestly for his own benefit—or, the things that are good (τὰ ἀγαθὰ) for him. Accordingly, it is part of human nature "to love nothing so much as its own interest."[13] For this reason, loving others—whether father, brother, children, friend, country, or God—is no more than the result of one's pursuit for their own good, for "the nature of the rational animal [is] such that it cannot obtain any one of its own proper interests, if it does not contribute something to the common interest."[14] When the individual finds themselves in a position when the other's interest conflicts with their own, then they must align their interests with their will, which in Stoicism, needs to be intentionally pointed towards virtue. For Epictetus, this is where love intersects with ethics; for it is only a virtue-bound volition that enables altruistic love.[15] The ultimate goal, however, is happiness (εὐδαιμονία), which is obtained through virtue. Thus, like in Plato and Aristotle, love for the Stoic is self-oriented.

Although there are differences in the way these three philosophical treat- ments deal with the subject of love, they all seem to share at least three features. First, whether finding its source in the pursuit of happiness or in the pursuit of virtue, love is generated within the individual, and from the individual's voli- tion. Second, love is self-oriented and reflexive. The goal of love is ultimately the benefit of the lover—or more specifically, the lover's εὐδαιμονία —even when it is aimed at the other or the common good. In these contexts, therefore, love originates in and ultimately points to the individual. Finally, since the ultimate

13. *The Discourses of Epictetus, with the Encheridion and Fragments*, trans. George Long (London: George Bell and Sons, 1890), 2.22.4.

14. *The Discourses of Epictetus, with the Encheridion and Fragments*, trans. George Long (London: George Bell and Sons, 1890), 1.19.4.

15. See William O. Stephens, *Stoic Ethics: Epictetus and Happiness as Freedom* (London: Bloomsbury, 2007), 82–83.

goal is happiness, love has an immediate focus, participating in the ongoing pursuit of the good in the present.

Even a cursory reading of Rom 12–13 shows that Paul's ethical understanding of love is significantly different from contemporary philosophy. First, instead of focusing on the individual's happiness, the ethical life unfolds in the believer's experience of God's good, pleasant and perfect will (12:2). While "discerning God's will" could be seen as a version of εὐδαιμονία, it is clear that the emphasis for Paul lies on God's will, not on the believer's happiness. In fact, that the term εὐδαιμονία, so popular among the philosophers, does not occur once in Paul's writings indicates that happiness, as conceived in Greek philosophy, is not part of Paul's ethical framework. Instead, the discernment and experience of God's good, pleasant and perfect will is the result of "presenting your bodies as a living sacrifice" (12:1)—a self-giving, rather than a self-oriented act.

Second, love in Paul is oriented outwards, expressed in concrete ethical attitudes towards brothers and sisters, and even enemies. In Rom 12–13 love is not reflexive, as in the philosophers. Rather, love is described as solely oriented towards the other. While it is true that, as in the philosophers, love is closely related to the pursuit of the good (12:9), it is not understood as a benefit to the one who loves, but relates exclusively to the good of others, expressed even counterintuitively in "blessing those who persecute you" (12:14) and "conquering evil with good" (12:21).

It is, however, a third distinction that stands out as the reason for the unique orientation of love in Paul's ethics. When we consider Rom 12–13 as the landing zone of Paul's theological argument, it becomes clear that ethical love flows out of the work of God in Christ. Rather than finding its *raison d'être* in happiness or virtue, in a rather existentialist pursuit of the good, Pauline ethical love is derived from a grammar of love determined by the love of God revealed in Christ Jesus. To this now we turn.

The Grammar of Love in the Larger Context of Romans

If Rom 12–13 with its focus on love indeed functions as the landing zone for Paul's theological argument, then it is important to understand how Paul's love paraenesis relates to his use of ἀγάπη in the first part of the letter. The orientation of love in both sections is different. While in Rom 12–13 Paul speaks of love primarily in the horizontal plane—namely, love for others[16]—in Rom 1–8 the apostle deals with love exclusively in the vertical plane—namely, God's love for the believers and the believers' love for God.[17] Despite the different orientations, the logic of the argument affords the conclusion that one stems from the other.

---

16. The only exception is 15:30.

17. Paul speaks of love in the first section primarily using first person plural pronouns (Rom 5:5, 8; 8:35, 37, 39).

Love features right at the outset of the letter in Paul's identification of his audience—they are "beloved by God and called to be saints" (1:7).[18] By employing the epithet in conjunction with covenant language (κλητοῖς), the apostle makes the love of God for the believers in Rome a matter of primary identity. It is only in Rom 5:1–10, however, that Paul will spell out whence this identity originates. Having described the plight of humanity—whereby sin has brought both Gentiles and Jews under the wrath of God (1:18–32; 2:2–5, 9, 12)—and God's solution by manifesting his righteousness apart from the law and by faith in Jesus Christ to all who believe (3:21–22), Paul describes the result of Christ's justifying and reconciling work.

> Therefore, since we have been justified by faith, we have peace (εἰρήνην) with God through our Lord Jesus Christ. Through him we have also obtained access by faith into this grace in which we stand, and we boast in hope of the glory of God . . . and hope does not put us to shame, because God's love has been poured into our hearts through the Holy Spirit who has been given to us. (5:1–5)

Being reconciled with God is the grounds for boasting (καυχώμεθα) in the hope of the glory of God. Paul has used the language of "boasting" to refer to the Jewish reliance on Torah, which ironically has not resulted in honoring God or upholding the law (2:23). Now Paul establishes the true grounds for boasting: the hope of eschatological vindication, when those who believe will not be put to shame (5:5). This eschatological hope is in contrast to present sufferings (5:3), which somewhat counterintuitively becomes the grounds from which hope eventually sprouts. And it is at this point that ἀγάπη features for the first time in Paul's theological argument.

Different from mere optimism, the eschatological hope has the value of absolute certainty in the midst of present sufferings, for it does not put the believer to shame (καταισχύνει); and the reason is that it is anchored not in human merit but in the reality of God's ἀγάπη poured in the hearts of the believers through the Holy Spirit (5:5).[19] By tying hope and love together, Paul makes the believer's experience of God's love the accomplished and ongoing reality which nurtures eschatological hope.[20] In "already-not-yet" terms, love

---

18. Paul seems to use the epithet ἀγαπητοῖς θεοῦ as a substitute for the more personal "my beloved", which he uses in relationships closer to him (cf. 1 Cor 4:14, 17; 10:14; 15:58; Phil 2:12; 4:1; 1 Thess 2:8; 2 Tim 1:2).

19. Contra Ceslas Spicq, *Agape in the New Testament*, 3 vols. (Eugene, OR: Wipf & Stock, 2006), 2:227. Despite the lack of a definite article, the reference to the Holy Spirit is best understood as God's Holy Spirit rather than a general reference to sanctification. See James D. G. Dunn, *Romans 1–8*, WBC 38A (Dallas: Word, 1988).

20. Paul uses the perfect ἐκκέχυται to express the pouring of God's love through the Spirit, which indicates a continuous aspect. The statement most likely refers to

is the "already" reality that points to and guarantees the "not yet" actualized reality of future vindication—a dynamic made possible by the agency of the eschatological Spirit. Paul will further describe this already-not-yet dynamic using expiatory imagery in 5:9: "Since, therefore, we have now (νῦν) been justified by his blood, much more shall we be saved (σωθησόμεθα) by him from the wrath of God" (5:9). Love, therefore, participates in the dynamic of accomplished justification and future salvation with eschatological overtones. This implication of the eschatological orientation of love should not be lost on the reader—God's love poured in our hearts through the Spirit is a concrete proleptic experience of the eschaton.

The ἀγάπη that informs the present and future of the believer in such a definitive way finds its thrust in its incongruity. The evidence (cf. συνίστησιν, 5:8) that gives this love its assuring character is Christ's sacrifice on behalf of undeserving sinners. As Barclay puts it,

> This gift [of love] is neither a trivial token, tossed to whomever it might reach, nor a costly gift carefully targeted at the highly deserving. It is the costliest gift, given with the deepest sentiment and the highest commitment to those who, at the time of its giving, had nothing to render them fitting recipients.[21]

Interestingly, the incongruous nature of God's love is described against the foil of an ethical discussion about "dying for a righteous (δικαίου) or good (ἀγαθοῦ) person" (5:7). While this would hardly happen, Paul says, God's love is shown in that Christ died for us while we were still sinners. The statement is reiterated in 5:10 highlighting the enmity overcome by the death of Christ, which guarantees future salvation: "For if while we were enemies (ἐχθροὶ) we were reconciled to God by the death of his Son, much more, now that we are reconciled, shall we be saved by his life" (5:10). The love of God which is expressed towards his enemies and the consequent peace it brings conveys the very meaning of reconciliation. This is the blueprint that will inform the believer's own practice of love towards others in Romans 12–13. The former enemies who have experienced this reconciling love are to demonstrate it towards others, including their own enemies.

The next reference to love in the letter, for the first time in verbal form (ἀγαπῶσιν), is 8:28, where Paul highlights the believer's love for God. As in 1:7, love is coupled with the notion of covenantal election (κλητοῖς). Just as being loved by God is part of their identity and calling, loving God is a result of God's purposeful election. Once again, there is an already-not-yet dynamic in play. The eschatological framework that Paul uses previously to speak of justification

---

God's love rather than the believer's love for God. See Spicq, *Agape in the New Testament*, 2:225.

21. Barclay, *Paul and the Gift*, 478.

now frames the reality of "life in the Spirit" (8:1–30). In the tension between the sufferings of the present time and the glory that is to be revealed (8:18), the Spirit intercedes according to the will of God, leading to the working together of all things towards the good (ἀγαθόν) of those who love (τοῖς ἀγαπῶσιν) God (8:26–28). As seen above, the "good" is understood in contemporary philosophical discourse primarily in relation to virtue. In this passage, however, the "good" refers to the conformity to the image of Christ (8:29), which, being the work of the eschatological Spirit, has both a present and a future dimension.[22] Therefore, love once again features in the dynamics of the eschatological work of the Spirit in a dialogical manner. The love poured through the Spirit into the hearts of believers, now is directed back to God, as the same Spirit intercedes for them to be conformed to the image of Christ, according to God's will.

The brief mention of the believer's love for God quickly gives way to another extended exposition on God's love for the believer. In a breathtaking discourse which ties themes previously associated with ἀγάπη, Paul builds up momentum for his most powerful claim about God's love: "[nothing] can separate us from the love of God in Christ Jesus." Once again, the experience of God's love is tied with covenantal language (ἐκλεκτῶν, 8:33), explained in terms of Christ's sacrificial death (8:34), contrasted with suffering (8:35–37), and painted on a cosmic and eschatological canvas (8:38–39). Paul's final statement in 8:39 then stands as the ultimate shout of victory that closes the first section of the letter. The unfailing love of God is the origins and the climax of God's redemptive work.

Paul's consistent use of love is quite evident in these passages. Developing ἀγάπη in the vertical plane, Paul works with an underlying grammar of love. The covenantal love of God, effected in the expiatory death of Jesus Christ is infused into the life of the justified believer through the Spirit. This love is the manifestation of the accomplished reconciliation with God, the reality in which believers participate in the present, and that which feeds the hope of ultimate eschatological vindication in the future. Given this consistent grammar, repeated at key moments in Paul's theological argumentation, it is clear that ἀγάπη has an internal meaning in Romans that goes beyond semantics. Paul's apotheotic claim at the end of the first part of his theological argument keeps echoing throughout the rest of the letter, used in both the covenantal language of 9–11 (cf. 9:13, 25) and the ethical language of 12–13. In light of this pregnant meaning of ἀγάπη, it is highly implausible that Paul has some other sense of love in mind in his ethical section. Rather, although there is a shift from

---

22. On the eschatological reading of the passage see Dunn, *Romans 1–8*, 483–84. For an alternative reading, see Douglas J. Moo, *The Epistle to the Romans*, NICNT (Grand Rapids: Eerdmans, 1996), 529–30, who includes the "good things in this life that contribute to that final salvation and sustain us on the path to that salvation."

the vertical to the horizontal plane, love is the same. Genuine love (Ἡ ἀγάπη ἀνυπόκριτος, 12:9), which fulfills the law (13:10) originates in and is patterned upon "the love of God in Christ Jesus."

Love and Ethics in Romans 12:9–13:10

Having looked at the role of love in the context of philosophical ethical discussions and in the context of Paul's theological argumentation in the first part of Romans, we can now evaluate how Paul develops his ethics of love in 12:9–13:10.

The Context of Ethical Love: Christoformity and Ecclesial Unity

Paul's love ethics in Rom 12–13 are situated in two fundamental theological contexts, outlined in two introductory appeals (12:1–2; 3–8). First, love flows out of the work of the Spirit, by which believers are transformed in the image of Christ. The first appeal, grounded in the mercies (διὰ τῶν οἰκτιρμῶν) of God, is to a transformed life and renewed mind (12:1–2). The appeal is comprised of two requests. First, the apostle urges the believers to "present their bodies (παραστῆσαι τὰ σώματα ὑμῶν) as a living sacrifice" (12:1), echoing the cultic language of 6:13–19 where he established a contrast between "presenting your members (παριστάνετε τὰ μέλη ὑμῶν) to sin" and "presenting yourselves (παραστήσατε ἑαυτοὺς) to God." Far from a mere image, offering oneself as a sacrifice has a concrete expression, which Paul will unpack in his paraenetic segment.

The second request, perhaps more forceful given the imperatival nature of the verbs, envisions a contrast between life conformed to "this age" (τῷ αἰῶνι τούτῳ), which is to be rejected, and a transformed life by the renewal of the mind (μεταμορφοῦσθε τῇ ἀνακαινώσει τοῦ νοός). The phrase should be interpreted in light of Rom 8:26–30— the renewed mind is the mind of the Spirit (cf. also 8:5–8), and transformation is towards conformity (συμμόρφους) to the image of Christ.[23] This "Christoformity" is concretely expressed in the ethics of love.[24]

Paul, therefore, assumes the same theological grammar of the first section of his letter· the believers, who do not live according to "this age" but live in

---

23. Admittedly, Paul uses two different words for "mind": νοῦς and φρόνημα. However, Paul uses both words in his discussion of the mind of the Spirit in Rom 7–8 (cf. 7:23, 25; 8:5–6), which suggests they are interchangeable in his discourse.

24. The two requests are linked by a symmetrical triad of adjectives. The worshipful sacrifice is "living, holy, and pleasing to God" (ζῶσαν ἁγίαν εὐάρεστον) and leads to the discernment of the will of God, "good, pleasing and perfect" (τὸ ἀγαθὸν καὶ εὐάρεστον καὶ τέλειον). The qualifiers give an ethical connotation to the appeal, preparing the way for the ethical admonitions of 12:9–13:10.

the new eschatological age inaugurated by the Spirit, are now to reject confor-mity with this age in order to live a transformed life towards Christoformity. This transformed life is concretely expressed in the ethics of love. Ethical liv-ing, therefore, flows out of the redemptive work of Christ and the work of the eschatological Spirit.

Second, Paul's love ethics have an ecclesiological thrust. In his second prefa-tory appeal (12:3–8), this time grounded in the "grace of God" (διὰ τῆς χάριτος), Paul situates his ethical commands in the context of the unity of the body of Christ (ἐν σῶμά ἐσμεν ἐν Χριστῷ) and the exercise of the gifts (χαρίσματα) of the Spirit (12:3–8). Even though Paul will address internal (12:9–13, 14–21; 13:8–10) and external (13:1–7) relationships in his admonitions, the overall par-aenesis is founded in the ecclesiological identity and unity of the people of God. The predominant focus is the ecclesial "one another" relationship, which becomes the ethical foundation for interaction with society at large.[25] In the context of the body of Christ, different gifts are given, and similarly to 1 Cor 12–13, the discussion on gifts culminate with an emphasis on love (12:6–9).[26] Therefore, Paul theologically anchors his love-shaped paraenesis in Romans 12–13 in Christoformity and ecclesial unity.

Love and Ethics

With 12:9–13:10, we arrive at the ethical section proper. This section is com-prised of various admonitions, sometimes expressed in a rather asyndetic form. However, the rhetoric should not distract us from noticing an overall thematic consistency in the address.[27] The sequence is comprised of bookending subsec-tions with references to ἀγάπη (12:9–10; 13:8–10), and two paraenetical sub-sections prescribing ethical behaviors towards enemies and authorities. Thus,

12:9–13: Genuine Love
12:14–21: Living in peace with all men, including enemies
13:1–7: Living in peace with authorities
13:8–10: Love as the fulfillment of the law

---

25. See Barram, "Romans 12," 424, where he notes that Paul's ethics in Rom 12 is essentially corporate ethics, envisioning a "communal response to God's grace."

26. Victor Paul Furnish, *The Love Command in the New Testament* (London: SCM Press, 1973), 103, points out this similarity. See also David Alan Black, "The Pauline Love Command: Structure, Style, and Ethics in Romans 12:9–21," *Filología Neotestamentaria* 2.1 (1989): 15.

27. Black evaluates Paul's rhetoric in the passage affirming that "the quick-fire verbalization of ethical duties serves to emphasize both the importance of his theme and the immensity of what is involved in genuine love. Black, "The Pauline Love Com-mand," 5–6.

The phrase ἡ ἀγάπη ἀνυπόκριτος in 12:9 functions as a kind of thesis state-ment, introducing the subsequent ethical prescriptions.[28] As David Alan Black suggests, "the entire composition is dominated from the initial utterance by the theme 'Let love be sincere.'"[29] Conversely, 13:8–10 functions as a concluding remark: "therefore (οὖν) love is the fulfillment of the law," which affirms all ethical commands prescribed in the Torah as subsumed under ἀγάπη. The fact that the two subsections dealing with potentially conflicting relationships are enveloped by ἀγάπη references suggests that all the ethical attitudes prescribed stem from and culminate in ἀγάπη. Thus, love in the passage is not merely part of a passing asyndetic command; it is the very context in which ethics develop.[30] Genuine love is supposed to nurture all ethical attitudes and represents the fulfillment of all ethical commands.

The Ethical Expressions of Sincere Love

12:9–13. The first subsection is marked by a *staccato* rhythm. Three adjectival constructions mark the main accents, while participial phrases provide further explanation.

12:9a: Ἡ **ἀγάπη ἀνυπόκριτος**
9b: *ἀποστυγοῦντες τὸ πονηρόν*
9c: *κολλώμενοι τῷ ἀγαθῷ*
12:10a: τῇ **φιλαδελφίᾳ** εἰς ἀλλήλους **φιλόστοργοι**
10b: τῇ τιμῇ ἀλλήλους *προηγούμενοι,*
12:11a: τῇ **σπουδῇ** μὴ **ὀκνηροί**
11b: τῷ πνεύματι *ζέοντες*
11c: τῷ κυρίῳ *δουλεύοντες*
12a: ῇ ἐλπίδι *χαίροντες*
12b: τῇ θλίψει *ὑπομένοντες*
12c: τῇ προσευχῇ *προσκαρτεροῦντες*
13a: ταῖς χρείαις τῶν ἁγίων *κοινωνοῦντες*
13b: ἣν φιλοξενίαν *διώκοντες*

---

28. Contra Runar M. Thorsteinsson, "Paul and Roman Stoicism: Romans 12 and Contemporary Stoic Ethics," *JSNT* 29.2 (2006): 145, who contends that the phrase is a mere part of a series of maxims, rejecting any structural function. However, the book-ending function highlighted above suggests otherwise. See Dunn, *Romans 9–16*, 739; Furnish, *The Love Command in the New Testament*, 103.

29. Black, "The Pauline Love Command," 6.

30. On the significance of the love command to the more direct ethical commands in the passage see Dorothea H. Bertschmann, "The Good, the Bad and the State: Rom 13.1–7 and the Dynamics of Love," *NTS* 60.2 (2014): 242–43.

The accents (9a, 10a, and 11a) are parallel. The nouns ἀγάπη and φιλαδελφία are related, which likely indicates that σπουδῇ should be understood along the same lines (cf. 2 Cor 8:7–8).[31] Genuine love, devoted brotherly love, and zeal are the catalysts of the ethical actions.

The concern with a genuine or sincere love is found elsewhere in the NT (2 Cor 6:6; 1 Tim 1:5; 1 Pet 1:22). The adjective ἀνυπόκριτος, also used in reference to faith and wisdom, is associated with ideas of purity (2 Cor 6:6; 1 Tim 1:5; James 3:17; 1 Pet 1:22), good conscience (1 Tim 1:5), and impartiality (James 3:17). In context, the genuineness of love flows from the transformed life (12:1–2) which entails a holy and pleasing sacrifice to God. Sincere love, therefore, implies integrity, both before God and others.

The qualification, "sincere," is particularly important given Paul's focus on ethics. As we mentioned above, love is not presented as a subjective feeling, but as concretely expressed in certain ethical actions.[32] However, it is impossible to judge the motivations behind one's actions. One may show honor to a neighbor, for example, for self-interested reasons. Therefore, the emphasis on the genuineness of love put concrete boundaries around the ethical actions. Only a love that is pure, devoid of pretense or hidden interests, can foster the kind of ethical attitudes Paul has in mind. By beginning the paraenesis with this important statement, Paul makes sure his audience understands that, even though there are concrete actions that are expected of those who have been transformed by the Gospel, it is imperative that these actions find their origins in pure, sincere love, and not a mere sense of moral duty.

Following the thesis statement about love, we find the first couple of participial phrases emphasizing the ethical nature of love in reference to the believers' attitude towards good and evil. The verbs are weighty and extreme. The genuineness of love is demonstrated in the believers' absolute hatred (ἀποστυγοῦντες) for what is evil and absolute attachment (κολλώμενοι) for what is good.[33] This would seem to put Paul's discourse close to the philosophers surveyed above, who value the pursuit of the good as the essence of ethics. However, rather than a moral virtue benefitting the individual, the good is spelled out by Paul as brotherly love and showing honor to one another, being therefore outwardly oriented—the good is the good of the other. This outward orientation derives its thrust from the grammar of love in the first section of the letter, more specifically in the incongruity and self-sacrificing nature of God's love for sinners expressed in Christ and through the Spirit.

---

31. Furnish makes the same observation based on the quick succession from vv. 10–11. See Furnish, *The Love Command in the New Testament*, 104.

32. See Moo, *Romans*, 423–24.

33. The more literal meaning of κολλάω is "to bind closely." See BDAG s.v. κολλάω (555–56).

Finally, zeal, informed by love, is the motivation for a devoted life (12:11–13), expressed in a list of seven items. Here we see elements of Paul's grammar of love outlined above. The reference to the Spirit in the context of love recalls 5:5 and 8:27–28, where the love of God and the love for God is tied with the activity of the Spirit. Similarly, the emphasis on hope (ἐλπίδι) in the context of suffering (θλίψει) echoes Paul's grammar in 5:3–5, 8:18–28, and 8:35–39. The same resilience and hope anchored in God's love poured out in the heart of the believer by the Spirit continues to furnish the believer's ethical actions. Finally, prayer, fellowship in the needs of the saints, and hospitality end the list with actions characteristic of a transformed life.

12:14–21. While it is clear that 12:9–13 envisions the life of the believer in relation to the church community, there is significant debate about whether Paul shifts his focus to outsiders in 12:14–21.[34] On the one hand, Paul refers to "persecutors" (τοὺς διώκοντας) and "enemies" (ἐχθρός) at the beginning and end of the paragraph (12:14, 20), which are designations more clearly applicable to outsiders.[35] Moreover, the mention of "not avenging yourselves" and "overcoming evil with good" also seem better understood as instructions regarding dealings with antagonists. On the other hand, the reference to "rejoicing with those who rejoice" and "weeping with those who weep," along with the appeal to "think the same with one another" (τὸ αὐτὸ εἰς ἀλλήλους φρονοῦντες) seem to indicate an internal focus (cf. Phil 2:5). It is also true that Paul's advice "not to think proudly" is similar to what he says in his admonitions regarding relationships within the church in 12:3.

While it may sound strange that Paul would hold such high standards for the social engagement of Christians with outsiders, there is nothing in the speech that necessarily prevents this conclusion. To "think the same with one another" may be read as having an eirenic disposition which leads to harmonious living (12:18). Moreover, it is not surprising that Paul would hold believers to the same standards in relation to outsiders that he does in relation to insiders. It is indeed in the radical nature of Christian love that the believers would act toward their enemies with the same grace and generosity they would extend to their fellow neighbors. Thus, the believers who are told to extend hospitality to the saints (12:13) are also commanded to extend it to enemies (12:20).[36]

More importantly, Paul's admonitions concerning enemies is firmly grounded in his understanding of the love of God. The apostle urges believers to live peaceably (εἰρηνεύοντες) with all, and not to avenge themselves, but to

34. Although the term φιλοξενία in 12:13 typically refers to hospitality to strangers, it is likely used here in reference to other Christians, given the mention of the needs of the saints, which is a reference to the saints in Jerusalem (cf. 15:26).

35. For an assessment of this possibility see Black, "The Pauline Love Command," 10.

36. On Paul's likely dependence on the Jesus tradition in these verses see Black, "The Pauline Love Command," 10–18.

give place to "the wrath"—likely a reference to the "wrath of God"—and to treat their enemies well. Read against the theological framework of Rom 5:1–10 (see above), the instructions are striking. Just as God's love is demonstrated towards his enemies, making peace with them, this same love, which has been poured out into the believer's hearts through the Spirit, now requires the believer to practice hospitality to their enemies and live in peace with all people.[37]

13:1–7. Paul then moves on to a more specific set of instructions regarding civil authorities. A full exegetical treatment of 13:1–7 is beyond the limits of this study. However, it should be highlighted that the reference to "doing good" (τῷ ἀγαθῷ, 13:3) recalls 12:9, where clinging to what is good is an expression of genuine love. While Paul does not use the language of love to talk about the believer's relationship with civil authorities, the ethical living expected is still a result of living in genuine love.[38] This seems corroborated by the fact that Paul moves seamlessly from his admonition for believers to "pay what they owe (τὰς ὀφειλάς)" (13:7)—whether taxes, fear, or honor—to his instructions for them to "owe (ὀφείλετε) *no one* (μηδενὶ) anything, except for love" (13:8).

13:8–10. Finally, Paul closes the paraenesis coming back to the theme of ἀγάπη. Just like in 12:9, when love is spelled out with concrete ethical commandments, so now it is once again expressed in ethical terms. However, the apostle now frames his love paraenesis within a framework familiar to the readers of his letter: the law.

Throughout Rom 1–8, Paul deals with the law in reference to justification. The apostle first establishes that the law is not just an election badge, but contains prescriptions meant to be observed by those who want to rely upon it for justification (2:13). Therefore, Gentiles who do not know the law and do what the law requires by nature become a law to themselves (2:14), while Jews who boast in the law but break it are condemned (2:17–24). Here Paul cites two of the commandments he cites in 13:1–8—adultery and stealing. Observing the law, therefore, comes down to practicing the specifics of what the law prescribes. And the ethical observance of these prescriptions reveals whether one is a true Jew, to the extent that circumcised Jews who are nevertheless lawbreakers are still condemned (2:25–29).

---

37. While Paul does not refer back to his theological argument at this point, the shared grammar of love establishes the link. In this context, giving place "to the wrath" might in fact envision the salvation of the enemies, since the wrath of God is overcome by his love shown in the sacrifice of Christ on behalf of sinners. See Spicq, *Agape in the Epistles of St. Paul*, 2:228.

38. As Bertschmann, "The Good, the Bad, and the State," 247–48, states: "The Christian paradigm of love, then, is the greater reality which encloses almost as a 'by-product' good and generally approved behaviour in the civic and political world." See Bertschmann, "The Good, the Bad and the State," 247–48. See also Dunn, *Romans 9–16*, 781.

Paul's point, however, is not to affirm the observance of the law as the actual means of justification—something he categorically denies later in the letter (3:20)—but to establish the common predicament of both Jews and Gentiles under sin. However, it is significant, in light of what the apostle will affirm concerning love and law in his ethical section, that it is the lack of observance of the commandments, namely the ethical failure itself, that exposes one's sinful state.

This is reaffirmed in 3:9–20. Quoting LXX Ps 13:1, Paul makes the case that all are under sin and "no one does good (χρηστότητα)" (3:12). The word can have a sense of "uprightness" or a more ethical sense of "kindness" or "generosity."[39] Although Paul highlights "righteousness" (δίκαιος) in the beginning of the quote, he also goes on to contrast the "good" with evil acts, which he brings forward by stringing together different parts of Scripture where such acts are emphasized (3:13–18).[40] This leads Paul to bring back the law into focus in his affirmation of the universality of sin, including those who possess the law, and to affirm faith in Jesus Christ as the sole means of justification (3:21–26).

Having established the insufficiency of the law for justification, insofar as no one is capable of actually upholding it, Paul goes one step further. The law not only cannot justify, but also creates an opportunity for sin to come alive (7:7–10). Citing the commandment not to covet as an example (7:7), Paul describes the conundrum the law creates in the lives of those under sin (7:12–25). The conundrum is resolved in Christ, whose sacrifice causes the requirements of the law to be fulfilled (πληρωθῇ) in the believers who walk according to the Spirit (8:1–4).

In summary, in Rom 1–8, the failure to uphold the ethical prescriptions of the law make evident that all are under sin—both Jews and Gentiles—and that the law, although an expression of the perfect character of God, cannot produce justification, given the sinners' inability to uphold it. It is only through faith in Christ and his expiatory sacrifice, and by the transformative work of the Spirit, that the requirements of the law are fulfilled in the life of the believer.

This is the essential background that informs Paul's love paraenesis in 13:8–10. Citing the commandments, specifically those with ethical implications towards one's neighbor, Paul hones in on ἀγάπη as the center point of ethics. Once again, love is not presented as a subjective feeling, but as concrete ethical actions. Love is the fulfillment of the law insofar as the ethical commands towards the neighbor are subsumed under the command to "love your neighbor as yourself"—or "to do nothing evil towards them" (13:10). Paul here cites Lev

---

39. BDAG s.v. χρηστότης (1090).
40. Moo argues this is "not directly related to Paul's purpose", alluding to the possibility of it being part of a pre-Pauline collection. See Moo, *Romans*, 134. However, the string of quotations is fairly long and could have been edited out by the apostle, were it not part of his purpose. Paul seems consistent with the ethical emphasis of 2:17–24. The mention of specific sins will prompt him to transition to speak about the law.

19:18, where the command to love one's neighbor is the last in a series of ethical commands, which includes instructions to care for the poor and the sojourner, not to steal, lie, bear false witness, oppress, curse the deaf or cause the blind to stumble, do injustice in court, slander, stand up against the life of the neighbor, take vengeance or bear a grudge (Lev 19:9–18). Significantly, this passage is one of the very few in the LXX where ἀγαπάω is used in social relations with ethical implications (cf. also Lev 19:34; Deut 10:18–19).[41] Love, in this context, is expressed in very concrete and practical actions oriented towards the other. It is worth noticing once again that Paul's teaching here is diametrically opposed to the philosophical tradition, where love has a self-oriented nature. It is a mistake to relate Paul's reference to loving "as yourself" to Aristotle's concept of self-love. The two could not be more distant. For while Aristotle unashamedly places the love of self as the priority, Paul sees love as a debt to others (13:8).

Significantly, the concluding statement—"love is the fulfillment of the law"—stands as the capstone of the whole argument Paul developed throughout the letter regarding the law. The fulfillment of the law, accomplished by the sacrifice of Christ, and enacted in the life of the believer by the agency the Spirit, is now expressed "ethically" in love.[42] Read against the first part of Paul's argument about the law in Rom 2–3, the statement comes as a fitting conclusion. Those who found themselves entrapped in sin, unable to uphold God's commandments, now fulfill God's law through love.

Conclusion

It is clear that the ethical section, with its emphasis on ἀγάπη is a fundamental part of Paul's argument in Romans, indeed its necessary "landing zone." Love, expressed in a concrete ethical way of living towards both fellow Christians and enemies, is the visible result and manifestation of God's work of justification and the transformative work of the Spirit towards Christoformity in the life of the believer. In a context where love is often seen as a means to a self-interested

---

41. The vast majority of occurrences of the verb refer to God's love (Exod 20:6; Deut 4:37; 5:10; 7:8–9, 13; 10:15, 18; 23:6; 33:12; 2 Sam 12:24; 1 Kgs 10:9; 2 Chr 2:10; 9:8; Neh 1:5; 13:26; Pss 10:7; 32:5; 36:28; 46:5; 50:8; 77:68; 86:2; 118:159; 145:8; Prov 3:12; 15:9; Isa 41:8; 43:4; 48:14; 60:10; 61:8; 63:9; Jer 12:7; 38:3; Dan 9:4; Hos 3:1; 9:15; 11:1; 14:5; Zech 10:6; Mal 1:2; 2:11), or one's love of God (Deut 6:5; 10:12; 11:1, 13, 22; 13:4; 19:9; 30:6, 16, 20; Josh 22:5; 23:11; Judg 5:31; 1 Kgs 3:3; Pss 5:12; 17:2; 30:24; 68:37; 96:10; 114:1; 118:132; 144:20; Isa 5:1; 56:6). Other "horizontal" forms of love include marital or sexual love (Gen 24:67; 29:18, 20, 30, 32; 34:3; Deut 21:15–16; Judg 14:16; 16:4, 15; 1 Sam 1:5; 18:20, 28; 2 Sam 13:1, 4, 15; 1 Kgs 11:2; 2 Chr 11:21; Eccl 9:9; Song 1:3–4, 7; 3:1–4; Lam 1:2; Ezek 16:37; Hos 3:1) and familial love (Gen 22:2; 25:28; 37:3; 44:20; Ruth 4:15; Prov 13:24).

42. Anselm L. Bencze, "Analysis of Romans 13:8–10," *NTS* 20.1 (1973): 90–92, argues that the passage is structured rhetorically to show a movement from law to love.

end, Paul presents it as the result of God's redemptive action, the fulfillment of the very intention of God when he gave his people his commandments, and the concrete expression of the Gospel.

The way the apostle develops this theme across the letter highlights the seamless integration of theology and ethics in his thought. The rich and deep realities of God's justifying act in the life of the believer are to be fully expressed in the day-to-day relationships of the church.

The discussion about the relationship between theology and ethics in Paul and in Christian theology in general is often fraught with difficulties. If on the one hand, we miss much of Paul's theology when we ignore its ethical implications, on the other hand we lose the significance of Pauline ethics altogether if we ignore its theological source, ending up with a baptized version of philosophical ethics. Notions such as virtue or the common good, as valuable as they are, fall short of conveying the intended goal of the Christian ethical discourse. Different from the philosophers, virtue is not an end in itself for Paul, but an expression of God's work in Christ in the life of the believer. If one bypasses the Christ event, love loses its unique Christian thrust.

On the other hand, Paul's love paraenesis reminds us that love is not an afterthought, or an optional appendix in Romans. Love is the necessary "so what" of the Gospel, expressed in concrete actions towards fellow believers and even enemies. The non-negotiable implication of "who can separate us from the love of God in Christ Jesus?" is "let love be genuine." Thus, ethical love is the necessary landing zone of Paul's Gospel of justification by faith. Without love and its concrete ethical expressions, the theological and doctrinal plane never lands.

Bibliography

Barclay, John M. G. *Pauline Churches and Diaspora Jews*. Tübingen: Mohr Siebeck, 2011.

———. *Paul and the Gift*. Grand Rapids: Eerdmans, 2015.

Barram, Michael D. "Romans 12:9–21." *Int* 57.4 (2003): 423–26.

Bencze, Anselm L. "Analysis of Romans 13:8–10." *NTS* 20.1 (1973): 90–92.

Bertschmann, Dorothea H. "The Good, the Bad and the State: Rom 13.1–7 and the Dynamics of Love." *NTS* 60.2 (2014): 232–49.

Black, David Alan. "The Pauline Love Command: Structure, Style, and Ethics in Romans 12:9–21." *Filología Neotestamentaria* 2.1 (1989): 3–22.

Danaher, James P. "Love in Plato and the New Testament." *European Journal of Theology* 7.2 (1998): 119–26.

Donfried, Karl P., ed. *The Romans Debate*. Grand Rapids: Baker Academic, 2011.

Dunn, James D. G. *Romans 1–8*. WBC 38A. Dallas: Word, 1988.

————. *Romans 9–16.* WBC38B. Dallas: Word, 1988.

Fitterer, Robert J. *Love and Objectivity in Virtue Ethics: Aristotle, Lonergan, and Nussbaum on Emotions and Moral Insight.* Toronto: University of Toronto Press, 2008.

Furnish, Victor Paul. *The Love Command in the New Testament.* London: SCM Press, 1973.

————. *Theology and Ethics in Paul.* Nashville: Abingdon, 1968.

Hays, Richard B. *The Moral Vision of the New Testament: Community, Cross, New Creation: A Contemporary Introduction to New Testament Ethic.* New York: Harper Collins, 1996.

Hooker, Morna D. "Interchange in Christ and Ethics." *JSNT* 25 (1985): 3–17.

Horrell, David G. *Solidarity and Difference: A Contemporary Reading of Paul's Ethics.* London: T&T Clark, 2016.

Jewett, Robert. *Romans: A Commentary.* Hermeneia. Minneapolis: Fortress, 2007.

Long, George, trans. *The Discourses of Epictetus, with the Encheridion and Fragments.* London: George Bell and Sons, 1890.

Moo, Douglas J. *The Epistle to the Romans.* NICNT. Grand Rapids: Eerdmans, 1996.

Novenson, Matthew V. *The Grammar of Messianism: An Ancient Jewish Political Idiom and Its Users.* Oxford: Oxford University Press, 2017.

Nygren, Anders. *Agape and Eros.* New York: Harper & Row, 1969.

Schrage, Wolfgang. *The Ethics of the New Testament.* London: T&T Clark, 1988.

Spicq, Ceslas. *Agape in the New Testament.* 3 vols. Eugene, OR: Wipf & Stock, 2006.

Stephens, William O. *Stoic Ethics: Epictetus and Happiness as Freedom.* London: Bloomsbury, 2007.

Thorsteinsson, Runar M. "Paul and Roman Stoicism: Romans 12 and Contemporary Stoic Ethics." *JSNT* 29.2 (2006): 139–61.

Wedderburn, A. J. M. *The Reasons for Romans.* London: T&T Clark, 2004.

CHAPTER 24

What Does Romans 16 Say about the Ministry of Women in the Earliest Church?

M. Sydney Park

Introduction

While it is common for Paul to send greetings to and from believers at the end of his letters, Rom 16 is unparalleled among his letters by the vast number of greetings he sends to the Roman congregation.[1] There are 27 named individuals, plus 2 unnamed individuals (Rufus' mother; Nereus' sister).[2] Of the 27 named individuals, only 2 (Narcissus; Aristobulus) do not receive a direct greeting as Paul greets their family. Apart from individuals, Paul greets 6 groups.[3] It is also common for Paul to send greetings on behalf of others to the addressee(s); but again, the Romans list is longest (16:21–23): 8 individuals, plus one group.[4]

By comparison, Paul sends greetings to individuals and groups only in 2 Tim 4:19, Col 4:15, and 1 Cor 16:19–20. In 2 Timothy, 2 individuals receive greetings from Paul (Prisca; Aquila) along with the household of Onesiphorus; in Colossians: the lone individual he greets is a woman named Nympha, along with the church that meets at her house and the Laodicean brothers. In 1 Corinthians, only the Corinthians receive greetings. As for greetings sent from individuals, there are 8 named persons in Col 4:10–14;[5] 5 in Phlm 23–24;[6] 4 in 2 Tim 4:21;[7] and 2 in 1 Cor 16:19 (Prisca and Aquila).[8]

---

1. See also Douglas J. Moo, *The Letter to the Romans*, 2nd ed., NICNT (Grand Rapids: Eerdmans, 2018), 928, for the unusual closing warning against false teachers (16:17–19).

2. Phoebe, Prisca, Aquila, Epaenetus, Mary, Andronicus, Junia, Ampilatus, Urbanus, Stachys, Apelles, Aristobulus, Herodion, Narcissus, Tryphaena, Tryphosa, Persis, Rufus, Asyncritus, Phlegon, Hermes, Patrobas, Hermas, Philologus, Julia, Nereus, and Olympas.

3. Church at Prisca's and Aquila's house (16:5); family of Aristobulus (16:10); family of Narcissus (16:11); brothers (16:14); all the saints (16:15); and Romans (16:16).

4. Timothy; Lucius (Acts 13:1); Jason (Acts 17:5–9); Sosipater, Tertius (letter writer); Gaius (host; Acts 19:29; 20:4; 1 Cor 1:14; 3 John 1); Erastus (city treasurer; Acts 19:22; 2 Tim 4:20); all the church; and Quartus.

5. Onesimus, Aristarchus, Mark, Barnabas, Jesus/Justus, Epaphras, Luke, and Demas.

6. Epaphras, Mark, Aristarchus, Demas, and Luke.

7. Eubulus, Pudens, Linus, and Claudia.

8. There are no greetings in Galatians, Ephesians, 1–2 Thessalonians, 1 Timothy, or Titus (only reports of activity). General greetings are sent in 2 Corinthians and Philippians.

In terms of women's participation in the nascent church, and specifically, Paul's perspective of women's ministry, Rom 16 offers extraordinary evidence. While women appear in the greetings to and from Paul in his letters (Prisca appears in both 2 Tim 4:19; 1 Cor 16:19; and Nympha in Col 4:15), there are 8 named and 2 unnamed women in Rom 16.[9] Given the small number of named individuals in the rest of Paul's letters, the anomaly of the greetings in Romans 16 lies in Paul's description of two specific women, namely Phoebe as deacon and Junia as apostle, rather than the aggregate sum of mentioned women.[10] Indeed, Rom 16:1–2 and 16:7 appear to be indisputable evidence of women's *official* leadership in the nascent church, recognized and endorsed by Paul himself. The complication lies in the fact that Paul's approval of these women's leadership in the church is seemingly at odds with Paul's injunction against teaching roles and eldership of women in the church (1 Tim 2:11–15; 3:1–7). Below, I will concisely address prominent exegetical issues regarding Phoebe and Junia with brief attention to Prisca, then explore the implications of the analysis.

Phoebe

In Paul's commendation of Phoebe, three words are noteworthy: ἀδελφή, διάκονος, and προστάτις. First, Paul calls her "our sister" (ἀδελφὴν ἡμῶν) to signify her authentic faith, which is the fundamental basis of his endorsement of Phoebe to the Romans.[11] She is not only a sister in faith to Paul, but also to the Romans—note the inclusive pronoun "our" (ἡμῶν)—thus, the Roman believers should "welcome her in the Lord in a manner worthy of saints" (16:2). As Frank Thielman saliently notes, commendation of Phoebe as well as the long list of greetings to members of the Roman church is to "promote the mutual, familial love that Paul has been encouraging explicitly within the Roman community since 12:1."[12] Authentic demonstration of Christ's love within the body of Christ is without gender discrimination. Paul's unambiguous endorsement of Phoebe's sound faith illustrates the very love of Christ that he prescribes in the letter.

---

9. Phoebe, Prisca, Mary, Junia, Tryphaena, Tryphosa, Persis, and Julia plus 2 unnamed (Rufus' mother; Nereus' sister).

10. In greetings *to* individuals, Paul mentions only Nympha in Col 4:15, and he mentions Prisca before Aquila in 2 Tim 4:19. In greetings *from* individuals, he mentions Claudia among three other men and a general reference to "the brothers" (2 Tim 4:21), and Prisca before Aquila (1 Cor 16:19). In Romans, the percentage of women in the greetings is slightly under 30 percent.

11. Ἀδελφή "sister" occurs less frequently (26x in NT) than ἀδελφός "brother" (343x in NT). Ἀδελφός is often used to refer to both genders coherent to androcentric world view and linguistics; e.g., 1 Cor 3:1; Rom 1:13; Eph 6:23.

12. Frank Thielman, *Romans*, ZECNT 6 (Grand Rapids: Zondervan Academic, 2018), 704.

Second, Paul states that she is a "deacon [διάκονος] of the church in Cenchreae" (16:1). Διάκονος occurs only twenty-nine times in the NT,[13] and generally conveys 3 different senses: 1) a servant to a master (hierarchical);[14] 2) an emissary, go-between with the sense of representation, agency; an intermediate (non-hierarchical);[15] and 3) an official capacity in the church—a deacon/ deaconess. With respect to the last sense, it could be argued that the only clear instances of an official sense of "deacon/deaconess" are found in Phil 1:1 and 1 Tim 3:8, 12, whereas the rest of the occurrences of διάκονος simply mean either "servant" in a hierarchal relationship or "agent" in non-hierarchal context. Clearly, passages such as Rom 15:8 (Christ as servant), Eph 3:7 (Paul as a servant of the gospel) and Col 1:7 (Epaphras as servant of Christ) cannot mean that each is a "deacon" in the church. Thus, it is argued that Rom 16:1 also conveys "servant" rather than a church official.[16] However, as well noted by Thomas Schreiner, "[Rom 16:1] is the only instance where διάκονος is linked with a particular local church;"[17] hence διάκονος carries an official sense in 16:1. Such a reading, in Schreiner's view, is coherent to 1 Tim 3:11 where Paul permits women to serve as deacons.[18]

---

13. The cognates are equally limited in the NT: διακονὶα "service" and (34x) διακονεῖν "to serve" (37x). Διακόνισσα the feminine form ("deaconess") does not appear in the NT as it is a later development; see Moo, *Romans*, 930n193.

14. Mark 9:35; 10:43; Matt 20:26; 22:13; 23:11; including the sense of a waiter at a meal (John 2:5, 9); cf. *TDNT* 2:88–93.

15. Cf. John N. Collins, *Diakonia: Re-interpreting the Ancient Sources* (Oxford: Oxford University Press, 1990), 77–95. Cf. BDAG s.v. διάκονος 1 (230); Thielman, *Romans*, 710; Lynn H. Cohick, *Women in the World of the Earliest Christians: Illuminating Ancient Ways of Life* (Grand Rapids: Baker Academic, 2009), 312–13; Richard N. Longenecker, *The Epistle to the Romans: A Commentary on the Greek Text*, NIGTC (Grand Rapids: Eerdmans, 2016), 1064–65; and Carolyn Osiek and Margaret Y. MacDonald with Janet H. Tulloch, *A Woman's Place: House Churches in Earliest Christianity* (Minneapolis: Fortress, 2006), 215.

16. Cf. Kazimierz Romaniuk, "Was Phoebe in Romans 16,1 a Deaconess?," *ZNW* 81 (1990) 132–34, esp. 134; Wilhelm Michaelis, "Kenchreä (Zur Frage des Abfassungsortes des Rm)," *ZNW* 25 (1926): 144–54.

17. Thomas R. Schreiner, *Romans*, BECNT (Grand Rapids: Baker Academic 1998), 787. Further, he notes that the masculine form of διάκονος signifies office, rather than the general sense of service. Adolf Schlatter, *Gottes Gerechtigkeit: Ein Kommentar zum Römerbrief*, 2nd ed. (Stuttgart: Calwer Verlag, 1965), 396, assumes Phoebe is a church official without argumentation.

18. Thomas R. Schreiner, "The Valuable Ministries of Women in the Context of Male Leadership: A Survey of Old and New Testament Examples and Teaching," in *Recovering Biblical Manhood and Womanhood: A Response to Evangelical Feminism*, ed. John Piper and Wayne Grudem (Wheaton, IL: Crossway, 1991), 209–24, esp. 213–14. But cf. also Robert W. Yarbrough, *The Letters to Timothy and Titus*, PNTC (Grand Rapids: Eerdmans, 2018), 206, who affirms Phoebe as deaconess, but sees women in 1 Tim 3:11 as wives rather than female deacons based on justified syntactical and morphological ambiguity in 1 Tim 3:11.

The second sense of "agency" or "representation" is a recently minted meaning from the seminal work of John N. Collins that examines usage of διάκονος in ancient Greek sources. According to his investigation, the context of menial service accounts for approximately half of all the instances of διάκονος.[19] Yet, he surmises that the root of διάκονος never expressed the notion of service, but rather one of "go-between," intermediary, or agency.[20] With this sense of intermediary, the focus shifts from the traditional sense of practical service rendered in a hierarchical structure to roles that may impart more dignity and status without any hierarchical sense; the difference, simply put, is that of a courier from a waiter.

Richard N. Longenecker elaborates the implications of Phoebe's plausible role as the letter courier *and* her status as "patroness" or "benefactor" (προστάτις) to Paul and others. He contemplates that given Phoebe's long-term relationship with Paul, she would have privileged knowledge of Paul's thoughts contained in the letter and therefore be able to represent Paul, indeed, even *interpret* Paul for the Roman Christians. Phoebe would "explain to the Christians at Rome (1) what Paul was saying in the various sections of his letter, (2) what he meant by what he proclaimed in each of those sections, and (3) how he expected certain important sections of his letter to be worked out in practice in particular situations at Rome."[21] Based on these assumptions, Phoebe would be, in Longenecker's words, "the first commentator" on Paul's letter to the Romans.[22]

To imbue more agency and status to the role of deacon is both misguided and moot. First, the appropriate word for the thorough representation Longenecker advocates in the sense of "envoy" or "ambassador" is not διάκονος, but ἀπόστολος, ἄγγελος, or πρεσβευτής in Greek diplomatic and epistolary literature.[23] For reasons writ large, Paul never uses any of these terms to signify diplomatic roles of ambassador or envoy. In the NT, ἀπόστολος predominately carries the sense of authoritative agents of Jesus Christ with the commission of evangelism and pedagogy for the churches (cf. Matt 28:16–20; Eph 2:20; 4:11).[24] Ἀπόστολος appears most frequently in Pauline epistles with the sense of God's (rather than human) agents, apart from two instances.[25] The sense of envoy ap-

---

19. Collins, *Diakonia*, 75.
20. Collins, *Diakonia*, 194, 335.
21. Longenecker, *Romans*, 1064.
22. Longenecker, *Romans*, 1065.
23. Margaret M. Mitchell, "New Testament Envoys in the Context of Greco-Roman Diplomatic and Epistolary Conventions: The Example of Timothy and Titus," *JBL* 111.4 (1992) 641–62, 652.
24. Cf. *TDNT* 1:407–47, esp. 420–30.
25. Lexical spread in the NT is as follows: ἀπόστολος appears 80x in NT (twice in 1 Cor 15:9); once in Matthew; twice in Mark; 6 times in Luke; once in John; 28 times in Acts; 34 times in Paul; 5 times in the General Epistles; and thrice in Revelation.

pears only in Phil 2:25, where Paul describes Epaphroditus as the Philippians' messenger (ὑμῶν δὲ ἀπόστολον) and in 2 Cor 8:23 Paul designates "our brothers" as "messengers of the churches" (ἀπόστολοι ἐκκλησιῶν).[26] New Testament usage of ἄγγελος also exhibits similar distinction from Greco-Roman usage; apart from few instances (Luke 7:24; 9:52; James 2:25), it routinely refers to supernatural messengers from God. Out of 175 occurrences in the NT ἄγγελος only appears 14 times in Paul and only once conveys the sense of human envoy (Gal 4:14). Πρεσβύτης, a variant of πρεσβευτής occurs just three times in the NT; twice it has the sense of "elder" or "old man," and only once possibly conveys the meaning of "ambassador" in Phlm 9.[27] The words used in the NT for "ambassador" are πρεσβεία (Luke 14:32; 19:14) or "I am an ambassador" (πρεσβεύω), which notably only appears in Paul within the context of evangelism (2 Cor 5:20 with respect to all believers vis-à-vis the world; Eph 6:20 with respect to his apostleship).

The closest parallel to what Longenecker describes may be Tychicus' role as "minister" and letter courier in Eph 6:21; and Col 4:7.[28] Paul uses διάκονος in both instances, the word itself does not necessarily convey "messenger" or "intermediary" as it appears in conjunction with other descriptors of Tychicus. In both passages Paul's portrayal of Tychicus' character is near identical: "the beloved brother and faithful servant and fellow slave in the Lord" (ὁ ἀγαπητὸς ἀδελφὸς καὶ πιστὸς διάκονος καὶ σύνδουλος ἐν κυρίῳ, Col 4:7); and "the beloved brother and faithful servant in the Lord (ὁ ἀγαπητὸς ἀδελφὸς καὶ πιστὸς διάκονος ἐν κυρίῳ, Eph 6:21). The phrase ὁ ἀγαπητὸς ἀδελφὸς (along with σύνδουλος and ἐν κυρίῳ) renders πιστὸς διάκονος as commendation of Tychicus' trustworthy, self-sacrificing character rather than his specific role as "messenger" to the respective communities. Indeed, given the notorious unreliability of strangers who functioned as couriers, Tychicus' proven character ensures the delivery of Paul's letter.[29]

That Tychicus functioned as Paul's courier is derived from, once again, virtually parallel phrases: "All the news concerning me Tychicus will tell you" (Τὰ κατ᾽ ἐμὲ πάντα γνωρίσει ὑμῖν Τύχικος, Col 4:7) and "So that you may also know my affairs, what I am doing, Tychicus will tell you everything" (Ἵνα δὲ

---

26. Cf. Murray J. Harris, *The Second Epistle to the Corinthians: A Commentary on the Greek Text*, NIGTC (Grand Rapids: Eerdmans, 2005), 611–12.

27. Cf. BDAG s.v. πρεσβύτης (863) and πρεσβευτής (861).

28. For either Phoebe and Tychicus, their role as letter courier is never explicit, but reasonably assumed.

29. As the postal system in first century Roman Empire was created for rulers, government and military, private citizens employed services of private courier service, trusted servants/slaves or strangers travelling to the same locale of the recipient. In the case of the latter, evidence suggests that theft and unreliability were familiar dilemma. For more, cf. John L. White, *Light from Ancient Letters* (Philadelphia: Fortress, 1986), 214–15, esp. footnote 133; Correspondence to Apollinarius (PMich VIII 499 and 500).

εἰδῆτε καὶ ὑμεῖς τὰ κατ᾽ ἐμέ, τί πράσσω, πάντα γνωρίσει ὑμῖν Τύχικος, Eph 6:21). In both instances, Tychicus' representation of Paul is narrowly limited to Paul's welfare (τὰ κατ᾽ ἐμέ [πάντα]) and not the content of respective letters. Likewise, while Paul's whole-hearted endorsement of Phoebe's faith and her extensive commitment to the gospel as deaconess and patroness is indisputable, and her role as courier (and reader) is indeed plausible, there is no indication that she served as Paul's interpreter or intermediary to the Romans.[30]

Second, if Longenecker's interpretation is to stand, the phrase would be "she is [also] my servant" (οὖσαν [καὶ] διάκονον μου/ἐμοῦ). Such construction never appears in Paul's letters perhaps *because* διάκονος conveys service within hierarchal relations in the NT. As evident from the examination above, Tychicus, as well as other co-laborers are typically portrayed in the egalitarian sense of siblings (ἀδελφός).[31] In the NT, including Paul, the identity of all believers as children of God equally saved by God's grace does not erode the authority of God's appointed ones; each is the necessary and coherent context for the other.[32] Regarding Phoebe, the construction is "deacon of the church in Cenchreae," if the notion of representation is applied to διάκονος, then she represents the Cenchreaen church and not Paul.

Third, when Paul deploys an agent with extensive representative function, he is explicit as to their purpose. Titus and Timothy serve as Paul's representatives on various occasions. In 2 Cor 8:16–24, Paul solicits an enthusiastic Titus to complete the financial collection for saints in need: "For he [Titus] not only accepted the appeal, but he himself being very eager went[33] to you of his own volition" (2 Cor 8:17). Further, there are two unnamed brothers sent with Titus (2 Cor 8:18, 22). The first one who has been expressly commissioned by the churches and sent by Paul represents the heart and mindset (monetary giving as "grace," χάρις, cf. 8:1, 6, 7, 9, 19)[34] behind the fundraising campaign—namely, his commission is to ensure glory to God with all probity (2 Cor 8:18–21)—the very concern of both

---

30. Reading the letter is, of course, not applicable with unfamiliar couriers, but in the stance of hired scribes as well as trusted literate servants, reading the contents of the letter is routine. Cf. White, *Light from Ancient Letters*, 216.

31. See footnote 11 above. The sole exception to this in Paul is Phlm 13 where διακονεῖν takes Paul as the direct object (ἵνα ὑπὲρ σοῦ μοι διακονῇ). The anomaly is one of many forceful rhetorical maneuvers in the letter to rebut and chasten Philemon's need to redress perceived injury from Onesimus' rebellious flight. Paul reminds Philemon that Onesimus is providing the service that he ought to provide, thus targeting Philemon's self-centered mindset, which contrasts with that of a servant in Christ as Onesimus demonstrates to Paul (cf. Matt 20:26; Mark 9:35; 10:43; for the mandate to serve one another, see Heb 6:10; 1 Pet 4:10).

32. For more on this issue, see below.

33. The Greek is ἐξῆλθεν as it would have already been a past action when the Corinthians read the letter. Cf. Mark A. Seifrid, *The Second Letter to the Corinthians*, PNTC (Grand Rapids: Eerdmans, 2014), 341n77.

34. Χάρις appears 18 times in 2 Cor (7 times in 2 Cor 8).

Paul and the churches. Although the function of the second unnamed brother is less explicit (2 Cor 8:22), that he and the first brother are called "messengers of the churches" (ἀπόστολοι ἐκκλησιῶν, 2 Cor 8:23) indicates that he has the same function. All three have a single function as envoys to represent the churches' and Paul's altruism rather than corruption of self-gain or deception to the Corinthians, so that the Corinthians not only complete their pledge of financial support for the poor (2 Cor 8:6–7; 10–11; cf. also 1 Cor 16:1–2), but therein participate in the fellowship of giving as modeled by Jesus Christ (2 Cor 8:9).[35]

Titus also appears to have played a critical role in the reconciliation between Paul and the Corinthians (2 Cor 7:5–16). At some point between the two extant Corinthian correspondences, Paul made a visit to the Corinthians, which he calls "painful" (2 Cor 2:1). In the aftermath of this visit Paul writes a "tearful" letter (2 Cor 2:4), of which we have no record, but most certainly delivered to the Corinthians by Titus. The postoperative report in 2 Cor 7:5–17 suggests the much-desired result of repentance and reconciliation was achieved by Titus' mediation between Paul and the Corinthians. The extent of Titus' representation of Paul is unclear as the letter is *in absentia*; yet, it appears that in this instance Titus not only carried the letter but, critically, conveyed Paul's heartfelt love as the motivation behind the injurious letter (2 Cor 7:7–9). Then, the concluding verses of 2 Cor 7:13b–16 relate not only Paul's anxiety in sending the harsh letter, but also delegating Titus as his courier and agent. Paul's conclusive boasts of the Corinthians were necessary for Titus' own hope of an efficacious mediation.[36]

More prominently, Timothy functions as Paul's representative for the Corinthians (1 Cor 4:17) as Timothy is able to faithfully portray to the Corinthians as a reminder of Paul's teaching and conduct ("my ways in Christ," τὰς ὁδούς μου τὰς ἐν Χριστῳ).[37] Such coherent depiction of Paul is necessary in order to buttress Paul's paternal imperative to the Corinthians: "Therefore, I urge you: be imitators of me" (1 Cor 4:16; 11:1; cf. also 4:15–16 on Paul's paternal role). Paul's whole-hearted confidence in Timothy as his emissary rests again on the fact that Timothy is a model of Christ's humility and self-sacrifice (2:6–8) in Phil 2:19–23.[38] For both Titus and Timothy, their role as Paul's agents in their respective context is explicitly articulated by Paul.

---

35. Paul also refers to the collection for the poor as "fellowship" κοινωνίαν in Rom 15.26.

36. On the complication of these verses, cf. Margaret E. Thrall, *2 Corinthians 1–7: A Critical and Exegetical Commentary*, ICC (London: T&T Clark, 1994), 497–99; and Seifrid, *Corinthians*, 311–13. Paul's boast of the Corinthians need not be disingenuous; rather, it is the certainty of God's faithful work even in the troubled believers.

37. One specific form of Paul's "ways" may be his description of the adversity and dishonor apostles faced in 1 Cor 4:9–13.

38. Although it is tempting to see Epaphroditus in similar capacity of Timothy in Phil 2:25–30, he is the Philippians' messenger (ὑμῶν . . . ἀπόστολον) to Paul rendering service to him on their behalf. Undoubtedly, he will relay news concerning Paul's

Their representation is not of Paul's theology per se, but of Christ's self-sacrificing mindset normative for all believers, which Paul personally embraces and proclaims. Even in the instance of the practical matter of financial collection, the fundamental rationale is Jesus' self-emptying sacrifice (2 Cor 8:9). Paul, at no point, designates these roles of representation as διάκονος. Titus is "my partner and coworker for your benefit" (κοινωνὸς ἐμὸς καὶ εἰς ὑμᾶς συνεργός, 2 Cor 8:23); Timothy is "my beloved and faithful child in the Lord" (μου τέκνον ἀγαπητὸν καὶ πιστὸν ἐν κυρίῳ, 1 Cor 4:17) and in Phil 2:22 "as a son with a father he has served with me in the gospel" (ὡς πατρὶ τέκνον σὺν ἐμοὶ ἐδούλευσεν εἰς τὸ εὐαγγέλιον). Despite the fact that both Titus and Timothy "represent" Paul in various ways, in no way do the terms κοινωνὸς or τέκνον function as substitutes for διάκονος in the sense of "intermediary."

Such detailed specificity with respect to envoys' function is coherent to Greco-Roman envoy tradition. John L. White notes the fluidity in the role of courier: "In the case of the messengers of the wealthy and eminent, we may assume that couriers tended to be even more conversant with the letter's contents and capable of adding supplementary news by word of mouth."[39] Yet, where more extensive duties of interpretation or representation are in view, the sender explicitly communicates the role of the envoy to the recipient, as White's example ably demonstrates. The conclusion of a letter from Simalē to Zēnōn (PCol III 6) specifies the courier's fuller capacity: "The rest [i.e., anything else that remains] learn from the one who carries the letter to you. For he is no stranger to us. Farewell."[40]

Paul uses the customary word in Greek recommendation letters "I recommend" (συνίστημι), which strongly suggests Phoebe is the courier of the letter.[41] Out of the 16 occurrences of συνίστημι in the NT, 14 instances appear in Paul and only here with a positive sense of "recommendation."[42] Yet, the type of clarity of envoy's function found elsewhere in Paul is absent in Rom 16:1–2. The ἵνα clause (16:2) attached to συνίστημι indicates a two-fold purpose: 1) to receive (προσδέξησθε) Phoebe in the Lord worthy of saints; and 2) to attend (παραστῆτε) to whatever matter she may need from the Romans. The second

---

welfare to the Philippians and he does model Christ's self-sacrificing mindset (Phil 2:6–8), along with Timothy in accordance to Paul's injunction in Phil 2:5.

39. White, *Light from Ancient Letters*, 216. See also D. Kienast, "Presbeia," PWSup 13:499–628, esp. 564–65.

40. See White, *Light from Ancient Letters*, 34: τὰ δὲ λοιπὰ πυνθάνου τοῦ φέροντός σοι τὰ γράμματα. οὐ γὰρ ἀλλότριος ἡμῖν ἔστιν. εὐτύχει. Also on the conventional formula of envoys, see Mitchell, "New Testament Envoys," 652.

41. See the salient example in Thielman, *Romans*, 710, as well as 2 Cor 3:1 cited in 710n6.

42. Over half of Paul's usage appears in 2 Corinthians, typically with the negative sense of *self*-commendation. BDAG s.v. συνίστημι 2 (972).

purpose clause would be the most appropriate juncture to articulate a more elaborate role of representation *if* Paul intended such a function for Phoebe. The wording of the clause is too vague for such conclusions. The construction ᾧ ἂν tied to πράγματι "deed, matter, undertaking," signifies contingency and indefiniteness, providing quite a bit of latitude for Phoebe, but lacks the specificity evident in both Titus' and Timothy's role of representation.

Finally, grievance over women's marginalization must contend with Jesus' own definition of discipleship as one that embraces degradation of servant/slave mindset and function over and against that of master (e.g., Mark 9:35; 10:43–44; Matt 20:26; 23:11). Indeed, humble service *is* the qualification for leadership (Luke 22:26).[43] Even though διάκονος does not appear in the election of the seven in Acts 6:1–7, the cognate διακονεῖν does appear in 6:2 in the context of serving at tables: "It is not right for us to lay aside (proclaiming) the word of God *in order to serve tables*."[44] The service certainly would not be limited to functions of a waiter but include logistics of planning and supervision. Yet, for the seven (as well as other disciples), *to spurn lowly service is to be disqualified from ministry*.[45] Simultaneously, these lowly servants exhibit impressive faith. For example, in Acts 6:5, Stephen is described as "a man full of faith and of the Holy Spirit;" in 6:8, he is "full of grace and power" performing "great wonders and signs." Following Robert Yarbrough, it is by no means a stretch of the imagination to suppose that Paul had Stephen in mind as he writes the qualifications of deacons in 1 Timothy since Paul witnessed Stephen's martyrdom (Acts 8:1).[46] Consequently, when Paul acknowledges Phoebe as "deacon" and "our sister," he attests to the strength of her faith and knowledge of the truth. If in similarity to Stephen, she is a woman "full of faith and of the Holy Spirit . . . of grace and power," it seems reasonable to conclude that much like Stephen, titles and status would not be her preoccupation, as they are seemingly for moderns.

The fact that Phoebe is also a patron (προστάτις) of Paul and others (καὶ γὰρ αὐτὴ προστάτις πολλῶν ἐγενήθη καὶ ἐμοῦ αὐτοῦ, Rom 16:2) bolsters the argument that she humbly serves because of her bona fide faith. Προστάτις is a *hapax* in both the NT and the LXX. Paul scrupulously rejected any financial support from two communities he established: the Thessalonians and the Corinthians. In Thessalonica, he and his colleagues were self-supporting to avoid any monetary impropriety and to model good work ethics for the new converts (1 Thess 2:9; 2 Thess 3:7–8) in direct contrast to popular, but unscrupulous, itinerant (Sophist

---

43. Despite Collins' conclusion that διάκονος in Greek literature does not convey service, he does recognize that in the NT, esp. in the Gospels the notion of humble service is prevalent, cf. Collins, *Diakonia*, 245–47.

44. Cf. Yarbrough, *Timothy and Titus*, 208, for commonality between the qualifications of deacons and the description of Stephen in Acts.

45. *TDNT* 2:84–85.

46. Yarbrough, *Timothy and Titus*, 208.

and Cynic) preachers of their day.[47] The gospel was pristinely proclaimed apart from Paul's self-gain. The same logic also applies to the Corinthians with an additional component. Paul steadfastly refused financial support from the Corinthians (1 Cor 9:6, 11–12, 18; 2 Cor 11:7; cf. also Acts 18:2–3) possibly because the Corinthians were still "fleshly" rather than spiritual in their modus operandi with respect to many issues; Christ had not yet infiltrated their hearts and minds to affect a radical approach to life.[48] Indeed, normative practice of patronage in Greco-Roman societies, such as Corinth, would find Paul's rejection of financial support offensive and suspect. Roy Ciampa and Brian Rosner state:

> his [Paul's] refusal to accept financial support from the Corinthians, preferring instead to ply his trade (see 9:1–27), would probably have offended some of the wealthier and more influential members of the congregation. Patronage, the giving of financial and other privileges to clients by leading figures in society, was an important feature of Greco-Roman social life. Respected teachers received such support. Paul took no part in this, and his refusal might have been construed as rejection of friendship.[49]

Yet, that hand of friendship in patronage-client system was extended with two critical factors. First, according to S. N. Eisenstadt and L. Roniger, these relationships are "based on a very strong element of inequality and of differences of power between patrons and clients."[50] Second, the motivation for patronage and various acts of benevolence is not altruism, but self-honor and glory.[51] Given the litany of misapprehension amidst the Corinthians that betray their "fleshly" rather than "spiritual" mindset (1 Cor 2:6–3:4), Paul judiciously rejects financial support from them that would facilitate the inappropriate patron-client hierarchy and self-glory.

Thus, the single instance of προστάτις, with all the implications of first century patron-client relations speaks volumes of Phoebe's character.[52] Whether

---

47. See the salient comments of Frank Thielman, *Theology of the New Testament: A Canonical and Synthetic Approach* (Grand Rapids: Zondervan, 2005), 241–42.

48. There are manifold issues outlined in 1 Corinthians (e.g., promotion of various leaders 1–4; incest, lawsuits, sexual immorality 5:1–6:20); foods offered to idols (8–11); disruptive worship and misunderstanding of spiritual gifts (11–14); abuse of the Lord's Supper (11); resurrection (15); etc.

49. Roy E. Ciampa and Brian S. Rosner, *The First Letter to the Corinthians*, PNTC (Grand Rapids: Eerdmans, 2010), 78.

50. S. N. Eisenstadt and L. Roniger, *Patrons, Clients, and Friends: Interpersonal Relations and the Structure of Trust in Society*, Themes in the Social Sciences (Cambridge: Cambridge University Press, 1984), 48–49; see also John H. Elliott "Patronage and Clientage" in Richard L. Rohrbaugh, ed., *The Social Sciences and New Testament Interpretation* (Peabody: Hendrickson, 1996), 144–56.

51. A. R. Hands, *Charities and Social Aid in Greece and Rome* (Ithaca: Cornell University Press, 1968), 49.

52. The masculine form προστάτης does not appear in the LXX or NT.

her benefaction included finances or merely social resources, it is clear on the evidence of 1 Cor 9:6, 11–12, 18; and 2 Cor 11:7, Paul would not accept her patronage nor commend her should she perceive it as means to gain power and self-glory. Given her status and wealth as patron, she, nevertheless, serves as διάκονος in Cenchreae. As Thielman notes: "This may reflect the transforming effect that the gospel had on the systems of honor and status that were so prevalent in the cultures where it first flourished."[53] Phoebe typifies the humble service and tremendous faith of Stephen (Acts 6:1–8).

Junia

What Paul has to say about Junia in Rom 16:7 is quite astounding as it seems to stand in stark contradiction to his own proscription of women's teaching and authority in the church in 1 Tim 2:11–15. Andronicus and Junia are a Jewish couple (τοὺς συγγενεῖς μου) much like Prisca and Aquila (τοὺς συνεργούς μου 16:3).[54] Apart from their Jewish descent, Paul describes them as "my fellow prisoners" (συναιχμαλώτους μου), "prominent among the apostles" (οἵτινές εἰσιν ἐπίσημοι ἐν τοῖς ἀποστόλοις), and those "who also were in Christ before me" (οἳ καὶ πρὸ ἐμοῦ γέγοναν ἐν Χριστῷ). The phrase "prominent among the apostles" is disputed because of Junia's gender. The concern here is not whether sexist bias or ideology drives the arguments, but textual as well as theological incoherence to Paul's view of women in ecclesial leadership elsewhere.

In the case of Junia, the Greek accent mark plays a vital role. As Schreiner notes, if the accent mark is a circumflex (Ἰουνιᾶν), then the name is masculine from Ἰουνιᾶς as contraction of Junianus.[55] However, if the accent mark is acute (Ἰουνίαν) the name is feminine.[56] Most modern scholars read Junia Ἰουνιᾶν as feminine rather than masculine as it had been previously assumed,[57] based on the fact that, as incisively noted by Linda Belleville, "Ἰουνιᾶς is absent from

---

53. Cf. Thielman, *Romans*, 712n23, citing Bruce W. Winter, *Roman Wives, Roman Widows: The Appearance of New Women and the Pauline Communities* (Grand Rapids: Eerdmans, 2003), 196.

54. While it is possible that they are brother and sister, non-marital relations are explicitly noted as such: Rufus and his mother (16:13) and Nereus and his sister (16:15). "Kinsmen" συγγενεῖς signifies common ethnic heritage rather than familial relations.

55. See Belleville's trenchant argument on contractions in "Re-examination," 239.

56. Schreiner, *Romans*, 795–96.

57. For an exception to this consensus, cf. Al Wolters, "IOYNIAN (Romans 16:7) and the Hebrew Name 'Yĕḥunnī'," *JBL* 127.2 (2008): 397–408. On feminine gender of Junia, see Elisabeth Schüssler Fiorenza, "Missionaries, Apostles, Coworkers: Romans 16 and the Reconstruction of Women's Early Christian History," *Word & World* 6.4 (1986): 420–33; Elisabeth Schüssler Fiorenza, "Women in the Pre-Pauline and Pauline Churches," *Union Seminary Quarterly Review* 33.3–4 (1978): 153–66. See also Linda L. Belleville, "Ἰουνιαν...ἐπίστημοι ἐν τοῖς ἀποστόλοις: A Re-examination of Romans 16:7

the Koine of the day. It does not appear in any inscription, letterhead, piece of writing, or epitaph."[58] Given the consensus on the gender of Junia, two other factors are challenged. First, given the different class of apostles in 1 Cor 15:3–11, "apostle" in 16:7 does not signify the same authority exercised by the Twelve. Second, the phrase "prominent among the apostles" (NRSVue) may not be inclusive but exclusive: "well known to the apostles" (ESV) as argued by Michael H. Burer and Daniel B. Wallace.[59] The first reading affirms their excellence as apostles, while the latter only indicates the apostles' knowledge of them.[60]

The most judicious and fair assessment of this issue comes from Thielman.[61] He anchors his reading on the oldest Greek commentators (e.g., Origen, Chrysostom) who acknowledge the inclusive reading of the disputed phrase.[62] Chrysostom in particular affirms the feminine gender of Junia as well as the inclusive sense of the disputed phrase:

> And indeed, to be apostles is a great thing. But to be even outstanding among the apostles—consider what a wonderful encomium this is! They were outstanding because of their works and virtuous actions. Indeed, how great is the wisdom of this woman as she was deemed worthy also of the title of apostles.[63]

On the kind of authority Junia may have exercised as apostle, there are two minimizing options: 1) "apostle" does not signify the authority of either Paul or the Twelve (1 Cor 15:3–11) and 2) her authority is directed to women.[64] On the first point, in 1 Cor 15:3–11, the classification is between the Twelve and the rest. And of the two, Paul relegates himself to the latter. The purpose of stratification is to discreetly isolate the authority of the Twelve as those who were discipled by Jesus. Such recognition of the Twelve's unique authority, according to Paul, clearly does not diminish authority of the rest in Gal 1–2. The latter point does

---

in Light of Primary Source Materials," *NTS* 51 (2005): 231–49; also from complementarian scholars: Thielman, *Romans*, 488; Moo, *Romans*, 938; and Schreiner, *Romans*, 796.

58. Belleville, "Re-examination," 240.

59. Michael H. Burer and Daniel B. Wallace, "Was Junia Really an Apostle? A Re-examination of Rom 16.7," *NTS* 47 (2001): 76–91; cf. Belleville's response in "Re-examination."

60. I will not rehash the arguments as I have no new arguments, but cf. Richard Bauckham, *Gospel Women: Studies of the Named Women in the Gospels* (London: T&T Clark, 2002), 172–80, who delivers a cogent argument against the methodology of Burer and Wallace; similarly, see Belleville, "Re-examination," 242–48.

61. Dr. Thielman is also a PCA ordained minister.

62. Thielman, *Romans*, 719–20.

63. Chrysostom, *Romans*, 489; PG 60.669–70 cited in Eldon J. Epp, *Junia: The First Woman Apostle* (Minneapolis: Fortress, 2005), 32; note also other ancient commentators in Epp, *Junia*, 32–36.

64. For the first, see Moo, *Romans*, 939–40; and for the second, Schreiner, *Romans*, 797.

have merit: it is logical that Junia's apostleship was primarily directed to women given the patriarchy of the first century for both Jewish and Greco-Roman cultures. Nevertheless, there is evidence in the NT, albeit singular, of a woman teaching a man: Prisca in Acts 18:27, along with her husband Aquila, teaches Apollos the more accurate way of God.

However, to be an apostle is not simply to exercise authority. If the notion of sending is the foundation of apostleship, then, as argued by Margaret M. Mitchell, that tradition begins with Jesus in the NT.[65] "Truly, truly I say to you, the one who receives whomever I send receives me, and the one who receives me receives the one who sent me" (John 13:20). The whole notion of apostleship depends on the integrity of Jesus' representation of God the Father: "The one who has seen me has seen the Father. . . . Do you not believe that I am in the Father and the Father is in me? The words that I say to you I do not speak on my own authority, but the Father who dwells in me does his works" (John 14:9–10). Likewise, the apostles are bound to similar representation of Jesus Christ, which requires strict obedience to his will. Paul is so wholly submitted to Jesus Christ that he embodies Christ's death (Phil 3:10; 2 Cor 4:10) and even represents him through the markings on his body (Gal 6:17). Indeed, absolute submission to the triune God is the apostle's authority. Junia as an apostle has no independent agency but must wholly be submitted to God's will and comprehensively represent Jesus Christ in her teaching and her life. In fact, she, along with Andronicus, demonstrates this in her willingness to endure imprisonment for the gospel—such submission to God's will is recognized and embraced by Paul (συναιχμαλώτους μου, Rom 16:7).

Prisca/Priscilla

At first glance, Paul's comments on Prisca (Rom 16:3–5a) do not seem to convey the kind of significance as those of Phoebe and Junia for female leadership. Yet, Prisca and Aquila receive the longest greeting as they are Paul's intimate acquaintances and co-workers. They appear in the greetings of 1 Cor 16:19 and 2 Tim 4:19. The background of their relationship to Paul is relayed in Acts 18. The married couple are Roman Jews, who encounter Paul in Corinth due to Claudius' edict against Jews in Rome (49 CE) (Acts 18:2); they are also tentmakers like Paul, and they work together in Corinth (Acts 18:3). Critically, they were most likely Christians prior to the expulsion.[66] Given the mention of the proconsul Gallio, whose tenure in Corinth was in 51–52 CE, Paul, Prisca, and Aquila lived, worked, and ministered in Corinth for a year and a half (Acts 18:11). The mutual devotion between them is marked by the fact that Paul takes

---

65. Mitchell, "New Testament Envoys," 644–45.
66. Cf. Thielman, *Romans*, 714.

them with him as he travels to Syria (Acts 18:18) after the coordinated attack on Paul and his co-workers (Acts 18:12–17). Paul's greetings to Prisca and Aquila are coherent to their mutual, affectionate constancy and united allegiance to the gospel. Paul says of them: "Prisca and Aquila . . . who, on behalf of my life, their own neck, they risked" (Πρίσκαν καὶ Ἀκύλαν . . . οἵτινες ὑπὲρ τῆς ψυχῆς μου τὸν ἑαυτῶν τράχηλον ὑπέθηκαν (Rom 16:3–4). My translation reflects the Greek word order to highlight the emphatic position of both clauses "on behalf of my life" and "their own neck." The emphatic word order reflects Paul's intense emotion in his knowledge of their unquestionable allegiance to him; something not to be overlooked in light of those who abandon him (such as Demas, 2 Tim 4:10). Hence, Paul says "to them I not only give thanks but also all the churches of the Gentiles" (Rom 16:4b) and greets also the church that meets in their house (16:5a).

In the six references that mention Prisca and Aquila, only twice is Aquila mentioned first (Acts 18:2; 1 Cor 16:19). Based on the four instances where Prisca precedes, some deduce that she is the more dominant of the couple. Perhaps the more accurate description of the couple is that there is no record of the individual activity of either. Prisca never appears apart from Aquila; simultaneously, Aquila never appears apart from Prisca. Even in their selfless courage, they are one—note that "neck" is singular in Rom 16:4 (τὸν ἑαυτῶν τράχηλον).[67] They work for the kingdom of God as one unit, a fact that Paul recognizes and affirms thrice in his letters.

The most significant point is one from silence. Given the intimacy of their affection and unity in ministry, it is unlikely that Paul was unaware of the fact that Prisca, along with Aquila, taught Apollos (Acts 18:27), presumably to great effect (Acts 18:27–28). Yet, there is not one instance of Paul's rebuke of either Prisca or Aquila nor any indication of fractured relations between Paul and the couple in the NT. When there is a critical challenge to the gospel message, Paul exercises no sensitivity to private feelings or public status, as he shockingly demonstrates in Gal 2:11–14 when he publicly opposes Peter.[68] Paul does not suffer any distortion of the gospel gladly. Yet, he does not correct either Prisca or Aquila. Finally, neither Prisca nor Aquila is ever designated as a leader in a formal capacity in the NT. Neither title nor official recognition is required for her and Aquila to teach Apollos.

---

67. Τράχηλος occurs only 6x in the NT (Matt 18:6; Mark 9:42; Luke 15:20, 17:2; Acts 15:10, 20:37; Rom 16:4); 86x in the LXX. Of the 6, Acts 15:10 is comparable to Rom 16:4, as "neck" is also singular with a plural modifier: "on the neck of the disciples" (ἐπὶ τὸν τράχηλον τῶν μαθητῶν)—the disciples are seen as a collective in this instance. By comparison, note Josh 10:24 (ἐπὶ τοὺς τραχήλους αὐτῶν); 2 Chr 30:8 (μὴ σκληρύνητε τοὺς τραχήλους ὑμῶν); Mic 2:3 (τοὺς τραχήλους ὑμῶν); and Jer 35:11 (ἀπὸ τραχήλων πάντων τῶν ἐθνῶν).

68. Paul's outright public exposure of Peter is, also now, permanent!

Conclusion

If as the exegesis indicates, the most faithful reading of Paul's description of the three women in Rom 16:1–7 is positive affirmation. In the case of Phoebe and Junia, Paul affirms their official, indeed, excellent leadership in the church. With respect to Prisca, despite the fact that she teaches a man, Paul has no words of rebuke but only praise in Romans and elsewhere. Perhaps two points can be briefly noted. First, it appears that Paul's gender boundary is more porous than often assumed. His commendation of women's agency in faith has equal weight to his proscription elsewhere. In light of this, the critical task for both sides of the gender debate is to avoid prostituting one passage for the sake of another; it is a disservice to Paul in either case. As such the solution will need to be multi-lateral rather than unilateral in its construction—how can two seemingly antithetical notions subsist within the church.

Second, to this end, I offer an initial proposal. The three women examined in Rom 16:1–7 exhibit the type of faith that Paul himself confesses and exhorts to his converts. All three have single-minded zeal for Jesus Christ and his gospel message. Phoebe demonstrates this through abdication of social status and power for humble service. Prisca, despite being financially privileged, risks her own neck for Paul. And Junia endures imprisonment for the sake of the gospel. They embody the discipleship Jesus commands: "If anyone desires to follow after me, let him deny himself and let him take up his cross and follow me. For whoever would save his life will lose it, but whoever loses his life for my sake and the gospel's will save it" (Mark 8:34–35). These women did not seek the comfort and security of their homes, of their social status and finances; they were not vain, frivolous creatures fixated on external adornment (1 Tim 2:9; 1 Pet 3:3–4); nor were they frenzied with their own spiritual gifts as to recklessly degrade men (1 Cor 11:2–16). All three are zealously submitted to the lordship of Jesus Christ. The three women have the kind of faith that Jesus commands and that Paul can affirm without reservation. This faith is what lies behind their leadership roles. To both sides of the debate, it is not gender alone, but faith that takes up the cross that justifies a person for service in the kingdom of God.

Yet, women's participation in ecclesial leadership still does not imply an egalitarian structure within Scripture. Male headship in both marriage and church is ordained by divine, creational fiat (cf. 1 Cor 11:8–9; 1 Tim 2:13; Gen 2:20–25), and as such is indispensable regardless of cultural trends. However, it may be claimed that where male headship is operative as intended, it leads to affirmation of women's agency and cruciformed faith. To this end, Yarbrough's savvy hermeneutical move on 1 Tim 2:11–15 offers a novel reassessment of Paul's motive—the end goal of 1 Tim 2:11–15 is not the exclusion but the edification of women.[69]

---

69. Yarbrough, *Timothy and Titus*, 170–81.

In Scripture, there is no equality apart from the framework of hierarchy. While this statement undoubtedly requires further elaboration, two concise observations will suffice. First, the unshakeable foundation for gender hierarchy is Jesus' appointment of the Twelve (Mark 3:13–19; Matt 10:1–4; Luke 6:12–16). The election of twelve men as Jesus' disciples and later apostles cannot be seen as simply a symbolic gesture for new Israel as correlation to the twelve tribes as argued by some.[70] Such a narrow and utilitarian hermeneutic fails to account for the fact that Jesus himself eschatologically represents Israel in terms of her history, God's promises and even male leadership (e.g., Matt 2:1–15, esp. v. 15; as well as the genealogy, Matt 1:1–17), which renders the Twelve's representation of Israel as coherent to Jesus, but less pivotal in and of itself. In ushering in the eschatological kingdom of God, Jesus violates various social protocol, especially with respect to women. In John 4, Jesus, in breach of the custom of his day, engages (the δεῖ in 4:4 may indicate divine appointment rather than mere coincidence) in a conversation with the Samaritan woman, apart from the company of others in broad daylight. Indeed, such radical departure from the norm shocked his disciples ("his disciples . . . were amazed that he was speaking with a woman," οἱ μαθηταὶ αὐτοῦ . . . ἐθαύμαζον ὅτι μετὰ γυναικὸς ἐλάλει, John 4:27). The disciples' reaction reflects Jewish rabbinic attitude towards women: "One should not talk with a woman on the street, not even with his own wife, and certainly not with somebody else's wife, because of the gossip of men" ('Abot 2 (1d)) and "It is forbidden to give a woman any greeting" (Qidd. 70a).[71] *Nevertheless*, Jesus does not appoint women as one of the Twelve. Alongside the Twelve's representation of Israel, the rationale must also be tethered to Adam's priority in creation in Gen 2. Under the apostolic leadership, which is firmly anchored to Christ's mindset of self-sacrifice, humility, obedience (Phil 2:6–8), and sinless life (Heb 4:15), women of same allegiance to Christ are not abused, oppressed, or marginalized, but find acceptance, praise, and equality.

Bibliography

Bauckham, Richard. *Gospel Women: Studies of the Named Women in the Gospels*. London: T&T Clark, 2002.

Belleville, Linda L. "Women in Ministry: An Egalitarian Perspective." Pages 19–103 in *Two Views on Women in Ministry*. Rev. ed. Edited by James R. Beck. Grand Rapids: Zondervan, 2005.

---

70. Cf. Linda L. Belleville, "Women in Ministry: An Egalitarian Perspective," in *Two Views on Women in Ministry*, ed. James R. Beck, rev. ed. (Grand Rapids: Zondervan, 2005), 69.

71. Hermann Strack and Paul Billerbeck, *Kommentar zum Neuen Testament aus Talmud und Midrasch* (München: Kessinger, 1922), 2:438.

————. "Ἰουνιαν . . . ἐπίστημοι ἐν τοῖς ἀποστόλοις: A Re-examination of Romans 16:7 in Light of Primary Source Materials." *NTS* 51 (2005): 231–49.

Burer, Michael H., and Daniel B. Wallace. "Was Junia Really an Apostle? A Reexamination of Rom 16.7." *NTS* 47 (2001): 76–91.

Ciampa, Roy E., and Brian S. Rosner. *The First Letter to the Corinthians.* PNTC. Grand Rapids: Eerdmans, 2010.

Cohick, Lynn H. *Women in the World of the Earliest Christians: Illuminating Ancient Ways of Life.* Grand Rapids: Baker Academic, 2009.

Collins, John N. *Diakonia: Re-interpreting the Ancient Sources.* Oxford: Oxford University Press, 1990.

Eisenstadt, S. N., and L. Roniger. *Patrons, Clients, and Friends: Interpersonal Relations and the Structure of Trust in Society.* Themes in the Social Sciences. Cambridge: Cambridge University Press, 1984.

Elliott, John H. "Patronage and Clientage." Pages 144–56 in *The Social Sciences and New Testament Interpretation.* Edited by Richard L. Rohrbaugh. Peabody, MA: Hendrickson, 1996.

Epp, Eldon J. *Junia: The First Woman Apostle.* Minneapolis: Fortress, 2005.

Hands, A. R. *Charities and Social Aid in Greece and Rome.* Ithaca: Cornell University Press, 1968.

Harris, Murray J. *The Second Epistle to the Corinthians: A Commentary on the Greek Text.* NIGTC. Grand Rapids: Eerdmans, 2005.

Kienast, D. "Presbeia." *PWSup* 13: 499–628.

Longenecker, Richard N. *The Epistle to the Romans: A Commentary on the Greek Text.* NIGTC. Grand Rapids: Eerdmans, 2016.

Michaelis, Wilhelm. "Kenchreä (Zur Frage des Abfassungsortes des Rm)." *ZNW* 25 (1926): 144–54.

Mitchell, Margaret M. "New Testament Envoys in the Context of Greco-Roman Diplomatic and Epistolary Conventions: The Example of Timothy and Titus." *JBL* 111.4 (1992): 641–62.

Moo, Douglas J. *The Letter to the Romans.* 2nd ed. NICNT. Grand Rapids: Eerdmans, 2018.

Osiek, Carolyn, and Margaret Y. MacDonald, with Janet H. Tulloch. *A Woman's Place: House Churches in Earliest Christianity.* Minneapolis: Fortress, 2006.

Romaniuk, Kazimierz. "Was Phoebe in Romans 16,1 a Deaconess?" *ZNW* 81 (1990): 132–34.

Schlatter, Adolf. *Gottes Gerechtigkeit: Ein Kommentar zum Römerbrief.* Stuttgart: Calwer Verlag, 1965.

Schreiner, Thomas R. *Romans.* BECNT. Grand Rapids: Baker Academic, 1998.

————. "The Valuable Ministries of Women in the Context of Male Leadership: A Survey of Old and New Testament Examples and Teaching." Pages 209–24 In *Recovering Biblical Manhood and Womanhood: A Response to*

Evangelical Feminism. Edited by John Piper and Wayne Grudem. Wheaton, IL: Crossway, 1991.

Schüssler Fiorenza, Elisabeth. "Missionaries, Apostles, Coworkers: Romans 16 and the Reconstruction of Women's Early Christian History." *Word & World* 6.4 (1986): 420–33.

————. "Women in the Pre-Pauline and Pauline Churches." *Union Seminary Quarterly Review* 33.3–4 (1978): 153–66.

Seifrid, Mark A. *The Second Letter to the Corinthians*. PNTC. Grand Rapids: Eerdmans, 2014.

Strack, Hermann, and Paul Billerbeck. *Kommentar zum Neuen Testament aus Talmud und Midrasch*. 6 vols. München: Kessinger, 1922.

Thielman, Frank. *Romans*. ZECNT 6. Grand Rapids: Zondervan Academic, 2018.

————. *Theology of the New Testament: A Canonical and Synthetic Approach*. Grand Rapids: Zondervan, 2005.

Thrall, Margaret E. *2 Corinthians 1–7: A Critical and Exegetical Commentary*. ICC. London: T&T Clark, 1994.

White, John L. *Light from Ancient Letters*. Philadelphia: Fortress, 1986.

Wolters, Al. "ΙΟΥΝΙΑΝ (Romans 16:7) and the Hebrew Name 'Yĕḥunnī.'" *JBL* 127.2 (2008): 397–408.

Yarbrough, Robert W. *The Letters to Timothy and Titus*. PNTC. Grand Rapids: Eerdmans, 2018.

Contributors

Michael F. Bird, Ridley College (Melbourne, Australia)

Christopher Bruno, Training Leaders International

Mateus F. de Campos, Gordon-Conwell Theological Seminary

Ardel B. Caneday, University of Northwestern, St. Paul

A. Andrew Das, Elmhurst University

Ben C. Dunson, Greenville Presbyterian Theological Seminary

Robert A. J. Gagnon, Houston Christian University

Benjamin Gladd, Reformed Theological Seminary

Joshua M. Greever, Bethlehem College and Seminary

Sigurd Grindheim, Western Norway University of Applied Sciences

Kevin McFadden, Cairn University School of Divinity

Benjamin L. Merkle, Southeastern Baptist Theological Seminary

Douglas J. Moo, Wheaton College Graduate School

M. Sydney Park, Beeson Divinity School

Charles L. Quarles, Southeastern Baptist Theological Seminary

Brian S. Rosner, Ridley College (Melbourne, Australia)

Eckhard J. Schnabel, Gordon-Conwell Theological Seminary

Patrick Schreiner, Midwestern Baptist Theological Seminary

Thomas R. Schreiner, Southern Baptist Theological Seminary

Mark A. Seifrid, Concordia Seminary

Frank Thielman, Beeson Divinity School

Jeffrey A. D. Weima, Calvin Theological Seminary

Kyle B. Wells, Christ Presbyterian Church (Santa Barbara, California)

Robert W. Yarbrough, Covenant Theological Seminary

Index of Subjects

wicked, wickedness, 35, 103, 155, 180, 182, 186, 191
wine, 183, 298, 299, 300, 304, 308, 312
wisdom, 41, 45, 117, 273, 295, 350, 368
wives, 72, 83, 84, 359
woman, women, 11, 12, 51, 52, 54, 55, 57, 58, 63, 67–84, 104, 158, 194, 200, 226, 306, 326, 357–59, 365, 367–69, 371–72
wordplay, 116, 124, 213
works. *See* law, Torah
worship, 60, 62, 156–57, 162–63, 188, 260, 269–71, 292, 294, 298, 304, 326, 366

wrath, 28, 34–46, 49, 66, 116, 121, 135, 139–40, 143, 147–49, 155, 156, 157, 160–61, 167, 190, 225, 227, 254, 259, 260, 262, 269, 271, 280, 340, 344, 345, 352. *See* power, revelation

Yahweh, 34, 87, 89, 90, 93–95, 98, 163–64, 166–68, 234–36, 238–39, 241

zeal, 204, 231–32, 236–37, 272, 350–51, 371
Zion, 89, 166, 167, 235, 243, 253, 254, 255, 256

Index of Ancient Sources

10:24 370
22:5 354
23:11 354
23:16 159

Judges
5:31 354
13–16 67
14:16 354
16:4 354
16:15 354

Ruth
4:15 354

1 Samuel
1:5 354
4:17 87, 88
12:7 23
15:22 276
18:20 354
31:9 87, 88

2 Samuel
1:20 87, 88
4:10 86, 87, 89
12:24 354
13:1 354
13:4 354
13:15 354
18:19 87
18:19–31 89
18:20 86, 87
18:22 86
18:25 86
18:26 87
18:27 86
18:31 87
22:9 280
22:12 280
22:50 127

1 Kings
1:42 87, 88
1:46 89
3:3 354
10:9 354
11:2 354

2 Kings
2:11 182
7:9 86, 89
18:2 159

1 Chronicles
10:9 87, 88

2 Chronicles
2:10 354
9:8 354
11:21 354

16:1–10 294
30:8 370

Ezra
6:20 299

Nehemiah
1:5 354
9:33 22
13:26 354

Esther
15:1 310

Job
20:20–29 39
21:27–34 39
36:18 155
37:16 303
41:12 280
41:13 280

Psalms
14:1 (LXX 13:1) 353
14:7 166
18:31 160
19:4 127
21:2 160
32 135
32:1–2 126
36:5–6 24
38:20 41
39:10 87
40:9 89
44:24–25 43
50:8–15 276
51:4 (LXX 50:6) 43, 261
51:14 23
67:12 87
67:19–20 166
68:11 89
68:25 35
69:10 (LXX 68:10) 278
69:22–23 127
71:21 23
72:1–4 26
73:2–8 (LXX 72:2–8) 155
73:6 (LXX 72:6) 155
77:49 35
90:7 36
90:9 41
90:11 36
90:13–17 36
94:8 157
95:2 87
96:2 89
98 20, 26
98:2 25, 29, 171
100:3 159
100:4 159
106 156

106:20 64, 156
110:1 94
110:5 39
117:1 127
118:6 262
119 22
145:7 24

Proverbs
3:12 354
11:4 39
11:5 155
13:24 354
15:9 354
17:15 120
25:21–22 280
30:4 238

Ecclesiastes
9:9 354

Song of Songs
1:3–4 354
1:7 354
3:1–4 354

Isaiah
1:9 127
1:11–17 276
2:3 254
5:1 354
5:22–23 120
5:24 280
7–8 234
7:4 35
7:9 234
8 235
8:14 166, 234, 235
9:18 35
10:22–23 127
11:10 127, 167
13:6–9 39
21:4 187
24:5 159
27:2 254
27:9 166, 253
28 235
28:15 235
28:16 127, 166, 167, 234, 236
29:10 127
29:16 45, 127
33:6 117
35:5 93
38:19 23, 24
40–66 23, 27
40:4–5 90
40:9 87
40:9–10 89
41:8 354
43:4 354
45:9 127

Cicero

De finibus
3.62   54

Dio Cassius

Roman Histories
67.14.1–2   224

Dio Chrysostom

Discourses
7.149–152   78

Diodorus

Historical Library
15.74.2   90

Diogenes Laertius

Lives of Eminent Philosophers
7.17   76

Epictetus

Diatribai
1.16.9–14   68
1.19.4   342
2.9.20   224
2.22.4   342
3.1.27–45   68

Euripides

Hippolytus
121–124   187

Phoenissae
1577–78   187

Homer

Odyssey
14.125   90
14.166   90

Horace

Satires
1.9.68–72   305

Hippocrates

On Regimen
1.28–29   76, 77

Isocrates

Aeropagiticus
7.10   90

Juvenal

Satires
2   72

Longinus

De sublimitate
9.9   302

Lucian of Samosata

Dialogues of the Courtesans
5   72

Pseudo-Lucian

Affairs of the Heart
4   72
5   79
9   79
19–20   56

Martial

Epigrams
1.24   72
12.42   72

Musonius Rufus
21   68

Ovid

Amores
219–220   305

Ars amatoria
1.75–76   305
1.413–416   305

Persius

Satirae
5.180–184   305

Plato

Charmides
155D   76

Laws
636C   55

Phaedrus
250E   55

Symposium
176A–B   187
180B   341
181D   71
183E   71
189C–193D   75
199E–200B   341
204C–D   341
205A   341
216–218   75

Republica
399B   274

Pliny the Elder

Natural History
28.99   79

Plutarch

Agesilaus
17.3   90
33.4   90

Dialogue on Love
751C   71
751D–E   55

Caesar
49.4   187

Galba
21.2   187

Moralia
347D   91

Sertorius
11.4   91

Pompeius
66.3   91

Polybius

Histories
1.51.6   187

Ptolemy of Alexandria

Tetrabiblos
3.14   72

Seneca

Epistulae morales (Letters)
4.6   228
95.47   305

Suetonius

Nero
6.10   288

Tacitus

Annals
13.50–41   288

Xenophon of Athens

Hellenica
1.6.37   90

Xenophon of Ephesus

An Ephesian Tale
3.2   72

7. Inscriptions

Priene inscription
  91

Oropos inscription
  91

8. Papyri

Columbia Papyri
III 6.14–16   364